Lecture Notes in Computer Science   11385

Commenced Publication in 1973
Founding and Former Series Editors:
Gerhard Goos, Juris Hartmanis, and Jan van Leeuwen

More information about this series at http://www.springer.com/series/7409

Manuel Gentile · Mario Allegra ·
Heinrich Söbke (Eds.)

Games and Learning Alliance

7th International Conference, GALA 2018
Palermo, Italy, December 5–7, 2018
Proceedings

 Springer

Editors
Manuel Gentile
Institute for Educational Technology -
National Research Council of Italy
(ITD-CNR)
Palermo, Italy

Mario Allegra
Institute for Educational Technology -
National Research Council of Italy
(ITD-CNR)
Palermo, Italy

Heinrich Söbke
Bauhaus-Universität
Weimar, Germany

ISSN 0302-9743   ISSN 1611-3349 (electronic)
Lecture Notes in Computer Science
ISBN 978-3-030-11547-0   ISBN 978-3-030-11548-7 (eBook)
https://doi.org/10.1007/978-3-030-11548-7

Library of Congress Control Number: 2018967685

LNCS Sublibrary: SL3 – Information Systems and Applications, incl. Internet/Web, and HCI

This Springer imprint is published by the registered company Springer Nature Switzerland AG
The registered company address is: Gewerbestrasse 11, 6330 Cham, Switzerland

Preface

The 7th Games and Learning Alliance (GALA) Conference, organized by the Serious Games Society (SGS) and the Institute for Educational Technology - National Research Council of Italy (ITD-CNR), was held in the all culturally unique, future-oriented, and inspiring ambience of the Sicilian city of Palermo, Italy, during December 5–7, 2018.

The GALA series of conferences provide an excellent opportunity to foster the discussion of relevant topics in the growing field of serious games. The conference is a venue for academic researchers, industrial developers, teachers, and corporate decision-makers to meet and exchange experiences and knowledge in this multidisciplinary and challenging area. GALA 2018 received 68 submissions. While the majority of authors are based in Europe, North and South America, Africa and Asia were also represented in the submissions. Each paper was reviewed by at least three Program Committee members. The Program Committee selected 37 of these papers for presentation at the conference and nine for presentation at a poster session of the conference. A total of 18 countries were represented at the conference.

The conference featured a tutorial session, a session for demos of serious games, and a serious game competition. It was an honor to have Dirk Ifenthaler, from the University of Mannheim, Germany, and Georgios Yannakakis from the University of Malta, Malta, as keynote speakers at GALA 2018. Dirk Ifenthaler vividly presented the basics, challenges, and chances of learning analytics in serious games. Giannis Yannakikis gave an inspiring overview of the possibilities of artificial intelligence in serious games. The momentum of both keynotes is likely to have a lasting influence on the work of the conference attendees. The conference featured nine paper presentation sessions. A number of paper presentation sessions focussed on the relation between serious games and a wide range of particular domains, such as computational thinking, energy conservation, musical perception, doorstep scams, meta-skills, health, nutrition, mobility habits, physics, and maths. Other sessions discussed gamification, game development, the assessment of games, game analytics, game design, the relation between games and learning and innovative game technologies, such as artificial intelligence, robotics, mixed reality, and haptics.

As in previous years, selected best papers of the GALA conference will be published in a dedicated special issue of the *International Journal of Serious Games*, the scientific journal managed by the Serious Games Society, which is a great reference point for academics and practitioners to publish original research work on serious games and be informed about the latest developments in the field. We thank the authors for submitting many interesting, field-advancing papers, the Program Committee for reviewing these papers, and the SGS and ITD-CNR for organizing the conference.

December 2018

Manuel Gentile
Mario Allegra
Heinrich Söbke

Organization

General Chair

Manuel Gentile   Institute for Educational Technology - National Research Council of Italy (ITD-CNR), Italy

Program Chairs

Mario Allegra   Institute for Educational Technology - National Research Council of Italy (ITD-CNR), Italy

Heinrich Söbke   Bauhaus-Universität Weimar, Germany

Exhibition Chair

Jannicke Baalsrud Hauge   BIBA, Germany/KTH, Sweden

Tutorials Chair

Remco C. Veltkamp   Utrecht University, The Netherlands

Awards Chair

Iza Marfisi-Schottman   University of Le Mans, France

Publication Chair

Riccardo Berta   University of Genoa, Italy

Communication and Promotion Chair

Manuel Ninaus   Leibniz-Institut für Wissensmedien, Germany

Administrative and Financial Chair

Francesco Bellotti   University of Genoa, Italy

Local Arrangements Chair

Simona Ottaviano   Institute for Educational Technology - National Research Council of Italy (ITD-CNR), Italy

Program Committee

Anissa All	University of Gent, Belgium
Alessandra Antonaci	OUNL, The Netherlands
Sylvester Arnab	Coventry University, UK
Aida Azadegan	The Open University, UK
Jannicke Baalsrud Hauge	BIBA, Germany/KTH, Sweden
Per Backlund	Högskolan i Skövde, Sweden
Sylvie Barma	Université Laval, Canada
Francesco Bellotti	University of Genoa, Italy
Riccardo Berta	University of Genoa, Italy
Rafael Bidarra	TU Delft, The Netherlands
Staffan Björk	Chalmers, Sweden
Lucas Blair	Little Bird Games, USA
Rosa Bottino	Institute for Educational Technology - National Research Council of Italy (ITD-CNR), Italy
Clint Bowers	University of Central Florida, USA
Maira Brandao Carvalho	Tilburg University, The Netherlands
Michael Coovert	University of South Florida, USA
Sylvie Daniel	University Laval, Canada
Alessandro De Gloria	University of Genoa, Italy
Kurt Debattista	University of Warwick, UK
Teresa de la Hera	Erasmus University Rotterdam, The Netherlands
Shujie Deng	University of Bournemouth, UK
Michael Derntl	RWTH Aachen, Germany
João Dias	INESC-ID and Instituto Superior Técnico, Universidade de Lisboa, Portugal
Frank Dignum	University of Utrecht, The Netherlands
Ioannis Doumanis	University of Middlesex, UK
Miguel Encarnação	University of Louisvillèe, USA
Samir Garbaya	ENSAM ParisTech, France
Manuel Gentile	Institute for Educational Technology - National Research Council of Italy (ITD-CNR), Italy
Junghyun Han	Korea University, Republic of Korea
Valerie Hill	Texas Women University, USA
Carolina Islas Sedano	University of Eastern Finland, Finland
Michael Kickmeier-Rust	University of Graz, Austria
Sotiris Kriginas	University of Athens, Greece
Ralph Klamma	RWTH Aachen, Germany
Silvia Kober	University of Graz, Austria
Niki Lambropoulos	Global Operations Division, Greece
George Lepouras	University of the Peloponnese, Greece
Theo Lim	Heriot-Watt University, UK
Sandy Louchart	Glasgow School of Art Digital Design Studio, UK
Katerina Mania	Technical University of Crete, Greece
Fabrizia Mantovani	University of Milan-Bicocca, Italy

Contents

Methods and Tools

Gamification and Innovative Game Approaches

Posters

Games for Skills Training

The Effect of Disposition to Critical Thinking on Playing Serious Games

Manuel Gentile[(✉)], Giuseppe Città, Salvatore Perna, Alessandro Signa,
Francesco Reale, Valentina Dal Grande, Simona Ottaviano,
Dario La Guardia, and Mario Allegra

Institute for Educational Technology, National Research Council of Italy,
Palermo, Italy
{manuel.gentile,giuseppe.citta,salvatore.perna,alessandro.signa,
francesco.reale,valentina.dalgrande,simona.ottaviano,
dario.laguardia,mario.allegra}@itd.cnr.it
http://www.pa.itd.cnr.it/

Abstract. This research is a first attempt to investigate the relationship between students' Disposition toward Critical Thinking (DCT) and their learning while engaging in the uManager serious game aimed at fostering the entrepreneurial mindset. Specifically, we will try to seek if the students' DCT influences their game-playing. To this aim, the uManager game was renewed to directly include game mechanics able to support the processes that are at the base of critical thinking like clarifying meaning, analyzing arguments, evaluating evidence. This paper shows the results of a trial conducted with 92 students of the 12th grade.

Keywords: Disposition to critical thinking · Serious games · Entrepreneurship education

1 Introduction

The current research in game-based learning [19,21,22] states that Serious Games (SG) are a widespread tool used to foster learning at different ages in a wide range of fields [2–4,24]. They are described as a tool allowing students to recall learning experiences in an engaging way [23] and involving players in tasks and activities conceived for knowledge and skills improvements [18]. However, there is no consensus on the effects that SGs may have in fostering students' 21st-century skill development and how they affect and support the teaching and learning of these skills is still a very controversial point [21]. Namely, although the SG field and research studies on learning and teaching through SGs are growing, very little is known about how SGs can affect the development of the so-called higher-level thinking skills such as, for example, critical thinking, problem-solving and creative thinking, that are classified as belonging to the 21st century skills [7]. Moreover, even more controversial in literature is the question of what degree of complexity should be achieved in the design of an SG to reach

© Springer Nature Switzerland AG 2019
M. Gentile et al. (Eds.): GALA 2018, LNCS 11385, pp. 3–15, 2019.
https://doi.org/10.1007/978-3-030-11548-7_1

meaningful indications about the role of the components mentioned above. In this paper, we aim to address these issues by focusing on a specific complex higher-level ability: Critical Thinking (CT).

CT is defined as a pervasive human feature thanks to which a thinker can, on the one hand, make judgments based on interpretations, analyses, evaluations and inferences and, on the other, provide explanations through reflections and arguments about concepts, methods or contexts. Briefly, it is an essential tool of Inquiry [7]. In literature, there are numerous definitions of this ability and each one highlights a specific aspect of such a complex phenomenon. Some of them focus on the cognitive characteristics and habits involved in critical thinking [5], others [13] focus on the critical thinking process (CT as problem-solving or decision making), while others direct their attention on the possible results of a critical thinking process [20]. Glaser [5] defines CT as "an attitude of being disposed to consider thoughtfully the problems and subjects that come within the range of one's experiences". Facione [6] describes it as "the ability to construct and evaluate arguments". Moore and Parker [20] suggest conceiving CT as the ability to judge specific assertions as plausible/implausible, evaluating evidence, assessing the logical aspects of inferences, elaborating and constructing counter-arguments and different hypotheses. Despite the heterogeneity of the definitions reported in the literature, the different perspectives are in agreement in judging the following components as essential for CT: clarify meaning, analyze arguments, evaluate evidence, judge whether a conclusion follows, draw warranted conclusions [10].

Our long-term goal is to investigate the effect/role that these core cognitive abilities of CT have in a context of a SG where game activities constantly involve problem-solving and decision making. In this paper, we will try to answer the following question: are there effects of cognizer's Disposition toward Critical Thinking (DCT) on game-playing? Namely, we will investigate the DCT as a starting mental attitude, as a particular "mental state of readiness organized through experience, exerting a directive or dynamic influence upon the individual's response to object and situation with which it is related" [11].

To this aim, the uManager game was renewed [9,17] to directly include game mechanics able to require the activation of the processes that are at the base of critical thinking like clarifying meaning, analyzing arguments, evaluating evidence. uManager is a serious game designed to foster the entrepreneurial mindset in young students engaging the students in a motivating and realistic learning path in which the user has to build and manage a resort village according to the preferences of the customers' needs. According to Krueger [15], the entrepreneurial mindset is a high-level concept that involves a complex set of attitudes, skills, and competencies (e.g., decision making, problem-solving and critical thinking).

In particular, for the aim of this paper we focus on the adaptation of a specific portion of the game connected to the choice of services and accommodations according to the customers' needs; the design objective was to link the customers' preferences and the available services according to an explicit knowledge provided to the students. In this way, we support the activation of reflective reasoning processes connected to the critical analysis of this information rather than rewarding instinctive decisions related to their previous and implicit knowledge. Focusing the DCT and its possible effect on serious-game-playing, according to our perspective, makes possible to extract some important information about the self-aware learning of students, about what in literature is called "meta-cognition".

In the following sections, we briefly describe the features of the uManager game and then focus on how we adapted the design of the game to facilitate the critical thinking processes. We then describe the method of analysis (sample, measures, and models) and, finally, we analyze the results.

2 uManager

The uManger game starts randomly assigning a specific customer typology as the target of the player. The goal of the student is to understand the needs of that customer typology and build up the village according, choosing which building to create and which services to provide in his resort, he also has to decide the best communication and marketing channels to promote the village.

The available customer categories are: *VIP, Senior, Low Cost, Young* and *Family*. Each category has different preferences concerning every aspect of the vacation in the resort and different spending power as well. Customer types are differently distributed in the market; each costumer type has different probabilities to be generated that are inversely proportional to the spending power of each segment. It is worth to specify that, despite the principal goal of the game is to satisfy the target customer typology, the village is open to all the customer categories. The resort will attract one or the other customer types based on the services offered.

The player starts the game with an initial amount of money and an empty terrain, including a beach. He/she can build the facilities in the available space of the map, hire employees and manage entrance costs and salaries. In case of a financial deficit, the player can ask for a loan, and he/she will repay the debt with interests in the next months. There is also a virtual assistant which guides the player sending him messages about the available feature of the game. uManager has a discrete time progression; this means that the simulation starts once all the decisions are made. Each interval simulates a quarter, during this time customers visit the resort and spend their money enjoying the structures inside the village.

Player's choices affect several aspects of the business simulation on which the game is based. In Fig. 1, we have reported a schema highlighting how the main game mechanics impact on the game variables. We represented the game mechanics as rectangles and the variables as circles. The dotted line identifies those mechanics which affect the cost variable, and the red line highlights those aspects we analyzed in this study.

The player can directly monitor many of these variables by the available tables and graphs in the game. Some of them, like the *Quality Price Ratio*

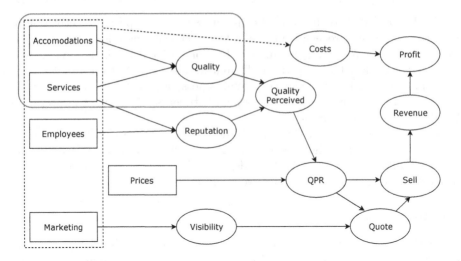

Fig. 1. Causal network of game mechanics and game variables in uManager (Color figure online)

(QPR), are hidden to the player and therefore do not appear in any of the explicit reports, so that the player must infer them. The game allows the player to view about ten linear graphs and see how the trend changes from quarter to quarter. The *Quality* graph, for example, indicates how much the target customer typology appreciates each service category offered in the village. The *Visibility* graph instead shows the marketing campaigns' efficacy regarding the village's notoriety to each customer typology. The student can also consult tables concerning financial recaps containing details about last quarter's costs and revenues.

During the game, the player has to understand and analyze the causal connections between his decisions and the game variables. For example, the student should realize that to increase the number of *Quotes* requested by potential customers he/she has to enhance the village's visibility. To get the best performance from each building in the village is crucial to understand which are the employees that fit better for that purpose, it's also possible to modify the standard employees' salary to enhance their productivity. There is a huge variety of available employees, and the player can hire specific staff for each service sector, from bungalow's or hotel's cleaner to tennis teacher passing by the receptionist or the restaurant's chef. To obtain the maximum profit from employees' work is essential to distinguish the helpful roles and invest in them only. Employees don't affect the village's quality directly, but they produce an indirect and delayed effect through the *reputation* variable. The reputation variable is built from consumer agents who "live" into the village after they buy the entrance. The goodness of their experience inside the resort contributes to the village's reputation which affects how other agents perceive the quality of the resort. This quality perception guides the customer which are about to evaluate the offering of a village for a vacation.

The *Quality Perceived* by each customer, which is defined by the total quality and the reputation, is evaluated together with the village entrance price to decide whether to buy the bundle or not. The player can modify the entrance price to give access to the village to the customers with less spending power or, otherwise, he/she can increase the prices and try to get more income from customers. Ultimately, to fully understand the game mechanics the student has to activate high-level inferential processes which are hard to identify and evaluate automatically by the designers.

3   The Design of uManager to Foster Critical Thinking

In this section, we discuss how the design of uManager supports the processes that are at the base of critical thinking. To comprehend how the critical thinking disposition affects the student's gaming capacity, we, therefore, limit our analysis focusing on the student's ability to choose services and accommodations preferred from the assigned customer typology.

As described in the previous section and highlighted in the causal network shown in the Fig. 1, uManager is a complex game in which the player's decisions on different aspects of management interact at different levels to define the level of success in the game. In order to better study the critical thinking processes used by the player, it was necessary to limit the analysis to a portion of the game (highlighted in the Fig. 1 with a red box) in which it was possible to analyze the direct cause-effect link between the player's choices and the *Quality* of the resort.

In particular, we will highlight how we created the matching function among the customer typologies and the game asset, to have the possibility to give specific hints and stimulate critical thinking processes during the gameplay. The Table 1 shows the available game assets for each category of Services (Accommodation, Food, Sport, Relax).

Table 1. Assets' categories schema

Accommodation	Food service	Sport	Relax
Tent	Market	Soccer	Umbrella
Camper	Self service	Tennis	Massage
Bungalow	Coffee shop	Bowls	Yoga
Duplex bungalow	Restaurant	Swimming pool	Seaview house
Hotel	Organic restaurant	Archery	Discotheque

For each service category, we identified a set of quality dimensions to categorize the game elements as well also the customer's preferences. For example, the accommodation service has been described according to the level of comfort they provide, the availability of external spaces, the level of cleaning service and room service from which they benefit, the level of privacy offered and the availability of other services (e.g., kitchen, laundry). By using the specific quality dimension of each service category, it is possible to represent both the game assets and the customer preferences as vectors in a multidimensional space and to calculate the distance between them. According to the values assigned to the quality dimensions, we provide a textual description for each customer cluster and asset. These descriptions allow the player to ground their decision-making processes not exclusively on his/her prior knowledge, providing explicit knowledge that has to be searched, read and critically analyzed. Furthermore, to lower as much as possible the chance of playing with the customer target they suppose to know and to put more emphasis on reading and analyzing the information available, we chose to assign the customer target randomly.

As a concrete example of this design approach let's consider one asset category (*accommodations*) and one customer cluster (*VIPs*). Table 2 shows the characterization of the various accommodations relative to the features identified for this category, while the Table 3 shows the characterization of the *VIPs* customers' needs and beliefs relative to the same set of features.

If we look at the vector characterizing the *Hotel* asset and the one characterizing the *VIPs* customer cluster a clear correlation is easily spotted. In fact, the needs and beliefs of the VIPs customer cluster in regards to the

Table 2. Characterization of accommodations buildings

	Comfort	External spaces	Cleaning service Room service	Privacy	Other services (kitchen, laundry)
Tent	−2	2	−2	−2	2
Camper	−1	2	−2	−1	1
Bungalow	1	1	1	2	2
Duplex bungalow	1	1	1	−1	1
Hotel	2	−2	2	2	−2

Table 3. Preferences of customers related to accommodations

	Comfort	External spaces	Cleaning service Room service	Privacy	Other services (kitchen, laundry)
VIP	2	−2	2	2	−2
Senior	2	1	1	2	0
Family	0	0	2	−1	1
Young	−2	2	−2	−2	2
Low cost	−1	1	0	−2	2

accommodations strongly match the Hotel. To bring this correlation from the implicit to the explicit level, as discussed above, we created the following textual description: *"VIPs choose **very comfortable, high-quality service accommodations**. Deeply jealous of their **privacy** they prefer **room service** over both open spaces and ancillary services."*; similarly, we formulated the following description for the Hotel: *"Inside the hotel, you can find the reception, some common areas, the refreshment zone and, certainly, rooms and apartments. These fulfill specific boundaries of refinement, elegance and **comfort** and offer **high quality services** (i.e. **room service**) to those who want to enjoy a vacation full of relax and **privacy**"*. We used bold-style in the above descriptions just to highlight the keywords that should stimulate the formulation of the associations through inference, while in the game the descriptions are reported as plain text to give to the player the goal to infer the quality dimensions. These descriptions are available in the game, and the players can review them anytime by explicit clicking on the button *"show more info"* of each game asset or customer description.

4   Methods

We conducted the trial in the fourth year classes of 2 Sicilian secondary schools: the "Istituto Girolamo Caruso" of Alcamo and the "Istituto Tecnico Economico per il Turismo Marco Polo" of Palermo. In total, five classes were involved, three from the Caruso Institute and two from the Marco Polo Institute for a total of 92 students. In Table 4 the distribution of students' gender across sampled schools.

Table 4. Distribution of students' gender across the sampled schools

	Caruso	Marco Polo	Total
Females	20	32	52
Males	29	11	40
Total	49	43	92

4.1   Critical Thinking Disposition

The students' critical thinking disposition was measured by the UF-EMI instrument [12]. The UF-EMI is composed of 25 Likert-type items measuring three latent constructs: engagement (range 11–55), cognitive maturity (range 7–35), and innovativeness (range 7–35). The English version of the UF-EMI has been validated in several papers [8,16]. There is also a Turkish version of it which has confirmed its validity [14]. Unfortunately, to the best of our knowledge, there is no validated version in Italian. The validation of Italian adaptation of the UF-EMI test is beyond the scope of this paper; this measure was then used to classify students into two groups, those with high DCT and low DCT. Nevertheless, a back-translation procedure was applied to improve the quality of the translation. One of the students did not complete the UM-EFI test even if was involved in the game activity, so the analysis focuses on 91 cases. In Table 5 the descriptive analysis of the UF-EMI constructs are reported.

Table 5. Critical thinking disposition scores

Variable	n	Mean	sd	Min	Max
Engagement	91	40.4	4.4	25	50
Cognitive maturity	91	25.6	3.6	17	33
Innovativeness	91	25.9	3.4	18	33
Total disposition score	91	91.9	9.3	60	110

Moreover, the internal consistency was checked by the Cronbach's alpha coefficients of the three constructs. The values obtained are not very satisfactory, in detail the latent construct Engagement has a value of 0.64, the latent construct Cognitive Maturity value of 0.49 and the construct Innovativeness a value of 0.56; of course, the low sample size ($n = 91$) affects the quality of the Cronbach alpha obtained.

However, the reliability obtained is sufficient for the aim of this work and the subsequent clustering analysis. In fact, after the values obtained, a cluster analysis was applied to group together the statistical units with common characteristics. For this purpose we used a non-hierarchical cluster, the k-means methodology with $k = 2$ in which each cluster is characterized by a centroid and each sample is assigned to the cluster whose centroid is closest.

Table 6. Scaled clusters centroids

	Engagement	Cognitive maturity	Innovativeness
Cluster 1	−0.66	−0.54	−0.65
Cluster 2	0.76	0.63	0.76

In the Table 6 the scaled centroids of the latent constructs of the 2 clusters are reported; cluster 1 (49 students) represents the group of low DCT while the cluster 2 (42 students) is the group with high level of DCT.

4.2 Game-Related Measures

The paper aims to verify how the critical thinking disposition impacts on the performance of the *Quality* game variable, that measures the player's ability to understand the particular consumer preferences. The overall quality of a resort is the average of the quality values of each category of services, that is calculated considering all the typologies of the game asset of the service the player has used. For each typology of the game asset used by the player, the cosine distance with the customer characteristic vector is calculated; the sum of all these distances is performed, and subsequently, a sigmoid function is applied to this sum to scale the measure of quality in the [0..1] range. The starting hypothesis is that the critical thinking disposition has a direct impact on the modes of play; in particular, we hypothesize that a high level of DCT leads the students to the exploration and critical analysis of the information provided by the game. To this end, a further game variable named *InformativeAction* was also taken into consideration; this measure, extracted from the game learning analytics, represents the number of the student's actions aimed at the information exploration. These measures are calculated automatically every quarter of the game. The observations are then collected by player, game and quarter. In fact, during the trial, some players started a new game since they could no longer recover the previous match.

4.3 Analysis

The observations of the outcome variables considered in this analysis are not independent because we have repeated measurements on the same subject; moreover, the users among them are not independent since theoretically there is a school effect that leads us to the application of a nested model. To cope with this condition, we rely on mixed linear models, that allowed us to reproduce the nested model and to define a specific variance term for the intra-subject analysis.

Let Q_{qvus} the level of quality perceived by the customer target of the qth quarter, within the vth village of the uth student of the sth school. First of all, we want to what is the best model that describe the hierarchical nature of the collected data. To this aim we have compared the following four models:

$$Q_{qv} = \beta_0 + \beta_{0(v)} + \epsilon_{qv} + \epsilon_q \tag{1}$$

$$Q_{qvu} = \beta_0 + \beta_{0(vu)} + \beta_{0(u)} + \epsilon_{qvu} + \epsilon_{qv} + \epsilon_q \tag{2}$$

$$Q_{qvus} = \beta_0 + \beta_{0(vus)} + \beta_{0(us)} + \beta_{0(s)} + \epsilon_{qvus} + \epsilon_{qvu} + \epsilon_{qv} + \epsilon_q \tag{3}$$

$$Q_{qvu} = \beta_0 + \beta_1 * school + \beta_{0(vu)} + \beta_{0(s)} + \epsilon_{qvu} + \epsilon_{qv} + \epsilon_q \tag{4}$$

We estimated these model using the lmer package (version 1.1.15) [1]. The Table 7 reports the Anova comparison of these models.

The model (4) shows the best fit. So there is an effect of the school on the quality, that is better described by a fixed effect than a random one, according to the expectations raised by the number of the sampled schools. Once we had verified the hierarchical nature of the data, we analyzed how three independent variables, such as the quarter, the number of *InformativeActions* and the different membership of the DCT cluster, affect the data. To this aim, we compared the following four models (Table 8).

Table 7. Anova comparison of the multilevel models

	Df	AIC	BIC	logLik	Deviance	Chisq	Chi Df	Pr(>Chisq)
Model 1	3	−2074.57	−2056.13	1040.29	−2080.57			
Model 2	4	−2878.28	−2853.69	1443.14	−2886.28	805.71	1	0.0000***
Model 3	5	−2877.33	−2846.59	1443.66	−2887.33	1.05	1	0.3060
Model 4	5	−2881.22	−2850.48	1445.61	−2891.22	3.89	0	0.0000***

***p<0.001

$$Q_{qvu} = \beta_0 + \beta_1 * school + \beta_2 * quarter + \beta_{0(vu)} + \beta_{0(u)} + \epsilon_{qvu} + \epsilon_{qv} + \epsilon_q \quad (5)$$

$$Q_{qvu} = \beta_0 + \beta_1 * school + \beta_2 * quarter + \beta_{0(vu)} + \beta_{1(vu)} * quarter + \beta_{0(u)} + \epsilon_{qvu} + \epsilon_{qv} + \epsilon_q \quad (6)$$

$$Q_{qvu} = \beta_0 + \beta_1 * school + \beta_2 * quarter + \beta_3 * InformativeActions$$
$$+ \beta_{0(vu)} + \beta_{1(vu)} * quarter + \beta_{0(u)} + \epsilon_{qvu} + \epsilon_{qv} + \epsilon_q \quad (7)$$

$$Q_{qvu} = \beta_0 + \beta_1 * school + \beta_2 * quarter + \beta_3 * InformativeActions$$
$$* DCTCluster + \beta_{0(vu)} + \beta_{1(vu)} * quarter + \beta_{0(u)} + \epsilon_{qvu} + \epsilon_{qv} + \epsilon_q \quad (8)$$

In the first one (model 5) we add the quarter variable to analyze the trend of the quality assuming a fixed effect. In the model 6, we added a random effect for the quarter to include a random slope for each student. In the model 7 we added the *InformativeActions* variable and in the last one, we also added the clustering variable assuming that there is a possible interaction between the number of Informative Actions and the group membership. The Anova among these models is reported in the Table 8. From the results shown in the Table 8 it is clear that model 7 shows the best fit.

Table 8. Anova comparison of the models with fixed and random effects

	Df	AIC	BIC	logLik	Deviance	Chisq	Chi Df	Pr(>Chisq)
Model 5	6	−1796.00	−1762.03	904.00	−1808.00			
Model 6	10	−2451.21	−2394.61	1235.61	−2471.21	663.22	4	0.0000***
Model 7	11	−2454.26	−2391.99	1238.13	−2476.26	5.04	1	0.0247*
Model 8	13	−2451.25	−2377.66	1238.62	−2477.25	0.99	2	0.6106

*p<0.05, ***p<0.001

5   Results

From the analysis of the model 7, it emerges that the variable quarter has a positive influence on the quality, specifically, as the number of quarters increases the total quality improves $\beta_2 = 0.015(p < 0.0001)$. This means a general improvement in the understanding of the dynamics of the game.

The *InformativeActions* variable also has an impact on quality $\beta_3 = 0.0060(p < 0.01)$; this means that as the number of information explored by the student increases, the total value of quality increases. Moreover, the Table 8 shows that adding the interaction between the cluster and informative action to model 7 does not lead to a better fit. To complete the analysis and verify how the *DCTCluster* membership effects on the amount of information the student accesses we fit the model 9.

$$
\begin{aligned}
InformativeActions_{qvu} = {} & \beta_0 + \beta_1 * quarter + \beta_2 * DCTCluster + \beta_{0(vu)} \\
& + \beta_{1(vu)} * quarter + \beta_{0(s)} + \epsilon_{qvu} + \epsilon_{qv} + \epsilon_q \qquad (9)
\end{aligned}
$$

The analysis of model 9 fit shows a coefficient $\beta_1 = -0.05(p < 0.001)$ which underlines how, with the progression of the quarters, the information read by the student decrease. It seems that the students tend to look less to the information provided by the game quarter by quarter. Finally, the coefficient $\beta_2 = 0.82(p < 0.01)$ for cluster 2, formed by the students with a high level of DCT, indicates that the students belonging to this cluster have a greater predisposition to explore and analyze the information.

6   Conclusion

This paper is a first attempt to investigated if the students' DCT influences the students' game-playing while they are using the uManager serious game. The analysis of results in a small sample trial conducted with 92 students of the 12th grade, seems to reveal that the disposition to critical thinking has an indirect impact on the users' performances measured by the *quality* variable. The effect of DCT is mediated by the number of information read by the student. Thus, the DCT influences the game-playing of the user who tends, in the presence of a high level of DCT, to search and analyze the available information of the game more than users with a low level of DCT; this greater attention to information reflects the overall performance of the users. Anyway, this work is the first step in a broader analysis of the relationship between DTC and the students' game-playing. In the future works, a trial with a larger sample will be carried out to confirm what suggested from this trial; moreover, we want to investigate how DCT affects the relationship between explicit and implicit knowledge and how it is possible to monitor these processes through learning analytics.

References

1. Bates, D., Mächler, M., Bolker, B., Walker, S.: Fitting linear mixed-effects models using lme4. J. Stat. Softw. **67**(1), 1–48 (2015). https://doi.org/10.18637/jss.v067. i01

2. Berta, R., Bellotti, F., van der Spek, E., Winkler, T.: A tangible serious game approach to Science, Technology, Engineering, and Mathematics (STEM) education. In: Nakatsu, R., Rauterberg, M., Ciancarini, P. (eds.) Handbook of Digital Games and Entertainment Technologies, pp. 571–592. Springer, Singapore (2017). https://doi.org/10.1007/978-981-4560-50-4_32

3. Boyle, E.A., et al.: A narrative literature review of games, animations and simulations to teach research methods and statistics (2014). https://doi.org/10.1016/j.compedu.2014.01.004

4. Connolly, T.M., Boyle, E.A., Macarthur, E., Hainey, T., Boyle, J.M.: A systematic literature review of empirical evidence on computer games and serious games. Comput. Educ. **59**(2), 661–686 (2012). https://doi.org/10.1016/j.compedu.2012.03.004

5. Glaser, E.M.: An experiment in development of critical thinking. Teachers Collage Rec. **43**(5), 409–410 (1941)

6. Facione, P.A.: Testing college-level critical thinking. Lib. Educ. **72**(3), 221–31 (1986)

7. Facione, P.A.: Critical Thinking: A Statement of Expert Consensus for Purposes of Critical Thinking: A Statement of Expert Consensus for Purposes of Educational Assessment and Instruction. Research Findings and Recommendations. American Philosophical Association, pp. 1–111 (1990). http://www.eric.ed.gov/ERICWebPortal/recordDetail?accno=ED315423

8. Friedel, C., Irani, T., Rudd, R., Gallo, M., Eckhardt, E., Ricketts, J.: Overtly teaching critical thinking and inquiry-based learning: a comparison of two undergraduate biotechnology classes. J. Agric. Educ. **49**(1), 72–84 (2008)

9. Gentile, M., et al.: Using the educational potential mapper to design an adaptive serious game: The "uManager" case study (2017)

10. Hitchcock, D.: On Reasoning and Argument: Essays in Informal Logic and on Critical Thinking. Argumentation Library, vol. 30. Springer, Heidelberg (2017). https://doi.org/10.1007/978-3-319-53562-3

11. Ibrahim, D.A.W., Yana, I.H., Yinusa, S.: Measuring attitudinal disposition of undergraduate students to English language learning: the Nigerian University experience. Int. J. Res. Engl. Educ. **3**(1), 28 (2018). https://doi.org/10.29252/ijree.3.1.28

12. Irani, T., Rudd, R., Gallo, M., Ricketts, J., Friedel, C., Rhoades, E.: Critical thinking instrumentation manual. Retrieved August 11, 2011 (2007)

13. Jenicek, M., Hitchcock, D.L.: Evidence-Based Practice: Logic and Critical Thinking in Medicine. AMA, Chicago (2004)

14. Kiliç, H.E., Sen, A.I.: Turkish adaptation study of UF/EMI critical thinking disposition instrument. Egitim ve Bilim **39**(176), 1–12 (2014)

15. Krueger, N.: Entrepreneurial education in practice-part 1 the entrepreneurial mindset. OCDE, Paris (2015)

16. Lamm, A.J., Rhodes, E.B., Irani, T.A., Roberts, T.G., Snyder, L.J.U., Brendemuhl, J.: Utilizing natural cognitive tendencies to enhance agricultural education programs. J. Agric. Educ. **52**(2), 12–23 (2011)

17. Gentile, M., La Guardia, D., Dal Grande, V., Ottaviano, S., Allegra, M.: An agent based approach to design serious game. Int. J. Serious Games **1**(2), 23–33 (2014). https://doi.org/10.17083/ijsg.v1i2.17

18. McDonald, S.D.: Enhanced critical thinking skills through problem-solving games in secondary schools. Interdisc. J. E-Learn. Learn. Objects **13**, 79–96 (2017)

19. Michael, D.R., Chen, S.L.: Serious games: games that educate, train, and inform (2005). https://doi.org/10.1021/la104669k

20. Moore, B.N., Parker, R.: Critical Thinking (2011)
21. Qian, M., Clark, K.R.: Game-based learning and 21st century skills: a review of recent research. Comput. Hum. Behav. **63**, 50–58 (2016). https://doi.org/10.1016/j.chb.2016.05.023
22. Romero, M., Usart, M., Ott, M.: Can serious games contribute to developing and sustaining 21st century skills? (2015). https://doi.org/10.1177/1555412014548919
23. Smith, J.W., Clark, G.: New games, different rules - millennials are in town. J. Diversity Manage. **5**, 1–12 (2010)
24. Van Eck, R.N., Guy, M., Young, T., Winger, A.T., Brewster, S.: Project NEO: a video game to promote STEM competency for preservice elementary teachers. Technol. Knowl. Learn. **20**(3), 277–297 (2015). https://doi.org/10.1007/s10758-015-9245-9

A Learning Path in Support of Computational Thinking in the Last Years of Primary School

Laura Freina[(✉)], Rosa Bottino, and Lucia Ferlino

Institute for Educational Technologies,
Italian National Research Council, Genoa, Italy
freina@itd.cnr.it

Abstract. A learning path supporting the development of Computational Thinking skills in students of the last years of Primary School was defined and tested in a case study involving a grade 5 class and their teacher for the whole school year. The project aimed at involving all the students regardless of their personal interest, as a standard school activity. The case study proved to be successful with respect to students' interest and their ability to reach the main project's objectives. Their skills increased along the project and students demonstrated to be on the right path to develop a complete and autonomous approach to Computational Thinking. Nevertheless, a longer time span would be needed to for students to master deeply the new concepts and tools. Sometimes abstraction can be difficult and concrete activities are needed to introduce new ideas. Furthermore, students showed little autonomy and a limited use of the social aspects of the chosen programming environment. Devoting a longer time to the learning path would help fostering these skills. Finally, a close integration of the learning path with the school curriculum is envisaged.

Keywords: Computational thinking · Game making · Coding ·
Primary education

1 Introduction

In 2006, Wing [1] first drew attention to the need in everyday life to be able to think computationally. Such a need, not limited to computer scientists, but for everyday life, was defined as Computational Thinking (CT): "the thought processes involved in formulating problems and their solutions so that the solutions are represented in a form that can be effectively carried out by an information-processing agent" [2].

The discussion on the introduction of CT in school curricula is currently one of the main topics on the educational policy agenda of many countries. For example, since 2014, in Italy there has been a discussion on the introduction of computational thinking in compulsory schools (age 6–16) led by the Ministry of Education. In 2015, the Italian National Plan for Digital Schools was launched as part of a general school reform (law n. 107/2015) [3]. This plan includes different activities oriented to the introduction of computational thinking, including a national project (not compulsory for schools) proposing coding in primary school. Even if successful (e.g. Italy is the country scoring the highest number of participants in the European Code week since its introduction),

© Springer Nature Switzerland AG 2019
M. Gentile et al. (Eds.): GALA 2018, LNCS 11385, pp. 16–27, 2019.
https://doi.org/10.1007/978-3-030-11548-7_2

this plan did not have a wide and substantial impact on classroom activities and teachers' involvement. It was therefore understood that the issue had to be dealt with in a more substantial way.

The Ministry of Education has recently released a document proposing the inclusion of CT in compulsory school curricula, clarifying that this will not imply the introduction of a new subject neither in primary school nor in lower secondary school. This will probably imply that CT will be handled as a transversal subject in primary school and within the existing subjects of Mathematics and Technology in lower secondary school. This situation is not unique in Europe: as an example France, Finland, Sweden, and Norway have recently completed curricula reforms following this path [4, 5].

These indications open up new opportunities but also a number of key challenges that schools will have to face, including the problem to scale-up teachers' competences, the necessity to identify CT key concepts in order to define objectives, assessment criteria, and possible synergies and differences with other school subject, the difficulty to accommodate a new topic in already full curricula. Furthermore, the modality of introducing a CT learning path in compulsory school classes and the evaluation of its feasibility and efficacy have also to be considered.

At present, CT has not been uniquely defined. Román-González, Pérez-González and Jiménez-Fernández [6] analyze several different definitions trying to determine the cognitive abilities underlying CT. They reported six different main concepts: logic, algorithms, decomposition, patterns, abstraction and evaluation. From their analysis, it stands out that even though CT is a wider concept than coding, some CT skills can be developed through a coding activity. Furthermore, one of the indications which derives from an analysis of the literature in the field [7] and which is present in the Italian Ministry guidelines, is that a simple and amusing way to develop CT skills is through coding in a gaming environment.

2 Introducing Computational Thinking in a Game Environment

Introducing games in a learning process has shown to be motivating and engaging, making learning more attractive, and effective. This approach can be carried further by considering the development of digital games [8]. This requires students to develop a technological fluency, which, according to Kafai, implies "not only knowing how to use new technological tools but also knowing how to make things of significance with those tools and most important, develop new ways of thinking based on use of those tools" [9, p. 39].

As a matter of facts, in order to be able to develop a simple digital game, most of the basic programming concepts have to be addressed. Such an activity would well support the development of the following abilities in the students [10]:

- Understand that computers have to be told everything they are meant to do;
- Know that programs execute by following precise and unambiguous instructions;
- Create and debug simple programs;

- Manage the abstraction needed to understand and represent the problem;
- Use logical reasoning to predict the behavior of simple programs;
- Know the basic programming blocks to produce sequences of commands, loops, variables, decisions, etc.

Furthermore, a collaborative approach to game making would give students the possibility to practice their workgroup skills. As reported by Bermingham et al. [11], many studies are based on individual game making activities and peers are involved only in the evaluation phase, playing with others' games and providing feedback. A closer collaboration is envisaged as a way to increase creativity, facilitate communication, as well as enhance a sense of classroom community, which encourages students to share findings and ask and give help to peers.

A research topic that has been investigated for years at the Italian National Research Council – Institute for Educational Technologies, is related to the use of digital games to foster the development of basic skills that are transversal to several subjects in primary school students [12]. With this respect, after previous works focused on logical reasoning [13, 14], a project was carried out with some classed of a primary school with the aim of promoting students' visuospatial abilities with digital, off-the-shelf games and understand how this would affect their mathematics performance [15]. During the development of these projects, even though students did like to play with all the selected games, they showed a deeper involvement in the cases when they could be more creative and active. For example, creating virtual houses in Minecraft (a sandbox digital game where players can build with a variety of different blocks in a 3D virtual world) was particularly appreciated by nearly all the students.

Starting from this observation and on the basis the results of previous research projects on collaborative programming with tangibles carried out with students of primary schools [16], a new project focused on fostering some CT abilities through a collaborative game making activity was set up with one grade five primary school class.

3 The Defined Learning Path

3.1 Description of the Learning Path

The current educational context, as stated in the introduction, motivates the opportunity to develop feasible proposals for introducing CT in compulsory education. This paper discusses a project aimed at defining and experimenting a learning path aimed at fostering CT in students of the last years of primary schools (aged 10–11). An exploratory case study was organized to verify if the learning path would be effective in a typical school environment. The case study was designed to involve all class students, regardless of their personal interest in the subject. At present, most activities linked to CT are organized outside school hours and participation is voluntary, which means that only those students who are already interested in computing take part to the activities.

The defined learning path was organized in two phases:

- A set of 10 lessons, about one hour long, to introduce some of the basic concepts of programming and the chosen programming environment;
- A role-play in which students, working in groups, play the role of game developers creating their own digital game. The role-play spans over 10 working sessions of about one hour and a half each.

In the design of the learning path, an iterative approach based on cycles of imagination, creation, reflections and refinement as described by Resnick [17] was chosen. This approach is supposed to be central to creativity. At each meeting, a new concept was introduced (see Sect. 3.3) and students were exposed to some examples of its application. Then some time was given to them in which they could explore and try freely the new concept.

In order to support abstraction, some concrete activities were also planned to help understanding specific concepts or algorithms. For example, to be able to understand the logic behind a memory game, a real life performance was devised, where the game was played with real cards while a researcher guided students in detecting what information was needed to understand when a pair of cards was found. Students took notes and then, working with the whole class, discussed their notes and managed to reproduce the algorithm in the programming environment.

Furthermore, to guarantee a full support to the students, a complete scaffolding structure was defined starting from a theoretical analysis of the envisaged difficulties in the game making activity. Students were asked to choose a game to develop from a restricted set of game types (which they could personalize to their wish). The list of the needed competences, the specific programming skills, and foreseen difficulties related to the proposed games gave the basis for the definition of a distributed scaffolding including unstructured help from peer and experts as well as structured support.

The structured support included a complete working sample of the proposed games and, for each game, a set of descriptions at different levels of detail. Furthermore, ready-made routines were provided for the most difficult parts of the games (e.g. in a jigsaw puzzle, the routine to check the distance of the actual position of a piece of the puzzle from its final destination). A specific meeting was also planned with the whole class to solve some of the most common problems (e.g. how to detect when all the pieces of a puzzle are in place).

3.2 Choice of the Programming Environment

Scratch [18], created by the MIT Media Lab (http://scratch.mit.edu), is especially designed for children from the age of eight up. Scratch is a playful visual programming environment, where instructions are given to the computer using programming blocks, which can be moved with the mouse and joined together like traditional building blocks. This approach avoids syntax errors and simplifies the programmer's work. Blocks are characterized by their color and are grouped according to their meaning. Moreover, Scratch can be accesses online, allowing students to continue their work outside the planned school activities.

Furthermore, Scratch is a social environment, where projects can be shared and commented, offering, in such a way, a wide collection of source code to copy from and stimulating ideas in support of creativity.

3.3 Programming Concepts

The learning path was oriented at introducing some of the basic CT concepts through a coding activity in a playful environment with the final aim of developing simple digital games. In the defined path, the developing activities have been focused on a limited set of games, addressing the following concepts:

- Variables, needed for the management of the player's score and in some games to be able to count the cards in order to understand when the game ends;
- The "if ... then ... else" block to manage different alternatives;
- Loops: for example, in the labyrinth there is a continuous check of the current position to avoid crossing walls;
- Synchronization of events to allow something to happen only when the game finishes or starts.

These concepts were chosen as they are at the basis of coding and are suitable to students of the chosen age. In the first part of the project, these concepts were presented along with several exercises to help students completely understand and remember them. In the second part of the project, a role-play was organized in which students, working in groups, played the role of game developers creating their own digital game. A restricted set of games, described in Sect. 4.3, was offered to choose from in order to limit the complexity of the coding activity.

4   The Case Study

4.1   Description

After the learning path was completely defined, a single explorative case study was set up to verify how effective it would be in an Italian school environment. The aim was to identify the main problems and issues in the use of the learning path, allowing for later adaptations to best match it to the school needs. The choice of testing the learning path through a case study was needed because the evaluation had to happen in a typical classroom, involving directly the class teacher, in the target context [19].

The case study, organized in a primary school in Genova (Italy), involved one grade 5 class (24 students, 13 boys and 11 girls). The class teacher was an active part in the whole project, along with four trainee teachers from the University of Genova who offered students some technical help and observed them at work during the meetings. Researchers, who were present at all the meetings, supported the class teacher in organizing the activities before the meetings and occasionally offered some technical support to the students.

4.2 Project Activities

Twenty meetings were organized, once a week, from November 2017 to April 2018. All the activities were part of the normal school curriculum and took place during school hours, either in the classroom or in the school computer lab.

The learning path was structured into two phases: an introduction to the Scratch programming environment during the first 10 meetings, followed by the role play in which students, organized into little groups, developed a simple digital game.

During the first phase of the project, after each meeting, students were asked to write a short diary of their experience. They were provided with a structured sheet where to report what they had done, state what they liked best, write about problems they had found and say something about their plans for the following meeting. They could also indicate their appreciation by choosing an emoticon (a smiley, a neutral or a sad face). Texts from all the collected diaries were typed and analyzed.

In the second phase of the project, students were organized in groups of four and played the role of software developers by building a complete and working prototype of a digital game, one for each group, including the basic game mechanics. The developed games were:

- **Labyrinth.** A typical labyrinth with coins to be collected before reaching the exit.
- **Memory.** A set of cards, containing two copies of each card, was shown with the cards upside down, and the player had to find the two cards that were the same (two different versions of memory games were implemented).
- **A jigsaw puzzle with no rotation.** An anime image was broken into pieces and the player had to put it back together by moving the pieces to their correct place.
- **A jigsaw puzzle with rotation only.** A football field was broken and the player had to fix it by rotating the pieces to make them match.
- **Educational Balloons.** Balloons of different color and shape raised in the air, when the player clicked a balloon, it burst and a question on a school subject was asked. The subject was linked to the looks of the balloons, for example, the blue M-shaped balloon triggered a Math question. If the answer was correct, the player got a point.

4.3 Collected Data

At the end of the project, students filled in a questionnaire addressing their appreciation of the Scratch programming environment and the project activities; their evaluation of the support received, including written materials, trainee teachers, class teacher, and researchers; their evaluation of the group work and an overall score out of 10 to the project (the final average score was 8.04).

Moreover, all students were interviewed at the end of the project by a researcher. The structured interviews aimed at verifying how much students were aware of the work done, if they remembered some problems they met and how they were solved, and if they would be able to solve those same problems independently. A sheet with 10 questions was used to guide the interviews, but students were free to add any observation or comment to their wish. All the interviews were recorded, typed and then analyzed.

Finally, a short multiple-choice test was given to the students to assess what they learnt of the Scratch programming environment.

5 Some Reflections on the Students' Work

5.1 Students' Autonomy

At the start of the project, a learning path was defined aimed at the collaborative development of a digital game by students. A creative project oriented approach was chosen, trying as much as possible to push students to be creative and to explore freely Scratch. Nevertheless, at the beginning of the case study, it was immediately noticed that students needed a closer guidance: when left free, they tended to stop working and were generally lacking the ability to pursue their own objectives. They became more positive and active as a larger number of specific exercises was assigned at each meeting.

The analysis of the texts from student diaries supports this observation. Diaries were organized into four sections: Report (what was done during the meeting), Like (something they particularly liked), Issues (a problem they met) and Next Time (plans for the following meeting). Texts from the diaries were coded by one researcher and two trainee teachers independently and then the results of the coding activity was merged. The identified topics were then grouped into the following categories:

- *Scratch* – all about coding and Scratch in general;
- *Work Management* – planning the work, finishing what was started, etc.;
- *Social Issues* – working with peers, sharing projects, looking at peer's work or working alone;
- *Attitudes* – attention and commitment, as well as generic difficulties (e.g. a girl wrote "mi sento confusa" – I feel confused);
- *Logistics* –problems with electricity, headphones, speakers, room, etc.;
- *Play activities* – playing with the finished games, either the student's own project or other's projects available on Scratch.

Diaries showed that in the Report, Like and Issues sections, more than 70% of the topics were about Scratch, against 27% in the "Next Time" section (Fig. 1). When students had to write about their plans for the following meeting, most of them did not think about the technical work they could do, but rather about attitudes ("I'll pay more attention", "I will not make mistakes", etc., for a total of 41%). This shows that most students tended not to have a specific plan for the following meeting.

In the second phase of the project, at the beginning of the game making activity, a free exploration, trial and error approach was pushed and help was given only when students asked for it. After a short time, as some groups showed the need for more guidance, written instructions were offered. At the end of the project, the interviews and the final questionnaire showed that while some students still felt the need to be guided, others were starting to be more independent.

In the final questionnaire, students were asked if they thought that the instructions they received were useful or not. Half of them affirmed that they would have liked to have them earlier and 20.83% said that they just followed the given instructions without completely understanding what they were doing. The remaining 29.17% of the students affirmed that they only used instructions partly, and did the rest autonomously (12.50%) or they would have preferred to continue without the instructions (16.67%) (Fig. 2). According to this result, nearly 30% of the students show a greater level of independence and autonomy in their work.

With this respect, the learning path should nurture more an autonomous and creative approach, by spending more time during the first phase in giving students a large set of short exercises and letting them approach each task with an incremental amount of autonomy, while gradually fading the given support, as stated in the theory of scaffolding [20]. Students need to learn gradually not to rely too much on a close guidance from their teacher and be more active in managing their own work.

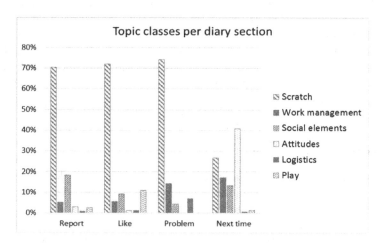

Fig. 1. Topics per diary section (from the students' diaries)

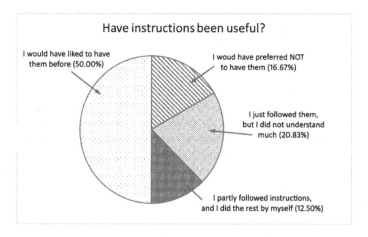

Fig. 2. Students' opinion about instructions (from the students' questionnaires)

5.2   Use of the Scratch Programming Environment

Scratch was chosen because it can be accessed both from school and from home, assuming that students would continue their exploration outside school hours, but this assumption was proven false. Only two out of 24 students actually connected outside school hours, and the class never went to the computer lab outside the hours devoted to the project. Consequently, more than one meeting was needed for every new concept and a number of exercises were added to help understanding and memorization. Likewise, those topics that were not central for the games to be developed were dropped or just outlined (animations, music, microphone and camera management, etc.).

In the final interview, less than half of the students affirmed that they looked at the existing Scratch projects for inspiration before starting to develop their game; none searched Scratch on-line environment with the aim of finding parts of code and most of the interest for other people's projects were related with the possibility to play with ready-made games.

This observation is closely linked to the students' autonomy in managing their own work. Most of them just did the task that was assigned, and their curiosity was limited. As stated earlier, spending more time on small tasks with an incremental request of autonomy may lead students to a more curious and creative approach as they increment their self-confidence and acquire a deeper knowledge of the programming environment.

5.3   Programming in Scratch

As for programming, all the groups demonstrated to be able to develop their game at the end of the project, even though most of them still needed some level of scaffolding. Different levels of fluency were noticed within the class, ranging from those who demonstrated to be able to solve simple problems without help, to others who still needed a close guidance. In general, students were observed during their work, noticing that often they were not immediately sure about how to overcome their technical problems. Nevertheless, they usually managed to find help from peers, and often found the solution without the intervention of the adults.

At the final test aiming at assessing what students learnt of the Scratch programming environment, 75% of the students managed to pass the test, showing to have memorized and understood the most common instructions.

Nevertheless, moving and rotating objects was considered a difficult task up to the end of the project. In the students' diaries, 48.19% of the reported issues related to Scratch were about objects and backgrounds, and 67.5% of these regarded moving or rotating objects. In the second part of the project, the issue was not completely solved. At the final test on Scratch, one question showed the script needed to move an object with the arrow keys, and 39.13% of the students still had problems in recognizing it.

Some students at this age still need to ground their concepts into concrete activities before moving to a virtual approach, which requires a certain level of abstraction. Before introducing the movement of objects on the screen, a tangible session based on moving a physical object by giving it the needed commands, would help understanding deeply the underlying concept. Students who worked on the Labyrinth game showed a greater confidence with respect to being able to move an object with the arrow keys, showing that they need a longer time to think about, try out and reason on the new concepts, and in those cases in which this has been possible, results were obtained.

All the developed games were a simplified version of the original games. However, in all cases, a complicated issue was considered and dealt with. To make the Memory games simpler, cards were not shuffled at the start of the game, but students had to devise a routine to detect the correct pairs of cards. Both jigsaw puzzle games had to check the position and rotation of the pieces and count the remaining cards to the end of the game. The Educational Balloons game requested to manage a list of questions and match them with the correct answer. All these concepts have been successfully turned into functioning algorithms by the students, even if often with some support from the adults. Students always participated actively and, in most cases, showed to have fully understood the algorithms.

5.4   Role of the Class Teacher

The class teacher was already ICT competent and was one of the reference teachers for the school ICT projects. Before the start of the project, she followed an online course on Scratch and analysed all the proposed activities in order to be well prepared for the meetings with the students. Nonetheless, this preparation was not enough to cope with the complexity of the project and sometimes she needed technical support. This is a key element to consider when organizing this kind of activities: teachers need to have a deep knowledge of CT and coding, which usually goes well beyond the basic skills usually required by the Italian schools.

During the meetings in the school computer lab, students worked in groups and, especially at the beginning, they often asked for help. One teacher is not enough to support the whole class. In the present experience, two trainee teachers and a researcher were present at each meeting with the objective of observing the groups at work, but they often had to provide help to the students, both with respect to coding issues and work organization. In order to manage correctly such a project, a group of CT competent teachers working together is recommended, possibly with specific knowledge of the chosen coding environment. This would allow for an adequate support both for students and for teachers themselves.

6   Conclusions and Future Work

A learning path fostering computational thinking skills through a game making activity in the last years of an Italian primary school was defined and then tested in a case study involving one grade 5 class. Unlike other experiences, participation was not on a voluntary base, but the whole class and their teacher played an active role in the project.

Results from the case study showed some strengths and weaknesses of the defined learning path. Among the main strengths, the role-play was proved highly motivating. Every group managed to create a complete game prototype, which was presented at an end-of-year meeting with the families and the head of the school with great satisfaction of all the students. Some difficult concepts or algorithms are best introduced with the use of tangible examples. This has been successfully done for some algorithms related to the games (e.g. in the Memory game, the identification of a pair of equal cards), and should be extended to other concepts to make them more easily understandable. For example, students may start moving a physical object on a grid on the floor before dealing with digital objects moving along virtual paths on the screen.

In the project, students' autonomous exploration of Scratch was rare, and most of them only did what they were asked to do. However, some improvement has been noticed during the project. In a future experiment, a larger number of easy activities based on a recursive learning cycle that can be completed in a short time may guide students towards a more autonomous, creative and active approach to learning. More time should be given to foster students' free creations after prompting them with a simple task. Sharing and discussing their work with peers should also be pushed more, in order to stimulate a reflection on their experience, and generate new ideas [17]. Furthermore, students need a lot of time and practice before being able to take full advantage of the social advantages offered by Scratch. They tend not to share their creations, look for inspiration or search for help to overcome specific issues, limiting peer support to classmates. In this case, intermediate steps may be devised, as the creation of a class level sharing space promoting search and discussion. With practice, students would learn how to productively search, share and comment in a constructive manner.

In order to support fully the whole class, more than one teacher needs to be involved, and all the staff is required to be competent with respect to the CT and coding.

The overall time available was too short with respect to the objectives that were initially planned. With respect to this problem, a one-year project may work better if focused on a limited range of concepts, aiming at the development of different versions of one game only. In future projects, the revised learning path will be tested more deeply, allowing for a longer periods of time, spanning over several school years, and concentrating each year on a smaller number of concepts.

References

1. Wing, J.M.: Computational thinking. Commun. ACM **49**(3), 33–35 (2006)
2. Wing, J.: Research Notebook: Computational Thinking - What and Why? The Link. Carneige Mellon, Pittsburgh (2011)
3. PNSD: Piano Nazionale Scuola Digitale. http://www.istruzione.it/scuola_digitale/allegati/Materiali/pnsd-layout-30.10-WEB.pdf. Accessed 22 June 2018
4. Bocconi, S., Chioccariello, A., Dettori, G., Ferrari, A., Engelhardt, K.: Developing computational thinking in compulsory education – Implications for policy and practice; EUR 28295 EN (2016). https://doi.org/10.2791/792158
5. Bocconi, S., Chioccariello, A., Earp, J.: The Nordic approach to introducing Computational Thinking and programming in compulsory education. Report prepared for the Nordic@-BETT2018 Steering Group (2018). https://doi.org/10.17471/54007

6. Román-González, M., Pérez-González, J.C., Jiménez-Fernández, C.: Which cognitive abilities underlie computational thinking? criterion validity of the computational thinking test. Comput. Hum. Behav. **72**, 678–691 (2017)
7. Kafai, Y.B.: Connected gaming: an inclusive perspective for serious gaming. Int. J. Serious Games **4**(3) (2017). https://doi.org/10.17083/ijsg.v4i3.174
8. Earp, J., Dagnino, F.M., Caponetto, I.: An Italian Pilot Experience in Game Making for Learning. In: Zhang, J., Yang, J., Chang, M., Chang, T. (eds) ICT in Education in Global Context, pp. 171–199. Springer, Singapore (2016). https://doi.org/10.1007/978-981-10-0373-8_9
9. Kafai, Y.B.: Playing and making games for learning: instructionist and constructionist perspectives for game studies. Games Cult. **1**(1), 36–40 (2006)
10. Zaharija, G., Mladenović, S., Boljat, I.: Introducing basic programming concepts to elementary school children. Procedia Soc. Behav. Sci. **106**, 1576–1584 (2013)
11. Bermingham, S., et al.: Approaches to collaborative game-making for fostering 21st century skills. In: European Conference on Games Based Learning, p. 45. Academic Conferences International Limited (2013)
12. Bottino, R.M., Ott, M., Tavella, M.: The impact of mind game playing on children's reasoning abilities: reflections from an experience. In: Conolly, T., Stansfield, M. (eds) Proceedings of 2nd European Conference on Game-Based learning, Barcelona, Spain, pp. 51–57. Academic Publishing Ltd, Reading (2008)
13. Bottino, R.M., Ott, M.: Mind games, reasoning skills, and the primary school curriculum: hints from a field experiment. Learn. Media Technol. **31**(4), 359–375 (2006)
14. Freina, L., Bottino, R., Ferlino, L., Tavella, M.: Training of spatial abilities with digital games: impact on mathematics performance of primary school students. In: Proceedings of the Game and Learning Alliance International Conference (GALA), Lisbon, Portugal, 5–7 December 2017
15. Freina, L., Bottino, R.: Visuospatial abilities training with digital games in a primary school. Int. J. Serious Games **5**(3), 23–35 (2018)
16. Bottino, R.M., Chioccariello, A.: Computational thinking: videogames, educational robotics, and other powerful ideas to think with. KEYCIT - Key Competencies in Informatics and ICT, pp. 184–189. University of Potsdam, Potsdam (2014)
17. Resnick, M.: All I really need to know (about creative thinking) I learned (by studying how children learn) in kindergarten. In: Proceedings of the 6th ACM SIGCHI Conference on Creativity & Cognition, pp. 1–6. ACM (2007)
18. Resnick, M., et al.: Scratch: programming for all. Commun. ACM **52**(11), 60–67 (2009)
19. Yin, R.K.: Case Study Research: Design and Methods. Sage, Thousands Oaks (2003)
20. Pea, R.D.: The social and technological dimensions of scaffolding and related theoretical concepts for learning, education, and human activity. J. Learn. Sci. **13**(3), 423–451 (2004)

ALF - A Framework for Evaluating Accelerated Learning and Cognitive Skills Development in Industry Through Games

Sobah Abbas Petersen[1(✉)], Manuel Oliveira[1], Kristin Hestetun[2], and Anette Østbø Sørensen[1]

[1] SINTEF Digital, Trondheim, Norway
{sobah.petersen,manuel.oliveira,
AnetteOstbo.Sorensen}@sintef.no
[2] Hydro Primary Metal Technologies, Årdal, Norway
Kristin.Hestetun@hydro.com

Abstract. Games have long been considered as a means to support effective learning, motivate learners and accelerate their learning. Several successful studies using game-based learning are reported in the literature. However, there appears to be a research gap on systematically evaluating accelerated learning in game environments. The main research question we address in this paper is how can we evaluate accelerated learning in game-based learning environments? The main contribution of this paper will be a framework for evaluating accelerated learning in games (ALF). We will illustrate the use of this framework by describing studies conducted in the Norwegian industrial project ALTT (Accelerate Learning Through Technology), aimed at capacity building in the aluminium industry, where we have co-designed a game for accelerating learning about the electrolysis process for extracting aluminium and heat balance in the aluminium production cells.

Keywords: Accelerated learning · Game-based learning ·
Cognitive skills · Workplace learning

1 Introduction

Many industries are experiencing significant changes due to digitisation of the workplace. As such, employees are faced with new demands for cognitive skills and challenged to acquire them rapidly. Many organisations have recognised this need and are looking at new means of engaging employees and using novel and digital solutions for accelerating learning in the workplace. Successful engagement of employees in their work are seen in organisations that invest in the employee experience [1].

The use of games, as a means to support effective learning, motivate learners and accelerate their learning; e.g. [2, 3], has gained increased interest by manufacturing and process industries in recent years. Although there is growing evidence in literature of successful studies using Game-Based Learning (GBL), there remains a research gap on systematically evaluating accelerated learning with GBL in workplaces. While GBL claims it can accelerate learning, there are no frameworks that explicitly address this.

© Springer Nature Switzerland AG 2019
M. Gentile et al. (Eds.): GALA 2018, LNCS 11385, pp. 28–38, 2019.
https://doi.org/10.1007/978-3-030-11548-7_3

Furthermore, the transferability of what is learned to the real world is often neglected in the evaluations. This paper presents a framework for evaluating accelerated learning in games, ALF. Our main research question is how can we evaluate accelerated learning in game-based learning environments at the workplace? We draw inspiration from the work done by the Serious Game community (e.g. [2, 4]) and the research in adult learning (e.g. [5, 6]). We illustrate the use of this framework by describing studies conducted in the Norwegian industrial project ALTT (Accelerate Learning Through Technology), aimed at capacity building in the aluminium industry, where we have co-designed a game for accelerating learning in the process industry – ALTT Heat Balance game. The project partners are the Norwegian aluminium producer Hydro, Attensi who develops gamified training solutions, Cybernetica who develops simulation models for dynamic process control and SINTEF.

Using the seven principles of accelerated learning from [6], we broaden the perspectives of learning traditionally adopted in serious games studies, where learning is considered beyond the knowledge retained after an intervention and considers the transformation of the learner's attitudes, motivation, confidence and reflection. As such, we discuss the potential to support accelerated learning in games and how to evaluate it.

The rest of this paper is organized as follows: Sect. 2 provides a background on accelerated learning; Sect. 3 presents the ALF; Sect. 4 describes the ALTT Heat Balance game and evaluation of learning; Sect. 5 discusses evaluation of accelerated learning using the ALTT Heat Balance game and finally Sect. 6 concludes the paper.

2 Accelerated Learning

Accelerated Learning has been defined as "faster attainment of skill and knowledge, and an increase in on-the-job performance with better retention of learning" [5]. Other definitions also focus on the time factor; e.g. "any learning system that attempts to optimize time spent learning versus content learned" [7]. Learning in the process industry as in any other, the amount of time spent by personnel in training corresponds to productivity loss and is usually associated to a cost rather than an investment. Consequently, there is a strong desire to reduce the time to competence [8]. In addition, the depletion of knowledge over time, or retention, is seen as an important factor [5].

Within the context of adult learning and training, accelerated learning takes a multidimensional approach and places the learner in the centre [9]. The origins of a "whole-body, whole-mind, whole-person experience" learning process was proposed by Meier [6]. This approach makes the use of multisensory learning environments, brings the ideas from Howard Gardner's multiple intelligences and makes use of both the right and left brain of a person. Meier's work has been used by several authors as the seven guiding principles of accelerated learning [10]: (i) learning involves the whole mind and body; (ii) learning is creation, not consumption; (iii) collaboration aids learning; (iv) learning takes place on many levels simultaneously; (v) learning comes from doing the work itself (with feedback); (vi) positive emotions greatly improve learning; and (vii) the image brain absorbs information instantly and automatically.

Several accelerated learning methods have been discussed in the literature and the evaluation of the learning outcome is important to determine the efficiency of the learning method. A set of features and characteristics proposed to evaluate the methods are based on three features: planning, application and deep understanding [3]. Planning involves engaging the learners when introducing new material and illustrating the use of the knowledge. Application involves the learner demonstrating the use of the knowledge and the consequences of applying the knowledge. Deep understanding involves engaging the learner on reflection upon her own learning and self-assessment of the application of the knowledge.

3   ALF - Framework for Evaluating Accelerated Learning in Games

Frameworks exist for the selection of an appropriate game for learning, e.g. [2], to help educators in choosing the right pedagogic approach and a game. The ideas from this framework by de Freitas et al. have later been developed as a framework for evaluating learning as immersive experiences [11]. This framework identified four dimensions: model or profile of the learner, the pedagogical aspects such as current knowledge of the learner, the context and the representation of it, such as the interactive nature. Mayor et al. proposed a comprehensive conceptual framework to support the design, data gathering and evaluation of serious games [4]. Mayor et al.'s framework takes into account the pre- and post-game conditions such as the learners' knowledge and attitudes; mediating variables such as learning styles and the context of learning. Furthermore, it provides guidelines for ensuring the quality of the intervention and data gathering for the evaluation. While these frameworks provide ideas for the evaluation of learning, they lack explicit support for the evaluation of accelerated learning using games, in particular, in adult learning at the workplace.

Based on the literature and existing frameworks for evaluating learning and serious games, we have identified three perspectives as central for supporting accelerated learning; the cognitive and affective domains [12] and the context of learning. Affective learning relates to the learner's emotions, interests, attitudes, and motivations [13, 14]. Bridging ideas from effective learning design, Vygotsky's ZPD [15] and Flow theory are important in the design of games for accelerating learning, to ensure that learners are engaged in an activity that is appropriately challenging to one's skill level. Gee uses the term "pleasantly frustrating" to describe the play to be challenging without being unmanageable for the learners [16]. Furthermore, contextualizing the learning so that the learners could practice in a relevant virtual environment and the potential to easily transfer what they have learnt to their work situations is important [17]. The synergy among these three perspectives is important for accelerating learning. These ideas and concepts are consolidated in ALF, which is illustrated in Fig. 1.

The cognitive-affective perspectives are relevant for determining good learning design, planning the learning progression and ensuring the right level of help or designing scaffolding. Similarly, the synergy between the affective domain and the learning context can support experiential learning and transferability of the learning to the work context. Finally, the synergy between the learning context and the cognitive domain can support the design of the appropriate learning content and activities to ensure deep understanding. These perspectives have similarities to the framework for evaluating learning as immersive experiences by de Freitas et al. [11]. By considering the synergy between two perspectives, we address all the dimensions identified by de Freitas et al. such as pedagogy and the learner profile and model; e.g. the learner profile will be relevant information in determining the appropriate content: synergy between the cognitive and context perspectives.

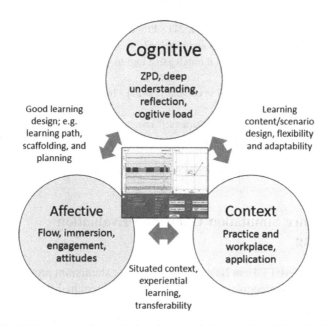

Fig. 1. Main concepts in evaluation framework for accelerated learning (ALF)

ALF, illustrated in Fig. 1, can be elaborated further to apply the ideas in the evaluation of accelerated learning. We have categorized the criteria and guiding principles for accelerated learning from the literature into the three perspectives, shown in Table 1. The criteria relevant for evaluating accelerated learning and types of activities that could be done in the evaluations are described. Some of the criteria address more than one of the perspectives; e.g. reflection is a cognitive support while it can reinforce the learning context. Similarly, feedback applies to both the cognitive and affective domains, e.g. a hint or clue is in the cognitive domain while a reward (as a feedback) is in the affective domain.

Table 1. ALF criteria for evaluating accelerated learning in games

Perspectives	Criteria and evaluation activities
Cognitive	Reflection and reflective practice [18] - In-game or post-game, through interviews and discussions
	Preferred learning Style [19] - Pre- and post-game: self-reported attitudes
	Creation, not consumption [6] - In-game: active learner through game logs, learner contributions
Affective	Emotional engagement [14, 20] - In-game: through game logs. Post-game: Self reported
	Attitudes and motivation [14, 21] - Pre- and post-game: Self reported
	Involves the whole mind and body [6]
	Feedback [6] - In-game: through game logs to see if the learner's play is affected by the feedback
Context	Learning by doing, and in context [22–24] - In-game: through game logs. Post-game: self reported
	Transferability [5] - Post-game: self reported
	Collaborative and social learning [6] - In-game: through game logs. Post-game: self reported
	Images, visuals [6] - In-game: through game logs. Post-game: self reported

4 Heat Balance Simulation Game and Evaluation of Learning

The context for the ALTT Heat Balance game was the aluminium production cells and the heat balance in the electrolysis process. The domain required the understanding of the dependencies among the parameters temperature, acidity, superheat and the liquidus temperature. Since the electrolysis process is a dynamic process, a key design decision was to implement a dynamic process model of the cell that could simulate future states of the cell. The actions in the game can be translated as parameter values for the dynamic process model. The gameplay is based on rounds, each corresponding to a 24-h time period, and the game environment calls the associated dynamic process model to obtain the new status of the model, based on the actions taken by the player.

As illustrated in Fig. 2, the game is designed around a 9 cell matrix, with axes showing the bath temperature and the superheat – the 9-box model. This is the essence of the conceptual model that captures the interdependencies of the aforementioned parameters associated to the electrolysis process. The current state of a production cell is shown as a dot position in the 9-box model. The other main GUI component is the cell's historical information, which is shown as a set of graphs, which include information on resistance, fluoride additions, acidity and bath temperature. The game is played by selecting one or more actions that will be taken on a cell, shown bottom right of the GUI. The actions available in the game are changing the resistance and the amount of fluoride (acidity) in the cell, wait without taking any action or add soda to the cell. Once an action is taken, the graphs and the 9-box model are updated with the new state of the cell, calculated using the dynamic process model.

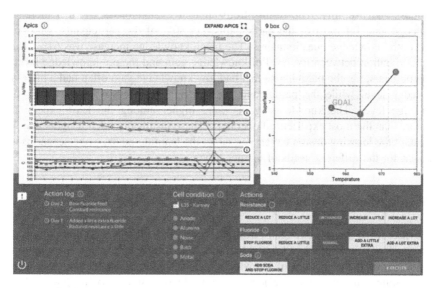

Fig. 2. Screenshot of a game session of the ALTT heat balance game

The game was co-designed with the operators and domain experts to ensure its relevance for the workplace and to understand the context of learning as well as to engage the end users from the beginning. Inspirations from Cognitive Task Analysis (CTA) methods, (e.g. [25]), were used to understand the typical problems faced during a working day, operators' cognitive challenges and the cues and hints that help them understand their tasks and the domain knowledge. Learning path and progression and functionality to support reflection and timely and appropriate feedback were explicitly considered during the design process; e.g. see [26].

4.1 Evaluation of Learning

The evaluation method was based on knowledge tests, combined with self-reporting (e.g. questionnaires) and in-game session log data [4]. We have conducted 4 summative evaluations with operators, across 4 aluminium production plants. Two of the evaluations (8 and 28 participants) were based on pre- and post-intervention evaluations, where questionnaires and interviews were used. The other two evaluations (12 and 16 participants) were conducted, where the game was used as a part of a classroom course to support reflection. In both these cases, the trainer was able to observe and interact with the participants during the course. The participants also completed questionnaires specifically designed for these courses. In addition, we have conducted numerous formative evaluations, where the operators were asked to play in pairs and talk aloud, play individually followed by a focus group discussion or individual interviews and observations by the project team.

The pre and post knowledge questionnaires were designed to evaluate the knowledge gain by playing the game. The pre-intervention background and post-intervention questionnaires included other aspects such as attitudes, perceptions, usefulness and usability. The results from all four evaluations show that there was knowledge gain for most of the participants, i.e. 80% of the participants, who completed both knowledge questionnaires. The mean knowledge increase was 61%. There was a correlation between the level of knowledge gain and the pre-knowledge level of the participants; i.e. the participants that had low knowledge gain often had a high pre-knowledge level while the participants with a high knowledge gain had less pre-knowledge level. The knowledge gains were higher among the least experienced operators than the most experienced operators. These results provided insights that will help adapt the learning design better; e.g. adapt the learning paths, game scenarios and feedback for the different needs of learner groups.

5 Evaluation of Accelerated Learning

The evidence of knowledge gain from the pre- and post-intervention knowledge questionnaires is not sufficient to establish that the learning took place faster than any other means or if the amount of knowledge gained or the understanding was indeed greater within that time. In our project, it was not feasible to use control groups due to operational reasons within the company. In response to the constraints of conducting evaluation studies within real industrial settings involving operators with different levels of expertise, we used the ALF framework to design the pre- and post-intervention questionnaires to ensure that the criteria and the principles of accelerated learning are taken into account. Questions were included that addressed the three perspectives of ALF. In the following paragraphs, we discuss how ALF has been used to evaluate accelerated learning using the ALTT Heat Balance game.

Cognitive Perspective: One of the most important feedback we have received from both formative and summative evaluations is that the game helped learners understand the dynamic process by seeing the causality of their decisions immediately, which was one of their cognitive challenges (note: in real life this could take days as the chemical processes in the aluminium production cells are slow). The learners expressed that the most important role of the game was "*to be able to see the consequences of your actions*", and "*learn from your mistakes*". The game was designed to encourage a **reflective practice**, where the operators are expected to review the current status by looking at the history of the cell and to anticipate the consequences of their actions on the cell [26] (in-game). Game logs show that learners use the support for reflection in the game. In addition, the post-intervention questionnaires from the studies show a positive response towards the functionalities in the game to support reflection, (see Fig. 3; the statement "the game can help me reflect better on what I have learned..."). The **preferred learning style** was evaluated by asking the learners if they think that games are a good way to learn and the data shows that over 80% of the participants either agree or strongly agree (Fig. 3). **Creation and not consumption** was considered in the interactive game design and by adding functionality to make the players take intentional actions and game logs confirm that they do.

Affective Perspective: Observations during all studies indicated engagement by the learners (note that observation and talk aloud were used as methods during most of the formative/iterative design related studies). **Emotional engagement, attitudes and motivation** were evaluated using questionnaire data which indicate a positive attitude towards learning about Heat Balance, an increase in the learners' confidence and perceived understanding. Several statements were included in the questionnaires and the responses show positive results (see Fig. 3). For the statement "I think games can be a good way to learn", over 80% of the learners agree or strongly agree, although the post-intervention results were less positive than the pre-intervention results. Over 70% agreed or strongly agreed that they understand the basic concepts and relationships better after playing the game and the statement related to learners' confidence show an improvement in the post-intervention results. Interviews and questionnaire data show that learners were positive towards the **feedback** and hints provided in the game. Feedback was provided within the game in many ways; e.g. by showing how the anticipated consequences of their actions differed from the actual consequences, and by letting them know when they were one or two turns away from winning the game. Hints were provided as information icons and suggestions when they were repeating the same mistake. Preliminary analyses of the play patterns from the game logs show play patterns where it is evident that learners respond to the feedback from the game to improve their scores. At the end of each game scenario, the player is provided a score and feedback as stars and glitter and several participants found this visual feedback encouraging.

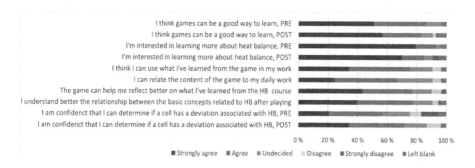

Fig. 3. Using ALF for evaluating accelerated learning

Context: **Learning by doing** was evaluated using open-ended questions in the studies where the game was a part of a classroom course, to support reflection. The data indicates that the game complements the theory by enabling the learners to experience trial and error in the game environment (see Fig. 3). One learner expressed that "*it's much easier to understand the theory when one gets to test oneself*". **Transferability** and a realistic game was a criterion and the iterative design and evaluation approach ensured this. The dynamic process model and the simulations from the model visualised by the graphs on the user interface made the game realistic, thus supporting easy transfer of what is learnt in the game to the real work situation. Post-intervention evaluations show that the learners think they can use what they've learned from the game in their work and they can relate the contents to their daily work, (see Fig. 3). Over 60% of the learners agreed or strongly agreed to the statement "I can relate the contents of the game to my work". Similarly, over 70% of the learners agreed or strongly agreed to the statement "I think I can use what I've learnt from the game in my work". The game is designed primarily for supporting individuals rather than **social and collaborative** learning. However, the participants have expressed that playing in pairs and using the game to support discussions and collective reflection among peers is helpful to their understanding. In addition, the expert users, who often take a mentor role for the novices, have identified the game as an important medium to help the novices understand the dynamic process and the complex dependencies and expressed a need for the game to support discussions at the workplace. The **visualisation** of the cell in different ways (e.g. the graphs, the 9-box model and others) that relate theory and operations (the graphs are what they use at work) support understanding and transfer of the knowledge.

6   Conclusions and Future Work

Frameworks for the design and evaluation of serious games exist and most of them focus on the evaluation of learning. While GBL claims it can accelerate learning, there are no frameworks that explicitly address this. This paper presents a framework for evaluating accelerated learning, ALF, where the cognitive, affective and contextual perspectives and the synergies among them were central concepts of the framework. The main research question addressed in this paper is how can we evaluate accelerated learning in GBL environments at the workplace? The use of the framework is described using the results from four summative evaluations with the end users.

The framework itself emerged simultaneously with the design of the game and the evaluation studies. This is perhaps not uncommon in industry and innovation projects. Nevertheless, since the game had an iterative design process, the central ideas of the framework influenced the design of the game and the evaluation method and material. Relevant results from the evaluations are discussed in the paper to illustrate how the ALTT Heat Balance game can support accelerated learning.

We are currently working on a comprehensive evaluation of the framework and a detailed analysis of the evaluation results. Based on the results we have so far, further evaluations studies are planned, with focus on accelerated learning using games and to address specific issues with specific user groups.

Acknowledgements. The authors would like to thank the Norwegian Research Council and the project participants from Hydro, Attensi, Cybernetica and SINTEF.

References

1. Morgan, J., Why the Millions We Spend on Employee Engagement Buy Us So Little. Harvard Business Review (2017)
2. De Freitas, S., Oliver, M.: How can exploratory learning with games and simulations within the curriculum be most effectively evaluated? Comput. Educ. **46**, 249–264 (2006)
3. Oliveira, M., Andersen, B., Torvatn, H.: Rapid competence development. In: Wild, F., Lefrere, P., Scott, P. (eds.) Advances in Technology Enhanced Learning. Open University Press, New York (2013)
4. Mayer, I., et al.: The research and evaluation of serious games: toward a comprehensive methodology. Br. J. Educ. Technol. **45**(3), 502–527 (2014)
5. Andrews, D.H., Fitzgerald, P.C.: Accelerating Learning of Competence and Increasing Long-term Learning Retention. U.S. Air Force Research Laboratory, Warfighter Readiness Research Division: Arizona (2010)
6. Meier, D.: The Accelerated Learning Handbook: A Creative Guide to Designing and Delivering Faster, More Effective Training Programs. McGraw-Hill Education - Europe, New York (2000)
7. Sottilare, R., Goldberg, B.: Designing adaptive computer-based tutoring systems to accelerate learning and facilitate retention. Cognitive Technology **17**(1), 19–33 (2012)
8. Serdyukov, P.: Accelerated learning: what is it? J. Res. Innov. Teach. **1**(1), 35–59 (2008)
9. Imel, S.: Accelerated learning in adult education and training and development. In: Trends and Issues Alert. Clearinghouse on Adult, Career, and Vocational Education (2002)
10. The guiding principles of accelerated learning. 2016 [cited 2018 8 May]. https://www.hma.co.nz/wp-content/uploads/2016/01/The-guiding-principles-of-accelerated-learning.pdf
11. De Freitas, S., et al.: Learning as immersive experiences: using the four-dimensional framework for designing and evaluating immersive learning experiences in a virtual world. Br. J. Educ. Technol. **41**(1), 69–85 (2010)
12. Bloom, B.S.: Taxonomy of Educational Objectives, Handbook I: The Cognitive Domain. David McKay Co Inc., New York (1956)
13. Bamidis, Panagiotis D.: Affective learning: principles, technologies, practice. In: Frasson, C., Kostopoulos, G. (eds.) Brain Function Assessment in Learning. LNCS (LNAI), vol. 10512, pp. 1–13. Springer, Cham (2017). https://doi.org/10.1007/978-3-319-67615-9_1
14. Picard, R.W., et al.: Affective learning—a manifesto. BT Technol. J. **22**(4), 253–269 (2004)
15. Vygotsky, L.S.: Mind in Society The Development of Higher Psychological Processes. Harvard University Press, Cambridge (1978)
16. Gee, J.P.: Good Video Games + Good Learning. Peter Lang, New York (2008)
17. Griffiths, T., Guile, D.: Pedagogy in work-based contexts. In: Mortimore, P. (ed.) Understanding Pedagogy and its Impact on Learning. Paul Chapman Publishing, London (1999)
18. Kolb, A.Y., Kolb, D.A.: The learning way: meta-cognitive aspects of experiential learning. Simul. Gaming Interdisc. J. **40**(3), 297–327 (2009)
19. Gardner, H.: Frames of Mind: Theory of Multiple Intelligences. Basic Books, New York (1983)
20. Csikszentmihalyi, M.: Flow: The Psychology of Optimal Experience. Harper, New York (1990)
21. Gardner, R.C., Smythe, P.C.: On the development of the attitude/motivation test battery. Can. Mod. Lang. Rev. **37**, 510–525 (1981)
22. Lave, J., Wenger, E.: Situated Learning: Legitimate Peripheral Participation. Cambridge University Press, Cambridge (1991)

23. Luckin, R.: Learning, Context and the Role of Technology. Institute of Education, University of London, London (2009)
24. Kolb, D.A.: Experiential Learning: Experience as a Source of Learning and Development. Prentice Hall, New Jersey (1984)
25. Militello, L.G., et al.: Applied Cognitive Task Analysis (ACTA) Methodology. Navy Personnel Research and Development Centre, San Dego (1997)
26. Petersen, S.A., Oliveira, M.: The use of reflection continuum model to support digital game-based learning for the development of cognitive skills. In: 11th European Conference on Game-Based Learning (ECGBL 2017). 2017: Graz, Austria

Musicality: A Game to Improve Musical Perception

Nouri Khalass[(✉)], Georgia Zarnomitrou, Kazi Injamamul Haque,
Salim Salmi, Simon Maulini, Tanja Linkermann, Nestor Z. Salamon,
J. Timothy Balint, and Rafael Bidarra

Delft University of Technology, Delft, Netherlands
n.m.p.khalass@student.tudelft.nl

Abstract. Musicality is the concept that refers to a person's ability to perceive and reproduce music. Due to its complexity, it can be best defined by different aspects of music like pitch, harmony, etc. Scientists believe that musicality is not an inherent trait possessed only by musicians but something anyone can nurture and train in themselves. In this paper we present a new game, named *Musicality*, that aims at measuring and improving the musicality of any person with some interest in music. Our application offers users a fun, quick, interactive way to accomplish this goal at their own pace. Specifically, our game focuses on three of the most basic aspects of musicality: instrument recognition, tempo and tone. For each aspect we created different mini-games in order to make training a varied and attractive activity.

1 Introduction

From personal experience we know there are different types of people interested in improving their ability to perceive and reproduce music for a variety of reasons. There are those who would like to learn to play an instrument, to sing, or to dance, but do not know where to start. Others strive to improve their tone hearing so they will be able to tune a guitar without help, to strike the right note while singing, or maybe even find the right notes to compose their own music. As dancers they want to have a really good perception of the tempo of a piece of music as well as its tempo changes. There are those who just enjoy listening to music, but ask themselves if they could enhance their perception of music somehow. Others are just curious to see how musically inclined they really are. In addition, there are people who are already taking music lessons and studying music at a university or consortium to become musicians or music teachers, who may be frustrated by boring theory lessons that repeat the same exercises again and again. All these people interested in music comprise the target audience of our game, whose goal is to provide a fun interactive way of testing and improving their musicality.

There is no widely agreed upon definition of musicality however most people agree that it is a term describing the feeling (or perception) of music [7,9].

© Springer Nature Switzerland AG 2019
M. Gentile et al. (Eds.): GALA 2018, LNCS 11385, pp. 39–48, 2019.
https://doi.org/10.1007/978-3-030-11548-7_4

Musicians are viewed as people with a high sense of musicality, but that does not necessarily mean they are born with it. While some people are musically inclined, it still requires practice and training to shape musical skills into something that can create respectable art.

The brain has a certain level of plasticity which allows this honing of skills [12]. Through exercises and training it is possible for a player to improve certain aspects of musicality, which is also the stated goal of our work. Specifically, we focus on three aspects of musicality: *instrument recognition, sense of tempo*, and *tone hearing*. These three aspects are usually considered among the most basic skills users need in order to start improving their musicality and, as mentioned above, they give valuable input to learn to play an instrument, to sing or to dance. For each aspect we have designed a set of mini-games that both train and assess the player's skills in that specific aspect. Our game shares the essence of several different musicality tests. However, it deviates by focusing on three general aspects instead of specific rote skills, targeting users of different skill levels. Through player testing, we confirmed our goal of creating an educational application that motivates the player to keep practicing on their musical skills.

2   Related Work

There already exist several musicality tests, most of them being used by universities as entry exams to test prospective students, e.g. the Seashore test, or PROMS (Profile of music perception skills) [8]. PROMS consists of tests for melody, tempo, accent, tone, tuning, rhythm, embedded rhythms, pitch and timbre. There was also a test conducted in the United Kingdom in 2011 [2], taken by more than 150,000 people, the largest ever investigation into the musical profile of an entire nation. It turned out there were some hidden musical talents in the population, and that many people seem to over or underestimate their musical abilities. A lot of people in the music business scored rather low at that test, so no real correlation exists between people who make money from music and their musicality. It was apparent that people who had undertaken musical training were better at remembering melodies and tapping out a beat in time, but not at detecting subtle differences in sound [1,2].

There are also commercial websites and applications that train a player's musical abilities or ear, respectively. These include Musical-u [3] and the Perfect Ear [4], which focus on music theory like interval hearing and other exercises for ear training. Pure ear training should however be differentiated from musical ear training. The website thetamusic [13] features several different, unconnected mini-games to train different aspects of musicality. In contrast, we strive to connect our created games to form a coherent product.

More developed music training applications also exists, such as Meludia [10]. Meludia is an ear training application that provides exercises in the form of simple games. Meludia covers many fundamentals aspects of music: recognition of melodies, forms, rhythm, intervals, chords, inversions, progressions. The development of the player ranges from the Discovery to the Expert modules. They also include a practice mode and provide feedback when a player makes a mistake. In the discovery mode the tasks are formulated in a way that no musical knowledge at all is needed, e.g. they ask for stable/unstable instead of harmonics: minor/major. All in all, we can say that Meludia is in far from our vision of a musicality enhancing game. Our work is meant for a more general audience and not only (amateur) musicians and people taking music lessons. We also focus on three aspects of musicality: *instrument recognition, tempo,* and *tone,* with several different mini-games for each. Specifically, we developed a *missing instrument* mini-game to recognize when an instrument is removed from an ensemble by listening to the same piece of music with and without the missing instrument.

3   Game Design

As mentioned in Sect. 1, the purpose of this game is to help train and improve the player's musicality over a time period. Our game is centered around a musicality test which is used to assign a level of musicality to the player over the three previously mentioned aspects (*instrument recognition, tempo,* and *tone*). Although more clinical musicality tests (e.g. [8]) could also have been implemented, we decided to focus on the three mentioned aspects as they are fundamental components of musicality. For each aspect, we develop several mini-games, listed in Table 1. To ensure the overall quality of each mini-game given the time frame of development, we focused on producing three to four games for each musicality aspect. We offer five levels of difficulty, each one accompanied with a title presented to the player. Specifically, these levels are: Level 1 - Beginner, Level 2 - Amateur, Level 3 - Professional, Level 4 - Rock star and Level 5 - Maestro. We use the same mini-games in our test and in the two training modes we present later in the section.

Table 1. Overview of mini-games per aspect

Aspect	Instrument recognition	Tempo	Tone
Mini games	Instrument recognition Missing instrument Instrument counting	Tapping along Continue tapping Tempo difference	Sorting tones Tone memory Matching tones Pitch difference
Purpose	Hear instruments in a arrangement	Build skills related to rhythm and pace	Distinguish frequencies and intervals

Each of our mini-games ranges in difficulty between Beginner (Level 1) and Maestro (Level 5). For our *instrument recognition* mini-games, we increase the number of instruments played in each track. We also increase the number of instrument options that are presented to the user. We use these tactics to challenge the player to clearly hear and distinguish the different instruments in a track in order to choose the correct answer. For our *tempo* mini-games, we reduce the acceptable threshold between the player's input and the tempo for a given composition. Specifically for the *tempo difference* mini-game, we shrink the change in tempo between the two presented tracks, making it more difficult to distinguish the difference between them. Finally we reduce the interval between the different notes or tunes the player has to distinguish in our *tonal* mini-games. By either reducing the difference between compositions or increasing the possibility in choices, each of our mini-games can become progressively more challenging and continue to assist the player in building their musicality skills.

To make our game accessible to a wide audience, we designed two training modes: "Story mode" and "Challenge Mode". Each mode leverages different player incentives in order to promote engagement. Story mode is a more traditional walk-through experience for players looking to improve their musicality through suggested games. Challenge Mode caters to a more competitive style of play, motivating players by completing achievements. Both modes contain the same mini-games and focus on the three aspects of musicality listed in Table 1.

3.1   Challenge Mode

Challenge mode allows a player to play all mini-games regardless of their musicality level. This mode exists primarily for those players who do not wish to follow a progression of levels, but rather enjoy quick, short games. The "Challenge Mode" also gives the player the opportunity to choose the specific mini-game they wish to play at any of the five levels of difficulty. Specifically, the player is presented with a list of all musicality aspects that they are able to train in and after selecting one they are shown a list with all games related to that aspect. After finishing three rounds of the mini-game, the player is presented with a score (in the form of stars) so that they can see how well they performed. The amount of stars that the player receives depends on how successfully they have completed the exercise. The game keeps track off the highest amount of stars a player has gotten for a specific mini-game at a particular level of difficulty. This presents the player with the goal to get three stars for every mini-game at every difficulty level. Additionally, the player is given the chance to take the musicality test whenever they wish to quickly determine their level without the need of collecting the required points to do a test as is required in Story Mode.

3.2   Story Mode

The player follows a minimal story to gradually increase their musicality in Story mode. A level is assigned for each musicality aspect and the overall musicality level is shown, e.g. if the player is assigned level one for all aspects then their overall level is 1.1.1 (where the first number is the level in *Instrument Recognition*, the second the level in *Tempo* and the third the level in *Tone*). In Story Mode, the player follows the character they created who is a beginner musician. This person wants to make a name for himself in the world of music. However, they lack the necessary musical skills and need training to acquire them.

The story is viewed from the perspective of the player and takes place in present day. In order to improve a particular aspect of musicality, the player must play mini-games (shown in Fig. 1) related to that aspect.

Successfully completing (part of) a mini-game earns the player notes for that aspect. Once the player has gathered enough notes they are allowed to take a quiz to increase their musicality level. This quiz is actually the musicality test with each aspect increased in difficulty by one level. We do this to check whether the player has improved their musicality. If the player fails the quiz, then they stay at the same level and are left with half of the musical notes that they had before taking the quiz. If, on the other hand, the player has improved in at least one aspect, they advance a level for that particular aspect. In addition to that, the player is shown playing at a music gig. Depending on their level, they either play a small bar gig, a large concert hall, or somewhere in between. The player's goal in Story Mode is therefore to complete the final concert for each aspect, achieving a musicality level equal to 5.5.5.

3.3   Technical Challenges

Because our game runs on mobile devices, there are a few limitations which we have to deal with. One of our goals was to ensure that our game could be accessed by as many people as possible. This goal influences how many devices we want to support. To make it possible for people with older phones to also run our game we chose to support Android devices which ran "Ice Cream Sandwich" (API 15) or higher. In practice this means that our application will run on 99.6% of all Android devices [6].

As many of our mini-games have the player compare pieces of a composition to determine differences, the mini-games require meta-data about the piece of music. For instance, the *missing instruments* mini-game requires the instruments in order to remove one instrument and display the removed instrument choices to the player, and the *tempo difference* mini-game requires timing information (such as BPM and a time signature). As we want to programmatically make these changes to the composition, we chose to use MIDI [11] instead of conventional MP3 files. MIDI files contain score information (note velocity, duration, pitch), as well as information about which instrument plays a certain note and timing information (BPM of the music and time signature). We can manipulate this information in order to play a composition at an exact BPM or pitch. However, MIDI files do not contain any information on how something should "sound". This means that we are unable to represent certain musical perception skills, such as *accent*. Usually a MIDI file is played by a MIDI sequencer which takes the timing and instrument information and plays a instrument sample at the right time. For this game, we use the Android MIDI sequencer "MediaPlayer" [5]. The overall pipeline of the MIDI System is shown in Fig. 2.

The process of analyzing a MIDI file for all of its information is the most resource intensive task in our game. Even though MIDI files are only a few kilobytes in size they usually contain at least 1000 MIDI events which all have to be processed. To reduce the amount of stutter of the game when reading

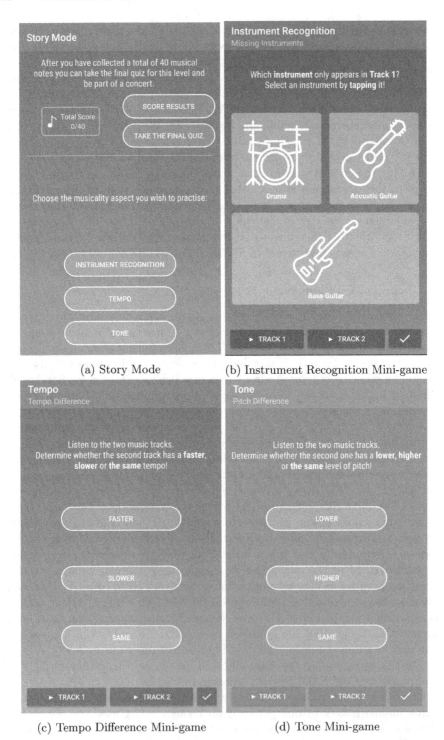

(a) Story Mode

(b) Instrument Recognition Mini-game

(c) Tempo Difference Mini-game

(d) Tone Mini-game

Fig. 1. Screen shots showing our game's story mode as well as a mini-game for each aspect of musicality we test.

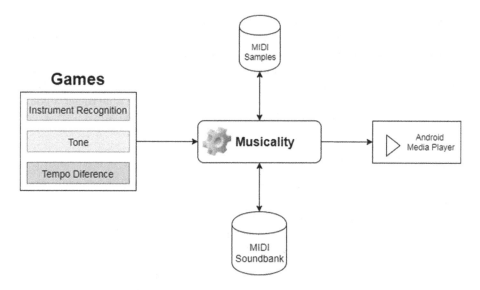

Fig. 2. MIDI System pipeline

and processing the MIDI data we decided to split the process in two parts. The MIDI file is first analyzed and all relevant information is extracted and stored. After this is done modifications can be made to (an abstract representation of) the composition without performance penalties. Then, once the player plays the music, the MIDI file is reassembled with all the updated information. The process of reassembling the MIDI file typically only happens once; if the player pauses and plays the music again and no modifications are made, the already assembled piece of music is loaded from a cache.

4 Evaluation

To evaluate the game during development, a test session was planned every week, making sure that newly implemented features worked and acted like intended. In this section we discuss our method of testing as well as some of the feedback obtained during testing.

4.1 Design of Test Sessions and Tests

We conducted weekly sessions with testers who evaluated our application. We allowed the testers to play the mini-games related to a certain musicality aspect, and we analyzed their play for: *difficulty, engagement, enjoyment,* and overall functionality of the mini-games. We used this analysis to determine direction that we would follow as the development progressed. It also allowed us to gain insight as to if the mini-games were meeting the expectations of the testers as well as if the testers felt the mini-games were improving their musicality.

We had a diverse testing group (56% male and 44% female), where a majority of our participants were young individuals (86% were between 21–30 years old). Moreover, one of the test players was a professional musician whose feedback played a vital role during the development phase of the prototype. Many of the test players also actively played the mini-games on a daily basis. We hoped that by looking at the two ends of the targeted group we would be able to get a good picture of what the needs and preferences related to our game are.

4.2   Result and Discussion

For our game, feedback from both the musician (people who have experience in playing at least one instrument) and non-musician group were indispensable as the "alignment" of such feedback from both groups depicts the extent of the success of the implementation. We received positive feedback from both groups concerning the design and the originality of some aspects of the game, especially *Missing Instruments*. The latter group also commented that they believe that it might help them improve their musical perception. Furthermore, players seemed to enjoy playing and most of them were motivated to continue playing in order to achieve better results themselves.

Since we were especially curious to know how the audio quality affected gameplay, we explicitly asked the participants during observations. Most of the testers said it is sufficient, but we also got some complaints that some of the instruments sounded too similar which made it unnecessarily difficult to recognize them. Moreover, testers suggested that they would like better audio quality instead of MIDI audio which is the motivation to incorporate better quality audio files in the game as a future step.

Some suggestions from the tester group provided insight into possible future additions to the existing prototype. For example, the players would like to be able to play the mini-games intuitively, without studying the instructions. Also, the aspect rated with the most disliked mini-games was *tempo*, as the tapping mini-games seemed to not always work properly or giving not the right guidance to follow the beat.

Furthermore, there is still room for improvement in terms of audio quality and responsiveness. The difficulty scaling of some of the mini-games still need tunning, which will require more player and test data. Additionally, there is also the possibility of adding new mini-games for the existing aspects and adding new aspects to further expand on the musicality topic.

While the implemented game is only a prototype we can conclude from the feedback that we have received that the overall design and functionality are at an acceptable stage. Based on the feedback received, we were able to achieve the creation of a fun and aesthetically pleasing educational game. Also, even though some additional tweaking is required, all the implemented mini-games work well and contribute to the learning process of the player.

5 Conclusion

We presented the design, development, challenges and evaluation of a game prototype aimed at improving a players' musicality. The game consists of mini-games to improve three aspects of musicality: *instrument recognition, tempo,* and *tone recognition*. These mini-games can be accessed through two different modes: A story mode, where the players are presented with games at a difficulty that is appropriate for them, and a challenge mode, where the player can pick an aspect, choose specific mini-games and difficulties in order to obtain maximum score in all of them. We used MIDI files, allowing us to quickly create and manipulate complex musical compositions with a slight decrease in audio quality when compared to acoustical or studio recordings. This is definitely a potential area for improvement to incorporate high quality audio files as audio is on the forefront of the game. Doing so will require solving new technical challenges, as we cannot remove instruments from an audio file. Keeping file size in check will be one of the bigger problems when increasing the number of compositions and games. Furthermore there are still some more possibilities to apply gamification techniques to, for example, encourage recurrent practice. Finally, since a person's musicality improves with practice over time and due to the short time frame this prototype has been in development we were not able to test how successful the game really was concerning the improvement of musicality. For further insights, thorough user studies must be conducted separately for different player groups. This should be one of the main concerns when moving forward with the further development of this musicality game. We hope that carrying out this more robust user study (by possibly examining different approaches for our two testing groups) will provide insight into the "alignment" of feedback by two groups. After such a study, we hope to determine if (i) the less musical group agrees that by playing the game it is possible to gain musical intuition, and (ii) the more musical group agrees that the game keeps them motivated to achieve better results.

Acknowledgements. We thank our commissioners Berend Glazenburg, Evert Rijntjes and Marc Stotijn for their invaluable guidance and contagious enthusiasm.

References

1. BBC: Musicality test reveals UK's 'untapped talent'. http://www.bbc.com/news/uk-18034617. Accessed 12 June 2018
2. BBC Lab UK: How musical are you? https://www.bbc.co.uk/labuk/experiments/how-musical-are-you. Accessed 12 June 2018
3. Easy Ear Training Ltd.: Musical-u ear training exercises. https://www.musical-u.com/ear-training-exercises/#beyond. Accessed 12 June 2018
4. EDuckApps: Perfect ear - ear trainer. https://play.google.com/store/apps/details?id=com.evilduck.musiciankit. Accessed 12 June 2018
5. Google: Android mediaplayer api. https://developer.android.com/guide/topics/media/mediaplayer. Accessed 12 June 2018

6. Google: Android usage data. https://developer.android.com/about/dashboards/. Accessed 12 June 2018
7. Honing, H., Ten Cate, C., Peretz, I., Trehub, S.: Without it no music: cognition, biology and evolution of musicality (2015)
8. Law, L.N.C., Zentner, M.: Assessing musical abilities objectively: construction and validation of the profile of music perception skills. PLOS ONE **7**(12), 1–15 (2012)
9. Marcus, G.F.: Musicality: instinct or acquired skill? Top. Cogn. Sci. **4**(4), 498–512 (2012)
10. Meludia. https://bit.ly/2l86o9e. Accessed 12 June 2018
11. MIDI: MIDI specification. https://www.midi.org/specifications. Accessed 12 June 2018
12. Scherder, E.: Singing in the Brain. Atheneaeum - Polak & van Gennep, Amsterdam (2017)
13. Theta Music Technologies, Inc.: Theta music trainer - music training games. https://trainer.thetamusic.com/en/content/music-training-games. Accessed 12 June 2018

Exploring Design Decisions in Interactive Narrative Games for Behaviour Change: A Case Study

Ivo Bril$^{(\boxtimes)}$ ⓘ, Nick Degens ⓘ, and Jef Folkerts ⓘ

Hanze University of Applied Sciences, Zernikeplein 11,
9747 AS Groningen, The Netherlands
{i.bril,d.m.degens,j.folkerts}@pl.hanze.nl

Abstract. Interactive Narratives (INs), usually within games, have the possibility to motivate users to change their attitude or behavior. The application of INs in healthcare has already shown promising results as opposed to traditional narratives. Yet, very little is known about the effect of each specific aspect of an IN or how to create an effective IN. Using the recent IN-model of Green and Jenkins, this paper explores the applicability of its constructs and exemplifies it through a case study. In doing so, this paper looks at the challenges one runs into when designing an IN. Subsequently it presents the way in which these problems were tackled for the case study. This results in new ways to look at the practical implications of Green and Jenkin's model, thus helping future IN designers and researchers to identify and avoid design pitfalls early. As gaps in the literature are discovered throughout the paper, possible future research topics are discussed.

Keywords: Interactive narrative · Behavior change ·
Healthcare · Persuasion

1 Introduction

The last decennium highlights an increased interest in the possibilities of interactive narrative (IN) for attitudinal change and persuasion [1–3], particularly in games. In INs, the persuasive power of a story is combined with agency and autonomy; these two are often seen as crucial in the behavior change process. Unlike a regular story, INs allow users to determine how the story unfolds, often at key moments in the story.

To formalize the research conducted on the topic so far, Green and Jenkins have proposed a theoretical model explaining the effects and possibilities of IN [1]. The model describes how adding interaction changes the way that users experience the narrative. For example, by increasing the amount of control users have on the flow of the story, the narrative will, as a result, become less linear and structured.

While useful for designers, the model is very conceptual, which is –mostly– due to a lack of empirical research. However, when designing an IN there are a lot of choices that have to be made that can have a significant impact on the effectiveness, usability, or perceived realism of the IN, which remain unmentioned in the current model.

© Springer Nature Switzerland AG 2019
M. Gentile et al. (Eds.): GALA 2018, LNCS 11385, pp. 49–59, 2019.
https://doi.org/10.1007/978-3-030-11548-7_5

To help designers with these choices, we will discuss the design choices of an IN using elements from Green and Jenkin's model. In doing so, we aim to identify and define the challenges involved in making an IN, whilst providing a vocabulary to discuss them.

The case presented in this paper aims to capitalize on the persuasive capabilities of IN, which have shown promise in health behavior interventions [2, 3]. The goal for the IN is to raise the awareness of, and lower the barrier for, improving and maintaining one's own mental and physical health. Specifically, this paper targets Dutch nurses in healthcare, as research shows that they suffer greatly from both physical and mental strain: 85% suffer from physical problems, such as back, neck, and shoulder pain [4], with 23% being unable to work due to these symptoms. Over half of the nurses also reported experiencing high psychosocial workload.

The excessive strain has led to high rates of sick-leave, short- and long-term, and a strong dependency on mental healthcare and physiotherapy. Causes often reported for these problems are: a high physical workload; time pressure; a lack of (qualified) colleagues; and the perceived need to put the patient's health before one's own [4, 5].

Throughout this paper we will describe the design of the IN to help these health-care professionals and describe other dimensions that have played a vital role in the design of this IN. The paper will conclude with future plans for the developed IN and its software, as well as summarize the lessons learned and how they relate to the model of Green and Jenkins.

2 Background Literature

Green and Jenkins [1] describe in their model a set of effects that interact with one another and influence aspects of the IN such as engagement, believability, and possible persuasive capabilities. We briefly summarize their work here to provide the vocabulary necessary to discuss the practical issues exemplified in the case study.

2.1 Narrative Immersion

Narrative Transportation. A mechanism of narrative persuasion [6, 7]. It describes the feeling of being immersed in the underlying world of the narrative. Successful transportation makes people more likely to alter their beliefs and attitudes due to experiencing the narrative [8]. These changes are positively influenced by narrative processes: the creation of vivid mental imagery [9], a reduction of counterarguing in users [9], and through connections with the story's characters (e.g. identification) [10–12].

Of these three processes, connecting with a story's character is particularly relevant for IN to provide a more enriching experience. Instead of passively taking in the story, IN allows users to 'become' the main character and take an active role in the story. This could heighten the impact of the story, increasing the persuasive effect [1, 13].

Perceived Realism. Preventing the persuadee from forming counterarguments to external claims is key for any persuasive endeavor [15], and providing a narrative perceived as realistic is one way of doing so. Narrative transportation is also easier if the user is not hampered in the construction of a mental model of the narrative's world, for which perceived realism is an important factor [16].

Perceived realism not only pertains to the content of the underlying world of the narrative, which could be realistic or fantasy-driven, but also to the structure of a story. Scenes need to be sequenced in a manner that is both understandable and at the very least plausible in terms of consistency with regards to the overall narrative and the character's actions. As the structure in IN is more fluid, attention should be spent to maintain coherent sequencing despite the emergent branching that occurs naturally in IN.

Processing Fluency. This effect describes the ease of use of the narrative, such as the readability of the font, or relatability of the narrative to users. Likewise, for a narrative, the writing style and word usage can influence the ease with which users can read and process the narrative. A narrative that is relatable to users and is easy to process, helps the narrative transportation process [17].

The interruptive nature of choice in IN could inhibit the processing fluency of the narrative. However, Green and Jenkins argue that this has not been apparent in their research so far [1, 14], and general theory on processing fluency would suggest that liking the option to make a choice in a story remediates the interruptive effect it could have [18].

2.2   Role of the Self

Going further into identification as a mechanism to support persuasion, the user's 'self' can become involved in the narrative in several ways.

Self-perception and Motives. A narrative with relatable characters can strengthen traits of both the user and an IN character, which can be used to reinforce behavior relating to those traits (e.g. healthy or responsible behavior) [19]. IN also allows the user to become inspired by what they could or want to be (i.e. their possible future selves), by exploring and experimenting with characters that portray such traits [20]. This has been shown to improve health behaviors [21].

Ideally, in health interventions, an IN stimulates users to make choices while referencing to their self (i.e. thinking about similar situations they encounter in their own life). Doing so can make the consequences of the actions chosen have more impact, as the user's self is closely involved [22].

Responsibility. In contrast to a traditional narrative, the interactive nature of an IN makes users largely responsible for the fate of the characters. This responsibility may lead to a conscious reflection on their actions and the consequences; this also increases the meaning attributed to a character's actions as they now reflect the user's.

In the domain of health care, appealing to internal attributions of responsibility has already been found as a method for behavior and attitudinal change [23, 24]. The feeling of control or agency found in IN appeals to the sense of responsibility of users and, initial research shows, can change the behavior or attitude of users [14, 25].

Participatory Responses. Although users cannot intervene or participate in a traditional story, users do psychologically react to a story's events (i.e. as if they were there) [26]. These *participatory responses* (p-responses) affect how users recall and feel about situations in which such a response has taken place [26].

Green and Jenkins posit that IN allows for users to act on their p-response, allowing a more engaging experience. However, it could also backfire as users may feel restricted by the responses provided by the IN, which could cause frustration (i.e. the response they would like to give is not a selectable option).

2.3 Individual Differences

The personal characteristics of the user have a crucial impact on their perception and interpretation of what happens in an IN. Four particularly relevant aspects are:

Need for Cognition. Individuals have differing preferences when it comes to the amount of effort they find enjoyable in their leisure activities [27, 28]. Studies show that INs are considered cognitively effortful to read through [14, 29], highlighting a possible limitation on the amount of people for whom an IN would be a fitting solution (as opposed to film or a traditional narrative).

Transportability. For traditional narratives, the tendency for narrative transportation to occur differs from person to person [30]. There's currently no empirical research on the effect on the transportation capabilities of IN. Green and Jenkins posit that there is little difference between how it affects INs and how it affects traditional narratives.

Need for Control. A high need for control describes people who like to take active control, whereas a low need describes people who find such control cumbersome. Similar to need for cognition, IN could be more engaging for people who prefer control, as they have control over the development of the story.

Comfort with Technology. Whereas a book only requires one to flip from page to page, IN requires more complex interaction. Being uncomfortable with such interactivity due to its complexity could negatively affect the impact IN can have.

3 Designing an Interactive Narrative

3.1 Purpose and Topic of the IN

The goal of this project is to design an IN to raise nurses' awareness about their own well-being. The IN also functions as a persuasive call-to-action, as it provides the means to act on this new-found awareness straight after the story ends. Ultimately, this empowers the nurses to maintain their own physical and mental well-being. One of the skills/competences deemed necessary for a nurse to maintain one's well-being is being able to 'provide constructive feedback' (based on competence documents of healthcare institutions and through discourse with two subject-matter experts (SMEs) [31])[1].

3.2 The Reasoning for IN

One's working behavior is not something that is constantly self-monitored, nor corrected. Thus, it is easy for unhealthy behavior to remain uncorrected or unnoticed until the consequences of said behavior emerge. IN allows its users the opportunity to not only learn more about situations they find challenging, but also to make users aware of the more subconscious choices involved in such situations.

Narrative transportation involves the user more in the situation. This is compounded by the nature of IN, which allows users to determine the way the story unfolds. Combined, these two factors help in making the consequences in the story more impactful as well as increase the relevancy of the feedback that is provided after the story.

Lastly, the real-life situations presented through IN tie the contents to the real-life context, making it easier to understand why certain knowledge is relevant and useful. Note that this reasoning is not exhaustive, as the scope of the paper is to discuss the design of the IN.

3.3 Narrative Structure and Level of Control

The most impactful element outlined in Green and Jenkins' model [1] (and elaborated upon in [2]) is the interplay between the amount of structure of the story and the amount of control users have in determining how the story unfolds.

The choice in balance for this interplay will determine what functionality the software needs and whether using something simple, like multiple-choice options for user interaction, are enough, or whether something more elaborate is required.

Elements such as the target audience's *need for cognition*, *need for control*, and *comfort with technology* also influence this choice. In our case, the age range of the target audience: broad, with varying levels of comfort with technology, and the amount of time available to read our INs is limited, presuppose a simple and intuitive interaction.

Aside from the user's perspective, there is the core question: "what is the goal that the IN is supposed to achieve?". For our case, the system behind the IN needs to acquire enough information of the user by the end of the story to be able to give proper feedback and advice. We need enough data points to show the competence of the user in different aspects of the to-be-measured skill.

In conclusion, our resources and constraints allowed little control to be in the hands of users. This led to a narrative structure that is mostly the same in terms of situations, but what can happen within those situations can differ due to choices made earlier in

---

[1] Both experts are from the healthcare sector, specifically from ergonomics and rehabilitation. One is specialized in healthcare ergonomics and communication in healthcare institutes, the other focuses on rehabilitation of nurses. Both also focus on the prevention of excessive mental and physical workload.

the story. This is an option to us, as users are unlikely to re-read the story and make different choices, as they have limited time and have already gained their personal feedback. Re-reading the story would give away the limited impact of the choices themselves, thus diminishing the *transportability* and sense of *responsibility*.

3.4 Interaction and Choice Design

Determining the most suitable type of interaction within the IN is strongly influenced by the same factors as the level of control; this is not surprising, as the amount of possible interaction is directly tied to the level of control. Even if we choose to limit the interaction to pivotal moments, there are still a lot of questions that need to be answered. These questions have proven to be difficult to answer through literature, even though they are vital for the success of an IN. We have identified several factors for each of these questions that have helped us in determining the answers to these questions.

What Do You Give the User a Choice in?

Types of Choices. The types of choices in an IN determine the way in which the user can exert influence over the story. Are the choice-options for example always action-oriented (e.g. go to *x* or do *y*) or more dialogue and text-focused (i.e. *how* you say something)? Depending on the type, you can focus on different aspects of a story, for example, a focus on dialogue emphasizes the relationships between characters.

For this case, the type of situations we want to give users a choice in relate to the competence we want to asses and raise awareness for. Thus, it requires us to break that competence down into its components. Doing so helps us identify the most important parts of the skill and how they can be measured: it gives a lens through which we can create a story about giving feedback. For example, in our IN, the first interaction moment is the initial reaction to seeing someone make a mistake: do you react immediately, or do you wait for the right moment? A more formalized way to create these interaction moments is through a (cognitive) task analysis.

Specificity. A measure involved in choosing these interaction moments is the specificity of the situation you allow users to interact in. The more specific a moment of choice is, the smaller the difference is between the choice-options. For our case, the component that is being assessed in a situation dictates this specificity: if the component is 'phrasing a negative message', the choice-options are limited to differently phrased pieces of feedback (i.e. a high level of specificity). However, a component such as 'timing of the message' is much more open-ended, and the choice-options reflect this by allowing users to, for example, decide to provide feedback much later.

When Do You Give the User a Choice?

Amount of Moments. The amount of choice-moments directly ties into the amount of perceived control, given that each choice-moment has relevance (i.e. not doing something inconsequential). The more moments that the user can influence the outcome of the story, the more it, or its designer, has to be able to manage the consequences. More choices also mean a higher demand on the cognition of the user, who has to reflect more often to determine the most preferable answer in a given situation.

Expectations. Humans are prone to create expectations, meaning that users will expect to be able to exert control in a situation similar to previous interactions. Thus, the types of moments in which they have to interact is best left consistent. Not being able to do so could lead to situations of frustration and a break in narrative transportation.

In our case, the competence *giving constructive feedback* was discussed with SMEs to determine common situations, conflicts, and errors made in the real-life work environment to use in the IN. The discussion gave us an overarching story: the protagonist is asked by one of her colleagues to help her out with a lifting procedure for a patient. The protagonist sees her colleague take the wrong stance and the story unfolds from there, eventually leading to a discussion during a team meeting.

Using the earlier identified story components as a lens, we can analyze these real-life examples to see when each component is most prominent, allowing us to build the IN from these moments. Ultimately, this helps us determine what types of situations users should get control over, something for which there is no empirical research so far (i.e. in a story, when do you give the user an option to interact?).

What Makes a Good Choice?

Choice Fidelity. As a traditional IN allows interaction only to take place through textual choices and actions, the types of possible choices and actions are limited to what words can convey. In choosing the type of interaction for a given situation, a balance must be struck between the expectations of a user when reading a given action and the to-be-expected consequences of said action.

During an early testing session of our IN, we had a situation in which one of the options was to give non-verbal cues as feedback (as means of giving feedback that is not noticed by the patient). Some of the participants showed signs of confusion after choosing the non-verbal option and stated that they expected it to go differently.

The issue here was that, even though the specific cues were described in detail, the execution of those cues was interpreted differently by these users. This raises an interesting point: the *fidelity* of the choice is limited by the medium with which it is conveyed and the breadth of interpretations possible. In this specific situation, the non-verbal cues were not shown to users through imagery, but through text. This requires users to mentally envision how the action would play out, which they will do from their own perspective, as they are portraying their own *self* on the protagonist. In the end this leads to an erroneous interpretation, as body language and non-verbal cues are too personal to generalize into one choice-option. Successfully using body language as a choice-option would have required a different *fidelity* in its representation.

To summarize: to promote transportation and identification, it is important that the fidelity of a choice-option *aligns* with the action of the choice-option. The more distance between the two, as seen in the example above, the greater the risk of erroneous interpretation and the possibility of a break in narrative transportation. As an example of aligned fidelity, choosing what the protagonist will say is less open to different executions. As such it does not lead to misinterpretation due to fidelity (although the outcomes may still be different than expected).

Identification. In theory, a real-life situation has a near infinite amount of possible actions. In an IN, it is impossible, and probably ill-advised, to show all these possible actions. Ideally, one filters through the entire scope of possible actions and selects a subset which allows users to always have a choice-option they can identify with. Being able to identify with one's choices is an important part of being transported into the narrative, as it allows users to relate with the protagonist and become more involved in the narrative itself. In terms of Green and Jenkin's model, this could be described as aiming for at least one of the choices for a situation to be the *participatory response* of users. In turn, this stimulates users to portray their own *self* in their choices.

Right or Wrong? When writing an interactive narrative, it is easy to lose track of the fact that users will determine the story. Especially when a story has an ulterior motive such as persuading its users, raising awareness, or assessing its users (as is the case here). In doing so, one runs the risk of thinking mostly through the lens of the 'right way', making it hard to create reasonable choice options that go differently. Early on in our design we fell into this trap: we focused too much on gathering data about 'right' and 'wrong' choices. As may be expected, life is hardly, if ever, so black and white. As such, the focus of our IN, with the goal of assessing a competence, came down to creating a narrative that allows users to show his or her working behavior as accurately as possible within the boundaries of the medium. This no longer forced us to think in terms of a multiple-choice test and provided a clear focus on providing realistic choices first and determining what they mean for our assessment second.

Thus, narrative transportation stimulating choices had to fit the following criteria:

- Make sure there is no clear right or wrong choice-option, i.e. each choice-option should be a realistically possible and plausible option;
- Every situation should have a choice-option that generally meets the participatory response of users;
- The choice-options should be aligned with the choice fidelity, i.e. users should clearly know how the protagonist will execute each choice-option;
- The reactions of other characters to the user's choices should be consistent and fit within the setting of your narrative (discussed below).

Note that this is not an exhaustive list of criteria for creating choice-options. Aspects such as using the right terminology and matching the language use of your setting are also essential, as well as processing fluency in general.

How Many Choice-Options Per Situation?

The number of choice-options is closely related to the earlier mentioned *identification* and *realism* discussed in the *right or wrong?* section. *Identification* strongly impacts the amount of options a situation can have while still maintaining that each option matches someone's *participatory response*. This would mean that, ideally, even the most personal participatory response is included to always attain *identification*. Understandably, this is unattainable, as the *processing fluency* of the IN prevents one from doing so. Adding more choice-options not only increases the amount of reading, it also increases the amount of consequences users have to envision and analyze. Although there is no empirical research on the consequences of too many choice-options, one can reason that adding options should be done sparingly and under great scrutiny. For our case, we ended up with, on average, four options per situation, with some situations being yes/no questions. Granted, there is little knowledge on what is optimal for this design choice.

3.5 Realism

For our case, it is essential that our options are realistic given the professional context of the nurses, as there are pre-existing conventions to providing feedback (e.g. giving colleague-to-colleague feedback in front of a patient is seen as rude). Aside from the options themselves, the story should be able to occur as it would in real-life (the story being: identifying a common problem and broadening the feedback to target the whole team instead of one individual). Within these constraints, the goal is to achieve the *perception* of realism: users *feel* in control and *feel* that the story is realistic. This is important to acknowledge, as there is a lot one can get away with while upholding this perception of realism. Below we describe a few practical aspects of maintaining this sense of realism.

Clarity of Consequences. In line with choice fidelity and interpretations, aligning the fidelity with the choice-options is only the first step. Even purely text-based, the choice-options should provide users with a sense of how the protagonist will act, how the other parties involved will (probably) react, and whether that fits with their perception of self (i.e. how they themselves would react). Essentially, if users cannot reason about the way other characters of the story will react, there will be a disconnect with the sense of responsibility of the user, as users can no longer control the fate of the protagonist or others (to a degree that achieves a perception of control).

This constraint demands of the designer to make sure that other characters are consistent in their behavior and that consequences and reactions maintain a sense of plausibility. In doing so one also has to strike a balance between matching the consequences that the users expect and providing impactful consequences that make a story interesting. For our case, it is important that users are confronted with the consequences of not providing feedback at all or providing it in a very crude manner.

Playtesting. An important step worth mentioning is the importance of testing the IN with the target audience. Throughout our design process, we have consulted people from the target audience to read through the story and comment on the choice-options, reactions, and general perception of realism and control. Multiple cycles, involving user evaluations, were necessary to achieve realism in the choice-options.

4 Conclusion and Discussion

In this case study, several practical design questions surrounding IN have been explored first hand and their design choices (i.e. answers) discussed. The aim was not to provide a definitive answer to these questions, but to link Green and Jenkin's model to these questions and identify any unexplained constructs that emerged (such as choice fidelity).

In doing so, we have made a next step in the formalization of the design process of an IN. The vocabulary provided through this case study hopefully lends itself well to designers and researchers of INs, further maturing and stimulating the design of, and discussion about, IN as a tool for learning and supporting long-term behavior change.

Although there is still limited empirical research into the working elements of IN in the context of behavior change, we believe that understanding the intricacies involved in designing one is a crucial step in understanding why, or when, an IN is effective.

The case outlined in this paper is currently being tested on its effectiveness in raising awareness and changing health-related intentions of behavior in its users. With its results we hope to shed some first empirical light on the aspects discussed in this paper.

References

1. Green, M., Jenkins, K.: Interactive narratives: processes and outcomes in user-directed stories. J. Commun. **64**(3), 479–500 (2014)
2. Christy, K.: Investigating the use of interactive narratives for changing health beliefs: a test of the model of interactive narrative effects. The Ohio State University (2016)
3. Yin, L., Ring, L., Bickmore, T.: Using an interactive visual novel to promote patient empowerment through engagement. In: Proceedings of FDG, pp. 41–48. ACM, New York (2012)
4. Bronkhorst, B., Ten Arve, A., Spoek, M., Wieman, D.: Gezond werken in de zorg. Onderzoek naar fysieke en psychosociale arbeidsbelasting onder zorgmedewerkers (2014). Stichting IZZ website. http://www.publicatiesarbeidsmarktzorgenwelzijn.nl/wp-content/uploads/2015/11/Rapport-Gezond-werken-in-de-zorg.pdf
5. Kuipers, D., et al.: iLift: a health behavior change support system for lifting and transfer techniques to prevent lower-back injuries in healthcare. Int. J. Med. Inform. **96**, 11–23 (2016)
6. Appel, M., Richter, T.: Transportation and need for affect in narrative persuasion: a mediated moderation model. Media Psychol. **13**(2), 101–135 (2010)
7. Murphy, S., Frank, L., Moran, M., Patnoe-Woodley, P.: Involved, transported, or emotional? Exploring the determinants of change in knowledge, attitudes, and behavior in entertainment-education. J. Commun. **61**(3), 407–431 (2011)
8. Green, M., Garst, J., Brock, T., Chung, S.: Fact versus fiction labeling: persuasion parity despite heightened scrutiny of fact. Media Psychol. **8**(3), 267–285 (2006)
9. Green, M., Brock, T.: The role of transportation in the persuasiveness of public narratives. J. Pers. Soc. Psychol. **79**(5), 701–721 (2000)
10. Slater, M., Rouner, D.: Entertainment—education and elaboration likelihood: understanding the processing of narrative persuasion. Commun. Theory **12**(2), 173–191 (2002)
11. Cho, H., Shen, L., Wilson, K.: Perceived realism: dimensions and roles in narrative persuasion. Commun. Res. **41**(6), 828–851 (2014)
12. Larkey, L., Hecht, M.: A model of effects of narrative as culture-centric health promotion. J. Health Commun. **15**(2), 114–135 (2010)
13. Cohen, J.: Defining identification: a theoretical look at the identification of audiences with media characters. Mass Commun. Soc. **4**(3), 245–264 (2001)

14. Jenkins, K.: Choose your own adventure: interactive narratives and attitude change. The University of North Carolina (2014)
15. Oinas-Kukkonen, H., Harjumaa, M.: Persuasive systems design: key issues, process model, and system features. Commun. Assoc. Inf. Syst. **24**(1), 485–500 (2009)
16. Busselle, R., Bilandzic, H.: Fictionality and perceived realism in experiencing stories: a model of narrative comprehension and engagement. Commun. Theory **18**(2), 255–280 (2008)
17. Vaughn, L., Hesse, S.J., Petkova, Z., Trudeau, L.: "This story is right on": the impact of regulatory fit on narrative engagement and persuasion. Eur. J. Soc. Psychol. **39**(3), 447–456 (2009)
18. Reber, R., Schwarz, N., Winkielman, P.: Processing fluency and aesthetic pleasure: is beauty in the perceiver's processing experience? Pers. Soc. Psychol. Rev. **8**(4), 364–382 (2004)
19. Klimmt, C., Hefner, D., Vorderer, P., Roth, C., Blake, C.: Identification with video game characters as automatic shift of self-perceptions. Media Psychol. **13**(4), 323–338 (2010)
20. Green, M., Tesser, A., Wood, J., Stapel, D.: Transportation into narrative worlds: implications for the self. In: Tesser, A., Stapel, D.A., Wood, J.W. (eds.) On Building, Defending and Regulating the Self: A Psychological Perspective, 1st edn, pp. 53–75. Psychology Press, London (2005)
21. Oyserman, D., Destin, M., Novin, S.: The context-sensitive future self: possible selves motivate in context, not otherwise. Self Identity **14**(2), 173–188 (2015)
22. Strange, J., Leung, C.: How anecdotal accounts in news and in fiction can influence judgments of a social problem's urgency, causes, and cures. Pers. Soc. Psychol. Bull. **25**(4), 436–449 (1999)
23. Rothman, A., Salovey, P., Turvey, C., Fishkin, S.: Attributions of responsibility and persuasion: increasing mammography utilization among women over 40 with an internally oriented message. Health Psychol. **12**(1), 39–47 (1993)
24. Harackiewicz, J., Sansone, C., Blair, L., Epstein, J., Manderlink, G.: Attributional processes in behavior change and maintenance: smoking cessation and continued abstinence. J. Consult. Clin. Psychol. **55**(3), 372–378 (1987)
25. Roth, C., Vermeulen, I., Vorderer, P., Klimmt, C.: Exploring replay value: shifts and continuities in user experiences between first and second exposure to an interactive story. Cyberpsychology Behav. Soc. Netw. **15**(7), 378–381 (2012)
26. Polichak, J., Gerrig, R.: "Get up and win!": participatory responses to narrative. In: Green, M.C., Strange, J.J., Brock, T.C. (eds.) Narrative Impact: Social and Cognitive Foundations, pp. 71–95. Lawrence Erlbaum, Mahwah (2002)
27. Cacioppo, J., Petty, R., Feng Kao, C.: The efficient assessment of need for cognition. J. Pers. Assess. **48**(3), 306–307 (1984)
28. Green, M., Kass, S., Carrey, J., Feeney, R., Herzig, B., Sabini, J.: Transportation across media: print versus film comparisons. Media Psychol. **11**(4), 512–539 (2008)
29. Vorderer, P., Knobloch, S., Schramm, H.: Does entertainment suffer from interactivity? The impact of watching an interactive TV movie on viewers' experience of entertainment. Media Psychol. **3**(4), 343–363 (2001)
30. Mazzocco, P., Green, M., Sasota, J., Jones, N.: This story is not for everyone. Soc. Psychol. Pers. Sci. **1**(4), 361–368 (2010)
31. Beverdam, A., Beverdam, L.: Beroepscompetentieprofiel Verzorgende IG in de branche VVT. Report of the Stichting Arbeidsmarkt- en Opleidingsbeleid Verpleeg-Verzorgingshuizen en Thuiszorg, Utrecht (2016)

MUV: A Game to Encourage Sustainable Mobility Habits

Salvatore Di Dio[1(✉)] , Enza Lissandrello[2] ,
Domenico Schillaci[1] , Brunella Caroleo[3] , Andrea Vesco[3] ,
and Ingwio D'Hespeel[4]

[1] PUSH Design Lab, p.za Sant'Anna 3, 90133 Palermo, Italy
s.didio@wepush.org
[2] Department of Planning, Aalborg University,
Rendsburggade 14, 9000 Aalborg, Denmark
[3] Istituto Superiore Mario Boella (ISMB),
Via P. C. Boggio 61, 10138 Turin, Italy
[4] LUCA School of Arts, Alexianenplein 1, 9000 Ghent, Belgium

Abstract. This working paper investigates the question of changing people mobility towards more sustainable habits involving them in an engaging gameplay. The work is performed within MUV H2020 research and innovation action. The game design, definition and features have been co-created through the involvement of different citizens and stakeholders in six European neighbourhoods. The paper discusses the game design as resulting from co-creation and co-design experiences with each neighbourhood communities involved in initial phases. The paper argues that the local co-design activities have influenced the game definition, together with the community engagement approach. The MUV gameplay approach results thus a demand-side measure able to encouraging people to sustainable mobility modes in the awareness of their potential role as agents of urban livability. The data collected by the players will be used to support a citizen-centric approach to facilitate equity and mobility justice in urban policies.

Keywords: Gamification · Urban sustainable mobility ·
Community engagement · Co-creation

1 Introduction

1.1 Urban Mobility: Supply-Side and Demand-Side Measures

How is it possible to realise more sustainable cities in an era of zero resources, rife social conflicts and unprecedented environmental issues? When it comes to discussions about urban sustainability, the focus is usually on the role of new technologies to improve the human habitat conditions. The general attempt is to innovate, in many different ways, the 'city hardware' or, in terms of sustainable urban mobility [1], to implement 'supply-side measures'.

However, this approach to urban mobility is very often proven hard to implement due to the lack of tools to value meaningful data in view of effective sustainable

© Springer Nature Switzerland AG 2019
M. Gentile et al. (Eds.): GALA 2018, LNCS 11385, pp. 60–70, 2019.
https://doi.org/10.1007/978-3-030-11548-7_6

mobility infrastructures, the time and economy needed for designing and developing those measures and to realise them in a time of rapidly aging technologies with high uncertainty of their actual positive impact.

This paper explores another angle that we call here "demand-side measures" to sustainable urban mobility. This alternative approach aims to a citizen-centric methodology focused on needs and new services, policies and solutions enabled through digital tools and gameplay development potentials. The research presented in this paper derives to a specific approach to gameplay as a means to involve people to "move" and to interact in their neighbourhood and city in a more active and sustainable way. The paper highlights the gameplay potential as a demand-side measure to effectively contribute to a urban mobility transition towards more sustainable cities also through digital technologies [2]. The paper elaborates from the research carried out in the context of "MUV – Mobility Urban Values" project [3], funded in 2017 by the European Commission under the call Horizon 2020 "Mobility for Growth". The research consortium consists of fourteen partners from eight countries and the action-research is piloted in six different neighbourhoods: Buitenveldert in Amsterdam, Sant Andreu in Barcelona, the old town of Fundão, Muide-Meulestede in Ghent, the new area of Jätkäsaari in Helsinki and Palermo Old Town.

1.2   Gamification and Urban Mobility

«Playing a game is the voluntary attempt to overcome unnecessary obstacles» stated philosopher Bernard Suits in his famous book "The Grasshopper: Games, Life and Utopia" [4]. Moving around the city in a more active and sustainable way - as walking or cycling or by public transport - means breaking a circle of solid routines that require valid reasons for people to change and do not give an immediate result to their action or effort in terms of gratification so that for many people it is really not considered necessary.

Nevertheless, according to Bernard Suits's quote, this is the perfect premise to design an engaging gameplay. Examples as digital services such as Empower [5], Sweatcoin [6], WeCity [7], RingRing [8] or TrafficO$_2$ [9], are basically mobile applications empowered by a game dynamic to stimulate users to commute in a more sustainable way. Activity recognition algorithms implemented by the mobile operating systems detect how people move and offer motivational rewarding to those who choose less polluting mobility systems.

The assumptions of these digital services are that by playing games, people for every trip on foot, by bicycle, by public transportation or by car-pooling systems, gain a certain amount of points. Points allow players to get rewarded. The data produced and collected through these services can have an impact on improving active mobility [10] and support data-driven approaches, such as evidence-based decision making, for mobility policies [11]. Experiences of this kind have been carried out in several contexts. TrafficO$_2$[9] has represented an important base for "MUV – Mobility Urban Values" research.

The interesting result from TrafficO$_2$ was that through a mobile app, almost 2,000 University students of Palermo (Italy) were engaged as testers of a game developed and tested in four different cycles (from 2013 to 2015), that has showed for active players an average CO_2 pollution reduction of 54% [12]. About 100 local businesses were involved as sponsors, with a total commercial value of product giveaways of €10,000. The game, during the four testing phases, different motivational strategies have been experimented and mixed within the game design:

(A) Social Motivation, through a leaderboard with all the students;
(B) Monetary Rewards, through the product giveaways from the sponsors;
(C) Intrinsic Benefits, mainly through the game narrative.

By interviewing active users, it was assessed that the gameplay successful strategies have been to not simply providing free gifts (B) to the highest ranked players, but rather engaging users as drivers and agents of the cultural change in their city (A) and, at the same time, provide an achievable personal challenge (C) which players can recognize individually. Such feedback has also been demonstrated valid by the data gathered during the last testing phase, when monetary rewards were completely removed. Despite the drop of students involved (from 342 and 161 active, to 65 and 46 active), the average results are easily comparable with those of previous experimentations.

TrafficO$_2$ main lesson has highlighted how this kind of mobility demand-side measures should not rely only on extrinsic incentives but, to become more effective, they might develop new motivational strategies to trigger intrinsic rewards.

2   MUV Action-Research Project

2.1   The Local Ecosystem Change: Citizens, Businesses and Authorities

These learning aspects of the use of gamification as a derived from TrafficO$_2$ in view of mobility demand-side measures have been elaborated further in the context of MUV [3], an innovative research action aimed to improve urban mobility at the neighbourhood level. Starting from an extensive network of cities and expertises on gamification, co-creation and open innovation, this EU project tries to address sustainable and active mobility by involving six neighbourhood communities (Table 1) and their challenges.

This paper elaborates into the co-design of self-rewarding game dynamics as an empowering tool able to develop wider interaction among citizens, local businesses and public authorities and to address new sustainable and active lifestyles [13].

The MUV gameplay model aspires to become scalable with an impact wider than the limited niche in which the service is actually enabled [14].

---

[1] TrafficO$_2$ was an action-research project, co-funded in 2012 through the call "Smart Cities and Communities and Social Innovation" promoted by the Italian Education, University and Research Ministry.

Table 1. City/Neighbourhoods/Challenges.

City	Neighbourhood	Mobility challenge highlighted by pilot managers
Amsterdam	Buitenveldert	Noise, pollution, traffic safety and more active mobility for elderly people
Barcelona	Sant Andreu	Decrease the use of private transport
Fundão	Old Town	Traffic jams in the working days
Ghent	Muide/Meulestede	Decrease the use of private transport amongst the non-Belgian communities
Helsinki	Jätkäsaari	A contemporary urban identity to propose in this new neighbourhood, with more sustainable and active mobility lifestyle and values
Palermo	Old Town	Traffic jams, illegal parking, noise and air pollution especially at night

2.2   MUV Roles: An Infrastructure to Co-create Value

In order to create a valuable synergy among the actors involved, MUV develops a mobile activity-based game here described as a sporty narrative: 1. citizens are engaged and involved as "athletes" (or MUVers) and get rewarded for their results of travelling on sustainable mobility through the city/neighbourhood (walking, cycling, public transit and car sharing); 2. local business owners act as "sponsors" and get data about their customers and through marketing campaigns; 3. public authorities act as "motivators", get data and insights about active and sustainable mobility behaviours and involve citizens in data-driven processes for co-creation of mobility policies.

This approach aims at defining a space where all the different actors can find their own value rationality about urban mobility (conscious behaviours, data, rewards, policies, creativity). Through gameplay, citizens, local businesses and public authorities engage and interact as diverse part of the community of place and neighbourhood identity improving the urban liveability. The game premise aims to create the potential infrastructure that supports the value creation process with local communities during MUV co-design process.

The sport metaphor serves to guide the horizon of MUV values (e.g. being active, sustainable and happy) to become accessible to common understandings and non-expert interpretations during co-creation processes as sport practices are carriers of values (e.g. fairness, team-building, equality, inclusion, respect, perseverance, healthy lifestyle, ambitions) to foster people's intrinsic benefits [15] and self-rewarding experiences in gameplay dynamics [16].

3   Shaping MUV Game: Results from the First Phase of the Co-creation and Co-design Methodology

3.1   Community Engagement and Self-rewarding Activities Insights

Community engagement in MUV has been inspired fundamentally by the work on public participation in planning and design studies and by Nabatchi and Leighninger's framework of citizen participation [17]. MUV methodology develops through diverse cycles of thick participation (involving groups of citizens) and thin participation (involving citizens as individuals).

MUV participatory method has been elaborated through diverse phases based on diverse cycles of co-creation (process-oriented) and co-design (solution-oriented).

Elaborating from an action-research approach [18], three different phases of co-design and co-creation activities have been planned in each city. Three co-creation iterations will take different shapes and forms in the six pilot neighbourhoods; the co-design phases aim to deliver comparable outputs, and will shape MUV gameplay features and dynamics:

- Phase 1 - co-design of general game features as linked to mobility issues;
- Phase 2 - co-design of specific game features and physical touch-points (e.g. monitoring stations) linked to the service system;
- Phase 3 - co-design of game features linked to generate data for enhancing future sustainable mobility policies.

For each pilot neighbourhood, MUV methodology has been developed around local stakeholders' engagement according to diverse communities of belonging: to the community of place (people living, working, frequenting the area), the community of practice (people working in local transport companies and authorities) and the community of interest (people that have economic, social, cultural interest in the neighbourhood) have been involved.

The first co-creation iteration was carried out from December 2017 to February 2018. About 130 participants among the six local communities attended the diverse participatory activities that have refined the MUV methodology for co-creation and co-design and the diverse tool-kits use. Among the different activities carried out in the six cities, workshops aimed at co-designing some of the game focuses have been structured according to new ways to interact with the topic of sustainable and active urban mobility adopting a playful approach (both physically and virtually). Through group activities, such as exercises and games, inputs were collected from each pilot neighbourhood, then outlined on special models and made available to R&D managers to be converted into game elements and app requirements.

Despite the different contexts, results show similar issues as related to personal mobility tracking issues and local mass transportation availability. As inspired by Jane McGonigal [19] categorization of self-rewarding (autolethic) experiences, game focuses have been addressed by clustering responses and insights from each MUV neighbourhood (Table 2) to: I - do a satisfying work; II - be successful; III - have social connections; IV - find meaning.

Table 2 shows that the mobility challenges in each neighbourhood under a framework of self-rewarding experiences can address specifically: (i) game focuses at the interface between the diverse problems at hand; (ii) the value of the playful experience to lever individual behaviour (e.g. personal reputation, identity building and antidote to frustrations), social practices (connectedness, community commitment, sense of community) and urban systems (safety and reliability).

Table 2. Neighbourhoods/Game focuses/Self-rewarding experiences.

Neighbourhood (city)	Game focuses	Self-rewarding experience			
		I	II	III	IV
Buitenveldert (Amsterdam)	Encourage social connectedness to be safer			X	
Sant Andreu (Barcelona)	Enhance individual personal reputation		X	X	
Old Town (Fundão)	Set common goals and improve the community commitment to change		X		X
Muide/Meulestede (Ghent)	Allow projecting a different personal identity	X	X		
Jätkäsaari (Helsinki)	Build the sense of community			X	X
Old Town (Palermo)	Provide an extensive playful experience to avoid frustrations	X			X

3.2   MUV Game General Features

In MUV local co-design activities influence the game focuses, but also the game features. As inspired by Jane McGonigal [19] an important elaboration of these game features depend from issues as: Goal, Rules, Real-Time Feedback, Voluntary participation (Table 3).

3.3   MUV New Dramatic Elements

Game insights have contributed to enriching the game modes as well as the interactions between the actors (both in and outside the game):

- MUV players, MUVers, have a real (achievable) sports career to cope;
- public authorities, from "motivators", have become MUVers' personal trainers;
- local business owners and supporting organizations will sponsor individual MUVers and their teams.

The MUV Experience. The MUV game experience has been designed around the four above-mentioned intrinsic motivation categories (do satisfying work, be successful, have social connections, find meaning). By playing the game, the player

Table 3. Game features/Links to local co-design sessions.

Game features	Links to local co-design sessions	Self-rewarding experience			
		I	II	III	IV
Goal					
Goal of the MUVers (the MUV players) is to gather points and *coins*	"Coins" are the currency of the game. They allow players to access some game experiences and customizations. They do not depend directly on mobility behaviours as such but could be earned also by participating in community (physical) meetings and events			X	
Rules					
MUVers score points via the app by moving sustainably: by walking they will have the maximum evaluation in points for the distance travelled, then by biking, then by using mass transportation systems and finally by private-vehicle pooling When players *move together* (by walking, by biking, by using mass transportation systems) they receive extra points	"Move together" has incentives linked to social interactions and improves traffic safety			X	X
Weather and traffic conditions might influence points attribution	"Weather and traffic conditions" work as points multipliers and they are designed t to address punctually local mobility issues and improve equity through the extra effort to reach common goals	X		X	X
MUVers earn coins by completing *Training Sessions*	"Training sessions" are mobility tasks to be accomplished. This game feature is co-designed locally by the community. Only by completing training sessions players can level-up. Training sessions aim to foster local interactions in defining common goals	X	X	X	X

(continued)

Table 3. (*continued*)

Game features	Links to local co-design sessions	Self-rewarding experience			
		I	II	III	IV
Coins can also be earned by achieving given *Tournaments* goals. To do that, players need to use the MUV mobile app and/or participate in specific community events	"Tournaments" are game features to be played as massive multiplayer, multiplayer and individually. Each game features has different characteristics that aim to enhance the sense of community and individual social benefits	X	X	X	X
Real-time feedback system					
Points collection is rewarded via the real-time improvement of *individual and local community statistics...*	MUV's core game features aim to co-create a community capacity of making cities healthier, this aim can include explicit players' "Stats" and MUV's "Cities' profile" where CO_2 equivalent emission are highlighted		X	X	X
...and the power index	"Power index" addresses the personal reputation and the social benefits Evaluates a player for his ability to play MUV and it's defined as the percentile rank of the score obtained by the user in a given time period within the group of scores obtained by all users in the same period It's meant to push		X		X
Tournaments and training sessions achievements are rewarded via the app with coins, *Levels of Experience (LoE)...*	"Levels of experience" are a measure of the volume of activity conducted by players and represent career steps: Newbie, Rookie, Pro, Star Only by scaling up the various LoEs players can experience all the game modes	X	X		X
...virtual badges, avatar customizations and discounts & gifts	"Virtual badges, avatar customizations" are co-designed with the local community This enhances the sense of the local ownership and allows also to push the sports metaphor into defining a completely new virtual world			X	X

(*continued*)

Table 3. (*continued*)

Game features	Links to local co-design sessions	Self-rewarding experience			
		I	II	III	IV
To enhance the performance, *Monitoring Stations* communicate weather, traffic and game info through the app and physically, once players pass nearby them, also visual feedback and cheerful sounds	"Monitoring stations" are physical devices located within the pilot neighbourhoods and hosted by the community of interest They represent a physical interface for MUVers that allows them to have useful information to improve their performances (like weather, air quality, traffic conditions) and actively interact with the community of interest			X	X
Voluntary participation					
The only way MUVers can play via the app is to *press a button* when they are starting to move in a sustainable way and then press it again when they stop	"Press a button" action allows at the same time the voluntary participation and the voluntary GPS tracking, coping the concerns of being tracked constantly	X			

collects points that will allow him/her to level up and gain access to new auto-rewarding game scenarios.

Like every career in sport, the experience of being a MUVer starts with tough trainings and ends with legendary triumphs. For this reason, at the very beginning, MUVers have to train to be ready to represent their cities at the city competition. By completing individual "Training Sessions", they learn how to play and how to measure their potential.

The second step will allow MUVers to be visible to the whole MUV international community by playing the "City Tournament". By playing together with their cities' community, MUVers can be recognized for their individual performance. But only by completing new additional Training Sessions, MUVers can jump to the next level.

The third step turns MUVers into professional players. Those who have achieved their individual goals are asked to join new teams, managed by sponsors, to play (in addition to the City Tournament) a new restricted tournament: the "Team Tournament". If they win with their teams they get rewarded with goods and services provided by the sponsors themselves. Again, only by selecting and finalizing more challenging Training Sessions MUVers can reach the final step.

The last phase of the MUVers' journey happens when they become international stars. They reach this point only when they achieved the most ambitious goals and demonstrated an outstanding impact in terms of sustainable mobility. At this moment, they are asked to join the "Stars Tournament", which consists of individual

Fig. 1. A peak into the MUVer experience (LTR): Phase 1 - a new MUVer started her first Training Session//Phase 3 - Team Tournament: MUVer Roberto and his friends are currently winning from their rivals of the 'Panaholics' team.

tournaments at an international scale. By playing in the Stars Tournament, they are individually sponsored and they can reach an international fame.

4   Conclusions and Future Work

The first release of the MUV game (Fig. 1) has been launched in the six neighbour-hoods during the European Sustainable Mobility Week (16–21 September 2018) through site-specific events. Moreover, during the CIVITAS annual congress (Umea, Sweden, 18–20 September 2018) an open call to select six new cities to join the project has been launched. The evaluation of MUV gameplay will be subject of further investigation in the coming months. Updates on MUV impact will be published on the MUV website and disseminated via the project newsletter [3].

Acknowledgments. This research has received funding from the European Union's Horizon 2020 research and innovation programme, under grant agreement No 723521.

References

1. SUMP Guide. http://www.eltis.org/it/guidelines/sump-guidelines. Accessed 30 Sept 2018
2. Vanolo, A.: Cities and the politics of gamification. Cities **74**(4), 320–326 (2018)
3. MUV project. https://www.muv2020.eu. Accessed 30 Sept 2018
4. Suits, B.: The Grasshopper: Games, Life and Utopia. Broadview Press, Peterborough (1978)
5. Empower. https://empowertoolkit.eu. Accessed 30 Sept 2018

6. Sweatcoin. https://sweatco.in. Accessed 30 Sept 2018
7. WeCity. http://www.wecity.it/en/. Accessed 30 Sept 2018
8. RingRing. https://ring-ring.nu. Accessed 30 Sept 2018
9. TrafficO$_2$. http://www.traffico2.com/en/. Accessed 30 Sept 2018
10. Weber, J., Azab, M., Riggs, W., Cherry, C.R.: The convergence of smartphone apps, gamification and competition to increase cycling. Transp. Res. Part F Traffic Psychol. Behav. **56**(7), 333–343 (2018)
11. Nakashima, R., Sato, T., Maruyama, T.: Gamification approach to smartphone-app-based mobility management. Transp. Res. Procedia **25**, 2344–2355 (2017)
12. Di Dio, S.: From Smart to Lean. Altralinea Edizioni, Firenze (2018)
13. Duhigg, C.: The Power of Habit. Why We Do What We Do and How to Change. Random House Books, London (2013)
14. Lissandrello, E., Morelli, N., Schillaci, D., Di Dio, S.: Urban innovation through co-design scenarios. In: Knoche, H., Popescu, E., Cartelli, A. (eds.) SLERD 2018 2018. SIST, vol. 95, pp. 110–122. Springer, Cham (2019). https://doi.org/10.1007/978-3-319-92022-1_10
15. Csikszentmihalyi, M.: Flow: The Psychology of Optimal Experience. Harper & Row Publishers, New York (1990)
16. Hamari, J., Koivisto, J.: Measuring flow in gamification: dispositional flow scale-2. Comput. Hum. Behav. **40**, 133–143 (2014)
17. Nabatchi, T., Leighninger, M.: Public Participation for 21st Century Democracy. Wiley, Hoboken (2015)
18. Manzini, E.: Design, When Everybody Designs. MIT Press, Cambridge (2015)
19. Mcgonigal, J.: Reality Is Broken: Why Games Make Us Better and How They Can Change the World. Penguin Group USA, New York (2011)

Putting the Long-Term into Behavior Change

Harmen de Weerd$^{(\boxtimes)}$ (i) and Nick Degens (i)

Research Group User-Centered Design, Hanze University of Applied Sciences,
Groningen, The Netherlands
{h.a.de.weerd,d.m.degens}@pl.hanze.nl

Abstract. Behavior change is a topic that is of great interest to many people. People can use apps to exercise more, eat healthier, or learn a new skill, but and digital interventions and games are also used by policy makers and companies to create a safe environment for the general public or to increase sales. Given this interest in behavior change, it is not surprising that this topic has seen a lot of interest from the scientific community. This has resulted in a wide range of theories and techniques to bring about behavior change. However, maintaining behavior change is rarely addressed, and as a result poorly understood. In this paper, we take a first step in the design of digital interventions for long-term behavior change by placing a range of behavior change techniques on a long-term behavior change timeline.

Keywords: Behavior change · Long-term effects · Behavior change techniques

1 Introduction

Behavior change is a topic that is of great interest to a wide audience: policy makers aim to encourage the public to exhibit behavior that results in a safe and comfortable environment, companies aim to have consumers buy their products, and many individuals use digital applications or games to change their own behavior by exercising more, eating a healthier diet, or ridding themselves of a bad habit. Given this interest in behavior change, it is not surprising that this topic has seen a lot of interest from the scientific community. This has resulted in a wide range of useful theories and techniques that are effective in bringing about behavior change [12, 14, 35].

However, many behavior change theories only consider the initial change of behavior and do not address the issue of maintaining behavior change. As a result, long-term behavior change is rarely achieved [18]. This is particularly unfortunate as common behavior change goals such as eating healthier, exercising more, or quitting smoking are intended to be long-term behavior changes.

In this paper, we take a first step towards a formalization for long-term behavior change interventions by taking a closer look at a number of behavior change techniques, particularly those that are used or that can be used in digital applications or games, and placing them on a long-term behavior change timeline. The goal of this timeline is to provide a clear picture of what behavior change techniques are most effective at different points in the behavior change process.

© Springer Nature Switzerland AG 2019
M. Gentile et al. (Eds.): GALA 2018, LNCS 11385, pp. 71–81, 2019.
https://doi.org/10.1007/978-3-030-11548-7_7

We discuss a number of behavior change techniques listed in the behavior change technique (BCT) taxonomy v1 [23]. These behavior change techniques differ in the way they approach behavior change by targeting different determinants of behavior. Across many theories on behavior, there appears to be a consensus that there are three main determinants of behavior; in this paper, we use the COM-B model of [22] and refer to these three determinants as motivation, capability, and opportunity. In Sects. 2, 3, and 4, we discuss the motivation, capability, and opportunity determinants of behavior, respectively, and discuss some of the behavior change techniques that target these determinants. In Sect. 5, we discuss our findings in the light of long-term behavior change, and place behavior change techniques on an intervention timeline. Finally, Sect. 6 concludes our paper and provides direction for future research.

2 Motivation

In the COM-B model [22], motivation is the total inclination of a user to engage in the target behavior. This includes voluntary considerations based on intrinsic motivators such as a sense of pleasure, achievement, or discovery, as well as extrinsic motivators such as monetary reward, verbal praise, or social recognition. In addition, motivation also includes involuntary processes that change the likelihood to perform the target behavior, such as habits, addiction, and emotional responses. However, although habits are explicitly included in the motivation determinant of behavior, we will delay discussion of habits until Sect. 4 on the opportunity determinant of behavior (Table 1).

Table 1. Summary of behavior change techniques through motivation considered in Sect. 2.

Technique	Effects
Extrinsic rewards	+ Can reduce costs of behavior change [7]
	− Low rewards may be counter-productive [13]
	− Effective rewards can have addictive properties [16]
Persuasive information	+ Social comparison can increase motivation [25]
	+ Vicarious experiences can increase motivation [21]
Fear appeal	+ Effective in many cases [33]
	− May be counterproductive for low self-efficacy users [15]
Punishment	+ Effective in reducing bad habits [1]
	− Limited effectiveness as a deterrence [19]
	− Concrete punishment may make bad behavior acceptable [11]
Social pressure	+ Monitoring by others increases adherence [24]
Long-term effects	− Motivators lose effectiveness over time

One of the reasons why people may fail to change their behavior is a lack of motivation. Perhaps the most obvious solution to this problem is to incentivize these people with additional (extrinsic) motivation in the form of rewards. Gamification elements such as points and achievements, but also likes on user-created content can be rewarding. Rewards even effect behavior change in people who do not receive the reward themselves; Ma et al. [21] show that children that observed peers who were rewarded for their honesty were more likely to be honest than those that observed honest peers that were not rewarded.

Social factors can also play a significant role in motivating behavior change in general. Nolan et al. [25] experimented with different energy conservation messages and found that Californians conserved more energy when they were told that their neighbors did so, even though respondents rated such normative information as the least motivating. Even the sense of being watched by others can affect motivation. Nettle et al. [24] show that participants were more likely to donate in the Dictator Game when a poster with a pair of eyes was present in the experimentation room.

While rewards may increase motivation, the use of rewards does not guarantee a beneficial effect. There are cases in which extrinsic rewards may actually suppress intrinsic motivation to perform a task. Heyman and Ariely [13] report on an experiment in which participants that were paid a low amount of money to perform a task put in *less* effort than those that were not paid at all. In addition, Kim and Werbach [16] argue that particularly strong gamified incentives can have addictive properties and unintentionally lead to physical or psychological harm to the user.

Extrinsic motivators can also be used to generate a positive association with the target behavior. For example, many medical treatments are boring to perform or have negative side effects that hinder adherence. By incorporating boring rehabilitation exercises in a game, such as the rehabilitation gaming system [7], the association of the rehabilitation with boredom can be changed into an association with fun.

Rather than rewarding behavior change, people can also be motivated to change their behavior by emphasizing the negative effects of failing to change behavior. Such *fear appeals* are an especially popular tool in campaigns to prevent or reduce smoking and binge drinking, or to improve road safety. While fear appeals have been shown to be effective [33], a threat alone is likely to be ineffective in encouraging behavior change and may even be counter-productive in users that feel incapable of changing behavior [15]. A threat should therefore be presented alongside concrete advice on how to avoid the negative effects mentioned in the threat. That is, a behavior change intervention that relies on fear appeals should have elements that target the motivation determinant, but also target the capability determinant of behavior (see Sect. 4).

If threats and fear appeals are not effective enough in discouraging negative behavior, behavior change techniques can attempt to remove the beneficial effects of the negative behavior or to add punishment. Examples of this type of behavior change technique are imposing fines for speeding by policy makers [19], applying a bitter creme to discourage nail biting [1], but also limited lives in a computer game.

Punishment may not be effective in reducing undesirable behavior. For example, Lawpoolsri and Braver [19] find that speeding tickets have a limited deterring effect. Gneezy and Rustichini [11] report a situation where a daycare center introduced a fine for parents that picked up their children too late, whereupon the number of late-coming parents *increased* rather than decreased. In this case, the fine may have been interpreted as a price for a service, making the negative behavior more acceptable.

In addition, rather than changing their behavior, people may put their effort in avoiding the punishment, such as installing a radar detector to avoid speeding tickets.

This is a particular challenge for game-based interventions, where a user may simply choose to stop playing to avoid punishment rather than engaging in behavior change.

A particular problem when trying to achieve long-term behavior change by targeting motivation is that the behavior is likely to revert back to the original once the intervention ends (e.g. when a player abandons a game). After all, if intrinsic motivation was not enough to encourage behavior change originally, it is likely to be insufficient once there are no more extrinsic motivators (cf. [5]). But even if the intervention can be continued indefinitely, repeated exposure to the same reward, threat, or punishment may lead to habituation or satiation, which may reduce its effectiveness. For example, users routinely disregard security warnings from their computer [2]. For long-term behavior change, an intervention based on rewards or threats should therefore also consider planning for habituation (see also Sect. 4).

3   Capability

In the COM-B model [22], capability refers to the user's perceived ability to perform the target behavior (i.e. self-efficacy, [3]), which includes physical ability and self-control, but also the knowledge and skill necessary to perform the task (Table 2).

Table 2. Summary of behavior change techniques through capability considered in Sect. 3.

Technique	Effects
Planning	+ Planning more concrete actions is more effective [8]
Instruction	+ Seeing peers perform behavior boosts self-efficacy [29]
	+ Testimonials can increase self-efficacy [34]
Task structuring	− Setting difficult goals can reduce self-efficacy [4]
	+ Scaffolding can gradually improve self-efficacy [36]
Feedback	− Data alone may not be effective [20, 30]
Identity	+ Identifying with the target behavior increases self-efficacy [28]

Conroy et al. [9] find that many top-ranked mobile apps for physical activity rely mostly on instructions or demonstrations of the target behavior. However, techniques that help users to transform their intentions into concrete behavior, for example through action planning, were rarely observed in these apps, even though these techniques have the potential to increase self-efficacy [8]. For example, a user that wants to exercise more is less likely to be effective when he commits to going to the gym this week than when he commits to go to the gym for an hour on Wednesday at 6 PM.

The successfulness of a behavior change intervention depends on whether concrete and manageable goals are set. Through chaining or scaffolding, complex goals can be achieved through a series of simpler tasks. For example, Dragonbox Algebra [36] starts teaching children how to solve algebraic equations by introducing a concept of zero. As the player progresses, the player receives incremental instructions on how to perform the more complex actions that are needed to complete later goals, while avoiding goals that are too complex. After all, a particularly challenging goal, even when the user does complete it, can reduce self-efficacy [4].

Schunk and Hanson [29] show that children that observed the subtraction skills of others were more confident that they could learn subtraction as well. This modeling effect was strongest when these children observed peers rather than teachers, which underlines that modeling is most effective when the model is similar to the target. A similar effect is shown by Ubel et al. [34], who report that testimonials of previous patients significantly influence the choice of treatment of a current patient. These effects can also be leveraged through multi-player elements in games.

A user's ability to change behavior can also be supported by feedback on or monitoring of the current behavior. For example, wearable activity trackers such as Fitbit provide continuous information on activity to help the user achieve their activity goals. However, Shih et al. [30] find that 17 out of 26 users stopped using the Fitbit within two weeks. Lazar et al. [20] report that athletic users found the data to be least useful, while other users believed the data to be more useful to athletic users. That is, while wearable devices provide a great opportunity to provide feedback on behavior, the presentation of this feedback should be designed with the end user in mind.

An important aspect of the capability determinant of behavior is that it refers to *perceived* ability to perform the behavior. The importance is exemplified by the fact that users tend to perform the behaviors that are associated with their perceived identity. For example, users that identify themselves as a smoker tend to smoke. If a smoker starts to identify as a non-smoker, for example through some success with quitting smoking, that person is less likely to relapse [28].

4   Opportunity

The third determinant of behavior in the COM-B model [22] is opportunity, which refers to external factors that facilitate or prompt the target behavior. Someone who is dedicated to dental hygiene and wants to floss more often may be helped by being prompted to floss at appropriate times. Similarly, notifications on a smartphone signal the opportunity for its user to interact with the smartphone (Table 3).

Table 3. Summary of behavior change techniques through capability considered in Sect. 4.

Technique	Effects
Habit formation	+ Relevant cues increase adherence and automaticity [26]
	− Adherence is not the same as automaticity [32]
	− Repetition alone is not enough [10]
Environmental restructuring	+ Distraction from cues can help to remove bad habits [27]

The opportunity determinant of behavior is strongly related to creating positive habits and removing negative habits, which in turn has strong ties with long-term behavior change. It is important to note that while repetition is an important aspect in habit formation, habits are not determined by frequency of behavior, but by automaticity in the presence of a given cue [10]. In order to form a habit, a relevant cue is therefore vital. Orbell and Verplanken [26] show their results of an experiment introducing a flossing habit in participants. They report that participants that were explicitly asked to write down a concrete cue to start flossing (e.g. after brushing teeth at night) flossed more over the four weeks of the experiment than control participants.

Habit formation relies vitally on the relevance of the cue. Ideally, the cue should only be present when the desired behavior is to be performed in order to ensure a strong connection between cue and behavior. For example, even though security warnings on a computer only occur in relevant situations, they are routinely ignored [2]. Interventions aimed at habit formation should therefore strive to select a relevant cue and make it more salient to the user, for example through prompts or reminders. Karppinen et al. [14] report that such reminders were perceived as especially beneficial features of behavior change support systems.

In addition, the cue should be salient enough to eventually trigger behavior without a prompt. Stawarz et al. [32] show that while time-based cues result in better adherence, context-based cues result in better automaticity. That is, while sending an SMS message every morning at 8 AM to floss may result in better adherence, a context-dependent cue at the end of breakfast is expected to result in better habit formation. However, it is more difficult to automatically send a message whenever a user finishes brushing their teeth than it is to send a message every day at 8 AM. When using prompts to help users change their behavior, the relevant cue should be salient enough for the intervention to detect. However, if the relevant cue is particularly salient, the user may not need a prompt. Sohn et al. [31] present a possible solution by prompting based on GPS location, which may be more salient for a device than for the user.

Some behavior change techniques are closely linked to both opportunity and capability. The antecedents group of behavior change techniques revolves around stopping negative behavior by avoiding the stimuli that encourage it. For example, people that want to eat healthier may decide to restructure their environment by filling their house with healthy snacks rather than unhealthy snacks, or even to buy only at stores that do not sell unhealthy food. Similarly, a student may decide to go to the library to avoid the distractions at home. By doing so, they avoid the stimuli that encourage the unwanted behavior (eating unhealthy snacks, being distracted from studying) while allowing ample opportunity to engage in the target behavior (eating healthy snacks, studying). For internal stimuli, such as cravings for smoking, distraction may provide a suitable technique to avoid giving in [27].

5 Designing Interventions for Long-Term Behavior Change

Behavior change techniques are typically described from a short-term point of view, in which the only significant influence on the user's motivation, capability, and opportunities can be assumed to be the technique itself. However, as time progresses, a user's motivation, capability, and opportunities may change, as well as the requirements a user has of the behavior change techniques that are offered by an intervention. In this section, we take a first step in placing behavior change techniques in a time frame specifically aimed at long-term behavior change.

In the process of behavior change, we identify four phases (see Fig. 1), which correspond to the four stages of competence [6]. In the earliest phase of behavior change, users of a behavior change intervention are *unconsciously incompetent*. A user in this phase is unable to implement the behavior change and does not recognize that such behavior change is necessary or beneficial. At this initial phase, the intended behavior change may even be actively opposed (e.g. in addiction), or already presumed to be achieved (i.e., an illusion of mastery).

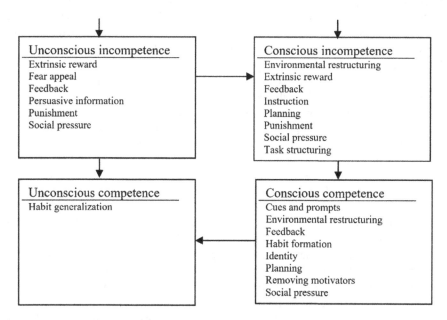

Fig. 1. Long-term behavior change timeline.

Users in this first phase will not knowingly engage in a behavior change intervention themselves but are rather entered into the intervention through outside forces. This could in the form of a game that requires its players to acquire certain skills to progress, or a government trying to dissuade negative behavior. Behavior change techniques that are expected to be effective in this phase mostly have an outcome that is attitudinal or results in declarative knowledge (cf. [17]). Users can be informed about the need for behavior change by information about the beneficial effects of behavior change, emphasizing the negative effects of failing to change behavior (e.g. fear appeals), or feedback on the user's performance on the target behavior. In addition, extrinsic rewards, punishment, and social pressure may also be persuasive.

A user that understands the importance of the behavior change, but is unable to realize this change, transitions to a phase of *conscious incompetence*. Most serious games and other behavior change interventions focus on this stage, in which the user attempts to increase his or her competence. Behavior change techniques that have a motivational or declarative knowledge outcome (cf. [17]) play an important role here.

Users that do not perceive themselves as capable of the behavior change can be assisted through instruction, task structuring, planning, and feedback. In addition, users may feel incapable of behavior change due to a disconnect between long-term goals and short-term urges or habits. For example, someone who wants to quit smoking may feel unable to resist the urge to smoke at specific moments. Behavior change techniques that target opportunity by reducing the opportunity to perform negative behaviors (i.e. environmental restructuring) may be particularly effective. Users may also benefit from extrinsic rewards, punishment, or social pressure. Note that while in the unconscious incompetence stage these motivation-centered behavior change techniques are aimed at increasing the perceived *benefit* of the behavior change (i.e. attitudinal outcomes), in the conscious incompetence stage they are aimed at reducing the perceived *cost* of behavior change (i.e. motivational outcomes). For example, rehabilitating within the context of a game does not make the outcome of the treatment more appealing, it makes the perceived cost of the rehabilitation process acceptable.

The third phase is characterized by *conscious competence*. A user in this phase is capable of performing the target behavior at any given moment, but it requires conscious effort to do so, which results in a risk for relapse. In this phase, extrinsic rewards and punishment may need to be removed in a controlled manner. After all, as mentioned in Sect. 2, habituation and satiation of the extrinsic motivator may eventually render it ineffective (cf. [5]). However, if these extrinsic motivators were instrumental in achieving behavior change, intrinsic motivators may not be enough to maintain the behavior change. Social support may be especially useful in compensating for the reduced effectiveness of other motivators (see also [14]).

To reduce the risk of relapse, the user may start to identify with the new behavior (e.g. a non-smoker). Planning and feedback may still be required to maintain the behavior change. Behavior change techniques with an automaticity or proceduralization outcome [17] will be especially effective in transitioning to the final phase.

The final phase is characterized by *unconscious competence*, where the behavior change is governed by habitual action. In this phase, the risk of relapse of the user is greatly reduced. However, this does not mean that the behavior change is persistent. A prolonged change in context may disrupt the habit that governs the behavior change. This is a particular challenge for game-based interventions, which have to ensure that skills acquired in the game context transfer to and persist in real-life scenarios. In this final phase, habit generalization may therefore be beneficial.

While these phases suggest a strong linearity in the process of behavior change, this is not the intended message. For example, users that knowingly engage in behavior change will typically be consciously rather than unconsciously incompetent, and therefore start the process in the second phase. Through conditioning, users may also go from unconscious incompetence straight to unconscious competence. In addition, at any point a user may relapse to an earlier phase.

6 Discussion

In this paper, we have taken a first step in creating a timeline for long-term behavior change by delineating what behavior change techniques are most likely to be effective in what phase of the behavior change. A behavior change intervention is more effective on the long run when it combines a variety of behavior change techniques that target motivation, capability, and opportunity. However, simply adding more behavior change techniques to an intervention does not guarantee its effectiveness will increase [37]. While some combinations of behavior change techniques show synergy, adding more behavior change techniques may reduce overall effectiveness. Unfortunately, it is currently poorly understood how different behavior change techniques interact. In addition, not all behavior change can be readily assessed.

To complicate matters, a particularly effective behavior change technique is tailoring [14], in which the intervention customizes itself to the needs of the user. Also, the effectiveness of behavior change techniques such as modeling as well as emphasizing personal susceptibility in fear appeals suggests that interventions that adapt to their user may be especially effective. Although it is known that different audiences have different needs, it is not clearly understood how the determinants of behavior and the effectiveness of behavior change techniques vary across audiences.

Behavior change is a complex interplay of motivation, capability, and opportunity, especially over longer periods of time. With the long-term behavior change timeline presented in this paper, we have taken a first step towards understanding how digital tools such as serious games need to be designed to ensure long-term effectiveness.

References

1. Allen, K.: Chronic nailbiting: a controlled comparison of competing response and mild aversion treatments. Behav. Res. Ther. **34**(3), 269–272 (1996)
2. Anderson, B., Jenkins, J., Vance, A., Kirwan, C., Eargle, D.: Your memory is working against you: how eye tracking and memory explain habituation to security warnings. Decis. Support Syst. **92**, 3–13 (2016)
3. Bandura, A.: Self-efficacy: toward a unifying theory of behavioral change. Psychol. Rev. **84**(2), 191–215 (1977)
4. Bandura, A., Cervone, D.: Differential engagement of self-reactive influences in cognitive motivation. Organ. Behav. Hum. Decis. Process. **38**(1), 92–113 (1986)
5. Bouton, M.: Why behavior change is difficult to sustain. Prev. Med. **68**, 29–36 (2014)
6. Burch, N.: The Four Stages for Learning Any New Skill. Gordon Training International, Solana Beach (1970)
7. Cameirão, M., i Badia, S., Zimmerli, L., Oller, E., Verschure, P.: The rehabilitation gaming system: a virtual reality based system for the evaluation and rehabilitation of motor deficits. In: Virtual Rehabilitation, pp. 29–33 (2007)
8. Carraro, N., Gaudreau, P.: Spontaneous and experimentally induced action planning and coping planning for physical activity: a meta-analysis. Psychol. Sport Exerc. **14**(2), 228–248 (2013)
9. Conroy, D., Yang, C., Maher, J.: Behavior change techniques in top-ranked mobile apps for physical activity. Am. J. Prev. Med. **46**(6), 649–652 (2014)

10. Gardner, B.: Habit as automaticity, not frequency. Eur. Health Psychol. **14**(2), 32–36 (2012)

11. Gneezy, U., Rustichini, A.: A fine is a price. J. Leg. Stud. **29**(1), 1–17 (2000)

12. Gourlan, M., et al.: Efficacy of theory-based interventions to promote physical activity. A meta-analysis of randomised controlled trials. Health Psychol. Rev. **10**(1), 50–66 (2016)

13. Heyman, J., Ariely, D.: Effort for payment: a tale of two markets. Psychol. Sci. **15**(11), 787–793 (2004)

14. Karppinen, P., et al.: Persuasive user experiences of a health Behavior Change Support System: a 12-month study for prevention of metabolic syndrome. Int. J. Med. Inform. **96**, 51–61 (2016)

15. Kessels, L., Ruiter, R., Wouters, L., Jansma, B.: Neuroscientific evidence for defensive avoidance of fear appeals. Int. J. Psychol. **49**(2), 80–88 (2014)

16. Kim, T., Werbach, K.: More than just a game: ethical issues in gamification. Ethics Inf. Technol. **18**(2), 157–173 (2016)

17. Kraiger, K., Ford, J., Salas, E.: Application of cognitive, skill-based, and affective theories of learning outcomes to new methods of training evaluation. J. Appl. Psychol. **78**(2), 311–328 (1993)

18. Kwasnicka, D., Dombrowski, S., White, M., Sniehotta, F.: Theoretical explanations for maintenance of behaviour change: a systematic review of behaviour theories. Health Psychol. Rev. **10**(3), 277–296 (2016)

19. Lawpoolsri, S., Li, J., Braver, E.: Do speeding tickets reduce the likelihood of receiving subsequent speeding tickets? A longitudinal study of speeding violators in Maryland. Traffic Inj. Prev. **8**(1), 26–34 (2007)

20. Lazar, A., Koehler, C., Tanenbaum, J., Nguyen, D.: Why we use and abandon smart devices. In: Proceedings of the 2015 ACM International Joint Conference on Pervasive and Ubiquitous Computing, pp. 635–646 (2015)

21. Ma, F., et al.: Promoting honesty in young children through observational learning. J. Exp. Child Psychol. **167**, 234–245 (2018)

22. Michie, S., van Stralen, M., West, R.: The behaviour change wheel: a new method for characterising and designing behaviour change interventions. Implement. Sci. **6**(1), 42 (2011)

23. Michie, S., et al.: The behavior change technique taxonomy (v1) of 93 hierarchically clustered techniques: building an international consensus for the reporting of behavior change interventions. Ann. Behav. Med. **46**(1), 81–95 (2013)

24. Nettle, D., Harper, Z., Kidson, A., Stone, R., Penton-Voak, I., Bateson, M.: The watching eyes effect in the Dictator Game: it's not how much you give, it's being seen to give something. Evol. Hum. Behav. **34**(1), 35–40 (2013)

25. Nolan, J., Schultz, P., Cialdini, R., Goldstein, N., Griskevicius, V.: Normative social influence is underdetected. Pers. Soc. Psychol. Bull. **34**(7), 913–923 (2008)

26. Orbell, S., Verplanken, B.: The automatic component of habit in health behavior: habit as cue-contingent automaticity. Health Psychol. **29**(4), 374–383 (2010)

27. Ploderer, B., Smith, W., Pearce, J., Borland, R.: A mobile app offering distractions and tips to cope with cigarette craving: a qualitative study. JMIR mHealth uHealth **2**(2), e23 (2014)

28. van den Putte, B., Yzer, M., Willemsen, M., de Bruijn, G.: The effects of smoking self-identity and quitting self-identity on attempts to quit smoking. Health Psychol. **28**(5), 535–544 (2009)

29. Schunk, D., Hanson, A.: Peer models: influence on children's self-efficacy and achievement. J. Educ. Psychol. **77**(3), 313–322 (1985)

30. Shih, P., Han, K., Poole, E., Rosson, M., Carroll, J.: Use and adoption challenges of wearable activity trackers. In: iConference 2015 Proceedings (2015)

31. Sohn, T., Li, K.A., Lee, G., Smith, I., Scott, J., Griswold, W.G.: Place-its: a study of location-based reminders on mobile phones. In: Beigl, M., Intille, S., Rekimoto, J., Tokuda, H. (eds.) UbiComp 2005. LNCS, vol. 3660, pp. 232–250. Springer, Heidelberg (2005). https://doi.org/10.1007/11551201_14

32. Stawarz, K., Cox, A., Blandford, A.: Beyond self-tracking and reminders: designing smartphone apps that support habit formation. In: Proceedings of the 33rd Annual ACM Conference on Human Factors in Computing Systems, pp. 2653–2662. ACM (2015)

33. Tannenbaum, M., et al.: Appealing to fear: a meta-analysis of fear appeal effectiveness and theories. Psychol. Bull. **141**(6), 1178–1204 (2015)

34. Ubel, P., Jepson, C., Baron, J.: The inclusion of patient testimonials in decision aids: effects on treatment choices. Med. Decis. Making **21**(1), 60–68 (2001)

35. Webb, T., Joseph, J., Yardley, L., Michie, S.: Using the internet to promote health behavior change: a systematic review and meta-analysis of the impact of theoretical basis, use of behavior change techniques, and mode of delivery on efficacy. J. Med. Internet Res. **12**(1), e4 (2010)

36. WeWantToKnow (2011). Dragonbox Algebra. http://dragonbox.com

37. Wildeboer, G., Kelders, S., van Gemert-Pijnen, J.: The relationship between persuasive technology principles, adherence and effect of web-based interventions for mental health: a meta-analysis. Int. J. Med. Inform. **96**, 71–85 (2016)

MainTrain: A Serious Game
on the Complexities of Rail Maintenance

David Alderliesten[✉], Kotryna Valečkaitė, Nestor Z. Salamon,
J. Timothy Balint, and Rafael Bidarra

Faculty of Electrical Engineering, Mathematics and Computer Science,
Delft University of Technology, Delft, The Netherlands
J.W.D.Alderliesten@student.tudelft.nl

Abstract. Commuters who travel by train often feel annoyed due to misunderstanding the causes of delays in train traffic. They oftentimes are unaware of the necessity of performing maintenance to stations, tracks, and trains. MainTrain is a serious game developed to teach commuters about rail-maintenance while simulating the difficulty of keeping passengers happy. It is a fast-paced strategy game with a top-down view in which a player can perform maintenance actions on stations, tracks, and trains. By using commuter happiness as a base metric, MainTrain attempts to elicit empathy from players dissatisfied with scheduled maintenance so that they gain a better appreciation of the need for scheduled maintenance. This is coupled with the need to schedule maintenance for several components of a rail network, encumbering a player while teaching them about different aspects of rail maintenance. To examine the effectiveness of the game, the results of a user study are presented.

Keywords: Serious game · Educational game · Rail maintenance

1 Introduction

Scheduled rail maintenance is a nuisance for any traveler. The additional waiting time created by maintenance can cause a delayed arrival time, missed connections, or even the inability to reach a destination. Some scheduling issues are the result of incidental failures of rolling stock or maintenance issues such as faulty junctions and signaling on semaphores, but many other delays arise due to planned maintenance. These types of scheduling conflicts do not restrict the ability to travel entirely, but do cause routes to have less capacity, less trains which can operate within a unit of time, or a requirement to travel through a different station to reach the desired destination [21].

Although these types of delays are usually announced as planned rail maintenance, many passengers do not understand why such maintenance must impact them. Passengers may be unable to understand what delays and issues arise in a rail network when this maintenance is not performed, thereby becoming unhappy when maintenance is

D. Alderliesten and K. Valečkaitė—Equal contribution.

performed on their routes. However, the effects of not maintaining a rail network include derailment, emergency maintenance, and wear and tear of assets. All these alternatives could cause bodily harm, more extreme issues with scheduling, or the entire cancellation of routes for a long period of time [20]. Therefore, passengers who deal with scheduled maintenance focus on current unhappiness as opposed to the greater potential unhappiness caused by not doing so.

MainTrain is a serious game meant to clarify and to show the effects of this planned & scheduled maintenance. It is meant to enable impacted customers of rail organizations to understand that, despite their frustration, the maintenance is required and not performing it could lead to longer inconveniences. MainTrain is also meant to expose players to the difficulties and conflicts with scheduling such planned maintenance, evoking possible empathy or understanding as to why they have been impacted while showing them that it was not possible to generate a maintenance schedule which avoids impacting any group of travelers or impact another group in a less negative manner.

The main aim of MainTrain is to provide players with the ability to manage a rail network with a selected set of features\regarding rail maintenance, as well as the ability to see the direct impact upon passengers and rolling stock (train cars). Moreover, to avoid extensive and tedious gameplay as it would occur in a real time simulation, MainTrain delivers the full experience in a maximum of five to ten minutes. The focus of MainTrain lies with imbuing an understanding to the players of the complexities of rail maintenance.

2   Related Works

The topic of planning and scheduling rail networks is not one lacking research, acting as the focus of significant algorithmic optimization efforts and decision support tools [4, 6, 8, 14]. Regardless of the effort on operational effectiveness, failures and delays are inevitable. Therefore, a significant amount of research is honed to minimize the passenger dissatisfaction (a recent review of the work is provided by [16]).

The perception of the train travel quality depends on many quantifiable (e.g. travel time, cost, reliability) and unquantifiable (e.g. comfort, passenger risk aversion) variables [15]. For instance, during a disruption event itself, the negative impact on the passengers' perception can be influenced by the type of information they are provided [18]. Tsuchiya et al. [18] show, that passengers appreciate being informed about the cause of the delay. However, in situations where the operator was responsible (rather than an unforeseen external factor), passengers experienced stronger negative emotions. Among such disruptions are train delays caused by the rail maintenance. Nonetheless, understanding the nature of the disruption alleviates stress experienced by the passenger [9].

Bringing it to serious games, interaction is one of the most important components of learning experience [7, 13]. One of the most effective ways of content-learner interactions have been provided by the relatively new medium of video games. Such games, focusing not only on the entertainment value, have been proven to work in a motivating, enabling manner [2]. Serious games allow people to actively participate and allow repetitive practicing. Even within a context of rail and transport planning, such games have been proven to be an excellent medium to explain complex concepts [3] and even explore radical innovations within transport planning [19]. These examples, Synchro Mania [3] and SprintCity [11, 12], do not explicitly deal with railway or rolling stock maintenance. The first one focuses on synchro modality and planning of freight transport. The second one primarily offers the possibility to create 'what-if' scenarios for infrastructure planning to support decision making.

On the one side of the spectrum lie games focusing on the economic aspects and optimization of railroad network use. The following examples are not considered serious games, but their core gameplay components illustrate the complexity of the railway design, scheduling and operating objectives. Among these are Simultrans [10], Railroad X [17], Sid Meyer's Railroads! [1]. Within this category of games, the player cannot schedule trains or funnel passenger movement paths but is able to make budgetary decision and can attempt to create a rail network design that most optimally funnels passengers to transfer locations. Looking at even more minimalistic games, such as MiniMetro [5], address the complexity of network design itself. MiniMetro places an emphasis on the design of the network and route capacities, with the requirement to transport a certain number of passengers within a given time limit. The game is open ended, with game difficulty increasing together with the growing rail network.

3   Game Design and Implementation

The purpose of the presented MainTrain game is to provide a player with an understanding as to why planned maintenance is required and why minimizing the negative impact on passengers is a difficult task. These insights are to be provided within the context of a short time period, such as a convention floor or on a station platform while waiting for a delayed train. The main purpose of the game is to:

- inform about the basic types of rail maintenance;
- make the player aware of the (dis)advantages of performing regular rail maintenance; and
- trigger the further interest in the topic.

For this, the game must provide a simple overview of a rail network with the essential features: stations, tracks, and trains. This system is not a representation of a real rail network to avoid overly complex starting conditions and possible player favoritism of known locations.

The core of the game is to perform maintenance tasks along a rail network, which is deteriorating over time. The player can perform rolling stock, station, and track maintenance. The player can perform these tasks by selecting the desired component (track element, station, rolling stock), and selecting one of the maintenance options provided. Track maintenance ensures trains can safely and quickly reach their destination, while also preventing accidents and a propagation of track damage. Rolling stock maintenance ensures that trains are clean and comfortable for passengers, increasing their tolerance for longer journeys and issues that arise while en-route. Station maintenance ensures that passengers are attracted to the idea of train travel and will tolerate longer delays and issues that arise before their journey begins. These three maintenance tasks were chosen as they are easily visible in both the game and real life. Most passengers interact with the trains and stations and can perceive repair being done on track if they pass by the track. Maintaining the rail system allows transporting larger quantities of passengers, as well as keeping them happy. For the first of the two, the user is rewarded by points and system complexity growth. Simultaneously, it is also essential to keep the passenger happiness high: if it drops below a set threshold, the game ends.

The simplicity of possible choices is counterweighted by the size of the provided network. Additionally, the inability to have a full overview of the system state at all times contributes to the complexity of decision making during the game session. Like in real world, situation the system operator needs to perform manual inspections of units. Furthermore, the user is presented with the knowledge at which points in time the routes will likely deteriorate. Making the game complicated is intentional: the player is supposed to feel discomfort as if to mimic the 'actual' situation. An overview of the presentation of these features is present in Fig. 1.

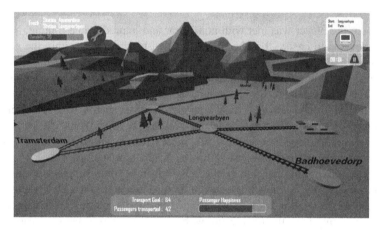

Fig. 1. A sample train layout, with *Tramsterdam* selected. In the upper left corner are stats related to the track reach the station. A train will soon run between two other stations, indicated by the card on the top right side.

3.1 Procedural Rails and Random Route Generation

MainTrain was developed to allow random station generation over time to increase the difficulty of the game for the player. To facilitate this, a method was developed to generate track pieces between randomly generated stations regardless of positions. A simple rail model was placed within the game and the stations were encoded to consist of track start and end points. Track would be generated by replicating the track model multiple times between these start and end points, generating a track that can be randomly created and allows for network expansion. The track's existence, including its length and direction between two stations, was implemented within a central array to allow for the simple addition of trains over the track, meaning they would travel over the procedurally generated rail segments. The players would be provided with an overview as seen in Fig. 2.

Fig. 2. Train cards with the route information and train properties.

To ensure the player was met with non-linear and unpredictable routing, a method had to be devised to ensure that the routes traveled by the trains within the game are random. Hence, an array of stations was created, and a random timer derived from the game engine determines whether an event should be generated at any random given moment. The routes generated take a start and end station, which can be connected directly but usually consist of at least a single stopover station between them. This utilizes more of the track, requiring more sections be operational to keep a high happiness score. The route uses the track pieces found within the game world to determine the most efficient route to get to the destination station.

Due to the possibility that a track piece is broken beyond the point of allowing a train to traverse it, the routing implementation also accounts for cases where a train cannot reach its destination or must be rerouted during its journey. This was done by continually iterating over the track array within the game world between each visited station and determines a new route to the desired destination if still possible. This solved the issue of random routing, as well as also the issue that could arise in which trains might be routed to move over broken track.

3.2 Passenger Satisfaction Coupling

The measuring of passenger satisfaction requires interplay between multiple variables within the game. These variables include: average cleanliness of stations, the durability of the track segment the train is moving over, and the cleanliness and repair status of the rolling stock itself. To ensure that the player notices the impact of these many variables, simple methods had to be found which could bind all associated variables together and impact a distinct set of variables that the player would notice. The Passenger Count and Passenger Satisfaction variables bind all associated values together to ensure the player is not tracking or noticing the interplay of elements but does receive understandable feedback when a train is generated to provide hints related to track status. The passenger count value is given when trains are generated and directly influenced by all variables related to the player performance, whereas the passenger satisfaction variable is shown as a percentage bar to provide an overview of passenger timeliness and comfort directly related to the actions of the player.

4 Evaluation

We assess the efficacy of MainTrain by performing a user-study. Testing was performed between groups on two different versions of the game: (i) one without a possibility to lose and without a clear indication of the score, named bare and (ii) one with both of these implemented and visual consequences amplified (i.e. track durability decrease would significantly impact the movement speed of the train) named full. We tested on this difference as the score and visual consequences most directly related to passenger happiness as well as visually explaining the variety of track maintenance. Our user study consisted of twelve one-on-one play-test and interview sessions, which occurred in a setting familiar to the participant (such as their home or office). On initiation, the participant was given no instructions apart from a request to interact with MainTrain. During the session, the interviewer provided only requested directions to the player, all of which were noted by the interviewer. After testing, the participants filled in a questionnaire. This questionnaire focused on user interface design, difficulty and immersiveness of the gameplay, as well as how well the game conveyed its intended purpose. Our user study was carried out with eleven participants from three age groups: 10–20 (1 participant), 20–30 (8 participants), and 30+ (2 participants), all of whom were familiar with computer games.

By examining the qualitative feedback on the questionnaire, we found that adding in a clear indication of score and visual degradation caused some players to feel overwhelmed by the amount of maintenance options available. This is most likely due to the fact that the full game allows the players to "see" what they could do as well as how those choices affect passengers and the rail network. Interestingly enough, this did not lead to a significant different between how players rated the overall enjoyment of the game ($p = 0.5$). Furthermore, showing player happiness as a scoring mechanism and allowing the participant to fail the game caused a shift in what each participant thought the goal of the game was. In the bare version of MainTrain, half the participants believed the goal was simply to transport people, with only one believing that customer satisfaction was the purpose. However, in the full version, half of the participants noted happiness as a goal, half noted transportation, with one saying that these were the two goals of the game. This makes sense as the full version of the game had happiness tied to success. While this does not mean that the game made the participants empathic to rail maintenance, it is a first step in determining if MainTrain will do so.

5 Conclusion and Future Work

In this paper we presented a game aiming to show the complexity and difficulty of rail maintenance to a varied audience in an exhibition or fair setting. The player is faced with a goal to allow as many passengers to be transported, keeping them happy whilst keeping up the stations, tracks, and the rolling stock.

While the player can theoretically burn through the game and never experience any of the issues - simulations do not reach a high level of complexity, MainTrain conveys the important concepts in rail maintenance, such as the three rail components that must be maintained.

Future versions of MainTrain will aim to introduce some required issues or problems as the game progresses, regardless of player performance (i.e. the breakdown of a train or a natural disaster). At this point in time, the player can play the entire game without experiencing any issues in track maintenance, whereas planned setbacks would ensure the player is shown the desired difficulties and complexities, which exist within the domain of rail maintenance.

Acknowledgements. Firstly, we would like to thank the project team, Kanav Anand, Floris Doolaard, Jesse Tilro, Tim Yue, for their time and patience whilst designing the MainTrain with us. Secondly, we are extremely grateful to Pawel Kolodziejczyk, who framed the project and gave insight into the world of rail maintenance. Lastly, we would like to express gratitude for the game testers - you provided us with the all too needed points of improvement.

References

1. 2K Games and Firaxis Games: Sid Meier's Railroads! Windows PC version (2006). https://www.2kgames.com/railroads/
2. Buckley, K.E., Anderson, C.A.: A theoretical model of the effects and consequences of playing video games. In: Vorderer, P., Bryant, J. (eds.) Playing video games - motives, responses, and consequences, pp. 363–378. Lawrence Erlbaum Associates Publishers, Mahwah (2006)
3. Buiel, E.F.T., et al.: Synchro mania - design and evaluation of a serious game creating a mind shift in transport planning. In: Proceedings of the International Simulation and Gaming Association's 46th International Conference, pp. 1–12 (2015)
4. Counter, B., Abu-Tair, A., Franklin, A., Tann, D.: Refurbishment of ballasted track systems; the technical challenges of quality and decision support tools. Constr. Build. Mater. **92**, 51–57 (2015). https://doi.org/10.1016/j.conbuildmat.2014.11.036
5. Dinosaur Polo Club. Mini Metro: Windows PC version (2015). https://dinopoloclub.com/minimetro/
6. Jamshidi, A., et al.: Probabilistic defect-based risk assessment approach for rail failures in railway infrastructure. IFAC-PapersOnLine **49**, 73–77 (2016). https://doi.org/10.1016/j.ifacol.2016.07.013
7. Jung, I., Choi, S., Lim, C., Leem, J.: Effects of different types of interaction on learning achievement, satisfaction and participation in web-based instruction. Innov. Educ. Teach. Int. **39**, 153–162 (2002). https://doi.org/10.1080/14703290252934603

8. Khouzani, A.H.E., Golroo, A., Bagheri, M.: Railway maintenance management using a stochastic geometrical degradation model. J. Transp. Eng. Part A Syst. **143**, 04016002 (2017). https://doi.org/10.1061/JTEPBS.0000002

9. Miller, S.M., Green, M.L.: Coping with stress and frustration. In: Lewis, M., Saarni, C. (eds.) The Socialization of Emotions. GB, vol. 5, pp. 263–314. Springer, Boston, MA (1985). https://doi.org/10.1007/978-1-4613-2421-8_12

10. Malthaner, H.: Simutrans - Transport Simulator. Windows PC version (1999). https://www.simutrans.com/en/

11. Meijer, S.: Introducing Gaming Simulation in the Dutch Railways. Procedia Soc. Behav. Sci. **48**, 41–51 (2012). https://doi.org/10.1016/j.sbspro.2012.06.986

12. Meijer, S.A., Mayer, I.S., van Luipen, J., Weitenberg, N.: Gaming rail cargo management. Simul. Gaming **43**(1), 85–101 (2012)

13. Moore, M.G.: Three types of interaction. Am. J. Distance Educ. **3**, 1–7 (1989). https://doi.org/10.1080/08923648909526659

14. Nunez, A., Hendriks, J., Li, Z., De Schutter, B., Dollevoet, R.: Facilitating maintenance decisions on the Dutch railways using big data: the ABA case study. In: Proceedings - 2014 IEEE International Conference on Big Data, IEEE Big Data 2014, pp. 48–53. IEEE (2015)

15. Ortúzar, J., Willumsen, L.G.: Modelling Transport, 4th edn. Wiley, Chichester (2011)

16. Parbo, J., Nielsen, O.A., Prato, C.G.: Passenger perspectives in railway timetabling: a literature review. Transp. Rev. **36**, 500–526 (2016). https://doi.org/10.1080/01441647.2015.1113574

17. Soft Pro Trend. Railroad X, Windows PC version (2014). http://www.railroad-x.com

18. Tsuchiya, R., Sugiyama, Y., Yamauchi, K., Fujinami, K., Arisawa, R., Nakagawa, T.: Route-choice support system for passengers in the face of unexpected disturbance of train operations. In: WIT Transactions on the Built Environment, pp. 189–197 (2006)

19. van den Hoogen, J., Meijer, S.: Gaming and simulation for railway innovation. Simul. Gaming **46**, 489–511 (2015). https://doi.org/10.1177/1046878114549001

20. Wallen, K.R.: How can improvements be made to the United States metrorail system (with a focus on the Washington metropolitan area transit authority metrorail system) to enhance safety for its riders. Technical report, US Army Command and General Staff College Fort Leavenworth, United States (2016)

21. Zhu, S., Masud, H., Xiong, C., Yang, Z., Pan, Y., Zhang, L.: Travel behavior reactions to transit service disruptions. Transp. Res. Rec. J. Transp. Res. Board **2649**, 79–88 (2017). https://doi.org/10.3141/2649-09

Board Games for Training Computational Thinking

Katerina Tsarava[1]([✉]) ⓘ, Korbinian Moeller[1,2,3],
and Manuel Ninaus[1,3] ⓘ

[1] Leibniz Institut für Wissensmedien, Tübingen, Germany
{k.tsarava, k.moeller, m.ninaus}@iwm-tuebingen.de
[2] Department of Psychology, University of Tübingen, Tübingen, Germany
[3] LEAD Graduate School & Research Network,
University of Tübingen, Tübingen, Germany

Abstract. Computational thinking (CT) is a term widely used to describe algorithmic thinking and logic reasoning concepts and processes often related to computer programming. As such, CT as a cognitive ability builds on concepts and processes that derive from computer programming, but are applicable to wider real-life problems and STEM domains. CT has recently been argued to be a fundamental skill for 21st century education and an early academic success indicator that should be introduced and trained already in primary school education. Accordingly, we developed three life-size board games – *Crabs & Turtles: A Series of Computational Adventures* – that aim at providing an unplugged, gamified and low-threshold introduction to CT by presenting basic coding concepts and computational thinking processes to 8 to 9-year-old primary school children. For the design and development of these educational board games we followed a rapid prototyping approach. In the current study, we report results of an empirical evaluation of game experience of our educational board games with students of the target age group. In particular, we conducted quantitative analyses of player experience of primary school student participants. Results indicate overall positive game experience for all three board games. Future studies are planned to further evaluate learning outcomes in educational interventions with children.

Keywords: Computational Thinking · Unplugged activities · Board games

1 Introduction

Computational Thinking (CT) denotes the mental ability of creating a computational solution to a problem, by first decomposing it, and then developing a structured and algorithmic solution procedure [1, 2]. CT as a cognitive ability is argued to reflect the application of fundamental concepts and reasoning processes that derive from computer science and informatics to wider everyday life activities and problems but also STEM (Science, Technology, Engineering, and Mathematics) domains [3]. The construct of CT as a cognitive ability shares common concepts with computer programming as a practical skill. Central concepts in computer programming are the ideas of sequences,

© Springer Nature Switzerland AG 2019
M. Gentile et al. (Eds.): GALA 2018, LNCS 11385, pp. 90–100, 2019.
https://doi.org/10.1007/978-3-030-11548-7_9

operators, data/variables, conditionals, events, loops, and parallelism [4]. Respectively, CT draws on processes such as decomposition, algorithmic thinking, conditional logic, pattern recognition, evaluation, abstraction, and generalization, which reflect cognitive counterparts of central computer programming concepts [2, 5].

CT, as a rather general problem solving strategy applied to different domains, has been identified as a fundamental 21st century skill [1]. It has been suggested that the instruction on CT concepts may improve students' analytical skills and provide early indication and prediction of academic success [6]. Therefore, CT is considered a key competence for everyone and not just computer scientists [1], comparable to literacy and numeracy [7], that should be taught and acquired early in education.

Recent research focused on the benefits of CT and its integration into educational curricula, which has lately led to several adaptations and reformations of educational programs throughout all levels of education worldwide [8, 9]. Educational initiatives and governmental institutions all over the world have been working on the integration of CT into curricula of educational programs of primary, secondary, and higher education [10–13].

The societal relevance of CT led us to design and develop a CT training course for primary school children, introducing computer programming concepts and CT processes, applied to different STEAM (Science, Technology, Engineering, Art, and Mathematics) domains (for information on the overall course structure see [14]). Importantly, to offer a low threshold introduction to CT utilizing embodied learning [15], we developed unplugged life-size board games *Crabs & Turtles: A Series of Computational Adventures* (for a more detailed description of the games see [16]) for our CT training course.

Crabs & Turtles shares common ideas with concepts of Papert's educational Logo Turtle [17] and logo-inspired gamified educational activities [18]. Logo Turtle transferred to the real world conceptualized ideas of programing-like commands and algorithms, by applying them for the first time to a transparent moving and haptic object, the Turtle. The unplugged life-size game design allows embodied training (for the concept of embodied cognition [15]) of simple computational concepts and encourages active engagement and participation of students (for an overview see [19]). The games' target group are primary and secondary school students (8–12 years old) with no prior programming knowledge. We deliberately chose an unplugged mode of the game taking into consideration common concerns regarding the introduction of computer programming to young children [20, 21]. The unplugged mode fosters the understanding that CT processes do not occur only within digital contexts, but have a wider application in real-life problem solving.

Design and development of the game followed an iterative user-centered process [22]. More specifically, we tested first design ideas of the game with a custom-made life-size game as a pilot educational intervention with primary school children [23]. Later on, we developed and tested usability of an early prototype with primary school students during a short workshop session. After integrating feedback from both previous stages, we continued with the examination of users' game experience quantitatively with an adult population to ensure the games' appropriateness for children before evaluating the game with the target age group [16]. Feedback from this study was integrated again and resulted in the latest version of the games. The final version of the games was evaluated for its game experience in the target age group. Results of this evaluation are reported in the current article.

2   Games Description

Crabs & Turtles [16] consists of three different games: i. *The Treasure Hunt*, ii. *The Race*, and iii. *Patterns*. The games are designed for children at primary school level, focusing specifically on 3rd and 4th graders. They are intended to be used as integrated educational interventions in the classroom. Teachers play a central role in their implementation by acting as the game master in all three games, which can be played independently from each other and at any order of preference. The games aim at introducing and training processes related to CT, like abstraction, algorithms, decomposition, evaluation and patterns. In particular, they focus on mathematical (i.e., addition, multiplication, subtraction, and angular degrees) and coding (i.e., conditionals, constants and variables, events, loops, operators, and sequences) concepts related to those processes.

Fig. 1. *The Treasure Hunt* game/grid board: 1. Sequence of commands created by the players, 2. Pawn, 3. Treasure collection point, 4. Pawn with food treasure items and badges that are collected by the players.

The Treasure Hunt (see Fig. 1) is the first game of *Crabs & Turtles*. Players have to strategically move the pawn in teams of two on a grid board to collect food treasure items for their pawns (either crabs or turtles). To do so, teams of two have to efficiently build sequences of instructions, consisting of specific card commands to move their pawns across the board to gather treasures. They also need to obey specific rules and restrictions on movements indicated by the environment. For example, crab and turtle pawns can move only across specific colored tiles on the grid, water or stone and grass or stone, respectively. The main learning objective of the game is the general introduction to algorithmic thinking and sequential problem solving, as well as the consideration of restrictions and the use of simple conditional orders. Coding concepts explicitly addressed in this game are sequences and loops. For successful application of coding concepts players are awarded badges during the game (e.g. loop badge, sequence badge, etc.). Along with coding concepts, students get familiar with handling angular degrees in spatial orientation. The winner of the game is the team that first collects a specific number of food treasure items.

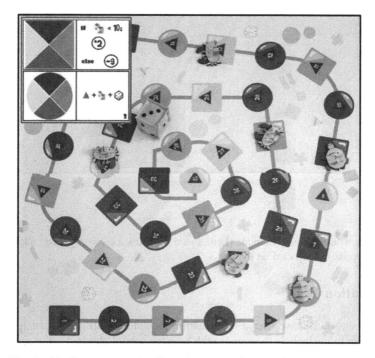

Fig. 2. *The Race* game board (Inner upper panel: example of game cards).

The Race (see Fig. 2) is the second game of *Crabs & Turtles*. In this game, players in teams of two have to reach the end of the game board by solving math/related riddles and handle the changing characteristics of variables (e.g. in-/decreasing of values). This game specifically focuses on coding concepts related to mathematics. In particular, coding skills explicitly addressed in this game are constants and variables, conditionals, events, and operators. During the game, players are awarded badges related to their achievements like variable badge, addition badge, etc. Mathematical abilities trained in the game relate to addition, subtraction, and multiplication. Consequently, the riddles of the game consist of equations related to mathematical operations and variables. The winner of the game is the team of two that first reaches the end of the race in the center of the game board.

Patterns (see Fig. 3) is the third game of *Crabs & Turtles*. In this game children play individually, trying to match as fast as possible two types of cards based on visual patterns depicted on them. In order to do so, they have to read color codes, recognize patterns, and follow specific restrictions. The color codes consist of colors, a shape, and an arrow that indicates the order of reading the color code (see Fig. 3, left). The patterns consist of colorful shapes which are depictions of a star, a square, a circle, and a triangle (see Fig. 3, right). The order of the shapes as well as their color is different on each card matching in this way only one specific color code. The main learning objective of the game is the introduction to the concept of patterns, by identifying color and shape patterns. The winner of the game is the player that succeeds in collecting the most cards.

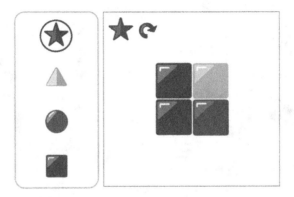

Fig. 3. *Patterns* card pairing example (Left: a card depicting a colorful pattern; Right: a color code matching the pattern card on the left).

3   Evaluation

After a successful 2-phase user test evaluation procedure with adult participants [16] we moved on to evaluating the games with primary school children – the actual target group of the games. In our 45-minute gaming sessions, main focus was on assessing game experience quantitatively to identify potential dysfunctionalities during game-play, which then can be addressed before integrating the games into our CT course and evaluating their educational potential. To validate the design approach, participants consisted of different grades of primary school. Instructors and game masters in those sessions were the creators of the games.

3.1   Participants

We collected data from 79 primary school students aged between 8 and 12 years of age from 6 different schools in Greece and Germany. Due to missing data on more than

10% of the items, we excluded data of 9 participants from further analysis. For another 4 participants who completed more than one game we had to exclude some of their questionnaires for specific games, because responses were missing due to local organizational issues. Missing values for fewer items in the questionnaires were replaced by the mean score for the respective item computed from other participants. As such, data of a final sample of 70 participants was considered in the analyses. (age in years: *mean* = 9.44, *SD* = 0.845; male: 42, female: 20, not indicated: 8).

3.2   Procedure and Materials

In separate teaching sessions, we evaluated game experience of primary school students. Most of the participants played all 3 games of *Crabs & Turtles*. Before participants started playing each of the games, we provided oral and visual instructions. After playing each game, participants were asked to complete the Game Experience Questionnaire (henceforth GEQ) [24]. We used a translated version of the Core (33 items) module in Greek and German to assess overall game experience. The Core module consists of seven subscales addressing i. Immersion, ii. Flow, iii. Competence, iv. Positive Affect, v. Negative Affect, vi. Tension, and vii. Challenge. For each subscale we used the average scores of the respective items as dependent variable in our analyses. Each item had to be responded on a 5-point Likert-scale (1 = not at all; 2 = slightly; 3 = moderately; 4 = fairly; 5 = extremely). For example, the fourth item of the Core module reads as follows: *"I felt happy"* and participants had to rate their experience of content on the aforementioned Likert scale by crossing an answer from 1 to 5 (e.g. crossing 4 would mean *"I felt fairly happy"*).

Furthermore, we used 4 additional items to further evaluate overall game experience, which also employed a 5-point Likert-scale: *Q1. I would explain my experience as playing*; *Q2. I would explain my experience as learning* (Q1 & Q2: 1 = not at all; 2 = not really; 3 = undecided; 4 = somewhat; 5 = very much); *Q3. I would recommend the games to a friend*; *Q4. I would like to play the games again in the future* (Q3 & Q4: 1 = not at all; 2 = not really; 3 = undecided; 4 = likely; 5 = very likely). We added these 4 items to the questionnaire with the intention to measure the experience of the game as learning and/or playing, because the GEQ aims at evaluating game experience more broadly and not game experience for educational games in particular.

Finally, to evaluate specific design elements of *The Treasure Hunt* and *The Race*, such as boards, cards, game pieces, inventory items, and rules, 5 more items (e.g. *Q: How much did you like the inventory items?*), again using a 5-point Likert-scale (1 = not at all; 2 = slightly; 3 = moderately; 4 = fairly; 5 = extremely), were used. For *Patterns* only cards and rules were evaluated.

3.3   Results

The analyses of the questionnaires were conducted for each game separately. Current results are presented in the following three sections. We used a conservative approach of analyzing each subscale of the GEQ by conducting one sample *t*-test comparing means of subscale ratings to the middle value of the scale (3 = mediocre) of the 5-point Likert scale. Internal consistency (Cronbachs's Alpha) of the GEQ as reported by [24] is presented in Table 1 (column α^*). In addition, Cronbach's alpha as obtained in the current sample is also reported in Table 1 (column α). The observed internal consistency indicated acceptable reliability for most subscales with $\alpha > .70$. However, this was not the case for subscales *Tension/Annoyance* (for games 2 and 3), *Challenge* (for games 1, 2 and 3) and *Negative Affect* (for game 1). For the analyses of overall game experience and the specific design elements we again ran *t*-tests against the middle of the respective scale. Descriptive results and inferential statistics for the GEQ subscales are summarized in Table 1 and Fig. 4.

3.3.1 The Treasure Hunt

Game Experience. Participants rated this game significantly above mediocre on the subscales *Competence, Sensory & Imaginative Immersion,* and *Positive Affect.* In contrast, ratings were significantly below mediocre for the subscales *Tension/Annoyance, Challenge,* and *Negative Affect.* We did not find a significant difference from mediocre for *Flow* (see Table 1).

Overall Experience. Participants experienced *The Treasure Hunt* somewhat as playing (Q1: *mean* = 4.22, *SD* = 1.10; $t_{(17)} = 6.29$, $p < 0.001$) as reflected by ratings significantly above mediocre and not so much as a learning activity (Q2: *mean* = 2.98, *SD* = 1.51; $t_{(17)} = -.09$, $p = 0.929$). Additionally, participants reported that they would likely recommend the game to a friend (Q3: *mean* = 3.74, *SD* = 1.37; $t_{(17)} = 3.05$, $p = 0.005$), and would likely play the game again in the future (Q4: *mean* = 4.29, *SD* = 1.08; $t_{(17)} = 6.71$, $p < 0.001$), as indicated by ratings significantly above mediocre.

Design Elements' Evaluation. The design elements of *The Treasure Hunt* scored a mean of 4.13 (*SD* = 1.02) on the 5-point Likert scale. More specifically, users rated all five design elements of *The Treasure Hunt* (Board: *mean* = 4.09, *SD* = 1.17, $t_{(17)} = 5.27$, $p < 0.001$; Cards: *mean* = 3.88, *SD* = 1.24, $t_{(17)} = 4.00$, $p < 0.001$; Game Pieces: *mean* = 4.50, *SD* = .84, $t_{(17)} = 10.07$, $p < 0.001$; Inventory items: *mean* = 4.16, *SD* = 1.17, $t_{(17)} = 5.61$, $p < 0.001$ and Rules: *mean* = 4.02, *SD* = 1.35, $t_{(17)} = 4.27$, $p < 0.001$) significantly above mediocre.

3.3.2 The Race

Game Experience. Participants' ratings for this game were significantly above mediocre for the *Competence, Sensory & Imaginative Immersion,* and *Positive Affect* subscales of the GEQ Core module. In contrast, participants rated the game significantly below mediocre on the subscales *Tension/Annoyance, Challenge,* and *Negative Affect.* Also, we did not find a significant difference to mediocre for the *Flow* subscale.

Overall Experience. For *The Race* ratings significantly above mediocre indicated that participants rated their game experience somewhat as playing (Q1: *mean* = 4.16, *SD* = 1.03; $t_{(16)} = 5.64$, $p < 0.001$) and not as a learning activity for which there was no significant difference from mediocre (Q2: *mean* = 3.21, *SD* = 1.41; $t_{(17)} = 0.74$, $p = 0.467$). Furthermore, ratings significantly above mediocre reflected that they would likely recommend the game to a friend (Q3: *mean* = 3.91, *SD* = 1.12; $t_{(16)} = 4.09$, $p < 0.001$), and also would likely play it again in the future (Q4: *mean* = 4.09, *SD* = 1.15; $t_{(16)} = 4.72$, $p < 0.001$).

Design Elements' Evaluation. Overall, all five design elements of *The* Race were positively rated scoring a mean of 4.02 (*SD* = 1.01). More specifically, participants liked all five design elements (Board: *mean* = 4.08, *SD* = 1.08, $t_{(16)}$ = 5.03, p < 0.001; Cards: *mean* = 3.75, *SD* = 1.20, $t_{(16)}$ = 3.13, p = 0.005; Game pieces: *mean* = 4.42, *SD* = 1.08, $t_{(16)}$ = 6.58, p < 0.001; Inventory items: *mean* = 3.91, *SD* = 1.22, $t_{(16)}$ = 3.72, p = 0.001 and Rules: *mean* =3.96, *SD* = 1.27, $t_{(16)}$ = 3.76, p = 0.001) as reflected by ratings significantly above mediocre.

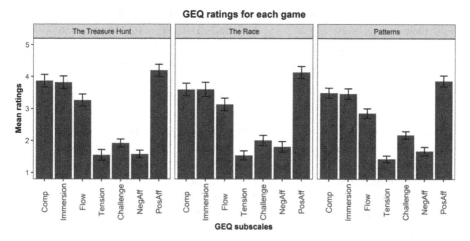

Fig. 4. Students' rating of GEQ subscales for each of the three games. On the y-axes mean ratings of each subscales of the GEQ is represented. The y-axes refer to each of the subscales of the GEQ (Comp = Competence; Immersion = Sensory & Imaginative Immersion; Flow = Flow; Tension = Tension/Annoyance;   Challenge = Challenge;   NegAff = Negative   Affect; PosAff = Positive Affect). Error bars depict 1 standard error of the mean.

3.3.3   Patterns

Game Experience. Similarly to the results of the other two games, participants' ratings for *Patterns* were significantly above mediocre for the *Competence*, *Sensory & Imaginative Immersion*, and *Positive affect* subscales of the GEQ Core module. Again, ratings for the *Tension/Annoyance*, *Challenge*, and *Negative Affect* subscales were significantly below mediocre. Also, we did not find a significant difference to mediocre for the subscale *Flow*.

Overall Experience. Participants perceived the *Patterns* game somewhat as a playing experience (Q1: *mean* = 3.93, *SD* = 1.24; $t_{(15)}$ = 4.92, p < 0.001) which was again reflected by ratings above mediocre and with a marginally significant score as a learning activity as well (Q3: *mean* = 3.42, *SD* = 1.43; $t_{(17)}$ = 1.94, p = 0.059). Moreover, according to ratings above mediocre, participants reported that they would likely recommend it to a friend (Q3: *mean* = 3.74, *SD* = 1.29; $t_{(15)}$ = 3.75, p = 0.001), and also play the game again (Q4: *mean* = 4.10, *SD* = 1.30; $t_{(15)}$ = 5.58, p < 0.001).

Design Elements' Evaluation. The design elements in *Patterns* scored a mean of 3.98 (*SD* = 1.01) on the 5-point Likert scale. The two design elements in the questionnaire for *Patterns* scored positively as indicated by ratings significantly above mediocre (Cards: *mean* = 4.00, *SD* = 1.05, $t_{(15)}$ = 6.27, $p < 0.001$; and Rules: *mean* = 3.95, *SD* = 1.09, $t_{(15)}$ = 5.72, $p < 0.001$).

Table 1. Mean scores for core module of GEQ at phase 2, per game-based activity.

The Treasure Hunt							
Competence	3.86	1.09	31	4.48	0.000	.923	.826
Sensory & imaginative immersion	3.82	1.11	31	4.17	0.000	.910	.891
Flow	3.26	1.07	31	1.39	0.174	.813	.866
Tension/annoyance	1.55	.96	31	−8.57	0.000	.890	.811
Challenge	1.92	.70	31	−8.76	0.000	.560	.745
Negative affect	1.58	.69	31	−11.69	0.000	.640	.712
Positive affect	4.20	1.06	31	6.38	0.000	.956	.797
The Race							
Competence	3.60	.98	24	3.05	0.006	.799	.826
Sensory & imaginative immersion	3.60	1.09	24	2.77	0.011	.876	.891
Flow	3.13	.99	24	.676	0.506	.759	.866
Tension/annoyance	1.54	.71	24	−10.34	0.000	.546	.811
Challenge	2.00	.80	24	−6.20	0.000	.673	.745
Negative affect	1.81	.82	24	−7.28	0.000	.745	.712
Positive affect	4.13	.95	24	5.98	0.000	.938	.797
Patterns							
Competence	3.49	1.03	42	3.12	0.003	.865	.826
Sensory & imaginative immersion	3.46	1.08	42	2.82	0.007	.871	.891
Flow	2.86	.99	42	−0.95	0.345	.771	.866
Tension/annoyance	1.43	.66	42	−15.72	0.000	.625	.811
Challenge	2.18	.75	42	−7.21	0.000	.592	.745
Negative affect	1.67	.87	42	−10.06	0.000	.752	.712
Positive affect	3.86	1.12	42	5.07	0.000	.928	.797

4 Discussion and Future Work

The present study aimed at evaluating game experience of primary school students in the three games of *Crabs & Turtles* and thus complements a previous evaluation of game experience in adults [16]. After evaluating the game experience in adults and gathering overall positive results and valuable feedback, we completed the design of the final prototype for our games and tested user experience in the actual target group. We play-tested the games and collected data using the GEQ. Quantitative analyses on the game users' experience provided promising results regarding the validity of our approach.

Student participants rated their game experience after playing each game. Results indicated an overall positive reception of the games. In particular, students reported feeling competent and immersed while playing all three games, as well as experiencing positive affect. On the other hand, the overall challenge was rated low. Importantly, tension and negative affect ratings were also low for all three games. In addition, all three games of *Crabs & Turtles* were experienced as a playing activity and students would likely be willing to play again all three of them and recommend them to their friends. Additionally, evaluation of the quality of design elements for each game was rated highly positive. In summary, this indicates that we managed to implement CT concepts into three gaming activities while achieving overall positive game experience in children. However, the actual educational value of each of the games needs to be investigated comprehensively and evaluated empirically in separate studies, which, in fact, are currently being conducted in Germany.

The main aim of this study was the quantitative evaluation of primary school students' game experience in *Crabs & Turtles* to extend a previous evaluation in adults [16]. The overall positive evaluation of game experience replicated in the target group now allows for a comprehensive evaluation of cognitive and educational benefits when playing the games. Although the overall results were positive, the rather low scores in challenge and flow in all three games may not be optimal. Therefore, we plan to provide a set of game instructions with multiple adaptations. For example, we will facilitate selection of difficulty levels based on the number of players, so that the game becomes adaptive to classroom conditions (e.g. few or many students) and to students' game understanding (e.g. in case the game is understood well and game play seems easy, rules could become gradually more challenging while playing). We also plan to adapt a challenging game mechanic in *The Race* that will foster competition between the teams at every round of the game by allowing all the teams to solve the riddle as fast as possible.

Future studies are planned with primary school students of 3rd and 4th grade to evaluate learning outcomes of the three games and their educational effectiveness on training CT-related skills. The three games, as part of a structured curriculum dedicated to training CT [14], will be evaluated through a pre-/post-test study design using a randomized field trial with a control group in 20 Hector Children's Academies in Baden-Wuerttemberg, Germany. Moreover, this forthcoming evaluation will aim at investigating cognitive abilities underlying CT and possible transfer effects of the course, using standardized cognitive tests to allow a diverse approach and definition of CT. Finally, we aim at developing digital versions of our board games to allow for individual dynamic adaptation of – for instance – the difficulty of the games.

References

1. Wing, J.M.: Computational Thinking. Theor. Comput. Sci. **49**(3), 33 (2006)
2. Wing, J.M.: Computational Thinking: What and Why? The Link - The Magazine of the Carnegie Mellon University School of Computer Science (2010)
3. Wang, P.S.: From Computing to Computational Thinking, 1st edn. Chapman and Hall/CRC, New York (2015)

4. Brennan, K., Resnick, M.: New frameworks for studying and assessing the development of computational thinking. In: Annual American Educational Research Association Meeting, Vancouver, BC, Canada (2012)
5. Astrachan, O., Briggs, A.: The CS principles principles project. ACM Inroads 3(2), 38 (2012)
6. Haddad, R.J., Kalaani, Y.: Can computational thinking predict academic performance? In: Integrated STEM Education Conference Proceedings. IEEE (2015)
7. Yadav, A., Mayfield, C., Zhou, N., Hambrusch, S., Korb, J.T.: Computational thinking in elementary and secondary teacher education. ACM Trans. Comput. Educ. 14(1), 5 (2014)
8. Tuomi, P., Multisilta, J., Saarikoski, P., Suominen, J.: Coding skills as a success factor for a society. Educ. Inf. Technol. 23(1), 419 (2018)
9. Brown, N.C.C., Sentance, S.U.E., Crick, T.O.M., Humphreys, S.: Restart: the resurgence of computer science in UK schools. ACM Trans. Comput. Educ. 14(2), 9 (2014)
10. European School Network Homepage: https://www.esnetwork.eu/. Accessed 6 May 2018
11. European Coding Initiative Homepage: http://www.allyouneediscode.eu/. Accessed 6 May 2018
12. Code.org Homepage: https://code.org. Accessed 6 May 2018
13. National Science Foundation Homepage: https://www.nsf.gov/. Accessed 6 May 2018
14. Tsarava, K., Moeller, K., Pinkwart, N., Butz, M., Trautwein, U., Ninaus, M.: Training computational thinking: game-based unplugged and plugged-in activities in primary school. In: 11th European Conference on Games Based Learning Proceedings, ECGBL, ACPI, UK (2017)
15. Barsalou, L.W.: Grounded cognition. Ann. Rev. Psychol. 59, 617 (2008)
16. Tsarava, K., Moeller, K., Ninaus, M.: Training computational thinking through boar games: the case of crabs & turtles. Int. J. Serious Games 5(2), 25–44 (2018)
17. Papert, S.: Logo Philosophy and Implementation (1999)
18. Papert, S., Solomon, C.: Twenty Things To Do With a Computer (1971)
19. Echeverría, A., et al.: A framework for the design and integration of collaborative classroom games. Comput. Educ. 57(1), 1127 (2011)
20. Grover, S., Pea, R.: Computational thinking in K-12: a review of the state of the field. Educ. Res. 42(1), 38 (2013)
21. Pea, R.D., Kurland, D.M.: On the cognitive effects of learning computer programming. New Ideas Psychol. 2(2), 137 (1984)
22. Fullerton, T.: Game Design Workshop: A Playcentric Approach to Creating Innovative Games. CRC Press, Boca Raton (2008)
23. Tsarava, K.: Programming in Greek with Python. Aristotle University of Thessaloniki (2016)
24. Poels, K., de Kort, Y.A.M., Ijsselsteijn, W.A.: D3.3: game experience questionnaire: development of a self-report measure to assess the psychological impact of digital games. Technische Universiteit Eindhoven, Eindhoven (2007)

Dungeons and Dragons as a Tool for Developing Student Self-reflection Skills

Samantha Clarke$^{(\boxtimes)}$, Sylvester Arnab, Luca Morini,
and Lauren Heywood

Disruptive Media Learning Lab, Coventry University, Coventry, UK
samantha.clarke@coventry.ac.uk

Abstract. The practice of self-reflection for some students is often thought of as tedious and more often than not, even though the benefits of self-reflection have long been documented, little time is given (to the fault of both students and educators) to building upon the necessary skills required for aiding this process. *Dungeons and Dragons* (D&D), a table-top roleplaying games system developed by Gygax and Arneson, utilises a host of game mechanics such as, but not limited to: character creation, customisation, skills development, leveling over time, story-telling and a game-masters feedback. Many of the game mechanics in D&D, require the player to self-reflect on behalf of their character and continually assess how they wish their character to develop for future game sessions. Coupled with interactive feedback (visual/written/auditory/narrative-development) that is provided throughout each game session from a game master who leads the players through a pre-developed story, the basis of the mechanics provides some similarities to a facilitator leading learners through an assignment. In this paper, the authors present a playful example of how role-playing games can be used to facilitate student self-reflection. A discussion of the design, method and mid-pilot feedback of n = 11 students undertaking the Dungeons & Dragons Self-Reflection Tool is presented alongside next stage pilot trials and considerations of future work.

Keywords: Dungeons and Dragons · Self-reflection · Role-playing

1 Introduction

Self-reflection in education has been a prominent topic since Dewey [1] highlighted the importance and affect that it can play in other areas of a learner's development, such as critical thinking, self-led learning and personal and professional development skills. Dewey defined reflection in the context of education as;

"active, persistent and careful consideration of any belief or supposed form of knowledge in the light of the grounds that support it and the further conclusion to which it tends" [1].

Other definitions of reflection [2, 3], offer up differing ideas on what reflection should encompass, however they all agree, that to achieve deeper learning of a subject, an understanding through critical analysis is required. Outside of this understanding that reflection is an important method to develop connections between materials, taught

© Springer Nature Switzerland AG 2019
M. Gentile et al. (Eds.): GALA 2018, LNCS 11385, pp. 101–109, 2019.
https://doi.org/10.1007/978-3-030-11548-7_10

matters and even episodes of failure, Moorefield [4] also indicates that self-reflection is required as it involves the recognition and regulation of behaviour by taking the time to think about it. Self-reflection as observed through the literature, is considered an essential element of the learning process.

However, an issue commonly reported in regards to self-reflection development in learners, is the lack of knowledge or time to achieve reflection in terms of Dewey's set out definition; that it should be active and persistent [5]. If a learner exhibits reflective practice, all too often it is not a consistent custom in which the learner leads the exercise. There is a need to ensure that reflection is built into the learning materials in a way that makes it a crucial element to the learning process, and in short that the learners accept that it is a valuable component of their learning. Following on from this, Zimmerman [6] believed that in order for students to become self-regulated learners, it is imperative that reflection skills are developed and honed in an effort to sustain this practice.

Role Playing Games (RPG's) are currently being utilised in educational settings, but mainly seem to be developed or used through the medium of digital games closer to the style of *World of Warcraft,* a Massively Multi-Player Online Role-Playing Game (MMORPG) [7]. One such example of such games is that of *ClassCraft* [8], a game designed in this digital style for primary school age learners. *ClassCraft* employs a range of RPG mechanics such as the building and development of characters, levels, quests and goal setting and layered reward structures. *ClassCraft* has been seen, to be hugely popular with this age group and has shown that these types of game mechanics can engage and help students on their learning journey [9]. Other studies have shown that University level students playing RPG's in place of traditional lecturers found that 81% of 230 students would use this method again [10]. This lays a foundation in which to try and understand in greater depth what and which RPG mechanics are useful for supporting students and which are not so accepted, especially with students in a higher education setting.

In light of the theory and their own practice observations, the authors were therefore keen to explore methods that could make the process of self-reflection more appealing and that could be built into a module from a position of a primary functional role, rather than a secondary afterthought. It was essential that whatever was developed, would fit easily and be relevant to their teaching within a University setting.

Dungeons and Dragons (D&D) by Gygax and Arneson [11], is a table top role-playing game in which players are asked first and fore mostly to create their character. During this process, a player reflects on who they want to play during the game, selecting a series of skills and feats that makes up their character's composition. Players are asked to roll a number of dice to then determine how many points they have to put towards their character's attributes. These attributes are: Strength, Charisma, Intelligence, Wisdom, Constitution and Dexterity. Throughout the game, these attributes are used to allow player characters to do actions; the higher the point score in each attribute, the more chance a player has on accomplishing a task that they want to do.

It is this method of creating a character, reflecting on attributes and using the D&D 'Monster Manual' system, that the authors have chosen to develop into a gamified reflection process that is used to help students assess their strengths and weaknesses at the start of a module and then actively troubleshoot through their progress through the module. This D&D method was chosen for the use of several interesting game elements, including both the character attributes which were first implemented in D&D systems and the 'Monster Manual' system that could support the reflection of student issues. This paper provides an overview of the design process and midway pilot feedback from participating students of a second-year University module on Design Thinking. It also presents a first look at an online tool that supports the 'monster' reflection process which was developed using a participatory approach to design and development.

2 Dungeons and Dragons Reflection Tool Design

Using the Disruptive Media Learning Lab's, GameChangers: 'Remixing Play into a Gameplan' [12] open course workshop, the authors set about developing the main principles of D&D into a system that could be used to help facilitate student self-reflection in an interesting and entertaining way.

The design of the tool started out with an inspection of the mechanics of D&D and a planning session of how it was to work in a University module setting. Character development via character sheets, character attributes, enemies and team-based role-play/narrative were some of the main factors that make up the game of D&D.

Nine stages of design considerations (documented below) were then put together to make up the basis of the self-reflection tool. This tool was developed to encourage group working within a problem-based scenario delivery style setting [13].

2.1 Journals and Character Sheets (Step 1)

A popular reflection method to help students critically review their progress over a period of time is that of a journal. Journal writing is thought to enable students to process their learning and help them to reflect and build their own strategies to help towards personal development [14–16]. The idea of giving the students a journal to write their reflections in, fits the theme of D&D quite well, as the game is all about documenting progress over time. Journals given to students would be thematically and aesthetically pleasing to help develop students sense of ownership with the journal writing tasks. Journals would also be used to keep the students character sheets in safely and provide a chance for ongoing reflection that could be used as evidence (by the student) to support their final assessment. It was designed so that it would support lecturers to use the journals as an opportunity to provide written feedback, formative assessments and view progress on a weekly basis.

Character development is a core component of the D&D game and all the information relating to a character is kept on a player's character sheet. In consideration of this, it was required to develop a modified character sheet that could be used for students to self-reflect upon and to keep with them over the course of the module. Traditional D&D attributes such as Strength, Dexterity and Wisdom, would not be suitable for the practice of self-reflection in relation to the learning content proposed and were therefore developed to have more real world meaning to the students. Attributes such as Creativity, Collaboration and Motivation replaced the original attributes on the modified character sheet. To encourage students to assess what they want to achieve by the end of a module, the authors developed a section on the sheet to include 'Epic Quest', where students could write down their main goals that they wanted to achieve by the end of the module.

2.2 Roll Character Attributes (Step 2)

Students would be required to roll dice (just like D&D) and come up with a series of stats for their character attributes that related to themselves. Students would be asked to reflect on their current strengths and weaknesses and assign their dice stats to each attribute, depending on how skillful they felt in each area. Attributes in the D&D world are equal to Strength, Dexterity, Wisdom, Charisma, Intelligence and Constitution. In this version, these attributes are assigned a real-world context into the following: Motivation, Multi-Disciplinary Working, Creativity, Collaboration, Subject Knowledge and Mental/Physical Wellbeing. This task is to help learners reflect on what skills they currently have and what skills they would like to develop throughout the modules course and was developed with the theoretical approach of using SWOT analysis for reflection [17, 18]. Using the classic method for rolling attribute scores, students would be required to roll four six-sided dice (4d6), dropping the lowest and adding the rest together, giving an overall score. This is repeated six times with students then tasked with completing the reflection task by arranging the numbers wherever they thought was applicable next to the modified attributes.

2.3 Define Epic Quest and Outline Attributes to Work Towards (Step 3)

Students would be next required to think about what they wanted to achieve by the end of the module. This would be known as their 'Epic Quest'. Again, following the method of SWOT analysis [17] but in a gamified capacity, this element would be used for students to identify the 'opportunities' that lay ahead of them and identifying key skills to develop. They are also required in this step to identify two attributes that they wish to work on improving during their time on the module. The completion of the 'Epic Quest' can form part of the final reflection task at the end of the module and should be done with the Dungeon Masters (Lecturers) guidance and supervision. Students would be encouraged to convince the Dungeon Masters (DMs) that they have succeeded in their quests, providing their journals as evidence.

2.4 Weekly Self-reflection (Step 4)

Each week, students will be asked after each lesson to independently choose and reflect on each of the following in their personal journals:

Monsters
Students will be asked to identify at least one problem concerned with the ongoing module work (this could be a personal development, team or project related problem) and re-imagine it as a monster. They must reflect on why this 'monster' is causing

issues for their learning and then pose solutions to overcome in order and defeat said monster. This is a creative exercise for re-imagining self-reflection tasks.

Example: A student's team has a problem with deciding on a particular issue to address with their project. Their monster is the 'sludge of indecision'. The student then suggests that in order to overcome this monster, the team must meet on another day and make a firm decision on which issue they are going to concentrate on.

Journal and Epic Quest Reflection

Students will be required to update their journal each week with the above sections including reflections on problems and resources. Alongside these, comments and reflections of their personal progress in class, with emphasis on how they are moving forward in pursuit of their 'Epic Quest' goals and how they are working on approving their chosen and/or other attributes. DMs can feedback in these journals and offer guidance and a bit of story (if creative enough) on each student's journey. They can also award skill points that can be spent in the Feat Tree and/or offer suggestions in other ways providing formative feedback each week.

3 Pilot

After obtaining ethics through Coventry Universities internal process, the pilot was undertaken as part of a self-reflection task for a second year undergraduate, Advantage + module. Advantage + modules are unique to Coventry University, and are optional modules that undergraduate students can pick to complement their core studies. These modules have a particular focus on developing employability and personal development skills. These modules run for a course of eleven weeks and are flexible for the first three weeks in that students can have a taster of the module and if they wish to try something else then they can move to different module. Due to the nature of the course flexibility and timeframe limitations, selected elements from the tool were used to trial within the pilot study. The authors choose to trial the modified character sheet, journal and 'monster' reflection elements of the tool. The module that the pilot was to be run in was titled 'Design Thinking'. The module ran for 2 h on a Wednesday evening for 11 weeks. Students on the 'Design Thinking' course are expected to develop and produce a concept design for a playful, game or gamified solution for a 'real world' problem of their choice. They must present their concept to the rest of the class at the end of the 11 weeks and are marked on research and empathy, creativity and practical application.

In week 1 of the module, following a welcome and introduction to the study via a Power Point presentation, each student (n = 11) was given a modified character sheet as shown in Fig. 1. Self-reflection was explained and highlighted to the students how it was an important aspect of their learning process. Each aspect of the sheet was explained, and the students were instructed on how to fill out each part of it. Students were asked to roll dice to and come up with a series of stats for their character attributes. It was made clear that their character sheets equaled them at the point they are at now in their learning journey. Students were given the option of whether they wanted to roll their attributes or take a baseline set of 15, 14, 13, 12, 11, 10.

Most students took the baseline with only 3 wanting to roll the dice. Students were asked to reflect on their current strengths and weaknesses and assign their dice stats to each attribute. The process was used to get the students thinking about themselves more critically and used to highlight the student's strengths and weaknesses. Once attributes had been placed, the students were asked to think about why they chose the module and the main thing that they wish to achieve at the end of it i.e. 'Epic Quest'. They were asked to identify two attributes that they were to work on improving during their time on the module.

In week 2 of the module, students were presented with thematic journals for the reflection task. They were told to place their character sheet inside and to bring the journal each week to the class. The students were told that 20 min each lesson would be set aside specifically for the reflection task. Each subsequent week till the end of the module, students were asked to identify at least one problem concerned with the ongoing module work in these 20 min sessions (they were told that this could be a personal development, team or project related problem) and they were asked to pose a solution in order to defeat the monster. A series of different monsters developed by the authors were colour coded to the attributes as listed on the modified character sheet. Students could pick and choose as many and whichever monsters that were relevant to them that week. 20 min were then set aside each week in which the students conducted a period of reflection using the monsters as the basis of the reflection task. They carried out this task using their journals to write notes in.

4 Results

Early findings gained from mid-point group focus interviews from the pilot indicate that the students ($n = 11$) overall found the process of using D&D as a reflection tool useful, with comments such as: "It helps with motivation and I can reflect about it when the class is finished", "Help you to realise what's there. Helps you to see things that you should" and "Organises your thoughts and gives them a certain meaning so you can follow them up step by step and at the end create something". Those that had no background in gaming, felt that the process had just enough gaming elements to make it an interesting experience. However, those who had more experience in playing games, wanted more from the game experience citing that there needed to be more of a leveling up component to the process and that "It is interesting but it needs to be expanded". Other comments on this element included: "It was easy to understand but it needs to be corrected to make time to improve the stats" and "If the stats were modified by the person who knew about knowledge and learning it would be better". Although it was mentioned that the journals were "really nice", all students who took part in the group interviews indicated that they would have preferred an online version citing "Instead of a physical journal, an electronic survey would be better. To do it in class" and "We could edit points through a digital system that would be easier to manage". As a pilot, the findings are rudimentary, however it has offered some basic insight into student acceptability and perceived use of some of the gamified elements of this study, particularly surrounding the 'monster reflection' and the 'character attributes'. These two areas, were the two that were commented on positively the most by the students, with a clear desire for better access to the 'monster reflection' as an online tool. In order to ensure more quality data is available on these game elements and the approach, a larger study is needed for an in-depth analysis of student acceptance, perceived use and usability.

5 Bothersome Beasties Online Self-reflection Website

In a response to the mid-point pilot feedback that the students would prefer an online version of the 'monster' reflection task, the authors developed the tool 'Bothersome Beasties (and how to deal with them!) see Fig. 1 [21]. The tool is a free, open source website that students can use anonymously to document their monsters. Redefined as 'Beasties', the tool acts as an online version of a 'monster manual' in which students are asked to reframe their issues as 'Beasties'. This was taken directly from the activity of selecting a 'monster' to reflect on in class and updated to reflect the students desire for an online tool. Students can now build and create their own 'Monster' to better reflect on their needs and are not limited to the original six that were developed for the classroom activities. The compendium then acts as a guide in which students from across any number of modules can view other student's issues and comment on them in a helpful way. Further development and refinement on this approach is needed and hoped to be used as part of the next version of trials. Currently the Bothersome Beasties tool can be found here: http://creditcontinue.coventry.domains/beasties/

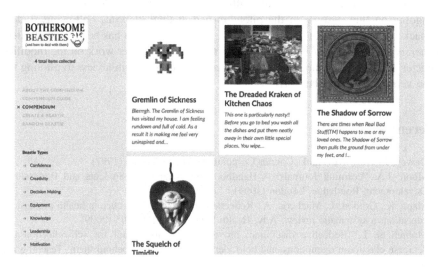

Fig. 1. Bothersome beasties website for self-reflection.

6 Conclusions

The authors have presented an overview of the design of the Dungeons & Dragons reflection tool, method of pilot and delivery and mid-point findings. Although early feedback from the students suggest that there are some positive results to using this method for reflection, there are several areas that need revising, including additional development of a gamified or full game system to accompany the character sheets and an online method of delivery/editing of reflections (addressed via Bothersome Beasties). However, since the pilot only focused on some aspects of the tools design, it is possible that the addition of some of the other game elements such as the leveling up system that was originally designed, would have addressed the student feedback regarding additional structure and modification of the attribute stats. More time and adequate attention to develop the leveling up approach in the style of D&D could help to address this area of the study in line with student feedback, and further development in general of all of the steps taking into account student desires for these tools to be easily accessible online. The desire for easy access has been one of the key insights to this project as traditional D&D is usually managed through a paper-based system. However, this was an area where students felt they needed more control of access and management of the system.

Taking this mid-way feedback into consideration, the authors will look to develop further on these insights with the project and iteratively work the student suggestions into the next design and testing phase. Key to this early feedback through is that there is evidence to suggest that there is some use in using this method as a more engaging alternative to aid and build reflection skills with higher education level students. Work is ongoing on this study with the pilot finished at time of print. Following student feedback, an online version of the 'monster' reflection process has been created titled: 'Bothersome Beasties and how to deal with them' [21]. Further work on the modified character sheet and the game process is currently underway with a view to piloting the online version in September 2018.

References

1. Dewey, J.: How We Think. Courier Corporation, Massachusetts (1997)
2. Moon, J.A.: Learning Journals: A Handbook for Academics, Students and Professional Development. Routledge, London (1999)
3. Mann, K., Gordon, J., MacLeod, A.: Reflection and reflective practice in health professions education: a systematic review. Adv. Health Sci. Educ. 14(4), 595 (2009)
4. Moorefield, L.: Reflective discipline: providing students a tool for self-reflection can decrease classroom disruptions–and help identify the problems behind them. Teaching Pre K-8 36(1), 70–71 (2005)
5. Quinton, S., Smallbone, T.: Feeding forward: using feedback to promote student reflection and learning–a teaching model. Innovations Educ. Teach. Int. 47(1), 125–135 (2010)
6. Zimmerman, B.J.: Becoming a self-regulated learner: an overview. Theor. Pract. 41(2), 64–70 (2002)
7. Blizzard Entertainment: World of Warcraft [Video game]. California: Activision Blizzard (2004)

8. Shawn, Y., Devin, Y., Lauren, Y.: ClassCraft [Video game]. Montreal, New York & QC: ClassCraft (2013)

9. Papadakis, S., Kalogiannakis, M.: Using gamification for supporting an introductory programming course. the case of classcraft in a secondary education classroom. In: Brooks, A.L., Brooks, E., Vidakis, N. (eds.) ArtsIT/DLI -2017. LNICST, vol. 229, pp. 366–375. Springer, Cham (2018). https://doi.org/10.1007/978-3-319-76908-0_35

10. Randi, M.A.F., Carvalho, H.F.D.: Learning through role-playing games: an approach for active learning and teaching. Revista Brasileira de Educação Médica 37(1), 80–88 (2013)

11. Gygax, G., Arneson, D.: Dungeons and Dragons, vol. 19. Tactical Studies Rules, Lake Geneva (1974)

12. GameChangers. http://gamify.org.uk/workshop-remixing-play-into-a-gameplan/. Accessed 29 April 2018

13. Kilroy, D.A.: Problem based learning. Emerg. Med. J. 21(4), 411–413 (2004)

14. Gleaves, A., Walker, C., Grey, J.: Using digital and paper diaries for assessment and learning purposes in higher education: a case of critical reflection or constrained compliance? Assess. Eval. High. Educ. 33(3), 219–231 (2008)

15. Hiemstra, R.: Uses and benefits of journal writing. New Dir. Adult Continuing Educ. 90, 19–26 (2001)

16. McCrindle, A.R., Christensen, C.A.: The impact of learning journals on metacognitive and cognitive processes and learning performance. Learn. Instr. 5(2), 167–185 (1995)

17. Humphrey, A.: SWOT analysis for management consulting. SRI Alumni Newslett. 1, 7–8 (2005)

18. Valentin, E.K.: SWOT analysis from a resource-based view. J. Mark. Theor. Pract. 9(2), 54–69. Vancouver (2001)

19. Martin, G.A., Double, J.M.: Developing higher education teaching skills through peer observation and collaborative reflection. Innov. Educ. Train. Int. 35(2), 161–170 (1998)

20. Gareau, T.P., Smith, R.G., Barbercheck, M.E., Mortensen, D.A.: Spider plots: a tool for participatory extension learning. J. Extension 48(5), 5TOT8 (2010)

21. Credit Continue. https://seriousgameslife.wordpress.com/2018/03/26/the-compendium-of-bothersome-beasties-a-splot-for-self-reflection-formative-feedback/. Accessed 10 May 2018

A Serious Game for Training Verbal Resilience to Doorstep Scams

Laura M. van der Lubbe[1(✉)], Charlotte Gerritsen[2], Daniel Formolo[1],
Marco Otte[1], and Tibor Bosse[3]

[1] VU Amsterdam, De Boelelaan 1081, 1081 HV Amsterdam, The Netherlands
{l.m.vander.lubbe,d.formolo,m.otte}@vu.nl
[2] NSCR, De Boelelaan 1077, 1081 HV Amsterdam, The Netherlands
cgerritsen@nscr.nl
[3] Radboud University Nijmegen, P.O. Box 9104, 6500 HE Nijmegen, The Netherlands
t.bosse@ru.nl

Abstract. People are frequently confronted with scams; swindlers trying to gain your trust to get hold of your personal information, money or belongings. Elderly people are especially vulnerable to these tricks, that typically occur at the front door, street or on the phone. We have developed a virtual training environment to teach people how to handle these situations and learn them to increase their verbal resilience. The training is implemented as a tablet application and consists of six scenarios that are likely to occur in daily life. Participants are placed in a dialogue with a virtual character and may interact by choosing an answer from a fixed multiple-choice menu or by speaking the answer aloud. A speech recognition module is able to detect the level of assertiveness and provides immediate feedback to the user's performance. In this paper, we present the implementation of the virtual training application. To evaluate the prototype a focus group was organized, consisting of potential end users. The outcomes were mainly positive and the provided feedback will be incorporated into the final version.

Keywords: Serious gaming · Learning · User study

1 Introduction

When a con artist tells you a convincing but fraudulent story in order to enter your house and/or rob you this is called a doorstep scam. Doorstep scams frequently happen, numerous news reports about different stories exist. Since doorstep scams often have a high (emotional) impact, various campaigns try to educate people on this topic in order to prevent doorstep scams from happening (e.g. 'Spot it, Stop it'[1]). Such campaigns focus at behavioral aspects of the prevention of doorstep scams. Doorstep scams are acknowledged by the Dutch ministry of Safety and Justice as high impact crimes. Because of this,

---

[1] www.ageuk.org.uk/information-advice/money-legal/scams-fraud/doorstep-scams/.

© Springer Nature Switzerland AG 2019
M. Gentile et al. (Eds.): GALA 2018, LNCS 11385, pp. 110–120, 2019.
https://doi.org/10.1007/978-3-030-11548-7_11

and because existing campaigns are not enough, they funded research towards a virtual doorstep scam resilience training. This research is executed in collaboration with a large Dutch elderly organization called KBO-PCOB[2]. In a previous paper [8], we proposed the idea of a serious game for training of verbal resilience to high-risk doorstep scams. That paper describes how a virtual training can be used to improve people in their verbal resilience in order to prevent doorstep scams from having negative outcomes. The target group for this virtual training is high-risk victims; for doorstep scams these are elderly people. A training with virtual agents offers multiple advantages, among which are the low costs and the repeatability, comparing it to training with actors. This has already been shown in research in other domains, such as [1,2].

The current paper describes the implementation of the serious game and is organized as follows: First, an overview of related work is given, followed by a detailed description of the different aspects of the implementation. A first evaluation of the prototype is described in Sect. 4. The paper ends with the conclusion and discussion.

2   Related Work

Doorstep scams mostly happen at the front door, on the street, or on the phone. The goal of a doorstep scam is often to rob or get sensitive information from the victim. The content of doorstep scams is studied in [8]. A list of frequently encountered doorstep scam stories was created, based on a field research, which lies at the basis of the created scenarios. From all the discussed scenarios, the six most encountered scenarios are chosen for the application. Two scenarios take place at the front door, two scenarios take place on the street, and two scenarios take place on the phone. The scenarios are described in more detail in [8].

A specific skill that is beneficial for the resilience against doorstep scams is assertiveness: behaving confident and daring to say what you think or believe[3]. Various interventions exist to improve people in their assertiveness. Increasing the refusal of an unreasonable request can be done by verbal modeling and therapist coaching [9]. Being able to refuse such a request is an important skill for doorstep scams. Refusing can be done in various ways, among which are simply saying no, but also refusing by changing the subject [12]. Both the different verbal strategies that can be used as well as the need to be assertive while refusing, need to be present in a prevention program in order to teach students to resist indirect and direct pressures to engage in negative behaviors [10]. It is important that the verbal strategies are practiced in specific situations, although nonverbal assertive skills can be used for different situations [12].

Being assertive is also reflected in the way someone speaks, which will also be addressed in the application that is built. For example, speaking firmly or authoritative [11] or the medium latency of the response [4] are associated with an assertive way to use your voice.

---

[2] www.kbo-pcob.nl.

[3] Definition: dictionary.cambridge.org/dictionary/english/assertive.

However, so far no comparable interventions for elderly people have been found to improve their resilience against (doorstep) scams. Serious games for elderly are often exergames, games in which the player has to perform some sort of physical activity. These games promote active aging or aim to help people with physical problems, such as balance or postural control problems with the use of Nintendo Wii Fit, together with the Balance Board (e.g. [7]) or the Xbox Kinect (such as [14]). Besides exergames, there are serious games for elderly people that help to improve their cognitive abilities, via brain training games such as Smart Thinker [3]. Other serious games for elderly aim to promote social activities, e.g. SilverGame [13].

3   Implementation

The three dimensional environment, which is described in more detail in Sect. 3.2, as well as the user interface for the application are created in the game-engine Unity[4]. In order to program the application various C# scripts are written.

The application starts with a main menu with four different options: scenarios, scores, explanation, and credits. On the scores pages the player can find their top ten scores and the average number of stars received for each scenario. It is also possible to reset all the scores. How the scores are calculated is described in Sect. 3.3. The scenarios, both their content as their functioning, are described in Sect. 3.1.

3.1   Scenarios

The player can choose from six scenarios described in [8], these are played from a first person perspective. The gender of the avatar is chosen randomly by the application. Besides this, the player can choose to play using speech analysis or not, in order to train the assertiveness of his/her voice. The speech analysis is only available when playing with a network connection and is, if connected, by default turned on. The speech analysis is further explained in Sect. 3.4.

Figure 1 shows the flow of the application when playing a scenario. First, the scenario is set up: the camera is moved to the correct location in the environment, and the gender of the avatar and/or voice are randomly chosen. When the scenario needs an avatar (this is the case when it is not a phone scenario), this avatar is activated. Finally, the intro animation is played. For each type of scenario (door, street or phone) another intro is used. In the case of the door scenario the doorbell is rang, the door is opened and the camera moves a bit forward. For the street scenarios the camera and an animated dog, placed close to the camera to represent the players dog, move towards the avatar. In case of the phone scenarios a ring tone is played after which the screen of the phone placed in the environment changes, representing an incoming call.

The scenario always starts with the virtual opponent, the speech is played together with face and body animations (if needed). After the turn of the virtual

---

[4] www.unity3d.com/.

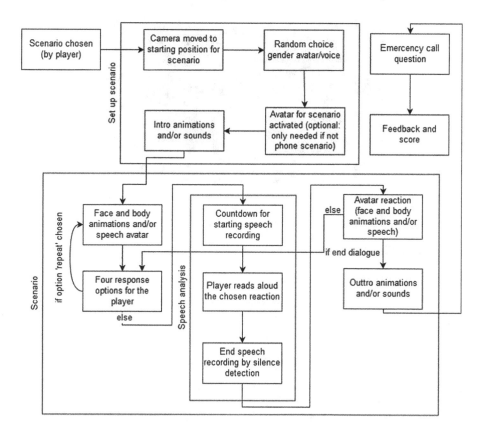

Fig. 1. Flowchart of the application when playing a scenario

opponent the player generally has four possible responses to choose from. One of these responses is to repeat the last turn (this response is only available if the virtual opponent has said something in the previous turn). This response is added to accommodate the target user group. The other responses influence the progress of the scenario.

Figure 2 shows a screenshot of the application when the player has reached a choice moment, during the energy scenario at the door. At the bottom of the screen the four possible reactions are visible, the bottom one is the repeat option, the other three options are randomly ordered. In the upper right corner the gauge for the speech analysis, showing the players last speech analysis score.

The scenarios can be represented in flowcharts, Fig. 3 shows such a flowchart for a scenario. The blue rectangles show the avatar's dialogue, the red rectangle shows a negative end state with the dialogue of the avatar. The rounded rectangles show the possible reactions of the player, the color of the rectangle represents the rating of the response. For some reactions of the player there are two outgoing arrows with conditions. These conditions are used by the speech

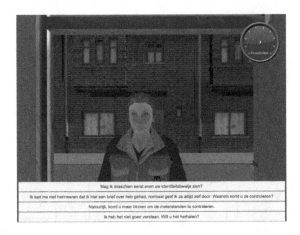

Fig. 2. Screenshot of a choice moment in the application

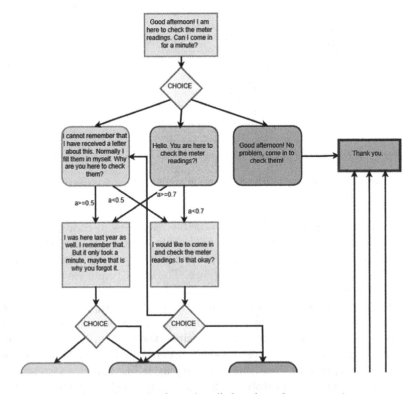

Fig. 3. Part of a (translated) flowchart for a scenario

analysis and indicate what the influence of the assertiveness of the players voice is on the progress of the scenario.

When the speech analysis module is turned on, a few more steps are taken before continuing with the scenario.[5] Right after choosing a response (other than the repeat option) all the other responses disappear and a countdown is shown, after which the recording automatically starts. The player is instructed by the game to read their response aloud. The recording automatically stops after a certain time of silence. The reaction of the virtual opponent in the next turn is determined by the response the player made and the score of the speech analysis (more on this in Sect. 3.4). If the reaction of the virtual opponent is not an end dialogue, the player will again be able to choose from different reactions. If an end dialogue is played the outtro of the scenario is played after that dialogue. This can either be closing the door (door scenarios), walking away (street scenarios), or a hung up sound (phone scenario).

When the scenario has ended the player is asked whether or not he/she would call the emergency number in such a situation, the rationale behind this is described in [8]. After this the player will receive feedback on their choices and see its score. This feedback is divided in three categories: general feedback, extended feedback and tips. For all feedback a 'read aloud' option is available. Section 3.3 discusses how the feedback and score are established.

The flow of the application is programmed in a general way, so that it is easy to add or change the content of the scenarios. The scenario specific content (avatars, dialogues, responses, tips, and feedback) are therefore stored in a database. By linking the code to the database the specific content is shown within the application. An overview of all the databases and the data stored in these databases can be found in Table 1.

3.2   Virtual Avatars and Environment

For each scenario at the doorstep and on the street, a male and female avatar are created, resulting in a set of eight different avatars. For the two scenarios at the front door the company uniform of two Dutch companies is manually recreated. For the scenarios on the street modern clothes are chosen for the avatars.

In order to animate the avatars iClone[6] is used. Both default animations and manually created animations are used as body animations. For the face animations, Facial Motion Capture[7] software, with a plug-in for iClone, is used. During two recording sessions a male and a female actor their face expressions were recorded while also recording the voice for the different dialogues. Their voices are also used for the scenarios that are not using a virtual agent (phone scenarios). After recording the facial animations, some further editing was needed in order to improve the animations. This was necessary because the results from the Facial Motion Capture were insufficiently realistic.

The three dimensional environment used for the application features a small part of a residential area and a partly decorated house. The environment is

---

[5] Note: sometimes a response is an action instead of a verbal response, in these cases the speech analysis step is always skipped.

[6] www.reallusion.com/iclone/.

[7] www.facewaretech.com.

Table 1. Overview of all used databases

Database	Description
Avatar	This database contains the names of all the available avatars and links them to the right scene (location) and scenario number
Dialogue	This database contains all the turns of the virtual opponent. Storing:
	- Scene number, scenario number and the dialogue ID
	- Text of the dialogue
	- The tip variable IDs that is turned false in this dialogue (if applicable, more details on this in Sect. 3.3)
	- The type of end state (if applicable)
	- The body animation of the virtual avatar (if applicable)
Responses	This database contains the responses that are linked to the dialogues. Storing the following:
	- Scene number, scenario number and the ID of the dialogue that the response is corresponding with
	- Text of the response
	- The ID of the default next dialogue
	- The threshold for the speech analysis score (if applicable)
	- The ID of the next dialogue when the speech analysis score is below the defined threshold, and the ID of the next dialogue when the score is above the threshold (if applicable)
	- The action (animation) linked to the response (if applicable)
	- The type of response (2 = good, 1 = average, 0 = bad)
	- A boolean if there is speech analysis for this response (default = true)
Tip	This database contains the tip variable IDs (corresponding with the dialogue table), their name and text
Feedback	This database contains the different types of outcomes. The IDs correspond with the type of end state defined in the dialogue table. Furthermore, it contains the name and the feedback text of the outcomes

created in Unity, using various assets from the Unity Asset Store[8]. The virtual avatars, including their body and facial animations are exported to Unity and added to the environment.

3.3 Feedback and Score

After each scenario the player receives feedback. The general feedback, shown by default, tells the player whether or not he/she has become a victim of a doorstep scam. This feedback is therefore depending on the type of the end state of the

---

[8] https://assetstore.unity.com/.

scenario, which is stored in the feedback database (see Table 1). Furthermore, the general feedback encourages the player to further explore the other feedback.

The extended feedback includes a paragraph that is specific for the scenario. It is therefore independent of the outcome reached by the player. Furthermore, the extended feedback includes feedback on the choice the player made for the call question. There are three different feedback texts available for this. The first is for players who chose to call the emergency number, the second is for people who did not choose to call the emergency number but did have a negative outcome, and the last is for people who did not call the emergency number but did also not become a victim in the scenario.

The most tailored feedback are the tips. In each scenario a number of variables are defined, who are by default true. If a specific dialogue that is linked (which is stored in the dialogue database) to a variable is played during the scenario, this variable is set to false. For the variables that are still true at the end of the scenario a tip is given to the player. The tips are showed in such an order that they follow the progress of the scenario. An example is a variable about asking the identification, this is linked to the dialogue where the virtual opponent shows its identification. If this dialogue is not played during the scenario (so the variable is still true and not set to false), the player receives feedback about this afterwards.

Besides feedback the player also receives a score at the end of each scenario. The higher the score of the player, the better the performance during the training was. The highest score is 105. The score is calculated using the average score for the choices, the average score for the voice, a score for the result of the scenario, and a bonus (of 5 points) if the emergency number is called.

Next to a score a player also gets a number of stars (0–5) for a scenario. A player will receive one star if he/she earned more than 11 points during the game, two stars for more than 33 points, three stars for more than 55 points, four stars for more than 77 points, and the maximal number of five stars is achieved when more than 100 points are earned during the game.

3.4 Speech Analysis

The speech analysis module is based on the Interpersonal Stances theory. This concept stems from social psychology, and can be defined as 'the ways in which speakers and writers linguistically demonstrate their commitment to or attitudes about a person or proposition' [6]. The module classifies the speech in 2 types of attitudes: Dominant (normally referred to as Above) and Submissive (Below).

A modified version of the openSmile[9] toolkit extracts the voice features, while an SVM algorithm classifies the extracted features into the categories. The SVM model was built using 4-fold cross validation over a dataset with 681 sentences of four people instructed in how to act into both categories. Details about the algorithm and the SVM tuning are described in [5]. The final accuracy of the module is 86.56%.

---

[9] https://audeering.com/technology/opensmile/.

The recorded voice of the player is analyzed by the algorithm. The application detects silence to determine when the recording ends. The ambient noise is measured while people are using the application. Silence is defined as a period of 3 s in which the volume is 20 decibels above the ambient noise volume maximum. The recording stops after 10 s or if silence is detected. The module runs on a server, it receives the user's voice and returns the classification status. In case of communication failure, the client application ignores the voice information and continues the dialogue without the speech analysis. The output of the module is the confidence percentage between the 2 categories. The application uses those values in the dialogue tree as described in Sect. 3.1. Figure 1 shows how the speech analysis is embedded in the flow of the application.

4 Evaluation Prototype

To obtain feedback from potential end users on the prototype, we organized a focus group at KBO-PCOB in Utrecht. This focus group consisted of five security advisors voluntarily working for KBO-PCOB. All participants belong to the group of potential end users, namely elderly. Two of the participants were female and three were male.

The focus group started with general instructions about the application. We explained how to start the application, introduced the different scenarios, and told the participants how to use the speech analysis module. After the instructions, all participants were provided a private practice space and a tablet. They each had 30 min to test the application and try different options. After this, we had a group discussion about their findings. This group discussion was based on open questions to get qualitative feedback.

The participants all responded positively about the application. They believed it is a nice addition to existing education on safety for elderly. They recognized the scenarios as being most common to experience in daily life. They especially saw added value of the application for group meetings in which elderly can work together on the application and afterwards discuss this with the group. They had some minor comments as well. For instance, they would like to see a progress bar in the scenarios with speech analysis so they know how much time they have left for recording their voice. Within those scenarios, they also wanted the time the system takes to detect the end of their spoken input to be shorter. Additionally, they would like to be able to go back within a scenario, to alter their answers, and to go back to the tips/feedback menu when clicking a scenario in the score screen. Finally, they would like to see more scenarios and they preferred lighter colors. Based on these suggestions, we are currently working on improving the application.

5   Conclusion and Discussion

In this paper, a serious game for verbal resilience training was presented. The training is specifically developed for elderly in order to teach them how to deal with scams. Elderly form a high-risk demographic group, and are relatively often confronted with scams, either on the phone, the street or at the front door. The training allows them to practice different scenarios on a tablet. Within the scenarios, the trainee is confronted with a virtual scam artist trying to convince the trainee to either pay money, provide personal information or let him/her inside the house. The trainee can interact with the virtual agent by choosing an option from the fixed multiple-choice menu and by either clicking on this answer or speaking the answer aloud. In the latter case, the speech recognition module is able to detect the level of assertiveness in the recorded voice, providing real-time feedback. Next to this, the trainees receive their score and feedback on their performance including tips at the end of a scenario and they can view the top ten scores and the average numbers of earned stars on a score page.

To evaluate the prototype we organized a focus group with potential end users. They reacted positively towards the developed environment. They especially saw the added value in the possibility to train scenarios in larger settings in which they can guide other users. They had some small remarks regarding the speech recognition module, which will be addressed in the final version.

References

1. Bosse, T., Gerritsen, C.: Towards serious gaming for communication training - a pilot study with police academy students. In: Poppe, R., Meyer, J.-J., Veltkamp, R., Dastani, M. (eds.) INTETAIN 2016 2016. LNICSSITE, vol. 178, pp. 13–22. Springer, Cham (2017). https://doi.org/10.1007/978-3-319-49616-0_2
2. Bosse, T., Gerritsen, C., De Man, J.: An intelligent system for aggression de-escalation training. In: ECAI, pp. 1805–1811 (2016)
3. Chi, H., Agama, E., Prodanoff, Z.G.: Developing serious games to promote cognitive abilities for the elderly. In: 2017 IEEE 5th International Conference on Serious Games and Applications for Health, SeGAH 2017, pp. 1–8 (2017)
4. Eisler, R.M., Miller, P.M., Hersen, M.: Components of assertive behavior. J. Clin. Psychol. **29**(3), 295–299 (1973)
5. Formolo, D., Bosse, T.: Towards interactive agents that infer emotions from voice and context information. EAI Endorsed Transactions on Creative Technologies **4**(10) (2017)
6. Gales, T.: Identifying interpersonal stance in threatening discourse: an appraisal analysis. Discourse Stud. **13**(1), 27–46 (2011)
7. Konstantinidis, E.I., Billis, A.S., Mouzakidis, C.A., Zilidou, V.I., Antoniou, P.E., Bamidis, P.D.: Design, implementation, and wide pilot deployment of FitForAll: an easy to use exergaming platform improving physical fitness and life quality of senior citizens. IEEE J. Biomed. Health Inform. **20**(1), 189–200 (2016)
8. van der Lubbe, L.M., Bosse, T., Gerritsen, C.: Design of an agent-based learning environment for high-risk doorstep scam victims. In: Bajo, J., et al. (eds.) PAAMS 2018. CCIS, vol. 887, pp. 335–347. Springer, Cham (2018). https://doi.org/10.1007/978-3-319-94779-2_29

9. McFall, R.M., Lillesand, D.B.: Behavior rehearsal with modeling and coaching in assertion training. J. Abnorm. Psychol. **77**(3), 313–23 (1971)
10. Miller-Day, M.A., Alberts, J., Hecht, M.L., Trost, M.R., Krizek, R.L.: Adolescent Relationships and Drug Use. Lawrence Erlbaum Associates, Mahwah (2014)
11. Nichols, T.R., Birnel, S., Graber, J.A., Brooks-Gunn, J., Botvin, G.J.: Refusal skill ability: an examination of adolescent perceptions of effectiveness. J. Primary Prevent. **31**(3), 127–37 (2010)
12. Nichols, T.R., Graber, J.A., Brooks-Gunn, J., Botvin, G.J.: Ways to say no: refusal skill strategies among urban adolescents. Am. J. Health Behav. **30**(3), 227–36 (2006)
13. Senger, J., et al.: Serious gaming: enhancing the quality of life among the elderly through play with the multimedia platform SilverGame. In: Wichert, R., Eberhardt, B. (eds.) Ambient Assisted Living. ATSC, pp. 317–331. Springer, Heidelberg (2012). https://doi.org/10.1007/978-3-642-27491-6_23
14. Taylor, L.M., Maddison, R., Pfaeffli, L.A., Rawstorn, J.C., Gant, N., Kerse, N.M.: Activity and energy expenditure in older people playing active video Games. Arch. Phys. Med. Rehabil. **93**(12), 2281–2286 (2012)

Game Design

Designing an Intrinsically Integrated Educational Game on Newtonian Mechanics

Anne van der Linden[(✉)], Wouter R. van Joolingen,
and Ralph F. G. Meulenbroeks

Freudenthal Institute, Utrecht University, Utrecht, The Netherlands
a.vanderlinden@uu.nl

Abstract. In the current paper we present the design process of an intrinsically integrated educational game on Newtonian mechanics. The design is based on a guiding frame in line with the intrinsic integration theory, which states that in a game, learning goal and game goal should be aligned. This also results in an alignment between a pedagogical approach and game mechanics. Our findings suggest three guidelines within this guiding frame. First, the guiding frame works in a specific order starting with forming a learning goal and ending with the game goal. Also, to optimize the alignment between the learning goal and the game goal, it should only be possible for players to reach the game goal when the desired learning goal is reached. Finally, during the iterations of the design process the focus is on aligning the pedagogical approach with the game mechanics. This proved to be an essential but difficult step.

Keywords: Educational game · Intrinsic integration · Newtonian mechanics

1 Introduction

When we look at a person who is gaming, we see a person fully immersed to master the game. Mastering the game means learning how to play the game. This learning occurs whilst the player, fully immersed in the gaming experience, loses the sense of time and surroundings, resulting in a state of flow [1]. This learning in a state of total immersion is in sharp contrast with the commonly observed lack of engagement in formal education. So, could it be possible to use this immersed learning that occurs whilst playing a game in formal education?

In the past decades, research focusing on using educational games has increased [2]. Research focusing on motivational effects show that educational games sometimes show an increase in intrinsic motivation of students as compared to participating in other instructional activities. However, a meta-analysis [3] shows that educational games in general do not yield positive motivational effects on students. Research focusing on cognitive effects of educational games, on the other hand, show promising results in general [2, 4]. However, the results of individual educational games remain inconsistent. This leads to the question why some educational games yield learning effects and others do not. Of course there could be many factors contributing to the absence or presence of a learning effect. In this paper we investigate the influence of the game design itself.

© Springer Nature Switzerland AG 2019
M. Gentile et al. (Eds.): GALA 2018, LNCS 11385, pp. 123–133, 2019.
https://doi.org/10.1007/978-3-030-11548-7_12

Several studies have been devoted to gain insight on the design process and different design elements of an educational game [2, 5–7]. Although this research has led to some interesting insights, much of how to design a good educational game remains unclear.

In the present study we aim to elucidate some design principles by describing the design process of an educational game on Newtonian mechanics. In our analysis of the step by step design process, we search for overarching design guidelines that can be transferred to the design process of other educational games.

The next section presents the theoretical substantiation of the designed educational game, which leads to the research question. Subsequently, the research question will be addressed in a case study that will describe the design process of the game.

2 Theoretical Substantiation

2.1 Educational Game Goals

Every game has a game goal, for instance, freeing a princess, collecting stars or simply surviving. To reach the game goal, players interact with the game through game mechanics and game attributes. Sicart [8] defines game mechanics as 'methods invoked by agents, designed for interaction with the game state' [8]. Examples of game mechanics are jumping, trading and climbing. Game mechanics thus describe an interaction between the player and the game. Game attributes are visualizations of game properties, such as stamina. For instance, a player is only able to climb a wall with enough stamina. In this case the player needs a visualization of their stamina, in a meter for instance, in order to make a decision to continue climbing. Game attributes and game mechanics are strongly connected and essential in reaching the game goal.

In an educational activity, students need to reach a certain learning goal. This means that if a game is to be used as an educational activity, it should always have two goals. So apart from the game goal, the learning goal of an educational game is that players need to learn something of value outside the game context. Within the game context players learn in order to master the game, whereas an educational game aims at learning for a broader context.

2.2 Intrinsic Integration

When designing an educational game, most educators or educational researchers tend to focus on the educational aspects of the game, making sure that the educational content is all there [9]. Then an educator usually adds game properties (such as adding points or a narrative) to make the game more engaging. This approach, however, can easily lead to a discrepancy between learning goal and the game goal. This could result in an unsuccessful educational game [5]. To make this discrepancy as small as possible, the additional educational learning should be integrated with the learning that occurs anyway whilst playing a game, the learning of how to play the game.

This integration of educational learning with the game mechanics is referred to as intrinsic integration. Intrinsic integration in a game is thus defined as subject matter and game mechanics being integrated within the same game idea [10]. Several studies focused on integrating learning content with game environments [5, 6, 11, 12]. However, it proves to be quite challenging to integrate learning with game mechanics while not affecting the enjoyability of games [11].

2.3   Pedagogical Approach

Any educational activity requires an underlying pedagogical approach. A pedagogical approach describes the steps that are seen as important in achieving the learning goal of the game. This means that the game mechanics should be designed in such a way that students will perform thinking activities relevant for learning. For instance, the game mechanics may be such that a real-life situation is mimicked, or that some kind of planning is required that has relevance for the learning goal.

The aim of the current paper is to investigate the way intrinsic integration can be reached, by aligning game goal and learning goal as well as game mechanics and pedagogical approach. We did this in the context of designing a game for learning elementary Newtonian mechanics.

2.4   Research Question and Hypothesis

The main research question in this paper is: How can an educational game be designed where learning is integrated with the game mechanics?

Our hypothesis on designing an intrinsically integrated game is shown in Fig. 1. To optimize the learning effect of an educational game, it is important to align the learning goal with the game goal. Only if the desired learning goal is reached should it be possible for players to reach the game goal. This alignment is in line with the intrinsic integration theory [10]. To optimize this effect, we propose an additional alignment between a pedagogical approach and game mechanics.

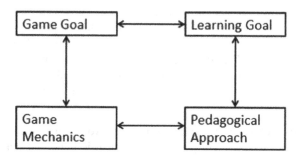

Fig. 1. Guiding frame on alignment between the game goal, learning goal, pedagogical approach and game mechanics.

3 Design Process: Newton's Race

3.1 Concretize the Hypothesis

The design process followed the basic hypothesized elements. First the hypothesis was made concrete by instantiating the learning goal, pedagogical approach, game mechanics and game goal. The results lead to an initial design that was tested on a small scale in two iterations leading to several modifications. The final design was pilot tested on a group of 73 9th grade students, using a pre- and post-test quasi-experimental design.

Learning Goal. The guiding frame (Fig. 1) is used from an educators point of view. As with designing any learning activity, we started with determining the subject matter and thus establishing the learning goal. The subject of Newton's laws was chosen not only because of their importance in the secondary school curriculum but also because the persistence of student's preconceptions resulting in conceptual challenges [13]. In the present research, we define preconceptions as pre-existing ideas based on daily life experiences. One of the conceptual challenges within Newton's laws is that force is proportional with acceleration, not with speed [14]. This means that an object can move without working forces on it and if there is a net force working on an object the object is not just in motion, it is accelerating (or decelerating). The learning goal that matches with this conceptual challenge is that students can understand the effect of forces on different motions. This implies that students can predict motions with given forces and that they can explain the effects of forces when given a certain motion.

Pedagogical Approach. Research has shown that in the case of force and motion, student's preconceptions are quite persistent [13]. Therefore the need to face students with their preconceptions is essential [15–17]. This lead to the choice for the problem posing approach as the pedagogical foundation. In the problem posing approach situations are created in which preconceptions are no longer adequate explanations [18]. The key element of this approach is that students put their preconceptions into the learning activity and experience the effects of those preconceptions. When they are confronted with something that counters their expectations, ideally, they should see the need for new theories to alter their preconceptions.

However, in our real world, students are not able to test all preconceptions, because our world provides a single case in which parameters of the general physical theories, such as friction, are fixed. The advantage of a digital environment is that the effects of students actions can be simulated with high precision, including movements without friction. In this case, students should be able to alter forces working on an object resulting in different motions.

Game Mechanics. A brainstorm session resulted in two possible genres for our game: puzzle and race. For the problem posing approach, it is important that players truly experience the consequences of their ideas and concepts. Therefore, the game mechanics should provide a so-called *setting phase* where players can incorporate their own ideas. Therefore, the game mechanic of setting a force on an object is needed. Then players need to experience the effects of their choice, thus a design is needed were players can clearly see the effects of those forces on the motion of the chosen object. Therefore, a race-like environment seemed fitting with our chosen pedagogical approach. Some other game mechanics that fit with a race game are: navigating through levels and steering.

Game Goal. Traditionally, the goal of a race game is to reach the end of a level as soon as possible. However, that would not fit our chosen learning goal, as the mimicking of a realistic, rather than a fast, movement is paramount. A more fitting game goal then would be to just finish a trajectory. To truly show effects of forces, a non-motorized object, a ball, was chosen for students to complete the trajectory with. A ball is a very familiar object that everybody knows. Thus, players will have experiences with possible motions a ball can make (after one kick, the ball will start to move, followed by a decrease in speed). A conflict with this expectation should occur when players select an scientifically incorrect setting in the setting phase. Ideally, this conflict results in failure to reach the end and this should prompt alteration of their preconception to scientific reasoning. This means that the learning goal of understanding the effects of forces resulting in different motions should be reached. Players then should select the scientifically correct setting and only then are able to finish the trajectory.

3.2   Initial Game Design and Playtesting

In order to seek balance between students' skills and the challenges of the game and thus trying to reach the desired state of flow [1] eight levels of increasing difficulty were included to the game. Each level consists of a different trajectory, starting with easier levels (no friction, straight path) building op to levels with turns, multiple surfaces (different frictions) and green and red platforms where the ball receives additional kicks respectively in the direction of motion or against the direction of motion. For each level the same game goal applies (get the ball to the finish line).

In the setting phase at the beginning of each level players decide if there is a constant force ($F_{constant}$) working on the ball to keep it moving after receiving an initial kick. They can set a value for that force by using a scrollbar. Whenever the ball receives a kick, a pow-icon is shown (see Fig. 2), so that students could see how and where a force is working on the ball. If a scientifically incorrect setting is chosen, the speed of the ball will be too high in turns of the trajectory. Therefore, the ball will fall off and that the game goal cannot be reached.

To strengthen players' experience of motions resulting from their preconceptions, it is important that the kind of motion (acceleration, deceleration, constant speed) of the ball is clearly visible. To make sure players could see the type of motion, several game attributes were added. As shown in Fig. 3, an accelerometer, speedometer and a tail proportional with speed were added to the game.

In order to complete trajectories, players need to be able to change the balls direction. This action must be scientifically correct. Therefore, players can give the ball a sideways kick (using arrow keys), perpendicular to the direction of motion.

To make the game more interactive and add some competition, the challenge of collecting coins was added. The coins were placed in such a way that the trajectory should become more difficult. For instance, coins were placed at harder to reach places, such as the inside of turns. Also, as conventional in race games, an overview map was added for players to anticipate on the trajectory.

In summary, the game design consists of two game mechanics within each level: setting a force and changing direction of the ball. The first mechanic is essential for the alignment with the pedagogical approach. To strengthen the effect of the pedagogical approach, game attributes were added to make the kind of motion visible. The second mechanic is needed to reach the game goal, since there are turns in the trajectories. In addition to the turns, collecting coins and green and red platforms were added to provide challenge for the players.

At this point a demo version (four levels) of the game was tested. Note that with every iteration bugs were eliminated, the game's interface was optimized and difficulty adjustments were made to optimize flow. Only results regarding the game's content will be discussed. This playtest showed a problem with the introductory texts in the setting phase of each level. Due to the length of the texts players were reluctant to read it or did not read it at all, resulting in not knowing what to do in a level.

Fig. 2. The pow-icon when the ball receives a kick

Fig. 3. A snapshot of level 3 with the setting: $F_{constant} = 0N$. In the upper left corner, the accelerometer is visible, the speedometer in the down left corner and the tail is visible behind the ball. The overview map is visible in the upper right corner.

3.3   First Version

For the next version of the game (eight levels) the introductory texts were adjusted so that they only contained important information regarding completing a level. This version was tested with thirty 10th grade students, aged between 15 and 16.

Results showed three issues with the game. First, none of the players could finish level eight. In this level students were also able to set a value for the mass of the ball. This extra setting provided players with too many options, making the level too difficult. A mass adjustment was not essential to our learning goal, therefore this level was deleted for the following version of the game.

Second, there were doubts as to if students saw the difference between a motion with $F_{constant}$ (acceleration or constant speed, depending on the value of friction) and without $F_{constant}$ (deceleration). In the next version students played the level twice, once with each setting. A fitting adjustment would be playing the same level twice, with these different settings.

Finally, most importantly, it appeared to be unclear for the players that by using the arrow keys to change the balls direction of motion, a small force was exerted on the ball. This indicates a discrepancy between the pedagogical approach and game mechanics. For the pedagogical approach it is necessary that students understand that they need to exert a force on the ball in order to change its direction. To make this more explicit, giving the ball a force needs to be visible. In an attempt to show this, another pow-icon was added whenever the arrow keys are used change the ball's direction, shown in Fig. 4. With this added icon students are more likely to link changes in direction due to a kick, instead of an internal steering system, as is traditional in a racing game.

Fig. 4. The pow-icon when the ball receives a sideways kick.

3.4   Pilot

The three adjustments were implemented for the pilot study. A quasi-experimental pre- and post-test design was used to evaluate the latest version on learning and motivational effects. The game was tested in three groups (73 9th grade students in total). The control group followed a traditional lesson, the game group only played the game and the test group played the game followed by a classroom discussion. The duration of the experiment in all groups was one lesson of 40 min including a pre- and post-test.

Results of the pilot showed a significant motivational effect between the two groups who played the game and the control group. All groups did not yield a learning effect. However, the game group scored significantly lower on the post-test than the other two groups. The complete results of the pilot study go beyond the scope of the present paper, these results are elaborated on elsewhere [19].

However, during the pilot we also found four important issues regarding the design of the game:

1. The learning goal and the game goal are not sufficiently aligned. More experienced gamers (with other games) could finish certain levels without the scientifically correct setting, thus reaching the game goal. This probably means that these players did not reach the desired learning goal.
2. Also, an issue was found with the alignment of the pedagogical approach and the game mechanics. When a ball receives a sideways kick, the ball makes a parabolic movement. This does not become clear in the game. This is probably due to the fact that the trajectory is quite small, therefore there is no room for players to see the parabolic movement. Also players still associate a change of the balls direction with internal steering, not with acting forces. This indicates that a more clear game attribute is needed to visualize acting forces.
3. As mentioned above, students who only played the game scored significantly lower than students who played the game followed by a classroom discussion. This indicates the importance of embedding the educational game in other learning activities.
4. Players did not read texts, resulting in not understanding what to do in the setting phase of the game.

The effects of the four issues on the game design and the relation with our hypothesis will be elaborated on in the next section.

4   Discussion and Conclusion

4.1   Design Process

Our research question was: How can an educational game be designed where learning is integrated with the game mechanics?

A guiding frame was presented (Fig. 1) fitting with the intrinsic integration theory. Then we designed a game by concretizing this guiding frame. During this design process we found three main guidelines fitting with the guiding frame. Firstly, we used the guiding frame in a specific order. From an educators' point of view, any design process starts with forming a learning goal (step 1) and then finding a fitting pedagogical approach (step 2). Then we chose a suitable game genre from game mechanics that strengthened the pedagogical approach (step 3). From these game mechanics followed a game goal (step 4). The main implication is that in order to reach goal alignment, alignment of the game mechanics with the pedagogical approach is essential.

Secondly, to truly align the learning goal to the game goal, it is necessary that the game goal depends on the learning goal. This means that players must reach the learning goal before as a necessity for reaching the game goal. Results of the pilot study show that this is not trivial at all. Experienced gamers are able to finish a level without the scientifically correct setting ($F_{constant}$ = 0N), whereas less experienced gamers have difficulties finishing a level even with the correct setting. To make the discrepancy as small as possible, the scrollbar in the setting phase could be changed to a setting system with less options. Then it will not be possible for experienced players to set a small $F_{constant}$ close to 0N and thus are not able to finish a level with a small constant force. Finally, we also found that aligning the pedagogical approach with the game mechanics was the most essential and difficult step. Therefore, this alignment was the focus during the iterations. In our case a big challenge is the visualization of movement and forces. With the learning goal on the relationship between forces and motion, it is important that players understand when forces are working on the ball and what type of movement (acceleration, deceleration or constant speed) the ball makes. Despite our efforts during the pilot study, we found that the added sideways pow-icons for instance, still did not reach the desired effect of understanding that a force is acting. Another challenge lies in the setting phase. Setting $F_{constant}$ is an essential game mechanic in order for our pedagogical approach to work. However, with players reluctance of reading text in the setting phase, this game mechanic is not optimally used. Even with the reduced text in the pilot study, a trial and error approach is opted by most players.

To our knowledge, few educational games are made with a specific focus on the alignment of game mechanics with a pedagogical approach. However, a clear pedagogical approach is needed to reach any learning goal. Therefore, we recommend giving this alignment explicit attention during the design process. All this applies to integrating the pedagogical approach *within* the game. In addition, with our hypothesis (Fig. 1) in mind the pedagogical approach can also be (partly) offered *outside* the game in additional learning activities. In this case the game should align with the other learning activities, thus alignment between game mechanics and a pedagogical approach is still necessary.

4.2   Further Research

Newton's Race is an educational game still in development. The game can be improved by adjusting mentioned issues. However, additional information is needed on how players interpret and use the game attributes (such as the accelerometer and speedometer) in order to improve the game further. In addition, research is needed on the influence of objects exerting forces on the ball to improve the visualization of acting forces.

Also, if Newton's Race is going to be used in educational practice, additional learning activities are needed. In line with Wouters and colleague's [3] we found that embedding the game in other learning activities is necessary for students to reach the learning goal. However, it remains unclear what additional learning activities that should be. Research is needed to suggest possible effective additional learning activities.

Acknowledgements. The authors gratefully acknowledge the fruitful discussions with Dr. Nico Rutten. The present paper was made possible by funding from the Dutch Ministry of Education, Culture and Science, OCW/PromoDoc/1065001.

References

1. Csíkszentmihályi, M.: Flow: The Psychology of Optimal Experience. Harper & Row, New York (1990)
2. Clark, D.B., Tanner-Smith, E.E., Killingsworth, S.S.: Digital games, design, and learning: a systematic review and meta-analysis. Rev. Educ. Res. **86**(1), 79–122 (2016)
3. Wouters, P., van Nimwegen, C., van Oostendorp, H., van der Spek, E.D.: A meta-analysis of the cognitive and motivational effects of serious games. J. Educ. Psychol. **105**(2), 249–265 (2013)
4. Ke, F.: Computer games application within alternative classroom goal structures: cognitive, metacognitive, and affective evaluation. Educ. Tech. Res. Dev. **56**(5–6), 539–556 (2008)
5. Denham, A.: Improving the design of a learning game through intrinsic integration and playtesting. Technol. Knowl. Learn. **21**(2), 175–194 (2016)
6. Ke, F.: Designing and integrating purposeful learning in game play: a systematic review. Educ. Tech. Res. Dev. **64**(2), 219–244 (2016)
7. Lameras, P., Arnab, S., Dunwell, I., Stewart, C., Clarke, S., Petridis, P.: Essential features of serious games design in higher education: linking learning attributes to game mechanics. Br. J. Edu. Technol. **48**(4), 972–994 (2017)
8. Sicart, M.: Designing game mechanics. Int. J. Comput. Game Res. **8**(2) (2008). http://gamestudies.org/0802/articles/sicart. Accessed 27 Sept 2018
9. Van Eck, R.: Digital game-based learning: it's not just the digital natives who are restless. EDUCAUSE Rev. **41**(2), 16–30 (2006)
10. Kafai, Y.: Learning design by making games: children's development of strategies in the creation of a complex computational artifact. In: Kafai, Y., Resnick, M. (eds.) Constructionism in Practice: Designing, Thinking and Learning in a Digital World, pp. 71–96. Erlbaum, Mahwah (1996)
11. Vandercruysse, S., Elen, J.: Towards a game-based learning instructional design model focusing on integration. In: Wouters, P., van Oostendorp, H. (eds.) Instructional Techniques to Facilitate Learning and Motivation of Serious Games. AGL, pp. 17–35. Springer, Cham (2017). https://doi.org/10.1007/978-3-319-39298-1_2
12. Habgood, M.P.J., Ainsworth, S.E.: Motivating children to learn effectively: exploring the value of intrinsic integration in educational games. J. Learn. Sci. **20**(2), 169–206 (2011)
13. Halloun, I.A., Hestenes, D.: Common sense concepts about motion. Am. J. Phys. **53**(11), 1056 (1985)
14. Driver, R., Squires, A., Rushworth, P., Wood-Robinson, V.: Making Sense of Secondary Science: Research into Children's Ideas. Routledge, Oxen (1994)
15. Vosniadou, S.: Capturing and modeling the process of conceptual change. Learn. Instr. **4**, 45–69 (1994)
16. Duit, R., Treagust, D.: Conceptual change: a powerful framework for improving science teaching and learning. Int. J. Sci. Educ. **25**, 671–688 (2003)

17. Schumacher, R.S., Hofer, S., Rubin, H., Stern, E.: How teachers can boost conceptual understanding in physics classes. In: Looi, C.K., Polman, J.L., Cress, U., Reimann, P. (eds.) Transforming Learning, Empowering Learners: The International Conference of the Learning Sciences, ICLS, vol. 2, pp. 1167–1168. International Society of the Learning Sciences, Singapore (2016)
18. Klaassen, K.: A Problem-Posing Approach to Teaching the Topic of Radioactivity. Cdβ Press, Utrecht (1995)
19. van der Linden, A., van Joolingen, W.: A serious game for interactive teaching of Newton's laws. In: Proceedings of the 3rd Asia-Europe Symposium on Simulation and Serious Gaming - 15th ACM SIGGRAPH Conference on Virtual-Reality Continuum and Its Applications in Industry, VRCAI 2016, pp. 165–167. Association for Computing Machinery, New York (2016)

Games and Learning: Potential and Limitations from the Players' Point of View

Donatella Persico(✉) , Marcello Passarelli , Francesca Dagnino ,
Flavio Manganello , Jeffrey Earp , and Francesca Pozzi

National Research Council of Italy, Institute for Educational Technology,
via de Marini 6, 16149 Genoa, Italy
{persico,passarelli,dagnino,manganello,
earp,pozzi}@itd.cnr.it

Abstract. In recent times, numerous researchers and educators have been exploring playful learning with digital games in both formal and informal contexts. This study explores the point of view of players on the relationship between digital games and learning, based on a set of semi-structured interviews and two workshops involving relevant stakeholder groups (players, teachers, trainee teachers, and parents). Analysis of the gathered qualitative and quantitative data reveals that both players and educators agree that games have educational potential, but the assumption of blanket learner enthusiasm for game based learning is not always accurate. In particular, players have some resistance towards serious games, which are seen as less appealing than "real" videogames. In addition, some players and some teachers feel that the use of games in formal learning contexts contradicts the fundamental freedom intrinsic to the act of playing. Players are aware of the risks video-gaming presents, but they do not appear to be fully aware of its learning potential, as most mention lower order skills (memory, attention, reaction time) rather than academic knowledge and soft skills. Some mention game potential for the development of their social, cultural and gender identity, with consequential positive effects on their ethical beliefs. Players also point out the importance of videogame education for teachers, parents and for themselves. Lastly, they feel the need for innovation in games that, through innovative game mechanics and narratives, enhances the cultural and artistic component of games.

Keywords: Game-Based Learning · Players' attitudes · Serious games · Entertainment games · Informal learning · Formal learning

1 Introduction

Researchers and educators are increasingly interested in leveraging the potential of digital games to boost student motivation and support learning. This is largely based on the assumption that, as Gee puts it, "[games] allow people to recreate themselves in new worlds and achieve recreation and deep learning at one and the same time" [1]. As a field of research, game-based learning (GBL) involves the study of learning through

© Springer Nature Switzerland AG 2019
M. Gentile et al. (Eds.): GALA 2018, LNCS 11385, pp. 134–145, 2019.
https://doi.org/10.1007/978-3-030-11548-7_13

both educational (serious) games and entertainment games deployed in both formal and informal contexts. The Holy Grail of this quest is to identify the "fundamentally sound learning principles" [1] that make games so motivating and effective and grasp how to incorporate them effectively in learning and teaching processes in schools [2], workplaces, homes and other contexts where learning motivation and engagement cannot be taken for granted.

Accordingly, many experimental studies seek evidence that, when compared to "traditional" approaches and practices, GBL leads to increased learner motivation and (hence) better learning. For example, Clark, Tanner-Smith and Killingsworth [3] provide empirical evidence of the effectiveness of digital games and gamification on learning in formal education, and identify a number of moderating variables. Indeed, acceptance of the educational use of games and recognition of their potential for learning seems to depend on a number of factors, some of which are target-related, such as gender or age [4], while others are related to game features [5]. In addition, some researchers [6] found a wear out effect of playful experiences in the classroom, although this is mitigated by the competitive factor. At the same time, studies focusing on gaming as a leisure activity reveal how learning can occur 'incidentally' through gameplay. For example, Granic and colleagues [7] report extensive evidence for the cognitive, social, emotional, and motivational benefits of gaming.

When it comes to serious games deployed in formal settings, countless experimental studies claim positive results in terms of boosting the motivation to learn [8, 9]. However, Wouters and colleagues' [10] meta-analysis of serious gaming found it to be effective in terms of learning and retention, but not actually more motivating. Indeed, while there appears to be a general implicit assumption that students welcome GBL, some studies challenge this notion [11–13]. Although these authors use different methods and terminology, they basically identify a common set of reasons why students' acceptance of GBL cannot be taken for granted. These can be grouped into two categories: student perceptions of the usefulness, relevance, and opportunities video games offer for learning; and perceived ease of use, media affinity, personal experience and self-efficacy beliefs. All in all, these studies suggest that not all students respond positively to GBL, highlighting individual differences in this regard.

Additionally, video gaming per se is held by some to entail certain risks, such as inducing compulsive and even addictive play habits, hindering social interactions [14], and fostering aggressive attitudes and behavior [15]. Leaving aside the question of whether these risks are real or not, this paper investigates players' beliefs about learning through games and how they consider the idea of harnessing digital gaming for learning [12].

Some researchers have investigated the perspective of teachers and parents [16]. By contrast, the focus here is on the perception of players, including some who are (or are training to be) teachers themselves. Accordingly, our data collection activities involved adult players[1] and gained a sense of minors' perspective by proxy via teachers and parents. Our overarching research question was:

- What perception do players have of learning with digital (entertainment or serious) games, whether in informal or informal learning contexts?

  More specifically:

- Do they believe that some kind of learning takes place when they play for fun? What benefits do they perceive, if any? Do they report issues related to videogame play that may offset any perceived gains in terms of learning?
- What do they think about the use of games for learning in formal learning contexts? What are the main factors that fuel their beliefs and possible resistances?

The study is based on qualitative and quantitative data collected in 2017 as part of Gaming Horizons, a European research project funded by the Horizon 2020 program[2]. This addressed broad issues of interest to a wide range of stakeholder groups. At the same time, it yielded evidence providing new insights into how players in particular view the potential that digital games offer for learning and the adoption of digital gaming in teaching practice. In the following sections, we describe the context of the study, the methods used, the results obtained and, finally, the conclusions reached.

1.1 Context

As mentioned above, this paper focuses on only one aspect among those studied in the Gaming Horizons research project, namely the point of view of players on the relationship between games and learning. The overarching aim of Gaming Horizons was to challenge the current prevailing vision of the role games occupy in society and in learning, and to propose alternative framings [17]. Hence, the project included, but was not limited to, the activities described in the following sections. It started with a meta-literature review of educational, psychological and ethical aspects concerning the role of digital games in society and their cultural and educational value [18]. Subsequently, 73 interviews were conducted with various stakeholders (game developers, policy makers, teachers, players, and researchers selected at international level) on these same themes [19]. Furthermore, a series of 15 workshops was held in Italy and UK, involving representatives of the above stakeholder categories, plus parents. Alternative framings were then formulated and presented in the form of online scenarios[3] and a manifesto [20].

The project activities that mostly inform this study are 25 interviews carried out with players and educators, with further input coming from two of the workshops. Thus, in the following section, we describe the method adopted for performing these activities and for analyzing the data obtained. In the subsequent sections, we discuss results and provide conclusive remarks.

---

[1] Project funding regulations did not permit the involvement of minors.

[2] https://www.gaminghorizons.eu/.

[3] https://www.gaminghorizons.eu/scenarios.

2 Method

2.1 Interviews

The interviews were one-on-one semi-structured interviews covering a wide range of topics connected to project themes. They were carried out online and involved the use of visual stimuli, namely the presentation of selected keywords intended to prompt interviewee responses on certain key issues. Players and teachers were shown slightly different keyword sets: while the former were mostly prompted to talk about their relationship with games, what they like about them and what they believe can be learnt from them, the focus of the teacher interviews was primarily on views and experiences concerning the relationship between games and learning. Care was taken to ensure that the visual stimuli did not imply a positive or negative position towards games and gaming. That said, the interviewers actively sought interviewee responses in either direction. The interviews lasted from 60 to 90 min, and were all recorded and transcribed. The transcripts were subsequently analyzed using a common codebook and coded with the NVivo qualitative data analysis software package.

Out of the 25 interviews, 13 were with adult players and 12 with teachers with solid experience in the use of games for learning. The interviewees were recruited through calls on relevant Facebook group pages, via other social networks, and also from personal contacts. Care was taken to ensure acceptable gender representativeness and a range of nationalities. Players' age bracket was also considered as was school level for teachers. Project regulations disallowed the involvement of people under 18, so school students' opinions of GBL could not be gained first-hand. However, the interviews with teachers did yield observations about their students' reactions to games in education. It is for this reason that we included teachers interviews in our dataset.

2.2 Workshops

The aim of the 15 workshops carried out in Gaming Horizons was to elicit further evidence on the positions of the project stakeholders about the themes that had emerged in the interviews [19]. Out of these workshops, only two yielded information relevant for this study. The first involved players and parents (not the players' parents), while the second addressed a population of trainee teachers, many of whom also described themselves as players. In the following, we briefly outline the format of these two workshops, referring to them respectively as the P&P and the TT workshop.

The P&P workshop was held in Genoa and participants were recruited locally. Attendance was limited to players of adult age and parents of children who play videogames. The workshop involved 13 participants (7 parents and 6 players), who were divided into two groups with equal player/parent representation; these were moderated by project researchers. To facilitate and scaffold interaction, each group was invited to produce a poster that represented their discussion in the form of a flower (see Fig. 1). The center of the flower was the core theme assigned to the group for exploration; this was an Area of Tension (AoT), i.e. a contentious issue that had emerged from the interviews. The two AoTs chosen for the P&P workshop groups were (a) games and socialization and (b) regulation of gaming. Participants were asked to discuss the AoT and add post-its with their various positions and experiences, subsequently grouped together in thematic petals around the center. They were also asked to add a slogan encapsulating the overall thrust of the discussion (the stem) and some recommendations for other stakeholders (the leaves). To conclude the workshop, rapporteurs from each group presented and explained their poster, with space for further comment and discussion from participants.

The data sources that project researchers later analyzed comprised (a) recordings of the group discussions, (b) the outcome of the group work (the flower posters), and (c) recordings of the rapporteurs' presentations.

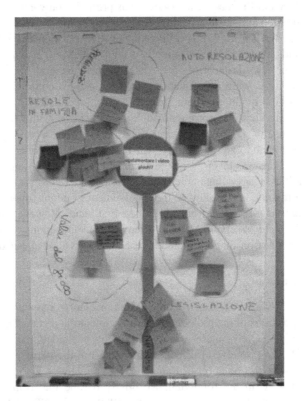

Fig. 1. Poster produced by one of the groups in the P&P workshop.

The TT workshop involved 70 trainee teachers from Genoa University's School of Education. Given the audience size, the Kahoot! application was used to collect participants' opinions on seven hot topics concerning the AoT: "Gaming and formal education: a difficult marriage?". Participants were asked a set of questions for profiling purposes, and then presented with a list of contentious statements on which they were required to express their level of agreement on a four-point scale. These stimuli provided a springboard for subsequent discussion, which also encompassed similar statements proposed by workshop participants themselves. After the event, data were downloaded from the Kahoot! database and quantitatively analyzed.

3 Results

3.1 Interviews Results

The outcomes from full analysis of all Gaming Horizons interviews are described in detail by Persico and colleagues [19]. Here we focus on the positions expressed by player interviewees, and also on student behaviors and beliefs as reported by interviewed teachers. Analysis revealed three main interconnected areas of concern: the potential of games (for learning and cultural/psychological development), their motivating power and players' acceptance of GBL, and risks connected to gameplay.

Potential. Analysis revealed that the potential of games for learning and development is undisputed by the educators and players alike. However, while the former see this potential mostly in the development of higher-order thinking skills (e.g., problem solving, critical thinking, decision making), the latter mainly mention aspects like improvement in memory, attention, reaction times and motor coordination. Only a few, on second thoughts, recognize that games can stimulate higher order skills too (*"I always thought gaming had no influence on skills, or problem solving, but now that I'm older I've seen it's not like that. I mean, some kinds of games can help a lot in the external strategy of how to act, and also on external perception agility"*).

Prompted about their experience with knowledge acquisition in academic terms, the players mostly mention applications for learning languages and scientific/technical disciplines. Among transversal skills, collaboration and competition are the main focus. (*"They [games] have taught me both about the positives and the negatives for competition I think."*). This clashes with the generally cautious attitude of the teachers, who tend to shun competitive games in the classroom.

Several players advocated the cultural and artistic value of some games (*"it's kind of like a new artistic medium that has yet to be fully experimented [...] there are a lot of [...] lovely interactive experiences that are very hard to define [...] those are very much like pieces of art that you could put in a gallery"*).

Last but not least, interviewee responses point to the strong influence games can have on the development of the cultural and gender identity of young players, with consequential effects on ethical beliefs concerning social inclusion/exclusion in terms of gender, race, ethnicity, religion, or sexual orientation (*"[in] Clash of Queens the strongest character is female and I'm really happy to finally see a woman who's strong and not just pretty. And that says it all"*).

Acceptance and Motivation. With regard to games and learning, the players mostly focus on informal learning through entertainment games, however some considerations about acceptance of GBL in formal learning also emerged, and these mostly align with teachers' perceptions. Of course, acceptance and motivation depend on several aspects, such as how and what games are proposed in the learning process, and the individual preferences of students. For example, in line with the findings of Wang and Wang [4], some teachers surmise differences between genders.

One player mentioned the need to strike a balance between free exploration and guidance from teachers: (*"the biggest mistake is [when] the player just has, like, an open sand box and they don't learn anything [...]. You need some sort of guided thing in order to get something out of it [...] [but]in my classes [the games] were too guided, [...] [like] watching a video*").

In contrast with the widespread assumption that games foster motivation to learn, few players supported this position. What is more, both teachers and players suggest that acceptance of GBL in formal education cannot be taken for granted. Players especially expressed skepticism towards serious games, characterized as being far less engaging than commercial video games, to the point of not being "real" games: ("*Playing educational games that try and gamify learning, I think they really missed the mark, because they're not fun*"). Some teachers share this opinion: ("*Young people nowadays are so used to a certain kind of gaming experience, that if you put a different kind in front of them [...] you don't engage them*"), adding that by definition play is a free activity and so cannot be assigned as a task to perform: ("*Imposing games on a school or a school district or a curriculum is the wrong way of approaching it*").

Both interviewee groups viewed the use of commercial games for learning purposes more favorably.

Risks. Many of the interviewees also discussed risks connected to gameplay and their (un)educational implications. While neither the players nor the teachers seem to share concerns expressed in the media that violent videogames can foster aggression (a link not conclusively proven by scientific evidence), they discussed other perceived downsides of videogame play at some length. Again, these concern entertainment games more than serious games. Addiction is probably the foremost of these, and the need to develop the skills required to self-regulate play time is frequently mentioned by both interviewee groups. Prompted about ethical issues in gaming, players mentioned the "toxicity" of interactions within some gamers' communities ("*Players calm down. Stop insulting*") and the need for better regulation to prevent children's access to games with unsuitable content.

As already mentioned, the influence of videogames on the development of players' personal and cultural identity is perceived by some as rather strong, but this potential is double edged ("*Actually in the end it's always the pretty girl who flirts with the protagonist and does little else*"; "*I'm playing a game, my character is black, woo, if it's a woman, woo, if it's a transgender, woo. I don't care*"; "*there are some big ethical issues around the depiction of contemporary events, like recent invasions of the Middle East*").

The interviewees see parents and educators as pivotal for favoring much-needed "*videogame education*" that should be a part of media education but is often missing due to the "*generation gap*". In this regard, they recommend that parents share the gaming experience with their kids ("*If you play games with your kids you get this beautifully shared experience with them [...] It's a great bonding experience*"). They also think teachers should increase their familiarity with digital games, recognizing their cultural and artistic value. They believe educators should try and reduce the generation gap with their students in order to better harness the educational potential of all types of games, equip their students with the skills needed to protect themselves from the risks, and get to know their children and students much better by "*meeting them where they are*" for so much of their time.

3.2   Workshops Results

P&P Workshop. As mentioned above, the areas of tension addressed in the P&P workshop were "the role games play in socialization" and "regulation of gaming". Participants interpreted the themes very broadly and, during the discussion, their beliefs about the educational value of games emerged, with learning being treated in wide-ranging terms that encompassed informal and lifelong processes.

On socialization aspects, participants underlined the role that games often assume as tools for exchanging knowledge between players. Several visions emerged. Some participants discussed games as tools to create narratives collaboratively ("*group storytelling*"). Some highlighted the opportunities that online games offer to get to know people of different ages and that have different backgrounds, languages and culture. According to the participants, this provides the opportunity to "*speak other languages*" in a literal and in a broad sense, while appreciating similarities and differences. Some also saw games as a way to "*stay in touch*" with friends who had moved far away. Others considered gaming as escapism, pointing out that play can be a way to escape from everyday problems, to delve into "*another world*" that is not necessarily illusory, but possibly one that is "*inside us*".

In this regard, games were seen as a medium for exploring attitudes and the self. One parent claimed that her child's aptitude for what later became his profession emerged thanks to the games he enjoyed playing most. In general, the group agreed on the capability of games to unveil personal attitudes that could guide decisions for the future, such as a course of study or career. This introspective power of games seems to be facilitated by the opportunity they offer players to leave behind daily issues and find time and space for self-reflection.

The "regulation of gaming" AoT turned attention to the other side of the coin, i.e. some of the parents' positions on the perceived negative effects of videogames on young people. What emerged from the discussion is that such concerns often overshadow the benefits seen in videogames. According to players, parents are able to recognize the benefits of other leisure activities such as playing a musical instrument, but not those of playing videogames. The group agreed that the main reason for this is parents' lack of familiarity and understanding of games. In line with the interview results, children and parents playing together was seen as a desirable and instructive activity. Players, however, were also very clear about the need for adolescents to be able to play without parental presence, as for other identity-forming activities. However, unfortunately, this can increase parents' suspicions and fears. The group concluded that parents would benefit from better understanding of the positive effects of videogame playing, while greater awareness of the risks of videogame play would be important for players.

TT Workshop. The data collected from the TT workshop with trainee teachers yielded a structured picture of their positions about the integration of games in formal education. Their opinions were deemed significant in that they represent a sample of teachers of the future, whose "generation gap" with today's students is presumably narrower than that of our teacher interviewees. Not surprisingly, 68% of participants described themselves as present or past players, and 42% had experienced GBL as students. Half of them had already had some teaching experience and about 85% stated that they had already used - or intend to use - games in their teaching.

Contrary to our expectations, the responses provided by the players and non-players in this workshop to the Kahoot! statements did not differ significantly (X2 ranging from 0.50 to 5.90 for the six questions we posed; p-values ranging from .12 to .92). Therefore, in the following, we will only report and comment on results from the player group (Fig. 2), which is the focus of the present study.

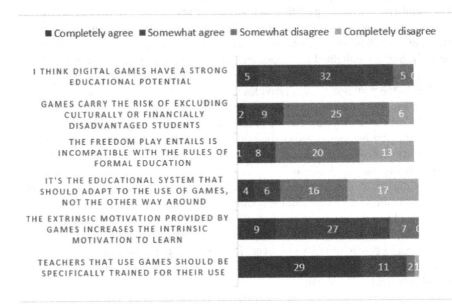

Fig. 2. Response of player trainee-teachers to the assertions concerning games for education.

Most of the trainees agree that games have strong educational potential (88% of complete or partial agreement vs. 12% who partially disagree with the notion). The overall vision remains positive if we consider only those who had the opportunity to play digital games at school for educational purposes: almost all the players who had played digital games at school (85%) agreed ("Completely" or "Somewhat") on games' educational potential. This is also reflected in the relative skepticism that games may exclude culturally or financially disadvantaged individuals (74% in complete or partial disagreement) and the alleged incompatibility between games and formal education (79% in complete or partial disagreement). Moreover, the player teacher-trainees were mostly in agreement with the assertion that the *extrinsic* motivation games provide may increase students' *intrinsic* motivation to learn (86% agreement). However, most of the player group disagree with the notion that the school system should re-shape itself to accommodate the integration of gameplay (79% completely or partially disagree). Lastly, an overwhelming majority of participants agree that suitable training is necessary in order to successfully deploy game-based activities (95% agreement).

4 Discussion and Conclusions

The aim of this study was to investigate players' opinions about the potential of digital games for learning. In some cases these opinions are compared with research results and teachers' opinions.

When prompted to discuss digital games and learning, players tend to focus on a range of effects deriving from informal play, rather than on GBL in formal contexts. Accordingly, most of our results (except for those of the TT workshop) pertain to attitudes towards entertainment games rather than serious games. In any case, results from both the interviews and the workshops lead us to believe that players have an eminently positive vision of the potential of digital games for learning, especially for the enhancement of transversal skills, cultural and artistic development and ethical thinking. This vision is shared by teachers, especially the pre-service ones.

As for the motivating potential, teachers' beliefs tend to align with the literature on GBL, which generally sees games as effective in motivating students to learn, with reservations in this regard about serious games [2, 10]. Indeed, some teachers revealed that their classroom experience with these games led to student disillusionment or even boredom. Players did not offer much significant input on the motivating potential of games. However, some expressed resistance towards the introduction of serious games in the classroom and, to a lesser degree, of videogames per se. The reason given was that serious games are generally less engaging than videogames but also that teacher-assigned and supervised gaming contradicts the very essence of gameplay itself.

General agreement also emerged on the need for greater "videogame literacy" to bridge the generation gap between young people and their teachers, and also their parents. This would allow teachers to make more informed choices in designing GBL activities and would give parents a better understanding of the benefits and risks of play. Media literacy would also better equip players to face some of the risks involved. Last but not least, players say that they look forward to playing games that incorporate innovative game mechanics and narratives, with special regard for the artistic component of games.

The main implications of this study concern the design of game-based educational interventions: greater awareness of players' attitudes and preferences should inform teachers' choice of games and the way they plan to deploy them for learning. One example would be for teachers to grant students some degree of freedom as to when and what games to play, a strategy that would concur with the perceived nature of gameplay as a voluntary activity. As for policies on game development, research funding programmes could grant more support for the development of innovative and artistically-oriented games, games that can stimulate learners with wide-ranging opportunities for reflection, discussion and growth, rather than pursing the transfer of specific curriculum contents.

Among the limitations of this study, we acknowledge that (a) the meaning of the term "game" adopted here is very wide and more research is needed on individual types of games for more specific findings, (b) for compliance reasons, the players involved in this study were exclusively adults, and (c) as a consequence of slow uptake of GBL in schools, only a limited number of our informants had engaged extensively in GBL as learners in formal education.

Acknowledgements. The Gaming Horizon project has received funding from the European Union's Horizon 2020 research and innovation programme under grant agreement No 732332.

References

1. Gee, J.P.: What video games have to teach us about learning and literacy. Comput. Entertain. (2003)
2. Passarelli, P., et al.: On the surmised motivating power of games. New Trends Issues Proc. Hum. Soc. Sci. (2018)
3. Clark, D.B., Tanner-Smith, E.E., Killingsworth, S.S.: Digital games, design, and learning: a systematic review and meta-analysis. Rev. Educ. Res. **86**, 79–122 (2016)
4. Wang, H.Y., Wang, Y.S.: Gender differences in the perception and acceptance of online games. Br. J. Educ. Technol. **39**(5), 787–806 (2008)
5. Hamari, J., Shernoff, D.J., Rowe, E., Coller, B., Asbell-Clarke, J., Edwards, T.: Challenging games help students learn: an empirical study on engagement, flow and immersion in game-based learning. Comput. Human Behav. **54**, 170–179 (2016)
6. Wang, A.I.: The wear out effect of a game-based student response system. Comput. Educ. **82**, 217–227 (2015)
7. Granic, I., Lobel, A., Engels, R.C.: The benefits of playing video games. Am. Psychol. **69**, 66–78 (2014)
8. Marina, P.: Digital game-based learning in high school computer science education: impact on educational effectiveness and student motivation. Comput. Educ. **52**, 1–12 (2009)
9. Huizenga, J., Admiraal, W., Akkerman, S., Dam, G.: Mobile game-based learning in secondary education: engagement, motivation and learning in a mobile city game. J. Bus. Psychol. (2009)
10. Wouters, P., van Nimwegen, C., van Oostendorp, H., van Der Spek, E.D.: A meta-analysis of the cognitive and motivational effects of serious games. J. Educ. Psychol. **105**, 249 (2013)
11. Martí-Parreño, J., Galbis-Córdova, A., Miquel-Romero, M.J.: Students' attitude towards the use of educational video games to develop competencies. Comput. Human Behav. **81**, 366–377 (2018)
12. Bourgonjon, J., Valcke, M., Soetaert, R., Schellens, T.: Students' perceptions about the use of video games in the classroom. Comput. Educ. **54**, 1145–1156 (2010)
13. Ibrahim, R., Masrom, S., Yusoff, R.C.M., Zainuddin, N.M.M., Rizman, Z.I.: Student acceptance of educational games in higher education. J. Fundam. Appl. Sci. **9**(3S), 809–829 (2017)
14. Sioni, S.R., Burleson, M.H., Bekerian, D.A.: Internet gaming disorder: social phobia and identifying with your virtual self. Comput. Human Behav. **71**, 11–15 (2017)
15. Ferguson, C.J., Kilburn, J.: The public health risks of media violence: a meta-analytic review. J. Pediatr. **154**, 759–763 (2009)
16. Henriques, S, Sousa, C., Costa, C.: Drivers and motivations to game-based learning approaches – a perspective from parents and teachers. In: Proceedings of the 11th International Technology, Education and Development Conference, INTED2017, pp. 5722–5730. IATED (2017). https://doi.org/10.21125/inted.2017.1342
17. Perrotta, C., et al.: Final research report, Gaming Horizons Deliverable D1.8 (2018). https://www.gaminghorizons.eu/deliverables/. Accessed 10 Oct 2018

18. Persico, D., et al.: Systematic review and methodological framework, Gaming Horizons Deliverable D2.1 (2017). https://www.gaminghorizons.eu/wp-content/uploads/sites/18/2017/05/D2.1-State-of-the-Art-Literature-review.pdf. Accessed 10 Oct 2018
19. Persico, D., et al.: Report on interviews with experts and informants, Gaming Horizons Deliverable D2.3 (2017). https://www.gaminghorizons.eu/deliverables/. Accessed 10 Oct 2018
20. Haggis, M., et al.: A Manifesto for European Video Games. CNR Edizioni, Rome, Italy. https://doi.org/10.17471/54006

Balancing Realism and Engagement for a Serious Game in the Domain of Remote Sensing

Daniel Atorf$^{(\boxtimes)}$, Ehm Kannegieser, and Wolfgang Roller

Fraunhofer IOSB, Fraunhoferstr. 1, 76131 Karlsruhe, Germany
{daniel.atorf, ehm.kannegieser,
wolfgang.roller}@iosb.fraunhofer.de

Abstract. This paper elaborates on the development of a serious game in the domain of remote sensing. It describes the challenges of defining the target group and keeping them motivated over several weeks in order to achieve specific learning objectives. Furthermore, the paper states the integration of the game into the pedagogical concept. The paper illustrates in detail how the balance was found between realistic learning objectives and engaging gameplay following the ideas of Immersive Didactics and Digital Game-Based learning. It depicts on how to find close correlation between learning objectives and game objectives while keeping engagement and immersion. In addition, the paper outlines the support for educators and trainers via the implemented editors. Finally, the paper will report about the current evaluation of the game's learning outcome and user experience.

Keywords: Balancing realism · Game design · Pedagogical design · Training · Remote sensing · Digital game-based learning · Immersion

1 Introduction

One of the huge challenges in today's classrooms is to keep students motivated and engaged over a period of time long enough to get them to learn the desired objectives [1]. A training school of the German Armed Forces in Fürstenfeldbruck is faced with this challenge. Their students are now mostly so-called Millennials [2], which are considered as the first generation of digital natives [3]. This generation has grown up using technology and playing games. They expect the use of technology and games in their world of work and education [1].

The school offers various trainings in the remote sensing domain, mainly teaching image analysis and reporting included in the so-called Reconnaissance Cycle. Image analysis is about finding and identifying objects like buildings, vehicles, infrastructures, etc. in aerial or satellite imagery. The imagery is not limited to electro optical images, which are comparable to Google Earth images. Image analysts also have to deal with imaging sensors using the electromagnetic spectrum, like infrared or radar.

Reporting is about formally describing the identified objects in the imagery using specific terms and answering to specific tasks.

© Springer Nature Switzerland AG 2019
M. Gentile et al. (Eds.): GALA 2018, LNCS 11385, pp. 146–156, 2019.
https://doi.org/10.1007/978-3-030-11548-7_14

This training domain is rather complex to teach, therefore individual training courses last several months and the school has a high interest in keeping the students motivated over a long time. A large part of the courses is to repeat image analysis tasks over and over again while learning to deal with software tools, official forms and workflow restrictions. In addition, trainers cannot monitor every individual student for the whole time of the course. However, how can the school keep students motivated in repeating image analysis tasks over several weeks? Moreover, how can the training be motivating on one hand, but stay realistic with task, tools, workflows and forms on the other hand?

This paper addresses the challenge on how to develop a serious game for the training school, keeping their students motivated over the time of the courses. The paper presents how the balance was found between realistic learning objectives and engaging gameplay following the ideas of Immersive Didactics and Digital Game-Based learning.

2   Learning Objectives

In cooperation with the school, the first step was to define all key learning objectives, which should be addressed in the serious game. The objectives are described using Bloom's revised taxonomy of educational objectives [4] (see Table 1).

The main objective is in the knowledge-based cognitive domains of Analyzing and Evaluating. The verb "report" is not meant in the sense of the taxonomy, as this would hint to only the domain of Understanding. The verb is used because the students will actually have to fill out an empty form according to their analysis and evaluation of the image. This form is called a "report", thus the verb. In addition to the main objective, the training should involve a couple of minor learning objectives as well.

Table 1. Main and base learning objectives

Type	Cognitive domain	Description
Main objective	Evaluating, Analyzing	Analyze real electro optical images from either air-borne or space-borne platforms in order to select, judge, identify and eventually report objects according to the briefing task
Base objectives	Understanding	Describe the Reconnaissance Cycle
	Understanding	Explain the main advantages and disadvantages of the sensor platforms
	Understanding	Explain the main advantages and disadvantages of the sensor types
	Applying	Apply basic image analysis knowledge of electro optical images to infrared images

As those learning objectives are in rather high levels of the taxonomy, it is crucial how the serious game is embedded in the overall pedagogical concept and principles of the school. Figure 1 shows the principal structure of an average course day at the school.

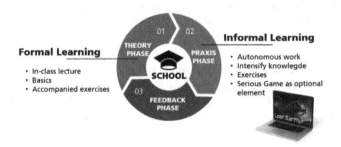

Fig. 1. Serious game course integration

The structure is separated in three phases. The first phase is formal learning, thus in a standard in-class lecture the trainer teaches theoretical basics. These basics are supplemented by accompanied exercises, meaning, that the trainer gives example images and explains the respective sample solution.

The second phase is informal learning, usually scheduled in the afternoon and evening. In this phase, the students learn autonomously without the trainer being around. Students are motivated by the trainer to do certain image analysis exercises on their own or together in groups in order to intensify their knowledge and train image analysis by seeing and interpreting lots of real life image examples. The serious game is located in this phase as it is meant to help achieve exactly that premise of seeing and interpreting lots of images. Using the game is optional in order to address the recommendations of Prensky [1], that all learning content should always be available for everyone. Therefore, the exercises in the serious game are also available as standard exercises, so no one is forced to play the game.

Phase 3 is the constructive feedback phase. In this phase, usually in the next morning, students discuss, evaluate and correct their outcomes and solutions with the trainer. This feedback is the base for the new formal learning phase.

3   Approach

3.1   Methods and Theory

The development of the serious game is based on the goal to enable and enhance intrinsic motivation for learning success [5]. The meta analysis of Schiefele et al. [6] shows that the intrinsic learning motivation correlates significantly positive with learning strategies and more importantly with learning results. In other words, if you succeed in activating and stimulating the intrinsic motivation of a student you'll get better and lasting learning results. Possible solutions on how to stimulate the intrinsic motivation are found in Marc Prensky's Digital Game-Based Learning [1] and Immersive Didactics mentioned by Matthias Bopp [7]. The basic idea of both is that people play games voluntarily and keep playing them because of their intrinsic motivation to do so, thus implementing learning goals in a game will lead to better and more long-term learning outcomes.

Bopp describes the so called Immersive Didactics. Immersive Didactics mean that the game design tries to immerse the player thoroughly into the game world and to keep him this way at all times. This especially applies to the parts of the game where the player has to learn something. The game design has to avoid the blatant exhibition of learning objectives in the game.

This idea is very similar to what Prensky calls stealth learning [1]: "The learning would happen almost without the learners' realizing it, in pursuit of beating the game. We would give them 'stealth learning'." As stated before digital natives expect to find a blend between traditional learning environments and learning through games, according to Prensky. The method to address this is Digital Game-Based Learning.

Prensky states that "good Digital Game-Based Learning does not favor either engagement or learning, but strives to keep them both at a high level". Putting too much emphasis on the learning part will lead to boredom. The player will stop playing the game and thus stop learning. On the other hand, putting too much emphasis on the engagement will make it a regular entertainment game and players will not achieve the learning objectives.

When developing a serious game following these concepts, there is a strong need to balance realism and engagement. The realism is found in the learning objectives, as these have to be accurately transferred from the real world into the game.

3.2 Procedure

The goal was to develop a serious game that fully immerse students into a fictional world and story. Therefore, it should "feel" like playing an entertainment game, but implicitly teach learning objectives.

In order to achieve this goal an iterative procedure was developed (see Fig. 2). The procedure merges processes recommended by Prensky [1] and common development milestone processes from the gaming industry [8].

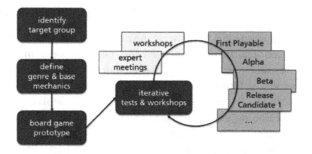

Fig. 2. Development procedure

The first step was to identify the target group. According to Prensky not everyone in the target group will be willing to play the game [1]. This might be due to a general aversion to gaming or due to disfavoring the genre. Therefore, it is not possible to get the entire target group into playing the game, but it is crucial to identify the target audience and to meet the majority of their preferences.

After the identification of the target group, the second step was to define the best suiting game genre and base game mechanics with regard to the elaborated preferences of the target group. These core mechanics were documented in a concept paper, which evolved to the game design document during the project [8]. This game design document contains the detailed documentation of the games genre, target audience, premise, backstory and game world, gameplay mechanics, character descriptions, mission and story progression, as well as the art and audio description. The main addition to the game industry's standard game design document was a detailed description of the mapping of learning objectives and game objectives. A base version of this mapping is found in the concept paper as well.

The next step was creating a board game prototype featuring the game genre and a basic mapping of the learning objectives to the base game mechanics. This prototype served as a rather quick tool to evaluate if the genre and base game mechanics were suitable for the majority of the target group and if the base mapping of learning objectives and game objectives work.

The next steps were derived from the board game step. These were iterative tests and workshops. On the one hand, there were several workshops with teachers and user group experts in order to define the specific images and image analysis tasks that should be implemented in the game. Expert meetings were held to evaluate the learning outcomes of the implemented tasks and to adjust the level of difficulty, the task description, feedback, etc. were necessary. On the other hand, there were common development milestone tests, like Alpha tests and Beta tests with their respective evaluation of game functionality and user experience (GUI, story, characters, and fun). Of course, expert meetings, workshops and milestone tests were combined.

In all these steps, the school was closely involved. A liaison teacher was defined as single point of contact for close communication and feedback.

4   The Game

4.1   Balancing Realism and Engagement While Keeping Immersion

A vital part of the development is to immerse the player into the game while finding the right balance between realism and engagement. On one side, there are learning objectives, which should be kept realistic. This includes dealing with realistic software tools and using the official forms and workflows when handling the task. On the other side, there is the need to present an engaging, immersive gameplay.

The first steps in finding the right balance were to identify the main target group and to find a suitable genre, as stated in the presented procedure before. The main genre employed in the game, is a combination of 4X strategy and adventure with a strong emphasis on the 4X part. 4X, introduced by Emrich [9], means explore, expand, exploit and exterminate and "[...] players must rise from humble beginnings, finding their way around the map [...]". This core feature is very similar to the task of an image interpreter: to explore and analyze unknown via aerial or satellite imagery.

The next step was to find a suitable setting. Ideally, the setting should feature realistic everyday work and experiences. Yet the impression had to be avoided, that the German Armed Forces develop a game simulating anything related to real world nations. Therefore, after some discussions and previous work with the school, which showed quite strong affinity to science fiction, a respective game premise was developed: Starting at his home planet, the player explores planets in the galaxy colonized by humankind. He takes on the role of an avatar, who is a member of a rebel organization trying to deliver all colonies from an evil, suppressive cult. On each colony, the player will face a more and more challenging mission.

Regarding realism, this sci-fi premise had a huge downside. The main learning objective was about analyzing real imagery, but the game should took place in a future setting. It would be fatal to let students analyze images with futuristic structures and units on alien worlds with regard to the learning objective. Thus a story was developed, which considered both sides. The cult was not only evil and suppressive; they also banned further technology advancement when they came into power. The takeover happened in the present when large parts of the galaxy where colonized using alien arks, "copying" nowadays structures from earth to colonies. In 2307, a rebellion arises against the cult and the story of the game "Lost Earth 2307" begins. This way the game could take place in the far future, letting the player experience an extensive story arc, while presenting image analysis tasks with original images from today. Furthermore, the liberation of colonies and having to perform image analysis tasks beforehand is still relatively close to the everyday work of an image analyst.

In order to keep the balance between realism and engagement, learning objectives and game objectives were correlated very closely. Therefore, the better the image interpretation results, the more successful the liberation mission. Two different kinds of liberation missions were developed in order to incorporate all learning objectives properly: reconnaissance missions and deployment missions.

The reconnaissance mission primarily maps the main learning goal. The player has to perform an image interpretation task according to the problem of a tasker, for example if a bridge is still passable. By doing so, the player passes through the original Reconnaissance Cycle, starting with the tasker as stage one. The next stage is tasking the appropriate sensor and platform. Initially only a selection of reconnaissance systems is provided by the game, showing an original tasking form used in everyday work. The player has to choose the appropriate realistic sensor, platform and flight parameters according to conditions at the target site to accomplish the current mission. This stage also features the minor learning objectives of the pros and cons of sensors and platforms.

Once the tasking and planning has been completed, the player has to analyze the recorded images. These images are from a pool of real images provided by the German Armed Forces. By using an adapted real image analysis tool (see Fig. 3, left), the player has to annotate and align images. Eventually he has to report the results back to the tasker using the original reporting form and using the original terms. A debriefing stage (see Fig. 3, right), provides detailed feedback on the quality and unlocks rewards

Fig. 3. Left: adapted image analysis tool integrated into the game; Right: feedback on report in reconnaissance mission

or penalties according to the results – for example providing additional resources that can be used to upgrade or develop new reconnaissance assets.

The deployment missions primarily map the minor learning objectives. They illustrate the advantages and disadvantages of sensors and platforms. The player has to build structures and especially sensor platforms. He will equip platforms with different sensor types and try to find the opponent using the sensors before the enemy finds the player. Realistic parameters, such as weather, daytime, material of objects, altitude as well as type and technology level of sensors and platforms influence the visibility of target objects. Hence, the player has to manage the influences on sensors and platforms skillfully in order to succeed in this kind of mission.

Fig. 4. Left: screenshot of bridge & tasker dialogue; Right: screenshot of ark

The mapping of learning objectives represented how the learning objectives could be integrated in realistic ways into the game, along with original adapted software tools, forms, workflows, images and tasks. In addition non-learning objective related game mechanics, like resource management, were integrated to facilitate even more engagement. This means that typical 4X mechanics, like technology advancement, colony management, etc., were implemented. Furthermore, a great emphasis was put on the narrative elements and story to engage and entertain the player. In this game world, the player is able to experience tales and avatar development, which would not be possible in real life, like for example fast promotions in rebellion forces. The storytelling uses cut scenes, dialogues (i.e. comic relief), interacting characters (i.e. antagonists, love interests, sidekick etc.), atmospheric graphics as well as high quality sound and music in order to support the immersion and engagement (see Fig. 4).

During the story campaign, the level of difficulty is increased continuously, to adapt the game to growing player skill (i.e. more complex weather conditions), thus triggering even more intrinsic motivation and eventually leading to total immersion as defined by Cairns [10].

Immersion refers to spatial immersion and emotional immersion. Spatial immersion (synonymous with Presence) is the psychological sense of perceiving a virtual reality as real while being physically located in another one [11], while emotional and engagement-based immersion deals with the intensity of user engagement with a task. Cairns defines engagement-based immersion as a three-level construct [10]. Cheng further improves Cairns' theory and adds dimensions to the three layers [12]. Table 2 illustrates how the game implemented the immersion aspects.

Table 2. Implementation of Cairns'/Cheng's immersion aspects in the serious game

Immersion level	Dimension and implementation
Engagement	**Attraction**: Target group identification yielded affinity to 4X computer games and science fiction scenarios
	Time investment: Informal learning phase during the seminar encourages participants to choose learning methods to their liking (i.e. autonomous work, exercises, serious games, etc.)
	Usability: The game provides a consistent operating concept (i.e. similar designed user interfaces, intuitive controls, story is told through a dialog system instead of block text, etc.)
Engrossment	**Emotional attachment:** Participants can identify with the game's main protagonist, which is in a similar situation (military, tries to specialize to gain accomplishments)
	Decreased spatial/temporal perception: The game confronts participants with motivating challenges, which are tailored to meet and exceed participants' skill level
Total immersion	**Loss of spatial awareness/presence**: Strong presence effects were not observed but could be accomplished by the latest VR implementation
	Empathy: Participants not only identify with the main character, but also are carried along by the story told and the fates of friends, love interests and antagonists

The overall goal of the balancing challenge was that learning objectives and game objectives are more or less the same. Thus, while the player tries to meet the game objectives he will automatically meet the learning objective.

4.2 Support for Educators and Trainers

The game features two modes, "campaign" and "free campaign". The campaign covers in chapters the respective remote sensing courses of the school and represents the default usage in the described course integration. The free campaign was implemented in order to enable and support trainers to create custom missions or even whole campaigns, with a different conceptual or content-related focus in mind.

The free campaign mode features three graphical editors: the first allows for creating new missions in a WYSIWYG environment where the base XML-structure of a mission can be created semi-automatically, displayed, modified and aerial images can be inserted. The second editor is used to create maps, which allows customizing the look and feel of the galaxy. The third editor allows to create and change the underlying mission structure and to place missions from the mission pool onto the newly created map, in certain places (colonies) and order (linear, parallel).

Third-party editors or even simple text editors may substitute these three editors, as XML was chosen to represent the game's data model in a human- and machine-readable format.

Additional support is provided by the player's manual, which details every aspect of the game in 64 pages, complemented by the 14-page teacher's manual with special emphasis on content structure and creation.

5 Evaluation

As described before, the game was constantly evaluated during the tests in the iterative phase of the project. The tests were always conducted by the school, led by at least one trainer and supported by additional image analysis experts. The test group size was between four and eight students new to the project. The participants' age ranged from 25 to 50 years. 20% of the students were female. All students had completed at least the first remote sensing training course when participating in the test. Overall, eight tests with students were executed in the iterative phase.

One main focus of the evaluation was on the learning outcomes of the implemented tasks. The trainer and the experts monitored the students play and rated the learning results. If applicable this monitoring led to adjustments of the difficulty level or the correction of errors, ambiguities in the task itself or the task description and task feedback. At the last test, the school confirmed, that all learning objectives can be achieved in the way intended.

Another focus of the evaluation was on game functionality and user experience. Besides bug reports, it was monitored how users accepted and experienced the narrative elements, GUI and game mechanics. The survey was done having the students take notes freely about the topics mentioned above. At the end of each day the students were interviewed in order to elaborate on their notes and to discuss their experience.

The results were used to continuously improve the game and raise acceptance. Especially the final test strongly indicated a high acceptance and fun while playing. While the male groups expressed their joy in the 4X strategy elements, the female groups expressed their joy in the narratives and how the story evolved. One of the groups made a strong comment at the end of the test: "I'd love to take the game home with me now and play the next chapters."

As stated before, these tests were executed with relatively small test groups, so the outcomes can be regarded as indicators. To further verify the indicators it is planned to do formal surveys once the game is fully deployed at the school.

6 Conclusion

The paper presented a process how to develop a serious game for a training school in the domain of remote sensing. It focused on how to balance necessary realism for learning objectives and engagement demanded by the concepts of Immersive Didactics and Digital Game-Based learning. A first evaluation proved that all learning objectives can be achieved and indicated, that the game was engaging.

Future work will focus on a formal evaluation of engagement with larger test groups, using for example NASA TLX, SUS and IPQ in order to further approve the balancing of realism and engagement.

A conclusion for developing a good serious game could be to take a strong and immersive story and add game mechanics suitable to the target group. Players will then try to meet the game objectives and will automatically meet the learning objective.

References

1. Prensky, M.: Digital Game-Based Learning. Paragon House, St. Paul (2007)
2. Strauss, W., Howe, N.: Millennials Rising: The Next Generation. Vintage Original, New York (2000)
3. Prensky, M.: Digital natives, digital immigrants part 1. On Horiz. **9**(5), 1–6 (2001)
4. Anderson, L.W., Krathwohl, D.R. (eds.): A Taxonomy for Learning, Teaching, and Assessing: A Revision of Bloom's Taxonomy of Educational Objectives. Longman, New York (2001)
5. Stipek, D.: Motivation to Learn: From Theory to Practice, 4th edn. Allyn & Bacon, Needham Heights (2002)
6. Schiefele, U., Schreyer, I.: Intrinsische Lernmotivation und Lernen. Ein Überblick zu Ergebnissen der Forschung. In: Zeitschrift für Pädagogische Psychologie, vol. 8, pp. 1–13 (1994)
7. Bopp, M.: Immersive Didaktik und Framingprozesse in Computerspielen. In: Neitzel, B., Nohr, R.F. (eds.) Das Spiel mit dem Medium. Partizipation-Immersion-Interaktion. Zur Teilhabe an den Medien von Kunst bis Computerspiel, pp. 170–186. Schüren, Marburg (2006)
8. Chandler, H.M., Chandler, R.: Fundamentals of Game Development. Jones & Bartlett Learning LLC, Sudbury (2011)
9. Emrich, A.: MicroProse's strategic space opera is rated XXXX. In: Computer Gaming World, Issue #110, pp. 92–93. Golden Empire Publications, Anaheim Hills (1993)

10. Cairns, P., Cox, A., Berthouze, N., Jennett, C., Dhoparee, S.: Quantifying the experience of immersion in games. In: Cognitive Science of Games and Gameplay Workshop at Cognitive Science (2006)
11. Zhang, C., Perkis, A., Arndt, S.: Spatial immersion versus emotional immersion, which is more immersive? In: 2017 Ninth International Conference on Quality (2017)
12. Cheng, M.-T., She, H.-C., Annetta, L.A.: Game immersion experience: its hierarchical structure and impact on game-based science learning. J. Comput. Assist. Learn. **31**(3), 232–253 (2015)

Extending a Digital Fraction Game Piece by Piece with Physical Manipulatives

Kristian Kiili[1]([⊠]) [iD], Antti Koskinen[1] [iD], Antero Lindstedt[1],
and Manuel Ninaus[2,3] [iD]

[1] Tampere University of Technology, Pori, Finland
{kristian.kiili,antti.koskinen,
antero.Lindstedt}@tut.fi
[2] Leibniz-Institut für Wissensmedien, Tuebingen, Germany
m.ninaus@iwm-tuebingen.de
[3] LEAD Graduate School, Eberhard-Karls University, Tuebingen, Germany

Abstract. This paper reports results from an ongoing project that aims to develop a digital game for introducing fractions to young children. In the current study, third-graders played the Number Trace Fractions prototype in which they estimated fraction locations and compared fraction magnitudes on a number line. The intervention consisted of five 30 min playing sessions. Conceptual fraction knowledge was assessed with a paper based pre- and posttest. Additionally, after the intervention students' fraction comparison strategies were explored with game-based comparison tasks including self-explanation prompts. The results support previous findings indicating that game-based interventions emphasizing fraction magnitudes improve students' performance in conceptual fraction tasks. Nevertheless, the results revealed that in spite of clear improvement many students tended to use false fraction magnitude comparison strategies after the intervention. It seems that the game mechanics and the feedback that the game provided did not support conceptual change processes of students with low prior knowledge well enough and common fraction misconceptions still existed. Based on these findings we further developed the game and extended it with physical manipulatives. The aim of this extension is to help students to overcome misconceptions about fraction magnitude by physically interacting with manipulatives.

Keywords: Game-based learning · Fraction · Number line ·
Conceptual change · Manipulatives · Serious games · Mathematics

1 Introduction

In recent years, mathematics has been the most researched discipline in the field of game-based learning in primary education [1]. Moreover, a recent meta-analysis [2] indicated that using game-based learning in mathematics is, in general, significantly more effective than other instructional methods. Game-based math trainings founded on number line based mechanics have been particularly successful in improving rational number magnitude understanding [e.g. 3–5].

© Springer Nature Switzerland AG 2019
M. Gentile et al. (Eds.): GALA 2018, LNCS 11385, pp. 157–166, 2019.
https://doi.org/10.1007/978-3-030-11548-7_15

While these studies paint an overall positive picture on game-based interventions to also foster fraction magnitude understanding, students generally struggle with fractions. Importantly, fraction magnitude understanding was found to be a relevant predictor for later knowledge of rational numbers, such as the density of rational numbers [6] and arithmetic operations with rational numbers [7]. Children's problems in understanding fraction magnitude [for a review, see 8] often originates from the tendency to treat denominators and numerators of a fraction as two separate whole numbers instead of considering their relation to each other [e.g., 9] - often referred to as whole number bias [10] or natural number bias [11]. Consequently, children often infer that the value or numerical magnitude, respectively, of a fraction increases when either the numerator or the denominator increases. For instance, 2/3 (0.667) is larger than 3/8 (0.375) although its numerator 2 is smaller than 3 and the denominator 3 is smaller than 8. According to conceptual change theories, these misconceptions originates from the fact that children form an initial conception of numbers as counting units before they encounter fractions, and later they draw incorrectly on this initial understanding to make sense of fractions and rational numbers [9, 12]. Therefore, conceptual change seems to be required in the acquisition of the concept of a fraction, because radical changes in the pre-existing concept of number magnitude is needed [12].

1.1 Conceptual Change

Conceptual change refers to situations in which a new information to be learned conflicts with learner's prior knowledge and thus changes in the prior knowledge are needed. Dole and Sinatra [13] have argued that radical changes in student's thinking are usually difficult to attain. The creation of cognitive conflicts has been a dominating instructional strategy in supporting conceptual change [14]. Cognitive conflict is a term used to describe a situation in which a new information makes a learner dissatisfied with his or her existing conception of a phenomenon. The perception of this contradiction between prior knowledge and new information may lead to radical changes in learner's thinking. In order to explain why cognitive conflict does not always support conceptual change, Merenluoto and Lehtinen [15] proposed a theoretical model of the dynamics of motivational, cognitive, and metacognitive processes in conceptual change. The model distinguishes three possible learning paths: the experience of conflict, the illusion of understanding, and having no relevant perception.

In the experience of conflict path, the conflict may lead to radical conceptual change. The experience of conflict reduces learner's certainty about the phenomenon and thus the learner is ready to change his or her knowledge beliefs. If learner's tolerance of ambiguity is high, the learner may feel that the conflict is solvable. However, if the tolerance of ambiguity is low, sensitivity to perceive novel features of the tasks may decrease or the situation leads to a loss of trust, resulting in avoidance behavior.

In the illusion of understanding path, the learner does not notice the conflict because of overconfidence. The learner recognizes some familiar elements in the new phenomenon, but his prior knowledge is not adequate for paying attention to the novel aspects. Familiar elements of the phenomenon arouse an illusion of understanding, which leads to an enrichment of existing naïve models or the construction of synthetic models.

In the no relevant perception path, the learner misses the conflict because of his or her broad cognitive distance to the phenomenon to be learned. Cognitive overload usually confuses the learner and may lead to avoidance behavior or routine activity that does not involve processing of the aspects of the new phenomenon. These learners can be supported by providing them with information that is needed to understand the phenomenon and consequently increase the probability to perceive a cognitive conflict. One aim of this paper is to consider how physical manipulatives could be integrated to a digital game to trigger reflective processes leading to conceptual change. Reflection refers to an activity in which a learner recaptures his/her experience, think about it, mull it over, and evaluate it. The outcome of reflection in game-based learning may be personal synthesis of knowledge, validation of a hypothesis laid during the formation of a playing strategy or a new strategy to be tested.

1.2   Present Study

The present pilot study builds on previous research that has proposed new game mechanics for learning fractions [16]. We report results from an ongoing project that aims to develop a digital game for introducing fractions to young children. We present the results of a pilot study in which we studied the effectiveness of the Number Trace: Fractions (NT Fractions) game among students who are new to fractions. Moreover, with self-explanation prompts we explored students' fraction comparison strategies to identify possible misconceptions. Based on the results we present an extension to the game in which physical manipulatives are integrated to the game. Physical manipulatives refer to concrete objects (e.g. base-ten blocks, colored counters, patterning materials, and different sized elements) that aim to help learners to better understand abstract mathematical concepts or properties by allowing them to manipulate the objects. The aim of the physical manipulatives is, in case of existing misconceptions of fraction magnitude, to create more explicit cognitive conflicts in students and help them to solve these conflicts by interacting with manipulatives.

2   The NT Fractions Prototype

The aim of the NT Fractions game is to introduce fractions to young children with limited previous knowledge of fractions. The core gameplay is based on number line estimation and magnitude comparison mechanics. In the game, players control a dog character and have to trace bones a cat has hidden in a forest (see Fig. 1). The locations of the bones are shown as symbolic or non-symbolic fractions (target number; left book in Fig. 1) reflecting locations on a number line ranging from zero to one. Players are supposed to direct the dog to the correct location on the number line and dig out the hidden bones by pressing the answer button (bone button in Fig. 1). The estimation accuracy determines whether players find a bone and get points or loses health. Accuracy is visualized also with the size of the found bone and the correct location of the bone is shown on the number line. The number line may also contain hidden obstacles that players have to avoid. The locations of the obstacles are indicated with symbolic or non-symbolic fractions (obstacle number; right book in Fig. 1). Some estimation tasks have monsters wandering around that players have to avoid or destroy. Most of the monsters have mathematical meaning. For example, monsters can move by jumping unit fractions and that way provide hints for the player. The aim of the monsters is to motivate players to observe the game world more mathematically.

The magnitude comparison task is implemented according to a recently proposed mechanic that integrates a comparison task into a number line estimation task to draw users attention to the spatial locations of fractions in a comparison task [17]. This combined task starts with a dialog in which a mole character asks players whether removing the obstacle is required. In case the obstacle is located between the dog and the bone – i.e. the obstacle number 1/6 is smaller than the target number 4/6 (see Fig. 1) - removing the obstacle is necessary. In contrast, removing obstacle is not necessary when obstacle is located beyond the bone. In practice, players have to compare explicitly the two values and answer either "Yes" or "No". Players get immediate feedback about correctness of their answer. Feedback to a correct answer: (a) If the obstacle is on dog's way to the bone, it is removed and the location of the removed obstacle is shown on the number line. (b) If the obstacle is not on dog's way to the bone, the location of the obstacle is shown on the number line. Feedback of an incorrect answer: Players lose health, the obstacle is removed, and the location of the inactive obstacle is shown on the number line. After the comparison dialog the task continues as a basic estimation task. However, players can utilize the location of an obstacle that is marked on the number line in estimating the location of the bone. Ninaus et al. [16] have argued that the strength of this novel number line based comparison task is the feedback, which is visually linked to the number line. In other words, the feedback allows players to see the relation of the compared magnitudes on the number line.

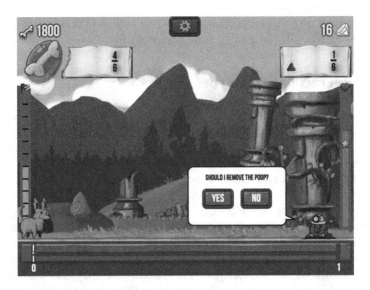

Fig. 1. An example of the task that consists estimation and comparison task mechanic; left book = Target number; right book = obstacle number.

When players progress in the game they earn special skills that are designed to support the development of conceptual fraction knowledge and to help them to perform well in the game. Players can activate these skills using in-game currency (diamonds). In each level, players can use only a limited number of diamonds. The skills influence either the mathematical or general gameplay challenges. Mathematical skills can be used to reveal the approximate location of the bone, divide the number line into convenient sections, transform a fraction number into a pie chart, reduce the fraction to lowest terms (e.g. 4/8 -> 1/2), see player's latest answer on the same task, and limit dog's movements only to unit fraction jumps (1/b of a fraction a/b). Gameplay skills make the tasks easier by removing obstacles, monsters or time pressure. Watch a video for more complete description of the features at https://youtu.be/xrL2kOR4-yU.

3   Method

3.1   Participants

Eleven Finnish third graders with no previous knowledge of fractions participated in the study (N = 11; 6 females; mean age = 9.18 years; SD = 0.40 years).

3.2   Measures

Pre- and Posttest
We created two versions of a paper-based conceptual fraction test. Only fractions between 0 and 1 were used. The tests included eight number line estimation items (e.g. Indicate the position of 1/5 on the number line below ranging from 0 to 1), six magnitude comparison items (e.g. "Circle the larger fraction. When the fractions are equal circle both.", e.g., 3/9 vs. 2/3), and three magnitude ordering items (e.g. "Put the numbers in order from smallest to largest": 1/2; 5/8; 2/6). Each item was scored as correct or incorrect. Estimations that were performed at least with 90% accuracy were considered as correct. The test versions were balanced according to difficulty (e.g. distance between compared magnitudes, whole number consistency).

Fraction Comparison with Self-explanations
The magnitude comparison task of the Semideus game [4] was extended with self-explanation prompts and used to explore students' fraction comparison strategies. In the comparison task, students had to arrange stones with fractions depicted on them in ascending order (left to right). In the case of equivalent fractions, students were instructed to pile up the stones. The items in the fraction comparison task were designed in a way that identification of students strategies that are incorrectly based on whole number properties is possible. Students played through one level that included four training items and eight test items with self-explanation prompts. After each comparison the game prompted a recording dialog and the students were asked to explain their solution. The spoken explanations were converted to text by Speech API of IOS and the texts were recorded to a server. In order to make the explanation

of comparisons easier, the colors of the fractions to be compared were different. With self-explanations we aimed to explore what kind of misconceptions students have about fraction magnitudes and what kind of strategies they use to compare magnitudes.

3.3 Procedure

First, two lessons about fractions were given to the students by their own teacher. Second, the students completed the paper based pretest. Third, students played the Number Trace game for five times 30 min during a two-week period. During the playing phase students did not get any other teaching about fractions. Fourth, students completed the posttest. Finally, students completed the Semideus based fraction comparison level along with the self-explanations.

4   Results of the Pilot Study

4.1   Learning Gains

During the intervention students played on average *(SD)* 276 (47) estimation tasks and 62 (16) comparison tasks. On average *(SD)* students used special skills 109 (19) times. From these skills 26% were math based skills and the rest were gameplay skills. The fact that gameplay skills were cheaper and more often available than math based skills might partly explain the difference. Figure 2 shows students' mean performance in the pre- and posttest according to task types. Students' performance seem to have improved from pre- to posttest in each task type. The overall mean *(SD)* accuracy also increased from 42.25% (20.81) to 64.17%. The student who used math based skills most, also improved most from pretest (24%) to posttest (82%). Due to the small sample we decided to not follow up our descriptive analysis with inferential statistical tests.

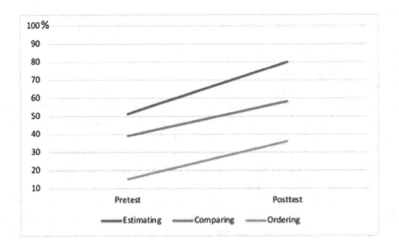

Fig. 2. Mean percentage scores in the pre- and posttest according to task types

4.2   Results from the Self-explanation Phase

Self-explanations

Students' explanations of their fraction comparison solutions showed that students relied on several faulty strategies or misconceptions, respectively. One of the most common comparison strategies was the missing pieces strategy, while 6 out of 11 students tended to use it. For example, one student explained that 1/9 is smaller than 1/6 based on the following reasoning. "There needs to be eight so that it makes a whole and the other needs only five to make a whole.". In this case, the missing pieces strategy worked, but in some cases it did not work. For example, one student failed to compare 3/9 and 1/3 while he or she reasoned that "It requires two to make three and other requires more." When solving the same tasks another student explained that "The red one is bigger [3/9] while it has bigger numbers than the blue one [1/3]". This strategy originates from clear whole number bias as the student do not understand fraction as a ratio between numerator and denominator, but considers numbers componentially as whole numbers. Popularity of the missing pieces strategy may have resulted from the fraction introduction that the students got in the beginning in which only part-whole interpretation was emphasized.

Two out of 11 students used a strategy that was based on pieces, but in an advanced way as they did not calculate the missing pieces, but based on pieces they compared fraction magnitudes to common fractions that they understood. For example, "If one is added to red [2/6] it makes only half, but if one is added to blue [5/6] it makes a whole." In fact, based on our observations, it seems that half was well understood among students and some students could utilize the half when making sense of compared magnitudes. For example, One student explained that "Two parts of three is much over half way and four parts of seven is maybe only little more than half."

We identified some occasions in which students noticed that they had used their strategy only superficially without thinking enough and when they explained their solution they realized that the strategy that they used did not eventually work. That is, self-explanation might have worked as a cognitive conflict and the explanation led students to think critically about their conceptions. However, self-explanation based conflicts did not lead to conceptual change in our study, because the game did not provide feedback that would have helped students to understand the fraction concept. For instance, one student who realized that the missing pieces strategy does not always work, did not experience this conflict as solvable, leading to confusion and consequently continued playing by guessing the right order.

5   Extending the NT Fractions Game with Manipulatives

The current results indicate that when young students reason about fraction magnitudes they may rely on faulty strategies as they do not understand the concept of fractions. For example, some of the students used component-based strategies and compared nominators and denominators separately. Moreover, the feedback of our game seems not be enough to cause cognitive conflicts and consequently facilitate conceptual change in students with very low prior knowledge in fractions. One problem of fraction comparison tasks is that some false comparison strategies such as missing pieces strategy may work with some comparison items leading to strengthening the naive conception of fractions and illusion of understanding. Consequently, for example an overconfident player who has an illusion of understanding the subject, may ignore the feedback (miss the conflict) that the game provides, because the same strategy has worked earlier in a different context and thus the player tends to rely on his/her prior experiences. Therefore, to support conceptual change we need to create stronger cognitive conflicts, provide enough information about fractions for students to facilitate perception of the conflicts, and motivate students to solve the conflicts. One way to reach this is to supplement gameplay with other instructional methods. In fact, a recent meta-analyses about game-based learning [2] supports this idea as the results indicated that, players learned more, relative to those taught with conventional instructional methods, when the game was supplemented with other instructional methods. Because a meta-analysis about math manipulatives indicated that manipulatives can be effective particularly in learning fractions [17], we extended the game with physical manipulatives. We modified the game in a way that fraction manipulatives can be used along the game to provide more direct and explicit support for fraction magnitude reasoning. In practice, color coding is used in the panels showing the locations of the bones and obstacles (Fig. 3) and through this color coding the game elements can be linked to fraction manipulatives that use the same color coding.

Fig. 3. Student comparing fractions with manipulatives along with the game providing more explicit and physically graspable support for fraction magnitude reasoning.

Each unit fraction (e.g. 1/2, 1/3,…) has its own color. In our example (Fig. 3), 1/4 is coded with blue color and consequently 2/4, 3/4 and 4/4 are blue as well. Figure 3 also shows how a student has used paper-based physical manipulatives to decide whether he should remove the obstacle (4/5) or not. Using the physical manipulatives the player can reason that 4/5 (four pink units) is larger than 3/4 (three blue units) and that it is not necessary to remove the obstacle with the mole. Let's assume that the player has earlier used the missing pieces strategy – the most common strategy in the current study. According to missing-pieces reasoning the player assumes that the fractions are equal and he or she should remove the obstacle. However, now when the player uses manipulatives along with the game, he or she notices that the fractions are not equal and it is not necessary to remove the obstacle. At the same time the manipulatives provide visual information that players can utilize to solve the conflict which might help players to understand why the missing pieces strategy cannot be used and how units can be used to reason about magnitudes. Therefore, future versions of the NT Fractions game can be accompanied with a set of physical manipulatives that may support players who need more concrete experiences to make sense of fraction magnitudes. The manipulatives are only addons and the use of manipulatives are not required to play the game. Furthermore, we will also implement virtual manipulatives into the game and study the usefulness and differences of these different manipulative approaches.

6 Conclusion and Future Work

The current study explored the usefulness of the NT Fractions game prototype for introducing fractions to students. In general, results of the pilot study are promising as students' performance in fraction tasks improved. It seems that our new task, combining mechanics of number line estimation and number magnitude comparison tasks, can be used in number line based games. However, we noticed that many students used false fraction magnitude comparison strategies after the intervention. It seems that the used game mechanics and the feedback that the game provided did not support conceptual change processes well enough and some misconceptions remained. Thus, based on the results we further developed the game and extended it with physical manipulatives. The aim of this extension is to trigger students to reflect on their conception of fraction and help them to overcome possible misconceptions of fraction magnitude.

The results also indicated that players utilized game character's special skills quite a lot, but, unfortunately, the use of the gameplay skills were more popular than math based skills designed to support the development of conceptual fraction knowledge. Thus, we will redesign the gameplay skills in a way that they are better integrated to the learning content. Furthermore, we are currently implementing adaptive features to the game. In fact, the game already detects students' misconceptions and the next version of the game will automatically activate math based skills that should support conceptual change processes.

Future studies need to study (i) learning effectiveness of the game with and without manipulatives, (ii) how students use in-game special skills and how the use of the skills influence learning outcomes, (iii) what game elements or interaction patterns lead to conceptual change and in what kind of context, and (iv) compare the effectiveness of in-game digital manipulatives and physical manipulatives used along a game.

References

1. Hainey, T., Connolly, T.M., Boyle, E.A., Wilson, A., Razak, A.: A systematic literature review of games-based learning empirical evidence in primary education. Comput. Educ. **102**, 202–223 (2016)
2. Wouters, P., Van Nimwegen, C., Van Oostendorp, H., Van Der Spek, E.D.: A meta-analysis of the cognitive and motivational effects of serious games. J. Educ. Psychol. **105**(2), 249–265 (2013)
3. Fazio, L.K., Kennedy, C.A., Siegler, R.S.: Improving children's knowledge of fraction magnitudes. PLoS ONE **11**(10), e0165243 (2016)
4. Kiili, K., Moeller, K., Ninaus, M.: Evaluating the effectiveness of a game-based rational number training-In-game metrics as learning indicators. Comput. Educ. **120**, 13–28 (2018)
5. Riconscente, M.M.: Results from a controlled study of the iPad fractions game Motion Math. Games Cult. **8**(4), 186–214 (2013)
6. McMullen, J., Laakkonen, E., Hannula-Sormunen, M., Lehtinen, E.: Modeling the developmental trajectories of rational number concept(s). Learn. Instr. **37**, 14–20 (2014)
7. Van Hoof, J., Vandewalle, J., Verschaffel, L., Van Dooren, W.: In search for the natural number bias in secondary school students' interpretation of the effect of arithmetical operations. Learn. Instr. **37**, 30–38 (2015)
8. Siegler, R.S., Fazio, L.K., Bailey, D.H., Zhou, X.: Fractions: the new frontier for theories of numerical development. Trends Cogn. Sci. **17**, 13–19 (2013)
9. DeWolf, M., Vosniadou, S.: The representation of fraction magnitudes and the whole number bias reconsidered. Learn. Instr. **37**, 39–49 (2015)
10. Ni, Y., Zhou, Y.-D.: Teaching and learning fraction and rational numbers: the origins and implications of whole number bias. Educ. Psychol. **40**(1), 27–52 (2005)
11. Alibali, M.W., Sidney, P.G.: Variability in the natural number bias: who, when, how, and why. Learn. Instr. **37**, 56–61 (2015)
12. Stafylidou, S., Vosniadou, S.: The development of students' understanding of the numerical value of fractions. Learn. Instr. **14**(5), 503–518 (2004)
13. Dole, J.A., Sinatra, G.M.: Reconceptalizing change in the cognitive construction of knowledge. Educ. Psychol. **33**(2–3), 109–128 (1998)
14. Limn, M.: On the cognitive conflict as an instructional strategy for conceptual change: a critical appraisal. Learn. Instr. **11**, 357–380 (2001)
15. Merenluoto, K., Lehtinen, E.: Number concept and conceptual change: towards a systematic model of the processes of change. Learn. Instr. **14**, 519–534 (2004)
16. Ninaus, M., Kiili, K., Siegler, R.S., Moeller, K.: Data-driven design decisions to improve game-based learning of fractions. In: Dias, J., Santos, P.A., Veltkamp, R.C. (eds.) GALA 2017. LNCS, vol. 10653, pp. 3–13. Springer, Cham (2017). https://doi.org/10.1007/978-3-319-71940-5_1
17. Carbonneau, K.J., Marley, S.C., Selig, J.P.: A meta-analysis of the efficacy of teaching mathematics with concrete manipulatives. J. Educ. Psychol. **105**(2), 380–400 (2013)

A Fun-Accuracy Trade-Off in Game-Based Learning

Simon Greipl[1][(⊠)], Manuel Ninaus[1,4] [iD], Darlene Bauer[2], Kristian Kiili[3], and Korbinian Moeller[1,2,4]

[1] Leibniz-Institut Für Wissensmedien, Tübingen, Germany
{s.greipl,m.ninaus,k.moeller}@iwm-tuebingen.de
[2] Department of Psychology, Eberhard-Karls University, Tuebingen, Germany
[3] TUT Game Lab, Tampere University of Technology, Pori, Finland
kristian.kiili@tut.fi
[4] LEAD Graduate School and Research Network, University of Tuebingen, Tübingen, Germany

Abstract. The present paper illustrates that the game-based implementation of a learning task - here to train basic math skills - entails benefits with strings attached. We developed a game for learning math with its core element based on the number line estimation task. In this task, participants have to indicate the position of a target number on a number-line, which is thought to train basic numerical skills. Participants completed both the game on a mobile device and a conventional paper-pencil version of the task. They indicated to have significantly more fun using the game-based environment. However, they also made considerably higher estimation errors in the game compared to the paper-pencil version. In this case, more fun in a math-learning task was ultimately bought at the expense of lower reliability, namely lowered accuracy of estimations in the learning game. This fun-accuracy trade-off between adding elements for enjoyment and clarity of content is discussed together with the consequences for game-design.

Keywords: Game-based learning · Reliability · Enjoyment · Number-line estimation · User-experience · Mathematics

1 Introduction

Game-based learning is thought to create, amongst other positive effects, increased motivation and special situational interest (e.g., for an overview see [1]) in the game and therefore in the topic to be learned. There is ample empirical evidence indicating that (math) games for learning had positive educational effects in terms of better learning outcomes or higher academic achievement [2–10]. While motivation and interest are part of the foundations of game-based learning [11] and contribute, amongst others, to the beneficial effect of the use of games for learning, we may sometimes turn a blind eye to the fact that these benefits may not come without any strings attached.

Trade-Offs in Game-Based Learning? The current scenario does not refer to pragmatic setbacks like the high costs of developing and implementing a game in

© Springer Nature Switzerland AG 2019
M. Gentile et al. (Eds.): GALA 2018, LNCS 11385, pp. 167–177, 2019.
https://doi.org/10.1007/978-3-030-11548-7_16

educational or similar non-profit settings. We rather want to delineate that the gamification or game-based setup of a task or educational content can be detrimental in various aspects regarding the very subject matter. For instance, the implementation of a storyboard to, for instance, create interest, identification or emotional value may be deployed at the expense of (learning-)time and energy as well as potentially distracting the player from the core topic.

An illustrative example showed that the implementation of games in education seemed to have elicited enjoyment during class as well as for the topic itself, but has not necessarily entailed a measurable cognitive advancement regarding the content to be conveyed [12]. Pittman used the commercial game *Portal 2*, which is basically a sequence of physics puzzles allowing to create individual experiments to teach physics in 11th grade high school. The author repeatedly proclaimed the bilateral enjoyment of the lessons, the engagement of students, and the opportunity of such methods to create "memorable, teachable experiences" [12]. Nevertheless, inexperience with gameplay, mainly regarding the required handling of the first-person navigation, were the biggest setback and major obstacle. This in turn led to "unimaginative experiments" and problems even in simple tasks. Finally, exam results at the end of the year did not reveal additional general improvement in learning outcomes traceable to the use of the game.

In another study, researchers tried to implement the content to be learned in a game by tightly coupling a math task with the core game mechanic, namely in-game combat. What is called *intrinsic integration* aims to minimize extrinsically engaging elements and rather making them an intrinsically motivating part of the game [13]. However, the authors also observed a decline in accuracy due to the implementation/operationalization of their task. Nevertheless, compared to an extrinsic counterpart of the game (non-mathematical combat and math-quiz between levels) and a control condition, students who played the intrinsic version achieved the best learning results.

It is imaginable that the use of a complex, enriched (digital) learning environment can also state a negative influence on the content to be learned. Other than through handling and interface related obstacles, this seems also feasible through the accumulation of game-elements unrelated to the content and thereby blurring the subject matter or diverting player's attention. In other words, the relationship between (game elements used for) motivation/engagement and reliability seems reciprocal and may even be negatively correlated. In this vein, we would have to look for a *sweet spot* between engagement and reliability.

Game-Based Math-Training. To shed some light on this relationship, the current study focused on the outcomes of a math game to objectively assess potential drawbacks of a game-based learning situation. Manipulating numbers in general is a necessity to deal with everyday life demands. For instance, the decision whether a purchase is still within budget or the percentage of savings of a discount requires addition/subtraction, multiplication and division and percentages as well as a general understanding of number magnitude. Difficulties in understanding and manipulating numbers have negative impacts on school career and can later lead to behavioural as well as societal problems like delinquency and in turn have "adverse consequences for cognitive function throughout life" [14]. In other words, numerical competences play a significant role in successful development.

For instance, Whyte and Bull [15] name nonverbal representation and manipulation of numbers as core competencies for developing adequate arithmetic abilities. Such basic numerical competencies in turn can be assessed by various tasks like enumeration, magnitude comparison, estimations, and the positioning of number magnitudes on a mental number-line [15]. The latter describes an often used metaphor to describe our mental representation of number magnitude according to which number magnitude is represented spatially along a number line in an analogue manner with magnitudes increasing from left to right (for an overview see [16]). It was observed repeatedly that arithmetic competencies can be predicted by more precise mental representations of number magnitude already in early childhood ages [17]. Therefore, fostering understanding of number magnitude is a crucial step in developing higher mathematical abilities.

In the current study, we examined the relationship between enjoyment and reliability of a well-known paper-pencil math task, the number-line estimation, and an in-house developed math game using the very same core task mechanic (see Fig. 1). In the following, we describe how the game was developed and which methods were employed to compare the two learning tasks to each other. Subsequently, the evaluation of subjective and objective measurements of task interaction is presented and lastly interpreted and discussed against the background of motivational, educational, and game design aspects.

2 Methods

We compared estimation accuracy as well as enjoyment between the game-based version and conventional number line estimation tasks on paper to investigate the relationship between enjoyment or fun, respectively, and answer accuracy.

2.1 Participants

18 adult student participants (10 females, mean age 22.72, $SD = 2.56$, range 19 to 30) were randomly recruited at the library of the University of Tübingen.

2.2 Design

Paper-pencil and game version of the number line estimation task were randomly assigned to participants, so that 10 participants started with the paper-pencil version, while the other 8 participants started with the game *Shoot The Number Line*. The main dependent variable for comparison was estimation accuracy in terms of absolute estimation error.

2.3 Measurement

We created a game for the use on tablets called "Shoot The Number Line" to examine the relationship between enjoyment and reliability within game-based learning (see Fig. 1). As the name suggests, the game uses the so-called number-line estimation task

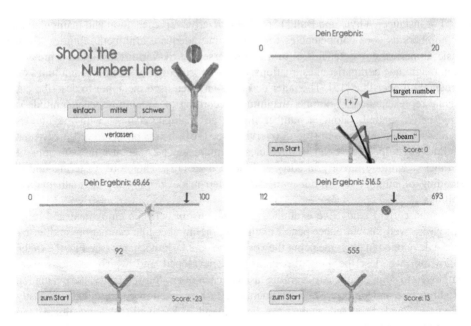

Fig. 1. Screenshots of "Shoot The Number Line" with target numbers displayed above the slingshot: top-left: startup screen with level choice; top-right: level "easy" with stretched slingshot, showing the "beam" as an indicator of shooting direction; bottom-left: level "medium" and negative feedback; bottom-right: level "hard" and successful estimation.

as the core game mechanic. In this task, participants must indicate the spatial position of a target number by slinging a ball as accurately as possible to the correct position along a number-line with only its endpoints specified (e.g., where goes 28 on a number line ranging from 0 to 100).

Accordingly, the current game focusses on the mental representation of magnitude on a number line. Usually, number line estimation tasks are implemented as paper-based tests. Accordingly, learners use a pen to mark the position of target numbers (e.g. with a cross or a simple stroke) on several number-lines printed on a multi-page document. Even though training number line estimation in such a way was found to be successful [18], the procedure itself seems rather tedious. Yet, the number-line estimation task is a suitable candidate for embedding into a game-based learning environment (see also e.g. [19, 20]) aiming at making the task more enjoyable and engaging. Likewise, through a comparison between in-game training and conventional paper-pencil methods, we can directly compare both methods in detail. *Shoot The Number Line* was developed in *Unity 3d*, which takes care of basic processes like model animation and physics interaction and is at the same time platform independent. The basic mechanics of the game comprise a slingshot with a ball that the player must shoot at the position of the respective target number – displayed right above the slingshot – on the number-line with highest possible accuracy. The moment the player touches the ball and stretches the slingshot, a beam is displayed to indicate the position where the ball will land on the number line. For a trial to be successful players need to hit the position of target numbers accurately. The maximum deviation from the target position/number allowed is held constant at 7%. Target numbers can vary from a simple number to a calculation problem. After a start-up menu, the player can choose between three difficulty levels *easy, medium,* and *hard.* On the easy level, the target number is a simple calculation within the 0 to 20 number range. On the medium level, participants had to estimate the position of a target number in the 0 to 100 range. Finally, the hard level employed the number range from 0 to 1000 and starting and endpoint of the range varied from trial to trial. In the current study, only the medium level was used. When the target was hit with sufficient accuracy, the player scored 20 points minus the ADT (absolute deviation from target). In case of a miss, the player's score is reduced by the ADT.

The paper-pencil version comprised a multiple-page document with number lines and target numbers between *0* and *100*. The game ran on a 10" Medion Touch-Netbook operated on Windows 8. Additionally, a questionnaire assessing user experience of the game was developed and had to be answered by participants (Example question: *How much fun did you have playing the game? – [1: not at all -> 5: very much];* see Appendix A).

2.4   Procedure

The experiment took about 10 min. After receiving oral and written instructions, participants were introduced with an exercise to either the digital game-based or paper-pencil version of the number line estimation task to get used to task requirements (onboarding phase). The game was played on medium difficulty level only with target numbers covering the whole range of the number line (0 to 100). Correspondingly, the same procedure was used in the paper-pencil version of the task. Each participant then had to indicate the position of 23 different target numbers in each version (in the order of presentation, paper-pencil targets: 56,16, 49, 3, 23, 95, 45, 31, 14, 73, 54, 91, 82, 76, 37, 51, 2, 98, 62, 69, 87, 28,8; game targets: 48, 39, 65, 81, 67, 52, 4, 12, 97, 1, 21, 43, 93, 26, 58,19, 89, 96, 35, 53, 74, 6, 78). After completion of both tests, the questionnaire had to be filled out. There was no time limit during the whole procedure. For the paper-pencil version, estimates on the number line were measured with a ruler and converted to the corresponding relative number to evaluate the estimation error. Afterwards, the single-factor-design allowed for *t*-tests to analyse all comparisons of interest.

3   Results

Estimation accuracy differed significantly between the game-based and the paper-pencil version of the number-line estimation tasks $[t(17) = 11.41, p < .001]$. The results showed, that participants estimated the target numbers more accurate and with less dispersion on the number line when they were performing the paper-pencil version [paper-pencil: $M = 2.16$, $SD = 0.05$; game: $M = 5.28$, $SD = 1.88$; see Fig. 2]. Conforming to this objective difference, participants also judged their own performance between the two trainings to differ significantly [$t(17) = 1.82$, $p = .043$]. In particular, they thought that their outcome was better in the paper-pencil version [$M = 3.67$, $SD = 0.97$] than in the game [$M = 3.11$, $SD = 1.08$] which was in consonance with the accuracy data. According to the questionnaire, participants seemed to have significantly more fun completing the game-based version [$M = 4.06$, $SD = 0.83$] than the paper-pencil version [$M = 2.28$, $SD = 0.83$; $t(17) = 8.59$, $p < .001$]. Moreover, design [$M = 3.83$, $SD = 0.62$] as well as clarity of the game [$M = 4.56$, $SD = 0.62$] were positively evaluated by participants. Overall, participants indicated a few problems operating the slingshot [$M = 3.12$, $SD = 1.04$]. This was substantiated by qualitative feedback. Some participants reported that they encountered problems handling shots close to the ends of the number line (see also Fig. 2). Feedback that the game provided was primarily perceived as helpful rather than disturbing [$M = 3.89$, $SD = 1.02$, see Fig. 3].

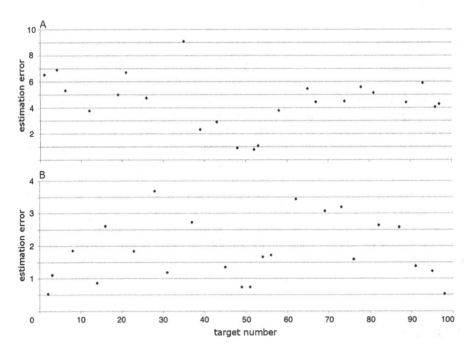

Fig. 2. Estimation errors in the game (top/A) and the paper-pencil test (bottom/B). These errors illustrate the average accuracy per target number across subjects. Higher values mean greater deviation from the target position on the number-line.

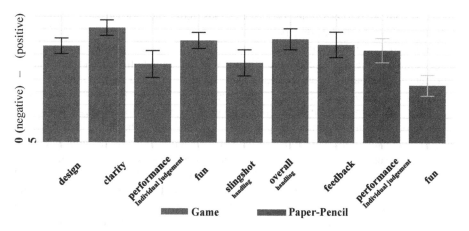

Fig. 3. Mean results of the questionnaire on various facets regarding user experience of the game-based as well as the paper-pencil learning task. Lower values (0) represent negative while higher values (5) represent positive experience. Error-bars at the top represent standard errors.

4   Discussion and Conclusion

The current study compared the performance of participants in two versions of the number line estimation task. Even though participants had more fun using the game-based version, accuracy was significantly higher in the paper-pencil based version of the task. In the following, we discuss these findings and the implications of enriching learning tasks with game elements.

Design of the game and its overall handling did receive very positive user-feedback. Yet, participants sometimes stated that there is still room left for improvement. For instance, they found targets on the very left or right side on the number-line explicitly hard to hit (see also Fig. 2A). This seems to be reflected in the only low positive evaluation of the slingshot-handling.

Obviously, there are some pitfalls that come along with an enriched digital learning environment. While there are a few issues – we already mentioned for instance problems with the slingshot handling – we want to focus on those that became apparent in the comparison between the game and paper-pencil training. Most strikingly, there was a difference in estimation errors participants made during the task. They obviously had more problems accurately hitting the target in the game-based than in the paper-pencil version, which seemed particularly apparent for target numbers close to start and endpoint of the number line (see Fig. 2). Because of very accurate performance in the paper-pencil-training, we must assume that participants have decent representations of number magnitudes. Therefore, we may infer that the significantly worse performance in terms of estimation accuracy in the game-based version originated from a property of the game itself. The shooting mechanism, in particular the rather short visualization of the beam in the game, is a very likely reason causing these performance deviations. Accordingly, the visual distance to target positions in the middle of the number line is smaller as compared to positions towards the ends, requiring more visual extrapolation of the trajectory of the slingshot ball.

Importantly, while this mechanic increases some levels of uncertainty and consequently difficulty it also decreases the reliability of the game with respect to estimation competence. Uncertainty is an important factor in engaging and motivating (e.g. [21]) players but may also improve learning outcomes due to its related release of dopamine (e.g., [22, 23]). Some degree of reliability however is needed to determine and foster players understanding of number magnitude. Importantly though, participants rated the game to be considerably more fun than the paper-pencil-task. Consequently, while the rather short visualization of the beam might have been a major contributor to participants' enjoyment, it might have also led to the worse performance in the game-based task as compared to the paper-pencil version. Similarly, Kiili and Ketamo [24] found that although participants performed significantly better in a paper-pencil based math test than in a game-based math test, the game-based test was more engaging.

Thus, the current results indicate that we may swapped a part of task accuracy and reliability, respectively, in favour of task enjoyment. It is additionally conceivable that an unknown amount of attention during the game is unwantedly shifted away from the core task – and presumably towards the shooting mechanism. Future studies may consider more exercises before the actual training to minimise the risk of handling-biases originating from participants' inexperience with a new interface. In line with this, Kiili and Ketamo [24] have proposed that an appropriate onboarding phase should be included in learning games to decrease mistakes caused by unfamiliar user interfaces, which should lead to smaller assessment errors in turn. In our case, some inaccuracies may have been caused by the inexperience with the new interface (i.e., slingshot mechanic), in particular targeting numbers on both ends of the number line (see Fig. 2A). We may at this point hint to a similar mobile math training game, *Semideus*, that needs an avatar to walk to the right place along the number line using tablet-based tilt-control [25]. The game therefore implemented the same core task – the number line estimation – but uses different control mechanics that enable high accuracy and thereby maintaining reliability of the task. Although the developers faced a similar effect as the tablet-based mechanics led to overall longer response times, hallmark effects of number magnitude processing were successfully replicated [25, 26]. Based on the study in which Semideus was used to train rational numbers, Lindstedt and Kiili [27] showed that user interface checkpoint tasks revealing participants' true controlling ability through trivial tasks can be used to increase the validity of math assessments by reducing effects of the user interface. The latter supports the validity of this instantiation of a game-based number line task as an assessment and learning tool [19].

In sum, these examples show that game-based task realisations can inherit a trade-off. In the present case this was reflected by heightened enjoyment at the expense of accuracy. Careful and sophisticated game-design can cushion or minimize such a fun-accuracy trade-off and simultaneously keep the clarity as regards content. Ultimately, the person in charge of training or assessment is obliged to evaluate in how far positive effects may outweigh negative ones, if existent, and which audience he/she intends to reach. Training and assessment comprise the main applications of game-based learning. and these two applications may come with different requirements. It would be rather inacceptable when reliability issues bias the outcome of a game-based (math) test, for instance, when introducing game elements for enjoyment may cause uncertainty with respect to performance, which may ultimately be reflected in an official examination (grade). In a training, however, such problems may be irrelevant when they evidently do not impede actual learning. For instance, even if such a fun-accuracy trade-off occurs in game-based learning, studies showed that the learning achievement was not necessarily lowered [12], or it was regardless the most successful learning strategy [13].

The latter even speaks in favour of the perspective that motivation – especially when intrinsically integrated – may potentially outweigh reliability issues. *Semideus* is again an example where the constraints caused by the game-based implementation of a task does not always lead to vital restrictions affecting the quality of the training nor the assessment power of the game [25]. Last, as mentioned before, for some audiences the motivational and engaging benefit originating from games designed for learning can provide the critical impulse that tips the scales in advance for a topic that is negatively connoted, tedious, boring, or otherwise difficult to approach (see e.g. [11]). To conclude, in some situations, depending on audience and/or game-design, trading reliability for fun can be a good deal.

The present work outlines that game-based learning environments can induce a setback that has to be evaluated carefully. In our case, however, there are some restrictions hindering a more detailed evaluation of this phenomenon. We already mentioned, for instance, handling issues, mainly regarding the slingshot and its beam. It is also likely that the onboarding phase was too short to make sure that participants were prepared enough to minimize interface induced biases. Because the paper-pencil method produced high accuracies despite a short introduction to the task, our findings suggest employing an appropriate adjustment of the onboarding phase when interacting with a new interface. Other criticism can be pointed out about the rather small sample size and the age of participants. In particular, we did not assess participants previous experience with tablet/touch-devices or even digital games, which might have affected our results.

Future studies will have to clarify the fun accuracy trade-off present in this and in other games and its theoretical and practical relevance. This entails the direct comparison of games for learning to conventional learning methods individually as well as in long term and for different skill/interest levels in the respective learning domain. Different skill and interests may have differential implications with respect to a continuum, in which seemingly a part of precision/reliability is given up for motivation or engagement. For instance, an engaging but less accurate learning game may act as a door opener for a child who struggles in the respective domain, but a child with high intrinsic motivation may not benefit from – or even be demotivated by – such a learning environment.

Appendix

See Table A.

Table A. Items to examine user experience

Item		1	2	3	4	5	
How appealing was the design of the app?	not at all	O	O	O	O	O	very much
Was the app clearly arranged?	not at all	O	O	O	O	O	very much
How good do you think your performance was in the game?	not at all	O	O	O	O	O	very much
How much fun did you have playing the game?	none	O	O	O	O	O	very much
How well did you manage to handle the slingshot?	not at all	O	O	O	O	O	very much
How well did you in general manage to handle the app?	not at all	O	O	O	O	O	very much
Was the feedback (explosions, arrows etc.) helpful?	not at all	O	O	O	O	O	very much
How good do you think was your performance in the paper-pencil test?	not at all	O	O	O	O	O	very much
How much fun did you have doing the paper-pencil test?	none	O	O	O	O	O	very much
Do you have other remarks?							

References

1. Plass, J.L., Kaplan, U.: Emotional design in digital media for learning. In: Emotions, Technology, Design, and Learning, pp. 131–161. Elsevier (2016)
2. Boyle, E.A., et al.: An update to the systematic literature review of empirical evidence of the impacts and outcomes of computer games and serious games. Comput. Educ. **94**, 178–192 (2016)
3. Hainey, T., Connolly, T.M., Boyle, E.A., Wilson, A., Razak, A.: A systematic literature review of games-based learning empirical evidence in primary education. Comput. Educ. **102**, 202–223 (2016)
4. Gee, J.P.: What Video Games Have to Teach Us About Learning and Literacy. Palgrave Macmillan, New York (2003)
5. Prensky, M.: Digital Game-Based Learning. Paragon House, St. Paul (2007)
6. Wouters, P., van Nimwegen, C., van Oostendorp, H., van der Spek, E.D.: A meta-analysis of the cognitive and motivational effects of serious games. J. Educ. Psychol. **105**, 249–265 (2013)
7. Li, M.-C., Tsai, C.-C.: Game-based learning in science education: a review of relevant research. J. Sci. Educ. Technol. **22**, 877–898 (2013)
8. Wouters, P., van Oostendorp, H., ter Vrugte, J., Vandercruysse, S., de Jong, T., Elen, J.: The effect of surprising events in a serious game on learning mathematics. Br. J. Educ. Technol. **48**, 860–877 (2017)
9. Vandercruysse, S., et al.: The effectiveness of a math game: The impact of integrating conceptual clarification as support. Comput. Hum. Behav. **64**, 21–33 (2016)

10. Seaborn, K., Fels, D.I.: Gamification in theory and action: a survey. Int. J. Hum.-Comput. Stud. **74**, 14–31 (2015)
11. Plass, J.L., Homer, B.D., Kinzer, C.K.: Foundations of game-based learning. Educ. Psychol. **50**, 258–283 (2015)
12. Pittman, C.: Teaching with portals: the intersection of video games and physics education. Learn. Landscapes **6**, 341–360 (2013)
13. Habgood, M.P.J., Ainsworth, S.E.: Motivating children to learn effectively: exploring the value of intrinsic integration in educational games. J. Learn. Sci. **20**, 169–206 (2011)
14. Beddington, J., Cooper, C.L.: The mental wealth of nations. Nature **455**, 3 (2008)
15. Whyte, J.C., Bull, R.: Number games, magnitude representation, and basic number skills in preschoolers. Dev. Psychol. **44**, 588 (2008)
16. de Hevia, M.D., Girelli, L., Macchi Cassia, V.: Minds without language represent number through space: origins of the mental number line. Front. Psychol. **3**, 466 (2012)
17. Opfer, J., Siegler, R.: Representational change and children's numerical estimation. Cogn. Psychol. **55**, 169–195 (2007)
18. Geary, D.C., Hoard, M.K., Nugent, L., Byrd-Craven, J.: Development of number line representations in children with mathematical learning disability. Dev. Neuropsychol. **33**, 277–299 (2008)
19. Kiili, K., Moeller, K., Ninaus, M.: Evaluating the effectiveness of a game-based rational number training - in-game metrics as learning indicators. Comput. Educ. **120**, 13–28 (2018)
20. Kucian, K., et al.: Mental number line training in children with developmental dyscalculia. Neuroimage **57**, 782–795 (2011)
21. Howard-Jones, P.A., Demetriou, S.: Uncertainty and engagement with learning games. Instr. Sci. **37**, 519–536 (2009)
22. Fiorillo, C.D.: Discrete coding of reward probability and uncertainty by dopamine neurons. Science **299**, 1898–1902 (2003)
23. Lisman, J.E., Grace, A.A.: The hippocampal-VTA loop: controlling the entry of information into long-term memory. Neuron **46**, 703–713 (2005)
24. Kiili, K., Ketamo, H.: Evaluating cognitive and affective outcomes of a digital game-based math test. IEEE Trans. Learn. Technol. 1 (2017)
25. Ninaus, M., Kiili, K., McMullen, J., Moeller, K.: Assessing fraction knowledge by a digital game. Comput. Hum. Behav. **70**, 197–206 (2017)
26. Schneider, M., Siegler, R.S.: Representations of the magnitudes of fractions. J. Exp. Psychol. Hum. Percept. Perform. **36**, 1227–1238 (2010)
27. Lindstedt, A., Kiili, K.: Evaluating playing experience and adoption of a math learning game. In: Proceedings of the 1st International GamiFIN Conference, pp. 39–46 (2017)

Integrating Self-Determination and Self-Efficacy in Game Design

Hossein Jamshidifarsani[1]([⊠]) (iD), Paul Tamayo-Serrano[1] (iD),
Samir Garbaya[2] (iD), Theodore Lim[3] (iD), and Pierre Blazevic[1] (iD)

[1] END-ICAP Laboratory - INSERM, University of Versailles
Saint-Quentin-en-Yvelines - Paris-Saclay, Versailles, France
{hossein.jamshidifarsani,paul.tamayo-serrano,
pierre.blazevic}@uvsq.fr
[2] END-ICAP Laboratory - INSERM, ENSAM, Arts et Métiers ParisTech,
Paris, France
samir.garbaya@ensam.eu
[3] Heriot-Watt University, Edinburgh, UK
t.lim@hw.ac.uk

Abstract. Video games have been known to increase the levels of player's motivation. This initiated the emergence of serious games and gamification to exploit game elements and mechanics for increasing the motivation in non-game contexts. The research reported in this paper used psychological theories of Self-Determination Theory (SDT) and Self-Efficacy Theory (SET) to design three versions of a game. The first version was based on SDT, the second on SET and the third version was based on a combination of these two theories. The objective is to investigate the impact of each game design on the user motivation and performance. An experiment of playing the games designed with these features was conducted. Surprisingly, the results on the objective evaluation revealed that there is no significant difference among the groups in terms of engagement and performance. Furthermore, these findings were confirmed by the results on the subjective evaluation of player's perceived motivation, which showed no significant difference between the three experimental conditions.

Keywords: Self-determination · Self-efficacy · Game design · Motivation · Engagement

1 Introduction

Motivation is the driving force of all of our actions. Deficiencies to motivation can lead to undesirable consequences. In extreme cases, it can cause severe problems such as hypophagia and starving to death [1]. Finding novel and effective ways to influence and increase the motivation can help humans to overcome countless problems. Hence, there have been plenty of efforts to improve our recognition of its nature and underlying mechanisms. Psychological theories such as Self-Determination Theory (SDT) attempted at explaining the building blocks of motivation and what drives us to action [2]. SDT argues that the need for three factors of relatedness, competence and

© Springer Nature Switzerland AG 2019
M. Gentile et al. (Eds.): GALA 2018, LNCS 11385, pp. 178–190, 2019.
https://doi.org/10.1007/978-3-030-11548-7_17

autonomy generates the intrinsic motivation that can push us to accomplish our goals [3]. However, SDT is a macro theory of human motivation and its three outlined components are really broad [4]. Thus, some researchers have decided to investigate the effect of integrating SDT with other psychological theories such as Self-Efficacy Theory (SET) to create a more concrete and practical theory, as well as increasing its effectiveness [5, 6].

Video games have been known for a long time to produce a surge in motivation and engagement levels [7, 8]. The motivational boost produced by video games motivated scientists and researchers to exploit game elements and mechanics for non-game purposes. This led to the emergence of fields such as gamification and serious games [9–11]. However, there exist plenty of game elements and mechanics, and it is important to recognize which game design produces the most motivation. One solution can be to test the engagement and motivation of the users with multiple game designs each based on different motivational theories.

The objective of this study is to investigate the integration of self-determination and self-efficacy theories in game design and compare the integrated design with the designs based on self-determination and self-efficacy individually. For this objective, three variations of a simple video game were developed, and each of the variations was based on one of the mentioned theories (SDT, SET and SDT+SET). Forty-six participants were involved in the experiment and they formed the three experimental groups. The data related to their performance and engagement were automatically recorded. The outcome results were analyzed to test the hypothesis of this study, which supposes that integrating self-determination, and self-efficacy theories in game design would lead to enhanced levels of motivation and performance.

The paper is organized as the following: Sect. 2 introduces SDT and SET and the related studies reported in the scientific literature. Section 3 presents the developed game and three variations of the game design based on each of the theories and the combined version integrating SDT and SET. Section 4 presents the methodology of the experiment design. In Sect. 5, the results from the analysis of the effect of each game design on the levels of engagement and performance are presented with the discussion. Finally, Sect. 6 presents the outcome of this study, its limitations and the conclusion with the future research.

2   Related Works

2.1   SDT, SET and SDT+SET

Self-Determination Theory (SDT), is a macro-theory framework for studying human motivation, it was first proposed by Deci and Ryan [2, 12, 13]. SDT defines psychological needs that need to be satisfied to foster motivation. The three psychological needs are Autonomy, Competence and Relatedness. Autonomy concerns with the sense of free will and being the agent of our own decisions. Competence is the need of being effective and competent in a task. Relatedness is the need of interacting with people, feeling attached or belonging to some groups.

Bandura [5] has defined self-efficacy as "the conviction that one can successfully execute the behavior required to produce the outcomes". Therefore, in this theory, the self-perceived judgment of one's capabilities is more relevant than the actual capability of the individual [14]. Bandura suggested four different sources for self-efficacy, which are Performance Accomplishments, Vicarious Experience, Verbal Persuasion and Emotional Arousal. Performance accomplishment is more related to the past successes and failures on a certain task and the perceived capability of accomplishing it. Vicarious experience happens when people see other people similar to them performing that specific task without too much hardship, this adds to the self-perceived capabilities. In addition, verbal persuasion from others can add to this perceived self-efficacy, although, the effect might be limited. Finally, emotional arousal relates to the emotional and physiological state of the person in face of a task, and people rely on their emotional arousal state to judge their self-efficacy.

Techatassanasoontorn and Tanvisuth [15], integrated SDT and SET to examine the influence of self-determined motivation on Information and communications technology (ICT) training outcomes and acceptance with emphasis for internet skill of a Thai community. They found that the individual with a higher self-determined motivation to participate in ICT trainings, are more predisposed to develop their Internet self-efficacy, training satisfaction and usage intention.

Sweet et al. [6], integrated and tested SDT and SET in the context of physical activity. In their work, they proposed an integration based on SDT's three psychological needs, where they replace Competence with SET and rename it as Confidence. They found that the integrated model was favorable over the individual theory models, but they warn that such conclusions warrant caution.

Sweet et al. [16], integrated SDT and SET and made a longitudinal test on post-cardiac patients for physical activity. They denote the need for physical activity for post-cardiac patients whom they present low adhesion to this activity. Hence, they proposed to fuse the two motivational theories for motivating patients to perform the necessary activities. In their experiment, they used questionnaires to assess both SDT and SET, and then they analyzed the results. Although their motivational construct was not able to predict physical activity change in a period of four months, the results suggested that it is possible to combine both theories.

2.2 SDT and SET-Based Game Mechanics in Serious Games

Peng et al. [17] presented one of the few works that actually implemented SDT through game features. In their work, they implemented autonomy and competence but not relatedness, hence implementing only two out of the three core constructs of SDT. Three features were identified and manipulated to relate them to the concept of autonomy: character customization, virtual currency to buy power-ups and freedom of dialogue interaction with non-player characters. To support competence, another three features were implemented: dynamic difficulty adaptation, progress bar and achievement in the form of badges. Although they were unable to measure the impact of each feature individually, they found evidence that both groups of autonomy-supportive and competence-supportive features led to greater game enjoyment, greater motivation for future gameplay, higher likelihood of recommending the game and greater game rating.

Francisco-Aparicio et al. [18], implemented SDT through gamification to satisfy users' three psychological needs. For Autonomy, they used profiles, task selection, configurable interface, privacy control and notification control. For competence: karma system, positive feedback, badges, real-time information, challenges and leaderboards. For Relatedness; working groups, messages, blogs and connection with social networks.

Although it was not implemented nor tested in a real system, Prouxl et al. [19] proposed to map SDT to a theoretical framework for designing serious games aimed at learning. The selected theoretical framework was the Learning Mechanics and Game Mechanics (LM-GM) [20, 21]. This work relates learning mechanics to game mechanics and classifies them according to different extrinsic and intrinsic motivation levels.

In their work, Richter et al. [22], analyzed several motivational theories and mapped them to game mechanics. Some of these theories include SDT, hierarchy of needs, SET, need achievement theory, goal setting theory, social comparison theory, Personal investment theory, expectancy value theory and skinner's principle of partial reinforcement. For SET, they proposed the following mechanics: audio/verbal/visual/music/sounds effect, progress bar, points/bonus/dividend, mini games/challenges/quests, badges, virtual goods, leaderboard, rewards-choosing colors, power, achievements and levels. However, this work lacks an experimental design to test the proposed approach.

3 Hypothesis

In the context of the research and based on the previous psychological findings, it is hypothesized that combining self-determination and self-efficacy will lead to enhanced motivation and better performance. In order to confirm this assumption, the following research question is stated: Does the integration of self-determination and self-efficacy enhance motivation and performance?

4 Developed Approach

In order to study the effect of SDT and SET on the player's in-game performance, a video-game system was developed. To keep the rules and interaction as simple as possible for the player, a platformer infinite-running type of game was developed. In this kind of game, the objective of the player is to accumulate maximum points possible by lasting as much time as possible while avoiding the obstacles. The interaction of the player is limited to pressing one button to command the in-game character to jump to avoid both the obstacles and falling.

To speed up the development, the video-game was adapted from the one presented in the tutorial "Let's Make a Game: Infinite Runner" presented at Unity Tutorials [23]. In this game, as shown in Fig. 1, a series of platforms were randomly generated in front of the player. The platforms were aligned to create three height levels, the player can jump between platforms while picking up coins and avoiding bombs. The score of the player is increased based on how much time he keeps his character alive and the number of coins he collects. The game session lasts until a bomb is touched, or the character falls to a pit. The player controls the jump of the character and he can even perform a mid-air jump, but he cannot control the force nor modify the starting trajectory of the character. Three different levels of difficulty were presented to the player to select: easy, normal and hard. The difference between the three levels of difficulties is an increase in the speed of the game and hence faster player reactions are required at harder levels.

Fig. 1. (**A**) User playing the game. (**B**) Screenshot of the game containing the player's character, the three height level platforms, bonus coins and hazardous bombs

Changes to the game mechanics were made in order to implement the different features that could foster either SDT or SET. These modifications resulted in three different game modes, one mode related to each of the theories of SDT and SET and a mode for the integration of SDT and SET. This represents the three experimental conditions of this study. The implementation and the difference between the developed game mechanics are shown in Fig. 2, they are explained as follows:

- Profiles, score and levels: These three mechanics were implemented in the same way for the three game modes. To create a profile, the user has to provide his nickname, age, sex, dominant hand, whether he wears glasses and his prior experience with infinite runner type of videogames. The objective of entering the player profile is to identify and save the data of the user for further analysis. In addition, the profiles helped to implement the leaderboards mechanic. Points are constantly shown to the player as his total score while playing the game and at the end of the session. The scores increase with the time that the character is alive and by obtaining coins. Finally, three levels were implemented, easy, normal and hard. The difference between these levels is that the speed of the game is increased and hazards are spawned more often.
- Character selection and environment configuration: To fulfill the player's need for Autonomy, character selection and environment configuration mechanics were provided. At the start of the experiment and later at the in-game personalization option, the player is asked to select one of seven different characters, one of four possible backgrounds and one of two different songs. These options are presented in

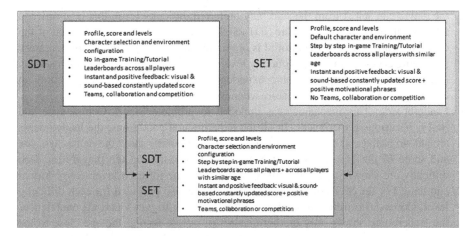

Fig. 2. Game mechanics implemented for SDT, SET and the integration of SDT+SET

the game session and can be changed at any time when desired by the player. In terms of gameplay, all the options are merely aesthetic, as they do not confer any advantage or disadvantage in the game session. These two mechanics exist in the SDT and SDT+SET game modes, but not in the SET mode where the player has to keep the default options.

- Training/Tutorials: Tutorials, particularly interactive tutorials are a very appropriate way to achieve SET's Mastery Experiences. In the SET game mode, the player is unable to play the game session in any difficulty level until he first completes the tutorial. The tutorial is divided in five successive stages; each stage aims at teaching the player a single gameplay rule of the game. Unlike the game sessions, the tutorial stages have a starting point and a goal, reaching the goal will open the access to the next tutorial. For completing the tutorial stages, the user has to understand a gameplay rule and apply it to proceed. The first tutorial stage is aimed to teach the player how to jump; simple obstacles and pits are present. To complete the stage the player has to avoid them. The second tutorial stage aims at teaching the mid-air jump, which is very similar to the first stage; but the obstacles and pits are larger, hence requiring the use of mid-air jumps to proceed. The third stage is for understanding the bonus represented by coins. By obtaining coins, the user will understand how they increase his score and why it is important to take as many as possible in order to reach higher scores. The fourth stage is about hazards, namely the bombs. If the player touches a bomb, he loses and he has to restart the tutorial. To reach the goal, the user has to avoid all the hazards. The fifth and final tutorial stage is a combination of the first four stages. By combining all the learnt lessons in a single mission, the player is requested to correctly make use of all the knowledge presented in the tutorials to reach the goal. After completing the final tutorial stage, the player is able to play the game session in easy difficulty, once he played at least one easy session, he can select normal difficulty and then, the same process is devised for hard difficulty mode. In the SDT mode, the tutorial is not present and the player can select from the start, any preferred difficulty level, this is in order to avoid limiting his autonomy. The SDT+SET mode presents the combination of the other two game modes. The tutorial is provided, but its completion is not necessary for having access to the three difficulty levels of game sessions. Hence, the user can benefit from mastering the game experience, without limiting his autonomy in choosing to play the game sessions whenever he wants.

- Leaderboards: This mechanic was included to promote SDT's Competence and SET's Vicarious Experiences. In all the experimental conditions, the leaderboards are shown at the end of each game session. Leaderboards show the name, age, sex and score of the top players. For SDT game mode, the top ten players for each difficulty are shown, there are three leaderboards, one for each level: easy, normal and hard. For the SET condition, leaderboards are also provided for each difficulty level. However to differ from SDT condition and to trigger vicarious experiences the leaderboard shows only the high scores of people having the age close to the player's age. Vicarious experience can be triggered in people when they are informed about the people that they consider similar to them and they completed the task at hand successfully. Since the developed system does not include multiplayer capabilities, it was assumed that leaderboards defined by the age could implement this experience. The reason behind choosing this mechanic in the infinite runner game, which is mainly based on quick reaction time, is by considering that older people generally have a slower reaction time than younger players. Hence, it was decided that comparing older and younger players will not produce the feeling of having similar people achieving a task, but comparing similar-aged people could produce the feeling of vicarious experience. For creating the sense of similarity between players, a range of three years for each player was considered to identify similar-aged players. The player under this experimental condition will only see the scores of people of their age group, which is denoted inside the game as "highscores in your range of age". The SDT+SET condition shows both of the two types of leaderboards described previously.
- Instant and positive feedback: This mechanic was used to strengthen the SDT's Competence and SET's Social Verbal Persuasion. In all three game modes, instant and positive feedback is shown under two conditions: first by increasing the player's score based on how much time he/she stays active. The player can see his/her score increasing in the upper left part of the screen; the second condition is when the player picks up a coin, in this case, a number (+200) is shown in the position were the coins are displayed. A positive sound is played and the score is increased likewise. As previously stated, the developed game does not include multiplayer mode, hence, social interaction is limited. In order to implement social verbal persuasion, voices of natural spoken speech were recorded, saying positive motivational phrases such as "well done" and "perfect". These voices are randomly played when the player obtains between three and five coins.
- Teams, collaboration and competition: These mechanics were selected to fulfil the player's psychological need for Relatedness in the SDT and SDT+SET game modes. At the start of the experiment, to foster the sense of belonging, the player has to choose to be part of the yellow or the red team; this decision cannot be changed later. Belonging to a team allows collaboration with teammates and

competing against other teams. For collaboration, when the player completes a game session, his score in the specified difficulty level is added to his team's total score. Hence, there are three scores for each team; they are based on each difficulty level. The team score is shown at the end of the game session. In order to create the sense of competition, the score of the adversary team is also shown. In addition to being a member of a team, the player feels motivated to collaborate for increasing his/her teams' score in order to beat the adversary team, thus promoting competition.

It is important to note, for implementing the leaderboards and team mechanics, fictive data was included in the game. The objective is to provide a starting point for the participants to have a "fake player" to beat individually and as a team. To avoid bias in the experimentation by players trying harder to beat the latest highscore, the leaderboard data was kept the same for all players. The fictive data is excluded from the data analysis of the experimental study.

In addition to the data captured during the user's profile creation, in each of the selected game sessions, the game automatically captures the score and the time spent in the session.

5   Methods

5.1   Participants

Forty-six volunteers participated in this experiment and assigned randomly, 16 to SDT condition, 15 to SET, and 15 to SDT+SET. The subjects are researchers, personnel and students from the university community. The sample was comprised mainly of females (59%). Ages ranged between 17 and 70 years (Mean = 30.93, SD = 13.78). Forty-five subjects are right handed (98%). 28 participants wear glasses (61%). All the participants were asked to rate their prior experience with infinite runner type of video games in a scale ranging from 0 to 10 (where 0 represents no experience and 10 represents a very experienced user). The reported prior experience has a Mean = 3.22 and SD = 2.83.

5.2   Procedure

Three experimental conditions were tested: SDT, SET, SDT+SET. An infinite-runner game was created based on a tutorial and different game mechanics were devised for each experimental condition.

The experiment was conducted individually in equal set-up conditions across the three experimental conditions. All participants where positioned in front of the same laptop where the game was running. The laptop was a Lenovo B50-80, with a processor of Intel Core i5 2.20 GHz, 8 GB RAM, Intel HD Graphics 5500 graphics card, 15.6″ HD screen and integrated speaker set to a comfortable volume. All participants were sitting on the same chair at the same height (40 cm). The laptop was set on a desk at 80 cm of height and to 15 cm from the edge of the desk. For the interaction, a mid-size mouse was set to a side of the laptop, participants were allowed to move the mouse to any position they found most comfortable for them.

A between subjects design was adopted for this experimental design. The volunteers were assigned to the experimental conditions randomly and they arrived according to their availability. In order to avoid the bias that might be caused by the intention of completing the experiment in rush, the subjects were asked to be available for 30 min, although the experimentation time for each subject was expected to be a maximum of 15 min. Each subject was assigned to one of the three experimental conditions randomly. The basic rules of the game were briefly explained to each subject prior to starting the experiment: "one click to jump, one click to perform a mid-air jump, try to collect coins, avoid bombs and pits, and the playing time is not limited". Subsequently, they were assisted to create their profiles in the game. Then, they played the game until they decided to finish the experiment.

5.3   Measures

Objective Evaluation:

- Player performance: At the end of each game session, the total score of the player was automatically saved to a file, which was eventually used for the analysis.
- Player engagement: In addition to saving the total score of the player at the end of each session, total time was also saved. Total time for each session and the number of sessions played in each difficulty level, were used to assess the player's engagement.

Subjective Evaluation:

- Player's perceived motivation: In order to capture the perceived motivation, the Situational Motivation Scale (SIMS) was applied [24]. This scale measured the player's own self-perception on Intrinsic Motivation, Identified Regulation, External Regulation and Amotivation. This test was administered in the form of pre-test post-test.
- Player's perceived system usability: The Usability of the system was assessed by applying a short version of the System Usability Scale (SUS). This test was applied in the form of post-test [25].
- Game mechanics and their impact on the player's motivation: A questionnaire was devised to assess whether each of the implemented game mechanics was perceived as motivating or demotivating.

6   Analysis of Data and Results

The 46 participants formed the three experimental groups of SDT, SET and SDT+SET with 16, 15 and 15 subjects respectively. For each subject, a set of subjective and objective data was captured. The subjective data was obtained via questionnaires, and the objective data was captured automatically from the game experience of each participant. For each subject three main outcome of the objective data were extracted: Total Sessions (sum of the number of sessions played for each difficulty level), Total Time (sum of the duration of times spent in playing each difficulty level), and Max Score (maximum of recorded high scores throughout all the difficulty levels).

For each of these dependent variables normality test of Shapiro-Wilk was conducted. The results of this test showed that the data belonging to Total Sessions and Total Time were not normally distributed for any of the experimental groups. P-values of this test for the variable of Total Sessions were: $p = 0.0002$ for SDT group, $p = 0.001$ for SET group and $p = 0.0001$ for SDT+SET group. For Total Time, $p = 0.002$ for SDT group, $p = 0.001$ for SET group and $p = 0.001$ for SDT+SET group. However, the results of Shapiro-Wilk test for Max Score confirmed its normality throughout the experimental conditions ($p = 0.679$ for SDT, $p = 0.287$ for SET and $p = 0.263$ for SDT+SET). Additionally, Levene's test of homogeneity of variances was conducted for Max Score, and the results confirmed the homogeneity of this data across the different groups ($p = 0.433$).

The test of Shapiro-Wilk was applied to the data of these variables based on independent variables of Age Group, Gender and Experience Level. They all followed the same pattern for the normality test, in which the data groups belonging to Total Sessions and Total Time were not normal, but the data groups belonging to Max Score was normally distributed. Hence, for the normal data One-Way ANOVA, as well as Post-Hoc test of Scheffe, was conducted and for not-normally distributed data the non-parametric test of Kruskal-Wallis was applied.

The results of Kruskal-Wallis test on the variables of Total Sessions and Total Time between the three experimental groups (SDT, SET and SDT+SET) were not statistically significant ($H(2) = 0.422$, $p = 0.810$ for Total Sessions, $H(2) = 0.666$, $p = 0.717$ for Total Time). In addition, the result of One-Way ANOVA on the variable of Max Score among the three experimental conditions (SDT, SET and SDT+SET) was not statistically significant ($F(2,45) = 0.987$ and $p = 0.381$). Moreover, the same tests of One-Way ANOVA and Kruskal-Wallis were performed on the data of each variable categorized based on Age Group, Gender and Experience Level. The only statistically significant result that was found belongs to the One-Way ANOVA test on data of Max Score categorized based on Experience Level ($F(2, 45) = 8.713$ and $p = 0.001$). This indicates a logically expected positive relationship between the prior experience in this type of games and the performance. However, no significant effect of Gender and Age group was found on these three variables.

The results from pre-test post-test questionnaires were extracted for the variables of Intrinsic Motivation, Identified Regulation, External Regulation and Amotivation. The difference between pre-test and post-test was calculated and the outcome was tested for the normality and homogeneity. The variable of External Regulation did not pass the Shapiro-Wilk test for normality. Hence, One-Way ANOVA test was conducted for the other variables and the results did not indicate any significant difference among the three experimental groups: Intrinsic Motivation $F(2,45) = 0.243$ and $p = 0.785$, Identified Regulation $F(2,45) = 0.356$ and $p = 0.703$, and Amotivation $F(2,45) = 0.080$ and $p = 0.923$. Furthermore, the non-parametric test of Kruskal-Wallis was applied for the data of External Regulation. The results showed no significant difference among the three experimental groups ($H(2) = 0.716$ and $p = 0.699$). Finally, the Paired-Samples

T Test was conducted to analyze the difference in the level of intrinsic motivation before and after the experiment. This test was carried out separately for each of the experimental groups and the results showed a unique significant difference for SET ($t(14) = -2.559$ and $p = 0.023$), which was not observed in the other experimental groups. Cohen's d effect size value ($d = 0.66$) suggested a moderate to high effect size.

The usability was assessed with the short post-test of SUS. The used scale ranged from one to five. On average, when the participants were asked if they would like to use the system frequently if it is available, produced a score of 3.3. When they were asked if they think that the game was easy to use, they produced an average score of 4.39. Participants gave an average score of 4.60 when they were asked if they think that most people will learn to use the game quickly. Finally, a score of 3.86 was given when they were asked if they felt confident when using the game.

Finally, a questionnaire was included to assess which game mechanics were perceived as more motivating for the players. The scale ranged from -3 (Very demotivating) to 3 (very motivating). The game mechanics that were perceived as more motivating were: watching the highscore in the player's range of age (mean = 2.36), being able to choose between doing and not doing the tutorial (mean = 2.2) and being able to select your character (mean = 2.12). The least motivating game mechanic was: being forced to complete the tutorial before being able to play the game (mean = 0.66).

The results did not confirm the hypothesis that combining self-determination and self-efficacy in game design would lead to enhanced motivation and performance. However, this does not imply that the hypothesis is not plausible. Specific attributes of the experiment design in this research (e.g. type of game, game design, and environment of the experiment) might have contributed to the results of the experiment. Thus, additional investigation and experimentation are necessary to confirm this research outcome.

7 Conclusion and Research Perspectives

Motivation is not a simple construct and recognizing its underlying mechanisms has been the subject of a plethora of scientific research. This paper aimed at investigating the impact of combining self-determination and self-efficacy theories in game design on performance and user engagement. Three variations of a game were designed based on each of these theories and a combination of them.

The statistical analysis revealed that there is not any significant difference between the experimental groups in terms of maximum score, number of sessions and total time spent in playing the game. These results did not confirm the hypothesis considering that integrating self-determination and self-efficacy would lead to enhanced performance and engagement. Additional analysis did not show any significant difference in terms of engagement among different levels of prior experience in this type of games. However, prior experience was shown to have a significant positive impact on the performance (Max Score).

Additionally, the analysis of the user feedbacks obtained through questionnaires did not reveal any significant difference among the experimental conditions in terms of Intrinsic Motivation, Identified Regulation, External Regulation and Amotivation.

However, a significant difference was found between the pretest and posttest questionnaires of SET condition on Intrinsic Motivation. This effect was not observed in the other experimental groups. Finally, the participants perceived the developed system as easy to use. The most motivating feature was to compare highscores between players of the same range of age; the least motivating feature was being forced to complete the tutorial before being able to play the game.

More investigations are necessary to check the validity of the results obtained in this study. Future experiments should involve bigger sample size of subjects. In addition, future experiments could include multiple games and allow the participants to choose among them, in order to increase their sense of autonomy. Additional indicators, such as emotion recognition should be included to evaluate the effect of the emotional state of the user during the gameplay. This could confirm the interplay between self-determination and self-efficacy in game design.

Acknowledgement. This research has been conducted with the financial support of the European Union through the Beaconing project (Horizon 2020-Grant Number 687676). The authors acknowledge the financial support of the EU, Hands-Free Computing Ltd and the National Council of Science and Technology of Mexico (CONACYT).

References

1. Szczypka, M.S., et al.: Feeding behavior in dopamine-deficient mice. Proc. Natl. Acad. Sci. U.S.A. **96**(21), 12138–12143 (1999)
2. Ryan, R., Deci, E.: Self-determination theory and the facilitation of intrinsic motivation, social development, and well-being. Am. Psychol. **55**(1), 68–78 (2000)
3. Ryan, R., Deci, E.: Self-determination theory: an organismic dialectical perspective. In: Deci, E.L., Ryan, R.M. (eds.) Handbook of Self-Determination Research, pp. 3–33. University of Rochester Press, Rochester (2002)
4. Deci, E.L., Ryan, R.M.: Self-determination theory: a macrotheory of human motivation, development and health. Can. Psychol. **49**(3), 182–185 (2008)
5. Bandura, A.: Self-efficacy: toward a unifying theory of behavioral change. Psychol. Rev. **84**(2), 191–215 (1977)
6. Sweet, S.N., Fortier, M.S., Strachan, S.M., Blanchard, C.M.: Testing and integrating self-determination theory and self-efficacy theory in a physical activity context. Can. Psychol. **53**(4), 319–327 (2012)
7. Gee, J.P.: What video games have to teach us about learning and literacy. Comput. Entertain. **1**(1), 20 (2003)
8. Ryan, R.M., Rigby, C.S., Przybylski, A.: The motivational pull of video games: a self-determination theory approach. Motiv. Emot. **30**(4), 347–363 (2006)
9. Deterding, S., Sicart, M., Nacke, L., O'Hara, K., Dixon, D.: Gamification. using game-design elements in non-gaming contexts. In: Proceedings of the 2011 Annual Conference on Extended Abstracts on Human Factors in Computing Systems - CHI EA 2011, p. 2425 (2011)
10. Deterding, S., Dixon, D., Khaled, R., Nacke, L.: From game design elements to gamefulness: defining 'gamification'. In: Proceedings of the 2011 Annual Conference on Extended Abstracts on Human Factors in Computing Systems - CHI EA 2011, p. 2425 (2011)

11. Susi, T., Johannesson, M., Backlund, P.: Serious games: an overview (2007)

12. Deci, E.L., Ryan, R.M.: Intrinsic Motivation and Self-Determination in Human Behavior. Springer, Boston (1985). https://doi.org/10.1007/978-1-4899-2271-7

13. Deci, E.L., Ryan, R.M.: The 'What' and 'Why' of goal pursuits: human needs and the delf-determination of behavior. Psychol. Inq. **11**(4), 227–268 (2000)

14. Bong, M., Clark, R.E.: Comparison between self-concept and self-efficacy in academic motivation research. Educ. Psychol. **34**(3), 139–153 (1999)

15. Techatassanasoontorn, A.A.: The integrated self-determination and self-efficacy theories of ICT training and use: the case of the socio-economically disadvantaged. In: Development (2008)

16. Sweet, S.N., Fortier, M.S., Strachan, S.M., Blanchard, C.M., Boulay, P.: Testing a longitudinal integrated self-efficacy and self-determination theory model for physical activity post-cardiac rehabilitation. Heal. Psychol. Res. **2**(1), 1008 (2014)

17. Peng, W., Lin, J.H., Pfeiffer, K.A., Winn, B.: Need satisfaction supportive game features as motivational determinants: an experimental study of a self-determination theory guided exergame. Media Psychol. **15**(2), 175–196 (2012)

18. Francisco-Aparicio, A., Gutiérrez-Vela, F.L., Isla-Montes, J.L., Sanchez, J.L.G.: Gamification: analysis and application. In: Penichet, V., Peñalver, A., Gallud, J. (eds.) New Trends in Interaction, Virtual Reality and Modeling. HCIS, pp. 113–126. Springer, London (2013). https://doi.org/10.1007/978-1-4471-5445-7_9

19. Proulx, J.N., Romero, M., Arnab, S.: Learning mechanics and game mechanics under the perspective of self-determination theory to foster motivation in digital game based learning. Simul. Gaming **48**(1), 81–97 (2017)

20. Arnab, S., et al.: Mapping learning and game mechanics for serious games analysis: mapping learning and game mechanics. Br. J. Educ. Technol. **5**, 19 (2014)

21. Lim, T., Carvalho, M.B., Bellotti, F., Arnab, S., De Freitas, S., Louchart, S.: The LM-GM framework for serious games analysis (2015)

22. Richter, G., Raban, D.R., Rafaeli, S.: Studying gamification: the effect of rewards and incentives on motivation. In: Reiners, T., Wood, L.C. (eds.) Gamification in Education and Business, pp. 21–46. Springer, Cham (2015). https://doi.org/10.1007/978-3-319-10208-5_2

23. Unity: Lets Make a Game: Infinite Runner. Unity Tutorials (2018)

24. Guay, F., Vallerand, R.J., Blanchard, C.: On the assessment of situational intrinsic and extrinsic motivation: the Situational Motivation Scale (SIMS). Motiv. Emot. **24**(3), 175–213 (2000)

25. Brooke, J.: SUS - a quick and dirty usability scale. Usability Eval. Ind. **189**(194), 4–7 (1996)

Linking Learning Outcomes and Game Mechanics in the Early Stages of the RU EU? Project

Elizabeth Boyle[1(✉)], Jannicke Baalsrud Hauge[2,3], Murray Leith[1], Duncan Sim[1], Hans Hummel[4], Petar Jandrić[5], and Athanassios Jimoyiannis[6]

[1] University of the West of Scotland, Paisley, UK
{liz.boyle,murray.leith,duncan.sim}@uws.ac.uk
[2] Bremer Institut fur Produktion und Logistik (BIBA), Bremen, Germany
baa@biba.uni-bremen.de
[3] KTH-Royal Institute of Technology, Stockholm, Sweden
[4] Open Universiteit Nederland, Heerlen, Netherlands
hans.hummel@ou.nl
[5] Tehničko veleučilište u Zagrebu, Zagreb, Croatia
pjandric@tvz.hr
[6] University of Peloponnese, Corinth, Greece
ajimoyia@uop.gr

Abstract. The issue of national and European identity is driving many of the issues that are currently of concern to European citizens. The Erasmus+ funded RU EU? project aims to develop an innovative online game, the RU EU? game, that will help students across Europe to develop a better understanding of their own National and European identity and values, as well as those of others, and to challenge them about their attitudes and prejudices by tackling problem solving dilemmas relating to identity. It is hoped that the game will provide an engaging platform for young Europeans to confront some of the complex and confusing issues surrounding National and European identity at a time of change and increasing tension across Europe. This paper describes the early stages of the game design and focuses on characterizing the learning outcomes and game mechanics for the RU EU? game and bringing these together.

Keywords: Serious games · European identity · RU EU? Project · Learning outcomes · Game mechanics

1 Introduction

We are once again living at a time of increasing uncertainty in Europe with respect to how European citizens get on with each other and it is acknowledged that there is a need to increase civic and intercultural understanding. Despite the European project, there is a lack of development of a sense of European-ness among many member states (Leith and Soule 2017; Sim and Leith 2014). Identity remains rooted in the national rather than the European, and the European Experiment is under challenge as a result.

© Springer Nature Switzerland AG 2019
M. Gentile et al. (Eds.): GALA 2018, LNCS 11385, pp. 191–200, 2019.
https://doi.org/10.1007/978-3-030-11548-7_18

At a time of change across Europe, it is very important to try and understand why European citizens have very different views of themselves and others and what motivates these differences. It is against this background that the RU EU? Project was proposed. The main objective of this project is to develop an innovative online game, the RU EU? game, that will help students across Europe to develop a better understanding of their own national and European identity and values. The idea for the game emerged from discussions about the recognized advantages that games can offer in providing engaging activities that can support learning in difficult subject areas (Boyle et al. 2012). Serious games are a relatively new area of interest but hard evidence is beginning to emerge that they support longer term retention and deeper learning of subject material (Wouters, Van Nimwegen, Van Oostendorp and Van Der Spek 2013).

Given the complexity of the political situation in Europe it was thought that a game might provide an active method for helping students to think in more constructive ways about these issues. Serious games can provide engaging activities while also supporting learning in challenging content areas (Boyle et al. 2012). Consequently it is hoped that the RU EU? game can provide an engaging platform for young Europeans to explore their own views as well as those of others, to examine and reflect upon the impact of their own identity and values on their interactions with others and to challenge them about their attitudes and prejudices in tackling problem solving tasks involving national and European identity. Since young people will play a key role in the determining the future of Europe, it is especially important to find out what they think and how they can work together.

This paper describes the early stages in the design of the RU EU? game, focusing on the learning outcomes and game mechanics for the game, how these were specified and brought together. The topic fits well as a case study within the "Mapping pedagogical goals, outcomes and principles into serious game mechanics" strand of the serious games design track for the GALA conference.

2   Game Design Models and Learning Outcomes

Designing serious games is a complex, interdisciplinary enterprise which is typically regarded as an iterative process, where ideas are proposed and developed into prototypes and then refined, amended or rejected at different stages depending on how well they work (McGrath 2011). While there is still no universally accepted model of serious game design, it is clear that the central factor in effective game design requires consideration of how instructional content and game characteristics are integrated to create the game activities, which in turn lead to clear learning outcomes (Garris et al. 2002). Generally it is not very clear what game attributes support what kind of learning. As Wilson (2009) said "little is known about what components of these games (i.e., game attributes) influence learning outcomes". Arnab et al. (2015) proposed a similar but more detailed model for the analysis and design of serious games, the Learning Mechanics-Game Mechanics (LM-GM) model, that endorsed the need to integrate learning (LM) and game mechanics (GM). Arnab et al. identified 31 learning mechanics (such as explore, identify, analyse) and mapped these into appropriate game mechanics (such as game turns, movement, feedback), providing a useful model for game design. Garris, Arnab and others make it clear that it is imperative to be clear about the learning outcomes sought for the game, and how these can be realized in gamified learning activities. Identifying learning outcomes for games can be difficult and authors have categorized them in different ways (Wouters, van der Spek and Oostendorp 2009).

3   The Design of the RU EU? Game

3.1   Learning Outcomes for the RU EU? Game

The general aim of the game activities in the RUEU? Game is to increase players' awareness of the complex nature of EU and national identity. The original project proposal for the RU EU? game identified 4 main learning outcomes for the game as: knowledge acquisition, attitudes, application of knowledge and collaboration.

Knowledge acquisition: players will extend and test their knowledge about Europe, European customs, values and traditions. This will be assessed via Multiple Choice Questions.

Attitudes: players will test their own attitudes to national and European identity and this will be fed back to the player to reflect upon. A very simple easy-to-administer measure that assesses both positive and negative attitudes towards the EU simultaneously is the evaluative space grid (Maier, Maier, Baumert, Jahn, Krause and Adam 2015).

Application of knowledge scenarios: players will solve challenging, ill-defined problems surrounding issues that are rooted in notions of identity. This was viewed as the main substance of the game where players encounter problem scenarios that tackle some of the difficult dilemmas concerning conflicting national and European identities. The aim of the dilemmas is to encourage players to consider and understand both sides of the argument in order to progress in the game. Since much of the information we have about identity is conveyed in the things that people say about their attitudes and opinions, it would appear to be useful for the player to interact in the game with a range of people (non-player characters) in different scenarios who express differing views about aspects of European identity. The players would then need to carry out a range of activities with the information that they had collected about the different viewpoints and for example organize statements into higher order categories, match the statements to higher order categories, rank them in terms of importance and evaluate them for relevance. Given all the text involved there was a concern that this risked being a bit boring, so the gameplay would need to be engaging.

Collaboration: players will collaborate in teams to tackle the problem solving and decision making scenarios. Our current thinking is that this element of the game will be located in the student support materials attached to the game.

3.2   What Is European Identity?

The first hurdle to emerge in designing the RU EU? game was to agree what European identity meant. As with many constructs in social science it was not very clear what this key construct meant and even our literature review that aimed to provide clarity about European identity concluded that "there is no real agreement on what it actually is" (Sim et al. 2018)! However Van der Zwet and Leith (2017) proposed that our understanding of the key components of European identity as involving: (1) Functional/instrumental considerations regarding the costs and benefits of European integration, (2) Value-based considerations that relate to shared beliefs and norms often expressed through political institutions (3) Cultural considerations which are often a more emotive identification to Europe as a shared cultural entity (4) Biological/geographical considerations which are more ethnic driven identification markers. Designing the game based on these components of identity will ensure that the game has theoretical integrity with respect to European identity.

It was thought to be important to convey the complexity of EU identity in the game and some understanding of its components. Since much of the information we have about identity comes from the things people say, it became evident that it would be useful for the player to interact in some way with varied non-player characters who express differing views about European identity. Players would then need to do something with this information, since it could be challenging to maintain interest in discussion of EU related issues. The game will be available in the languages of the 5 project partners: English, Dutch, German, Greek and Croatian.

4   What Game Activities/Game Mechanics Can Provide the Desired Learning Outcomes?

4.1   Game Genre

As Arnab et al. (2015) "It can be readily seen from entertainment gaming that certain genres, such as role-playing, action, adventure and simulation, share similar interaction models and game-play dynamics". Since the game is dealing with knowledge, attitudes and decision making, it seemed likely that the RU EU? game would involve aspects of simulation and role playing games. The game would simulate scenes where different individuals express varied opinions as they put forward their arguments about various issues related to the EU. Since positions on EU identity are frequently expressed as pro or anti EU, there seemed to be an option to have an argument set up where players took one of two roles – pro or anti EU – and then came to some kind of resolution.

Role play games specify further that the player would take on the function of a specific character. Initially we thought of characters role playing in a meeting to negotiate and resolve problems with differing opinions. However, as the Brexit discussions illustrate, negotiating outcomes in this area seems to be very difficult. We then had the idea that the player would be a journalist trying to acquire a better, more balanced and more critical understanding of the topic of national and European identity.

4.2   Narrative and Player's Brief

A good narrative in a game helps to provide a rationale for carrying out the game activities and structure the game activities into a coherent whole. The suggested overarching narrative for the RU EU? game is that the player takes on the role of a freelance research journalist who writes for a number of local, national and European newspapers. Like most journalists, he also writes a blog.

For the RU EU? game the player's brief is to help the readers of these newspapers to gain a better understanding of European and national identity. The player will carry out a number of assignments reporting about various issues relating to European identity and values that readers of the newspapers are struggling with. The player has access to material from a variety of sources including interviews with non-player characters (NPCs) and he will also have information coming into him via emails, texts and Twitter. He will carry out activities similar to those that a journalist might do, such as tracking down, sifting through and organizing material and collating and compiling this material into a draft article for later publication.

4.3   Setting

While he is carrying out these activities the journalist (player) will be located in front of his desktop computer in his office (Fig. 1).

Fig. 1. Work environment of main character

4.4   Scenarios for the Game

Most of the gameplay for the game was regarded as being located in the problem-solving scenarios. The literature review suggested that there are a number of themes that could be developed into scenarios and 5 scenarios have been identified as relevant:

1. The balance between national and European identities
2. Who is European? Different attitudes between nations
3. The rights of citizens to work in different partner countries

4. Changes to European identity over time
5. Immigration and the rights of migrants to travel throughout Europe

The scenarios provide the main guts of the game. They have been structured in a similar way using an agreed template to provide a common systematic approach to describing: (a) the tasks or assignments the player will do, (b) the knowledge and skills the player acquires in doing these tasks, (c) who is there to help the player, (d) at what stage in the overall game that scenario is played, and (d) what are the entry and exit conditions for that scenario.

For each scenario there are 4 different scenes that the journalist will access which depict the interviews carried out with the different stakeholders. The scenes will be represented on another screen that the journalist will access by clicking on it. The scenes depicted will differ from one scenario to another, but they will always illustrate the varied views that different stakeholders have about EU issues. The scenes in the balance scenario for example would include (1) a discussion in a pub, (2) a debate in a TV studio, (3) an interview with a manager of a recruitment firm and (4) incoming tweets. For every scene for ever scenario, the journalist will carry out research to compile a short article (composed of bullet points) at the end of mini-game play. As a good journalist, pros and cons from various resources will be reflected in these articles.

The Learning Objectives for the scenarios are:

1. To be exposed to, understand and appreciate different viewpoints and opinions about EU and national identity
2. To understand that people have pro, anti, balanced or neutral views with respect to EU identity
3. To start to identify what the stakes in the balance debate are, i.e. the varied influences that determine people's opinions
4. To understand why different people may feel the way they do
5. To adopt a critical approach to what they read.

To address these learning objectives the player (as journalist) will (1) access interviews from NPCs; (2) organise selected interview statements into higher order categories (e.g. pro and anti EU); (3) match statements to higher order stakes; (4) rank statements in order of importance; (5) evaluate the relevance or quality of statements or texts with respect to the debate, decide appropriate headlines for a story.

4.5   Scenario 1: Balance Between EU and National Identity

The first scenario will be slightly different from the other four and can be seen as a "learning" scenario, where the player is learning that many people's views about the EU are pro or anti EU. In addition the player learns about the reasons that motivate what people say about EU identity (stakes).

Suggested Games for Scenario 1. The balance game and the stakes game both require the categorisation of statements to higher order categories.

(1) *Balance game.* The aim of this activity is to understand the differing views that exist with respect to EU identity. In this activity the player will go to one of the

scenes (e.g. the pub scene) where he will observe and hear a heated discussion between participants on both sides of the "balance debate" about the pros and cons of leaving the EU. The player will then see 12 statements, representing both pro and anti views of the EU, extracted from that conversation. At the bottom of the screen there will be a scale with markings from 1 to 7 where 1 is strongly disagree, 4 is neither agree nor disagree and 7 is strongly agree. The statements will be presented to the player to consider one at a time and the player will be required to assign each statement to one of the grades to indicate the extent to which he agrees or disagrees with that statement. Examples of these statements are shown in Table 1, where the bold statements are essentially anti EU and the italic ones are pro EU.

Table 1. Assignment of statements in terms of strength of support for the EU

In my experience the different European countries do not subscribe to a set of shared beliefs and values
If my country had a referendum I would definitely vote to leave the EU
Immigrants have taken our jobs and these are jobs that should go to the people who have lived here for a long time
In the EU the different nations do not all implement the EU rules fairly
It's only a matter of time before one of the EU countries really decides to turn against the others
Some people have no insight into how good the UK could be on its own
I think that Europeans have more shared beliefs and values than they do differences
The EU is not perfect but I firmly believe that the best way forward is for EU member states to work together to make the EU better
Many employees from other EU countries are very worried that they will have to return home after Brexit
It is universally acknowledged that the EU provides very high standards for treating its citizens fairly
For me, one of the main benefits of the EU has been to prevent war between the nations of Europe
Voting to leave is a huge leap of faith and, quite honestly, I am not prepared to gamble with the future prospects of the people of my country

Players' responses on each of the 12 items will be totaled to provide a score (between 12 and 84). Players will be given feedback about whether their score indicates whether they are generally pro or anti EU or somewhere in the middle.

(2) *Stakes game.* We argue that an important idea underlying the statements made by NPCs is the idea of stakes. Stakes represent the motives that drive the statements that people make and explain why people feel the way that they do about issues related to EU/national identity. Stakes are a higher level constructs a bit like "themes" in qualitative research and the stakes that we propose are relevant to EU identity are shown in Table 2.

Table 2. Interview with the boss of an international recruitment company

Higher level stakes	Statements by the boss of an international recruitment company
Democratic human rights, values & freedoms	The common values of the EU, such as respect for human rights, democracy and equality, have definitely had a positive impact in our workplace
Locus of power/control/anti establishment – populism	I'd rather have the EU in charge than any of the populist parties in my country
Economy/money/jobs	Some of our employees from other EU countries are very worried that they will have to return home in the event of a Brexit vote
Equity - fairness, equality	It's only right that if you are an EU citizen you should have just as much right to work in my company as someone born in the UK
Security	The EU provides some security for our employees working abroad
Change and uncertainty	To be brutally frank I am really worried that we will vote to leave the EU, because our company has made no plans whatsoever about what to do in the event of a Brexit vote!
Feelings/emotions	The opportunities I've had to work with colleagues in Europe have definitely made me feel much more European
History and culture	In one way or the other Europeans share a common history that unites us

In the Stakes game the player will be given a set of 8 higher level stakes and a set of 8 statements (Table 2) and his task is to assign each statement to a higher level stake via a drag and drop mechanism. In this example the statements represent the views of a boss of an international recruitment company who has pro EU views.

(3) *Ranking game*. In the ranking game the player will take the same statements and will rank these in terms of how important/relevant he sees them to this issue of the balance between national and European identity. The game will employ a drag and drop mechanism where the player drags his 4 selected statements to the top 4 places and these will constitute the top four bullet points that he will include in his final report.

Feedback on Rankings. For each scene the player's ranked statements will be evaluated by the editor of the newspaper who will then provide the journalist with (automated) feedback about his top 4 selections from the ranking game. The feedback from the 'editor' will illustrate where the emphasis of the prospective journalistic output was, pro, anti or balanced, and suggest other areas of the classifications scheme that could be focused upon to take account of readers' views. The feedback would also attempt to assess the more 'personal focus' (bias) within the work and provide feedback on that too.

In-line with Arnab et al. (2015) we applied the LM-GM model in the design of the game play described above since its pedagogy-game mechanic mapping provided seems beneficial to inform the selected mechanics of RU EU? Game (Fig. 2).

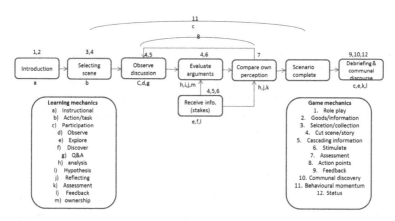

Fig. 2. LM-GM mapping of RU EU? European vs national scenario

4.6   Application of Knowledge to Other Scenarios

The last four scenarios are "application" scenarios, where players will "apply" the knowledge that they have acquired in the balance scenario to the working rights, immigration, differences between nations and changes over time scenarios. In these scenarios players will come to realise that many people's views are more nuanced than simply pro or anti EU.

5   Conclusion

We are on our way to developing a game that will support students in thinking more deeply about national and EU identity by presenting them with scenarios that illustrate the complex nature of EU identity and the varied and conflicting opinions expressed by different individuals about this. Designing the game has been a difficult process partly due the intrinsically fuzzy nature of the key concept, EU identity, and partly because the game helps the player to explore this in an implicit rather than an explicit way. The game content experts made a very interesting observation - that trying to design the game has helped them to consider the issues in a new way. We are hopeful that playing the game will also help players to understand EU identity in a new way. By December we aim to have more to report as well as a working version of the game.

Acknowledgements. The present work was carried out as part of the "RU EU? A game-based approach to exploring 21st century European Identity and Values" project. This project is partially supported by a KA203-Erasmus+ Strategic Partnerships for higher education, grant; KA2, Cooperation for Innovation and the Exchange of Good Practices; Grant Agreement no: Grant

Agreement no: 2017-1-UK01-KA203-036601. This presentation does not represent the opinion of the European Community, and the European Community is not responsible for any use that might be made of its content.

References

Arnab, S., et al.: Mapping learning and game mechanics for SG analysis. Br. J. Educ. Technol. **46**(2), 391–411 (2015)

Boyle, E.A., Connolly, T.M., Hainey, T., Boyle, J.M.: Engagement in digital entertainment games: a systematic review. Comput. Hum. Behav. **28**(3), 771–780 (2012)

Garris, R., Ahlers, R., Driskell, J.E.: Games, motivation, and learning: a research and practice model. Simul. Gaming **33**(4), 441–467 (2002)

Maier, M., Maier, J., Baumert, A., Jahn, N., Krause, S., Adam, S.: Measuring citizens' implicit and explicit attitudes towards the European Union. Eur. Union Polit. **16**(3), 369–385 (2015)

Leith, M.S., Soule, D.J.P.: Political Discourse and National Identity in Scotland. Edinburgh University Press, Edinburgh (2017)

McGrath, J.: The game development lifecycle - a theory for the extension of the agile project methodology (2011). http://blog.dopplerinteractive.com/2011/04/gamedevelopment-lifecycle-theory-for.html

Sim, D., Leith, M.S.: Scottish diasporic identities in the Netherlands. Natl. Identities **16**(2), 139–155 (2014)

Sim, D., Boyle, E.A., Leith, M., van der Zwet, A.: European identity: a literature review. Deliverable 01 for the RUEU? Project (2018)

Van der Zwet, A., Leith, M.: Presentation at the Kick Off meeting for the RU EU? Project, Paisley, October 2017

Wilson, K.A., et al.: Relationships between game attributes and learning outcomes: review and research proposals. Simul. Gaming **40**(2), 217–266 (2009)

Wouters, P., Van der Spek, E.D., Van Oostendorp, H.: Current practices in serious game research: a review from a learning outcomes perspective. In: Connolly, T.M., Stansfield, M., Boyle, L. (eds.) Games-Based Learning Advancements for Multisensory Human Computer Interfaces: Techniques and Effective Practices, pp. 232–255. IGI Global, Hershey (2009)

Wouters, P., Van Nimwegen, C., Van Oostendorp, H., Van Der Spek, E.D.: A meta-analysis of the cognitive and motivational effects of serious games. J. Educ. Psychol. **105**(2), 249–265 (2013)

Auditory Attention, Implications for Serious Game Design

Nikesh Bajaj[1,2] , Francesco Bellotti[1(✉)], Riccardo Berta[1],
Jesùs Requena Carriòn[2], and Alessandro De Gloria[1]

[1] Dipartimento di Ingegneria navale, elettrica, elettronica e delle
telecomunicazioni, University of Genoa, Genoa, Italy
[2] School of Electronics Engineering and Computer Science,
Queen Mary University of London, London, UK
n.bajaj@qmul.ac.uk

Abstract. Auditory attention is fundamental also in serious games. This paper synthetizes the results of a recent statistical analysis of auditory attention of non-native learners and proposes indications for serious game design. We propose a 3-dimensional difficulty level model that can be applied both for designing game levels and adaptivity to keep a player in the flow. The model suggests using background noise level as a prime factor to increase the difficulty of the game, followed by the length of the stimulus and the semantic complexity of the message. We also propose the concept of a mini-game format specifically aimed at training auditory attention and performance. As a format, it could be easily customized in different context domains and implemented as a service or a game engine plug-in.

Keywords: Serious game · Auditory attention · Language skill ·
Non-native learners · Attention score · Learning environment · Adaptivity

1   Introduction

Attention is one of the primary factors affecting the performance of any tasks, and it has been considered to play a vital role in learning [1]. Among other kinds of attention neuroscientists and cognitive psychologists have taken interest in selective attention for a long time to understand how brain select one stimulus over other. The selective attention includes basically two types of attention namely; auditory and visual, however, there are few studies conducted with task-oriented attention [2]. For auditory selective attention, the most popular experimental setting is the dichotic listening task, in which two different messages are presented to the participant and instructed to pay attention to one of them, after completion of listening, participants are asked to write as much as they can remember [3]. Most of the studies nowadays use different versions of the dichotic listening task in the simulated multi-message environment [4].

The mechanism of selective attention has been explained by many theories, widely accepted theories are namely; filter theory, early and late selection theory and load theory. Filter theory suggests the filtering of useful information, which is further explained by early selection and late selection theory [5]. Both theories indicate the

© Springer Nature Switzerland AG 2019
M. Gentile et al. (Eds.): GALA 2018, LNCS 11385, pp. 201–209, 2019.
https://doi.org/10.1007/978-3-030-11548-7_19

selection of information before or after processing hence named as early selection and late selection theory [6]. The contradiction of these two theories was resolved by load theory, which correlates the dependency of early and late selection on cognitive load, that is in low cognitive load, brain process all the information and then select useful one, whereas in high cognitive load, brain select the useful information first then process it [7].

Working in this field, we designed an experiment based on the dichotic listening task and the above-mentioned theories to investigate auditory attention for the design of interactive learning environments. The objective of the experiment was to quantify the effect of auditory conditions on auditory attention for non-native speakers. The experiment is described in detail in a companion paper [8] and synthesized here in Sect. 3. The focus of this manuscript, instead, is to discuss the implications of those results for the design of serious games.

The rest of the article is organized as follows. Section 2 presents the previous work published in the literature. In Sect. 3, we syntactically report on our abovementioned auditory attention experiment. In Sect. 4, we discuss implications and propose indications for serious game design. Finally, we conclude and discuss possible future work in Sect. 5.

2 Related Work

Serious games have been used in different areas, targeting different skills [9, 10]. Games improving motor skills are used for physical training [11, 12], cognitive skills are used in education [13–15], social and psychological skills are used in the treatment of patients to improve their physical and mental health [16–18].

Attention has also been the key interest in the serious game community. The increased interest in the attentional study was to help children and adults with Attention Deficit Hyperactivity Disorder (ADHD) [19]. Since then games have been treated as an alternative treatment of ADHD [20–23] to extend the attention span [24] and improve the attention [25]. Other technologies have also combined with serious games to improve attention of children with ADHD e.g. Augmented Reality [26]. The attention of children with movement disorder (cerebral palsy) was assessed with serious game incorporated with Electroencephalography (EEG). Games have also been designed to improve the attention of ordinary people. The attention development was studied specifically for children [27] and older adults [28]. A study was conducted to improve the attentional behavior of school students with the computerized system [29]. A mobile game *TrainBrain* was also designed to improve the attention [30]. Many aspects of attention were studied with games namely visual selective attention [31–34], knowledge acquisition and retention [35] and the limited capacity model of attention [36]. A computer-based cognitive therapy software is designed, named as *RehaCom*, which is used by the expert to help improve various aspects of attention and memory [37].

3 Experiment

3.1 Experiment Design

For evaluating auditory attention for learning environments, we designed an experiment based on dichotic listening task, where participants were presented audio stimuli and asked to write the text message presented in the audio file. As in interactive environment, attention is affected by many factors that were mapped as independent variables in the experiment, to analyze their effects on the auditory attention. In the experiment, we explored three variables, namely; Noise, Length of stimulus and Semanticity. Noise is mapped from environmental distractions such as background noise, elements of User Interface (UI), multiple voices in the environment and tiredness of learner. Even though audio noise has no direct relation to distracting UI elements or tiredness of learner, we considered it for an analogy. Other two experimental features are related to the language skills of the learner. The length of the message is mapped from the amount of information given in the presented statement or message and Semanticity is mapped from the learners' language understanding.

A total of 5000 semantic English language audio files along with their corresponding text were obtained from the Tatoeba Project [38]. Each audio file has only one spoken sentence and all the sentences range from 3 words to 13 words per sentence. Non-semantic audio files were generated by suitably inserting random word(s) in the semantic files. A total of 1700 new non-semantic stimuli were thus generated.

Six different sets of stimuli were created by adding different levels of background noise to semantic and non-semantic stimuli. The level of background noise used are; signal to noise ratio (SNR) of −6 dB, −3 dB, 0 dB, 3 dB, 6 dB and no noise (∞ dB).

3.2 Participants

A total of 25 (4 female and 21 male) non-native student speakers was selected from the science and technology department with no known auditory processing disorder. The age of participant ranges from 16 to 34 years. The majority of nationalities among participants were Indian and Italian and the majority of first languages were, Arabic, Italian, and Malayalam. None of the participants had the first language as English. Even though nationalities of some participants were different but they had the same first language e.g. Arabic and the other way round was also the case for Indian nationality. The focus on non-native speakers reflects the fact that, in several domains, instructional tools are in English only, on the other hand, it introduces the difficulty that might be assimilated to the difficulty for a novice to become familiar with a technical language/jargon.

3.3 Results

Results detailed in [8] show that attention score always increases when we move from −6 dB to ∞ dB SNR, independent of length or semanticity. Similarly, attention score almost always decreases with the increase of the length of stimuli. This general trends can be visualized as box and whisker plot in Fig. 1.

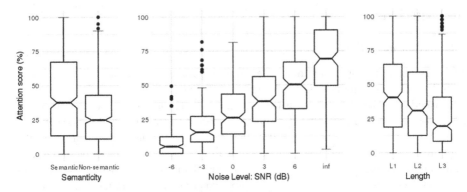

Fig. 1. Attention score with respect to Semanticity, Noise level, and Length of stimulus.

The effects of all the three independent variables are apparent in Fig. 1. Non-semanticity makes listener distracted and listener loses the auditory attention. Similarly, increasing noise level (or decreasing SNR) makes it harder to pay attention, while shorter sentences are easily acquired by listeners. The figure also highlights that noise has a strong impact on attention score, however, ANOVA reveals that all the three independent variables are significantly ($p \ll 0.0001$) affecting the attention score and $\eta^2_{partial}$ also shows that at least 75% of the differences in experimental conditions are explained by the respective independent variables.

4   Discussion and Indications for Serious Game Design

Serious games for learning languages are a major application target for the above-presented analysis. However, those results may be applied to other training/instruction context, and not only because of the specific jargon typical of some domains (which represents a barrier, especially for novices). With the wide diffusion of 3D environments and natural interaction modalities, auditory attention has gained ever more relevance also in the world of serious games, as-imitating reality - a lot of information relevant to training/instruction can be conveyed by means of speech. Non-player characters (NPCs) are a key mechanics in this regard [39].

The presented experiment highlights that noise, length of message and semanticity are key factors for a player's auditory performance. This information, qualitative and quantitative, can be exploited for designing levels and, similarly, to adapt (also dynamically) the game environment to the player's actual capabilities, in order to keep him in flow [40, 41]. The difficulty of the different levels – and player performance alike - can be estimated through the quantitative information provided by the experiment. A 3-dimensional difficulty level model can be designed for games, with the noise level, length of messages and semantic complexity of message at each dimension, as shown in Fig. 2. At every level of noise, a player can be subjected to longer messages and semantically more difficult messages to increase the difficulty of the game. The noise level axis of the model can be treated as the primary axis of difficulty, as statistical analysis demonstrated noise as the strongest factor affecting auditory attention. The length of the message can be considered as a secondary axis to increase the difficulty of the game, as an increase in the length of the message is quantitatively easier than increasing the semantic complexity of the message, which can be regarded as the last axis of difficulty.

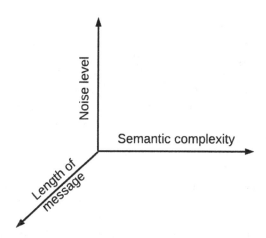

Fig. 2. Difficulty level model for game design.

The same concept can be used for the sake of game adaptivity, as the user performance might be continuously profiled along the three axes to get reference values to assess his auditory attention level. This construct could be an enhancement to the learning/gaming analytics profilers that are spreading also in the world of serious games [42–44]. The developed knowledge might be applied also to serious games specifically aimed at training auditory attention. This might be done by featuring player interaction with NPCs in the plot, or by developing a set of generic mini-games [45], each one targeting a specific factor. We could think of a very simple format, with a customizable NPC and environment/background. The target of the player, in a conversation, could be to catch the meaning or identify one or more wrong/specific words. The difficulty of the trial could increase in terms of environment noise (e.g., environmental noise and/or overlapping voices by specific "competing" NPCs), length and meaning of NPC messages. This could be implemented as a service, in a service-oriented architecture perspective (e.g., [46]), or even a game engine plug-in [47], and supported through an authoring tool for efficient development.

For a game design, considering a whole scale of semantic complexity has advantages over considering only two distinct categories of semanticity (i.e., semantic/non-semantic information). Semantic complexity of a message can be treated as a complex grammatical structure of language (English as an example), which serves the purpose of the game to improve the attention of player on language. In this scenario, the player will learn to process complexly structured messages. On the other hand, if just two distinct categories of semantic and non-semantic are used, learners will practice paying attention to non-semantic sentences which are not as useful as to learn complex grammatical structures of a language. Moreover, the game designer will have two levels of difficulty in the dimension of semanticity unlike the whole scale of semantic complexity, which can have more levels of difficulties.

5 Conclusion and Future Work

Auditory attention plays a fundamental role in instruction, also concerning serious games. In this paper, we have synthesized the results of a recent statistical analysis of auditory attention of non-native learners [8] and discussed them to devise indications for serious game design. Of course, indications are important also for teachers/instructors that should control application in class (or in the field).

We propose a 3-dimensional difficulty level model, that can be applied both for designing game levels and adaptivity to keep a player in the flow. The model suggests using background noise level as a prime factor to increase the difficulty of the game, followed (not closely) by the length of the stimulus and the semantic complexity of the message. Application of the model is expected to improve the auditory attention of the player, especially, but not exclusively, for learning a language. For example, international students can be targeted to improve the auditory attention with the English language. A similar model can be used to design a game with the Italian language for non-Italian students to improve their auditory attention on the Italian language. Other potential applications of the proposed model could be in designing of SG for Auditory Processing Disorder (APD) patients (adults and children) to improve the attention on auditory stimulus. Children, at an early age, can be trained with customized games to improve their attention on different languages. Similar games can be designed to complement the treatment of ADHD for auditory aspects.

We also propose the concept of a mini-game format specifically aimed at training auditory attention and performance. As a format, it could be easily customizable in different context domains and implemented as a service or a game engine plug-in.

There are a few aspects which can or should be explored in future research work. The impact of specific distracting elements should be studied, for example, distraction by UI, player's tiredness and emotional state. As the current study is focused on non-native learners, a similar study could be conducted for native learners. Visual and task-oriented attention should be explored as well. Concerning the design part, sample implementations should be made in order to check and tune the proposed model.

References

1. Kail, R.: Speed of information processing: developmental change and links to intelligence. J. Sch. Psychol. **38**(1), 51–61 (2000)
2. Anderson, J.R.: Chapter 3: Attention and Performance: Cognitive Psychology and its Implications, 8th edn. WH Freeman/Times Books/Henry Holt & Co., New York (1985)
3. Spence, C., Santangelo, V.: Auditory attention. In: Plack, E.C. (ed.) Oxford Handbook of Auditory Science: Hearing, vol. 3, p. 249. Oxford University Press, Oxford

4. Ingram, J.C.: Neurolinguistics: An Introduction to Spoken Language Processing and its Disorders. Cambridge University Press, Cambridge (2007)
5. Treisman, A.M.: Monitoring and storage of irrelevant messages and selective at-tention. J. Verbal Learn. Verbal Behav. **3**, 449–459 (1964)
6. Deutsch, J.A., Deutsch, D.: Attention: some theoretical considerations. Psychol. Rev. **70**(1), 80–90 (1963)
7. Lavie, N.: Distracted and confused? selective attention under load. Trends Cogn. Sci. **9**(2), 75–82 (2005)
8. Bajaj, N., Bellotti, F., Carriòn, J.R., Berta, R., De Gloria, A.: Analysis of factors affecting the auditory attention of non-native speakers in learning environments. Submitted for review (2018)
9. Susi, T., Johannesson, M., Backlund, P.: Serious games: an overview (2007)
10. Carvalho, M.B., et al.: An activity theory-based model for serious games analysis and conceptual design. Comput. Educ. **87**, 166–181 (2015)
11. Chatham, R.E.: Games for training. Commun. ACM **50**(7), 36–43 (2007)
12. De Gloria, A., Bellotti, F., Berta, R.: Serious games for education and training. Int. J. Serious Games **1**(1), 43–58 (2014)
13. Stege, L., Van Lankveld, G., Spronck, P.: Serious games in education. Int. J. Comput. Sci. Sport. **10**(1), 1–9 (2011)
14. Read, J.C.: Serious games in education. EAI Endorsed Trans. Serious Games **2**(6), 1–5 (2015)
15. Hamdaoui, N., Khalidi Idrissi, M., Bennani, S.: Serious Games in Education towards the standardization of the teaching-learning process. Adv. Educ. Technol. **174**, 174–181 (2014)
16. Read, J.L., Shortell, S.M.: Interactive games to promote behavior change in prevention and treatment. JAMA **305**(16), 1704–1705 (2011)
17. Burke, J.W., McNeill, M., Charles, D.K., Morrow, P.J., Crosbie, J.H., Mc Donough, S.M.: Optimising engagement for stroke rehabilitation using serious games. Vis. Comput. **25**(12), 1085 (2009)
18. Fleming, T.M., et al.: Serious games for the treatment or prevention of depression: a systematic review (2014)
19. Barkley, R.A., DuPaul, G.J., McMurray, M.B.: Comprehensive evaluation of attention deficit disorder with and without hyperactivity as defined by research criteria. J. Consult. Clin. Psychol. **58**(6), 775 (1990)
20. Wegrzyn, S.C., Hearrington, D., Martin, T., Randolph, A.B.: Brain games as a potential nonpharmaceutical alternative for the treatment of ADHD. J. Res. Technol. Educ. **45**(2), 107–130 (2012)
21. Chan, P.A., Rabinowitz, T.: A cross-sectional analysis of video games and attention deficit hyperactivity disorder symptoms in adolescents. Ann. Gen. Psychiatry **5**(1), 16 (2006)
22. Fròlich, J., Lehmkuhl, G., Doepfner, M.: Computer games in childhood and adolescence: relations to addictive behavior, ADHD, and aggression. Zeitschrift fur Kinder-und Jugendpsychiatrie und Psychotherapie **37**(5), 393–402 (2009)
23. Shaw, R., Grayson, A., Lewis, V.: Inhibition, ADHD, and computer games: the inhibitory performance of children with ADHD on computerized tasks and games. J. Atten. Disord. **8**(4), 160–168 (2005)
24. Pope, A.T., Bogart, E.H.: Extended attention span training system: video game neurotherapy for attention deficit disorder. Child Study J. **26**(1), 39–50 (1996)
25. Colombo, V., Baldassini, D., Mottura, S., Sacco, M., Crepaldi, M., Antonietti, A.: Antonyms: a serious game for enhancing inhibition mechanisms in children with attention deficit/hyperactivity disorder (ADHD). In: 2017 International Conference on Virtual Rehabilitation (ICVR), pp. 1–2. IEEE (2017)

26. Rivera, L.A.: Augmented reality serious games design to improve attention of children with ADHD. In: IEEE 11CCC (2016)
27. Berger, A., Jones, L., Rothbart, M.K., Posner, M.I.: Computerized games to study the development of attention in childhood. Behav. Res. Methods Instrum. Comput. **32**(2), 297–303 (2000)
28. Ku, C.-H., Huang, S.-L., Li, T.-Y.: The design and study of a serious game for attention training of the older adults. In: Vaz de Carvalho, C., Escudeiro, P., Coelho, A. (eds.) Serious Games, Interaction, and Simulation. LNICST, vol. 161, pp. 50–57. Springer, Cham (2016). https://doi.org/10.1007/978-3-319-29060-7_9
29. Navarro, J., Marchena, E., Alcalde, C., Ruiz, G., Llorens, I., Aguilar, M.: Improving attention behaviour in primary and secondary school children with a computer assisted instruction procedure. Int. J. Psychol. **38**(6), 359–365 (2003)
30. Fontana, E., Gregorio, R., Colussi, E.L., De Marchi, A.C.B.: Trainbrain: a serious game for attention training. CEP 99052, 900 (2017)
31. Green, C.S., Bavelier, D.: Action video game modifies visual selective attention. Nature **423** (6939), 534 (2003)
32. Green, C.S., Bavelier, D.: Effect of action video games on the spatial distribution of visuospatial attention. J. Exp. Psychol. Hum. Percept. Perform. **32**(6), 1465 (2006)
33. El-Nasr, M.S., Yan, S.: Visual attention in 3d video games. In: Proceedings of the 2006 ACM SIGCHI International Conference on Advances in Computer Entertainment Technology, p. 22. ACM (2006)
34. Dye, M.W., Bavelier, D.: Playing video games enhances visual attention in children. J. Vis. **4**(11), 40 (2004)
35. Ricci, K.E.: The use of computer-based videogames in knowledge acquisition and retention. J. Interact. Instr. Dev. **7**(1), 17–22 (1994)
36. Lee, M., Faber, R.J.: Effects of product placement in on-line games on brand memory: a perspective of the limited-capacity model of attention. J. Advert. **36**(4), 75–90 (2007)
37. Song, K., Lee, S., Pyun, S.-B., Kim, L.: Comparative study of tangible tabletop and computer-based training interfaces for cognitive rehabilitation. In: Antona, M., Stephanidis, C. (eds.) UAHCI 2016. LNCS, vol. 9739, pp. 414–424. Springer, Cham (2016). https://doi.org/10.1007/978-3-319-40238-3_40
38. Trang Ho, A.S.: Tatoeba: open collaborative multilingual "sentence dictionary". https://tatoeba.org. Accessed 16 Jan 2017
39. Subramaniam, S., Aggarwal, P., Dasgupta, G.B., Paradkar, A.: Cobots-a cognitivemulti-bot conversational framework for technical support. In: Proceedings of the 17th International Conference on Autonomous Agents and Multiagent Systems, International Foundation for Autonomous Agents and Multiagent Systems, pp. 597–604 (2018)
40. Csikszentmihalyi, M.: Toward a psychology of optimal experience. Flow and the Foundations of Positive Psychology, pp. 209–226. Springer, Dordrecht (2014). https://doi.org/10.1007/978-94-017-9088-8_14
41. Perttula, A., Kiili, K., Lindstedt, A., Tuomi, P.: Flow experience in game based learning–a systematic literature review. Int. J. Serious Games **4**(1), 57–72 (2017)
42. Peddycord-Liu, Z., Cody, C., Kessler, S., Barnes, T., Lynch, C.F., Rutherford, T.: Using serious game analytics to inform digital curricular sequencing: What math objective should students play next? In: Proceedings of the Annual Symposium on Computer-Human Interaction in Play, pp. 195–204. ACM (2017)
43. Georgiev, A., et al.: The RAGE advanced game technologies repository for supporting applied game development. In: Bottino, R., Jeuring, J., Veltkamp, Remco C. (eds.) GALA 2016. LNCS, vol. 10056, pp. 235–245. Springer, Cham (2016). https://doi.org/10.1007/978-3-319-50182-6_21

44. Bellotti, F., Kapralos, B., Lee, K., Moreno-Ger, P., Berta, R.: Assessment in and of serious games: an overview. Adv. Hum. Comput. Interact. **1**, 1–11 (2013)
45. Bellotti, F., Berta, R., De Gloria, A., Dùrsi, A., Fiore, V.: A serious game model for cultural heritage. J. Comput. Cult. Herit. (JOCCH) **5**(4), 17 (2012)
46. Carvalho, M.B., Bellotti, F., Berta, R., De Gloria, A., Gazzarata, G., Hu, J., Kickmeier-Rust, M.: A case study on service-oriented architecture for serious games. Entertain. Comput. **6**, 1–10 (2015)
47. Carmosino, I., Bellotti, F., Berta, R., De Gloria, A., Secco, N.: A game engine plug-in for efficient development of investigation mechanics in serious games. Entertain. Comput. **19**, 1–11 (2017)

How to Set the Game Characteristics, Design the Instructional Content and the Didactical Setting for a Serious Game for Health Prevention in the Workplace

Julia Rapp$^{(\boxtimes)}$, Julia Rose, Susanne Narciss, and Felix Kapp

Faculty of Psychology, Technische Universität Dresden, Dresden, Germany
julia.rapp@tu-dresden.de

Abstract. The game "simkult" is a serious game for health prevention in the workplace. The design process focused on three key aspects of serious games derived from the Input-Process-Outcome model of learning with games by Garris and Driskell. In order to introduce knowledge, skills and attitudes with regard to safety and health at the workplace we systematically developed (a) the instructional content, (b) the game characteristics and (c) the context of use, which defines how the game is used and how the debriefing can be realized. As a result, "simkult" is a multi-player simulation game for five to 20 persons which addresses work teams in small and middle sized companies. By putting each player in the position of a restaurant manager the complex interplay of important areas towards safety and health at work (e.g. work climate, leadership) are displayed. Two core aspects within the game are the non-player characters and critical incidents which represent quests for the players in the simulation. These were developed with regard to the target group's needs in order to create an engaging and effective serious game.

Keywords: Serious game · Health prevention · Learning

1 Introduction

Several reviews and meta-analysis show that serious games have a great potential to influence both the motivation and the knowledge acquisition of learners in a positive way [7, 8, 10, 11]. According to Garris and Driskell's [6] Input-Process-Outcome model learning with serious games is characterized as a process consisting of cyclical phases (for an adapted version see Fig. 1) in which the learner has to analyze the game (user judgement), act based on his analysis (user behavior) and receives feedback with regard to his actions (system feedback). How this process is happening depends on (A) the instructional content implemented in the game and (B) the specific game characteristics. These two input variables influence the game experience of the players and define what can be learned by playing the game. The game process is therefore influenced by the decision to teach a certain subject (e.g. math, health education) and the design of the game (e.g. single- vs. multiplayer). Garris and Driskell [6] furthermore point out that in order to successfully reach the learning outcomes (such as declarative

M. Gentile et al. (Eds.): GALA 2018, LNCS 11385, pp. 210–220, 2019.
https://doi.org/10.1007/978-3-030-11548-7_20

knowledge, skills) (C) a debriefing phase is crucial in order to ensure a transfer from the game context to the real world.

In a further development of the Input-Process-Outcome model Mattheiss et al. [12] point out that the players themselves determine to what extent they engage in the game process and show a certain behavior within the game.

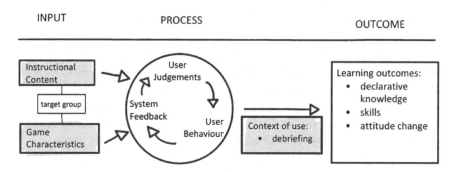

Fig. 1. An adapted version of the input-process-outcome model by Garris and Driskell [6]. Pointing out the three core aspects of the design of games: the instructional content, the game characteristics and the context of use have to match the target group's needs.

In this paper we present the design process of the serious game "simkult" which addresses health prevention in the workplace. Based on the above mentioned assumptions we thereby will focus on (A) the instructional content, (B) the game characteristics and (C) the context of use, which defines how and when the debriefing can be realized. The decisive influence of the player's characteristics (such as prior knowledge) emphasizes the need to integrate the target group in the design process and make decisions according to their needs.

2   The Project "Simkult" – Simulation Game Culture of Prevention

The serious game "simulation game culture of prevention", in short "simkult", addresses health prevention in the workplace. The overall aim is to communicate a holistic approach towards safety and health at work and by that foster a culture of prevention. The game shall raise awareness as to what extent daily work processes (e.g. concerning leadership) can influence the well-being, health and safety of working people and teach concrete activities to enhance the safety and health of one's company (e.g. short brake system). Scientific research shows that fostering a culture of prevention can buffer negative effects of work stressors on the physical, mental and social well-being of workers as in addition positive organizational outcomes like enhanced performance and work quality arise [1, 3, 9] and has been therefore a topic for interventions in this area (e.g. current campaign of the german statutory accident insurance, DGUV).

To develop the game "simkult" we conducted two studies which we will present here in short to give an overview. In a first study in form of semi-structured interviews we assessed the target group's characteristics (e.g. current working conditions, prior knowledge). In a second study in form of an online-survey with the target group we evaluated first design elements of the game (e.g. setting, non-player characters). In the next sections the results of the studies which contributed to the design of the instructional content, the game characteristics, and the context of use will be highlighted.

Table 1. Overview of the two studies executed during the developmental process of the serious game "simkult" to involve the target group.

Studies	Participants	Research topic
1. Semi-structured interviews	• N = 31 • 17 managers, 14 employees • 11 women, 20 men	Assessment of the target group: • current working conditions • prior knowledge and attitudes
2. Online-survey	• N = 114 (sometimes reduced N due to missing values) • 86 women, 28 men • 53 executive, 60 non-executive employees (missing value n = 1) • broad range of industries (e.g. services sector, public institutions, industry)	Evaluation of first design elements: • restaurant setting • non-player characters • critical incidents

3   Instructional Content

The german statutory accident insurance (DGUV) has identified the following areas of action in which interventions for health prevention in the workplace can be carried out: Leadership, participation of employees, communication, work climate, error culture and safety and health as a strategy [5]. These six areas will be addressed in the game "simkult". The aim of "simkult" is to reach the following three levels of learning goals in the six areas: First level learning goals address declarative knowledge, e.g. by introducing the concept of participation of employees in operational decision processes which will heighten their motivation and satisfaction at work. Second level learning goals aim at fostering skills such as knowledge about action alternatives for operational practice, e.g. by giving the player the possibility to actively try out different actions followed by feedback about the consequences. Third level learning goals consist of raising awareness and changing attitudes towards a positive understanding of health and safety promotion in the workplace, e.g. by giving arguments why these topics are important not only for the health of the employees but also for the company and the managers themselves.

Study 1 (see Table 1) was conducted to get to know information about the current working conditions and the prior knowledge and attitudes of the target group.

Current Working Conditions: We asked the participants to rate given statements for each of the six intervention areas presented above indicating how the person judges the situation in his/her current workplace. As an example in the area "leadership" the participants were asked to rate the following statement: "The executive manager considers health and safety to be important topics." The answers indicate how the interviewees rate the six areas at their workplace. A high number indicates satisfaction whereas a low number stands for safety harassment. The results for the six areas are displayed in Fig. 2. Afterwards we asked the person to elaborate how she/he got to her/his ratings naming incidents that substantiate his/her judgments. The combined results of these information indicate that though the persons judge the current situation in their workplace as substantial (with interpersonal differences), they also see possibilities of improvement. The game "simkult" hence could be of help to promote declarative knowledge, skills and attitude changes to encourage improvement processes concerning health prevention in the workplace.

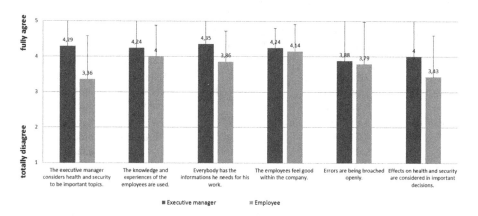

Fig. 2. Results of semi-structured interviews with executive managers (N = 17) and employees (N = 14): approval of the statement (indicated by a high value) means that their company is well prepared in the correspondent area (e.g. leadership).

Prior Knowledge and Attitudes: We analyzed the incidents that were mentioned to describe the participant's judgements of their current working conditions. Findings were f. ex. that "health" was often simply defined as the absence of disease. Just few people would link "culture of prevention" with aspects like "lively social climate" or "work-life balance". Five people couldn't derive any ideas about the term. Prevention at work was not seen as relevant to certain industries like IT-services.

Based on the results of the two studies and the theory driven structure containing the six areas of action mentioned above we formulated 14 main learning goals for the six areas. Thereby we covered up the three goal levels described above (see Table 2).

Concerning the example from the area "safety and health as a strategy" the findings from the interviews resulted in the learning goal "definition of health" which can be specified further into gaining a holistic understanding of health in sense of the definition of the WHO that describes health as "a state of complete physical, mental and social well-being" [14] – learning goal on the first level declarative knowledge. In addition, in this area the learning goal on the second level - fostering knowledge about action alternatives for operational practice contains knowledge about appropriate management approaches for workplace health promotion and possible actions in sense of behavior (e.g. relaxation or sport programs) or conditional (e.g. forms of work time and work breaks) prevention at work. To promote the third level learning goals – attitude change - the benefits of an effective culture of prevention are pointed out, as f. ex. financial benefits on the long run and a positive reputation of the company.

Table 2. Overview of the six areas of action addressed in "simkult" and correspondent 14 main learning goals exemplarily assigned to the three goal levels declarative knowledge, skills and attitude change.

Areas of action	Main learning goals	Declarative knowledge	Skills	Attitude change
Leadership	1 Managers as s role model	Social learning, Bandura	Reflection on leadership	Importance of own actions
	2 Health promoting leadership	Def. Presenteeism	Take care on one's health	Consequences on health, quality
Participation	3 Participation in decisions	Levels of participation	Use of instruments	Satisfied and productive employees
Communication	4 Annual one-on-one meeting	Content and aims	Procedure, preparation	Benefits, personal relationship
	5 Regular interchange, meetings	Principles team meetings	–	Quality of meeting decisive
	6 Appreciation of employees	Communication model	Possible actions, authenticity	Employees as "human beings"
Work climate	7 Facets of work climate	Def. work climate	–	–
	8 Relation to health/safety	–	–	Impact on health
	9 Actions to foster work climate	Possible actions	How to choose adequate actions	Awareness of risks and benefits

(continued)

Table 2. (*continued*)

Areas of action	Main learning goals	Declarative knowledge	Skills	Attitude change
Error culture	10 Errors as learning opportunity	Def. errors	Steps of error analysis	Working conditions as possible cause
	11 Mention errors openly	Aspects error culture	Create atmosphere of openness	Accident prevention and learning
Safety/health as strategy	12 Understanding of "health"	WHO definition "health"	–	Importance mental and social health
	13 Management systems	Approaches	Actions (behavior, conditions)	Return on prevention
	14 Good reputation as benefit	–	–	Recruitment skilled workers

4 Game Characteristics

The game characteristics determine how the players engage in the game process and what behavior they show within the game. The game "simkult" puts the player in the position of a restaurant manager responsible for the well-being of the employees and the economic success of their restaurant.

4.1 Multi-player

The game "simkult" is designed as a multi-player for work teams of five to 20 people. This design decision is based on one of the main aims of "simkult": to raise awareness of managers as well as their employees for health prevention and to initiate an attitude change. Playing the game in one's work team can initiate attitude changes as social psychology points out that group processes are helpful to change attitudes and behaviors and are of particular importance when companies want to instigate change processes [4]. Furthermore, the semi-structured interviews of study 1 revealed that 77% of the sample could imagine to play with coworkers whereas only 26% could imagine to play alone or against the computer.

Within the game, players have various ways of interacting with each other – resulting in both cooperation and concurrence. As manager of their restaurant they compete with respect to employees and clients on the job market and at the same time they can cooperate by introducing interventions for their workers together (e.g. joined time-management trainings). Baranauskas et al. [2] point out that cooperation and concurrence are both important for the game experience and to raise the motivation to play the game and to subsequently deal with the instructional content. In line with that assumption is the empirical finding that success in learning takes place especially when the players can work together in groups [15].

4.2 Simulation

In particular simulation games have potential when it comes to communicate complex topics. "Simkult" faces such a complex topic: The game needs to illustrate the complex interplay of the six areas decisive for the own prevention culture and the consequences that derive with regard to health and safety at work. We decided to design "simkult" as a simulation game that contains the economic consequences of healthy workers and displays the interdependences between the six areas addressed in the game (e.g. leadership) and the wellbeing of the employees. Every player in "simkult" leads his own restaurant in the position of an executive manager. The higher goal of the game is to manage the restaurant successfully – which means not only to have economic success but also take care that the employees are healthy and satisfied and that safe working conditions are established (e.g. by participation of employees in decisions [13]). The players can choose between different actions to enhance the well-being and health of their employees (e.g. participation of employees in decisions) while financial resources and time are restricted. So the employees can take over the perspective of the executive manager and try out different strategies in the six relevant areas addressed within the game and experience which consequences derive.

4.3 Game Setting and Game Phases

In the introductory phase of the game the players can design their restaurant in line with their own preferences. They can choose a name, the type of restaurant (f. ex. a café or a pizzeria) and place it on a map. The restaurant as game setting was evaluated in study 2 which was conducted to evaluate first design elements (for an overview see Table 1). Results show that the majority of the participants could imagine to play in the setting of a restaurant (21 = "in any case", 38 = "rather yes", 30 = "maybe", 18 "rather no", 6 = "on no account"). We furthermore asked them to describe which tasks have to be carried out in order to manage a restaurant and the results indicate that the participants have a sufficient knowledge of managing a restaurant so that we opted for that setting.

After the introductory phase the game follows an iterative cycle. Each cycle consists of four phases that give the players further possibilities to actively engage in the learning process. In the first phase the players plan the current calendar week, f. ex. personnel planning. In the second phase they play a "minigame on time" where daily working routine is displayed in the game and money is earned. In the third phase a so called "critical incident" takes place (e.g. a working tool breaks down) and the players have to react to it. In the fourth phase of the game the players get feedback as to their actions and can reflect on the consequences (e.g. satisfaction of employees, economic success).

4.4   Non-player Characters – the Employees in the Game

All players have to put together their working teams within the game. They have to hire employees at the beginning and adapt their leadership according to the needs of their virtual staff. The design of non-player characters that are perceived as authentic to the players is a critical success factor in designing an engaging educational game. In study 2 the participants were asked to rate eight developed non-player characters with regard to their authenticity (e.g. Fig. 3).

The participants were asked to rate how realistic, interesting and unforeseeable they perceive the characters to be (5-point scale; e.g. 1 – "boring", 5 – "very interesting"). Beside the name and facts about their salary, productivity and satisfaction with their job further information about the character was delivered. This additional information allows addressing certain topics (e.g. "two children" - combining work and family life) and contributes to the narrative of the game. All characters were rated as rather authentic. The character shown in Fig. 3 was assessed as "realistic" (M = 4.25, SD = 0.80, n = 112), more or less "interesting" (M = 3.63, SD = 0.88, n = 112) and rather less "unforeseeable" (M = 2.41, SD = 0.88, n = 112). The results give us information on how further authentic characters can be designed.

Fig. 3. One of the characters that can be employed in one's restaurant in the game "simkult".

4.5   Critical Incidents

"Critical incidents" are used in the game to actively engage the learners in the learning process and to demonstrate the complexity of certain decisions when it comes to topics concerning health prevention in the workplace, such as considering the cost-value ratio. Critical incidents pop up during the game play and challenge the player to react to them in an appropriate manner. For an illustration, the wording of one such incident description is:

"The cooker in your restaurant has just broken down. You have to purchase a new one. Therefore you have to find out which model fulfills the requirements you need.

The cooks work with the cooker every day. Each day you need to take the decision costs you money because in that time you cannot serve your clients warm dishes."

Subsequently, the players have to decide how they can solve the problem and act on the problem. They can buy the same cooker again, choose a new model or let their employees participate in the decision to a differing degree (e.g. ask them which model they would prefer).

The critical incidents should be authentic and challenging in order to create game engagement in the players. Within study 2 participants were asked to rate ten critical incidents as to how realistic, interesting and unforeseeable they perceive them to be (5-point scale; e.g. 1 – "boring", 5 – "very interesting"). All critical incidents were rated as authentic, differing slightly to the degree of the rating of the incidents as "unforeseeable". The incident "cooker broke" illustrated above was rated as highly "realistic" (M = 4.48, SD = 0.90, n = 58), "interesting" (M = 3.84, SD = 1.25, n = 56) and rather not "unforeseeable" (M = 2.96, SD = 1.41, n = 56). Authentic and challenging critical incidents were embedded in the game.

5   Context of Use

In order to introduce knowledge, skills and initiate an attitude change with respect to health and safety the game must be played at work. It is therefore crucial to consider the future utilization scenario while designing the game. That contains aspects like when and under what condition the game will be played as well as how the debriefing can be realized in order to secure transfer.

Managers and employees are restricted to working schedules. The game must therefore allow players to choose when and how to play it within a certain time window. Study 2 indicates that the target group would like to play the game either one to two times per week or per month and invest up to 30 min each time. On that basis "simkult" is designed to be played during 10 weeks for around 30 min each week.

Empirical evidence shows that success in learning takes place especially when the game is embedded into a didactical concept [11, 15]. The so called debriefing after the game play illustrated in the Input-Process-Outcome model [6] is realized with additional information material and central questions which can be used in team meetings and pick up aspects of the game "simkult" relevant to the team's real work setting. As such the actual prevention culture of one's company can be discussed and improved collectively.

6   Conclusion

One approach to design serious games is to systematically develop (A) the instructional content, (B) the game characteristics and (C) the context of use, which defines how the game is used and when the debriefing can be realized. In order to create a good serious game the involvement of the target group is crucial. Along the developmental process of the game "simkult" we conducted two studies to assess characteristics of the target group (such as prior knowledge, attitudes) and to evaluate first design elements (such as non-player characters, critical incidents). The results informed the game design with regard to the instructional content and give concrete information on how interesting, authentic or challenging the target group judges first concrete design elements of the game "simkult".

Forthcoming experimental evaluation with a digital prototype will investigate to what extent the design of (A) the instructional content and (B) the game characteristics lead to player's engagement, game experience and effective learning. We therefore will compare a game playing group to a control group studying a text about the topic. Engagement in learning will be measured using a questionnaire that gathers game experience. The participants will be asked to draw a mind map on the topic "safety and health in the workplace" before and after the experimental trial to asses if declarative learning took place and to check for learned relations between variables (e.g. connection between satisfaction and productivity). We will finally also check for (C) how the additional information material can initiate debriefing processes.

Acknowledgements. This research was supported by the german statutory accident insurance (Deutsche Gesetzliche Unfallversicherung e.V., DGUV). The authors are responsible of the content of this contribution.

References

1. Bakker, A.B., Demerouti, E.: The job demands-resources model: state of the art. J. Manag. Psychol. **22**(3), 309–328 (2007)
2. Baranauskas, M., Neto, N., Borges, M.: Learning at work through a multi-user synchronous simulation game. In: Proceedings of the PEG 1999 Conference, Exeter, UK, pp. 137–144. University of Exeter, Exeter (1999)
3. Doi, Y.: An epidemiologic review on occupational sleep research among Japanese workers. Ind. Health **43**, 3–10 (2005)
4. Doppler, K., Lauterburg, C.: Change Management – den Unternehmenswandel gestalten. Campus Verlag, Frankfurt, New York (2014)
5. Ehnes, H., Eggert, B., Hundeloh, H., Portuné, R., Prüße, H.M., Bollmann, U. et al.: Fachkonzept für die nächste gemeinsame Präventionskampagne der DGUV und ihrer Mitglieder (2015). https://www.dguv.de/medien/inhalt/praevention/kampagnen/praev_kampagnen/ausblick/fachkonzept.pdf
6. Garris, R., Driskell, J.E.: Games, motivation, and learning: a research and practice model. Simul. Gaming **33**(4), 441–467 (2002)
7. Giessen, H.W.: Serious games effects: an overview. Procedia-Soc. Behav. Sci. **174**, 2240–2244 (2015)
8. Girard, C., Ecalle, J., Magnan, A.: Serious games as new educational tools: how effective are they? A meta-analysis of recent studies. J. Comput. Assist. Learn. **29**(3), 207–219 (2013)
9. Halbesleben, J.R.B., Buckley, M.R.: Burnout in organizational life. J. Manag. **30**(6), 859–879 (2004)
10. Ke, F.: A qualitative meta-analysis of computer games as learning tools. In: Ferdig, R.E. (ed.) Handbook of Research on Effective Electronic Gaming in Education, pp. 1–32. IGI Global, Hershey (2009)

11. Kerres, M., Bormann, M., Vervenne, M.: Didaktische Konzeption von Serious Games: Zur Verknüpfung von Spiel- und Lernangeboten. MedienPädagogik. Zeitschrift für Theorie und Praxis der Medienbildung (2009)

12. Mattheiss, E., Kickmeier-Rust, M.D., Steiner, C.M., Albert, D.: Motivation in game-based learning: it's more than flow. In: Schwill, A., Apostolopoulos, N. (eds.) Lernen im Digitalen Zeitalter – Workshop-Band Dokumentation der Pre-conference zur DeLFI 2009 – Die 7. E-Learning Fachtagung Informatik der Gesellschaft für Informatik e.V. (2009)

13. Wagner, J.A.: Participation's effects on performance and satisfaction: a reconsideration of research evidence. Acad. Manag. Rev. 19(2), 312–330 (1994)

14. World Health Organisation: Preamble to the Constitution of WHO as adopted by the International Health Conference 1946 entered into force on 7 April 1948 (1948)

15. Wouters, P., van Nimwegen, C., van Oostendorp, H., van der Spek, E.D.: A meta-analysis of the cognitive and motivational effects of serious games. J. Educ. Psychol. 105(2), 249–265 (2013)

Co-created Design of a Serious Game Investigation into Developer-Centred Security

Manuel Maarek[1]([⊠]) , Sandy Louchart[2], Léon McGregor[1] ,
and Ross McMenemy[2]

[1] Heriot-Watt University, Edinburgh, UK
{M.Maarek,L.McGregor}@hw.ac.uk
[2] Glasgow School of Art, Glasgow, UK
S.Louchart@gsa.ac.uk, R.McMenemyl@student.gsa.ac.uk

Abstract. The cyber security context requires to better understand how developers write (in)secure code and to assist them in their software developments. We have developed a secure coding experiment and serious game intervention. In this paper, we report on the design of a serious game to investigate developer-centred security. We used a combination of approaches to shape discussions and support the serious game co-creation.

Keywords: Serious game · Serious game design · Cyber security ·
Software security · Developer-centred security

1 Introduction

Cyber security is a growing concern in a world of ever-increasing connectivity. Our activities and lives depend on software systems that are vulnerable as recent attacks have shown (e.g. impact on the UK health service of the WannaCry worldwide cyberattack). This results in a need to raise the awareness of software security issues and to train the developers of software systems, whether they are professionals or hobbyists.

As part of a project funded by the Research Institute in Science of Cyber Security (RISCS) in association with the National Cyber Security Centre (NCSC) and the EPSRC, we started to investigate how serious games could impact developer-centred security. In this paper, we report on the co-design of a serious game for code security. We used different serious game approaches to shape the discussions and the exploration for a serious game intervention. We focus on the steps we took to facilitate dialogue and the type of support we put in place in order to design a solution that fits the purpose of the experimentation. We present the process we implemented and provide a contribution to other serious game designers as to how a number of different methodologies can be used in order to provide an ad-hoc solution to a domain problem.

Plan. In Sect. 2, we give the background and motivation for the overall cyber security research project. Sections 3 and 4 focus on the serious game design and implementation. In Sect. 5, we present the experimental setting surrounding the serious game. Finally, Sect. 6 concludes and draws future perspectives of this work.

© Springer Nature Switzerland AG 2019
M. Gentile et al. (Eds.): GALA 2018, LNCS 11385, pp. 221–231, 2019.
https://doi.org/10.1007/978-3-030-11548-7_21

2 Serious Game Investigation into Developer-Centred Security

While software systems become more ubiquitous and we are increasingly reliant on their use in our everyday lives, accessibility of mobile and cloud programming platforms makes software development and deployment more democratically available. This combination creates security challenges as software code could be deployed without having the security vetting or level of scrutiny that the end-users expect. The project in which this work takes place, proposes to investigate how serious game could play a role in evaluating and training the security skills of *the masses* of software developers. This project is part of the RISCS community for *developer-centred security* research. In our work, we focus particularly on serious games for secure software development and aim at identifying activities that could effectively persuade developers to improve their cyber security skills and increase the security of their code.

Background. A recent study has explored the software development security skills of GitHub users [1]. In this online experiment, the participants were invited to undertake three secure programming exercises in Python, their programming was then evaluated with regards to security properties. The experiment revealed that the self-reported security knowledge level or the professional or student status of the participants was not statistically related to the security grading of their programming solutions.

Serious Game Intervention Project. We chose to build our investigation as an extension to this base study, giving us some grounds to compare our results. We framed the experiment as an embedding of the programming exercises of the base study inside a game. The base study [1] evaluated the participants' ability to write secure code using three Python script tasks (URL Shortener, Credential Storage and String Encryption). A secure solution would for instance involve using a strong encryption algorithm or would prevent code injection. We complemented these exercises with three additions which have no obvious security focus (Image Analysis, Time Tool and Search & Replace), with the intention to compare the specific impact gamification has on security.

The base study [1] has found that developers often program insecure solutions regardless of their background. Developers will often have knowledge of security related concepts but fail to implement them or use an outdated or insecure standard. A game could be used to remind and raise awareness of security, while not necessarily instruct on the concepts or methods. As our primary purpose is to evaluate developers' security, the game intervention should replicate the base study with a control group. The game should motivate players to perform the programming tasks well. The key developer-centred security issues that the game could target are therefore: lack of awareness, outdated knowledge of standards, lack of experience, motivation or reasoning to implement proper security. To target these issues, the game could put the following potential processes in use: presenting an in-game context and motivation to build secure solutions, providing information on secure standards, challenging players with the effects of insecure solutions while maintaining neutrality to meet the evaluation aim.

Related Research. Recent surveys of game-based cyber security training [2, 3] show a growing interest in designing games for security. In [4], the authors show the benefits of security exercises and competitions in cyber security training based on a survey of experiments. In [5], the authors used a game to study security decisions. Coding games such as *Code Hunt* are being adapted for secure coding [6], while secure coding competitions such as *Build It, Break It, Fix It* are organised as a *Catch The Flag* game [7]. Another coding game, *Code Defenders* [8], was primarily designed for crowed-sourcing purposes but also served in training [9]. In [10, 11], the authors advocate the use of dialectics and games for raising developers' security. Gamifications within software engineering has been studied and used [12], for example as a means to incite developers to remove compilers warning [13]. However our research aims at going beyond gamification, as other researchers also suggested in [14].

3   Design Methodology

To handle the complexity of cyber security and software programming, we chose to combine the LM-GM (Learning Mechanics – Game Mechanics) framework [15] with the Triadic Game design approach [16] to facilitate domain and serious game experts' discussions. The Triadic game design approach was initially used to explore the domain and range of potential intervention areas. The LM-GM framework was used to support the concrete definition of meaningful gameplay loops when determining the meaning of the intervention and the exact nature of the learning outcomes and gameplay experience. This section details how we used these approaches for the game co-creation.

3.1   Reflection on the Triadic Game Design Approach

The Triadic game design [16] is an approach to designing serious games through balancing three constituent parts. The worlds of; *Reality*, *Meaning* and *Play* are put forward as these parts and reflect balancing between serious aspects and gameplay. *Reality* describes the context behind the game and rely heavily on the domain expert to map out potential issues and problems within the target domain, often demanding some real-world features be reflected in the game. Secondly, *Meaning* is the phase of the design that focuses on exploring one or several intervention areas and lead to the identification of clearly intended outcomes for the player. intended outcomes of the game. We used the LM-GM framework in order to establish a clear link between learning and gameplay outcomes during this phase of the design. Finally, *Play* is a measure of interaction and fun within the game and represents the phase of the design when the game is actually designed according to pedagogies in line with the intervention's learning outcomes. Gameplay loops are created to match and map onto identified pedagogies and design the game aspects of the intervention. Balancing theses aspects can help a game to execute on its intended outcome, while being both believable and enjoyable to play. In our context, the *Reality* aspect of the game design framework had already been explored through the base study [1] and overseen by the cyber security co-creator of the game. As such, this phase of the design had already been completed and discussions focused on establishing a dialogue between serious games and cyber security researchers on the precise nature and meaning of the intervention.

Table 1. Learning verbs associated with the development of the serious game intervention

Verb	Gameplay mechanic	Implementation	Task usage/motivation	
Instruct	Tutorial	Teach player the game	Context for tasks	A
Respond	Feedback	Provide feedback on a mistake	Give players contextual hints towards successful task completion	B
Act	Intervene	Allow players to react to situations where they lose control	Reflect methods of security prevention/response	C
Choose	Strategize	Task completion order enables gameplay strategy	Motivate players to complete task they perceive as impactful	D
Construct	Task embodiment	Players will be able to interact with objects that are analogous to a task's process	Provide an in-game context and motivation for why the task should be performed	E
Present	Text	Tasks related information displayed within the game	Show hints towards a secure task	F
Situate	Provide context	Have tasks completion affect the players abilities in game	Show how good and bad implementations of the task affect the game	G
Reward	Rewards	Give in-game rewards for good play and task performance	Motivate through extrinsic rewards	H

3.2   Exploring Meaning Through the LM-GM Framework

LM-GM [15] is a game analysis and design model that allows for game mechanics to be studied and discussed in parallel with learning mechanics. We chose it for its simplicity and focus on semantics. The model helps to relate a set of standardised learning mechanics to another set of standard game mechanics. It allows for designers to investigate how the mechanics interact and to ensure that a game is grounded from a pedagogical and entertainment standpoint. Finally, it allows the definition of contextualised Serious Game Mechanics (SGM) that bridge the blending of leaning outcomes and gameplay elements. In our context, we used the framework to determine the nature of learning outcomes, feeding into the *Meaning* part of the Triadic game design approach.

Learning Mechanics. Game verbs [17] are a method of mapping learning and game mechanics by quantifying player actions. Table 1 gives the verbs used and their implementation. The aim of this exercise is to identify verbs relevant to the domain and tasks to frame a range of possible interventions based on pre-determined learning outcomes. The list of verbs with their meaning has been compiled from established learning theories (e.g. Piaget, Bloom's revised Taxonomy etc.) [17]. We decided to focus on using verbs that add potential for a motivational as well as learning impact.

Game Mechanics. The LM-GM framework proposes a set of standardised game mechanics for use with analytics, drawn from the SCVNGR set [18]. There are however many other useful game mechanic resources available and, from a purely design perspective, this exercise served as a framing device for design discussions and engaging stakeholders from disparate disciplines to discuss the overall game approach. As such, any game mechanics set can be used for this stage of the process. We later designed the game through the use of game bricks [19]. Table 2 gives the game mechanics we chose.

Table 2. Game mechanics of the game

Game mechanic	Description	
Selecting collecting	The player scores and collects points based on their performance	1
Tokens	Players earn tokens to track their task progression and show the task-to-game mechanical interaction	2
Infinite gameplay	The game is designed to infinitely loop replaying a level, in order to facilitate hi-score chasing and illustrate player progression	3
Strategy	Players can pick and choose how they want to play the game by utilizing and upgrading certain mechanics over others	4
Resource management	Player actions have associated resources that must be balanced to make effective use of all mechanics	5
Eliminate	The game presents security threats that must be eliminated to perform	6
Time pressure	The main level has a set number of waves, which appear at certain time intervals	7
Meta-game	The tasks are integrated within the game through a meta element that links an out of game mechanism to the game	8
Tutorials	The gameplay is taught through an instructional tutorial	9
Competitions	A fake leader board and core systems encourage hi-score chasing and game replaying	10
Rewards penalty	Players are rewarded based on their in-game and task performances	11

LM-GM Relationships. Figure 1 displays the LM-GM diagram which describes how each set of mechanics relates to the game flow. It describes the specific game mechanics varying with game progression and how they relate to the LM and GM and the coverage of learning outcomes within the overall serious game approach. We see that both the macro and meta gameplay loops have roughly equal number of mechanics. Having sufficient mechanics relating to the tasks helps integrate task performance into the game.

3.3 Conceptualising Play Through Gameplay Loops

We can restructure the gameplay loops [20] to also take LM-GM into account, see Fig. 2. This should help illustrate what mechanics are most important to the serious game intervention and how game mechanics are linked to the learning mechanics. Here we can see that strategizing is an important aspect for the macro gameplay loop (left diagram of Fig. 2), which is completely overlooked in the game map (Fig. 1).

If a new threat was to be added, it must be highly relevant to the security concerns, such as to target Act (C) and Situate (H). In addition, it should have certain strategies and resources needed to eliminate it. Security relevance is important to the loop, mainly through Construct (E) which presents text information. However, this game is intentionally limited to allow for a control group. If the game was to be a learning tool, this element could be strengthened through increased presence and specificity.

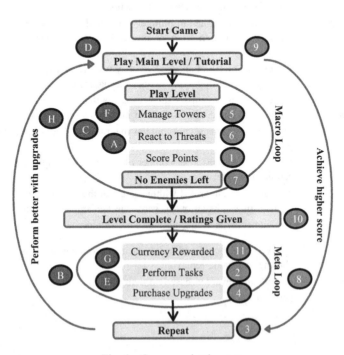

Fig. 1. Game mechanics map

The goal of having players complete programming tasks relies on the idea of a meta-game. In this context, the meta-game takes on two of its common meanings: having external elements (the tasks) affect the game state and enabling strategic trends to develop by allowing player to choose what task to perform. To strengthen the tasks, the Construct (E) learning mechanics could increase the immersive and motivational factors to complete tasks. This would be by having highly relevant and contextual upgrades presented. Another method would be to increase the play mechanics of the meta-game by adding game elements to the tasks or more strategic depth to the upgrades.

The map and loops show that an upgrade could be used to strengthen motivation through a meta loop element – as all in-game mechanics strengthen only macro or micro abilities. An upgrade that targets either the currency or task completion tokens could support the motivational factors provided by Reward (G) in a virtuous cycle, by motivating players to increase their own motivational incentives.

Finally, adding threats can be expanded to consider how its relevant upgrades are developed. In this case, mechanics can be either security or non-security relevant, provided that its integration into the game share strong relations with the corresponding tasks. The upgrade must enable or strengthen a mechanic, but also have a clear comparative strength to other upgrades. These enable the strategic game mechanic, but also the meta-game strategy of choosing the strongest upgrades to purchase. Weak upgrades need to exist to enable the meta-game and players discovering dominant strategies.

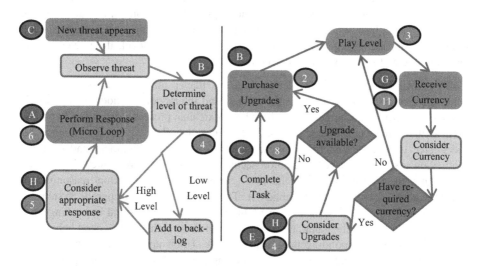

Fig. 2. Macro loop (left) and Micro loop (right). Dark green represents in-game mechanics while light green represents an out-game cognitive response. (Color figure online)

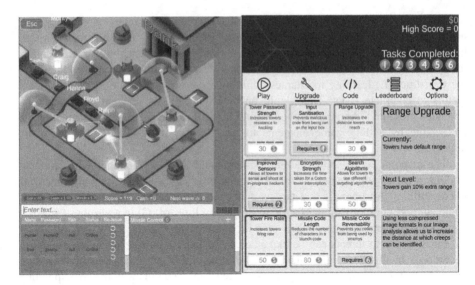

Fig. 3. The game showing standard gameplay (left) and the upgrade system for the game (right)

4 Game Implementation

The games basic genre is that of a *Tower Defence*, sub-genre of strategy games and well known for being approachable and having players improve their abilities over time. The player manages static defences and traps to defend from an invading enemy. The game takes place in a situation where the player is defending a bank from cars and trucks that are attempting to rob it. Before playing the next level, the player spends bank currencies to improve the security systems.

Context and Integration. In order to situate a player for tasks performance, core game mechanics and tasks share some context and interaction methods. Game text is written primarily to strengthen these shared contexts than present a narrative. Typing is used as the main game interaction method to draw parallels with programming. All tasks have in game counterparts, presenting reasons for development and example motivations. Similarly, several common security concerns are represented through the effects they have on the game mechanics – giving players a contextual reasoning for developing tasks with a security mind-set. The game features an upgrade system, in which several gameplay elements can be upgraded – improving and expanding on a player's ability to play the game. However, each of these elements is locked behind the completion of a corresponding programming task. Upon upgrading, the player's in-game abilities are noticeably improved – allowing them to score higher and play better. The motivational drive to continue to achieve higher scores and explore new gameplay options is directed into the completion of tasks.

Gameplay Mechanics. Mechanics follow similar structure, interaction methods and appearance, such that a player can quickly learn and understand a new mechanics after being introduced to a related one. The player is working to defend the bank from

Creeps of several kind that are trying to reach it. The creeps have to travel along a winding road to reach the bank. Under the players control are serval *Towers* which will damage and destroy the creeps by shooting them. Between levels the player is able to improve their in-game abilities through an upgrade system, which increases the effectiveness of the towers or increases defences to a threat. Table 3 gives the four kinds of towers of the game and their relations with the programming tasks and motivations.

Table 3. Table relating the towers to tasks and task motivations.

Tower	Player interaction blocks	Task integration	Integration mechanics	Task completion motivation
Standard	Write, Match, Select, Manage	Credential Shortener, Time Tool, Search & Replace, Image Analysis	Creep hacking and password resetting	To decrease how often the player has to manage the tower
Communication	Select, Create, Manage	String Encryption	Encryption laser communication	To decrease how often the player has to manage the tower
Laser	Write, Match, Select	Credential Storage	SQL codes having adverse effects	To allow player to select tanks without having to weigh the pros and cons of entering SQL
Missile	Write, Match, Select, Shoot	URL Shortener	Generating codes and shorten them	To shorten the time taken to write codes To prevent the code entering time from being wasted

Game Heuristics. While a tutorial is in place, the layouts of the game elements instruct players how to play [21]. Directional heuristics help direct a player to specific elements: the player needs to read potentially moving words and write them into a text box. Figure 3 shows the game being played, and the upgrade system. Positional heuristics give the player feedback: for example, a bar shows progress when a tower is being hacked.

5 Design of the Experiment

Our choice has been for an online experiment. The experimental platform consists of a Web-browser extension, the game, a Web-API server and an online questionnaire. Participants are invited to log into the GitHub website and install the extension which guides them through the experiment and provides a programming environment for the tasks. We chose to base the interface on the GitHub website as it is a natural developers' codebase. Participants can follow the tutorial to familiarise themselves with the game. Within the game, participants would choose to take on the programming tasks. Completing an individual task activates the corresponding upgrade. After playing the game the participants are invited to fill out an online questionnaire that combines the questionnaire used by the base study [1] with game-related questions inspired by [22]. A Web-API server performs software tests on the participant solutions to the programming tasks and collects gameplay data for analysis. The platform includes a no-game mode to be able to replicate the base study with a control group. After an early pilot of the experiment we improved and explained better to the participants the flow between the game and the programming environment. We are in the process of inviting participants for the experiment, so we cannot report results at this stage.

6 Conclusion

We have presented the combination of serious game design approaches we used in the co-creation of a serious game to investigate developer-centred security. We have also described the mechanics and gameplay loops of the serious game we have developed and how we integrated the programming tasks within the game. We have given an overview of the experimental platform which we have built for this ongoing experiment. This work is an initial step which shows the potential that serious game for software engineering and secure coding could offer to assist and engage developers with a specific concern such as cyber security.

References

1. Acar, Y., Stransky, C., Wermke, D., Mazurek, M.L., Fahl, S.: Security developer studies with GitHub users: exploring a convenience sample. In: Symposium on Usable Privacy and Security (SOUPS) (2017)
2. Tioh, J.N., Mina, M., Jacobson, D.W.: Cyber security training a survey of serious games in cyber security. In: IEEE Frontiers in Education Conference (FIE), pp. 1–5 (2017). https://doi.org/10.1109/FIE.2017.8190712
3. Hendrix, M., Al-Sherbaz, A., Bloom, V.: Game based cyber security training: are serious games suitable for cyber security training? Int. J. Serious Games 3, 53–61 (2016)
4. Sommestad, T., Hallberg, J.: Cyber security exercises and competitions as a platform for cyber security experiments. In: Jøsang, A., Carlsson, B. (eds.) NordSec 2012. LNCS, vol. 7617, pp. 47–60. Springer, Heidelberg (2012). https://doi.org/10.1007/978-3-642-34210-3_4
5. Frey, S., Rashid, A., Anthonysamy, P., Pinto-Albuquerque, M., Naqvi, S.A.: The good, the bad and the ugly: a study of security decisions in a cyber-physical systems game. IEEE Trans. Softw. Eng. (2018). https://doi.org/10.1109/TSE.2017.2782813

6. Xie, T., Bishop, J., Tillmann, N., de Halleux, J.: Gamifying software security education and training via secure coding duels in code hunt. In: Symposium and Bootcamp on the Science of Security, pp. 26:1–26:2. ACM (2015). https://doi.org/10.1145/2746194.2746220

7. Ruef, A., Hicks, M., Parker, J., Levin, D., Mazurek, M.L., Mardziel, P.: Build it, break it, fix it: contesting secure development. In: ACM SIGSAC Conference on Computer and Communications Security, pp. 690–703 (2016). https://doi.org/10.1145/2976749.2978382

8. Rojas, J.M., White, T.D., Clegg, B.S., Fraser, G.: Code defenders: crowdsourcing effective tests and subtle mutants with a mutation testing game. In: International Conference on Software Engineering, pp. 677–688. IEEE (2017). https://doi.org/10.1109/ICSE.2017.68

9. Rojas, J.M., Fraser, G.: Code defenders: a mutation testing game. In: International Conference on Software Testing, Verification and Validation Workshops (ICSTW), pp. 162–167 (2016). https://doi.org/10.1109/ICSTW.2016.43

10. Weir, C., Rashid, A., Noble, J.: Reaching the masses: a new subdiscipline of app programmer education. In: ACM SIGSOFT International Symposium on Foundations of Software Engineering, pp. 936–939 (2016). https://doi.org/10.1145/2950290.2983981

11. Weir, C., Rashid, A., Noble, J.: I'd like to have an argument, please : using dialectic for effective app security. In: European Workshop on Usable Security (EuroUSEC) (2017)

12. Pedreira, O., García, F., Brisaboa, N., Piattini, M.: Gamification in software engineering – a systematic mapping. Inf. Softw. Technol. **57**, 157–168 (2015). https://doi.org/10.1016/j.infsof.2014.08.007

13. Arai, S., Sakamoto, K., Washizaki, H., Fukazawa, Y.: A gamified tool for motivating developers to remove warnings of bug pattern tools. In: International Workshop on Empirical Software Engineering in Practice, pp. 37–42. IEEE (2014). https://doi.org/10.1109/IWESEP.2014.17

14. Barik, T., Murphy-Hill, E., Zimmermann, T.: A perspective on blending programming environments and games: Beyond points, badges, and leaderboards. In: IEEE Symposium on Visual Languages and Human-Centric Computing (VL/HCC), pp. 134–142 (2016). https://doi.org/10.1109/VLHCC.2016.7739676

15. Lim, T., et al.: Serious game mechanics, workshop on the ludo-pedagogical mechanism. In: De Gloria, A. (ed.) GALA 2014. LNCS, vol. 9221, pp. 174–183. Springer, Cham (2015). https://doi.org/10.1007/978-3-319-22960-7_17

16. Harteveld, C.: Triadic Game Design: Balancing Reality, Meaning and Play. Springer, London (2011). https://doi.org/10.1007/978-1-84996-157-8

17. Arnab, S., et al.: Mapping learning and game mechanics for serious games analysis. Br. J. Educ. Technol. **46**, 391–411 (2014)

18. Schonfeld, E.: SCVNGR's Secret Game Mechanics Playdeck (2010). http://social.techcrunch.com/2010/08/25/scvngr-game-mechanics/

19. Djaouti, D., Alvarez, J., Jessel, J.-P., Methel, G., Molinier, P.: A gameplay definition through videogame classification. Int. J. Comput. Games Technol. **2008**, 4:1–4:7 (2008). https://doi.org/10.1155/2008/470350

20. Guardiola, E.: The gameplay loop: a player activity model for game design and analysis. In: ACM International Conference on Advances in Computer Entertainment Technology (2016). https://doi.org/10.1145/3001773.3001791

21. Fullerton, T.: Game Design Workshop: A Playcentric Approach to Creating Innovative Games, 3rd edn. A K Peters/CRC Press, Natick (2014)

22. IJsselsteijn, W.A., de Kort, Y.A.W., Poels, K.: The Game Experience Questionnaire. Technische Universiteit Eindhoven, European Community - New and Emerging Science and Technology (NEST) Programme (2013)

Conceptual Factors for the Design of Serious Games

Christina Tsita[✉] and Maya Satratzemi

Department of Applied Informatics,
University of Macedonia, Thessaloniki, Greece
{c.tsita,maya}@uom.edu.gr

Abstract. Serious Games (SGs) are widely used in a variety of fields, because they have been shown to effectively facilitate learning in an engaging and entertaining manner. In recent years, there is discussion on how valid evidence of SGs efficiency can be increased, in order to further promote their use. Thus, numerous SG design and evaluation frameworks have been introduced, many of which have proved useful for SGs developing teams. Despite this, however, for novice designers, this vast array can be daunting. The aim of the present paper is to combine well-known frameworks and extract the conceptual factors that need to be considered when designing an SG. Having in mind that the proposed aspects are not in their essence independent, a classification of these aspects is presented, along with suggestions regarding their use and the dependencies among them. Although the various frameworks might have many common factors, there are some that highlight specific aspects of a particular factor. For instance, those frameworks that apart from the descriptive factors provide aspects regarding application, measurement, and assessment.

Keywords: Serious Games · Framework · Conceptual design

1 Introduction

In the last few decades, many design frameworks have been introduced as tools within the research community for the development and implementation of Serious Games (SGs). At the same time, the latest discussions regarding SGs focus on increasing their effectiveness. The intention of this study is to understand, on the one hand, the existing frameworks, and on the other, the factors that need to be taken into consideration in SG design that reinforce efficiency, implementation, and evaluation. Some frameworks provide generic guidelines on how to design an effective SG [1, 2], while others present processes and best practices on how to apply learning and gaming theories and methods to the gameplay [3–6]. A few models provide some relatively distinct factors for consideration, while others offer extensive schemas on how these elements interact with each other. Concepts regarding learning (e.g. target group, learning styles, curriculum, intended learning outcomes, learning strategies, etc.), entertainment (e.g. user interface, aesthetics, music, etc.), and gaming (e.g. game mechanics: rules, levels, game goals, etc.) are connected in order to formulate a conceptual scheme of how these concepts work together in game design [7, 8]. Such frameworks can inspire researchers

© Springer Nature Switzerland AG 2019
M. Gentile et al. (Eds.): GALA 2018, LNCS 11385, pp. 232–241, 2019.
https://doi.org/10.1007/978-3-030-11548-7_22

that want to develop SGs intended for different use cases. It should be pointed out that following a framework can be very useful for a team, which may lack a deep understanding of learning theories and/or game mechanisms, as it secures a certain level of efficiency for the creation of the SG. However, the selection of the most appropriate model for a particular case may be a difficult task, especially for someone who is new in the field. Subsequently, the aim of this study is to provide an overview on existing frameworks by synthesizing their key conceptual factors.

Taking into account the fact that the proposed aspects are basically not independent, the classification presented (as derived from the frameworks under review) includes the dependencies among them, as well as suggestions regarding their use, which can act as a tool for decision-making support during the early phases of game design. One of the main aspirations is to support the systematic and effective design of SGs, which can subsequently assist a systematic selection of metrics to evaluate the initial goals of the SG. The paper is structured as follows: after the introduction in section one, the SG design model concepts are presented in detail in section two, and the conclusions in section three.

2 SGs Design Model Concepts

The first step of the research was to identify the frameworks for the design of SGs. This was followed by compiling the selection of frameworks to be examined in this study. The aim was to come up with frameworks that provide a different perspective to the various factors, and even if these might be based on common models, they bring something new to the discussion on SGs. This phase resulted in the selection of the following well-known frameworks: the Four-Dimensional Framework (4DF) [3], the Experiential Gaming Model (EGM) [9], the Exploratory Learning Model (ELM) [10], the Flow Model (FM) [12], and a Task Annotation Model (TAM) [11]. In addition, the Conceptual Framework (CF) [2] was included because of its simple structure and the fact that it is based on earlier well-structured models, such as [8], the CMX framework which is based on additional earlier models [13], and finally, a framework that was described by Fisch in [1], was included as it provides a more empirical perspective on various factors. The third step was to focus on the factors stated as essential for effective SG design, for which lists were compiled for each framework. Next, depending on the aim/purpose of each factor, four conceptual units were formed. *Learners' specifications,* which comprise those factors concerning the requirements of learners; *learning intentions,* regarding the goals of the game in terms of learning; *game attributes,* the games' features; and *facilitating learning,* those factors that make learning easier.

An explanation is here given regarding the six tables, which are presented in each of the following subsections comprising the four conceptual units. The first column lists the frameworks examined, and the most common factors appear in the top row. In more detail, in the case where the factor gave its name to the column, a check-mark (✔) was made in the corresponding cell. In the rest of the cases, the factors are presented in the way they were identified in the given framework. This is done in order to provide the reader with the information about what was identified and how the grouping was conducted.

2.1 Learners' Specifications

Learners' specifications (Table 1), we refer to the game's target audience, including demographics, previous game and technology use experience & skills learning styles, and preferences [3]. In this case, the game should be interesting for players and delivered in an appealing way. The activities should also be aligned with their previous knowledge and skills, both at the beginning and as the game progresses [10, 12]. What is more, there should be a balance between the challenge that the user is called to execute and the skillset that they already have. In other words, if the challenge is too difficult for the user to successfully complete, they will feel anxiety, in contrast, if there is no challenge because the activity is too easy for the user, they will feel bored [14]. Thus, as the user progresses in the game, the difficulty should increase accordingly.

Table 1. Factors related to learners' specifications

Framework	Learning styles	Needs & interests	Learners experience/skills
Fisch [1]			
EGM [9]			
4DF [3]	Learner profiling	Learners' specifications - preferences	Demographics, ICT skills, gaming experience
CM [2]	✔	Situated & authentic learning	
ELM [10]			Based on experience, challenges aligned with learners' skills
TAM [11]	✔	Needs/preferences	Skills
FM [12]			Challenges aligned with learners' skills
CMX [13]		User profiles	User – initiatives inside the game & knowledge to support reflection

2.2 Learning Intentions

The *Learning intentions* are defined according to users' needs (Table 2). The decision on the *pedagogy* used is essential for carrying out the next steps which concern the design/selection of activity types. The pedagogy may be associative (a): task-based learning, mainly for skills and training - learning a skill through practice in the game; cognitive (c): built on experience, reflection, abstraction and experimentation - forming a new cognitive model through experimentation; and situative (s): social - learning through social interaction and collaboration with others [3, 10]. In Table 2, these pedagogical approaches are referred to as a, c, and s, respectively. The *learning context* may include economic or political factors (macro-level factors), the available spaces, technological means [13], as well as media and sources (micro-level factors) [1]. The context of use would affect which game will be used and which game type would be most appropriate [3]. The *learning content* is the subject the learner is intended to learn [2]. [1] emphasises the proper integration of the educational content in gameplay. Having a strategy where the appealing elements are inserted alongside the educational content to form the SG is not as effective as having the educational content integrated into the gameplay so that the users employ the targeted skills and knowledge as part of the game's progress. The *intended skills* are the cognitive, psychomotor and affective skills which the learner is targeted to develop as a result of playing the game [2]. Skills may be cognitive (c): recall, analysis, synthesis, evaluation; psychomotor (ps): well-timed, fluid execution; or affective (a): identifying, adopting, valuing appropriate attitudes and points of view. In Table 3 these skill sets are referred to as c, ps, and a, respectively. The combination of learning content and intended skills forms the *learning objectives*, meaning the game's specific educational goals (e.g. "Users should be able to recall the date of the battle of Thermopylae") [1]. Thus, the learning objectives refer to a specific verbal formulation of what we target to do. Learning intentions may include *teaching support* which refers to whether the game will play an additional role supporting the teacher's or author's work and what kind of support it will be [11]. If teaching support is available, the authoring tool should help the teacher organise the learning material into units and set the educational goals [13].

Table 2. Factors related to learning intentions

Framework	Pedagogy	Learning context	Learning content	Intended skills	Learning objectives	Teaching support
Fisch [1]		Media	Educational content	Targeted skills		
EGM [9]				Skills	✔	
4DF [3]	Pedagogy (a, c, s)	Context				
CM [2]			Instructional content	Capability (c, ps, a)	Intended learning outcomes	
ELM [10]	a, c, s					
TAM [11]	Educational aspects		Content	Skills	✔	Teaching patterns
FM [12]						
CMX [13]	✔	Infrastructure	✔	Skills	Learning objectives, goals	Authoring tool

2.3 Game Attributes

The most appropriate *game genre* (strategy, adventure etc.) should be selected according to previous decisions and needs, which will lead to the proper inclusion of rules and *game mechanics* (Table 3). The intended learning activities and educational content affect the selection of the proper game mechanics that should support learners' specifications [2]. The *narrative structure* is also related to game genre [11]. The educational content of the game should be properly integrated into the story [1]. The game scenario and activities establish the game plot, and subsequently the overall navigation of the user. The story links the educational and entertainment factors of the game [13]. The way that the story unfolds, should be aligned to the pedagogical strategy and learning objectives. As the flow theory proposes [14], the game *activities* (challenges) should be aligned with users' skills, in order for them not to feel bored (if the tasks are too easy), nor anxious (if the tasks are too difficult to solve) [9, 10, 12]. In the case of an authoring tool, different task types, as well as different possible combinations of tasks can support the various needs [11]. *Interactivity* is the extent to which the game activities require responses and engagement from the learners [2], while the interactivity level should be defined in accordance with the users' specifications (prior gaming experience, skills, preferences etc.). The decisions as to what extent the user will interact with the game is based on the learning objectives, outcomes and the way that the user learns [3].

Table 3. Factors related to game attributes

Framework	Game genre & mechanics	Narrative structure	Activity	Interactivity	Rewards
Fisch [1]			Content - gameplay		
EGM [9]			Challenges		
4DF [3]				Level of interactivity	
CM [2]	Genre, mechanics & rules		Learning activity	Interaction	Rewards, achievement
ELM [10]			Challenges		
TAM [11]	Sandbox, mechanics	✔	Tasks	Method/level of interaction	✔
FM [12]			Challenges		
CMX [13]	MMORPG, mechanics	Game plot	Activities	Interactivity	Awards, game achievement

Furthermore, there should be coherence between the interaction modalities and the game's educational strategy [11]. Different types of games and activities offer diverse opportunities for interaction. The type of *rewards* encourages the users to continue playing, while keeping their motivation high [2]. What is more, the frequency of the rewards and the time they are given are important in making the users feel that they have been rewarded as a result of their actions.

It is important for users to feel that they have control over their actions in the game (*sense of control*) [9, 10, 12] (Table 4). The extent to which the user can direct the actions in a game need to be defined. To enhance this feeling of control, users may be able to play at their own pace and define their own sequence of gameplay (level of linearity) [2]. The *graphical user interface* (GUI) is also important regarding the impact that the game will have on the users. It should be aligned with the game genre and user preferences [3]. The GUI is not only essential in making the game appealing to the target audience through the use of certain colours, styles and animations, but also carries elements of the learning strategy [11]. For example, a clear background with elements that are appropriately contrasted, has the effect of focusing the user's attention to the targeted spot in the game, or elements and animation can be used to indicate hints. The level of graphic fidelity is associated to the level of immersion. In a serious game, the appropriate *level of immersion* should be defined as a highly immersive environment may, in some cases, distract from learning, while in others, it may be supportive [3, 10]. Level of immersion is related to the technological means and the context of use. *Usability* is a major factor of success for any game [9], which should have been tested to ensure playability as well as minimise any software weaknesses (errors, bug, latencies etc.) [13]. *Clear goals* are important to make the user feel confident and enable them to achieve one goal at a time (incremental learning). Needless to say, the goals should be related to the learning objectives, in order to increase the educational effectiveness of the game [2, 9, 10, 12].

Table 4. Factors related to game attributes (continued)

Framework	Sense of control	GUI	Level of immersion	Usability	Clear goals
Fisch [1]					
EGM [9]	Control over the game			✔	✔
4DF [3]		Level of fidelity	Level of immersion		
CM [2]	Learner control, linearity				Incremental learning
ELM [10]	Sense of control		Immersive learning		✔
TAM [11]		Presentation pattern			
FM [12]	✔			Playability	✔
CMX [13]				Infrastructure	

2.4 Facilitating Learning

Numerous ways to facilitate learning through gaming have been presented (Tables 5 and 6). Users need to be able to *focus their attention* (Table 5) on the particular activity of a game as a high attention level is of paramount importance for learning in any context [9, 12]. An appropriate graphical user interface design helps users concentrate on particular elements and activities [11]. Not only should they be able to focus visually, but also mentally on the specific game activity at hand for optimal learning [9]. Users should receive *feedback* on each action they perform so that they know that it has been executed (interaction feedback), and the extent to which every interaction provides feedback should be defined (intermittent feedback). Feedback may be delivered immediately or on demand [10, 12], and cognitive feedback may be provided to users in various forms (simple answers, virtual character discussion, explanations, guidance etc.) to support reflection [9, 12]. This means that the game should not provide the right answer immediately, but rather guidance for the user to think in order to head in the right direction [11]. Support, hints, help, explanations, adapted feedback and social communities are important means/models in providing scaffolding opportunities [1, 2, 11–13].

Table 5. Factors related to facilitating learning

Framework	Focused attention	Feedback	Reflection activity	Schemata construction	Experimentation activity	Transfer of knowledge
Fisch [1]		Feedback, hints				
EGM [9]	✔	✔	Reflection observation	✔	Active experimentation	Transfer new knowledge
4DF [3]						
CM [2]	Attention span	Intermittent, scaffolding	Reflection			Transfer learned skills
ELM [10]		Immediate feedback	Reflection – meta-reflection	Forming abstract concepts	Experimentation	Contextual transfer
TAM [11]	Presentation pattern	✔	Metacognitive support			
FM [12]	Concentration	Feedback, Immediate	Cognitive feedback			
CMX [13]		Scaffolding	Reflection			

By integrating Kolb's theory [15] into serious games, users would have the opportunity to observe the results of an experience and to *reflect* on their actions (think about what has happened), and form new *cognitive schemata* (think about what can be done – abstract concept, hypothesis) in order to test it (*experiment*). To support effective learning, the user should be able to transfer and use their knowledge in different contexts (*transfer knowledge*). This may include the use of knowledge from a previous level to the next, or the use of a skill in different activities during gameplay [2, 9, 10].

Repeating activity (Table 6) refers to the frequent assignment of the same task inside the gameplay [11]. Those activities may be supportive especially when practicing skills is the goal of the game. The tasks should become increasingly harder to maintain a balance between the player's skills and the game challenges [2]. An explorative game environment, such as a 3D world, gives the user a higher sense of control, and can be used with the intention of increasing the user's exploratory behavior (*exploration activity*) [10–12]. The *flow state* is different to attention and immersion. Attention is needed for the user to concentrate on an activity and consciously think and act in order to learn. Immersion is a state where the user feels that they are part of the environment. A flow state is when the user has all of their attention on an activity; as such they do not have a sense of their surroundings or self and their sense of time has been altered. This apparent loss of who or where one is due to being fully engrossed in the game does not mean that the user cannot consciously learn in the game's environment. In fact, the user feels that the actual activity is highly rewarding [12]. It has been shown that a high level of user engagement can increase both playing time and learning performance, as well as motivate the user to play the same game again and also enhance their willingness to play a game with similar content or cause [11, 13]. *Social interaction* is an important source of learning, especially when situative learning is intended [3]. Social interaction can support scaffolding, while members of a group engage in social learning through interaction [10].

Table 6. Factors related to facilitating learning (continued)

Framework	Repeating activity	Exploration activity	Flow state	Social interaction	Level of entertainment	Assessment
Fisch [1]						
EGM [9]			Flow			
4DF [3]				Situative learning		
CM [2]	Practice & drill					
ELM [10]		Exploration		✔		
TAM [11]	Repetition	Exploration	Engagement	✔	Entertainment value	
FM [12]		Exploratory behaviour	Flow state			
CMX [13]			Engagement	Collaboration tools	Entertainment features	Learning outcomes

This kind of learning strategy is supported by collaboration tools, such as chat, forum etc. [13]. The intended *level of entertainment* in a game needs to be well-defined, while there should be a balance between the entertainment and educational factors, which is the foundation of any serious game (edutainment) [11, 13]. Finally, the ways in which the learning outcomes are *assessed* should be defined during the design phase, so as to incorporate the corresponding tools and techniques within the game's architecture, and the gameplay. Defining the goals of the game, its attributes, content, activities, user interface etc., should correspond to the evaluation strategy, as well as the source of data provision between intended and actual outcomes [13].

3   Conclusions

The aim of this study was to combine and classify the conceptual factors that have been proposed for the creation of a Serious Game from existing frameworks. This study resulted in a comprehensive set of concepts that can be used in the design phase of an SG as a guide for decision making, regarding learning and gaming factors. Not only is this decision phase crucial for the success of an SG, but also in the final assessment phase, will the effectiveness of the SG be measured in accordance with the initial intentions.

Feedback is the most common factor suggested in all the frameworks examined. In fact, it is proposed that interaction feedback be delivered immediately, as this is how the user knows that their action has been executed in the game world. Feedback regarding the learning process should also be delivered but on demand, when the user needs help for instance. Most of the frameworks, but especially those based on experiential learning and Kolb's theory [15] suggest that the feedback must allow the user to reflect on their actions in order for them to form new cognitive structures. Then they should test their hypothesis in activities that support experimentation and new virtual experiences that allow the transfer of knowledge in different contexts. Most of the frameworks, and particularly those inspired by the flow theory, suggest that a serious game should incorporate focused attention, clear goals, and a sense of control as standard assets [14]. These factors, together with the game's challenges should be balanced with the user's skills, not only at the beginning of the game, but also during the gameplay, as the user increases both their skills and knowledge. Most of the frameworks also consider scaffolding to be essential. The proposed scaffolding mechanisms, such as hints, help, forum, chat, virtual characters etc. help the user to reach an optimal level at a particular time that would otherwise not have been possible without external stimulus [16]. Interestingly, the assessment factor was not a common reference in the frameworks examined. One reason could be that there are various frameworks for SG assessment. Nevertheless, it is practical to define both the intended outcomes and the way they will be measured. In sum, we propose that all the evaluation strategies should be defined in the early design phase, in order to incorporate the corresponding tools and techniques within the architecture of the game itself, as well as in the gameplay (e.g. log data, recordings, analytics etc.). Furthermore, we believe that the findings of the current study can be used in future as guidelines in the design of Serious Games for different case studies.

References

1. Fisch, S.: Making educational computer games educational. In: Proceedings of the 2005 Conference on Interaction Design and Children, pp, 56–61. ACM, Colorado, USA (2005)
2. Yusoff, A., Crowder, R., Gilbert, L., Wills, G.: A conceptual framework for serious games. In: Ninth IEEE International Conference on Advanced Learning Technologies (ICALT), pp. 21–23 (2009)
3. De Freitas, S., Jarvis, S.: A framework for developing serious games to meet learner needs. In: Interservice/Industry Training, Simulation, and Education Conference (I/ITSEC), Florida (2006)
4. Catalano, E.C., Luccini, M.A., Mortara, M.: Best practices for an effective design and evaluation of serious games. Int. J. Serious Games 1(1) (2014)
5. Arnab, S., et al.: Mapping learning and game mechanics for serious games analysis. Br. J. Educ. Technol. 46(2), 391–411 (2015)
6. Carvalho, M., et al.: An activity theory-based model for serious games analysis and conceptual design. Comput. Educ. 87, 166–181 (2015)
7. Roungas, B., Dalpiaz, F.: A model-driven framework for educational game design. In: de De Gloria, A., Veltkamp, R. (eds.) GALA 2015. LNCS, vol. 9599, pp. 1–11. Springer, Cham (2016). https://doi.org/10.1007/978-3-319-40216-1_1
8. Garris, R., Ahlers, R., Driskell, J.E.: Games, motivation, and learning: a research and practice model. Simul. Gaming 33(4), 441–467 (2002)
9. Kiili, K.: Content creation challenges and flow experience in educational games: the IT-Emperor case. Internet High. Educ. 8(3), 183–198 (2005)
10. De Freitas, S., Neumann, T.: The use of 'exploratory learning' for supporting immersive learning in virtual environments. Comput. Educ. 52(2), 343–352 (2009)
11. Bellotti, F., et al.: Designing serious games for education: from pedagogical principles to game mechanisms. In: Gouscos, D., Meimaris, M. (eds.) 5th European Conference on Game-Based Learning, October 2011, Athens, Greece, pp. 26–34. Academic Publ. Ltd., Reading, UK (2011)
12. Kiili, K., De Freitas, S., Arnab, S., Lainema, T.: The design principles for flow experience in educational games. Procedia Comput. Sci. 15, 78–91 (2012)
13. Malliarakis, C., Satratzemi, M., Xinogalos, S.: Designing educational games for computer programming: a holistic framework. Electron. J. e-Learn. 12(3), 281–298 (2014)
14. Csikszentmihalyi, M.: Flow: The Psychology of Optimal Experience. Harper Perennial, New York (1991)
15. Kolb, D.A.: Experiential Learning: Experience as the Source of Learning and Development. FT Press, London (2014)
16. Vygotsky, L.: Interaction between learning and development. Read. Dev. Child. 23(3), 34–41 (1978)

Teaching and Learning with Escape Games from Debriefing to Institutionalization of Knowledge

Eric Sanchez[✉] and Maud Plumettaz-Sieber

University of Fribourg, CERF, P.-A. de Faucigny 2, 1700 Fribourg, Switzerland
{eric.sanchez,maud.sieber}@unifr.ch

Abstract. Educators have now introduced the so called escape-games into their teaching or training practices. During a limited time, a team of learners collaboratively solves puzzles related to educational content. For learners, the aim consists of "escaping" from a room. For educators, an escape-game contextualizes an educational content into a meaningful and inspiring experience based on game-based and collaborative learning. This paper deals with the implementation of what we call educational escape game with the focus on the process dedicated to decontextualize the knowledge after a game session. We want to get a better understanding of debriefing so that practice can improve. The paper is based on an empirical study carried out with teachers/trainers experienced in implementing educational escape games. The paper is organized as follow. We (1) provide with a brief review of literature on debriefing and we argue for the adoption of the term "institutionalization", a concept enabling to take into consideration the transformation of knowledge after a game session. We (2) propose a definition for educational escape-game based on a literature review and the systematic analysis of 2 French databases of educational escape games and (3) we discuss the results of an empirical work aiming at understanding how educators carry out the debriefing session which follows the time dedicated to play. According to our theoretical framework, debriefing consists of a process aiming at the transformation of the subjective and situated knowledge developed during the game into objective and transferable knowledge. Interviews and questionnaires conducted with three teachers enable to describe this process in terms of time (*chronogenesis*), role played by participants (*topogenesis*) and the settings (objects and relationships between objects) in which this process takes place (*mesogenesis*). These findings offer the opportunity for new guidelines for the design of debriefing sessions.

Keywords: Escape game · Game-based learning · Debriefing · Institutionalization · Chronogenesis · Topogenesis · Mesogenesis

1 Introduction

The success met by escape games is attested by the increase of the number of companies who propose players to be locked in a room where they must seek clues and solve puzzles tied to a storytelling to escape before time runs out. We can hypothesize that this success results from the two core dimensions that are not specific to escape

© Springer Nature Switzerland AG 2019
M. Gentile et al. (Eds.): GALA 2018, LNCS 11385, pp. 242–253, 2019.
https://doi.org/10.1007/978-3-030-11548-7_23

game but are combined in a same game: the sense of reality due to the fact that the players are locked in a room, seek tangible objects, and playing by team and experiencing social relatedness.

Innovative educators, teachers or trainers, have been inspired by these games and they adapted the concept to education. They created escape games focused on educational content – called educational escape games in this paper - and their students or trainees participate to a game-based and collaborative one hour learning session. Today, this phenomenon is visible for secondary school education but also at university level and for adult education.

However, we know from research on game-based learning that there is a difference between mastering the rules of a game and learning from the game content. Learning requires reflection on the actions performed during the time devoted to play and we know that game-based learning requires debriefing. There is a risk that educators involved in implementing educational escape games miss this important phase. There is a risk that they face difficulties to implement it so that debriefing meets its purpose: making explicit and transferable the knowledge developed during the session dedicated to play.

Thus, this paper deals with debriefing practices with educational escape games. We want to get a better understanding of how debriefings are carried out by teachers/trainers who have introduced educational escape-games into their teaching practices. We want to understand how they make possible that knowledge is processed and learnt by the students. First we propose a literature review and a theoretical framework for debriefing. We also provide with a definition for educational escape games. Second, we describe the methodology used for an empirical study on teachers/trainers practices. Third we discuss the data collected and we conclude on the importance to provide educators with theoretical models and tools.

2   From Debriefing to Institutionalization of Knowledge

There is a difference between mastering the rules of the game and recognizing the ways those rules structure our perception of reality [1]. Thus, learning from a game occurs only after reflection and debriefing [2] and debriefing is an integral part of a game-based learning experience [3]. Debriefing plays different roles. First, debriefing fosters reflection and metacognition. The implicit knowledge dedicated to play becomes explicit during an after-playing debating session. Second, debriefing is recognized to be crucial for the transfer of knowledge and the learning experience is undermined if the players are not aware of the learning elements [4]. For some authors, the game-based learning experience is transferable if the teacher clarifies the purpose of the simulation [5]. However in 2010, Crookall [6] stated that the concern with debriefing seems to have been lost in a majority of research studies. This assertion seems to be still true ten years later.

Lederman proposes [3] a literature review on debriefing and a description of this "post-experience analytic process". For Lederman, debriefing is "a process in which people who have had an experience are led through a purposive discussion of that experience" (p.146). Her literature review shows that debriefing may have different purposes: to gather experience from subjects [7], to inform subject on the purpose of the lived experience [8] and, within an educational context, to provide learners with insight into the activity in order to help them to learn from their experiences [9]. According to this review of literature, debriefing relates to the learning, the emotional or the behavioral content and, depending on the purpose of the game, the content of debriefing, different scenario might be used by debriefers. In the education setting, guided discussions seem to be favored. Lederman's work is focused on a methodology for carrying out a debriefing and different elements are identified. However, her work is focused on the participants to the debriefing and knowledge is not explicitly mentioned.

Another approach comes from the theoretical work carried out by Brousseau [10] in the field of didactics of mathematics. This approach stresses the difference made in French language between savoir and connaissance both translated by knowledge in English. Savoir means objective and institutionalized knowledge while connaissance refers to subjective and situated knowledge. Savoirs refers to concepts, models and theories. They results from the questioning of reality and they are produced by institutions (e.g. University). Connaissances are individual explanations that emerge from the lived experience. Thus, Warfield [11] proposes to distinguish the verbs connaître (to be familiar with) and savoir (to know a fact). The differences stress the status of universal, formalized and transferable knowledge with statements precisely known and knowledge non-formalized and tied to a specific context (connaissance). Institutionalization, relates to the change of the status of knowledge during a debriefing session. The subjective and situated knowledge becomes objective and context-free. This transformation occurs when the situated knowledge needed to win the game is made explicit and validated by an official external source (the teacher or trainer as debriefer) and becomes universal and transferable. Thus, the term debriefing is focused on the cognitive, behavioral and psychological dimensions of the game experience while institutionalization is more focused on the transformation of knowledge.

According to Sensevy [12], as a transformation, institutionalization encompasses different productions. Topogenesis refers to the place occupied by the participants (teacher and learners, trainers and trainees) and the roles that they play during the process. Who is involved? Who is in charge of the verbalization of the knowledge? Who is asking questions? Who is answering? Chronogenesis refers to the position and the evolution of knowledge on the timeline for teaching and learning. How is the knowledge expressed and described at a specific moment? Mesogenesis refers to the design of the setting of the debriefing. Space and objects are organized by the teacher/trainer in order to establish constraints. The learners will have to address these constraints and evolve. What are the objects used by the teacher? How does he/she set up the situation?

While the term debriefing mostly refers to pragmatic issues, institutionalization stressed that knowledge needs to be transformed after a time dedicated to play and these transformations encompasses explanation, validation and objectivation. In the following, we will refer to this concept to get a better understanding of the role taken by the phase dedicated to report the experience gained during the time dedicated to play. This work has been carried out for a project dedicated to understand the implementation of educational escape games for teaching or training. We want to develop a better understanding of debriefing and to improve debriefing practices.

3 Educational Escape-Games

Our study focuses on the debriefing session that follows the use of escape games for educational purposes. Although there are some evidences for stating that educational escape-games become more and more popular among educators. According to our knowledge, empirical researches are rare and systematic reviews on educational practices have not been conducted yet.

3.1 Toward a Definition

A search in research databases in English (ERIC, Google Scholar) and French (CAIRN) languages with keywords such as "escape game", "escape room" and "jeu d'évasion" provided with few results. Altogether, 70 articles were mentioned. However, only 6 were directly linked to our subject. We also found that there is a lack of empirical work related to the escape games. We didn't found research papers based on empirical evidences but merely papers that consist of experience feedbacks and develop arguments already well known from the game-based learning community such as students' motivation and collaborative learning [13].

According to Corkill [14], escape games, also mentioned as real escape games or escape rooms [15], come from Japan and appeared in 2007. Escape games were played in clubs and bars where players had to escape from the "room" by seeking clues and solving puzzles in less than 60 min. This is in line with the definition proposed by Nicholson [16]. Escape rooms are "live-action team-based games where players discover clues, solve puzzles, and accomplish tasks in one or more rooms in order to accomplish a specific goal (usually escaping from the room) in a limited amount of time." We also found similar definitions in papers published in French [13]. Escape games designed for educational purposes are sometime quoted with the expression "serious escape games". We prefer to use the expression *educational escape game* to describe an instructional method requiring the learner to participate in a playful activity aiming at collaboratively finding clues and solving puzzles linked to an educational content, in order to escape from a physical room. Based on the systematic review of the games described on website dedicated to display educational escape games among the education community and our literature review, we retain the following characteristics:

- *Unambiguous educational objectives*. By unambiguous we mean that designers and/or game masters have clear expectations in terms of learning and that the educational content is intrinsic, *i.e.* non-separated from the game mechanics [17]. These objectives are usually communicated to learners after the game session through a debriefing. They consist of concepts, competences and/or soft skills such as collaboration, communication or creativity.
- *A physical space dedicated to the game*. This space takes the form of a room where clues are present and must be seek and interpreted by players/learners. This physical space is usually tailored to creating a gaming context, for example with low light and music for mysterious atmosphere.
- *Clues and puzzles*. Players/learners address a challenge, "escaping" from the room. These clues and puzzles are based on a storytelling. This storytelling can take

different forms such as finding a specific password or object. For each clue or puzzle, the player/learner has to develop specific knowledge and/or skills. Usually, the links between the different puzzles are non-linear and it is possible to win with different approaches and strategies.

- *Team work*. Players/learners form a unique team. There is no competition with other teams but a conflict with the game itself [18]. The game requires collaboration of teammates (common objective, task sharing, communication and management).
- *Fantasy and play*. Play is subjective and the game requires interpretation from the players. Play is based on meta-communicative acts that frame patterns of behavior in time [19].

3.2   Teaching Levels and Educational Purposes

The French website *S'cape*[1] designed by three teachers is a database of 142 educational escape-games designed for primary and secondary students and also for training teachers. The website also provide with ideas and advices for the design and implementation of educational escape-games. Another French website *Escape n'games*[2] brings together 145 escape games from primary school to adult education. Universities have also implemented educational escape games with various objectives. For example, the Louvain Learning Lab (LLL) has developed an educational escape game dedicated to foster game-based approach in university courses. *Hellscape* is another educational escape game implemented into University Paris Sorbonne Nouvelle. *Hellscape* aims to help new students to develop digital and media literacy. In the University of Fribourg (CH), we teach technology enhanced learning and game-based learning to pre-service teachers with *Enigma*, an escape game designed by French teachers trainers.

An analysis of a sample of 25 educational escape games from the website *S'cape* shows that they are mainly designed for secondary education (23) and far less for primary education (1) or university (1). Various subjects are addressed: biology, geology, maths, physics, chemistry, history, geography, literature search, information and media education, citizenship education and foreign languages (Spanish and Italian).

According to this review, the purposes of the educational escape games are mainly learning or reviewing concepts and less about creativity or team building. Students engagement and students motivation are also often mentioned. Although the games are mainly based on the core idea that learners solve puzzles in a room and use tangible objects, digital tools are also often used: QR code reader, Learning Apps, augmented reality. *Genially*[3], a digital online platform which enables to create interactive content is also often used for the design of the games.

---

[1] https://www.scape.enepe.fr.

[2] https://www.cquesne-escapegame.com/.

[3] https://www.genial.ly/fr.

4   Research Questions and Objectives

The objectives of this preliminary work are to get a better understanding of how debriefings are carried out and how knowledge is institutionalized by teachers/trainers who have introduced educational escape-games into their teaching practices. This first step aims at preparing a more long term objective: modeling institutionalization as a process and designing a digital tool dedicated to support this process. Thus, we want to improve debriefing practices by getting a better understanding of debriefing and providing with guidelines.

These objectives cannot be reached without taking into account the way educational escape-games are introduced into teachers/trainers practices in terms of teaching objectives and game implementation. Thus, this study focuses on teachers/trainers' practices and we want to address the following research questions:

- A first category of questions is linked to the educational content and the way educational escape games are implemented: What kinds of objectives are addressed by the teachers/trainers? Are these objectives linked to a totally novel knowledge or do they implement educational escape games so that learners get the opportunity to assess their understanding of concepts previously taught? What measures should be taken so that the situation can be seen as a game by the learner? Which role is taken by the teacher/trainer during the session dedicated to play?
- The second category of questions is linked to the way the debriefing is carried out by the teachers/trainers. How is the knowledge verbalized and expressed on the timeline (chronogenesis)? What are the roles of the different participants (learners/trainees and teachers/trainers) during the debriefing session (topogenesis)? And how space and objects are organized by the teacher/trainer (mesogenesis)?

5   Research Settings

The research settings encompass a questionnaire. We selected 3 teachers/trainers (Z, Y and X) who have already a lot of experience in designing and implementing escape games for teaching/training. Indeed, they are both responsible for implementing educational escape games at various levels and for the design of a website displaying educational escape games among the education community. Y is a secondary school teacher for information and documentation. Z and X teach biology and geology at secondary school students. They are all teachers trainers on the use of digital technology at school and involved in teachers training sessions on the use of educational escape games. They also published articles, on the website about the design and the use of educational escape games for educational purposes. Thus, we consider them as experts.

For gathering this expertise we designed a questionnaire. The questionnaire encompasses 30 questions on:

- The teacher/trainer and her/his expertise and experience in designing educational escape games.

- The way she/he designs and implements escape games, what educational objectives are pursued, and which role is taken by the teacher during the time devoted to play.
- How the debriefing is performed in terms of chronogenesis, topogenesis and mesogenesis.

Mesogenesis encompasses questions about space and the tools used for the debriefing. Do they debrief learners in the room where the game took place? Do they use traces collected during the game? Do they use specific tools or representations such as *Post-it* or conceptual maps?

Topogenesis was assessed by questions about the roles of the different participants. What questions are asked by the teacher? What are the roles taken by the learners?

Chronogenesis encompasses questions about how knowledge is processed during the debriefing. What kind of knowledge? Do they aim to teach concepts or to develop skills? Is this knowledge made explicit? Decontextualized? Institutionalized?

The questionnaire also enables to consider the debriefing in terms of product (the knowledge involved), process (institutionalization) and roles (teachers/trainers and learners).

The questionnaire was tested with one of the participants during an online interview performed with SWITCHinteract, an online conference tool that allows to split screen and to share documents. SWITCHinteract also enabled to videotape the interview. This participant first filled the questionnaire and then she was asked to explain her answers during the interview. Thus, this interview enabled to gather information and also to revise the formulations of some questions that were not totally clear. The questionnaire was sent to the two other participants who filled it without being interviewed.

The research settings also encompass the implementation of Enigma, an educational escape game dedicated to train pre-service teachers to use digital technologies for educational purposes. We selected the game from S'cape, a French website dedicated to spread experience and material about educational escape games. Enigma was adapted for the training of pre-service teachers from our university and 3 sessions were organized. By implementing Enigma, we wanted to face common issues for the implementation of an educational escape game and to gain a concrete experience. Thus, the research settings of our research are design based [20].

6 Results and Discussion

In the following, we first describe the practices expressed by the teachers/trainers in terms of educational objectives, game design and game implementation. Second, we analyze how they describe the performing of the debriefing sessions.

6.1 Design and Implementation

Educational Objectives: The answers show that it is possible to distinguish 2 categories of educational escape games: (1) games dedicated to introduce a totally novel educational content and (2) games designed for the review of concepts supposed to be already known by students. For this last case, the game enables to "go further" (Y).

Each participant to the study considers that it is important to not communicate educational objectives to their students/trainees prior to the game session. Z explains "Lets the game be". For Y, there is a risk to "kill the game". The introduction to the game encompasses the presentation of the pedagogical approach (game-based learning), security rules and the importance of communication and collaboration. The descriptions of the game introduction show that this introduction aims to make possible that the students/trainees will experience a situation that they will interpret as a real game. In this way, an escape game sounds like what Brousseau call adidactical situation [10]. It means that the role of the teacher consists of arranging the set-up and standing back while the students construct their knowledge by overcoming challenges and difficulties while the teaching objectives are hidden. Hiding the teaching objectives makes possible that the players/learners take on the challenge offered by the game and perform according to their understanding of the situation rather than to the expectations of the teacher/trainer. Thus, students' engagement into the game becomes possible and they freely perform according to their understanding of the puzzle and their knowledge (or misconceptions).

Role of the teacher/trainer during the time devoted to play: The participants to the study identify themselves as game masters. They recall security rules, remaining time. They foster communication and collaboration and guide the players/learners to recall the concepts that might be useful. Sometime, provide learners/players with additional information but they expect that solutions come from the learners/players themselves. They expect them to be autonomous. However, they indicate that they also need to scaffold the learners/players activity. According to our own experience in implementing educational escape games. The joy of playing is an outcome from the tension between the frustration resulting from failure and the pleasure of success. Thus, there is a risk to kill the game if the learner/player feels that the puzzles are solved by the game master. The answers to the questionnaire show that the feeling of competence of the learners/players is an issue which needs to be addressed by teachers/trainers.

6.2 Debriefing

According to the answers from the 3 teachers/trainers, the design of the educational escape game always includes a debriefing session.

Chronogenesis. Based on the answers to the questionnaire, we identified 4 different steps for the debriefing session:

A. Feedbacks about the game experience. Teachers/trainers ask questions about the situation experienced by the learners/players. Did you enjoy the game? Why? Did you found the puzzles difficult to solve?
B. Feedbacks on learning. What did you learn from this experience? The learning content might be related to specific concepts; however, teachers/trainer seems to also consider skills to be important: scientific inquiry (X) and search for information communication and collaboration (Y).
C. Feedback on the game itself. Presentation of the organigram of the different puzzles, presentation of the game material.

D. Feedbacks on the link between the concepts, the content to be learnt and the puzzles. Errors are discussed. The concepts are named. For example, Y explains that "when [the students] talk about the puzzles, I rephrase in a scientific way so that each student understands".

E. Conclusion of the game. This is a way to assess the students' willingness to participate to a similar experience. Are you ready to start a similar experience?

According to Lederman's model of debriefing, A corresponds to "a systematic self-reflexive process about the experience", B, C and D to "the refocusing of participants' reflections onto their own individual experience and the meaning they have for them". Depending on the teacher/trainer, the debriefing follows the chronology A-B-C, A-C-B-D or A-B-C-D. Phase 3 of the Lederman's model [3] ("the exploration that takes the participants from their own individual experience to the broader application and implication of that experience") is missing. Thus, the institutionalization process is not totally complete.

The learners/players are lead to reflect to their past experience, the concepts involved are identified and named. Activities are also foreseen after the debriefing. They take the form of labwork (Z), exercises (Y) or other forms of school works. These activities are also opportunities to assess the students and to confirm that the transfer of knowledge is effective. Thus, the transfer is not taken into consideration during the debriefing but after the debriefing, during more traditional school activities. From this study it appears that an educational escape games and the debriefing which follows are not isolated. They are integrated into a global learning scenario.

Topogenesis. Each teacher/trainer explains that he/she splits the time with students. However, depending on the participant to the study the roles are distributed differently regarding the knowledge. Z explains that the debriefing is based on a Powerpoint presentation and this presentation helps him to be focused on the topic when the students tend to propose ideas that are far from the subject to be learnt. Y underlines the importance to take into consideration the students' proposals and to rephrase them. She seems to give a greater place to students' participation but she is responsible for a final summary of the concepts involved in the game. X describes herself as a guide. She organizes students' participation and takes care that everyone participates. For her, questions enable for the guidance of the students. The end of the debriefing depends on the available time (Z) or the end of the questions posed by learners/players. The limited time dedicated to the debriefing is also considered to be an issue. According to the different participants to the study there is a balance between students and teacher's roles regarding the knowledge involved in the game. Students provide feedback about their failure and success. They talk about their interpretation about what happen and ask questions. They make their knowledge (and misconceptions) visible. Teachers/trainers have three main roles. (1) They emphasize the importance of assessing learners/players. Either they assess them based on their answers to the questions asked; either the students are expected to self-assess their knowledge. (2) The teachers/trainers make possible that student's knowledge become visible and shared. They are also responsible to assessing and validating the knowledge expressed by the students. (3) They also name the concepts that emerged during the game and introduce scientific vocabulary. It means that they try to make possible the conversion of the individual and situated *connaissances* into shared and universal *savoirs*. (4).

Mesogenesis. The need for a clear distinction between the time dedicated to play and the debriefing emerges from the answers provided by the teachers/trainers. Y explains that it is sometime difficult to decrease the students' excitation and that he has already faced the difficulty to deal with two teams who wanted to compete with each other. There is a debate about holding the debriefing in the room where the game takes place (and then it is possible to look back, with learners/players, to the material that they used during the game) or to hold the debriefing in another room and then, to make clear the boundary between the game and the debriefing. Y explains that the "shift to paper and pencil activities is difficult. There is a gate to pass through".

Different settings are mentioned for setting up the debriefing. X and Y ask the students to seat down or to stand up around a table where all the clues collected are made visible. This is a "relaxing time" (Y), "one listens to each other and the discussion needs to be pleasant". The setting chosen by Z is more face-to-face and based on the use of a Powerpoint presentation.

Traces from the students' activity are not often collected and used. Z and Y do not gather any traces. Z provides the students with a "kit encompassing all game elements and additional information about the concepts involved in the game". Sometime, Y takes a picture from the concept map drawn during the debriefing. This picture is utilized during further activities. X carries out a brainstorming session with *Post-it*. She produces quizzes that are used latter on and an infography for the learners/players. She takes photos. She also audio or video-tapes the key moments of the game (search, cooperation, solving the puzzles, final solution found by the learners/players…). These traces are published on the website of the school.

7 Conclusion

Our study made visible that the debriefing refers to a diversity of practices and there is not a unique approach. However, beyond this diversity of practices, the answers from the participants of our study show that the main issue faced by educators relates to the transformation of knowledge developed during the game session so that this knowledge makes sense for the learners.

As a result, the term debriefing does not totally cover the complexity of the process which make possible that players become learners. The term fully reflected that learning occurs if players are engaged in a systematic self-reflexive process about the lived experience. The term also expresses the importance to helping players to envisage the broader application and implication of that experience. However, the term fails to describe how knowledge is or should be processed. This process relates to the decontextualisation of knowledge. The player develops skills and acquires knowledge during the game. The French word *connaissance* expresses that this knowledge and these skills are subjective and tied to a specific context. This knowledge and skills need to be processed so that they become *savoirs* that will be usable in contexts that are different from the context prevailing for their development.

Based on the information gathered from the participants to our study we conclude that this issue is addressed by experimented teachers/trainers. We underlined some difference in terms of teachers/trainers practices but we can conclude that they recognize the importance of institutionalization of knowledge by paying specific attention to organizing place and object (mesogenesis), time (chronogenesis) and distributing roles (topogenesis). However, due to the complexity of this process and the constraints faced by educators, there is a risk that is not fully addressed by less experienced educators. Thus, there is a need to go further and to get a better understanding of how knowledge should be processed to insure that the transfer will occur. This issue is not specific to game-based learning. However, the implementation of educational escape games make more apparent the need for a time dedicated to institutionalize knowledge. It also emphasizes the need to offer educator specific tool dedicated to carry out this process. Gathering traces from the gaming experience, making these traces visible for educators and learners, enabling players to participate to a discussion based on these traces, naming the underlying concepts and enabling learners to envisage how these concepts might be applied in different contexts are out of importance. This is why we are now involved in modeling this process and to develop digital tools that could help teachers/trainers to address this issue.

References

1. Jenkins, H., Clinton, K., Purushotma, R., Robison, A.J., Weigel, M.: Confronting the Challenges of Participatory Culture: Media Education For the 21st Century. The MacArthur Foundation, Chicago (2006)
2. Garris, R., Ahlers, R., Driskell, J.E.: Games, motivation, and learning: a research and practice model. Simul. Gaming 33, 441–467 (2002)
3. Lederman, L.: Debriefing: toward a systematic assessment of theory and practice. Simul. Gaming 23, 145–160 (1992)
4. Egenfeldt-Nielsen, S.: Overview of research on the educational use of video games. Digit. Kompetanse 1, 184–213 (2006)
5. Aldrich, C.: Learning by Doing. A Comprehensive Guide to Simulation, Computer Games, and Pedagogy in-Learning and Other Educational Experiences. Pfeiffer, San Francisco (2005)
6. Crookall, D.: Serious games, debriefing, and simulation/gaming as a discipline. Simul. Gaming 41, 898–920 (2010)
7. Walker, G.: Crisi-care in critical incident debriefing. Death Stud. 14(2), 121–133 (1990)
8. Tennen, H., Gillen, R.: The effect on debriefing on laboratory induced helplessness: an attributional analysis. J. Pers. Soc. Psychol. 217–224 (1979)
9. Lederman, L.: Intercultural communication, simulation and the cognitive assimilation of experience: an exploration of the post-experience analytic process. In: Conference of the Speech Communication Association of Puerto Rico, San Juan (1983)
10. Balacheff, N., Cooper, M., Sutherland, R.: Theory of Didactical Situations in Mathematics: Didactique des mathématiques (Didactique des Mathématiques, 1970–1990 - Guy Brousseau). Kluwer Academic Publishers, Dordrecht (1997)
11. Warfield, V.: Invitation to the Didactque. University of Washington, Seattle (2006)
12. Sensevy, G.: Théories de l'action et action du professeur. In: Baudouin, J., Friederich, J. (eds.) Théories de l'action et éducation. De Boeck, Bruxelles (2001)

13. Guigon, G., Humeau, J., Vermeulen, M.: Escape Classroom : un escape game pour l'enseignement. In: 9ème Colloque Questions de Pédagogie dans l'Enseignement Supérieur (QPES 2017), QPES 2017, Grenoble, France (2017)
14. Corkill, E.: Real Escape Game brings its creator's wonderment to life. Japan times (2009)
15. Borrego, C., Fernández, C., Blanes, I., Robles, S.: Room escape at class: escape games activities to facilitate the motivation and learning in computer science. J. Technol. Sci. Educ. **2**, 162–171 (2017)
16. Nicholson, S.: The state of escape: escape room design and facilities. In: Meaningful Play 2016, Lansing, Michigan (2016)
17. Habgood, J., Overmars, M.: The Game Maker's Apprentice: Game Development for Beginners. APress, Berkeley (2006)
18. Sanchez, E.: Competition and collaboration for game-based learning: a case study. In: Wouters, P., van Oostendorp, H. (eds.) Instructional Techniques to Facilitate Learning and Motivation of Serious Games. AGL, pp. 161–184. Springer, Cham (2017). https://doi.org/10.1007/978-3-319-39298-1_9
19. Bateson, G.: Steps to an Ecology of Mind. Ballantine, New York (1972)
20. Sanchez, E., Monod-Ansaldi, R., Vincent, C., Safadi, S.: A praxeological perspective for the design and implementation of a digital role-play game. Educ. Inf. Technol. **22**, 2805–2824 (2017)

Methods and Tools

Enhancing Energy Conservation
by a Household Energy Game

Jan Dirk L. Fijnheer[1,2(✉)], Herre van Oostendorp[1(✉)],
and Remco C. Veltkamp[1(✉)]

[1] Department of Information and Computing Sciences, Utrecht University,
Princetonplein 5, 3584 CC Utrecht, Netherlands
{J.D.L.Fijnheer, H.vanoostendorp, R.C.Veltkamp}@uu.nl
[2] Inholland University of Applied Science, Wildenborch 6,
1112 XB Diemen, Netherlands

Abstract. This paper presents the results of a study, comparing a game versus a dashboard with respect to energy conservation in the household. In a pretest-posttest design, an empirical study tested whether change in attitude, knowledge, engagement and behaviour with respect to energy conservation in the household was different for participants playing *Powersaver Game* compared to a control condition where participants used an energy dashboard with the same content, but excluding game features. The aim of this game (developed using an iterative user-centered game design methodology) is to influence household energy consumption by means of electricity and gas usage in the long-term. The intervention time was at least 5 weeks and pre and post measures based on 21 days intervals. All energy conservation activities that the application provides (e.g. washing clothes on low temperatures) take place in the real world and feedback is based on real time energy consumption. This inverse gamification principle aims to optimize the transfer between the game world and the real world. Energy consumption significantly changed in the game condition compared to the control condition, and the difference between both conditions is more than 33% after the intervention. In the game condition, knowledge about energy conservation was significantly increased, although no significant differences in increase of attitude and engagement were found. We conclude that *Powersaver Game* is effective in transfer of energy conservation knowledge, which leads to energy saving behaviour on the long term. It cannot be concluded that playing the game leads to a greater change in attitude, however, attitude scores of the participants were high from the start.

Keywords: Gamification · Energy conservation · Persuasive games · Behaviour change

1 Introduction

Gamification by incorporation of game features can be a valuable strategy for making non-game products, services, or applications, more motivating, and/or for engaging the user [6]. We expect that a persuasive application that aims to stimulate energy conservation is more effective when game features like missions, quizzes, narrative,

M. Gentile et al. (Eds.): GALA 2018, LNCS 11385, pp. 257–266, 2019.
https://doi.org/10.1007/978-3-030-11548-7_24

competition and rewards are implemented. Additionally, besides game features, the inclusion of reality by using reversed gamification principles in a persuasive application can be an outstanding effective means to change people's energy conservation behaviour [8]. Gamification research has shown that the integration of serious games into real life could have positive effects on attitude and behaviour [3, 4, 10, 11, 16, 20]. In a normal gamification process, game features are implemented in real world processes to stimulate desirable behaviour. In this research project, a different and novel approach is chosen. It takes the opposite approach by implementing real world processes like household energy activities into the game design itself. The aim of this approach is to optimize the transfer between the game world and the real world. When the transfer is optimized, the game is expected to be more effective in change of behaviour and attitude [13]. Implementing real world processes in a game design is still an emerging principle in gamification research [8]. When people are highly engaged, they are apt to adopt the attitude that is promoted in the application [17]. This can lead to a higher awareness of relevant factors involved in, for instance, energy conservation. In effect, attitude may positively change, and subsequently trigger a change in energy saving behaviour on the long term. The assumed chain of events that higher awareness (more accessible knowledge) leads to attitude change, which leads to behaviour change, is what persuasive games try to accomplish [2, 5, 19].

The persuasive application *Powersaver Game* is developed in an iterative user-centered design approach [8, 9] and is used as a tool in a larger research project that examines the influence of playing in the real world on attitudes towards energy conservation, and on energy conservation behaviour in the long term. The focus is specifically on energy consumption in households by means of electricity and gas usage. The aim is to contribute to the stimulation of individual sustainable behaviour by studying how gamification can be a positive incentive for people to change their behaviour regarding energy use at home. It also aims to study whether transfer from game play to real life behaviour has a long-term character. It is conducted over a longer period of time, measures changes in knowledge, attitude, engagement and behaviour also after delay, and includes an adequate control condition. Families have played *Powersaver Game* or used in the control condition the *Powersaver Energy Dashboard* version which contains no game features.

The research question is if there are changes in knowledge transfer, attitude towards energy conservation, engagement and energy conservation between the game and control condition. This is, basically, the effectiveness of a game focused on energy conservation. We hypothesize that knowledge, attitude, engagement and energy conservation of participants playing the game will increase more than that of participants in the dashboard control condition.

In the next section the research design is presented, with special attention to game design. In the third section the outcomes of the empirical data are discussed. Finally, we draw conclusions and discuss how we will continue our research with *Powersaver Game*.

2 Method

Media comparison research examines differences in learning the same content of a game – or as similar as possible - with conventional media, answering the research question: "Do people learn better with games or conventional media [15]?" Inspired by this approach, our focus is comparing a persuasive game (*Powersaver Game*) and control condition (*Powersaver Energy Dashboard*) within a computer-based medium. This prevents us for problems of possible media differences. In *Powersaver Game* several gamification features are incorporated and is a persuasive game that can be expected to stimulate energy conservation. *Powersaver Energy Dashboard* is a learning application that provides instruction and feedback on energy conservation. In both conditions every 2 days families receive the same information about energy conservation about a specific theme, e.g. washing clothes, and receive feedback. Besides knowledge transfer, i.e. learning results, we also measure attitude, engagement and behaviour, i.e. energy consumption.

2.1 Participants

In this study 21 households including 49 participants older than 12 years participated on a voluntary basis in this experiment. 6 Households dropped out during the intervention. The loss is 17 participants. From the remaining 32 participants who finished the application only 15 from 7 households in the game condition filled in all questionnaires.

2.2 Design

Powersaver Game is a web-based application and is played in households whereof the whole family is involved. The navigation by the player of *Powersaver Game* is done by point and click in the Internet browser. It is an Eco-feedback, Multiplayer, Roleplaying and Point & Click Adventure game [1] and has been designed in an iterative process [9]. A real time connection between the household energy meter and game server is accomplished by dataloggers with an Internet connection. The data of energy consumption is sent to a database of a server at Utrecht University.

Avatars of family members are the central characters of *Powersaver Game*. The family composition in the game is customized to the household. The game starts with an introduction of the story. A storyline in a game can be engaging because it can stimulate our emotions [7, 18]. A family arrives at a dilapidated country house where a professor had caused a failed experiment. The family enters the main hall of the house that contains several doors (Fig. 1). Behind each door a room is situated where a game character in the form of a confused electrical device is placed. A cat (former pet of the professor) called Kyoto guides the family in the game. In every mission session the family is asked to enter a preselected room. Before the door opens a quiz has to be played. A quiz contains questions about energy conservation that will prepare player's knowledge for the missions that are occurring in that specific room. When the family enters the room a character in the form of a device that is in a confused state is shown (Fig. 2). The family has to accomplish missions, which contain energy conservation knowledge, to help the device to return to a normal state. All missions (e.g. washing clothes on low temperatures) take place in the real world; this represents our inverse gamification principle. The total period of playing the game is at least 5 weeks if players end missions and start new ones in the given time. It takes approximately 2 days to complete a mission. The game has 13 missions, 8 quizzes and an end-battle/scene. The end condition is reached when all devices and the professor are brought out of their confused state. The player is getting feedback on energy use and savings during playing, which is based on average energy consumption in the 21 days before the intervention started. The results of the quizzes are shown and achievement of a completed mission is displayed with a badge. A household is in competition, another game feature, with 7 virtual households, but assumes to play against real households. Competition is simulated to stimulate households to achieve high scores and it was technically not feasible to implement a real and fair competition.

Fig. 1. Part of the main hall

Fig. 2. Scenes laundry; Bad State (on the left) and Normal State (on the right).

Control Condition

For our approach families used *Powersaver Energy Dashboard* in the control condition. The energy dashboard has an identical design style as the menu page of the game. It contains a screen where energy conservation recommendations and a timer are presented, and to give feedback two screens with energy consumption charts and energy conservation results are presented. The form, timing and content of the information the control condition receives are highly similar as in the game condition, but excluded game features such as missions, quizzes, narrative, competition and rewards [19].

2.3   Measurements

Participants completed an online pretest as well as an online posttest questionnaire to assess their attitude towards sustainable energy consumption related topics and knowledge level towards household energy conservation. For attitude measures both questionnaires included 30 statements rated on a 7 point Likert-scale ranging from strongly disagree to strongly agree. Different statements on the same topics are used in pretest and posttest. 15 Statements are regarding micro-level attitude topics (about sustainable energy consumption in a household) as well as 15 statements regarding macro-level attitude topics (10 statements about sustainable energy and 5 statements about sustainability). Macro-measures were composed partly based on previous research on attitudes toward sustainability [19]. With this approach we measure specific hierarchical attributes of the object of sustainable energy attitude [22]. Krosnick and Petty [14] describe that strength-related attributes of attitudes are categorized in affective, cognitive and behaviour intention components. In our questionnaire we only used statements from affective and cognitive categories, because behaviour intention to save energy in the household was already high by voluntary registration to participate in this experiment. For knowledge measures 12 multiple-choice questions including 4 answer options per question are used. The questions are related to the content about energy conservation from both applications. The same questions are used in the pretest and posttest.

Engagement measures were composed based on previous research on engagement in serious games [21]. To monitor engagement participants completed an online questionnaire in the second week and the last week of the intervention. Both questionnaires included the same 7 statements rated on a 7 point Likert-scale ranging from strongly disagree to strongly agree.

Behaviour, in the form of energy consumption, is monitored during 21 days before the intervention to set a good baseline of average energy consumption. In both applications the user is getting feedback (on energy use and savings) during the intervention. And after the intervention the energy consumption is monitored for 21 days to examine the impact of the intervention.

2.4   Procedure

Participants have been recruited using different methods and communication channels like social media, direct mail, digital newsletters and public lectures. Participants registered at the beginning of 2017 using an online form. They could participate when the technical situation of their energy supply (e.g. presence of smart energy meter) was adequate. In spring 2017, 49 participants from 21 households filled in the online pretest. To monitor real energy consumption in this period also hardware was installed in the households. It took at least 21 days of monitoring to set a firm baseline. All participants above 12 years replied to the pretest questionnaire about attitude and knowledge measurements and the first engagement questionnaire in the second week of the intervention. Participants were randomly assigned to conditions, however we took care that there was a global matching between conditions on the composition of the household (adults and children), attitude towards energy conservation (higher or lower than average compared to other participants) and energy consumption (higher or lower than average of the same type of households in The Netherlands). Knowledge scores are not used in this assignment process because all participants scored very low. All household types are equally represented in each condition. 11 Households are assigned to the game condition and 10 households are assigned to the control condition. The intervention started in June and ended in July 2017. Some households ended later due to delay in starting new sessions. From the 11 households that started in the game condition 6 households finished on schedule (Mean 5,5 weeks) and 4 households finished later (Mean 18 weeks). 1 Household did not finish the game. From the 10 households that started in the control condition 5 finished in mean 13 weeks and the other 5 households stopped halfway after 4 weeks.

When a household finished all the sessions they were asked to fill in the online posttest. Only 15 participants, a third of total, respond to the second questionnaire about engagement before the last week of the intervention and the posttest questionnaire about attitude and knowledge measurement after the intervention. These 15 participants that responded to all questionnaires are from 7 households in only the game condition.

The hardware was disconnected after at least 21 days from the end of the intervention.

3   Results

The effects on energy conservation and knowledge, engagement, and attitude measures are presented below. Energy conservation between the game and control condition is based on 6 households from the game condition that have finished on schedule (mean 5,5 weeks) and 5 households from the control condition that have finished (mean 13 weeks). 4 Households that finished the game later (mean 18 weeks) did not provide data on energy consumption within the time constraints for our study. Unfortunately the post-measurements fell in the heating season.

Only knowledge, engagement, and attitude measures from the game condition are discussed due to lack of sufficient observations in the control condition on the questionnaires.

3.1   Energy Conservation Measures

The results in energy conservation between households in the game and control condition are presented in Table 1. The average energy consumption per day from 21 days after the intervention is compared to the consumption over 21 days before the intervention. The difference in percentage change of total energy consumption ($\%\Delta$ kWh electricity + $\%\Delta$ m^3 gas/2) is presented as well as the percentage change in consumption in kWh electricity and m³ gas. An independent-samples t-test on the gain scores is performed to test if differences in percentages of change between the game and control condition are significant.

Table 1. Energy conservation: mean changes, standard deviations, t-statistic and significance levels of difference.

Energy conservation	Game		Control		Diff	t	p
	M	SD	M	SD	M		
Total	21,4%	7,7	−12,2%	18,5	33,6%	−4,081	<0,005
kWh Electricity	12,9%	7,9	−1,7%	16,6	14,5%	−1,915	<0,05*
M³ Gas	30%	12,1	−22,7%	38,3	52,7%	−3,211	<0,05

* one-tailed test

There is a significant major difference of 33,6% in total change in energy conservation between both conditions: $t (9) = -4,081$, $p < 0,005$: while the game condition consumes 21,4% less energy than before the intervention, the control condition consume 12,2% more energy. When we look specifically at conservation of kWh electricity there is a significant difference of 14,5% between groups: $t (9) = -1,915$, $p < 0,05$ (one-tailed test). The game condition consumes almost 13% less kWh electricity than before, while the control condition consumption is almost the same as before the intervention. The largest significant difference between the groups is 52,7% m³ gas consumption: $t (9) = -3,211$, $p < 0,05$. Notable is that in general the standard deviation of the control condition is high.

3.2 Knowledge, Engagement and Attitude Measures

The results in knowledge, engagement and attitude measures of participants are presented in Table 2. These fifteen participants who filled out all questionnaires (thirty percent of all participants), as explained above, are only from the game condition. A paired-samples t-test is executed to conclude if differences between the pretest and posttest are significant.

Table 2. Knowledge, engagement & attitude in the game condition: means, standard deviations, t-statistic and significance levels of difference.

	Pretest		Posttest		Post - Pre		t	p
	M	SD	M	SD	M	SD		
Knowledge*	4,27	1,62	5,8	1,93	1,53	1,81	−3,29	0,005
Engagement	5,35	0,94	5,29	0,75	−0,06	0,45	0,54	ns
Attitude								
Total	5,38	0,85	5,34	0,74	−0,04	0,4	0,391	ns
Micro-level	5,35	0,88	5,43	0,75	0,09	0,51	−0,662	ns
Macro-level	5,41	0,92	5,25	0,81	−0,17	0,4	1,609	ns

* Maximum score = 12, ns - not significant at 0,05 level

The average score on knowledge increased from 4,27 to 5,8 points. Although the average score in the posttest is not high (the maximum score possible is 12 points), knowledge about energy conservation increased significant: $t(14) = -3,29, p < 0,05$.

The engagement is high and constant during the intervention. There is no significance difference in engagement at the beginning and end of the intervention: $t(13) = 0,54, p > 0,05$.

All attitude scores are already high from the beginning and the intervention did not lead to a significant attitude change: Attitude total: $t(14) = 0,391, p > 0,05$; Attitude at micro-level: $t(14) = -0,662, p > 0,05$; Attitude at macro-level: $t(14) = 1,609, p > 0.05$.

4   Conclusion and Discussion

Based on the results of this study we conclude that there are differences in learning the same content of a persuasive energy conservation game, developed by using an iterative user-centered game design methodology, compared to a dashboard control condition. Furthermore, and most importantly, we conclude that energy consumption changed significantly on the long term. A persuasive game that includes reality by using reversed gamification principles is, thus, effective in learning people to save energy in the household and to actually do that for the long term, while an energy dashboard does not change that behaviour at all. Similar studies [e.g. 3; 4; 10; 11; 16; 20] also presented positive results but had some shortcomings; the lack of a control condition, the intervention time was short, no real consumption measurements are used, implementation of gamification could be better, limited number of variables is measured and/or the lack of pre-measurements & post-measurements [9], which altogether could explain that the positive effect on energy conservation in our study is higher than in previous studies.

From the beginning of the intervention, participants in the dashboard control condition had delay in starting missions (mean 13 weeks to finish while 5 weeks is possible), did not carry out missions (no energy conservation) or quit (50% in 4 weeks). Unfortunately, these participants in the control condition were not motivated to respond to questionnaires, so the resulting number of questionnaires is too small for meaningfully analyzing the data. It is possible that some participants are disappointed in that they are not assigned to the game condition and therefore less motivated. But there are also participants from the control condition who stated after the intervention that they did not prefer to be assigned to the game condition. In the game condition energy consumption (behaviour) changed and knowledge about saving energy at home increased. Also in this condition, despite of the long intervention time, engagement remained high during the whole intervention. These results align with the earlier mentioned chain of events that higher awareness (more accessible knowledge) for a longer period leads to increased knowledge, which leads to behaviour change on the long term. The attitude scores on micro-level and macro-level are extremely high, both nearly the same and the intervention did not change it. Because of this a ceiling effect regarding attitude could be the case, resulting in no-gain in attitude but still a positive change in energy conservation behaviour.

Krosnick and Petty [14] mention that the more extreme an attitude is, the more an individual likes the object of the attitude, and should be more likely to guide behaviour. It is surprising that during the intervention a substantial number of participants in the control condition, thus with an extreme attitude score, dropped out. It is possible that behaviour intention within the attitude diminished [14]. In future research questionnaires have to be modified to study this phenomenon. These results can have considerable implications for policymakers and companies in the field of smart energy meters. Now in practice only dashboard designs are used to give feedback on energy consumption (e.g. Nest) and our data seem to indicate that these designs are probably not effective on the long term [12].

Constraints in this study are that only from participants in the game condition all dependent variables (knowledge, attitude, engagement and behaviour) could be analyzed and that there is not sufficient data to look closely at the control condition. Independent of the preceding, the results also showed in the control condition no positive change was attained in the long run. Another constraint is the limited number of households participating in this study. This limitation also occurs in related studies [3, 4, 10, 16, 20]. Although the number of households was limited, still significant differences are found. There is a possibility to scale up the number of participants if the smart energy meter can be monitored without additional hardware and a large(r) campaign to recruit households is launched.

To bring the research field on energy reduction games a step further, the research question would be useful "Which persuasive features of a persuasive game exactly promote lasting changes in knowledge, attitude and behaviour regarding sustainable energy use of households?". For that purpose we will in a next phase of research apply a "value added" approach [15]. Here we examine the effects of the persuasive features personal relevance (by means of customized avatars) and social interaction (by means of competition) – separately and combined - on participants' knowledge, attitude and behaviour with respect to sustainable energy consumption with *Powersaver Game*.

References

1. Adams, E.: Fundamentals of Game Design, 3rd edn. Pearson, Peachpit, California (2014)
2. Aronson, E., Wilson, T.D., Akert, R.M.: Social Psychology. Pearson, Upper Saddle River (2013)
3. Bang, M., Gustafsson, A., Katzeff, C.: Promoting new patterns in household energy consumption with pervasive learning games. In: de Kort, Y., et al. (eds.) Persuasive Technology. LNCS, vol. 4744, pp. 55–63. Springer, Heidelberg (2007). https://doi.org/10.1007/978-3-540-77006-0_7
4. Bang, M., Svahn, M., Gustafsson, A.: Persuasive design of a mobile energy conservation game with direct feedback and social cues. In: Proceedings of the 2009 DiGRA International Conference: Breaking New Ground: Innovation in Games, Play, Practice and Theory (2009)
5. Chen, S., Chaiken, S.: The heuristic-systematic model in its' broader context. In: Chaiken, S., Trope, Y. (eds.) Dual Process Theories in Social Psychology. Guilford Press, New York (1999)
6. Deterding, S., Khaled, R., Nacke, L., Dixon, D.: Gamification: toward a definition. In: CHI 2011 Gamification Workshop Proceedings. ACM Press, Vancouver (2011)

7. Dickey, M.D.: Murder on Grimm Isle: the impact of game narrative design in an educational game-based learning environment. Br. J. Educ. Technol. **42**(3), 456–469 (2011)
8. Fijnheer, J.D.L., van Oostendorp, H.: Steps to design a household energy game. Int. J. Serious Games **3**(3), 16 (2016)
9. Fijnheer, J.D.L., van Oostendorp, H., Veltkamp, R.C.: Gamification in a prototype household energy game. In Connolly, T., Boyle, L. (eds.), Proceedings of the 10th European Conference on Game Based Learning - ECGBL 2016, pp. 192–201. ACPI, Paisley (2016)
10. Gamberini, L., et al.: Tailoring feedback to users' actions in a persuasive game for household electricity conservation. In: Bang, M., Ragnemalm, E.L. (eds.) Persuasive Technology, Design for Health and Safety. LNCS, vol. 7284, pp. 100–111. Springer, Heidelberg (2012). https://doi.org/10.1007/978-3-642-31037-9_9
11. Gustafsson, A., Katzeff, C., Bang, M.: Evaluation of a pervasive game for domestic energy engagement among teenagers. ACM Comp. Entertain. **7**(4), 1–19 (2009)
12. Hargreaves, T., Nye, M., Burgess, J.: Making energy visible: a qualitative field study of how householders interact with feedback from smart energy monitors. Energy Policy **38**(10), 6111–6119 (2010)
13. Kors, M., van der Spek, E., Schouten, B.: A foundation for the persuasive gameplay experience. In: Proceedings of the International Conference on the Foundations of Digital Games, CA, USA (2015)
14. Krosnick, J.A., Petty, R.E.: Attitude strength: an overview. In: Petty, R.E., Krosnick, J.A. (eds.) Attitude Strength: Antecedents and Consequences, pp. 1–24. Erlbaum, Mahwah (1995)
15. Mayer, R.E.: Multimedia learning and games. In: Tobias, S., Fletcher, J.D. (eds.) Computer Games and Instruction, pp. 281–305. Information Age Publishing, Charlotte (2011)
16. Reeves, B., Cummings, J.J., Scarborough, J.K., Yeykelis, L.: Increasing energy efficiency with entertainment media: an experimental and field test of the influence of a social game on performance of energy behaviors. Envir. Behav. **20**(10), 1–14 (2013)
17. Ruggiero, D.: The Effect of a Persuasive Game on Attitude towards the Homeless. Unpublished thesis, Purdue University (2013)
18. Schneider, E.F., Lang, M., Shin, M., Bradley, S.D.: Death with a story how story impacts emotional, motivational, and physiological responses to first- person shooter video games. Hum. Commun. Res. **30**(3), 361–375 (2004)
19. Soekarjo, M., van Oostendorp, H.: Measuring effectiveness of persuasive games using an informative control condition. Int. J. Serious Games **2**(2), 37–56 (2015)
20. Svahn, M.: Persuasive Pervasive Games: the Case of Impacting Energy Consumption. Dissertation, Stockholm School of Economics, Stockholm, Sweden (2014)
21. Van der Spek, E.D.: Experiments in serious game design: A cognitive approach. Dissertation, Utrecht University, Utrecht, The Netherlands (2011)
22. Watt, S.E., Maio, G.R., Haddock, G., Johnson, B.T.: Attitude functions in persuasion: matching, involvement, self-affirmation, and hierarchy. In: Crano, W.D., Prislin, R. (eds.) Attitudes and Attitude Change, pp. 189–211. Psychology Press, New York (2008)

Analyzing and Predicting Player Performance in a Quantum Cryptography Serious Game

Dilanga Abeyrathna, Srikanth Vadla, Vidya Bommanapally,
Mahadevan Subramaniam, Parvathi Chundi$^{(\boxtimes)}$, and Abhishek Parakh

Computer Science Department, University of Nebraska, Omaha 68182, USA
pchundi@unomaha.edu

Abstract. An adaptive 3D serious game, *QuaSim* for imparting to learners the fundamental concepts of quantum cryptography and their applications in designing computer security protocols is described. *QuaSim* emulates an often used instructional model of practice exercises followed by timed-tests (practice-timed-test) in a serious game setting by automatically designing timed-tests guided by models learned from data about the performance of players in practice exercises. *QuaSim* also automatically selects next practice exercises based on player performance in previous exercises. The game was played by 150 students and the results are highly encouraging. They show that the model learned by the game is able to select next practice exercises to improve player performance in the timed tests and is able to generate meaningful timed-tests.

1 Introduction

Serious games have been widely used to complement and assist traditional classroom instruction in various aspects of computer security [1, 2, 4–6, 11]. The immersive and engaging experience provided by serious games have made them highly pervasive in learning complex security concepts. The recent rapid advances in quantum computing and cryptography along with their inherent multidisciplinary nature involving concepts from quantum physics, mathematics, and computer science, pose formidable challenges for students to become proficient in this field. Inspired by the success of serious games in enhancing learning, we present an adaptive 3D game, *QuaSim*, that can supplement traditional instruction in imparting to learners the fundamentals of quantum cryptography and their applications in designing various computer security protocols.

A novel feature of the *QuaSim* game is its automated emulation of the often-used practice exercises followed by timed-tests *(practice-timed-tests)* instruction model within a serious game. A *QuaSim* game session consists of a set of lessons, which are comprised of a set of exercises. Each lesson is tagged with a set of concepts that the players are expected to learn using a finite set of resources provided for this purpose. The exercises in each lesson are interactive game scenarios (problems), classified into practice and timed-test scenarios. Players may engage in practice scenarios until they succeed, or their resources are exhausted. The timed-test scenarios are dynamically generated upon successful completion of practice scenarios and are parameterized by time and concepts. Appropriate values for time and concepts are automatically learned

© Springer Nature Switzerland AG 2019
M. Gentile et al. (Eds.): GALA 2018, LNCS 11385, pp. 267–276, 2019.
https://doi.org/10.1007/978-3-030-11548-7_25

by the game based on a classifier that is trained on player interaction data from the practice scenarios. The practice-timed-test model allows *QuaSim* to simulate a traditional instruction model that is customized for each student in a serious game setting that provides an immersive and engaging experience.

The *QuaSim* takes this emulation a step further, by choosing practice exercises dynamically based on observed player performance. To perform such a selection, each problem in each exercise is tagged with the associated concepts, and the next exercise chosen by the selection algorithm for a player ensures target concept coverage while maintaining a high degree of exploration of concepts. For instance, if the player has succeeded in concept *a*, and has had an unsuccessful attempt involving concept *b*, the game favors an exercise involving concepts *b* and a new concept *c* over an exercise involving a prior seen concept *a* and the concept *b*. The chosen next practice exercises manifest in the form of player hints that are either manual (*mhint*-displayed on players request), semi-automatic (*sahint*-displayed but are activated by player), or automatic (*ahint*-perform automatic selection). These hints are referred to as *adaptive gaming hints* which help players to navigate to the next problem they are eligible and are generated by an algorithm (For More details, please refer to [3]). The next problem generated by algorithm is based on the problems the player solved and the learning concepts covered up to that point. In the *sahint* and *mhint* modes, players have an option to accept or reject these hints. If a player accepts the hint, they are directed to the chosen problem. Otherwise, they continue to solve problems sequentially.

QuaSim game was played by 150 students (26 females and 124 males, 143 graduates, 7 undergraduate seniors). Our major objectives were to study the effectiveness of emulation of practice-timed-test instruction model in *QuaSim* and that of automatic selection of hints based on proficiency and exploration value of knowledge concepts. Three research questions we studied were – *RQ1*: what correlation, if any, does the pre-game knowledge acquired through lectures and prior gaming have on success in a timed-test scenario? *RQ2*: do the hints about next practice exercise affect the player success in a timed-test scenario? and *RQ3*: is it feasible to learn a model that can predict the player success in a timed-test scenario based on their performance in the practice scenarios?

Our results show that while there was no significant correlation between the pregame data and the performance on the timed-test scenarios, players with the automatic hints selecting the next exercise performed better than their counterparts in the timed-tests. Our results also show that we can train a multi-label classifier to accurately predict player proficiency in concepts based on their performance in practice scenarios, which can then be used to design meaningful timed-tests. Our preliminary results are highly encouraging and lead us to believe that incorporating a practice-timed-tests model in a push-button manner in a serious game about quantum cryptography can complement traditional instruction and result in positive learning gains.

2 Related Work

Several game-based systems have been designed in the computer security domain including those that teach concepts in quantum cryptography [2, 12]. Cone et al. [5, 6] present a highly interactive video game CyberCIEGE, a security awareness tool which enables users of an organization to accomplish security training objectives. Boopathi et al. [4] introduce a gaming method (interactive video quiz) to test students' knowledge in several computer security concepts with a final goal to provide computer security training. Labuschagne et al. [11] show an interactive web-based game that notifies and examines users about security threats and vulnerabilities, eventually making cyber security awareness. A shape changing cube and a bouncing ball game are used by Benjamin et al. to visually teach superposition, and qubit orientation in [2, 12].

Recently, there has been a lot of interest in integrating traditional instructional methods along with gaming to design serious games with high learning value. The mapping of learning mechanics to game mechanics (LM-GM mapping) is described by Arnab et al. [1] where they propose high level model to incorporate educational game elements in a serious game. In this context, Dicheva et al. [7] study gamification design principles, game mechanics, context of applying gamification based on educational level, academic subject and type of application etc. Smith et al. [13] discuss about their game for STEM education, game development strategy, and how it helped to improve the learning and engagement of student.

Our work in this paper is similar in spirit to the above works in terms of integrating traditional instructional elements into serious games. In this context, we have described how the practice-timed-test paradigm can be incorporated into serious games to teach quantum cryptography concepts. A novel feature of the proposed work is that it integrates traditional instruction with gaming in a customized manner driven by learning from player data. Further, our data driven next exercise selection based on tagged knowledge concepts, while preserving engagement tightly integrates the benefits of serious games and learning. Also, there are several studies conducted for the analysis and improvement of serious games using the machine learning techniques [8]. However, unlike these, the proposed approach performs predictive analysis using multi-label classification.

3 *QuaSim*: Quantum Cryptography Game

QuaSim is an interactive, multi-player, 3D game built using the Unreal Engine platform incorporating instructional components including videos, audio dialogues, auto-graded quizzes, and tests. Objective of this game is to teach the fundamental concepts of quantum cryptography and its applications in computer security protocols. The game scenarios occur at different high-rise buildings and open spaces in an urban setting. The scenarios are scored and can be continued to achieve success while resources are available. The game consists of two single player lessons targeting quantum cryptography basics, one single player lesson targeting quantum communication and two multi-player lessons involving the quantum key exchange protocols. Each lesson consists of several exercises that introduce new concepts and mathematical notations.

Each exercise consists of multiple problems that reinforce the associated concepts by varying the values. The Figs. 1(a) and (b) show an instance of the two lessons, Lesson 1 or polarization and Lesson 2 or superposition respectively. Refer [3] for more description about the game.

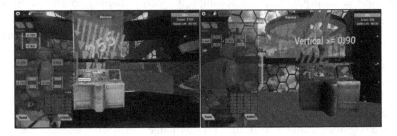

Fig. 1. (a): Lesson 1 screen shot shows a player firing a photon (qubit) at 255° to activate the detector. (b): Lesson 2 screen shot shows player firing a qubit such that the vertical component is greater than or equal to 0.9.

4 Experiments

We analyzed the data collected from play sessions to evaluate the proficiency achieved by players to program a qubit at different orientations using the matrix, ket, and linear combination notations. Those players that achieved proficiency in these concepts in the first three exercises were then given a timed-test problem from the fourth exercise in the same session. The data analyses focused the following three main research questions – **RQ1**: What influence, if any, do the prior knowledge and gaming experience of players, have on the successful completion of a timed-test problem in Exercise 4? **RQ2**: Do the gaming elements related to hints influence player's success in such a timed-test? **RQ3**: Can we predict the player performance in a problem in Exercise 4 with respect to the concepts involved in the problem?

Addressing these questions enables us to assess (*i*) utility of *QuaSim* in instructing players about programming qubits, (*ii*) the feasibility of emulating practice-timed-test instruction model in *QuaSim* and (*iii*) study the impact of automatic selection of next exercise by the game on player proficiency achievement.

4.1 Experimental Setup

The *QuaSim* game was played by 150 players (26 females and 124 males, 143 graduate students, 7 seniors) in a media lab. Of these, 23, played the game no hints, 43 played the *ahint* version, 42 played the *sahint* version, and 42 played the *mhint* version. Play sessions were about an hour long and were conducted on an Windows 10 Intel i7 @ 3.40 GHz processor machine, with 16 GB RAM, NVIDIA GeForce GT 730 graphic card. Each player completed a background demographics survey, and watched a short video introducing *QuaSim* features before start.

Dataset. *QuaSim* assigns each player a unique *PlayerID* and logs every action of the players in the *QuaSim* database (*SQLite3*). Players also completed a qualitative survey after completing the game. *QuaSim* logs player interactions in a game session as *time-stamped events*. In *QuaSim*, *SessionID* is a unique identifier which identifies all events from a *login* to *logout* of a player. Each event has an *EventID* and *EventData*. For example, if *EventID* is 1 (to display the problem and problem type information), then the corresponding *EventData* will be *'Angle:90 Problem Type: Orthogonal'*. *Event-Time* has the time at which an event is triggered and it is stored in format [yyyy-mm-dd hh:mm:ss:SSS]. A player session in *QuaSim* may generate over 100 distinct events most of which are analyzed in our experiments.

4.2 RQ1: Pre-game Data and Player Performance

To address **RQ1**, we studied the any possible correlation between the player pre-game data collected by *QuaSim* and their success in solving a problem from Exercise 4. The pre-game data collected from players consists of 15 attributes and includes the pre-requisite courses completed, knowledge and interest levels in classical, quantum cryptography, and mathematics, and prior experience with computer games. The completion status of prerequisite courses (9 courses in total) such as *Mathematical Foundations of Computer Science, Data Structures, Theory of Computation, Introduction to Algorithms* and *Cryptography*, is collected using check boxes provided (recorded as 1 or 0). To collect data about a player's interests and background knowledge, slide bars (0–100) are provided to collect the level of interest/knowledge in *classical cryptography*, *quantum cryptography*, *mathematics* and previous game experience. Using these 15 attributes, we compute a numerical score called the *pre-game strength*, representing the strength of the pregame knowledge of a student. We add the slide bar values and n × 100 where n is the number of prerequisite courses (to homogenize with other pregame data), to obtain *pre-game strength* of a player. High value of *pre-game strength* denotes student with good background knowledge. We also have computed the success of a player in a problem from Exercise 4 based on the time taken to correctly solve it *problem-completion time* (T_c). T_c is the time duration between the *EventTime* when the player reaches the problem-solving region to *EventTime* when the quantum receptor gets activated. Then, we obtain a normalized T_c value for each player as follows. Let *maxtime* be the maximum time taken by any player to solve a problem in Exercise 4 and *mintime* be the minimum time taken by any player to solve a problem in Exercise 4[1]. Then, *normalized problem-completion time* $NT_c = ((maxtime - T_c)/(maxtime - mintime)) * 100$.

In the first experiment, we determined the effect of *pre-game strength* measure on NT_c as follows. Pearson correlation method [10] was used on *pre-game strength* and the NT_c for 3 different groups group1, group2 and group3 which are divided based on the standard quartiles Q1, Q2 and Q3 of NT_c respectively. We used *Pearson correlation* method since it is a standard method to measure the linear correlation strength between two variables. Also, we have conducted hypothesis test where the *p* value

---

[1] In our experiments, *mintime* was around 70 s, and *maxtime* was around 6 min.

Pregame attributes	Group1		Group2		Group3	
	r	p	r	p	r	p
Prerequisite strength	0.236	0.074	-0.049	0.615	0.231	0.118
Knowledge in classical crypto	-0.04	0.595	0.305	0.031	-0.014	0.529
Knowledge in quantum crypto	-0.326	0.979	0.086	0.305	0.035	0.431
Interest in classical crypto	-0.173	0.854	0.285	0.042	-0.064	0.626
Interest in quantum crypto	-0.265	0.949	0.04	0.407	-0.057	0.613
Interest in mathematics	-0.34	0.983	0.027	0.436	0.167	0.198
Previous gaming experience	0.015	0.464	-0.055	0.629	0.24	0.11

Fig. 2. Pre-game data and NT_c correlation results

$(0 < p < 1)$ weighs the strength of the evidence of the correlation results. A small p value (i.e., $<=0.05$) indicates strong evidence against the null hypothesis and large p value indicates weak against the null hypothesis. From this experiment, we observed very small values of r and very large values of p for all the 3 groups ($r = 0.118$, $p = 0.236$ for group1, $r = 0.007$, $p = 0.483$ for group2, $r = 0.227$, $p = 0.121$ for group3) which denotes that there is no strong correlation between the *pre-game strength* and the success (NT_c) of the player and even the hypothesis test revealed no strong evidence about the results.

Similarly, we have done another experiment to see if there was any correlation between each pregame attribute related to a players interest/knowledge in classical/quantum cryptography, mathematics, and computer games, and prior gaming experience and NT_c (see Fig. 2). However, this experiment (see Fig. 2) also reported very small values of r and large values of p for almost all the pregame attributes among all the groups. From the Fig. 2, we can observe that only the attributes knowledge in classical crypto and interest in classical crypto for the group2 players has some positive correlation with the NT_c with strong evidence to reject the null hypothesis, and remaining attributes has no strong correlation results.

From these results, it is clear that *there is no significant linear correlation between player's pre-game knowledge and their success in solving problems from Exercise 4.* This experiment establishes that *QuaSim* game can be effective to teach quantum cryptography concepts to players with limited background in classical or quantum cryptography and previous gaming experience.

4.3   RQ2: Next Exercise Hints and Player Performance

For **RQ2** we analyzed the time taken by each player to complete a timed-test problem from Exercise 4 $(T_c)^2$ and his/her performance in Exercises 1, 2, and 3. For this analysis, we considered the average time taken by a player to complete Exercises 1, 2 and 3 and time taken for Exercise 4 for each player. Let T_l be the total time taken by a player to complete problems form Exercises 1 through 3. We can think of this time interval as the time taken by the player to learn the concepts. Let P be the number of

---

[2] Recall from previous section that players completed this test in around 70–420 s range.

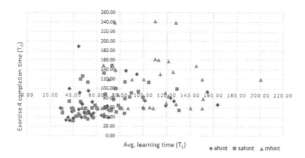

Fig. 3. Practice vs Test time vs Hints

problems the player completed from Exercise 1 to 3, then the average learning time say AT_l of a player to complete Exercises 1 to 3 is simply T_l/P.

We then categorized the players into 4 regions based on thresholds pertaining to ATl and T_c as suggested by the experts (the faculty members in the project). The threshold ATH_l for AT_l was set to 80 s and for T_c, the threshold TH_c was set to 100 s. The four regions being R_1: $AT_l > ATH_l$, $T_c > TH_c$ with 18% of players, R_2: $AT_l < ATH_l$, $T_c > TH_c$ with 8% of the players, R_3: $AT_l < ATH_l$, $T_c < TH_c$ with 48% of the players, and R_4: $AT_l > ATH_l$, $T_c < TH_c$, with 26% of the players. Those players in R_3 took less time to complete all exercises in the game and therefore, can be thought of as *successful* learners. Figure 3 shows this distribution of players in the four regions with X-Axis depicting AT_l and Y-Axis depicting T_c.

We then studied the types of hints – *ahint* mode, *sahint* mode, and *mhint* mode used by players. Of the Players in region R_3, 45% played *QuaSim* in *ahint* mode, and 37% in *sahint* mode. The rest of the players played *QuaSim* in *mhint* mode (See Fig. 3). To support the results a chi-square test of independence, with the null hypothesis, players' performance is independent of hints was performed to examine the influence of hints on players' success/failure. The null hypothesis is rejected as $\chi^2(2, N = 160) = 17.081$, $p < 0.001$. From this it is evident that hints had an influence on the players' performance, as the hints reduce the distractions that may be caused due to other gaming elements and keep the player engaged in a directed way towards achieving the targeted proficiency based on their performance. Whereas without hints players could choose random exercises irrespective of their result in the current exercise, they could lose engagement. Refer [3] for more details on how hints influenced the rate of proficiency achieved by the players. We also observed that players in *mhint* mode tend to use fewer hints (only 20% of the hints suggested) during the game when compared to players in *sahint* mode who followed around 75% of the hints. We also analyzed the pre-game data provided by the players in each region and observed that players that indicated less background knowledge in math and cryptography fall in region R_3 or R_4. This indicates that the game *QuaSim* was pretty helpful for players to learn the concepts despite their background.

4.4   Multi-label Classifier to Predict Concept Proficiency in Tests

In this experiment, we created a multi-label dataset having 150 records, 1 record per player consisting 23 features and 5 labels. Gaming activities measured during the learning process and *pre-game strength* is considered as the feature set. Concepts covered in Exercise 4 *Matrix, ket, linear combination, Same, Orthogonal, and opposite quadrant angle* are considered as label set of the data set. A concept label for a record is 1 if the player successfully completed that concept in Exercise 4. If a player quit Exercise 4 or could not complete the task within given time threshold, the concept label for the record is assigned 0.

There are 16 features related to the gaming activities namely, hint mode used *ahint, sahint, mhint,* number of attempts and time taken for each problem during Exercise 1 to Exercise 3, health remaining after completion of the game 0%–100% and counts of accepted hints. Rest of the features are pre-game attributes with number of prerequisite courses completed by the player which is in a range of [0–9], and knowledge in classical cryptography, knowledge in quantum cryptography, interest in classical cryptography, interest in quantum cryptography, interest in mathematics and previous experience in computer games which are measured in the range of [0–100]. Then, the data set split into training and testing sets for cross validation purposes. This holdout cross validation is done with stratified sampling-based technique to guarantee that each class is properly represented in training and testing sets. Sampling is done so that training set covers 70% of the dataset and the rest 30% used for testing the model computed from the training set. Finally, we used both binary relevance (BR) [9] and label powerset (LP) [14] methods to learn a multi-label model for the input data set. We used BR as it provides independent prediction of performances and LP as it provides classification performances by considering label dependencies. The goal of using multi-label classification is to use the demographic and game interactions of a player to predict if he/she can successfully demonstrate the knowledge of a fundamental concept during the solving of Exercise 4. The evaluation of models learned by multi-label learning methods requires different measures than those used in case of single label data. A unified presentation and categorization of existing evaluation measures for multi-label classification is given in [15]. The evaluation in this experiment is based on the popular and indicative **accuracy** and **micro-F1** measures. The main reason of using both evaluation measures is higher accuracy alone does not always determine the predictive power (Accuracy Paradox) of a classifier. We ran the experiment for different thresholds on T_c, (the time taken to successfully complete a problem in Exercise 4) to see if accuracy of the multi-label model changes with increasing threshold value. As the threshold value on Tc increases, the label set of input set can contain more 1's. Both BR and LP algorithms were trained using base-level learning algorithm, Support Vector Machine, for the training set and the predictive performance of the models was collected using the test data set. All the These steps were iterated for 10 times for each time threshold and the accuracy and micro-F1 measure values are collected for each run. Figure 4 shows classification accuracy and micro-F1 measures of two classification algorithms. The X-axis in the figure shows the different threshold values on T_c and the Y-axis plots the predictive accuracy in the chart on the left side (a) and plots micro-F1 measure in the chart on the right side (b). According to the Fig. 4(a) it is clear that

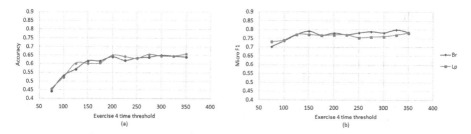

Fig. 4. (a) Classification accuracy for given time constraints, (b) micro-F1 measures for given time constraints.

predictive accuracy of the classifier ranges from 45% to more than 65%. It reaches the maximum predictive accuracy of 65% for $T_c = 150$ and stabilizes somewhat for higher threshold values, for both BR and LP methods. When we consider the micro-F1 measures (see Fig. 4(b)), it is observed that the results are almost remained constant between 0.7 and 0.8 for all the time thresholds. Hence, we can say that when the time constraint assigned is feasible (that is, it provides sufficient time for a normal player to complete Exercise 4), classification model can predict the outcome of Exercise 4 for a majority of players. Based on this we can infer that the player performance in the practice exercise scenarios can be used by *QuaSim* to automatically design timed test problems involving relevant concepts.

5   Conclusions

An adaptive, 3D serious game *QuaSim* for learning quantum cryptography and their applications in designing various security protocols is described. The multi-player game built using Unreal platform incorporated traditional instructional components into a serious game in a data driven manner. The data obtained from player interactions in the practice game scenarios were used to learn a model based on a multi-label classifier to identify player proficiency in associated knowledge concepts and were used to generate meaningful timed-tests to assess the players. The game also used a next practice exercise selection algorithm to automatically select practice problems based on player past performance in order to steer them towards the required target concept proficiency while preserving their engagement. Experiments involving 150 undergraduate seniors and graduate students were performed to study the effectiveness of the proposed approach.

References

1. Arnab, S., et al.: Mapping learning and game mechanics for serious games analysis. Br. J. Edu. Technol. **46**(2), 391–411 (2015)
2. Benjamin, S.C., Hayden, P.M.: Multiplayer quantum games. Phys. Rev. A **64**(3), 030301 (2001)
3. Bommanapally, V., Subramaniam, M., Chundi, P.: Navigation hints in serious games. In: Beck, D., et al. (eds.) Online Proceedings from Fourth Immersive Learning Research Network Conference, Technischen Universitat Graz, Missoula, Montana (2018)
4. Boopathi, K., Sreejith, S., Bithin, A.: Learning cyber security through gamification. Indian J. Sci. Technol. **8**(7), 642–649 (2015)
5. Cone, B.D., Irvine, C.E., Thompson, M.F., Nguyen, T.D.: A video game for cybersecurity training and awareness. Comput. Secur. **26**(1), 63–72 (2007)
6. Cone, B.D., Thompson, M.F., Irvine, C.E., Nguyen, T.D.: Cyber security training and awareness through game play. In: Fischer-Hübner, S., Rannenberg, K., Yngström, L., Lindskog, S. (eds.) SEC 2006. IIFIP, vol. 201, pp. 431–436. Springer, Boston, MA (2006). https://doi.org/10.1007/0-387-33406-8_37
7. Dicheva, D., Dichev, C., Agre, G., Angelova, G.: Gamification in education: a systematic mapping study. J. Educ. Technol. Soc. **18**(3), 75–88 (2015)
8. Frutos-Pascual, M., Zapirain, B.G.: Review of the use of AI techniques in serious games: decision making and machine learning. IEEE Trans. Comput. Intell. AI Games **9**(2), 133–152 (2017)
9. Gibaja, E., Ventura, S.: A tutorial on multilabel learning. ACM Comput. Surv. (CSUR) **47**(3), 52 (2015)
10. Hall, G.: Pearsons correlation coefficient. Other Words **1**(9) (2015)
11. Labuschagne, W., Veerasamy, N., Burke, I., Eloff, M.: Design of cyber security awareness game utilizing a social media framework. In: Information Security South Africa (ISSA), pp. 1–9. IEEE (2011)
12. Situ, H.: A quantum approach to play asymmetric coordination games. Quantum Inf. Process. **13**(3), 591–599 (2014)
13. Smith, K., Shull, J., Shen, Y., Dean, A., Michaeli, J.: Overcoming challenges in educational stem game design and development. In: 2017 Winter Simulation Conference (WSC), pp. 849–859. IEEE (2017)
14. Tsoumakas, G., Katakis, I.: Multi-label classification: an overview. Int. J. Data Warehouse. Min. (IJDWM) **3**(3), 1–13 (2007)
15. Tsoumakas, G., Vlahavas, I.: Random *k*-labelsets: an ensemble method for multilabel classification. In: Kok, J.N., Koronacki, J., de Mantaras, R.L., Matwin, S., Mladenič, D., Skowron, A. (eds.) ECML 2007. LNCS (LNAI), vol. 4701, pp. 406–417. Springer, Heidelberg (2007). https://doi.org/10.1007/978-3-540-74958-5_38

The RAGE Software Portal: Toward a Serious Game Technologies Marketplace

Wim Westera[1]([⊠]), Baltasar Fernandez-Manjon[2], Rui Prada[3],
Kam Star[4], Andrea Molinari[5], Dominic Heutelbeck[6], Paul Hollins[7],
Rubén Riestra[8], Krassen Stefanov[9], and Eric Kluijfhout[1]

[1] Open University of the Netherlands,
Valkenburgerweg 177, 6419 DL Heerlen, The Netherlands
{wim.westera, eric.kluijfhout}@ou.nl
[2] Universidad Complutense de Madrid,
Prof Jose Garcia Santesmases 9, 28040 Madrid, Spain
balta@fdi.ucm.es
[3] Instituto de Engenhariade Sistemas e Computadores,
Investigacao e Desenvolvimento em Lisboa,
Avenida Alves Redol 9, S Joao De Deus, 1000 029 Lisbon, Portugal
rui.prada@gaips.inesc-id.pt
[4] PlayGen Ltd., Princelet Street 42-46, London E1 5LP, UK
kam@playgen.com
[5] Okkam Srl, Via Segantini 23, Trento 38122, Italy
molinari@okkam.it
[6] FTK Forschungsinstitut für Telekommunikation und Kooperation Ev,
Martin-Schmeisser Weg 4, 44227 Dortmund, Germany
dheutelbeck@ftk.de
[7] The University of Bolton, Deane Road, Bolton BL35AB, UK
p.a.hollins@bolton.ac.uk
[8] Inmark Europa Sa, Av Llano Castellano 43, 28010 Madrid, Spain
ruben.riestra@grupoinmark.com
[9] Faculty of Mathematics and Informatics, Sofia University
"St. Kliment Ohridski", Sofia, Bulgaria
stefanov@fmi.uni-sofia.bg

Abstract. This paper presents the RAGE marketplace portal
(gamecomponents.eu), which is intended as a hot spot and neutral single point
of access for serious game technologies. The portal aims at fostering collaborations and the exchange of technical artefacts and associated knowledge and
resources between different stakeholders in the field of serious gaming (e.g.
educators, developers, researchers, publishers, policy makers and end-users).
After a brief introduction to the H2020 RAGE project, the flexible design of the
marketplace portal and its underlying software repository are presented.
A concise overview is given of the initial set of advanced game technology
components created by RAGE, that are currently exposed in the portal. For
empirical validation of these components, we have developed 7 serious games
based on subsets of these components, which were then tested in educational
practice with several hundreds of end-users. This game components portal want
to be a neutral hub not dependent on any technology or provider and therefore it

© Springer Nature Switzerland AG 2019
M. Gentile et al. (Eds.): GALA 2018, LNCS 11385, pp. 277–286, 2019.
https://doi.org/10.1007/978-3-030-11548-7_26

is open for new game technologies submissions. We envision this marketplace as a knowledge and game technologies hub to support and amplify serious game development.

Keywords: Serious games · Software components · Learning technology Marketplace · Education · Learning

1 Introduction

1.1 Serious Gaming as a European Priority

For serious game development to become an actual industry in Europe, a better transfer of knowledge and technologies from research to application (and especially to SMEs) is required. Among the priorities of the European Commission investments are the creation of new jobs and growth (a.k.a. the Juncker plan) and the transition to a more efficient digital single market. Accordingly, the European Commission has spent hundreds of millions Euros in the last decade to ICT-oriented research and innovation in the context of learning, from schools to higher education, workplace learning and life-long learning. This includes the priority of serious gaming, viz. the use of game approaches for non-entertainment purposes. However, the transfer of knowledge and technologies from research to societal sectors to create economic and social value is problematic. The process of knowledge valorisation often fails, thus demonstrating the "knowledge paradox" [1], which refers to the fact that increased public investments in science and technology do not translate into economic benefits and job creation, while leaving many scientific findings unused. This is even more painful in the case of serious game technologies, because of their dual role in both innovating the domain of education and contributing to raising skills levels in other domains. Upon the transition from FP7 to the Horizon 2020 programme (H2020), innovation was identified – in addition to research – as a separate priority, and the principal funding criterion of "excellent science" has been complemented with the criteria of "societal challenges" and "industrial leadership", highlighting the importance of impact beyond the scientific communities. This means that H2020-funded research projects should not only deliver relevant scientific output, but should also aim at the practical application of research outcomes by targeted end-users and even devise sustainable exploitation models for this.

1.2 Supporting an Emerging Industry

Notwithstanding the potential of serious games in education, training, health and other domains, the serious game industry displays many features of an emerging, immature business, e.g. weak interconnectedness, limited knowledge exchange, limited division of labour and insufficient evidence of the products' efficacies [2]. The industry is scattered over a large number of small independent players (SME's). Because of limited collaborations and limited interconnections between industry and research, these small companies display insufficient innovation power to open up new markets (e.g. schools, business, governments). Consequently, the reinforcement of a "gaming innovation ecosystem" is indicated, connecting and integrating research networks, networks of innovators and commercial parties across the entire value chain to reduce the entry cost and generate value [3].

1.3 The RAGE Project Supporting Serious Gaming

The H2020 RAGE project (www.rageproject.eu), combines advanced serious game technology research with a technology transfer mechanism. The technology research part focuses on creating advanced, reusable software components for serious games. These components cover a wide range of functionalities relevant for both the gaming domain and the technology-enhanced learning domain, including personalisation, adaptation, assessment, learning analytics, affective computing, among other topics [4]. The reuse of these dedicated components in new training applications would lead to higher quality solutions, reduced costs and reduced time-to-market. For the technology transfer part, RAGE establishes a marketplace portal to accommodate collaboration and exchange of knowledge and technologies among different stakeholders (e.g. educators, developers, researchers, publishers, policymakers and end-users). The marketplace portal would link supply and demand of knowledge and technologies and may ideally develop into a hot spot for (serious) gaming support, once a critical volume of users would be reached. The portal is readily positioned as an instrument to promote the formation of an "innovation ecosystem".

This paper presents the RAGE project as a driver of technology transfer in the serious gaming domain. First, its objectives and outcomes are presented. Thereafter, a brief overview is given of the software components and the games that were used for their validation, and a description of the marketplace portal. The paper is concluded with a discussion of critical factors.

2 The RAGE Project as a Driver of Innovation

2.1 Toward an Innovation Ecosystem

RAGE has launched a community portal that provides centralised access to a wide range of game technologies and knowledge resources. The project has created an initial collection of game software components (up to 40) and a multiple of associated knowledge and training resources, which are accessible at the portal. This collection of resources is complemented with community tools for annotation, rating, and social media integration, among other things. The portal addresses serious gaming stake-holders, which eventually will help to establish the desired innovation ecosystem. The software components and the marketplace portal are further detailed and explained in the next sections.

2.2 RAGE Reusable Software Components

To accommodate the easy integration and reuse of software in a wide diversity of development platforms, target platforms and programming languages, RAGE has prepared a component-based architecture [5] that assures compliancy with these different environments. This supports the wider uptake and applicability of the software. Even so, the marketplace portal should be "neutral" and would welcome any software that is relevant for technology-enhanced learning or serious gaming, whether or not it is compliant with this architecture.

The RAGE Component-Based Software Architecture

The RAGE architecture [6, 7] distinguishes between server-side components and client-side components. Remote communications of server-side components with centralised applications are based on a service-oriented architecture (SOA) using the HTTP-protocol (e.g. REST), which offers platform-independence and interoperability among heterogeneous technologies. In contrast, client-side RAGE components, which need to be integrated into client-machine applications (e.g. game engines), are likely to suffer from incompatibilities. Regarding the client-side, the RAGE component architecture omits dependencies of external software frameworks to avoid interference with the application code. Instead, it relies on a limited set of well-established software patterns (Bridge, Singleton, Publish/Subscribe) and coding practices aimed at decoupling abstraction from its implementation. This decoupling facilitates reusability of a component across different game engines and other client environments with minimal integration effort. The architecture was validated for multiple programming languages (C#, C++, Java, JavaScript) and proof cases have been established with real games developed with different technologies (e.g. C++, Unity3D, Cocos2D) [6, 7].

The Initial Set of Software Components

As explained above, RAGE has developed up to 40 initial software components, all of which offer pedagogically-oriented functionality to be integrated in digital learning solutions, such as serious games. Table 1 lists the various aggregate component packages that are currently exposed on the portal (http://gamecomponents.eu). All these components use the Apache 2.0 license (white label software), which allows for reuse by third parties both for commercial and non-commercial purposes, either under

Table 1. Initial set of RAGE software component packages

Package	# components
Game Analytics Suite	8
Player Competence Adaptation Pack	3
Player Motivation Adaptation Pack	2
Other Adaptation components	5
Real-Time Emotion and Arousal Detection	4
Easy Dialogue Integrator	2
Shared Data Storage	2
Performance Statistics	1
Social Gamification Framework	1
Social Agency	5
Natural Language Processing	6
Storytelling Framework (Role Play Character)	2
Evaluation	1

open source or closed source conditions. To promote the adoption and reuse of the software products exposed all products have been enriched with user guides, instructional materials, demonstrators and proof cases.

Validation of the Approach

To validate the approach, game studios within the RAGE consortium created 7 serious games based on the various software components, which were then tested and evaluated in real end-user pilots. The games focus on various social and entrepreneurial skills and address diverse educational contexts. Table 2 shows an overview of the games, their purpose, target groups, and the main component functionality used.

Table 2. Games used for testing and validation of RAGE components.

Game title	Purpose	Target group	Main component
Sports Team Manager	Leadership and management skills	Recreational sports leaders	Social Agency
Space Modules Inc	Customer helpdesk skills	Vocational IT students	Role Play Character
IT Alert	Collaboration skills	Vocational IT students	Social Gamification
Job Quest	Job application skills	Corporate candidates	Emotion Detection
Watercooler	Conflict management skills	Art and Design Students	Dialogue Integrator
Hatch	Creative Entrepreneurial skills	Art and Design students	Essay scoring
ISPO	Interrogation skills	Police officers	Text-to-speech

The games are used as proof cases of "components in action". As an example, Fig. 1 shows a screen of the Space Modules Inc. game, which is based on RAGE's role-play virtual character components. In this game on customer communication skills, the player takes on the role of a customer service representative working at the help desk of a spaceship part manufacturer. Customers with a variety of starting moods and emotional dispositions get in touch about faults they are experiencing. The player has to manage diverse situations and has to decide how best to respond.

RAGE's role-play virtual character components are used to model the decisions and emotional reactions of the diverse customers. In this process, the Emotional Appraisal Component evaluates how the virtual character's emotional state should change as a result of player actions, whilst the Emotional Decision Making component dictates the reaction of the character based on the changes to their emotional state. In the context of this game, the facial expression of the virtual character is determined by its mood, which is calculated using the values of their various emotional states as set by the Emotional Appraisal Component. Overall, the main purpose of the role-play components is to easily establish believable social behaviour of virtual characters.

Fig. 1. A screenshot from the Space Modules Inc. game, showing one of the customers.

More than 500 participants were involved in the first pilots to formatively evaluate the games with respect to usability, user-experience, motivation, learning outcomes, and costs versus benefits. After an iteration cycle based on the evaluations, improved versions of the games were used in a second pilot series, involving over 1500 participants in total. Results are being reported elsewhere. Gathering sound empirical evidence of both the effectiveness of the games for learning as well as the added value of diverse technology components is considered essential for devising relevant business cases and promoting wider adoption by the industry. Alongside RAGE pilot studies, a survey among software component developers and game developers has confirmed the practicability of the component-based architecture and the ease of integration and reuse of the components in diverse game engines. Details are in [8].

2.3 The Marketplace Portal

The RAGE marketplace portal, available at http://gamecomponents.eu, is the technical platform for exposing game technologies and resources. In contrast with existing marketplaces, which are either driven by commercial game platform vendors (e.g. Unity, CryTec, Unreal), by vendors of other creative software tools (e.g. Adobe), or general media stock asset marketplaces (e.g. graphicriver.net), the RAGE portal is "neutral", that is, not platform driven or game engine driven, but instead domain driven. With its focus on serious games it has a clear scope, not positioned as a by-product of leisure games. At the core of the portal is a digital repository of software objects and associated knowledge resources [9]. Figure 2 shows a screenshot of the software catalogue page.

The portal provides search functionalities and a high level categorisation of software into functional areas. The look and feel of the portal largely complies to what is common at existing marketplaces.

The submission process for new software is guided by a stepwise workflow (i.e. wizard) for entering the most relevant metadata and the associated artefacts (see Fig. 3). The software can either be uploaded as a separate zip archive or included as a

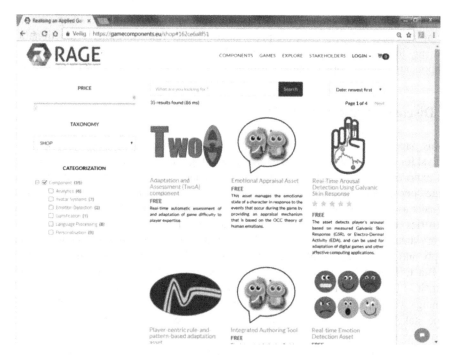

Fig. 2. A screenshot of the software catalogue at the marketplace portal (gamecomponents.eu).

Fig. 3. A screenshot displaying part of the software submission workflow.

reference to an external archive (e.g. Github). Also, associated artefacts (e.g. manuals, tutorials, videos, demos) can be provided. Integration with social media platforms such as Mendeley and Slideshare allow for easy import of pre-existing resources [9].

Finally, to support future sustainable exploitation of the portal including software pricing and paid subscriptions, the portal also includes full e-commerce functionality, allowing for secure financial transactions between parties. Still, all current RAGE components are free, open source software.

3 Discussion and Conclusion

In this paper, the H2020 RAGE marketplace portal was presented as a vehicle and a catalyst for amplifying the domain of serious gaming. Launching a portal, however, even if it exposes high quality technologies and associated knowledge resources, does not create "per se" an innovation ecosystem. An ecosystem should be a lively social system that acts as a catalyst among diverse stakeholders across the value chain: researchers, industries, education and government. To achieve this, it is needed to raise interest among stakeholders, engage them and demonstrate the value that the portal offers, so that supply and demand are amplified, and help to establish the self-sustained community.

But to have a successful marketplace, three critical factors need to be addressed. First, it is unclear if the initial set of RAGE technologies and related resources (e.g. training) would display sufficient critical mass to create traction among in the serious game stakeholders (e.g. game studios, developers, researchers). To increase its portfolio other research partners and projects are actively being approached and invited to expose their software at the portal. Already, visitors of the portal (at http:// gamecomponents.eu) can register and upload their own software for exposure at the marketplace. We have noticed that an exclusive focus on reusable software components in accordance with the RAGE architecture would be too restricted and might discourage third-part software developers to expose their software at the portal. Therefore, the portal allows for posting any software applications and platforms that are deemed relevant for serious gaming. Both production-level software and experimental software prototypes would be allowed, as well as associated knowledge resources.

Second, for professional users the quality of the exposed software and its associated resources is deemed crucial. This quality refers to correctness and style of coding, documentation of code, installation manuals, test suits, demos, evaluations, scientific evidence, maintenance info, and many more factors. In the concept of a community-driven marketplace, however, centralised quality control (i.e., checking and testing all the submitted products) is not a viable option. In the terms and conditions of the portal, it will be made explicit that all ownership, quality claims and liability of software products remain at the submitting parties. Still, to avoid low-quality software submissions four quality assurance mechanisms will be put in place:

- *Completeness of metadata*: In the submission workflow, completion of metadata is checked and indicated, as to make sure that submissions go with an appropriate set of metadata.
- *Self-assessed quality score*: In the submission workflow, the submitting party is asked to indicate the quality conditions of the software posted, such as the status of documentation, the availability of test suits and so on, which becomes visible for all users.

- *Community ratings*: To exploit the wisdom of the crowd, the portal includes a product rating system, which allows consumers to rate the products exposed. Weak software will be spotted soon and publicly disqualified. The overall software quality is raised by this reputation mechanism.
- *Automated quality checks*: To a limited extent, automated quality checks may be used to assess the submitted software. This may include generic test methodologies, such as using test suites, code coverage tests or error injection [10], but also tests specifically testing compliance with the RAGE architecture, for instance detecting incorrect implementation of software design patterns, or detection of component's API and bridge usage [6, 7].

Third, to effectively address the knowledge paradox RAGE also includes an exploitation and revenue model for the portal so that it can continue and grow beyond the lifetime of the project. Based on extensive stakeholder consultations, a Hybrid Multi-Sided Business Model has been selected as the best option, providing the flexibility and ability to eventually accommodate multiple revenue streams, such as subscription fees, e-commerce services, and premium services, and to adapt quickly to changing market conditions in the fluid and fractured serious game development landscape [11]. RAGE seeks active involvement with stakeholders who could support sustainable exploitation, either as technology users, technology providers or as participants in the governance of the platform. To continue the RAGE activities after the ending of the project (2019), a Foundation (legal entity) has been established, that is open to third parties, to look after the implementation and sustainable exploitation of the marketplace platform.

We expect that successful maintenance and exploitation of the marketplace may truly advance synergy and coherence in the serious gaming domain.

Acknowledgement. This work has been partially funded by the EC H2020 project RAGE (Realising an Applied Gaming Ecosystem; http://www.rageproject.eu/), Grant No 644187.

References

1. EC Green Paper on Innovation. European Commission, Brussels (1995). http://europa.eu/documents/comm/green_papers/pdf/com95_688_en.pdf. Accessed 15 Apr 2018
2. Stewart, J., et al.: The potential of digital games for empowerment and social inclusion of groups at risk of social and economic exclusion: evidence and opportunity for policy. In: Centeno, C. (ed.) Joint Research Centre, European Commission (2013). http://ipts.jrc.ec.europa.eu/publications/pub.cfm?id=6579. Accessed 15 Apr 2018
3. Jackson, D.J.: What is an Innovation Ecosystem. National Science Foundation, Arlington, VA, pp. 1–11 (2011). http://erc-assoc.org/sites/default/files/topics/policy_studies/DJackson_Innovation%20Ecosystem_03-15-11.pdf. Accessed 15 Apr 2018
4. Westera, W., Van der Vegt, W., Bahreini, K., Dascalu, M., Van Lankveld, G.: Software components for serious game development. In: Connolly, T., Boyle, L. (eds.) Proceedings of the 10th European Conference on Games Based Learning, Paisley, Scotland, 6–7 October 2016, pp. 765–772. ACPI, Reading (2016)

5. Bachmann, F., et al.: Technical concepts of component-based software engineering, vol. II. Carnegie Mellon University, Software Engineering Institute, Pittsburgh (2000)
6. van der Vegt, W., Westera, W., Nyamsuren, E., Georgiev, A., Martínez Ortiz, I.: RAGE architecture for reusable serious gaming technology components. Int. J. Comput. Games Technol., Article ID 5680526, 10 pages (2016). https://doi.org/10.1155/2016/5680526
7. van der Vegt, W., Nyamsuren, E., Westera, W.: RAGE reusable game software components and their integration into serious game engines. In: Kapitsaki, G.M., Santana de Almeida, E. (eds.) ICSR 2016. LNCS, vol. 9679, pp. 165–180. Springer, Cham (2016). https://doi.org/10.1007/978-3-319-35122-3_12
8. Gaisbachgrabner, K., et al.: D8.3 – First RAGE Evaluation Report. RAGE project (2018). http://hdl.handle.net/1820/8785. Accessed 18 Sept 2018
9. Salman, M., et al.: Integrating scientific publication into an applied gaming ecosystem. GSTF J. Comput. (JoC) 5(1), 45–51 (2016)
10. Rehman, M.J., Jabeen, F., Bertolino, A., Polini, A.: Testing software components for integration: a survey of issues and techniques. Softw. Test. Verif. Reliab. 17, 95–133 (2007). https://doi.org/10.1002/stvr.357
11. Hollins, P., Riestra, R., Griffiths, D., Yuan, L., Santos, P., Becker, J.: Potential business models report, RAGE-project (2017). http://hdl.handle.net/1820/7500. Accessed 18 Sept 2018

Improving Serious Games Analyzing Learning Analytics Data: Lessons Learned

Cristina Alonso-Fernández$^{(\boxtimes)}$, Iván Pérez-Colado ,
Manuel Freire , Iván Martínez-Ortiz ,
and Baltasar Fernández-Manjón

Facultad de Informática, Complutense University of Madrid,
C/Profesor José García Santesmases 9, 28040 Madrid, Spain
{crisal03, ivanjper}@ucm.es,
{manuel.freire, imartinez, balta}@fdi.ucm.es

Abstract. Serious games adoption is increasing, although their penetration in formal education is still surprisingly low. To improve their outcomes and increase their adoption in this domain, we propose new ways in which serious games can leverage the information extracted from player interactions, beyond the usual post-activity analysis. We focus on the use of: (1) open data which can be shared for research purposes, (2) real-time feedback for teachers that apply games in schools, to maintain awareness and control of their classroom, and (3) once enough data is gathered, data mining to improve game design, evaluation and deployment; and allow teachers and students to benefit from enhanced feedback or stealth assessment. Having developed and tested a game learning analytics platform throughout multiple experiments, we describe the lessons that we have learnt when analyzing learning analytics data in the previous contexts to improve serious games.

Keywords: Serious games · Learning analytics · Dashboards · Game-based learning · Stealth assessment

1 Introduction

Serious games are being successfully applied in multiple fields (e.g. military, health); however, their uptake in formal education is still poor, and usually restricted to complementary content for motivation [1]. Several reasons can explain this, including the high development cost of new games, or the difficulty for teachers to assess the acquired learning, and therefore to effectively deploy and apply games in their classes.

Moreover, very few serious games have a full formal evaluation, and those that have been evaluated are usually tested with limited numbers of users [2]. This is hardly surprising, as large-scale formal evaluations can become as expensive as creating the game. Also, the feedback from formal evaluations is often obtained too late to improve the games or their educational experience. We consider that information from In-game users interactions can benefit all phases of a serious game's lifecycle, including game design, development, piloting, acceptance, evaluation and maintenance; and should be used to improve the experience of all stakeholders involved (teachers, educators, and

© Springer Nature Switzerland AG 2019
M. Gentile et al. (Eds.): GALA 2018, LNCS 11385, pp. 287–296, 2019.
https://doi.org/10.1007/978-3-030-11548-7_27

students), providing each with the specific information that they need for their purposes. But this process is still too game-dependent, complex and expensive.

Analysis of in-game user interaction data has been used to improve games development in the entertainment industry, in a discipline called Game Analytics (GA). This requires data to be obtained via telemetry, and then analyzed to extract metrics, such as performance or user habits. However, the usual focus of GA is increasing user retention, playing time and revenue [3]; while serious games, particularly in education, instead seek to maximize learning or improve the learning experience.

Learning Analytics (LA) is "the measurement, collection, analysis and reporting of data about learners and their contexts, for purposes of understanding and optimizing learning and the environments in which it occurs" [4]. LA seeks to lay the groundwork to go from theory-driven to evidence-based education, where data can be used to improve educational scenarios [5]. This approach can be extended to serious games, where in-game user interaction data can benefit their creation and applicability in real environments, in a discipline that we call Game Learning Analytics (GLA) [6].

In this paper, we wish to go beyond the usual post-game session analysis, and focus instead on three scenarios where GLA can be especially helpful. First, the data extracted, if done in a systematic and standardized way, can be not only used for improving the games but also openly shared for research purposes. Second, in the context of applying games in education, all stakeholders involved could benefit from information from the actions taken in the game, directly during the session. Finally, after sufficient data has been gathered, deeper analysis can be helpful to obtain richer information for all stakeholders, and inform improvements in several stages of the game's lifecycle.

2 Obtaining In-Game User Interaction Data

The first step to gain insights from in-game user interactions is to ensure that all data with the potential to yield such insights is adequately collected. Experimental design and deployment should comply with all the legal regulations (e.g. users' consent). We consider three main pillars that data management must ensure:

- **Anonymization:** when possible, data must be adequately anonymized so no personal details are attached to the student data (e.g. using randomly generated codes). This will help to comply with regulations on data privacy [7].
- **Collection:** data collection must be non-intrusive and transparent, to avoid interrupting the students' gameplay. Collection can be greatly improved using a standard tracking model that simplifies and standardizes this process.
- **Storage:** data received from games should be collected in a server that can efficiently manage large amounts of data in a secure way. If data is collected in a specific format, the storage system should also be prepared to validate and handle that format.

Our research group has developed a GLA System that is currently been improved and extended as part of two EU H2020 projects (RAGE and BEACONING). With this analytics platform, we have already conducted several experiments that follow the above data-management guidelines, collecting data from thousands of game sessions. Some of the results and conclusions drawn from these experiences are detailed in the following sections, since we have used the resulting data for each of the three applications described in this paper: research, real-time reports, and deeper offline analysis.

2.1 Standardizing Data Collection: Experience API Serious Games Profile

To systematize and standardize data collection we propose the use of the Experience API Serious Games Profile (xAPI-SG for short), described in detail in [8].

As previously mentioned, it is mandatory to comply with all personal data privacy regulations, capturing only the relevant data and using anonymization whenever possible before storage, so no data can be traced back to specific students. For analytics, pseudo-anonymization techniques can be used, where the manager of a session assigns random tokens to players that use them to access the game. The tokens tie all data received from each player together, while providing no information of their identity. When required, teachers can retain the correspondence between anonymous tokens and students that use them; in such cases, this link must be managed outside the game and the analytics system. Additionally, best practices require informed consent forms disclosing both the intended experimental design and how collected data will be used.

Servers that can store xAPI data are usually called Learning Record Stores (LRS), and generally allow limited query capabilities. Every server and technology used in the tracking architecture should be ready to deal with large amounts of data (*big data*) as the number of traces generated by a single player may be large; and if the system is successful, large amounts of users generating many interactions per second can easily overwhelm low-capacity solutions. To ensure scalability, multiple servers that can share the load are an obvious choice; however, this also increases the chances of at least one of them failing or becoming unreachable, forcing truly scalable analytics implementations to be distributed, redundant, and fault-resistant.

Data tracked from serious games using an open format such as xAPI-SG, when suitably anonymized, can be easily shared with other researchers. Open sharing of research data and publications are among the tenets of the Open Science movement, with initiatives such as the European Commission's OpenAIRE [9] or CERN's Zenodo [10], which seek to ensure open access of research data and publications, respectively.

3 Uses of Analytics Data to Improve Serious Games

Users of serious games can benefit from collected data at several stages: (1) at real time, to provide real-time feedback to teachers and students, (2) after the session is finished, to provide detailed feedback, and (3) after sufficient data has been collected, through enriched feedback based on data mining. In this paper we are mostly interested in (1) and (3), since (2) is generally known and explored in many other resources.

Figure 1, has been adapted from the Learning Analytics Framework (LAF) described in [11], to add and highlight the use of open data, real-time feedback, and data-mining. The LAF did not envision serious games as sources for analytics data, and

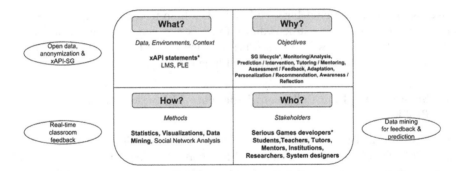

Fig. 1. Contributions of this paper (ovals), and an adapted version of the Learning Analytics framework, as described in [11]. Elements with an asterisk were not present in the original framework. Bold-face text highlights framework elements affected by our contributions.

predates the appearance of xAPI. As seen in the figure, the contributions described in this work have consequences for most if not all elements considered in the LAF. For each of the 4 questions considered in the LAF:

- **What** kind of data does the system gather, manage and use for analysis? While the LAF mentions e-learning systems as sources, we propose the use of xAPI anonymized statements from games.
- **Why** does the system analyze the collected data? We extend the goals of the LAF to improve serious games, from design to development, deployment, and maintenance. Real-time feedback is key for monitoring and classroom intervention, while data mining allows enhanced feedback once enough data has been gathered.
- **How** does the system perform the analysis of the collected data? We apply most of the methods envisioned by the LAF, even though our current focus is on single-player games.
- **Who** is targeted by the analysis? Stakeholders now include the actual game developers, in addition to the learners and teachers that gain, among others, feedback and assessment, or educational institutions that wish to know the outcomes of applying games in education. Researchers can also benefit from open research data.

4   Game Learning Analytics Real-Time Applications

Different stakeholders can benefit from (near) real-time feedback. In this section, we adopt the common scenario of using serious games in education as part of a lesson in a classroom environment, focusing on real-time feedback for teachers and students.

Real-time feedback is available as soon as the game starts to be played; to allow teachers to monitor and perform timely interventions, easy-to-understand feedback must be quickly generated. For example, a student that stops playing can trigger an alert that allows the teacher to walk over to find out the cause; or a student that is advancing much quicker than the rest of the class may benefit from the teacher suggesting additional tasks to attempt. Such simple scenarios illustrate real-time applications where the information collected from interaction data can help teachers and students. Certain types of visual analytics are particularly suited for real-time feedback, especially when combined in dashboards. The ideal content of these dashboards will depend on the game, delivery environment, and the metrics and KPIs that are most relevant to each stakeholder.

4.1 Real-Time Information for Teachers

For teachers, visual analytics provide an easy way to explore the information gathered from their students' interactions. Analytics dashboards present aggregations of individual visualizations, each providing insight into specific aspects, such as progress, errors, or choices taken. Visualizations can also display actionable feedback to locate students that get stuck, or suggest additional work that may interest advanced students.

We have conducted multiple experiments with students to test our data gathering, real-time analytics and dashboards; the latest, as of this writing, with over 1000 students, seeking to validate a serious game that raises awareness on cyberbullying [12]. Previous experiments include games that teach first aid techniques [13], or that were geared towards cognitively impaired users (e.g. with Down Syndrome or Autism) [14], where dashboards were the only option to follow the progress of players.

Figure 2 describes some of the visualizations included in the teacher dashboard used in the latest experiments to provide real-time feedback in classroom settings [15]. The dashboard uses xAPI-SG concepts such as *completables* (e.g. levels) and *alternatives* (e.g. multiple-choice questions). The visualizations depicted inform users on (a) *correct and incorrect alternatives selected*: the number of correct and incorrect answers selected as *alternatives* for each player, and therefore the general knowledge of players; (b) *total session players*: the number of students that have started the game; (c) *maximum progress of players per completable:* for each *completable*, the progress achieved by each player, and therefore whether students are finishing or struggling to continue; and finally (d) *games started and completed*: a pie-chart that displays the number of games that have been started and completed, providing an overview of the students that have started and finished; and indirectly, how many students are still playing.

These visualizations aim to provide general information from gameplays (e.g. progress, answers) to teachers, allowing them to understand it with minimal effort. Data can be used to trigger alerts or warnings in specific situations that require immediate action for teachers (e.g. a player has been inactive for too long). Figure 3 shows the general view of alerts and warnings; clicking on a specific student, teachers can see details of alerts and warnings triggered by that student's actions, and act accordingly.

Improvements are being considered for the visualizations in Fig. 2, based on the feedback collected from teachers. For example, simplifying the visualizations by adding clearer titles and legends, and showing general metrics that provide a quicker overview of the most critical information (e.g. questions failed most, critical areas in-game). We have also determined that providing additionally recommended actions is well-received by teachers (e.g. specific student needs help). These recommendations can help teachers to improve their classes, linking the information provided by LA with actions to support students learning [16]. For instance, teachers requested reports on the topics with the highest error ratios, to allow them to be reviewed before any others.

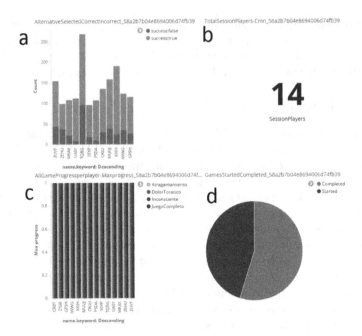

Fig. 2. Some of the visualizations included on the default teacher dashboard.

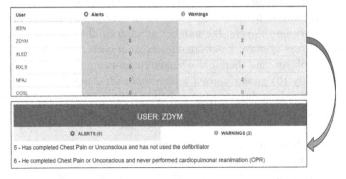

Fig. 3. Alerts and warnings general view (top part). Clicking on a specific student displays detailed information on the warnings and alerts triggered by that student (bottom part).

4.2 Real-Time Information for Students

Student dashboards provide information on performance and in-game outcomes, allowing them to easily assess their strengths and weakness. Current solutions for learners' dashboards present several issues that should be considered. It is common to compare the results of students with their class or with average results (e.g. scores, times-to-finish) from their classmates; however, some researches have pointed out that this may demotivate those students who do not reach at least average rankings [17]. Authors of [18] concluded that most educational concepts used to design LA dashboards focus on self-regulated training by displaying their own data to players. These dashboards generally fail to use awareness and reflection to improve competencies (e.g. cognitive, behavioral or emotional) and usually promote competition instead of knowledge mastery.

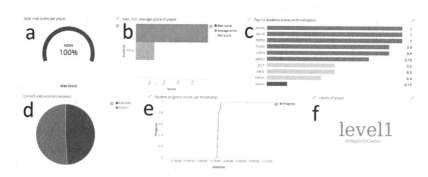

Fig. 4. Sample student dashboard showing information about scores, errors or progress.

Figure 4 provides a sample dashboard with typical information shown to students: maximum score achieved (visualization labelled *a*); maximum, average and minimum scores of the player (*b*); a comparison with other players in a leaderboard (*c*), which uses traffic-light colors to display ranges of players scores; correct and incorrect answers (*d*); student progress over time (*e*); and levels completed (*f*).

Another area where data can be exploited at real-time to benefit students is that of adaptive learning experiences. Games can adapt their difficulty in real-time in response to players' in-game performance. The authors of [19] described the results of experiments comparing adaptive, non-adaptive games and other non-adaptive learning activities, concluding that, although all activities reached equal levels of motivation, the adaptive game resulted in significantly higher learning outcomes.

5   Offline Data Analysis

Apart from displaying real-time information, data collected during several gameplays can be further analyzed to yield additional insights. Data mining processes can be applied to extract patterns of use, which can be leveraged to improve the game for future deployments. Educational institutions and higher-education administrations can also benefit from aggregated data that can quantify the extent to which the use of games in class benefits learning, allowing them to make evidence-based decisions on the value of using serious games in their classrooms.

Game developers and designers can obtain feedback from actual classroom gameplays to improve both the game and the learning design. For instance, they may find errors in the game, unreachable areas, levels that are too difficult or too easy for players, a more precise determination of average playing time, etc. In this sense, analysis can certainly help to improve the iterative design for subsequent versions of the game.

Data gathered can also be used to categorize players, creating different profiles for targeted feedback, a process which can be automated using data mining (considering some limits such as data complexity or the algorithms' efficiency). This feedback may include hints to help students or even changes in level difficulty to avoid a decrease in motivation [20]. Clusters of players that show different behaviors and characteristics may provide clues on how different learning elements affect each type of players [21]. In one experiment, we collected data for more than 200 students playing a serious game that teaches first aid techniques. Using data mining, we managed to classify players based on their actions and results to identify clusters of player profiles, and even the discovery of those in-game actions that had greater influence on player outcomes [13].

One of the latest steps we have carried out to improve the lifecycle of serious games using GLA data focuses on improving evaluation methods. So far, serious games are commonly evaluated using costly pre-post experiments [2]. We consider that their application in education would benefit from a quicker and cheaper evaluation process. To this end, we have proposed and tested the use of data mining to predict the results of the pre- and post- tests based on interaction data; while only possible once a sufficiently-large training set has been collected, the technique avoids the need of conducting tests – at least for players that are similar to those that the system was trained with.

This can be considered as another step in stealth assessment. Serious games can also become powerful assessment tools, even though the exact characteristics of games that best allow these assessments is still not entirely clear. Stealth assessment [22] is the practice of embedding assessment in a gaming environment in a non-intrusive way, analyzing gameplay actions to infer exactly what players know at each point in time; it is, in this sense, and extension of the evaluation without pre- and post-test described in the previous paragraph. For this discipline, it is still important to improve the serious games themselves, ensuring that their application is effective and making assessment more valid and reliable.

6   Conclusions

In-game users' interaction data from serious games can be exploited to provide a wide variety of insight on the educational process of different stakeholders. Developers can use it to improve the full lifecycle of games. Teachers can gain real-time insights of student behavior, allowing them to help students playing, or to summarize a session when discussing it with students once they have finished. Students can get feedback on their performance, including their strengths and weaknesses. Researchers can benefit from open access to shared research data. Educators can obtain metrics on the efficacy of games application on their institutions.

When collecting data, many issues need to be addressed, including anonymization, which is especially relevant when working with minors or to allow collected data to be openly shared for research purposes.

In real-time scenarios, visualizations, alerts and warnings can help teachers to gain insights of the whole classroom, while students can track their performance and compare it to that of their peers; both uses of data provide information that allows teachers and students to make better decisions while the games are still in play.

After data has been collected, data mining techniques can provide further information to improve game design, deployment and evaluation. To improve evaluation, the latest line of work continues with experiments that follow the usual evaluation structure (pre-test, gameplay, post-test) and track interaction data to later predict previous and subsequent knowledge; and compare those predictions against actual data collected in the tests.

Adoption of serious games in schools could greatly improve with the feedback retrieved from interaction data, ideally with a general game learning analytics system that standardizes data tracking, collection, analysis and visualization, extracting useful information to be given back to the stakeholders involved. Whichever the approach, we consider that data-driven solutions that take advantage of the power of game learning analytics are essential to guide the future application of serious games.

Acknowledgments. This work has been partially funded by Regional Government of Madrid (eMadrid S2013/ICE-2715), by the Ministry of Education (TIN2017-89238-R) and by the European Commission (RAGE H2020-ICT-2014-1-644187, BEACONING H2020-ICT-2015-687676, Erasmus+IMPRESS 2017-1-NL01-KA203-035259).

References

1. Popescu, M., et al.: Serious games in formal education: discussing some critical aspects. In: Proceedings of the 5th European Conference on Games Based Learning, pp. 486–493 (2011)
2. Calderón, A., Ruiz, M.: A systematic literature review on serious games evaluation: an application to software project management. Comput. Educ. **87**, 396–422 (2015)
3. El-Nasr, M., Drachen, A., Canossa, A.: Game Analytics: Maximizing the Value of Player Data. Springer, London (2013). https://doi.org/10.1007/978-1-4471-4769-5
4. Long, P., Siemens, G.: Penetrating the fog: analytics in learning and education. Educ. Rev. **46**, 31–40 (2011)
5. Bienkowski, M., Feng, M., Means, B.: Enhancing teaching and learning through educational data mining and learning analytics: an issue brief, pp. 1–57. SRI International, Washington, DC (2012)
6. Freire, M., Serrano-Laguna, Á., Iglesias, B.M., Martínez-Ortiz, I., Moreno-Ger, P., Fernández-Manjón, B.: Game learning analytics: learning analytics for serious games. In: Spector, M., Lockee, B., Childress, M. (eds.) Learning, Design, and Technology, pp. 1–29. Springer, Cham (2016). https://doi.org/10.1007/978-3-319-17727-4_21-1
7. European Union: Regulation (EU) 2016/679. http://eur-lex.europa.eu/legal-content/EN/TXT/?uri=CELEX%3A32016R0679. Accessed Sept 2018
8. Serrano-Laguna, Á., Martínez-Ortiz, I., Haag, J., Regan, D., Johnson, A., Fernández-Manjón, B.: Applying standards to systematize learning analytics in serious games. Comput. Stand. Interfaces **50**, 116–123 (2017)
9. European Commission: OpenAIRE. https://www.openaire.eu/. Accessed Sept 2018
10. CERN, OpenAIRE, EC: Zenodo. https://zenodo.org/. Accessed Sept 2018
11. Chatti, M.A., et al.: Learning Analytics: Challenges and Future Research Directions. E-Learning Education (2015)

12. Morata, A.C.: Videojuegos Como Herramienta Educativa En La Escuela: Concienciando Sobre El Ciberbullying (Master Thesis) (2017)
13. Alonso-Fernández, C.: Applying data mining techniques to game learning analytics (Master Thesis) (2017)
14. Cano, A.R., Fernández-Manjón, B., García-Tejedor, Á.J.: Using game learning analytics for validating the design of a learning game for adults with intellectual disabilities. Br. J. Educ. Technol. **49**, 659 (2018)
15. Alonso-Fernandez, C., Calvo, A., Freire, M., Martinez-Ortiz, I., Fernandez-Manjon, B.: Systematizing game learning analytics for serious games. In: IEEE Global Engineering Education Conference (EDUCON). IEEE (2017)
16. Bakharia, A., et al.: A conceptual framework linking learning design with learning analytics. In: Proceedings of the 6th International Conference on Analytics and Knowledge 2016, LAK16, pp. 329–338 (2016)
17. Gašević, D., Dawson, S., Siemens, G.: Let's not forget: learning analytics are about learning. TechTrends **59**, 64–71 (2015)
18. Jivet, I., Scheffel, M., Drachsler, H., Specht, M.: Awareness is not enough: pitfalls of learning analytics dashboards in the educational practice. In: Lavoué, É., Drachsler, H., Verbert, K., Broisin, J., Pérez-Sanagustín, M. (eds.) EC-TEL 2017. LNCS, vol. 10474, pp. 82–96. Springer, Cham (2017). https://doi.org/10.1007/978-3-319-66610-5_7
19. Sampayo-Vargas, S., Cope, C.J., He, Z., Byrne, G.J.: The effectiveness of adaptive difficulty adjustments on students' motivation and learning in an educational computer game. Comput. Educ. **69**, 452–462 (2013)
20. Shute, V., Ke, F., Wang, L.: Assessment and adaptation in games. In: Wouters, P., van Oostendorp, H. (eds.) Instructional Techniques to Facilitate Learning and Motivation of Serious Games. AGL, pp. 59–78. Springer, Cham (2017). https://doi.org/10.1007/978-3-319-39298-1_4
21. Loh, C.S., Sheng, Y., Ifenthaler, D.: Serious Games Analytics. Springer, Cham (2015). https://doi.org/10.1007/978-3-319-05834-4
22. Shute, V.J., Moore, G.R.: Consistency and validity in game-based stealth assessment. In: Technology Enhanced Innovative Assessment: Development, Modeling, and Scoring From an Interdisciplinary Perspective (2017)

A Toolkit for Creating Cross-Reality Serious Games

Telmo Zarraonandia[✉], Paloma Díaz, Andrés Santos,
Álvaro Montero, and Ignacio Aedo

Department of Computer Science, Universidad Carlos III de Madrid,
Leganés, Madrid, Spain
{tzarraon,pdp,andsanto,ammontes}@inf.uc3m.es,
aedo@ia.uc3m.es

Abstract. In this paper, we present a toolkit that aims at facilitating the design and implementation of serious games played in cross-reality environments. This type of systems interconnects a physical space with a virtual world. Its use as a platform for serious games will open the door to the design of collaborative learning experiences based on games played simultaneously by real and virtual players. However, due the wide range of technologies they require to integrate, their implementation could be complex and expensive. The toolkit aims at lowering the cost of building cross-reality serious games, so that the opportunities that this type of artefacts might offer in educational contexts can be more easily explored.

Keywords: Serious games · Cross-reality · Authoring tools

1 Introduction

A *cross-reality* or *xReality* [1] experience interconnects a virtual space and a real scenario via a network of sensors and actuators. The activities on both worlds can be mirrored or influenced with each other. In an Augmented Reality (AR) experience the real-world information is extended, and in Virtual Reality (VR) it is replaced by synthetic images generated by a computer. On the contrary, in a xReality (XR) experience the user might act either upon the real world or a virtual representation of it, having the opportunity to interact and collaborate with other users co-located in the same reality or in the counterpart one. This feature has been exploited in several XR systems that support collaboration [2, 3] and interaction [4] between geographically distant people. Instead of communicating via a 2D interface or a videoconference system, the distant collaborators interact through avatars in a 3D virtual space, which might use virtual replicas of the devices the collaborators in the real world are working with [2, 3]. The actions of these avatars are translated into real world representations via a network of actuators and sensors, which also capture the activity in the real scenario and translated it into the virtual world.

In this paper, we focus on the use of XR for educational purposes and, more specifically, as a platform for serious games. XR technology will give the educator the opportunity to create learning experiences based on games whose action can take place

M. Gentile et al. (Eds.): GALA 2018, LNCS 11385, pp. 297–307, 2019.
https://doi.org/10.1007/978-3-030-11548-7_28

in the real and virtual world simultaneously. This opens the door to the design of games whose different stages or missions take place in the type of reality that is more adequate for learning the concept linked to the mission. Also, it will possible to design multi-player games, in which virtual and real players collaborate or compete with each other from the "game reality" that best suits their needs or restrictions at the time. Furthermore, most traditional XR environments use multi-user virtual worlds, as Second Life, as a basis for supporting the virtual action [4]. However, it is now possible to develop XR systems that exploit the latest advances in VR, AR, and ubiquitous computing (UC). Each of these technologies offer unique opportunities for education. For example, VR allows to create immersive and realistic first-person learning experiences [5]. AR can be used to enhance the interaction with the learning content [6] and to support embodied cognition [7]. Finally, UC allows to design situated learning experiences [8]. An XR platform for serious games based on these technologies might allow to deliver educational experiences that combine the benefits of all those technologies with the ones provided by educational games.

However, in order to explore the possibilities of XR serious games, it is necessary first to reduce the cost associated to their design and implementation. Due the wide range of technologies integrated in an XR system, which might include ubiquitous devices, communication networks, and virtual worlds or game engines, its implementation is often costly and expensive. As a first step to understand the potential benefits of XR serious games it is necessary to be able to generate prototypes at a low cost [9] so that ideas can be quickly evaluated to get feedback on their real utility. In this paper, we introduce the XRSG Toolkit (XR-Serious Games Toolkit), a platform that aims at simplifying the design and implementation of this type of artefacts, and that provides a running environment for their execution.

The rest of the paper is organized as follows. In the next section, some related work is presented. Next, we describe the toolkit and the editors it provides. Next, and in order to clarify the potential of the toolkit's, we briefly describe a XR serious game example. The paper ends with some conclusions and future lines of work.

2 Related Work

One of the first examples of an XR environment is *ShadowLab* [10], a system that interconnects the *Responsive Environments Group* lab from *MIT* to a replica of itself in the virtual world *Second Life*. In this environment, real and virtual visitors could know the level of activity in their counterpart situated in the other reality. Graphical representations or avatars of the real visitors were included on the virtual world based on the information received from light, sound, and movement sensors situated in the real world. On the other side, the number of virtual visitors was represented in the real world using some specifically devised devices ("data ponds").

In the area of education, the *InterReality Portal* [3] supports the collaboration between students situated on distinct geographic positions during the construction of a IoT (Internet-of-things) device. While the students in the physical location used an electronic kit to build the *IoT* device, the students in the virtual world visualize and interact with its *IoT* counterpart by means of a "*xReality* object" which represented it.

With regards to its use for games, the most outstanding example is *TwinSpace* [2]. Although the original purpose of the environment was to support the collaboration between distributed teams, their designers also use it as a platform for a game in which players from teams compete for the collection of objects in a virtual environment that represents a fort. Some of the players take the roll of "soldiers" which control the virtual representation in a traditional way using the mouse and keyboard. Other players take the roll of "mystiques" or "phantoms", and control the actions of their avatars using tangible objects in interactive tables or by moving a cart with a tangible screen. Another example of *cross-reality game* is *LSInvaders* [11], a version of the "Space Invaders" game in which the action of the game is projected on a wall and a physical robot reproduces the movements of the ship in the virtual world.

3 The XR-Serious Games Toolkit (XRSG)

To support the design and development of XR serious games we developed a platform named XRSG. The platform has been developed as an extension of the X-Reality Toolkit (XRT) presented in [12]. In this section, we briefly introduced the XRT, and describe the functionalities of the new toolkit.

3.1 The X-Reality Toolkit (XRT)

XRT aimed at facilitating the implementation of cross-reality environments which combine interactions between electronic-incorporated objects and 3D virtual worlds. The toolkit was designed to address four different challenges when creating cross-reality experiences:

- Designing and building the virtual world.
- Augmenting the physical world by means of networked sensors and actuators.
- Managing the communication between the two worlds.
- Defining a mapping between the two worlds.

Taking into account these challenges, the toolkit provided four editors for simplifying the creation of cross-reality experiences:

- a *Virtual World Editor*, for designing 3D virtual scenarios. This editor allows to design a virtual 3D scenario by modifying and populating a pre-defined setting, or background scenery, with 3D models retrieved from the toolkit's 3D models warehouse. This process is carried out in a similar way as in Minecraft or other popular sandboxes: the designer walks around the environment, using a first-person perspective, and edits (e.g., rotate, shrink/enlarge, etc.) the elements on it.
- a *Real World Editor*, for helping to specify the scenario of the game in the real world, and describe where and how the player would interact with the objects in it.
- an *Electronic-Incorporated Object Editor,* for helping to build interactive objects. This tool provided visual hints that guided the user to correctly connect sensors and actuators to the pins of a microcontroller board.

- and an *Interaction Rules Editor,* for specifying high-level interaction policies that synchronize sensors and actuators in the physical room with digital entities in the virtual world. These policies were defined as *trigger-action rules,* that specify behaviors in the form *if something happens* (the trigger), *then do something* (the action). The rules were described by linking through connection lines representations of the virtual and physical objects specified using the two other editors.

The Toolkit also provided a *Cross-Reality Runtime Server,* which interpreted the designs specified with the editors, and provided a runtime environment for their execution, and a *Virtual World Client,* that provided a 3D virtual scenario for the experience.

The XRT's authoring tool were implemented using HTML and JavaScript. The Virtual World Editor and the Virtual World Client are extensions of the GREP (Game Rules scEnario) Platform [13], implemented in Unity 3D. More information about the different features of the toolkit and its implementation can be found in [12].

3.2   The XR-Serious Games Toolkit (XRSG)

The XRSG Toolkit extends the capabilities of XRT to support the design and implementation of a specific type of cross-reality environment, XR Serious Games. The creation of this type of technological artefact poses some additional challenges to the ones specific of generic cross-reality experiences:

- *Designing and specifying the rules of the game.* This is a common challenge when designing videogames. Having to describe the rules that govern the action of the game can be tedious and complicated and might make necessary to learn specific notations or design languages.
- *Designing and building a real scenario for the game.* This challenge is related to the challenge *Augmenting the physical world by means of networked sensors and actuators,* of the standard cross-reality environments. It is necessary to consider that to capture the action of a play, the extension and complexity of the network of sensors might be larger than in the case of a cross-reality environment designed to support one or two types of collaborations. Also, it will be necessary to specify the area of the physical world in which the game take place.

The XRSG platform responds to these challenges by adapting the original XRT's editors and runtimes to the requirements of the XR-Serious Games and providing some additional ones.

Virtual World Editor

This editor (Fig. 1) expands the original functionality of the XRT's virtual world editor. It not only supports the design of the 3D virtual space, but it also allows to specify the rules that govern the game action. This addresses the challenge *Designing and specifying the rules of the game.* To specify the game rules the toolkit implements the combinative design approach described in [12]: games are described as a combination of rules and mechanics of more simple games. Currently, the tool allows to use game rules derived from 4 classical games, *treasure hunt, avoid enemies, race* and *adventure.* The designer links rules taken from these games to the elements of the scenario (Fig. 2). As the four games are popular and well-known, the designer is not required to master new concepts or to learn a new language for describing the game action. For example, a *coin* could be linked to the rule "*collectable*" from the "*treasure hunt*" game, to specify that the player can pick it up. As another example, by linking a *fire* to the rule "*enemy*" from the "*avoid enemies*" game, the designer specifies that the contact of the player with the fire will produce damage. The *adventure* game provides the rule "*transform*", which can be used to specify that certain object can be combined with another one to produce a new one. For example, a *key* can transform a *closed door* into an *open door*.

Fig. 1. Screenshot of the virtual world editor

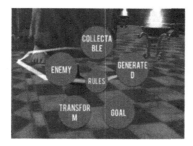

Fig. 2. Screenshot of the rules menu of the virtual world editor

Real World Editor

The Real World Editor addresses the challenge *Designing and building the real scenario for the game*. To hide the complexity of setting up connections between boards, sensors and actuators, the toolkit provides a set of predefined *Interactive Boxes*. Each box contains certain combination of sensors, buttons and leds connected to an ESP8266 NodeMcu board equipped with a WIFI module (Fig. 3). These boards are pre-programmed to send the information captured by the boxes' sensors to the cross-reality engine, and to activate or deactivate the leds on request. The game designer can use the

Interactive Boxes to enhance the objects in the real scenario with interaction capacities. For example, a box with a distance sensor placed in certain location can be used to detect when the user is close to that spot. For another example, a box with a button positioned close to an object could be used to permit the player to "select the object".

The process of defining a real scenario for the game is as follows. Firstly, the designer uploads to the platform a map or aerial view of the area where the game will be played (Fig. 3). Next, she selects from the editor's menu the *Interactive Boxes* to use in the game, and place them over the image at a position that approximates the location where the box should be placed in the real setting.

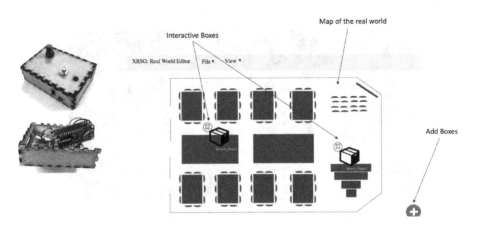

Fig. 3. Left- interaction boxes. right- screenshot of the real world editor

Interactive Boxes Editor

This editor is a new version of the *Electronic-Incorporated Object Editor* of the XRT. Its objective is to allow the user to build *Interactive Boxes* to be used in the Real World Editor. As in the original editor of the XRT, the user selects a micro-board (the ESP8266 NodeMcu) and a set of sensors, buttons and led to connect. The tool provides visual hints on how to connect all the elements to build an *Interactive Box* (Fig. 4). The user just needs to follow these instructions, and load into the micro-board a standard communication script provided by the toolkit. The design of the box is then exported as an XML file containing all the information about the input and output components added to the box, and the pines of the micro-board at which each of them is connected. To finish the process, she just need to provide a name for the box and it will be ready to be used in the real world editor.

Interaction Rules Editor

The *Interaction Rules Editor* version of the XRT has been adapted to the requirements of the new toolkit and expanded with more functionalities. Each time a game rule is attached to a virtual object, or an interactive box is added to the real scenario a new representation is added to the *Interaction Rules Editor*'s view. These representations take the form of rectangles with certain number of red and green circles (connections)

(Fig. 5). The red circles correspond to triggers (*if this happens...*) and the green circles correspond to actions (*...then do this*). The red and green circles are automatically generated by the toolkit based on the rules definition or the design of the *Interaction Box*. For example, the rules "collect" and "Transform" generate red circles labelled "when collected" and "when used", respectively. In a similar way, linking the rule "generate" to an object produces an object's representation with a green circle, meaning that this rule can be activated by a trigger, at the designer's choice. With regards to the *interaction boxes*, each button or sensor in the box generates a set of red circles ("when pressed", "when released", "when sensor activated", "when sensor deactivated"), while leds produce green circles representing their states ("led on", "led off").

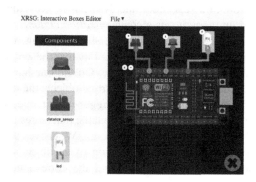

Fig. 4. Screenshot of the interactive boxes editor

To allow the designer to specify more complex interaction rules between virtual and real objects, the *Interaction Rules Editor* allows to apply the logical operations *AND* and *OR* to several inputs. This allows to define rules of the type "IF the player presses the button of the interactive box AND uses the key THEN transform the closed door into an open door".

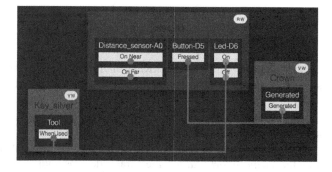

Fig. 5. Screenshot of the interaction rules editor (Color figure online)

XRSG Game Engine

Finally, the original *Cross-Reality Runtime Server* and the *Virtual World Client* of the XRT have been integrated into a game engine (*XRSG Game Engine*) that interprets the designs produced using the editors, and generates cross-reality game experiences based on them. More specifically the *XRSG Game Engine* is in charge of:

- *Generation of the Game's Virtual Scene*: The engine retrieves from the toolkit's 3D model warehouse the ones specified in the game design, and compose the Game's Virtual Scene by instantiating the model with the size, position and orientation specified in the design files.
- *Generation of the Game's Real Scene*: In a similar way, it retrieves from the game design the identifiers of the *Interaction Boxes* to be used in the game. Next, it obtains from the toolkit's repository the XML files containing the box design descriptions. Based on them, it sets a *communication channel* for each box to send and receive messages to control and manage all its components.
- *Management of the rules of the gameplay*: Finally, the engine is in charge of implementing and controlling the game logic. On the one hand, it configures pre-defined scripts with the game rules for the virtual objects the designer has attached rules to. On the other hand, it reads the *trigger-action* rules described with the *Interaction Editor* and it configures a look-up table that stores the links between the virtual objects rules and the boxes' components. Whenever the engine receives a message from a box's sensor or a notification of an object's rule activation, the engine checks the table. If a match is found the corresponding consequence is activated.

Currently the XRSG Game Engine has been implemented in two versions:

- *Tabletop*: this version aims to support XR mono-player Serious Games. The tablet provides the player with a portable "window" to the virtual scene of the game. This allows her to act both upon the real scene of the game and the virtual one.
- *Immersive VR*: this version aims to supports playing XR serious games in which a virtual player and real player participate. The virtual player will play the game using an Oculus Rift Head Mounted Display.

4 A XR-Serious Game for Learning About Cultural Heritage

In order to illustrate the possibilities of the XRSG platform, in this section we summarize the design of a *XR-Serious Game* implemented with the toolkit. Let's say a curator of the remains of a roman temple wants to create a game to enhance the visitors understanding of the site, and at the same time, to increase the interest in the site of other people at home. Following this idea, she decides to design a *XR-Serious Game* to be played by the visitor in the site and a friend at home simultaneously, this latter using VR technology. Using the *Virtual World Editor,* the curator designs a virtual replica of the temple, depicting the place as it was originally at the ancient time. The VR player will be able to move around this scenario, to observe all their elements with their original positions, size and colors, and to interact with some of them. On the other hand, she designs a real scene for the game that includes both the temple site as well as a temple's museum close to it. This museum exhibits figurines, cups, or any other object that the archeologists found in the site. The designer places some *Interactive Boxes* close to the glass-cabinets of the figurines and objects exhibited. In addition, she places another set of *Interactive Boxes* at some specific locations of the archeological site.

Next, she starts defining games which require the collaboration of two players. For example, in one game the virtual player is required to make an offer to please the temple's god. To perform the offering, she requires an offering dish and some gold coins, but these elements cannot be found in the virtual world. The real player needs to identify them in the museum's glass cabinets, and to press the buttons of their corresponding *Interactive Boxes* to "send them back in time" to the virtual world. Now the virtual player is ready to combine the two objects in front of the god's statue to complete the offering. But to do it correctly, it is necessary that the two players are positioned front of the temple's deity statue. As the deity statue has been destroyed in the real world, the virtual player needs to guide the real player to the position in which it used to be. Then, the real player activates an *Interactive Box* placed at that location to indicate she is at the right spot, and the virtual player can complete the offering.

With this simple game both players could learn some interesting facts about the temple. On the one hand, the real player would be required to go through the glass cabinets examining the objects exhibited to find the ones she need. On the other hand, she would also learn the precise spot of the temple's remains where the god's statue used to be. Moreover, by making necessary that the virtual player guides the real one through the temple, both would gain a better comprehension of the way the temple looked at the ancient times.

5   Conclusions

In this paper, we introduced a toolkit that aims at accelerating the design and implementation of *XR-Serious Games*: serious games that run in a cross-reality platform and can be played simultaneously in the virtual and the real world. Currently, the toolkit can support the design of mono-player XR-Serious Games played in a tabletop, and multi-player games that make use of immersive VR technology. Our current work focuses on exploring the uses and potential benefits of this type of artefacts for educational purposes. This line of work includes the collaboration with educators in the design and implementation of a set of game prototypes to be used in different educational contexts, and the evaluation of their effectiveness as educational tools. Also, and for the perspective of the design of the game experience, we plan to extend existing serious game models [14, 15] to tackle the definition of the real perspective of the play.

At the same time, we are also extending the toolkit functionalities to allow designing and implementing more complex *XR-Serious Games*. On the one hand, we are working on a new editor to allow creating games based on AR technology. On another hand, we are implementing more game rules for the designers to use in their games. Finally, we are increasing the number and type of sensors and actuators the *Interaction Boxes* could integrate, as depth sensors or LCD screens.

For the perspective of the design of the experience, we are also planning to extend existing serious game models as the one presented in [13] or [14], so that the definition of the real perspective of the game is also considered.

Acknowlegments. This work is supported by the project CREAx funded by the Spanish Ministry of Science and Innovation (TIN2014-56534-R).

References

1. Lifton, J., Laibowitz, M., Harry, D., Gong, N.: Metaphor and manifestation-cross-reality with ubiquitous sensor/actuator networks. IEEE Pervasive Comput. **8**, 24–33 (2009)
2. Reilly, D., Rouzati, H., Wu, A., Yeon Hwang, J., Brudvik, J, Keith Edwards, W.: Twinspace: an infrastructure for cross-reality team spaces. In: Proceedings of the 23rd Annual ACM Symposium on User Interface Software and Technology, pp. 119–128. ACM (2010)
3. Peña-Ríos, A., Callaghan, V., Gardner, M., Alhaddad, M.: Remote mixed reality collaborative laboratory activities: Learning activities within the interreality portal. In: Proceedings of the 2012 IEEE/WIC/ACM International Joint Conferences on Web Intelligence and Intelligent Agent Technology, vol. 03, pp. 362–366. IEEE Computer Society (2012)
4. Paradiso, J.A., Landay, J.A.: Guest editors' introduction: cross-reality environments. IEEE Pervasive Comput. **8**(3), 14–15 (2009)
5. Winn, W.: A conceptual basis for educational applications of virtual reality. Technical Publication R-93-9, Human Interface Technology Laboratory of the Washington Technology Center, University of Washington, Seattle (1993)
6. Chen, G.-D., Chao, P.-Y.: Augmenting traditional books with context-aware learning supports from online learning communities. J. Educ. Technol. Soc. **11**(2), 27–40 (2013)
7. Lindgren, R., Johnson-Glenberg, M.: Emboldened by embodiment: six precepts for research on embodied learning and mixed reality. Educ. Res. **42**(8), 445–452 (2013)
8. Hwang, G-J., Yang, T-C., Tsai, C-C., Yang, S-JH.: A context-aware ubiquitous learning environment for conducting complex science experiments. Comput. Educ. **53**(2), 402–413 (2009)
9. Klopfer, E., Squire, K.: Environmental detectives—the development of an augmented reality platform for environmental simulations. Educ—Technol. Res. Develop. **56**(2), 203–228 (2008)
10. Lifton, J., Laibowitz, M., Harry, D., Gong, N., Mittal, M., Paradiso, J.: Metaphor and manifestation cross-reality with ubiquitous sensor/actuator networks. IEEE Pervasive Comput. **8**(3), 24–33 (2009)
11. Fusté, A., Amores, J., Perdices, S., Ortega, S., Miralles, D.: LSInvaders: cross reality environment inspired by the arcade game space invaders. In: ACM/IEEE International Conference on Human-Robot Interaction, p. 399 (2013)
12. Bellucci, A., Zarraonandia, T., Díaz, P., Aedo, I.: End-user prototyping of cross-reality environments. In: Proceedings of the Eleventh International Conference on Tangible, Embedded, and Embodied Interaction, pp. 173–182. ACM, March 2017
13. Zarraonandia, T., Diaz, P., Aedo, I.: Using combinatorial creativity to support end-user design of digital games. Multimedia Tools Appl. **76**(6), 9073–9098 (2017)

14. Zarraonandia, T., Diaz, P., Aedo, I., Ruiz, M.R.: Designing educational games through a conceptual model based on rules and scenarios. Multimedia Tools Appl. **74**(13), 4535–4559 (2015)
15. Carvalho, M.B., et al.: An activity theory-based model for serious games analysis and conceptual design. Comput. Educ. **87**, 166–181 (2015)

TurtleTable: Learn the Basics of Computer Algorithms with Tangible Interactions

Iza Marfisi-Schottman[(✉)], Sébastien George, and Marc Leconte

Le Mans Université, EA 4023, LIUM, 72085 Le Mans, France
{iza.marfisi,sebastien.george,
marc.leconte}@univ-lemans.fr

Abstract. Computer programming has become a basic skill and is now part of the curriculum taught in middle school. In France, this educational reform was very sudden and many teachers are not yet trained adequately to teach this subject, leaving them in search of guidelines and tools to help them. It is in this context that we propose TurtleTable, an educational game, who has two main originalities. First of all, this game is not based on writing a computer program, like most of the other tools, but rather on executing a given program, step by step. These two approaches are complementary and essential to apprehend the logic behind computer programming. Secondly, TurtleTable is played in groups of three, by manipulating Tangible objects on an Interactive Tabletop (TIT). The players have to collaboratively move the objects on a grid, by following the instructions of the program on the screen. The game immediately indicates which instructions are executed correctly, allowing the learners to correct their mistakes. TurtleTable was tested by 59 middle school students. We developed four different interactions for TurtleTable (TIT, tabletop, tablet and computer) to compare their effects on motivation, collaboration and learning. The preliminary analysis show that the students really appreciated the game, especially the TIT version, that encouraged collaboration and gave them the impression they learned more.

Keywords: Tangible object · Interactive tabletop · Serious games · Learning games · Algorithm · Computer programming

1 Tools for Teaching the Basics of Computer Programming

Digital tools are an important part of our modern society and computer science is now considered as a basic skill that needs to be taught as early as possible, along with math and science. In many countries, such as France, the new official curriculum adopted in September 2016, that includes computer programming, was very sudden, leaving many teachers unprepared. Most teachers do not have any training on these new skills and are in need of guidelines and tools to help them. Many passionate teachers and associations have created blogs with examples of activities [1]. Most of these activities are "unplugged", meaning they can be done without a computer or specific digital equipment. Among these activities, one seems to be particularly appreciated: the *stupid robot* game. This game has many variations for 2 to 4 players but basically one player

© Springer Nature Switzerland AG 2019
M. Gentile et al. (Eds.): GALA 2018, LNCS 11385, pp. 308–317, 2019.
https://doi.org/10.1007/978-3-030-11548-7_29

writes a program with instruction cards (e.g. move forward, turn left, turn right) and the other player executes it like a computer by moving and turning on a checkered floor mat of tiles. Teachers can also use free digital tools to help their students learn how to program with drawings [2], diagrams [3], blocs [4] or even with real computer languages [5]. These digital tools have the advantage of correcting the students directly and offering many exercises with various difficulty levels. These digital games are based on activities that consist in writing a program to move a robot (or an animal) in an environment. These activities are often presented in a game-like environment, and challenge the students with tasks that progressively get harder (e.g. move the robot to collect all the candy, only use three lines of code). The basic concepts of computer programming (i.e. variables, conditions, loops and functions) are gradually introduced as the levels of the games get harder. This type of activity, based on the construction of a program, is essential to understand algorithms, but often leads learners to execute their code compulsively and irrationally, until it works. Indeed, this type of game doesn't encourage the players to simulate the program in their head, before pressing the execute button, to foresee how it's going to behave. Yet, this is a key competency to master computer programming. Many unplugged activities, such as the example given above, help develop this competency by working on the execution of a program step by step. However, these activities require the constant presence of the teacher to explain the activity and to make sure the students do not make mistakes.

In order to fill the gap, we propose TurtleTable, a digital game that teaches students how to execute a program, just like a machine. The goal is to help them understand how a computer program is executed and understand the logic of algorithms. In the third part of this paper, we detail the innovative Human Computer Interactions (HCI) with tangible objects and interactive tabletops, we designed for TurtleTable, in order to enhance motivation, collaboration and learning. We then discuss the results of a test lead with 59 middle school students, from 14 to 16 years old. In the last section, we provide insight on the improvements that could be brought to TurtleTable.

2 TurtleTable: Learn How to Execute a Computer Program

TurtleTable is complementary to other digital tools that teach computer programming. First of all, the game is based on executing an algorithm, step by step, whereas the other tools are based on building algorithms. TurtleTable is also meant to foster collaborative learning whereas more classical computer applications are typically played alone. In this section, we will present the TurtleTable's game, the programming concepts introduced in each level, and the functionalities that allow real-time corrections and scoring. TurtleTable was named after *turtle graphics*, a tool that was used to introduce computer programming, with the LOGO language [6] since the 1960s. It has since inspired generations of programmers and countless educational games. These games come in all shapes: card games, digital games, simulators, kits to build your own robot... and now this one, on an interactive table.

2.1 Game Objective

The objective the TurtleTable game is simple: execute the program on the left of the screen (Fig. 1, panel A) by moving the objects on the grid (Fig. 1, panel B). The program, written in a pseudo-language, is composed of basic instructions (e.g. *move obj_1 3 steps forward, turn obj_2 45° to the right*), and can contain variables, conditions, and loops. If the instruction is executed correctly (i.e., the object was placed on the right spot or turned correctly), the instruction is colored in green and the students can execute the next instruction. In addition, the movements of the objects are materialized by a line on the grid, that creates a drawing at the end of the level. On the top of the interface (Fig. 1, panel C), the players can access the 20 levels and see their scores.

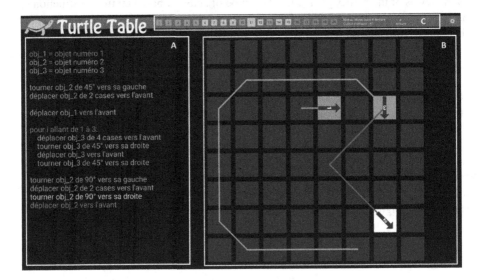

Fig. 1. Interface of TurtleTable, level 11

2.2 Introducing Basic Computer Programming Concepts

TutleTable has 20 levels that progressively introduce the basic concepts of computer programming. Level 4 introduces the notion of variables ($a = 4$), Level 8 introduces the repeat loop (*for i from 1 to 3 do {...}*), level 12 introduces the simple conditional instructions (*if i ==2 {...}*), level 14 introduces the conditional instructions (*if a < b {...} else {...}*) and finally, level 15 introduces the repeat until loop (*repeat {...} until a > 3*). These concepts were found in the official guidelines for teaching computer programming in middle school. The explanations to introduce these concepts and the order in which to present them were inspired by the tutorials in the CODE games [4] that are widely used in American schools. As the players get further in the game, these concepts accumulate. For example, level 16 has a conditional instruction in a loop and level 20 has a loop in another loop. The levels therefore get more complicated and challenging.

2.3   Real Time Correction and Scoring

If the students don't move an object correctly, the image of this object shakes and they have to execute the instruction again, until they get it right. TurtleTable offers several visual aids to help the learners execute the algorithm correctly: the current instruction is colored in white, the instruction executed correctly in green and the instruction executed with an error appears in red. All of these visual aids are optional and can be tuned off, making the levels substantially more challenging, especially those with loops.

TurtleTable keeps track of the number of errors for each level and shows them on the top right of the game interface (Fig. 1, panel C). If the level is finished without any errors, the level's button turns green. If the level is finished with one or more errors, it is colored in orange. The objective is to encourage players to take the time to think and discuss with each other, before moving the objects. Once all the instructions are done correctly, the next level automatically shows up. When the 20 levels are finished, the game shows a personalized message with the total number of errors, urging the players to improve their score by doing the levels again.

Now that we have described the TurtleTable game, the next section will present the innovative interactions it offers to increase motivation, collaboration and learning.

3   Tangible Objects with Interactive Tabletops

Our goal is to provide a tool that teachers can use in their classes, to introduce the basic concepts of computer programming to middle school students. Since programming is completely new to the students and most of the teachers, we wanted to create a fun and social activity that would encourage everyone to participation and collaborate. Research in Human Computer Interactions (HCI) offers empirical evidence that the use of Tangible objects on Interactives Tabletops (TITs) fosters student engagement and may enhance learning through collaborative learning methods [7, 8]. The use of TITs appears especially effective for children, who are used to learning by manipulating objects. We therefore choose to use this type of interaction for TurtleTable. In the next section, we provide details on why and how these interactions were designed.

3.1   Tangible Objects

Several studies have proven the fact that tangible objects help students collaborate and appropriate concepts, while making problem solving more fun and pleasant [9, 10]. In addition to the attractiveness of this new kind of interaction, the main advantage of tangible objects is that they are an invitation to action and physically engage the body in the activity. Toy manufacturers already make games for learning computer programming that are composed of software, installed on a computer, and tangible objects, that communicate with this software. These objects are either used for the construction of the program [11–13], or for the construction of the robot that will execute the program [14]. For TurtleTable, we decided to use tangible objects to execute a given program (Fig. 2). Apart from the first two levels, all the others require the use of two or three objects. The objective was for each player to participate by moving his/her object.

The objects were custom-made with a 3D printer. The top is hollowed out so that the players can see the screen underneath. The objects have exactly the same shape and therefore can be interchangeable and turned. After testing the game with a small group of students, we realized it was more intuitive to add a sticker that indicates a number and the front of the object that would correspond with the number and front of the virtual object it is on.

Fig. 2. Tangible objects manipulated to play TurtleTable

3.2   Interactive Tabletops

The use of an interactive tabletop also facilitates collaboration between team members [15]. The large work space allows students to visualize the interface and interact with it equally, unlike computers or tablets where, most of the time, one person interacts and the others observe. The interactive tabletop used for TurtleTable is a *ActiveTable* produced by Promethean. This model does not have RFID captors or a camera under the screen, that can detect *ARTags*. It is equipped with laser beams that swipe the surface of the screen. A touch on the screen is detected when a finger or an object cuts the lasers. We therefore designed the tangible objects with "legs" that could be detected by the table and wrote a protocol to recognize it, by detecting the space between the four legs, so that it would not be mistaken for fingers.

4   Tests Lead with Middle School Students

4.1   Objectives

The game objective in TurtleTable (i.e. correctly executing an algorithm) is based on unplugged activities that are largely used in class and that have proven their effectiveness for teaching computer programming. The main benefit of TurtleTable is the fact that it corrects the students automatically and therefore allows the teachers to spend more time helping those in need. Consequently, it does not seem very interesting to compare classes that use TurtleTable with classes that do not. The benefits of the innovative TIT interactions, however, remains uncertain. The aim of this first exploratory study is therefore to measure if the use of TITs has a positive effect on **motivation, collaboration** and **learning**. TIT interactions offer two original features: the tangible objects and the large workspace, offered by the interactive tabletop. In order to measure the effect of each of these features, we decided to set up two control groups: one without tangible objects, but with the big screen, and another without tangible objects or the big screen. In order to have a neutral control panel, we also wanted a group to play the game on a computer, with basic mouse and keyboard interactions. We therefore developed four versions TurtleTable (Fig. 3).

Fig. 3. Middle School students playing with the four versions of TurtleTable

- The **TIT** version is played with Tangible objects on an Interactive Tabletop. The players move and turn the object on the grid by placing the tangible object on top of it and doing the desired movement.
- The **Tabletop** version is played on an interactive tabletop, without tangible objects. The objects are moved with basic tactile interactions: click to select and then swipe to move forwards or backwards. We developed a two finger compass-like rotation movement to turn the objects.
- The **Tablet** version is played on a tablet. The tactile interactions are the same as the tabletop version.
- The **Computer** version is played on a computer. To move an object, the player must first click on it with the mouse and then press the UP arrow to move forward or the DOWN arrow to move backward. The LEFT and RIGHT arrows are used to turn the object.

4.2   Data Collection and Experimental Protocol

In order to measure the effect of the of TITs on motivation, collaboration and learning, we collected different types of data. First, we designed an individual **pre and post-test** to measure the knowledge of the subjects regarding the basic concepts of computer programing (variables, loops and conditions). This test is composed of 10 exercises that are similar to TurtleTable's levels: the goal is to execute a program by drawing the path that the objects do on a grid with a pencil. In order to evaluate if the subjects are capable of using the right syntax and writing optimized code, the two final exercises of the test consist in writing the algorithm for a given drawing on a grid. All the **usage tracks** of TurtleTable are also collected. This provides precise indications on the number of errors and the time it took to complete a level. We also **filmed all the sessions** in order to analyze the interactions between the subjects. In order to understand these interactions, we also set up **focus groups** during which we discussed these interactions. Finally, we designed a **final survey** to collect the subjects' insight on TurtleTable and it's HCI.

A first experimentation was led with 59 students of the La Salle middle school (Laval, France). There were 30 girls and 29 boys, from 14 to 16 years old. These students came to our research center for half a day in December 2017. This field trip was presented by their teachers as a first initiation to computer programming. The large majority of these students had no experience in computer programming or algorithms: only 5 subjects were familiar with scratch programming, as they went to a computer science workshop during their lunch break.

The students were separated in four groups and assigned different versions of TurtleTable: 16 in the TIT group, 16 in the Tabletop group, 15 in the Tablet group and 12 in the Computer group. Each group was composed of 4 teams of three to four students. We asked the teachers to prepare the groups and the teams so that the level of the students would be evened out. The experimentation was planned as such:

1. The subjects had 15 min to answer the individual pre-test.
2. The teams had 60 min to play with the version of TurtleTable they were assigned. We asked them to go at least up to the level 15, in order for them to have seen all the programming concepts. During this session, we explicitly asked the teachers not to help their students.
3. The subjects had 15 min to answer the individual post-test.
4. The teams had 20 min to test the other versions of TurtleTable. During this session, several teams were interviewed in focus groups.
5. The subjects had 20 min to individually answer the final survey.

4.3   Results

First of all, **TurtleTable was greatly appreciated by the students and the teachers**. Almost all the groups managed to finish the 20 levels of the game in the allotted time and were competing to get the lowest number of errors by redoing all the levels. The analysis of the post-test shows that more than half of the students mastered the two first concepts presented in the game: variables (6/8) and repeat loops (12/16). Considering only a few students had motions of algorithms, this is a good result for their first hour of programming class. In the next sections, we discuss the differences between the different HCI versions of the game, in terms of motivation, collaboration and learning.

Motivation

In the final survey, the subjects indicated the version of the game they preferred (Fig. 4). Almost **2/3 preferred the TIT version**, 1/5 preferred the Tablet version and very few preferred the Computer of the Tabletop versions. These results are confirmed by the words they used to qualify the versions of TurtleTable (word clouds in Fig. 4) and the discussions lead during the focus groups. The TIT version is mostly qualified as "fun" and "interesting", the Tablet version is viewed as "interesting" and "educational", the Computer version as "amusing" by half of subjects but "boring" by the other half and finally, the Tabletop version is seen as "difficult".

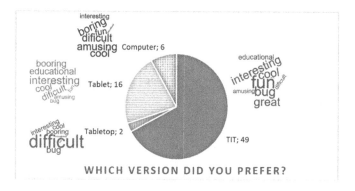

Fig. 4. Subjects preferred version of TurtleTable

Collaboration

The analysis of the videos shows that the teams using TITs and Tabletops had **much more interaction with each other** than the other groups. They talked more to each other and were all looking at the screen. In addition, the use of TITs facilitated collaboration: at least **two or three members of the team were engaged in the activity** by moving an object or helping the others move the objects. This is confirmed by the words used by the subjects in the final survey such as "convivial" and "group work", that only appear for the TIT version. With Tabletops, only one or two team members were engaged. With Tablets and Computers, the players would take turns playing the levels and the others would often look away while they were waiting for their turn.

Learning

Each pre and post-test was analyzed to determine the instructions that had been done correctly. The mean scores out of 100 for the pre-test was: TIT-14.00, Tabletop-15.42, Tablet-13.86 and Computer-15.54. For the post-test: TIT-28.38, Tabletop-27.85, Tablet-26.80 and Computer-26.85. The ANOVA test showed there was no significant differences between progression of the four groups. However, if we analyze the knowledge gain in each concept separately (bottom of Fig. 5), the subjects who used TITs seemed to have significantly better results for the "Repeat loop". The analysis of the questionnaires also revealed that more **subjects using TITs and Tabletops said they had learned a lot in the survey** (top of Fig. 5). In addition, the subjects qualified the TIT version with adjectives such as "educational" and "instructive", three times more than the other versions.

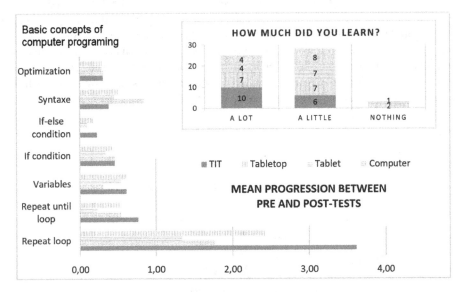

Fig. 5. Objective and subjective data to measure knowledge gain

5   Conclusion, Limitations and Perspectives

In this paper, we propose TurtleTable, a game that introduces the basic concepts of computer programming. The game is made to be used in class, in teams of three to four. It offers an original approach to apprehend the logic behind computer programming: the players have to execute a program by moving objects on a grid. The game offers real-time correction and a scoring mechanism that encourage players to take time to discuss the next move with the others. In order to maximize motivation, collaboration and learning, we designed TIT interactions: the students play by manipulating Tangible objects on an Interactive Tabletop. The first test, lead with 59 middle school students, was a success. In less than one hour, more than half of the students, with no prior knowledge in algorithms, had mastered the concepts of variables and the repeat loops. We developed four different versions of HCI (TIT, Tabletop, Tablet and Computer) to compare their effect on motivation, collaboration and learning. Even though the preliminary analysis did not show a significant increase in learning with TITs, this interaction definitely facilitated collaboration among the group and was a factor of great motivation.

Further analysis of the data collected during the test needs to be done. For example, we did not take into account the fact that some students were sitting and others standing when using the TIT and the Tabletop version of TurtleTable. In addition, we observed interesting behavior that needs to be analyzed. For example, with the TIT version, the students would rotate their bodies to help them turn the object in the right direction. We are currently looking into standardized interaction analysis to annotate the hours of videos collected during the teste. Finally, in order to test the effect of the size of the workspace, we intent on developing another version of TurtleTable that works with tangible objects on a tablet. We are looking into the possibility of painting the objects with conductive paint so that they are recognized by the tablet.

References

1. One of the main French website with various unplugged activities to help teachers teach computer science. https://pixees.fr/informatique-en-primaire-les-activites-debranchees/. Accessed 17 July 2018
2. LightBot. https://lightbot.com/. Accessed 17 July 2018
3. RobotProg. http://www.physicsbox.com/indexrobotprogen.html. Accessed 17 July 2018
4. Scratch. https://scratch.mit.edu/, https://code.org/learn. Accessed 17 July 2018
5. Logo Turtle. https://www.tortue-logo.fr/en/logo-turtle. Accessed 17 July 2018
6. Turtle Academy. http://turtleacademy.com/. Accessed 17 July 2018
7. Kubicki, S., Pasco, D., Arnaud, I.: Using a serious game with a tangible tabletop interface to promote student engagement in a first grade classroom: a comparative evaluation study. Int. J. Inf. Technol. **4**, 381–389 (2015)
8. Schubert, M., Serna, A., George, S.: Using collaborative activities on tabletops to enhance learning and knowledge transfer. In: Proceeding of the International Conference on Advanced Learning Technologies (ICALT), Rome, Italy, pp. 610–612 (2012)
9. Schneider, B., Jermann, P., Zufferey, G., Dillenbourg, P.: Benefits of a tangible interface for collaborative learning and interaction. IEEE Trans. Learn. Technol. **4**(3), 222–232 (2011)
10. Price, S., Pontual Falcão, T.: Where the attention is: discovery learning in novel tangible environments. Interact. Comput. **23**(5), 499–512 (2011)
11. Scharf, F., Winkler, T., Herczeg, M.: Tangicons: algorithmic reasoning in a collaborative game for children in kindergarten and first class. In: Proceedings of the International Conference on Interaction Design and Children, NY, USA, pp. 242–249 (2008)
12. Bers, M.U., Horn, M.S.: Tangible programming in early childhood: revisiting developmental assumptions through new technologies: Childhood in a digital world. In: Berson, I.R., Berson, M.J. (eds.) High-tech tots: childhood in a digital world Greenwich, Osmo (2009)
13. Magnenat, S., Ben-Ari, M., Klinger, S., Sumner, R.W.: Enhancing robot programming with visual feedback and augmented reality. In: Proceedings of the Annual Conference on Innovation and Technology in Computer Science Education (ITiCSE), Vilnius, Lithuania, pp. 153–158 (2015)
14. Lego Mindstorms. http://www.lego.com/en-us/mindstorms. Accessed 17 July 2018
15. Shaer, O., et al.: The design, development, and deployment of a tabletop interface for collaborative exploration of genomic data. Int. J. Hum Comput Stud. **70**(10), 746–764 (2012)

Modding Tabletop Games for Education

Daisy Abbott[(✉)] [iD]

The Glasgow School of Art, Glasgow, UK
d.abbott@gsa.ac.uk

Abstract. This paper describes a learning-objective-centric workflow for modifying ('modding') existing tabletop games for educational purposes. The workflow combines existing research for serious games design with novel systematic analysis techniques for learning and game mechanics and gameplay loops to improve the understanding and rigour of the process. A detailed worked example applies the workflow to the development of a serious tabletop game with the educational goal of increasing knowledge and confidence of performing postgraduate literature reviews. Systematic application of the workflow to a real example supports the value of this approach and provides a useful template for educators to follow for increasing the quality and feasibility of self-designed serious games.

Keywords: Serious games · Board games · Modding · Game-based learning

1 Introduction

It is now well evidenced that games can be engaging and effective tools for education but that the design of an intervention has as large an effect on success as the medium [1] and that designing effective game-based learning solutions requires significant expertise in both game-design and pedagogy [2]. Educational games which do not successfully combine game design with learning design are ineffective in terms of engagement, learning, or both (often known as a 'spinach sundae': a product which is neither appealing nor good for you [3]). Furthermore, research into game-enhanced learning demonstrates that the different characteristics of different games have discernible effects on the learning behaviours of players [4] and consequently on how well the game achieves its educational purpose [1, 5]. In short, educational game design is complex, resource intensive, and requires multiple interdisciplinary skillsets. Games designed for digital platforms also need significant technical expertise and the resources to support them. Despite these barriers, the well-documented advantages of game-based learning (GBL) drive demand for games for learning, training, or behavioural change (henceforth referred to as 'serious games') across a wide range of contexts [6–8]. However, as evidence of the efficacy of GBL grows, the discipline gains new advocates from a variety of backgrounds which increases the risk of GBL solutions being designed and implemented in isolation of the expertise and resource contexts necessary to make them effective. This paper presents a practical solution to the tension between the growing desire for serious games amongst students and educators and the barriers to effectively implementing them [9]. It is proposed that serious game design

© Springer Nature Switzerland AG 2019
M. Gentile et al. (Eds.): GALA 2018, LNCS 11385, pp. 318–329, 2019.
https://doi.org/10.1007/978-3-030-11548-7_30

can be streamlined and made cost-effective, without the loss of either learning objectives or game engagement and enjoyment, by developing educators' skill in modifying existing tabletop games.

1.1 Why Tabletop Games?

Tabletop games (e.g. board, card, and dice games) are under-represented in serious games literature; in fact, many definitions inexplicably restrict the concept to digital games. For clarity, this paper defines 'games' according to Juul's six game features (games have rules; variable, measurable outcomes with different values; players invest effort and are attached to outcomes; and consequences are negotiable) [10] and 'serious games' as games which have at least one characterizing goal as well as entertainment, *regardless of platform.*

Clearly, delivery platform (like game mechanics) affects interaction and therefore learning behaviours. Major advantages of digital games are their infinite reproducibility, scalability, and remote digital accessibility. However, if this is not needed – as is the case in some classroom delivery – the interaction behaviours of tabletop games can make them much more appropriate to a wide range of teaching situations. Tabletop interaction is kinaesthetic as well as mental, often involving players literally constructing maps, hands of cards, structures, or patterns on the game board where options are explored and solutions reinforced by physical movement and positioning. Unlike the typically isolated, human-computer-interaction gameplay of educational video games, tabletop games are usually social experiences where players analyse, learn from, and react to the strategies and actions of others. Furthermore, the educator is not only present but an active facilitator when students play educational tabletop games – allowing a more scaffolded learning experience that can be adapted on-the-fly to players' needs and also encourages further learning activities to take place in and around the game context. Enhanced scaffolding has been shown to have a significant improvement on acquisition of intended learning outcomes (ILOs) [1] and instructional support during gameplay is recommended [11]. These characteristics of tabletop games can increase the well-documented educational advantages of digital serious games, particularly for understanding complex systems [12] and collaborative group approaches [1] in tutorials or closely guided classroom contexts.

Furthermore, a common misconception that digital games are inherently engaging and motivating for learners is not supported by evidence. Even well-designed digital serious games can be disengaging, even intimidating, for some learners [7, 13] (particularly in Higher Education [14]) and there is evidence of lack of confidence for teachers using digital serious games, as learning to facilitate the game requires non-trivial additional expertise [13, 15]. This barrier is reduced (albeit not eliminated) for tabletop games, partly due to their lack of technological interface but also because rules and components are explicit and transparent [12]. Technical barriers to engagement should not be underestimated in educational settings. Not only do computer games require hardware, software, power, and often network connections to run at all (infrastructure that is often assumed but rarely smooth for educators to implement [13]), many digital serious games struggle to satisfy the user expectations created by the commercial game industry [13].

Finally, tabletop games require no programming skill and can be relatively quick and cheap to develop. This makes them considerably more achievable for educators who have games experience but limited time and money to devote to designing GBL activities. Nevertheless, for tabletop GBL to be successful, it still requires considerable pedagogical and game design expertise. This is the challenge this paper addresses.

1.2 Why Mod?

Flexibility and customisability are key features of tabletop games that can increase enjoyment [16] and potentially learning. The conceptual approach here assumes that pedagogy experts have familiarity with games, the desire to create GBL activities for their students, but not necessarily any applied game design expertise. It is concentrated on three principles:

1. Educators could focus on adapting ('modding') existing tabletop games, instead of creating a game from scratch. This approach reduces the game design expertise required (modding skill relies on recognizing/adapting rather than conceiving/designing appropriate game mechanics) and eliminates the need for lengthy testing, as the game being adapted is already commercially successful. Of course, adaptations for learning will still require evaluation and it is important to acknowledge that game literacy is important as misrecognition of game mechanics may impair learning. However, modding markedly reduces the expertise and resources required to produce an effective serious game.
2. Serious game design is made more manageable by adapting previous processes and workflows, concentrating on modding. This provides robust design principles that are easy to understand and follow, whilst also giving educators the framework for the baseline skills required for serious game design and a context for improvement.
3. The incorporation of analysis techniques that can be relatively easily understood and applied allows pedagogy experts to swiftly gain the minimum expertise necessary to produce and implement a serious game without too onerous a demand on their time.

The remainder of this paper presents a workflow for serious game modding, aimed at educators with some experience of GBL, which is critically applied via a worked example (identified as important for understanding [9, 15]). The game developed elucidates the process for a particular, real-world educational setting; increasing knowledge and confidence for Higher Education students about to undertake a literature review.

2 Workflow for Serious Game Modding

Figure 1 shows a workflow for effectively modding tabletop games for educational contexts. This workflow synthesises previous serious game development models [4, 5, 17–19], incorporating guidelines aimed at educators [13, 20], with a particular focus on tabletop GBL [6] and modding [12]. It further enhances previous research by categorising the steps by pedagogic and/or game design expertise and including gameplay

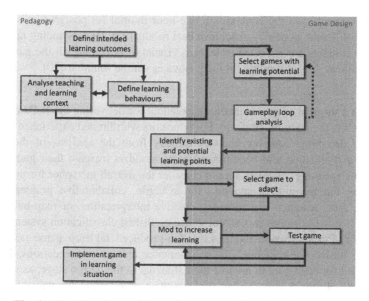

Fig. 1. Workflow for modding existing games for educational purposes

loop analysis [21] as a method to map learning mechanics to game mechanics [22] in order to inform both choice and adaptation of games. Each step is described below.

Define Learning Outcomes
The first (and most important) step is to define the overall purpose of the activity in terms of its intended learning outcomes (ILOs): i.e. what knowledge or understanding should be improved after playing? This may seem obvious but is worth making explicit that ILOs should be clearly defined and kept in mind throughout the design process. If this step is taken for granted, or subsumed into game design, it is likely that the game will either not be effective, or will teach something other than the lessons intended. This primary and central position of ILOs reflects previous research cited above.

Analyse Context and Define Learning Behaviours
The next, concurrent, steps are to consider the learning and teaching context and to define the intended learning behaviours [4, 17, 23]. Too often games are developed in isolation of their context and not enough thought is given to how they will be effectively integrated into teaching and learning practice [13, 17]. Is the game intended for quiet, independent study or will it be deployed in a classroom of 30 children? Will it be played once or repeated? Will players compete or co-operate? Who will lead the game and support the learning? A common mistake in designing serious games is to default to a 'question and answer' model, familiar to educators from quizzes and simple trivia games. This is perfect for demonstrating existing knowledge but ineffective for learning new information [5]. Therefore, if ILOs are centred around memorisation, the learning mode is behaviourist 'drill and practice', and the context is independent home study, a digital game with strong extrinsic rewards, high interest and replayability, or both, could be an effective solution [11, 24]. Conversely, if ILOs rely on collaborative, constructivist

learning behaviours and the context is a one-hour tutorial for postgraduates, this will require very different gameplay to achieve best results [23]. Understanding *how* as well as *what* the students are expected to learn is crucial to informing all the game design steps that follow. A useful guide for GBL novices can be found at [20].

Select Potential Games

Next, create a shortlist of games that have potential for delivering the ILOs defined, in the way that fits the learning situation. For educators with limited experience of games, this can be daunting, however it arises directly from the analysis of the learning behaviours and situation and becomes easier as modders increase their game literacy [12]. Broadly speaking, modders should consider the overall metaphor for the game as indicated by the learning behaviours, for example, collaborative problem-solving, competitive race, resource management, creative interpretation, or map-building. To then shortlist suitable games it is useful to use published classification systems such as the Gameplay/Purpose/Scope model [25], fan-produced tabletop game taxonomies[1] and (not to be overlooked) one's own experience and recommendations. It is also recommended for educators to involve their students in the design stage, as much as is possible, not only for acceptance but students themselves may have valuable insights. Importantly, the overall game format should arise from learning behaviours and context, not the subject matter. Whilst it may be tempting to search for games with similar content to the ILOs, it is the underlying game mechanics that support learning and there arises a risk that the game 'skin' (i.e. theme/narrative) will distract from the actual pedagogic goals.

Gameplay Loop Analysis, Identification of Learning Points, Game Selection

Gameplay refers to players interacting with the game and here explicitly includes cognition as well as physical actions influencing the game world. The gameplay loop follows Guardiola's definition [21] and builds on his pedagogic method: the loops represent gameplay as linked actions. This process breaks down and describes every game interaction, allowing educators to consider the types of behaviours involved and map them to learning behaviours. This stage is more easily understood using the worked example (Fig. 2), however the basic steps for analysis are as follows. Firstly, *play the game*. Whilst aspects of gameplay loops can be discerned from reading the rules, it is necessary to gain a more holistic understanding through play as this includes social and emotional elements of gameplay. Next, map the gameplay loops as a flowchart at a macro level, identifying In Game and Out Game actions [21] i.e. actions that have an immediate, measurable effect in the game such as moving a piece, and those that do not such as chatting to other players. As much as is productive, expand each sub-loop and categorise the types of interactions using an established concept map such as the Game Mechanic – Learning Mechanic framework [22]. This allows the identification of learning mechanics that happen in and between each interaction (not forgetting Out Game actions, where important scaffolding and metacognition takes place). Finally, highlight points that would easily support additional learning

---

[1] E.g. https://boardgamegeek.com/thread/581158/alternative-classification-board-games-long; https://www.boardgamegeek.com/image/3613899/rouie-a.

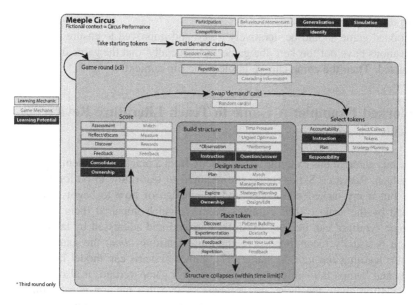

Fig. 2. Gameplay loop analysis of Meeple Circus, using an extension of the LM-GM model

mechanics, even when not currently present in gameplay. Based on these analyses, it is possible to see which games have the mechanics that best support the learning behaviours desired (or, to demonstrate that games do not support the overall purpose, in which case it may be necessary to return to the shortlisting stage or elect instead to create the game from scratch).

Modification for Learning

If analysis shows that all learning mechanics are already present and the game's theme can be mapped directly to the stated ILOs, modifying a game could be as simple as changing the theme content ('reskinning'). However, it is more likely that game mechanics will need to be added to or altered to enable or reinforce the desired learning mechanics and players' exposure to learning material (content) during gameplay. A simple example is creating a trivia game by adding 'question and answer' interaction which acts as a gateway to progression. Whilst this 'quiz' approach can be very effective for certain ILOs, it has limitations [5] whereas gameplay with intrinsically integrated learning content can be more effective for learning and motivation [26]. Therefore care should be taken to, where fruitful, embed learning mechanics into the core of gameplay without disrupting the overall game. In general, once gameplay satisfies the ILOs, context and behaviours defined, game mechanics should be altered as little as possible as every change affects the game system and balance and could lead to unwanted emergent behaviours or even risk undermining the ILOs.

Testing and Implementation
The modded game should be iteratively tested and improved to ensure firstly that the modifications have not 'broken' the game and, crucially, that the game does impart the ILOs stated. Then the game can be implemented in context.

3 Worked Example: A Game to Teach Literature Review Skills

The serious game in this example arose directly from a practical problem: students on a postgraduate Research Skills course are required to learn how to perform a literature review but many lacked confidence and knowledge of how to begin and felt overwhelmed by the scale of this complex process, which impaired their learning. This pedagogic 'vertigo' can be very fruitfully mirrored and addressed by tabletop games. Whilst it is usually recommended to minimise learning *about* the game in order to maximise learning *through* the game [27], games systems can model larger complex systems and "when the sim dissolves the player's game vertigo, it also dissolves his system vertigo about the large and complex system that the sim is modelling." [12] Therefore, a GBL approach was chosen to reflect the process of undertaking a literature review and to diffuse students' trepidation about starting this large and complex task.

Intended Learning Outcomes
Intended learning (and attitudinal) outcomes were defined as follows. After playing the game, students should: Understand the basic principles of searching, evaluating, and assimilating research sources; Be able to identify different types of source and understand when they are most useful; Be able to describe techniques for choosing sources and deciding what to read; Recognise that evaluation of sources has a time cost, but saves time and improves quality overall; Understand that literature search and review requires iterative refocussing and describe techniques for refining searches, and; Feel more relaxed and confident about the literature search and review process.

Teaching and Learning Context
Implementation is within a postgraduate tutorial context, therefore a face-to-face, instructor-supported tabletop game is suitable. Student numbers exceed 30 therefore the game should either be simple enough to not require direct supervision or engaging enough to maintain interest and learning as a spectator. An alternative is to implement the game with smaller groups in turn whilst the rest of the class are engaged in a different activity, requiring the game to be relatively short duration. Supporting smaller groups of players is an acknowledged limitation of non-digital tabletop games with implications for educators that must be considered.

Learning Behaviours
Learning behaviours were defined to mirror the real-life task of performing a literature review: exploratory, discovering, constructivist, independent, selective, refining/refocussing, consolidating, and non-linear. Overall comprehension of the process is more important than learning specific facts, therefore repetition is focussed

on refining understanding, not memorisation. Due to students feeling overwhelmed, it is also important to 'drip feed' content, using a Cascading Information learning mechanic [22].

Shortlist Games

Games were shortlisted based on a strategic construction overall mechanic (as a metaphor for exploring and constructing an understanding of a research topic through a literature review), including elements of selection and matching (representing selection of sources to match research topic), and repetition for both consolidation of knowledge/understanding and refining. Five games were shortlisted using BoardGameGeek's taxonomy and personal recommendations: *Blueprints, Meeple Circus, Best Treehouse Ever, Junk Art,* and *Rhino Hero.*[2] All five games involve literally constructing something and for four games, Dexterity is a core mechanic meaning game tokens are played thoughtfully and carefully. All are competitive (with the exception of one of the minigames within *Junk Art*), however in all cases except *Rhino Hero,* competition is via scoring each player's own structure rather than directly interfering with opponents' structures. All games except *Rhino Hero* explicitly involve repetition and Cascading Information is core to *Meeple Circus* and *Best Treehouse Ever.*

Gameplay Loop Analysis and Selection

Guided by the literature, gameplay loops were produced for each shortlisted game (including every minigame within *Junk Art*) and points of learning (and potential learning) were identified. This allowed a rigorous parity of comparison between each game.

Rhino Hero was rejected first as the lose condition is binary – when the tower collapses, the game ends for everybody – this halts learning. Analysis showed that this game relies heavily on Dexterity and Press Your Luck mechanics which were difficult to imagine being intrinsically integrated with the ILOs, and learning mechanics are restricted to planning which cards to use against your opponents. However, its simplicity, linearity, and quick repeatability would be highly appropriate for lower-order ILOs related to literature review, especially as the folded cards are reminiscent of books.

Junk Art was also rejected. Whilst several of the minigames were highly appropriate for the fictional context of performing a literature review, token design made balancing pieces more difficult which, considered alongside the core role of fallen pieces in most of the minigames' exit conditions and scoring, was felt to not contribute to the learning behaviours effectively. A further reason was that scoring rewards and penalties are explicitly comparative (e.g. who has the tallest sculpture and/or most fallen tokens), whereas the scoring of the remaining three games focusses more on how well each individual construction matches external scoring conditions. The latter situation was judged to be more appropriate to the literature review metaphor.

---

[2] https://www.zmangames.com/en/products/blueprints/;   http://www.matagot.com/en/catalog/details/family-games/3/meeple-circus/894;   http://www.greencouchgames.com/besttreehouseever;   http://www.pretzelgames.com/en/home/21-junk-art.html; http://www.habausa.com/rhino-hero/.

Blueprints, *Meeple Circus*, and *Best Treehouse Ever* were all suitable for modding for the ILOs and context defined. All three use repetition, strategic selection and management of resources, strategic placement of tokens/tiles in the overall construction, followed by a scoring phase which allows assessment, feedback, and reflection for players. Furthermore, all three involve design for pattern matching with strategic elements. Meeple Circus uses an elegant Cascading Information mechanic via game Levels to gently introduce complexity, thereby reducing game vertigo whilst also acting as a highly appropriate metaphor for the iterative refining process of exploring a research topic. Furthermore, overall its rules were felt to be simpler than the other two games, therefore *Meeple Circus* (Fig. 2) was selected as the game to be modded.

Mod Game to Increase Learning

The first step was to change the theme to match the learning situation. Instead of creating a circus performance, players are building their knowledge of a research area by finding, reading, and synthesising literature and other research sources. Strategic selection of game tokens becomes searching and evaluating sources, placing tokens in the structure represents understanding and synthesising knowledge, matching acrobatic feats becomes closeness of fit to the research question being investigated, and scoring indicates the quality of the literature review. In this way, the game functions as a simulation, allowing players to both identify with the content and generalise it to their individual situations (Fig. 2).

Care was taken when conceptually 'reskinning' the game to map components to ILOs which are supported by the game rules, particularly the scoring system. For example, a blue acrobat represents baseline knowledge sources used when starting a literature search – because it scores points for touching the ground it is much more useful in the first round than a red acrobat, which represents innovation and originality and scores highly in later rounds. 'Audience demand' cards score when a player matches their pattern – this represents the student's current use of sources to understand their research area – and changes between rounds, making it an excellent metaphor for iteratively developing an understanding of a specific topic. The change in game theme requires explanation to students, therefore an Instruction learning mechanic is required in the Select and Build phases.

The next step was to evaluate how well the reskinned game matches the ILOs. Each ILO was mapped to existing game mechanics to assess whether it was delivered. Where not effectively achieved, additional learning and/or game mechanics were devised using the points of potential learning already identified in the gameplay loop analysis. Additional game mechanics were required to deliver the Instruction, Question/Answer and Consolidate learning mechanic potential. To ensure all ILOs were satisfied, the following rules were added:

1. When taking any component, players must first draw the appropriate card for that component from the new deck of Instruction cards and read out the fact/tip to the group. Cards contain ideas for sources of this particular type, and techniques for evaluating sources and deciding what (and what not) to read. This builds knowledge which can be later demonstrated or discussed in 'out game' learning activities with direct relevance to the student's particular subject domain.

2. After component selection, players have the option of receiving a generic extra component (such as a 6-sided die) or of swapping one of their existing components for one of their choice (after considering a question from a new deck of Evaluate cards). This mechanic creates active engagement with the techniques of rigorous evaluation of sources. However, this mechanic in particular needed to be tested to ensure that swapping leads to higher scores than accepting the generic component.

3. During the 'swap demand card' phase, the two (as opposed to one) players with the lowest score can swap an 'audience demand' card. To do this each must read out a card from the new deck of Refine and Focus cards. This increases emphasis on techniques for refining and focussing research questions.

4. The final round contains performative 'challenge' cards. These cards were altered to allow players to demonstrate knowledge about specific aspects of the literature review process, as well as learning from each other. They move cognitive processes explicitly into the active mode by prompting recall, analysis, or interpretation of game content.

5. Finally, the name of the game was changed to *On the Shoulders of Giants* (Fig. 3).

On the Shoulders of Giants was then informally tested with small numbers of students and staff who teach research skills and feedback on gameplay and the content and phrasing of learning cards was incorporated. No major changes were required.

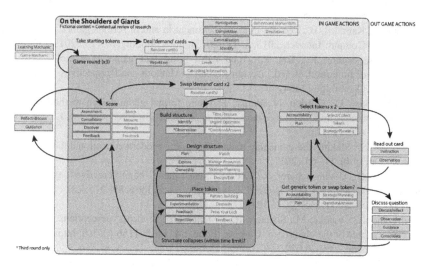

Fig. 3. Gameplay loop analysis of *On the Shoulders of Giants*: educational mod of Meeple Circus

4   Conclusion and Next Steps

This worked example of the development of a tabletop serious game shows the value of using a robust design workflow to modify an existing tabletop game. Reflection on the process demonstrates that close analysis using the LM-GM model, combined with gameplay loops, allows the identification of particular points within gameplay where educational content can be integrated to match the game's content to defined ILOs. This makes the process of game design significantly easier and more rigorous, especially for modders who do not necessarily already have a high level of game literacy.

Further steps are to formally evaluate this game with a larger cohort of students in order to demonstrate whether or not it is effective at delivering the ILOs and attitude change defined. Another avenue for future research would be to test this workflow with educators who have limited experience of game design, to establish if their experience supports the hypothesis that serious game design can be achievable (albeit still challenging) by analysing and modding tabletop games in a systematic and rigorous way.

Finally, incorporating feedback from the serious games research community has the potential to further improve and potentially streamline this workflow to increase its efficacy and ease of use.

Game rules and further information about this research is available at http://blog.gsofasimvis.com/index.php/research/games/.

References

1. Clark, D.B., Tanner-Smith, E.E., Killingsworth, S.S.: Digital games, design, and learning: a systematic review and meta-analysis. Rev. Educ. Res. **86**, 79–122 (2016). https://doi.org/10.3102/0034654315582065
2. Bellotti, F., Kapralos, B., Lee, K., et al.: Assessment in and of serious games: an overview. Adv. Hum.-Comput. Interact. **2013**, 1–11 (2013). https://doi.org/10.1155/2013/136864
3. Jenkins, H., Squire, K., Tan, P.: "You can't bring that game to school!" Designing supercharged! In: Laurel, B. (ed.) Design Research: Methods and Perspectives, pp. 244–252. MIT Press, Cambridge (2004)
4. Grey, S., Grey, D., Gordon, N., Purdy, J.: Using formal game design methods to embed learning outcomes into game mechanics and avoid emergent behaviour. Int. J. Game-Based Learn. **7**, 63–73 (2017)
5. Nicholson, S.: Making the gameplay matter: designing modern educational tabletop games. Knowl. Quest **40**, 60–65 (2011)
6. Sardone, N.B., Devlin-Scherer, R.: Let the (board) games begin: creative ways to enhance teaching and learning. Clear. House J. Educ. Strat. Issues Ideas **89**, 215–222 (2016). https://doi.org/10.1080/00098655.2016.1214473
7. Bourgonjon, J., Valcke, M., Soetaert, R., Schellens, T.: Students' perceptions about the use of video games in the classroom. Comput. Educ. **54**, 1145–1156 (2010). https://doi.org/10.1016/j.compedu.2009.10.022
8. Sandford, R., Ulicsak, M., Facer, K., Rudd, T.: Teaching with games. Bristol (2006)
9. Ney, M., Emin, V., Earp, J.: Paving the way to game based learning: a question matrix for teacher reflection. Procedia Comput. Sci. **15**, 17–24 (2012). https://doi.org/10.1016/j.procs.2012.10.053
10. Juul, J.: The game, the player, the world: looking for a heart of gameness. In: Copier, M., Raessens, J. (eds.) Proceedings of the Level Up: Digital Games Research Conference. University of Utrecht, Utrecht, pp. 30–45 (2003)
11. Hays, R.T.: The effectiveness of instructional games: a literature review and discussion. Naval Air Warfare Center Training Systems Division 1–63 (2005). citeulike-article-id:3089090

12. Castronova, E., Knowles, I.: Modding board games into serious games: the case of Climate Policy. Int. J. Serious Games **2**, 41–62 (2015). https://doi.org/10.17083/ijsg.v2i3.77
13. Marklund, B.B.: Working with educational games. University of Skövde (2014)
14. Whitton, N.: Encouraging engagement in game-based learning. Int. J. Game-Based Learn. **1** (1), 75–84 (2011). https://doi.org/10.4018/ijgbl.2011010106
15. Bourgonjon, J., De Grove, F., De Smet, C., et al.: Acceptance of game-based learning by secondary school teachers. Comput. Educ. **67**, 21–35 (2013). https://doi.org/10.1016/j.compedu.2013.02.010
16. Frapolli, F., Malatras, A., Hirsbrunner, B.: Exploiting traditional gameplay characteristics to enhance digital board games. In: 2nd International IEEE Consumer Electronic Society Games Innovation Conference, ICE-GIC 2010, Hong Kong. IEEE (2010)
17. Catalano, C.E., Luccini, A.M., Mortara, M.: Best practices for an effective design and evaluation of serious games. Int. J. Serious Games, 1 (2014). https://doi.org/10.17083/ijsg.v1i1.8
18. Marne, B., Wisdom, J., Huynh-Kim-Bang, B., Labat, J.-M.: The six facets of serious game design: a methodology enhanced by our design pattern library. In: Ravenscroft, A., Lindstaedt, S., Kloos, C.D., Hernández-Leo, D. (eds.) EC-TEL 2012. LNCS, vol. 7563, pp. 208–221. Springer, Heidelberg (2012). https://doi.org/10.1007/978-3-642-33263-0_17
19. Lui, R.W.C., Au, C.H.: Establishing an educational game development model. Int. J. Game-Based Learn. **8**, 52–73 (2018). https://doi.org/10.4018/IJGBL.2018010104
20. Torrente, J., Marchiori, E.J., del Blanco, A., et al.: Production of Creative Game-Based Learning Scenarios: A Handbook for Teachers (2011)
21. Guardiola, E.: The gameplay loop: a player activity model for game design and analysis. In: Proceedings of the 13th International Conference on Advances in Computer Entertainment Technology, Osaka (2016)
22. Lim, T., Louchart, S., Suttie, N., et al.: Strategies for effective digital games development and implementation. In: Baek, Y., Whitton, N. (eds.) Cases on Digital Game-Based Learning: Methods, Models, and Strategies, pp. 168–198. IGI Global, Hershey (2013)
23. Abbott, D.: "How to Fail Your Research Degree": A serious game for research students in Higher Education. Serious Games **9090**(1), 179–185 (2015). ISSN 0302-9743
24. Keller, J.M.: Motivational Design for Learning and Performance: The ARCS Model Approach. Springer, New York (2009). https://doi.org/10.1007/978-1-4419-1250-3
25. Djaouti, D., Alvarez, J., Jessel, J.-P.: Classifying serious games: the G/P/S model. In: Felicia, P. (ed.) Handbook of Research on Improving Learning and Motivation Through Educational Games: Multidisciplinary Approaches, pp. 118–136. IGI Global, Hershey (2011)
26. Habgood, M.P.J., Ainsworth, S.E.: Motivating children to learn effectively: exploring the value of intrinsic integration in educational games (2017). https://doi.org/10.1080/10508406.2010.508029
27. Sandford, R., Williamson, B.: Games and Learning: A Handbook from Futurelab. Bristol (2005)

HPGE: An Haptic Plugin for Game Engines

Nicolò Balzarotti[1,2] and Gabriel Baud-Bovy[1,3(✉)]

[1] Robotics, Brain and Cognitive Science Department,
Istituto Italiano di Tecnologia, Genova, Genova, Italy
`gabriel.baud-bovy@iit.it`
[2] DIBRIS, Università degli Studi di Genova, Genova, Italy
[3] Faculty of Psychology, Vita-Salute San Raffaele University & Unit
of Experimental Psychology, IRCCS San Raffaele Scientific Institute, Milan, Italy

Abstract. In this paper we present HPGE, an Haptic Plugin for Game Engines. Based on CHAI3D, it aims at providing an easy way to integrate haptics in game engines. HPGE provides `C` and `C#` bindings to be usable with almost any game engine or software. In addition, HPGE provides Unity3D `C#` scripts to facilitate the integration with Unity3D. Thanks to this plugin, it is possible to take advantage of the CHAI3D force-rendering algorithms and Unity3D Graphical User Interfaces to develop serious games. The paper goes through the requirements of such plugin, the issues that need to be addressed, to conclude with a description of the implementation and usage of the plugin.

1 Introduction

Serious Games are games whose primary purpose is to integrate educational objectives with specific evidence-based game mechanics known to support learning and its generalization [6,9]. A motivation for using haptic feedback in games with educational purposes is that sensory-motor experience and active exploration is beneficial for learning. This insight has been conceptualized in various theoretical frameworks, such as Constructivism and Embodied Cognition. Moreover, various Virtual Reality applications with force-feedback devices have shown promising results (review in [4]). The development of these applications is however hampered by the lack of easy-to-use tools to integrate force-feedback devices: a problem that the haptic plugin for game engines (HPGE) presented in this paper tries to address.

Haptics (from Greek *aptikos*, "suitable for touch") combines touch and manipulation. As a sensory modality, it includes the sense of touch based on skin receptors and proprioception (i.e. the sense of movement and force) based on muscle and joint receptors [10]. The generic term *haptic devices* refers to devices whose aim is to provide haptic sensations. Haptic devices can be divided in *force-feedback devices* interacting primarily with the proprioceptive system and *tactile devices* interacting primarily with the tactile system.

© Springer Nature Switzerland AG 2019
M. Gentile et al. (Eds.): GALA 2018, LNCS 11385, pp. 330–339, 2019.
https://doi.org/10.1007/978-3-030-11548-7_31

While games tend to privilege visual and audio sensory modalities, haptics is not completely neglected. In fact, common games controllers like the Nintendo Switch, Sony Playstation and Microsoft Xbox are able to produce vibro-tactile feedback.

However, games typically don't integrate *force-feedback devices* for two possible reasons. The first reason is the lack of low-cost force-feedback devices although this obstacle could in principle be overcome if a market and applications could support manufacturers. As a matter of fact, various low-cost force-feedback devices were commercially available in the past, such as Microsoft 2D SideWinder joystick and the Novint's Falcon, a 3D force-feedback device with a price below $250. The second reason is the complexity and hard real-time constraints of the control algorithms needed to simulate contact with virtual objects with a force-feedback device. For this reason, applications involving haptic devices are typically realized with specialized software libraries.

This paper is organized as follows. First, we review the requirements and characteristics of software libraries that are typically used to develop applications with a force-feedback device and explain some major differences with game engines. Then, we describe the architecture of the plugin and some issues that need to be addressed. Finally, we conclude by describing briefly some applications that were implemented with the HPGE plugin and discuss some of its limits.

1.1 Haptic Rendering Software

Haptic rendering allows users to feel objects haptically in a virtual environment [14]. It is the process that allows a computer to *display* a force through an *haptic device* [15]. Just like computer graphics, the user must specify *what* to render and *how* to render it. Depending on the type of rendering needed, different kinds of information about the objects' properties is required like their shape, texture or elastic properties.

Haptic rendering algorithms work by updating the haptic device position and orientation in space, by detecting an eventual collision between the device and virtual objects in the haptic scene, and then by computing the appropriate response to the collision (e.g. to push the device outside of the virtual object) [3]. Crucially, the force-rendering must be computed and updated at high frequency (>1 kHz) to avoid vibrations and ensure the *stability* of the interaction.

Various high-level haptic libraries are available (review in [11]). For the HPGE plugin, we choose CHAI3D [7] for a variety of reasons. First, CHAI3D is free and open source (revised BSD License). Second, CHAI3D supports a wide range of devices. Third, CHAI3D implements complex force-rendering algorithms. In particular, it is almost alone in having built-in support for haptic texture rendering. Finally, it has features such as hierarchical scene graph that are similar to ones defined in Unity3D, making it easier to mirror Unity3D scene in the plugin (see Sect. 2.3).

1.2   Game Engines

Game engines are software development environments designed to build computer games. While there are some similarities with haptic libraries that are used to develop applications with force-feedback devices (see Sect. 1.1), they also differ in important ways [12].

First, game engines such as Unity3D[1] or Unreal[2] provide advanced tools to write stories, animate characters and interact with users. Although game engines don't support force-feedback devices in a standard way (but see [8]), they support numerous other devices, such as motion trackers and head mounted displays. Second, game engines have typically more advanced graphical and audio capabilities than haptic software. Third, much of the application and/or game development can be done via a Graphical User Interface (GUI), speeding up the development time by avoiding tedious coding of low-level features. In contrast, haptic Software Development Kits (SDKs) provide much less tools to develop applications and no Integrated Development Environment (IDE). Finally, the community of developers for game engines is one or two orders of magnitude larger than the community of haptic device users.

For all these reasons, using a game engine to develop haptic-based applications and games would be a considerable benefit. However, connecting a force-feedback device to a game engine is challenging because of the complex algorithms that need to be implemented to simulate contact with virtual objects and the hard real-time constraints described in Sect. 1.1. In fact, to our knowledge, games engines have never been used to develop haptic based Virtual Reality applications for educational purposes (see [4]). To address this issue, the HPGE library comes with special scripts to integrate the haptic plugin in Unity3D.

Unity3D is a proprietary cross-platform game creation system with a very large developer basis. Its Personal edition is free to use for non-commercial applications. Its Integrated Development Environment allows a user to develop the game using built-in tools and the programming language C#. Physical simulation are performed using PhysX, a C++ physics engine developed by NVIDIA that can take advantage hardware capabilities of the graphical card.

2   Plugin Description

2.1   Objectives

The main objective of HPGE is to provide an easy way for the game developer to integrate a force-feedback device, with the final aim to increase the number of serious games that take advantage of haptic feedback.

While HPGE includes scripts for Unity3D integration, a secondary objective was to design the plugin so that it can be inter-operable with other game engines.

---

[1] unity3d.com.
[2] unrealengine.com.

2.2   Features

The range of applications and user experiences that a game might provide via the haptic plugin and device is very large. For example, the haptic plugin might allow the user to touch virtual objects, explore their shapes and feel the properties of their surfaces (e.g., stiffness, friction or texture). In addition, the force-feedback device can also be used as 3D (position) or 6D (position and rotation) input device to draw in space and to move or rotate objects for example. Some applications are described in Sect. 3.

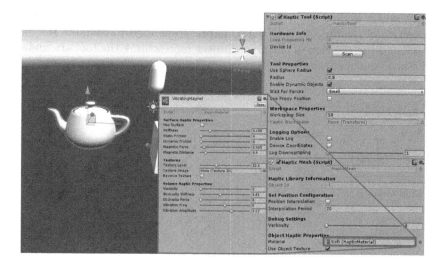

Fig. 1. HPGE haptic rendering parameters

Drag-and-Drop Support. For the game developer, the plugin provides scripts that can be dragged-and-dropped on GameObject in Unity3D IDE to make them touchable (see Sect. 2.4).

Graphical User Interface. All parameters of CHAI3D force rendering algorithm can be modified from the Unity3D GUI (see Fig. 1).

Haptic Textures. CHAI3D implements a haptic texture rendering algorithm, which modifies the force experienced when one explores the surface of an haptic object. It is possible to define the haptic texture by associating a bitmap image in Unity3D IDE to the object as well as to dissociate haptic and visual textures.

Custom Haptic Force-Feedback. The library provides a hook function that is called in the main haptic loop to define a custom haptic effect. The hook function can be used to compute the desired force as a function of the `position` and the `velocity` of the device, which are passed as parameters. In this manner, a custom haptic effect can be defined without having to modify the haptic plugin.

Device Logging. A logging mechanism allows the developer to save the position, velocity and force applied by the tool at the frequency of the haptic loop (typically 1 kHz). This makes it possible and easy to analyze the behavior of the user and the quality of interaction off-line.

2.3   Integration Principle

The integration between Unity3D and CHAI3D happens by duplicating part of Unity3D world into the haptic plugin (see Fig. 2). Such a duplication is necessary because the force-feedback must be computed at a high frequency to insure stability, which is done by a dedicated thread running at 1 kHz in the plugin. The position of the objects in CHAI3D haptic scene used to compute the force-feedback and the position of the GameObject representing the tool are updated at a lower frequency (see Sect. 2.4).

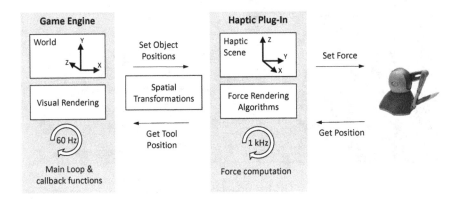

Fig. 2. Unity3D (left) left-handed vs CHAI3D (right) right-handed world coordinate systems

The haptic scene inside the haptic plugin is created automatically when the Touchable scripts is attached to a GameObject in Unity3D. Information about the object geometry is recovered from the Unity GameObjects and automatically transmitted to CHAI3D to create a mirror object.

Static Scenes. Static scenes are scenes where the objects do not move. This is the simplest scenario for haptic rendering. In this case, force rendering depends only on the movement of the user on the touchable objects. For visualization purposes, the position of device is automatically updated in Unity3D.

Animated Scenes. Animated scenes are scenes where touchable objects are moved by Unity3D in a manner that is *independent* from the interaction force applied to the object. In other words, animated scenes do not involve physical simulation besides the contact between the user and the touchable object. In these scenes, the object position that is computed by Unity must be communicated to the haptic plugin. We discuss this case in more details in the next section.

Interactive Scenes. Interactive scenes involve scenarios with physical simulations where the action of the user has a dynamic effect on the motion of the objects.

2.4   Implementation

Architecture. To make the haptic plugin compatible with different game engines and software, we adopted a layered architecture for HPGE (see Fig. 3).

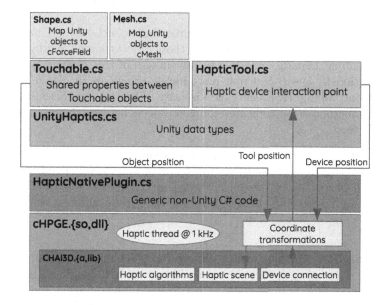

Fig. 3. Architecture details of the integration between HPGE and Unity3D. Names on the left upper corner are the filenames

- At the lowest level, cHPGE is a C library that wraps a light-weight version of CHAI3D where unnecessary dependencies (OpenGL, OpenAL and Theora) have been removed. The removal of unneeded dependencies reduces the size of the library, making it possible to compile and run it even on an Android device.
- HapticNativePlugin.cs is a C# wrapper that uses only C# data types in order to allow any C# program to use the library. This layer handles the conversion between native and managed code.
- The layers above are specific to Unit3D. UnityHaptics.cs take advantage of Unity3D data types to simplify the C# API.
- At the highest level, the HPGE library contain several scripts that extend the MonoBehaviour Unity3D class (see Sect. 2.4).

Unity3D Scripts. This section provides some information about the C# scripts that have been developed specifically for the integration of the haptic plugin in Unity3D[3]. As mentioned in Sect. 2.2, game developers can drag-and-drop these scripts on Unity3D `GameObjects` to endow them with haptic properties:

- `HapticTool.cs` is required and must be associated with a Sphere `GameObject` representing the haptic device in the game (another `GameObject` with a different shape can be attached to the sphere in Unity3D for visualization purposes if desired).
- `HapticMesh.cs` can be applied to any `GameObject` with a mesh. The object is rendered with CHAI3D implementation of the *Finger Proxy Algorithm* [2]. The algorithm is suited for complex 3D shapes but it is computationally expensive.
- `HapticShape.cs` can be applied to simple shapes such as the Unity3D Box or Sphere `GameObjects`. The surface of those objects is rendered by CHAI3D using a simple *Penalty method*. The advantages of this method is that it is computationally cheap and that more haptic effects are available, including Magnet and volumetric effects (like Viscosity, Vibrations and StickSlip). However, the method is not indicated for thin objects because the tool might pop through them.

The position and orientation of the tool is automatically updated when the user moves the device. To configure touchable objects, it is possible to change the material properties of the surface via Unity IDE (see Fig. 1). The haptic parameters are updated on-the-fly, also when the game is running, which allows fast prototyping.

Interoperability. The plugin encapsulates CHAI3D haptic scene and all force rendering computation inside a dynamic library with C bindings (see Fig. 2). Moreover, all spatial transformations between the game engine and the haptic device coordinate systems are implemented at this level. The C API allows one to manage the haptic scene that is used by the plugin to simulate contact with virtual objects without having to deal with real-time constraint explicitly. Keeping all crucial computation in the lowest level of the plugin and the choice of a C API make the integration with all sort software particularly easy[4]. For example, we have used Python and Julia to control the haptic device and test the plugin during its development. In principle, one might call plugin functions from Unreal C++ scripts to create new `Component` classes that can dropped on any `Actor` like the previously described C# scripts used in Unity3D to endow GameObjects with haptic properties.

Object Position Updating. Scenarios with moving objects (Animated Scenes) can present difficulties if the user is touching the object at the same

---

[3] https://www.youtube.com/watch?v=HVYiBpmMfeM.

[4] https://rosettacode.org/wiki/Call_a_function_in_a_shared_library#C.23.

time or if the object moves to a new position that englobes the tool. In both cases, the movement might result in an abrupt change of the tool position with respect to surface of the object, which leads to an abrupt change in the interaction force. The problem is particularly acute if the object stiffness is high.

This problem can however be mitigated by minimizing the size of the instantaneous displacements or, equivalently, by increasing the frequency at which the position is updated. In Unity3D, the `Update` callback is called once per visual frame and runs typically at 60 Hz (which corresponds to 16.7 ms period), which is relatively slow for a quick object displacement. In principle, the `FixedUpdate` can be called several times for each `Update` callback. To be able to take advantage of this possibility, the object (and tool) position in HPGE is updated inside the `FixedUpdate` callback. The frequency of the `Update` and `FixedUpdate` can be controlled by Unity3D `Time Manager` parameters.

Another (complementary) approach is to smooth the changes of the position. This second approach was also implemented in the haptic plugin by interpolating the object position between the actual position and the new position over a user-settable time period. This approach has the effect of slightly delaying the change of position but can be used with relative slow update rates.

Fig. 4. Left: Balloon Game. The objective is to pop the balloons in order to acquire familiarity with the 3D space and the haptic device. **Right**: SpaceShape Game. The game is divided in two phases: in the first one the children has to open all the cube faces and get rocket pieces hidden inside. The second part consists on assembling the rocket.

3   Conclusions

The plugin has already been used in several applications. First, the haptic plugin has been used into two *serious games* that have been developed to teach geometry to children (Screenshots in Fig. 4), in collaboration with game developers (LearnTPM[5]) for the weDRAW project[6]. For example, in the *HapticShape* game, the haptic plugin allows the child to touch the cube haptically inside and outside, as well as the rocket parts that must be assembled. We also used Unity3D with the haptic plugin to perform a psychophysical experiment on the

---

[5] learntpm.com.
[6] https://www.wedraw.eu/.

haptic perception of textures [1]. In this latter study, we explored the perceptual effects of CHAI3D parameters that control texture rendering to identify the most important ones. Besides educational applications, low-cost force-feedback devices might also be used in rehabilitation applications [5,13,16].

The HPGE library has currently some disadvantages and limits. First, the choice of using a haptic plugin entails some duplication between the game engine and the haptic plugin. In particular, there is a memory cost in duplicating the objects in the game engine and the plugin. Also, some computation such as detecting a collision between the tool and the objects are duplicated (done independently in Unity3D and in the library) if a `Collider` is associated with Unity3D `GameObjects`.

Second, the scenarios involving physical simulations (i.e., *Interactive Scenes*, see Sect. 2.4) are particularly challenging. The problem is fundamentally linked to HPGE integration principles, where the object position is updated by Unity3D, which requires that physical simulations be also run in Unity3D. In order to allow the user to interact physically with the virtual object, it is necessary to add the interaction force to the simulation. While Unity3D provides ways for doing it, preliminary experiments have revealed that the these scenarios are hard to implement satisfactorily.

Until the plugin is publicly released, people interested in evaluating it might contact the authors.

Acknowledgments. This work has received funding from the European Union's Horizon 2020 Research and Innovation Programme under Grant Agreement No. 732391 (weDRAW Project).

References

1. Balzarotti, N., Baud-Bovy, G.: Effects of CHAI3D texture rendering parameters on texture perception. In: Prattichizzo, D., Shinoda, H., Tan, H.Z., Ruffaldi, E., Frisoli, A. (eds.) EuroHaptics 2018. LNCS, vol. 10893, pp. 138–149. Springer, Cham (2018). https://doi.org/10.1007/978-3-319-93445-7_13

2. Barbagli, F., Frisoli, A., Salisbury, K., Bergamasco, M.: Simulating human fingers: a soft finger proxy model and algorithm, pp. 9–17, March 2004

3. Basdogan, C., Srinivasan, M.A.: Haptic rendering in virtual environments. In: Stanney, K.M., Hale, K.S. (eds.) Handbook of Virtual Environments, vol. 1, pp. 117–134. Lawrence Erlbaum Inc., Mahwah (2002)

4. Baud-Bovy, G., Balzarotti, N.: Using force-feedback devices in educational settings: a short review. In: Proceedings of the 1st ACM SIGCHI International Workshop on Multimodal Interaction for Education, MIE 2017, pp. 14–21. ACM, New York (2017)

5. Baud-Bovy, G., Tatti, F., Borghese, N.A.: Ability of low-cost force-feedback device to influence postural stability. IEEE Trans. Haptics **8**(2), 130–139 (2015)

6. Breuer, J., Bente, G.: Why so serious? On the relation of serious games and learning. J. Comput. Game Cult. **4**(1), 7–24 (2010)

7. Conti, F., et al.: The CHAI libraries. In: Proceedings of Eurohaptics 2003, Dublin, Ireland, pp. 496–500 (2003)

8. Cuevas-Rodriguez, M., Poyade, M., Reyes-Lecuona, A., Molina-Tanco, L.: A VRPN server for haptic devices using OpenHaptics 3.0. In: Penichet, V., Peñalver, A., Gallud, J. (eds.) New Trends in Interaction, Virtual Reality and Modeling. HCIS, pp. 73–82. Springer, London (2013)

9. Djaouti, D., Alvarez, J., Jessel, J.-P.: Classifying serious games: the G/P/S model. In: Felicia, P. (ed.) Handbook of Research on Improving Learning and Motivation Through Educational Games: Multidisciplinary Approaches, pp. 118–136. IGI Global, Hershey (2011)

10. Grunwald, M.: Human Haptic Perception: Basics and Applications. Springer, Basel (2008). https://doi.org/10.1007/978-3-7643-7612-3

11. Kadleček, P., Kmoch, S.P.: Overview of current developments in haptic APIs. In: Proceedings of CESCG. Citeseer (2011)

12. Paul, P.S., Goon, S., Bhattacharya, A.: History and comparative study of modern game engines. Int. J. Adv. Comput. Math. Sci. 3(2), 245–249 (2012)

13. Pirovano, M., Mainetti, R., Baud-Bovy, G., Lanzi, P.L., Borghese, N.A.: Intelligent game engine for rehabilitation (IGER). IEEE Trans. Comput. Intell. AI Games 8(1), 43–55 (2016)

14. Salisbury, K., Conti, F., Barbagli, F.: Haptic rendering: introductory concepts. IEEE Comput. Graphics Appl. 24(2), 24–32 (2004)

15. Srinivasan, M.A., Basdogan, C.: Haptics in virtual environments: taxonomy, research status, and challenges. Comput. Graph. 21(4), 393–404 (1997)

16. Tobler-Ammann, B.C., et al.: Exergames encouraging exploration of hemineglected space in stroke patients with visuospatial neglect: a feasibility study. JMIR Serious Games 5(3), e17 (2017)

Gamification and Innovative Game Approaches

Gamifying with OneUp: For Learning, Grades or Fun?

Darina Dicheva[✉], Keith Irwin, and Christo Dichev

Computer Science Department, Winston Salem State University,
Winston Salem, NC 27110, USA
{dichevad, irwinke, dichevc}@wssu.edu

Abstract. Gamifying learning is a challenging task assuming holistic thinking about the learning experience rather than focusing on specific game elements. Part of the challenges in this task stem from the fact that gamification represents a class of systems combining utilitarian and hedonic benefits. In addition, there is a lack of appropriate tools supporting gamification of learning. To bridge this gap, we developed OneUp, a course gamification platform. This paper examines the challenges associated with gamifying learning along with OneUp's support for overcoming them. It also presents a preliminary study of the impact of utilitarian and hedonic values in the context of a gamified Data Structures course.

1 Introduction

Gamification in education refers to the enrichment of learning environments with game design elements in order to reinforce desired behaviors through experiences typical of games. Although gamification has been actively explored in education, as evident from the fast growing number of gamification systems and related publications [1], it still faces a lack of sufficient empirical evidence confirming its benefits in educational contexts as well as of practical methods for its design and implementation [2]. There are no commonly accepted theoretical frameworks or general principles on how to apply gamification strategies to specific learning situations. This is not surprising, since gamifying learning is a complex task - it involves combining utilitarian benefits, such as learning efficacy, and hedonic benefits, such as enjoyment, in a single system.

Creating a gamified course fitting a particular course structure aligned with the vision of the course designer can be time-consuming and design limited without supporting tools. In addition, gamifying learning "from scratch" often requires some software development skills that many instructors lack. This entails a need for appropriate tools to support learning gamification. One possible solution is to bring educational gamification development closer to the educators, allowing them to realize their own approaches to gamified learning and experiment with them autonomously. However, our study [3] confirmed that there is a dearth of appropriate tools to support comprehensive gamification of learning, particularly in higher education. In addition, reports on how to gamify learning and, in particular, skill-based learning are scarce. To bridge this gap we developed OneUp Learning, a course gamification platform [3].

© Springer Nature Switzerland AG 2019
M. Gentile et al. (Eds.): GALA 2018, LNCS 11385, pp. 343–353, 2019.
https://doi.org/10.1007/978-3-030-11548-7_32

In this paper we examine challenges associated with gamifying learning. We also describe OneUp's support for overcoming them. Further, we present a preliminary evaluation of the impact of utilitarian and hedonic values in the context of a gamified Data Structures course.

2 OneUp: A Platform for Gamifying Learning Activities

The analysis of the current state of educational gamification and the barriers for its growth motivated us to develop OneUp Learning, an educational gamification platform aimed at facilitating the gamification of academic courses/learning activities and fostering experimental research on gamifying learning [3]. The main functionality of the platform includes: (1) support for instructors to integrate game design principles and mechanics in the instructional methods they use in their courses, (2) authoring of static and dynamic problems, and (3) learning analytics and visualization to inform students and instructors of the student performance and progress throughout the course. The platform enables instructors to define course activities and create exercises for practicing and self-assessment and quizzes or exams for testing knowledge and skills. Learning activities are supported by OneUp with immediate feedback including detailed progress information and possibly some kind of reward (e.g. badges or virtual currency).

The platform is highly configurable and enables tailoring gamification features to meet the vision of the instructor. Its configuration includes two parts: one related to the course structure and another to the gamification features to be used in the particular course. The course configuration includes specifying the course topical structure, the learning objectives (skills) targeted in the course, and the milestones and activities planned for the course (with their corresponding points), but none of these is required. The gamification related configuration includes the choice of the game elements to be used in the course along with specification of gaming rules for them. The system currently supports the following game elements: points (challenge points, skill points, and activity points), progress bar, virtual currency, badges, leaderboard, skill board, learning dashboard, avatars, and immediate feedback. The gaming rules define the conditions upon which certain game elements are applied (e.g. a specific badge is awarded). The rules are standard production rules in the form *IF <condition> THEN <action>*, where the condition is a Boolean expression of arbitrary complexity. The rules are served by a game rule engine, which is built in the platform.

The platform supports two types of challenges: warm-up challenges (for student practice and self-assessment) and serious challenges (graded course quizzes and tests). For each problem included in a challenge, the instructor specifies the challenge points earnable from that problem, i.e., the problem's points in the context of the specific challenge. The instructor could also specify skill points which indicate how the problem contributes to increasing the level of student mastery of related skills (from the pre-defined set of skills). The challenges are built of problems and OneUp supports two type of problems: static and dynamic. Static problems (for which the correct solution is given at creation) include multiple-choice questions, multiple answer questions, true/false questions, and matching questions. Dynamic problems are problems for which the system does not contain solutions entered by the instructor. These problems are short computer programs which use a random seed to generate a unique instance of a particular programming or calculating problem and then grade the correctness of the submitted answer. Somewhat in between are the Parson's problems. These are a type of code completion problems in which the learner must place given mixed up code lines/blocks in a correct order. By dynamically generating problem instances, the platform makes available a sufficient pool of exercises of a particular type for students to practice.

All elements of the OneUp platform - course topics, targeted skills, warm-up and serious challenges, activities, game elements and relations between them are configurable, which makes OneUp a course independent, customizable platform. Depending on the configuration, it can function as a full-fledged LMS or as a simple online practicing platform. Any game element can be turned on or off to allow studies on the effectiveness of various combinations of game elements.

3 Challenges to Gamifying Learning

Despite the growing number of gamified courses and learning activities, there are no established practices on how to gamify learning. While some publications (e.g. [4]) provide recommendations and guidelines, most implementations follow a simple reward-feedback pattern.

Learning is multifaceted and gamifying it is a difficult task for several reasons:

- Promoting behavioral change through gamification is based on psychological principles which implies understanding a range of underlying motivational factors and how they can be used in the gamification design [5] for achieving the desired behavior.
- Successful gamification of learning assumes holistic thinking about the whole learning experience rather than focusing on specific game elements and should result in well-planned activities incorporating intrinsic and extrinsic rewards.
- Unlike games, the primary aim of gamification in learning is not to entertain but rather to shape learners behavior through the use of game design elements which assumes a separate design approach.
- The enjoyment associated with playing games cannot be easily incorporated into learning activities to produce effective and enjoyable learning experiences. How a learner perceives the gamification is highly dependent on the nature of the activity and the contextual factors related to it, in addition to the individual's own personal and demographic characteristics [5].
- Evaluating the outcomes of gamifying learning is also a challenging endeavor. Typically the impact of gamifying a particular learning activity is measured by performance and less by behavioral and motivational metrics. While learning outcomes are easier to measure, they are not always the best indicators of what is valued in the gamified activity nor the best predictors for sustainable behavior.

All these challenges contribute to the complexity of the design and implementation of a gamified learning system. OneUp was built with the goal of addressing these challenges and facilitating the process of designing and implementing gamified learning activities. The following section describes how OneUp alleviates these challenges.

3.1 Addressing Difficulties of Gamifying Learning

Psychological Principles Backing OneUp Gamification. We have chosen the Self-Determination Theory (SDT) [6] as a theoretical framework guiding the design of the OneUp platform. According to SDT, the most self-determined form of behavioral regulation is intrinsic motivation, which denotes the pursuit of an activity for the sake of the activity itself. Extrinsic motivation refers to behaviors carried out to attain outcomes unrelated to the activity itself, such as rewards or praise. In line with SDT, humans have three fundamental psychological needs: autonomy, competence and relatedness. Satisfaction of these three needs is essential for an individual's intrinsic motivation. People experience more self-determined types of motivation when the activities in which they participate make them feel that they have *autonomy* (the power to make their own choices), *competence* (ability to effectively perform the behavior), and *relatedness* (social connections with others). The OneUp support for intrinsic motivation includes: non-required warm-up challenges and skill development (autonomy); immediate, multifaceted feedback and leveling challenges (competence); and sharing achievements and healthy competition (relatedness).

According to Goal Theory [7], the goal serves as a stimulator to motivate and direct the learners towards desired learning behavior. Learners are motivated by SMART goals: Specific, Measurable, Attainable, Realistic and Time-bound. This type of goal motivation is supported by OneUp learning analytics and the related learning dashboard.

Support for Holistic Gamification Design in OneUp. Since the most common form of educational gamification is course gamification, the discussion in this section will center on course gamification, which typically incorporates different types of learning activities. Gamifying learning with OneUp assumes more than decorating existing content with achievements and rewards mechanics.

The creation of a new course with OneUp includes specifying the course topics, targeted skills, and milestones, as well as the game elements to be used in the course. The instructor also has to enter warm-up challenges for student practice and self-assessment and serious challenges for course assessment (if desired). When defining a challenge, instructors can choose from problems available in OneUp's problem bank or create new ones. For each problem included in the challenge, they specify challenge points earnable from that problem and possibly skill points. The instructor can also enter activities, which will be manually graded. In this aspect, OneUp has pretty much the standard functionality of a Learning Management System (LMS).

The distinguishing feature of OneUp is that it empowers instructors with control over how to link learning activities to the intended game mechanics provided by the platform. The mere presence of game elements in the environment is not sufficient to produce an engaging experience for the learners. Making learning more compelling entails creative use of game design elements. Accordingly, through the course gamification interface, OneUp encourages the instructor to look at the entire course organization systematically and holistically, considering various aspects such as: which activities should give rewards and at what scale, how to organize feedback loops, which activities should award virtual bucks and how learners can spend them, which activities support autonomy, which activities strengthen competency, how to stimulate feeling of relatedness, how to reinforce goal orientation, etc. From a technical perspective, gamification rules are what links the learning activities to the game design elements, for example, the conditions upon which a badge is awarded or course bucks are earned. In fact, rules combine the learning activities (the utilitarian activities) with the game design elements (hedonic utilities) in a coherent gamified course. Another important difference from LMSs is that the instructor can specify how the problems contribute to increasing the level of student mastery of each related course skill.

Using the Rule Engine for Driving Motivation and Learners' Behavior. Gamification is commonly used for behavior change, as a meaningful use of game design elements can encourage certain behaviors to be exhibited. It has gained significant traction as a method of steering user behavior in a desired direction in a variety of domains, including education. Looking at the traditional educational practices, when instructors want to exert influence on students to encourage certain behaviors, they reward the positive behaviors and discourage the undesirable. OneUp supports an analogous strategy through the gamification rules. From a behavioral perspective, rules can be viewed as:

if_satisfy (action, condition) then offer (incentive),

where *action* denotes any measurable process performed by a learner and *incentive* denotes any award supported by OneUp. For example,

If a student completes more than 10 challenges in a given session award her a badge.

Using OneUp rules an instructor can define tactics similar to the traditional approach of steering learners' behavior. For creating meaningful rules an instructor has to decide first what behavior is to be encouraged and then what incentives are more compelling for the targeted learners. For example, if the goal is to encourage practicing, any measurable practicing action can be incentivized (extrinsically or intrinsically) with rules such as:

After your first five attempts you will receive a "Beginner" badge.
One of the first five problems is lucky: if you solve it, you will earn 5 course bucks.

While OneUp provides extrinsic mechanisms for steering learners' behavior, instructors can use also the intrinsic motivational factors. For example, making practicing a voluntary activity where students can choose which problems to solve will meet their need for autonomy. Similarly, showing students a comparison between points earned so far and the total amount of points that will be earned if the student keeps their current level of performance will aid their goal orientation and feedback needs.

Support for Gameful Experience and Enjoyment. Enjoyment can come in many different forms, including feelings of competence, overcoming challenges, creative accomplishments, experience of choice, personal triumph, amazement and surprise.

OneUp provides two levels of support for promoting gameful experience and enjoyment - through utilizing gameful activities and through incorporating appropriate rules.

Challenges in games are motivating experiences. Overcoming non-trivial challenges creates an experience of satisfying the competence need [8]. Deciding to approach a game challenge and then choosing which challenges to approach and which strategies and actions to apply satisfies the need for autonomy. Furthermore, the outcome of a non-trivial challenge is usually uncertain, stimulating curiosity and interest. An analogue of game challenges in learning contexts are exercise problems provided for students in various disciplines. First, choosing to exercise is typically a voluntary decision. Which problem to approach and how many is also a learners' choice. Second, solving a problem successfully engenders a sense of competence. Following this correspondence, OneUp offers a platform for deliberate practice that provides multiple opportunities for demonstrating competence and receiving immediate feedback in a risk-free environment. Creating and structuring learning exercises that make the practice interesting and engaging is at the heart of designing a motivating experience. In order to approximate the repetitive pattern of game play featuring instant feedback and freedom to fail, we included support for immediate assessment where the counterpart of game challenges are exercise problems with automatic checking. This is also in line with the value of deliberate practice for mastering particular skills, especially in sciences and mathematics, which assumes a rich pool of problems of different levels of difficulty. The latter is essential, since students are more likely to be motivated by the feeling of flow [9], experienced when challenges match their individual skills and knowledge level. This is achieved by offering a sufficient number of challenges with varying levels of difficulty, realized by the dynamic generation of problems from templates.

Exercise problems are probably as old as education itself. But, in general, they have not been considered as a gameful activity. The missing part is the game rules. The rules along with the challenges define the game-like experience. In fact, they combine the utilitarian (usefulness) values with hedonic (enjoyment) values. While practicing can be meaningful without rules, it would not be perceived as a game-like activity without appropriate rules. Rules are what can make an experience game-like, interesting, and intriguing. By defining rules with different conditions and game elements that are granted upon these conditions, instructors can induce different forms of enjoyment, such as, an experience of curiosity, surprise and novelty or experience of choice/autonomy as illustrated by the following examples:

One of the next five consecutive days is lucky: if you solve three problems in the lucky day you earn 3 course bucks.
You can choose to retake any quiz for 50 course bucks each.

4   What Are the Motivations for Using the OneUp Platform?

Systems or services, such as LMSs or videogames, can be classified as either utilitarian or hedonic in nature. Traditionally, utilitarian and hedonic systems were considered as separate entities. While utilitarian systems provide instrumental value (e.g., increased participation or learning performance), hedonic systems provide self-fulfilling value (e.g., fun or pleasurable experiences) [10]. In contrast, gamification combines both hedonic and utilitarian values in a new kind of motivational aggregate. The underlying assumption is that adding hedonic elements, such as those found in games to utilitarian activities, will create the level of engagement observable in games. However, this assumption has not received sufficient empirical support yet - a fact that reflects why this combination known as gamification is difficult to design in learning contexts. While the use of gamification is driven by both utilitarian (usefulness) and hedonic (enjoyment) benefits, we still lack sufficient understanding of which factors predict why learners use gamified systems. More specifically, how motivation to learn can be influenced by utilitarian and hedonic factors. Several studies have explored the reasons for using gamified systems [10] including in a learning context [11]. However, these studies do not explore learners' motives for using a gamified system in the context of a specific course, where factors such as course grades, exams, homework, and skills may impact the reasons for using the system. We aimed to bridge this gap with a focused study, stimulated also by the fact that this context is the most common way of utilizing OneUp.

In this section we report preliminary results, the initial part of a large scale study involving several STEM courses over a three year period. The first phase of the study was conducted in a Data Structures course during Fall 2017 and Spring 2018 semesters. Students in both groups were able to use OneUp during the entire semester where the goal was to motivate regular practicing with the provided warm-up challenges. Practicing was a voluntary activity. The students in the control group (17 students, Fall 2017) were using a non-gamified version of OneUp, while the students in the experimental group (12 students, Spring 2018) were using a gamified version. Based on predefined rules, students in the experimental group could earn experience points (XP), badges and course (virtual) bucks through practicing. Course bucks could be spent for course related "goods", such as buying an extension for an assignment, buying a resubmission, etc. Students from the experimental group could track their performance in their personal learning dashboard and compare it to the other students' performance on a customizable class leaderboard.

Tracking Students' Behavior. Using the data in OneUp's logs we compared the number of attempts for solving warm-up challenges of the control group with the number of attempts of the experimental group. The average number of warm-up challenge attempts for the control group was 4.5625, while the average number of challenges for the experimental group was 46.1667. The t test (t = −3.1574, p-value = 0.008895) showed that the difference was statistically significant. For the experimental group, we also looked at the distribution of warm-ups. The distribution shows peaks around the dates of the three course exams. These results signal that after the gamification intervention, students' practicing has intensified significantly. In this context and from the viewpoint of utilitarian and hedonic factors, the central question guiding the next part of our study was: *What are the reasons driving students to use OneUp?*

To answer this question we adopted a combined qualitative and quantitative approach: a focus group and a survey.

Focus Group. We used a focus group interview to seek input from students enrolled in the experimental group. Eleven students (seven males and four females, ranging in age between 19 and 31 years old) participated in the focus group discussion. The following questions (inspired by [11]) provided the basis for the discussion: *What was your reason to use OneUp? What prompted you to start a practicing session in OneUp? What made you continue a practicing session? Do you think using the system affected your behavior in any way?*

From the analysis of the discussion data, four themes emerged that encapsulated the experiences of the students:

1. *Utilitarian factors – the main driver for using the platform.* The majority of the participants expressed the opinion that they were using warm-up challenges to either improve their learning or boost their grades or to successfully pass exams or get extrinsic/intrinsic awards that help reaching their learning goals.

   I go there for learning. OneUp gives you, like, kind of confidence. I will do the questions, and I will try to do the implementations, and I will continuously do them until I know I can do the assignments and tests.

   My reason for doing it was that it did give me a lot of help for a lot of different concepts I did have troubles on. But also course bucks - there was a lot of things that was in the course store that really helped me as far as being able to resubmit stuff or being able to get extra time on something.

2. *Utilitarian values amplified by hedonic values take students on board.* For many participants, the typical factors triggering students to start a practicing session were improving learning and grades. However, for some students the triggering factors to start practicing session were game elements such as competition, rewards or goal-related.

   Knowing that it will help me with the tests and assignments I go and try the challenges until I learn how to solve them.

   I liked the incentives too, although I did always used to practice and stuff but I like the incentives too - to know that, hey, if I'm practicing I can get something for it.

3. *The effect arising from the interaction of utilitarian and hedonic values keeps students on board.* The majority of students noted that grades were a strong motivator for keeping them going when practicing in OneUp. At the same time, many participants shared that the game elements had also a positive effect on their motivation to continue. This suggests that when students practice in a gamified environment, utilitarian and hedonic values interact and form a specific motivational value impacting their experience.

   When you're getting questions correct it makes you more to continue, continue, more like you feel good. And when I am accumulating points towards getting rewards that would make me want to continue practice further if I'm accumulating something.

   I put both of those together. If I'm getting it wrong, I want to keep doing it. Also I know I'm getting compensation at the end. Not compensation, but rewards.

4. *Utilitarian and hedonic values have different motivational effects on different groups of students.* In several parts of the focus group discussion, a number of participants noted that improving learning or their grades were the major reason for

practicing in OneUp. In a similar fashion, a number of participants commented that various gameful features were the driving force for their practicing in OneUp.

If you have questions and want to find the answer by yourself. I guess practicing really gives you some clarity, and this just gives you additional ways for learning.
I don't know if this is a bad thing but sometimes, if you look on the dashboard and you can see like the different, like, you don't know who the people are, but you can see the icons and see what they're doing. I'm like, okay, I'm gonna keep going till I get to the top.

Student Survey. To gain a better insight into how the utilitarian and hedonic factors influence the use of OneUp practicing support, the focus group qualitative study was conducted in parallel with a quantitative study – a survey based on a standard Student Course Engagement Questionnaire administered to the experimental group at the end of the course. The survey was augmented with questions addressing the reasons for OneUp use inspired by [11]. The questionnaire uses a 5-point Likert scale. All students enrolled in the course responded to the questionnaire. The following is an excerpt from the questions and Fig. 1 presents a graph capturing students' responses.

1. A desire to boost my grades prompts me to start a new practice session in OneUp.
2. A desire to get new OneUp badges prompts me to start a new practice session.
3. A desire to earn more virtual currency prompts me to start a new practice session.
4. The learning experience with OneUp prompts me to start a new practice session.
5. The enjoyment I experience with OneUp prompts me to start a new practice session.
6. A desire to boost my grades encourages me to continue practice sessions in OneUp.
7. A desire to earn more OneUp badges drives me to continue practice sessions.
8. A desire to earn more virtual currency drives me to continue practice sessions.
9. The learning experience with OneUp drives me to continue practice sessions.
10. The enjoyment I experience encourages me to continue practice sessions.

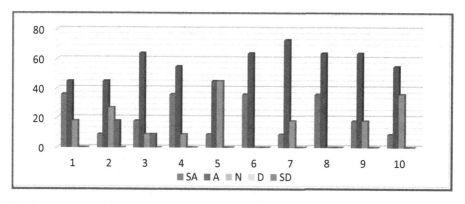

Fig. 1. Aggregated responses to the above questions (Strongly Agree (SA), Agree (A), Neither agree nor disagree (N), Disagree (D), Strongly Disagree (SD).

As illustrated by Fig. 1, the results of the questionnaire are in line with the preliminary findings from the focus group. The most frequent reported reason for starting (82% agree or strongly agree) and continuing (100% agree or strongly agree) a practice session are the grades. While the questions related to the desire to earn virtual currency yielded strongly positive responses, we interpret them as a further confirmation of the significant influence of the utilitarian value on using OneUp, since the earned virtual currency could be spent for buying resubmissions, time extensions or dropping the lowest homework grade – benefits with positive impacts on course grades. Interestingly, the questions related to the driving effect of game design elements on starting or continuing practicing sessions yielded also positive responses (more than half of the respondents either agree or strongly agree). We interpret these preliminary results as evidence that the motivational effects driving students to start or continue practicing sessions are generated through the interplay between the hedonic and utilitarian values, where the gamification plays a role of a mechanism reinforcing students' extrinsic (grades, rewards) and intrinsic (competency, goal orientation) motivations. It is backed by the fact that OneUp practicing support was available to all students in the control group (using the non-gamified version) but its use was very low. This result suggests that its utilitarian value (in terms of improving learning or grades) had an insufficient motivational power. Notably, our preliminary study does not confirm the motivational threshold effect reported in [11]. In summary, enhancing the practicing support with gamification results not only in hedonic enrichment but also in activating pre-existing intrinsic and extrinsic factors. This observation suggests also that learning activities, such as practicing, that are amenable to a gameful reconstruction can be transformed into motivating learning tasks.

5   Conclusion

Gamifying learning is a complex process that requires knowledge of motivational psychology and understanding how that knowledge can be used in the gamification design for achieving the desired learner's behavior. This implies a need for appropriate tools to support gamifying learning in order for the theoretical and practical fields of educational gamification to continue to grow. The OneUp platform was developed in response to that need with the purpose to facilitate the gamification of academic courses and to foster empirical studies aimed at understanding the effects of educational gamification.

Part of the design challenges of gamifying learning stem from the fact that gamification represents a class of systems combining utilitarian and hedonic benefits. Traditionally, hedonic design focuses on making interaction fun and enjoyable, while utilitarian design emphasizes utility. In contrast, gamification aims at motivating learners toward learning-related goals through hedonic drivers, essentially acting as a hedonic instrument for enhancing learning. From this perspective, the purpose of our preliminary study was to gain insight into utilitarian and hedonic motivational factors that drive the use of gamified learning environments. The results suggest that the motivational effect is created through interactions between utilitarian and hedonic factors of the gamified system and preexisting extrinsic and intrinsic learners' motivations.

Acknowledgments. This material is based upon work funded by NSF Project 1623236 "TIP: Increasing Student Motivation and Engagement in STEM Courses through Gamification" and partially supported by NSF DUE-1821189 Project.

References

1. Dicheva, D., Dichev, C., Agre, G., Angelova, G.: Gamification in education: a systematic mapping study. Educ. Technol. Soc. **18**(3), 75–88 (2015)
2. Dichev, C., Dicheva, D.: Gamifying education: what is known, what is believed and what remains uncertain: a critical review. Int. J. Educ. Technol. High. Educ. **14**, 9 (2017)
3. Dicheva, D., Irwin, K., Dichev, C.: OneUp learning: a course gamification platform. In: Dias, J., Santos, Pedro A., Veltkamp, Remco C. (eds.) GALA 2017. LNCS, vol. 10653, pp. 148–158. Springer, Cham (2017). https://doi.org/10.1007/978-3-319-71940-5_14
4. Kapp, K.M.: The Gamification of Learning and Instruction: Game-Based Methods and Strategies for Training and Education. Pfeiffer, San Francisco (2012)
5. Morschheuser, B., Hassan, L., Werder, K., Hamari, J.: How to design gamification? A method for engineering gamified software. Inf. Softw. Technol. **95**, 219–237 (2018)
6. Ryan, R., Deci, E.: Intrinsic and extrinsic motivations: classic definitions and new directions. Contemp. Educ. Psychol. **25**, 54–67 (2000)
7. Tondello, G., Premsukh, H., Nacke, L.: A theory of gamification principles through goal-setting theory. In: Proceedings of the 51st Hawaii International Conference on System Sciences (HICSS). IEEE (2018)
8. Przybylski, A.K., Rigby, C.S., Ryan, R.M.: A motivational model of video game engagement. Rev. Gen. Psychol. **14**, 154–166 (2010)
9. Csikszentmihalyi, M.: The flow experience and its significance for human psychology. In: Optimal Experience: Psychological Studies of Flow in Consciousness, pp. 15–35. Cambridge University Press, New York (1988)
10. Hamari, J., Koivisto, J.: Why do people use gamification services? Int. J. Inf. Manag. **35**(4), 419–431 (2015)
11. van Roy, R., Deterding, C.S., Zaman, B.: Uses and gratifications of initiating use of gamifed learning platforms. In: CHI 2018 Extended Abstracts, 2018 ACM CHI Conference on Human Factors in Computing Systems, Montreal, Canada. ACM, New York (2018)

Teaming up with Artificial Intelligence: The Human in the Loop of Serious Game Pathfinding Algorithms

Michael D. Kickmeier-Rust[1(✉)] and Andreas Holzinger[2]

[1] Institute for Educational Assessment, University of Teacher Education,
St. Gallen, Switzerland
michael.kickmeier@phsg.ch
[2] Holzinger Group, HCI-KDD, Institute of Medical Informatics,
Statistics and Documentation, Medical University Graz, Graz, Austria
andreas.holzinger@medunigraz.at

Abstract. Serious games' success depends on its capabilities to engage learners and to provide them with personalized gaming and learning experiences. Therefore, theoretically sound mechanisms for gaining a certain level of understanding of learning and gaming processes by the game is crucial. Consequently, AI and machine learning technologies increasingly enter the field. These technologies often fail, however, since serious games either pose highly complex problems (combining gaming and learning process) or do not provide the extensive data bases that would be required. One solution might be allowing human intelligence or intuition influence AI processes. In the present study, we investigated pathfinding algorithms with and without human interventions to the algorithms. As a testbed, we used a clone of the Travelling Salesman problem, the Travelling Snakesman game. We found some evidence that in this particular pathfinding problem human interventions result in superior results as the MAXMIN Ant System algorithm.

Keywords: Game AI · Ant colony systems · Human in the loop

1   Introduction

Serious games have arrived in mainstream educational settings at all level (school education, higher education, and even workplace learning). Serious games capitalize on their core strengths - distilled to its essence: fun, fantasy, curiosity, challenge, and control. These strengths lead to an enormous intrinsic motivational potential so that digital games can reach a broad audience. Also as a means of research, games have particular advantages. Many large machine learning/AI companies, for example, are designing experiments based on games [1]. A meta-review of Pieter Wouters and colleagues [2] revealed evidences about the effects of game-based learning along all dimensions, that is, primary (the intended learning outcome), secondary (side effects such as the improvement of attitudes), and tertiary (unpredictable positive and negative side effects). A recent meta-review by [3] yielded that digital games significantly

© Springer Nature Switzerland AG 2019
M. Gentile et al. (Eds.): GALA 2018, LNCS 11385, pp. 354–363, 2019.
https://doi.org/10.1007/978-3-030-11548-7_33

enhanced student learning relative to non-game conditions. More importantly, a substantial body of research reported that a key element of a serious game's success is a suitable personalization and balancing of learning and gaming experiences. This endeavor, however, requires a solid understanding of individual learning processes, strengths, weaknesses, knowledge gaps, and learning dispositions by a game as an autonomous tutorial system. In other words, individualized learning and gaming requires valid, reliable, and accurate assessments and meaningful personalized responses by the game. Consequently, the research body in the context of intelligent and adaptive tutorial systems and their relationships to serious games is very broad [4].

In every digital game, players both act in and interact with the game. They use the options of game mechanics to achieve certain goals. The quality and the results of interactions determine the performance, which makes it a complex construct, subsuming the learning dimension, the emotional-motivational dimension, as well as the gaming dimension. In the context of serious games, an important role of assessment is equipping the game system with a certain "understanding" of the individual learners in order to tailor learning experiences to their particular needs. [5] distinguish data-based decision-making (DBDM), assessment for learning (AfL), and diagnostic testing (DT). While DBDM is rather a summative approach, AfL heavily focusses on the learning process as such, rather than on outcomes. DT has a strong relation to the evaluation of problem solving processes in the context of learning [6] and thus have particular implications on the assessment philosophy in game-based learning scenarios. [5] describe a thoughtful integration of all approaches, leading to more valid evidence-based assessments.

Assessment must be based on simple identifiable indicators and it must be based on valid heuristics. The indicators, thereby, may be divided into performance related aspects, emotional-motivational as well as personality related aspects [7]. The performance related aspects include measuring, gathering, analyzing, and interpreting scores, task completion rates, completion times, success rates, success depths (the quality or degree to which a task has been accomplished), etc. The approaches to in-game assessment, stealth assessment, and non-invasive adaptation of games have been refined significantly over the past decade [8]. State-of-the-art methods include the concept of stealth assessment by [9], which is a method based on evidence-centered design, for embedding assessment seamlessly into games. There exist structural models, cognitive diagnostic models, Bayesian and latent variable models and also methods from the field of learning analytics. In addition to the psychometric approaches, more and more commercial game technologies and AI techniques from intelligent tutoring systems [10] and intelligent narrative technologies [11] entered the genre. The solutions range from real-time narrative planning and goal recognition to affective computing models for recognizing student emotional states. Intelligent game-based learning environments serve as an excellent laboratory for investigating AI techniques because they make significant inferential demands and play out in complex interactive scenarios.

1.1 Game AI

The development of intelligent features in order to improve gaming experiences has a long tradition in the context of entertainment games (cf. http://gameai.com). The techniques are manifold, however, the main goal is most often make non-player characters (NPC) more credible and more serious opponents. In an overview article, [12], mention following functions: (i) pathfinding algorithms for NPCs, (ii) Bayesian approaches for NPCs' decision making, and (iii) genetic algorithms to equip NPCs with learning mechanics. Pathfinding, for example, is a technique to determine how a non-player character (NPC) moves from one place to another, accounting for opponents, obstacles, and certain objectives. This technique is widely seen in real-time strategy games [13]. AI function specifically enable a credible movement of characters in dynamics environments [14].

Over the past years, sophisticated methods have been developed to increase the fidelity and credibility of computer game environments. The main inspiration is often the improvement of combat simulations. However, with the increasing importance of serious games, the techniques of game AI seeped into this genre. More importantly, in the context of serious games, game AI approaches merged with the traditional approaches to educational AI (from the communities of adaptive and intelligent tutorial systems as well as open learning modeling) and established a completely new field, the serious game AI research.

1.2 Serious Game AI

The increasingly important role of AI in serious games is reflected by AI being the main theme of this years' Serious Games Conference in the context of the famous CeBIT fair. Leading experts discussed the role of current and future AI technologies in serious games. An anchor point in the discussions was Google's *AlphaGo*, beating the world's best human player in the game Go [15]. Serious games present a fusion of smart technologies and applications of computer game mechanics in "serious" areas on the other side and therefore can provide learners with innovative functionalities, features and advances. As [16] pointed out, it is critical that intelligent (or smart, adaptive) educational systems and in particular serious games rely on important underlying pedagogical principles. [16] list four such principles: (1) employing sound game theory, (2) focusing on problem-based learning, (3) including situated cognition, and (4) including cognitive disequilibrium and scaffolding. Lester et al. [12] emphasize the utility of intelligent narratives in serious games and conclude: "because of their ability to dynamically tailor narrative-centered problem-solving scenarios to customize advice to students, and to provide real-time assessment, intelligent game-based learning environments offer significant potential for learning both in and outside of the classroom" ([12], p. 43).

In a comprehensive review of the literature, based on 129 papers, regarding AI functions of serious games, [17] summarize decision making functions, algorithms and techniques that are used for logical and rational decision-making processes on the basis of the available information about learners, and machine learning approaches. The former are subdivided into decision tree approaches, fuzzy logic techniques (specifically related to the control of NPCs), Markov systems, goal-oriented behaviors for NPCs, rule-based systems, and finite state systems.

A second aspect, listed by [17], is machine learning. [18] argue that machine learning in education will be the fourth revolution towards utilizing student data for improving learning quality and for accurately predicting academic achievements. Techniques for machine learning in serious games include Bayesian models, neural networks, case-based reasoning, support vector machines, and cluster analyses.

In a recent article, Cristina Conati and colleagues [19] added an important aspect to the conversation about AI in education, that is, transparency and an opening of underlying reasoning processes of AI functions. The community of open learner modelling (OLM) is attempting to enable learners and other stakeholders to look behind the processes of intelligent functions and perhaps even disagree with the conclusions (this is researched by the community of negotiable/persuadable open learner models). [19] argue that approaches for an interpretable and perhaps credible AI are necessary to increase the impact on learning.

This claim is in center of this paper, although from a different angle. We argue that it is not only necessary to open the reasoning processes and make them interpretable, it may be desirable also, that humans can directly and intentionally influence algorithms, in order to improve their efficiency.

2   Machines, Humans, or Both?

Machine learning algorithms became nearly omnipresent in today's online world. The basic idea is to develop techniques that reason over the existing vast amount of digital data and to "learn" from these data. An example is the breakthrough achieved with deep learning [20] on the task of phonetic classification for automatic speech recognition. Actually, speech recognition was the first commercially successful application of deep convolutional neural networks. Astonishingly, autonomous software is able to lead conversations with clients in call centers, or think about Siri, Alexa and Cortana. A game-related example is autonomous game play without human intervention [1].

Automatic approaches to machine learning have a number of disadvantages, though. They are for instance intensively resource consuming, require much engineering effort, need large amounts of training data, and they are most often black-box approaches. This opposes the aforementioned claim of transparency and interpretability, which is of particular importance in educational applications. Also in other sensitive domains, such as medicine or in the context of privacy/data-protection, intransparent AI is considered problematic and thus the topic is a matter of debate in the AI community [21]. Conventional machine learning works asynchronously in connection with a human expert who is expected to help in data preprocessing and data interpretation - either before or after the learning algorithm. The human expert is supposed to be aware of the problem's context and to evaluate and interpret specific datasets. This approach inherently connects machine learning to cognitive sciences and AI to human intelligence.

A different concept is Interactive Machine Learning (iML), which allows humans interactively intervene with the algorithmic processes of an algorithm [22]. The goal is capitalizing repeatedly on human knowledge and understanding in order to improve the quality of automatic approaches. The iML-approaches can be therefore effective on problems with scarce or overly complex data sets, when a regular machine learning method becomes inefficient.

3 The Travelling Snakesman Game

3.1 Problem Definition

The *Traveling Salesman Problem* (TSP) is one of the most famous combinatorial optimization problems, studied since the 18th century [23]. Ever since, the TSP has become a test bed for the development of new AI methodologies and algorithms in all disciplines, for example in medical research such as DNA sequencing [24]. TSP refers to the problem of finding the most effective (i.e., shortest possible) path between a given set of points. The name "travelling salesman" refers to the problem description where a salesman has to travel a number of cities and return to the starting point. The problem is a NP-hard problem in combinatorial optimization, which means that an algorithm for solving it can be translated into one for solving any NP-problem (non-deterministic polynomial time) problem. NP-hard therefore means "at least as hard as any NP-problem," although it might, in fact, be harder. In other words, for a NP-hard problem a polynomial time algorithm for solving all its cases has not been found by now and it is unlikely that it exists [25].

A popular and flexible algorithm is the MAXMIN Ant System [26]. This is a probabilistic technique for solving computational problems, which can be reduced to finding good paths through graphs. It is a multi-agent method inspired by the behavior of real ants. The pheromone-based communication of biological ants is often the predominant paradigm used for the computational optimization. MAXMIN Ant System exploits the best tour of an ant, it limits the excessive growth of the pheromones on good tours (which in some cases is suboptimal), by adding upper and lower pheromone limits (min and max). In addition, it initializes the pheromone amount of each edge to the upper pheromone limit max, which increases the exploration of new tours at the start of the search. Finally, each time, if there is a stagnation in some way or no improvement of the best tour for a particular amount of time, it reinitialize the pheromone trails.

3.2 Human Interventions

A fundamental idea of the study is to elucidate the impact of human interventions on the results of the pathfinding algorithm. When humans are facing a TSP, they automatically and intuitively gain a first-sight overview and they can identify certain patterns and global relationships. The psychological foundations can be seen, for example, in the fundamentals of Gestalt psychology [27]. Our hypothesis is that this initial global evaluation of the waypoints and the identification of certain cluster and patterns may give human strategies the edge over the computational approximations. For the present study, we implemented the possibility that humans can intervene in the path-finding process by intentionally altering the pheromone distribution. Basically, this is made by controlling the snake in the game manually. The human players may chose other apples than the algorithm might propose. By this means, the decisions of the algorithm are overruled and the pheromone distribution changes accordingly. In line with our hypothesis, the wayfinding should be superior to the results of the algorithm without the human intervention.

3.3 The Game

To investigate this hypothesis, the Holzinger group developed a Unity-based browser game, the *Travelling Snakesman* game (freely accessible at https://iml.hci-kdd.org/ TravellingSnakesmanWS). Their interest is in interactive machine learning with the human-in-the loop [28], which is a natural progression of the HCI-KDD approach [29]. Automatic approaches often are considered black-box approaches, that is, fully automatic. In certain cases, there is need though, for interactive approaches, for example in the medical domain, when only a small number of data sets, rare events, or highly complex problems are given. Automatic approaches may fail or deliver unsatisfactory results. Human intelligence or intuition can be beneficial in helping to solve such problems. Particularly, such a "human-in-the-loop" approach may be beneficial in solving computationally hard problems, where human expertise can help to reduce an exponential search space through heuristics. The main and central motivation is that by opening the black box the results can be made transparent, hence retraceable, which is essential for trust in AI [30]. As technical basis they used the Ant Colony Optimization (ACO) framework on the Traveling Salesman Problem (TSP) which is of high importance in solving many practical problems in health informatics, e.g. in the study of proteins. As a side note, AI for games constituted often the implementation of a set of algorithms and techniques from both traditional and modern artificial intelligence in order to provide solutions to a range of game dependent problems. The majority of such approaches, however, lead to predefined, static and predictable game agent responses, with no ability to adjust during game-play to the behavior or playing style of the player.

The game represents the original TSP by displaying apples on the screen. The human player controls a snake with the goal to eat all apples as quickly as possible (Fig. 1). Controls work via mouse or touchscreen inputs. The game is composed of three levels with increasing complexity. High scores for all levels are available on a daily, weekly, and an all time basis.

At the beginning of a level, an instance of the MAXMIN Ant System algorithm approximates the solution, that is, the minimal distance among the apples. To avoid delays due to computation times and to establish comparable conditions, the algorithm was restricted to 175 iterations of the pathfinding process. In the course of the human play, the algorithm includes decision of the player every 5 iterations. In other words, the human player changes the pheromone strength distribution of the algorithms and therefore significantly influences the optimization results of the algorithm.

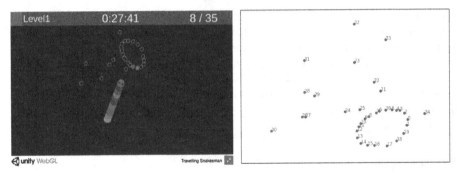

Fig. 1. The left panel shows a screenshot of the game. The right panel illustrates the pathfinding problem for level 1.

3.4 Results

In order to investigate the hypothesis, we set up a first exploratory online study. We invited people to play the game and instructed them to play it as effectively as possible in order to improve the high score. In total 95 games were played. In a first step, we investigated the results of the MAXMIN Ant System algorithm (C) with the results of the algorithm including the human interventions (CH). As dependent variable, the distances travelled on the screen was measured.

To quantify the difference between the C and the CH group, we computed an analysis of variance (ANOVA) for the independent variables level (game levels 1–3) and group (C, CH). The variable level (ranging from 1 to 3 with an increasing difficulty) is the repeated factor since all participants played the levels consecutively. The ANOVA yielded a significant main effect of the factor level [$F(2, 189) = 79546.172$, $p < .001$]. This result is expected since the levels with increasing difficulty require increasingly longer paths. More important is the factor group, where we found a significant main effect as well [$F(1, 189) = 33.951$, $p < .001$]. At level 1 the mean of group C was 4489802.48 (SD = 109628.351), the mean of group CH was 4376090.665 (SD = 94430.853). At level 2 the mean of group C was 36281284.86 (SD = 855204.253), the mean of group CH was 35839124.63 (SD = 722500.697). At level 3 the mean of group C was 44247653.59 (SD = 713300.268), the mean of group CH was 43233333.61 (SD = 865187.636). Across all levels, group CH resulted in somewhat shorter distances traveled.

In order to elucidate the differences of groups C and CH more in-depth, we looked into the path length differences between both groups. Instead of computing the differences in each trial – remember, for each trial, the algorithm approximated the shortest path, in parallel humans played the game and influenced the algorithm with their choices – we computed the difference between group CH and the average of all computer trials. For an equal comparison, we transformed the distances into a range between 0 and 1 (by [$CH - C_{min}$]/[$C_{max} - C_{min}$]), which can be considered as the relative improvement in group CH as opposed to the average of group C.

Table 1. Absolute minimum distances obtained across groups and levels.

	C	CH	Diff.
Level 1	4242192.5568	4215015.4717	27177.0851
Level 2	34178226.0850	34680651.6358	−502425.5508
Level 3	42529746.1429	41378863.0008	1150883.1421

The relative improvement for level 1 was 0.1394, for level 2 0.1021 and for level 3 0.0814. One-sample t-tests computed for each level yielded that this improvement is significant for each level. Level 1: $t(38) = 7.519$, $p < .001$; level 2: $t(26) = 4.310$, $p < .001$; level 3: $t(27) = 3.346424$, $p = .002$.

In general, the results of this study provide some evidence for our initial hypothesis that human interventions can improve the computer algorithm. The absolute distances are shown in Table 1.

4   Conclusions

Serious games are a mainstream educational medium and the repertoire of existing games is extremely broad. Growing communities and platforms successfully aim at making the genre ubiquitous. One example is the Serious Games Information Center (https://seriousgames-portal.org), hosted by the Technical University of Darmstadt. A number of studies and meta-review yielded that a serious game's success depends on it capabilities to engage learners and to provide them with personalized gaming and learning experiences. Therefore, theoretically sound mechanisms for gaining insight and a certain level of understanding of learning and gaming processes by the game, as an autonomously acting instance, are crucial. This refers to sound psychometric methods for an in-game assessment – ideally in an unobtrusive, stealth manner. This refers also to leading edge AI techniques, which increasingly become part of the tool sets of modern serious games. Serious game AI can and must support learners making their way through the game environment and the narrative, help them overcoming challenges and solve problems in a constructivist sense, and – ultimately – help them reaching the game's "serious" goal. In this study, we focused on one particular aspect of AI in serious games, that is, pathfinding algorithms. The goal of such features is to identify and suggest the most promising gaming paths and learning trajectories. The traveling salesman problem served as a well-known starting point and provided the game mechanics on the one hand and the research paradigm on the other. Machine learning features can capitalize on the results of each played episode and improve the learner support. In complex environments such as games, this is not trivial. Therefore, we investigated an approach of bringing artificial intelligence and human intuition together. The results provide some evidence that combing the strengths of machine algorithms and humans may result in better results and perhaps more credible than the AI features alone. This opens interesting and highly promising pathways to improve serious games by AI and, at the same time, new research directions for game-based assessments and personalization.

In this study, we used the MAXMIN Ant System as testbed. Of course, there are other algorithms. In the context of games, the A* search algorithm [31] is popular. There are pros and cons to the various algorithms, the MAXMIN Ant System appears more flexible in settings with varying costs functions, which is determined by the human interventions in this study. Future work will consider comparing the performance of different algorithms with humans in their loop. Also, future work will increasingly develop path finding scenarios on the basis of psychological theories.

References

1. Silver, D., et al.: Mastering the game of Go with deep neural networks and tree search. Nature **529**(7587), 484–489 (2016)
2. Wouters, P.J.M., van Nimwegen, C., van Oostendorp, H., van der Spek, E.D.: A meta-analysis of the cognitive and motivational effects of serious games. J. Educ. Psychol. **105**, 249–265 (2013)
3. Clark, D., Tanner-Smith, E., Killingsworth, S., Bellamy, S.: Digital Games for Learning: A Systematic Review and Meta-Analysis (Executive Summary). SRI International, Menlo Park (2013)
4. Kickmeier-Rust, M.D.: Balancing on a high wire: adaptivity, a key feature of future learning games. In: Kickmeier-Rust, M.D., Albert, D. (eds.) An Alien's Guide to Multi-adaptive Educational Games, pp. 43–88. Informing Science Press, Santa Rosa (2012)
5. Van der Kleij, F.M., Vermeulen, J.A., Schildkamp, K., Eggen, T.J.H.M.: Integrating data-based decision making, assessment for learning and diagnostic testing in formative assessment. Assess. Educ. Princ. Policy Pract. **22**(3), 324–343 (2015)
6. Crisp, G.: Integrative assessment: reframing assessment practice for current and future learning. Assess. Eval. High. Educ. **37**(1), 33–43 (2012)
7. Kickmeier-Rust, M.D., Albert, D.: Educationally adaptive: balancing serious games. Int. J. Comput. Sci. Sport **11**(1), 15–28 (2012)
8. Bellotti, F., Kapralos, B., Lee, L., Moreno-Ger, P., Berta, R.: Assessment in and of serious games: an overview. Adv. Hum. Comput. Interact. **2013**, 11 (2013)
9. Shute, V., Ke, F., Wang, L.: Assessment and adaptation in games. In: Wouters, P., van Oostendorp, H. (eds.) Techniques to Improve the Effectiveness of Serious Games, Advances in Game-Based Learning, pp. 59–78. Springer, Cham (2016). https://doi.org/10.1007/978-3-319-39298-1_4
10. D'Mello, S., Graesser, A.C.: Multimodal semi-automated affect detection from conversational cues, gross body language, and facial features. User Model. User-Adap. Inter. **20**(2), 147–187 (2010)
11. Si, M., Marsella, S.C., Pynadath, D.V.: Directorial control in a decision-theoretic framework for interactive narrative. In: International Conference on Interactive Digital Storytelling (ICIDS), pp. 221–233 (2009)
12. Lester, J., Ha, E.Y., Lee, S.Y., Mott, B.W., Rowe, J.P., Sabourin, J.L.: Serious games get smart: intelligent game-based learning environments. AI Mag. **34**(4), 31–45 (2013)
13. Yannakakis, G.N.: Game AI revisited. In: Proceedings of the 9th Conference on Computing Frontiers, pp. 285–292. ACM, May 2012
14. Cui, X., Shi, H.: A*-based pathfinding in modern computer games. Int. J. Comput. Sci. Network Secur. **11**(1), 125–130 (2011)
15. Silver, D., et al.: Mastering the game of go without human knowledge. Nature **550**(7676), 354–359 (2017)

16. Shute, V.J., Rieber, L., Van Eck, R.: Games . . . and . . . learning. In: Reiser, R., Dempsey, R. (eds.) Trends and Issues in Instructional Design and Technology, 3rd edn., pp. 321–332. Pearson Education Inc., Upper Saddle River (2011)

17. Frutos-Pascual, M., Zapirain, G.: Review of the use of AI techniques in serious games: decision making and machine learning. IEEE Trans. Comput. Intell. AI Games 9(2) (2015)

18. Ciolacu, M., Tehrani, A.F., Beer, R.: Education 4.0 — Fostering student's performance with machine learning methods. In: IEEE 23rd International Symposium for Design and Technology in Electronic Packaging (SIITME) (2017)

19. Conati, C., Porayska-Pomsta, K., Mavrikis, M.: AI in Education Needs Interpretable Machine Learning: Lessons from Open Learner Modelling. Cornell University Library (2018)

20. LeCun, Y., Bengio, Y., Hinton, G.: Deep learning. Nature 521(7553), 436–444 (2015)

21. Bologna, G., Hayashi, Y.: Characterization of symbolic rules embedded in deep dimlp networks: a challenge to transparency of deep learning. J. Artif. Intell. Soft Comput. Res. 7 (4), 265–286 (2017)

22. Amershi, S., Cakmak, M., Knox, W.B., Kulesza, T.: Power to the people: the role of humans in interactive machine learning. AI Mag. 35(4), 105–120 (2014)

23. Laporte, G.: The traveling salesman problem: an overview of exact and approximate algorithms. Eur. J. Oper. Res. 59(2), 231–247 (1992)

24. Karp, R.M.: Mapping the genome: some combinatorial problems arising in molecular biology. In: Proceedings of the Twenty-Fifth Annual ACM Symposium on Theory of Computing (STOC 1993), pp. 278–285 (1993)

25. Michael, R.G., David, S.J.: Computers and Intractability: A Guide to the Theory of NP-Completeness. Freeman, San Francisco (1979)

26. Stützle, T., Hoos, H.H.: Max–min ant system. Future Gener. Comput. Syst. 16(8), 889–914 (2000)

27. Wertheimer, M.: Productive Thinking, Enlarged edn. Harper & Row, New York (1959)

28. Holzinger, A.: Interactive Machine Learning for Health Informatics: When do we need the human-in-the-loop? Brain Inform. 3(2), 119–131 (2016)

29. Holzinger, A.: Human-Computer Interaction and Knowledge Discovery (HCI-KDD): What is the benefit of bringing those two fields to work together? In: Cuzzocrea, A., Kittl, C., Simos, Dimitris E., Weippl, E., Xu, L. (eds.) CD-ARES 2013. LNCS, vol. 8127, pp. 319–328. Springer, Heidelberg (2013). https://doi.org/10.1007/978-3-642-40511-2_22

30. Holzinger, K., Mak, K., Kieseberg, P., Holzinger, A.: Can we trust Machine Learning Results? Artificial Intelligence in Safety-Critical decision Support. ERCIM News 112(1), 42–43 (2018)

31. Hart, P.E., Nilsson, N.J., Raphael, B.: A formal basis for the heuristic determination of minimum cost paths. IEEE Trans. Syst. Sci. Cybern. 4(2), 100–107 (1968)

Shallow and Deep Gamification in Mathematics Trails

Iwan Gurjanow[1($\boxtimes$)], Miguel Oliveira[2], Joerg Zender[1],
Pedro A. Santos[2], and Matthias Ludwig[1]

[1] Institute of Mathematics Education,
University of Frankfurt, Frankfurt/Main, Germany
{gurjanow, zender, ludwig}@math.uni-frankfurt.de
[2] INESC-ID & Instituto Superior Técnico,
Universidade de Lisboa, Lisbon, Portugal
{miguel.oliveira.f, pedro.santos}@tecnico.ulisboa.pt

Abstract. Mobile Math Trails for Europe (MoMaTrE) is an ongoing project with the objective of conceptualizing and developing a fully gamified platform for creating, organizing and executing mathematics trails. We present some early experimental results concerning the introduction of shallow gamification techniques in the platform and discuss our plans for adding other gamification elements.

Keywords: Mathematics trails · Gamification · Mobile

1 Introduction

1.1 Shallow and Deep Gamification

The most basic distinction between types of motivation as given by self-determination theory was made by Ryan and Deci [1] by their subdivision of motivation into intrinsic and extrinsic forms. Many school activities, due to their obligatory character, require an external reason for the engagement of the student. However, even if an activity is initially externally motivated, inherently interesting properties of it can be experienced, leading to a motivation shift [1].

Gamification describes various techniques for controlling the behavior of users through game elements towards a specific goal, that is, the application of game elements in a possibly non-gaming context [2]. The overriding goal of gamification is to modify the affected activity, which was originally designed for a specific purpose, so that the user feels intrinsically more engaged, thus increasing their intrinsic motivation and commitment.

There are several experiences of gamification in education, using different approaches [3–5]. Techniques can be though at two different levels. In a *shallow* level or *thin layer* of gamification, the core teaching and learning processes are not substantially changed. There are still lectures, exercises, homework. But the language changes to making quests, crafting items, defeating bosses with the grade given in Experience Points. An example of such an approach applied to undergraduate studies is

M. Gentile et al. (Eds.): GALA 2018, LNCS 11385, pp. 364–374, 2019.
https://doi.org/10.1007/978-3-030-11548-7_34

given in [4]. Another possible shallow gamification technique is to give stars, badges and prizes for activities in the course, use leaderboards, or yet use game-like interface components. Shallow gamification has been the target of some criticism because it can be seen as manipulative and making excessive use of external motivation [6]. In fact, shallow gamification can be seen as a layer that is put above and on top of the core processes, without changing their essence.

In contrast to shallow gamification, deep gamification can be defined as introducing game elements that change the core processes of the activity [7]. A seminal example of that approach was given by Quest to Learn, an innovative school for grades 6 to 12 that started in 2009 in New York City [5], where the whole curriculum was planned using game design techniques. While shallow gamification needs mainly programing and visual design skills, deep gamification uses mainly game design skills, because it is necessary to rethink the activity and design game mechanics at its core.

1.2   Mathematics Trails, MathCityMap and the MoMaTrE Project

A maths trail is a trail where the participants can discover mathematics in the environment at predefined stations [8]. Blane and Clarke [9] were among the first to present the maths trail idea to a broad, scientific audience. Their concern at the time was the popularization of mathematics. Today, we see the benefits above all in the application of mathematics in real, authentic situations in reality, as well as the modeling that precedes the calculations.

The MathCityMap (MCM) project of the Goethe University in Frankfurt combines the idea of mathematics trails with the possibilities of smartphones [10]. The main idea of the project is to give the participants another perception and experience of mathematics. Maths takes place mainly indoors inside the school, inside the classroom. But all human concepts, including mathematical concepts, are based in the perceptual motor system experiences we have while interacting with the world around us [11]. Furthermore, the project addresses the advantages of the Web 2.0, to have users create content, which can be shared and reused. The MathCityMap website (www. mathcitymap.eu) is a portal, where (teachers) users can create tasks everywhere on the world map. These tasks can be published and if successful, they can be combined with tasks done by other users for a maths trail.

The objective is to bring mathematics outdoors more often, for students as well as every citizen. We seek for new forms of getting a mathematical view of one's neighborhood, of one's environment, see the questions and problems, which are everywhere, and on top of that, do it digitally with a smartphone.

In order to leave the borders of Germany and to further develop MathCityMap, a consortium was formed and an Erasmus+ Grant obtained, the MoMaTrE (Mobile Math Trails for Europe) project. The main target groups for this project are student teachers, in-service teachers and the public. Our approach contains a platform and a mobile application to create tasks and with these tasks, mathematical trails can be built by everybody, especially teachers. New ways of collaboration should be possible and we want to build a community of active maths trailers, who share their work and help each other to develop things further. Some shallow gamification elements are part of the app today. In this paper, we will present and discuss a study done to measure their effects and we will present ideas how to apply other gamification elements (including some deep gamifications) to the concept of mathematics trails.

1.3   Literature Results on the Impact of Gamification

Dicheva and Dichev [12] conducted a meta-analysis on gamification in education. Compared to the time span of over four years (from January 2010 to June 2014), where 34 papers related to this topic were published, and the time span from July 2014 to June 2015 (one year), the number of published papers has increased to 41. These findings indicate a growing interest in gamification in the area of education. Nevertheless, only about half of the publications can draw a positive conclusion [12].

The intrinsic motivation and experience associated with playing video games can be seen in gamified activities as well [13]. This is why gamification can benefit on a large array of areas when used correctly as is shown in several studies.

For instance tourism, [14] where the presence of game mechanics in a travel-related application and website resulted in an improvement in terms of engagement and made the experience more social and interactive. Another example is the introduction of gamification in higher education classrooms. One of these cases resulted in an increase in approval rating, interaction and attention in the classroom [15]. Other cases indicated positive effects on the engagement of students and a moderate improvement in learning outcomes, see for instance Ibáñez et al. [16] and Santos [7].

The gamification of a training module with fiction also showed a significant improvement of the satisfaction of the trainees. This same study [17] also shows that the declarative knowledge did not differ between the control condition and the gamified condition, but the procedural knowledge scores were higher in the control condition.

2   The Impact of Shallow Gamification Elements

2.1   Introducing Gamification Elements into MathCityMap

Besides many positive observations of students walking a maths trail, two negative observations lead to the addition of gamification elements to the MathCityMap app. Firstly, students often tried to guess answers, if their first attempt was incorrect. Secondly, there seems to be a motivational obstacle to begin working on the tasks, which is expressed by walking slowly to the first task and thus leading to a low ratio of doing mathematics to the time spent on the trail. Before a decision on the type of gamification was taken, we have analyzed the project as suggested by Morschheuser et al. [18] and defined gamification goals.

The mathematics trail activity as supported by the MathCityMap app focuses on secondary school students, who are familiar with using smartphones and apps. A maths trail is usually carried out on an irregular basis e.g. day's hike or project days. In our approach, students collaborate in groups of three (one is using the MCM app, one is responsible for measuring and the last person has the task to take notes) and walk the trail independently. To complete a maths trail students have to complete each task that is part of the trail. The activity to complete a task is divided into seven sub activities:

(1) finding the task's location; (2) reading the task's description; (3) collecting data; (4) transforming task into mathematical model; (5) calculating the answer; (6) entering answer into the app and getting feedback; (7) optionally, taking hints and retry. During the steps (1), (2), (6) and (7) students have to use the application. Finally, two gamification goals were defined.

1. Prevent students from guessing answers.
2. Increase intrinsic motivation for working on maths trail tasks (increase the number of tasks completed per hour).

Based on Lieberoth [19], who found shallow gamification in the form of a game-like design to have impact on the participants motivation, the first gamification elements added to the application were simple and fall into the category of shallow gamification. Following his suggestion to "break clusters of game elements down to individual functional units" [19], we have decided to create three different versions of the app. Each version adds further game elements to the application. To prevent guessing, a points system (G1) was added to the task activity, rewarding the students with up to 100 points for a correct answer. Additionally, each wrong answer after the first one decreases the value of the task by ten points. The second gamification approach is the local leaderboard gamification (G2). It augments the points gamification with the possibility to see the score of the user in front and behind you, so that users get into competition with each other. To not frustrate the last ranked group, we have added a computer player, who will be always ranked last (Table 1).

Table 1. Types of gamification in MathCityMap

G0: No gamification	G1: Points	G2: Local leaderboard

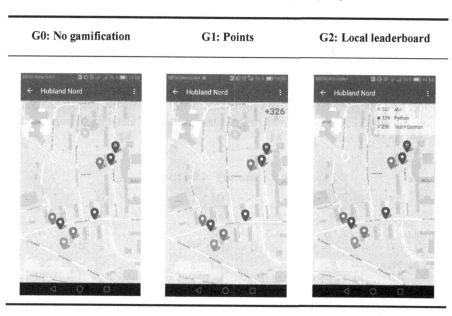

2.2   The Study

In a study with ninth graders, the following research questions were studied in the summer semester 2017:

- How does the gamification system influence the motivation of the participants?
- What effects does the gamification system have on the performance parameters (completed tasks per hour, incorrect entries per task) of the 9th graders when working on a maths trail?

Methodology. 196 ninth grade students (97 female, 99 male) from 14 different school classes took part in the tests. They were randomly assigned to the control group G0 (no gamification; N = 48; 19 female, 29 male), experimental group G1 (points gamification; N = 56; 24 female, 32 male) or experimental group G2 (local leaderboard gamification; N = 92; 54 female, 38 male). After a short introduction to the MathCityMap application and the use of measuring tools, the students were handed out a set of materials (smartphone, measuring tools and a paper trail guide) and walked a mathematics trail in groups of three. The trail's tasks focused on cylinder problems. Finally, they were asked to fill in a standardized questionnaire on intrinsic motivation We designed the intervention as close to real (German) mathematics classes as possible so that findings could be easily applied to the school context. For instance, teachers divided their students into groups of three themselves. Furthermore, we invited teachers and their students for a frame of 90 min that is a typical duration of mathematics classes (two classes with 45 min each). Subtracting the time for the introduction and the time for answering the questionnaire, about 70 min were left to walk the trail. The motivation questionnaire contained a subset of questions of the Intrinsic Motivation Inventory [20]. The questionnaire comprises 21 items that could be answered on a 7-point Likert scale. Additionally, all inputs that the students made (especially the number of completed tasks per hour and the number of incorrect entries) were logged by the smartphones.

Results. An earlier study indicated that the influence of gamification might be dependent on the gender of a person [21]. That is the reason why, besides the gamification, also the gender of the students was taken into consideration during the data analysis (Table 2).

Table 2. Summary of the results

	G0		G1		G2	
	M	F	M	F	M	F
Motivation	4.6 (±1.5)	4.2 (±1.3)	4.8 (±1.2)	4.8 (±1.3)	4.8 (±1.3)	4.9 (±1.3)
Tasks per hour	3.2 (±1.8)	2.7 (±0.8)	2.3 (±1.3)	2.4 (±1.5)	3.9 (±1.2)	2.8 (±1.1)
Incorrect entries per task	4.9 (±4.0)	3.7 (±2.7)	4.4 (±4.2)	4.0 (±4.4)	2.7 (±3.1)	1.9 (±1.7)

Multiple two-way analysis of variance were conducted on the influence of two independent variables and their interaction effect (gamification, gender, gamification * gender) on (a) the intrinsic motivation score, (b) completed tasks per hour and (c) number of wrong answers per task. Gamification included three levels (G0 – no gamification, G1 – points gamification, G2 – leaderboard gamification) and gender consisted of two levels (M – male, F – female).

(a) None of the effects were statistically significant ($F_{(5, 190)} = 1.041$, $p = .395$))

(b) All effects were statistically significant at the .05 significance level. The main effect for gamification yielded an F ratio of $F_{(2, 190)} = 9.417$, $p < .001$, partial $\eta^2 = .09$, indicating a significant difference between G0 (M = 3.0, SD = 1.5), G1 (M = 2.3, SD = 1.4) and G2 (M = 3.2, SD = 1.3). The main effect for gender yielded an F ratio of $F_{(1, 190)} = 6.2$, $p < .05$, partial $\eta^2 = .032$, indicating a significant difference between female (M = 2.7, SD = 1.2) and male (M = 3.2, SD = 1.5) students. The interaction effect was significant, $F_{(2, 190)} = 4.161$, $p < .05$, partial $\eta^2 = .042$.

(c) One effect was statistically significant at the .05 significance level. The main effect for gamification yielded an F ratio of $F_{(2, 190)} = 8.056$, $p < .001$, partial $\eta^2 = .08$, indicating a significant difference between G0 (M = 4.4, SD = 3.6), G1 (M = 4.2, SD = 4.2) and G2 (M = 2.2, SD = 2.4). The main effect for gender yielded an F ratio of $F_{(1, 190)} = 2.475$, $p = .117$, partial $\eta^2 = .013$, indicating that the effect for gender was not significant, female (M = 2.8, SD = 2.9) and male (M = 3.9, SD = 3.9). The interaction effect was not significant, $F_{(2, 190)} = 0.181$, $p > .05$, partial $\eta^2 = .002$.

2.3   Conclusions

The motivation of the groups that used a gamified app version tends to be higher but not significantly so. This result is in line with the analyzes of different studies on gamification by Dicheva and Dichev [12] and suggests that the actual activity is crucial for the motivational expression and the introduction of shallow game elements have at most a small impact on this. On the other hand, the speed of task resolution was significantly influenced by gamification. The leaderboard group G2 stands out with a higher number of tasks processed per hour and less mistakes per task. In particular, boys responded to the competitive nature of the leaderboard [22], addressing and solving an average of 3.9 tasks per hour. Girls work in all three settings a similar number of tasks, but pay attention to the Leaderboard Gamification, especially on the correctness of the results with just 1.9 incorrect entries per task. Zender and Ludwig [23] discuss further results on learning performance of students using the MathCityMap app.

3 MoMaTrE and Deeper Gamification

The above results support the idea of implementing and testing more complex gamification elements. These might not be, by definition, deep gamification elements but they are objectively more rich and elaborated than the ones presented so far. We propose the implementation of two types gamification. One regarding the use of narrative elements to improve the engagement of users and another which adds different types of objectives to the routes, making the use of the MathCityMap a more cooperative and/or competitive experience for the users (depending on the objective).

3.1 Narrative Approach

The addition of fiction elements to the routes in the application can potentially increase the interest and engagement of the students regarding math problems.

A study performed to 858 secondary school students [24] shows that their preference for video games in the classroom is affected directly by, amongst other things, their perception regarding the usefulness of videogames and their previous experiences with them. This could be favorable due to the demographic consisting of students below 18 years old, which recent studies show is more propitious to playing video games [25].

The introduction of narrative elements to the MathCityMap app brings some challenges. Several maths trails which utilize fiction [26, 27] commonly have narrative elements that are highly contextualized and integrated within the tasks themselves, due to the fact that there is only one route.

The MathCityMap app allows users to create and participate in several routes. As such, creating a narrative contextualized for each one is a challenge due to the necessary authoring effort. It is not our goal to force the user who creates a route to also create a narrative that fits said route.

As previously stated, the tradeoff of creating more specialized and contextualized fiction is that the authoring effort is highly increased. Therefore, two possible solutions to cover different approaches for this problem are being worked on:

Non-contextualized Narrative Nodes: The creation of a set of fiction nodes that between themselves are part of a bigger narrative but that are non-connected with the tasks or the route itself. The nodes could have different purposes:

- To introduce the narrative (these nodes would appear at the start of a route);
- To introduce each task;
- To replace the message of a correct or incorrect answer;
- To make the bridge between tasks;
- To conclude the narrative (these nodes would appear after the completion of the last task of the route);

The amount of nodes for each purpose should be enough to avoid repetition inside each route. This solution would be light in terms of authoring effort but at the cost of some disconnection between the tasks and the narrative.

Contextualized Narrative Nodes: This approach is similar to the one stated above but with more specified narrative nodes to fit the context of the tasks. The narrative would make references to the problems present in the tasks themselves instead of just present the narrative without mentioning the current task objective. This means that more specified nodes would have to be created to introduce a set of types of tasks, for example, nodes could reference some tasks available in the task wizard like:

- Determination of slopes of ramps;
- Number of stones in a rectangular wall;
- Volume of a cylindrical pool;
- Walk a certain distance or the shape of a geometrical object.

This solution requires a higher authoring effort when compared to the non-contextualized one, due to the fact that each task needs to have specific narrative nodes tailored to it, which implies a larger number of nodes. Also, it may be difficult to create a route where all the tasks have narrative nodes specific to their type. The higher authoring effort can be mitigated with the use of Procedural Content Generation techniques, in a similar way to what has been proposed for game level generation [28].

This approach will allow the tasks to have a more engaging narrative component since the nodes blend better with the tasks and close the disconnection gap between the narrative and the tasks which may exist in the non-contextualized method.

3.2 Gamified Activities

On top of the narrative approach, we propose the addition of objectives to tasks and routes. This also aims to improve the experience of the users and cooperation between them.

As proposed by Hauge et al. [29] context aware activities can be implemented in such a system, for example a Treasure Hunt, or a Conquer activity. Also, the routes can be made to work differently, not showing all the tasks at the start but instead upon the completion of a task, a clue is given regarding the location of the next one or, in some cases, the task itself would result in the finding of the next task. For example: one task may be "walk 50 m south", and upon arrival at the solution, the next task would be unlocked. This helps connecting the several tasks and making them less individual. On top of that, it also allows for a bigger pool of options in the integration of the narrative elements.

A factor that can be added to an activity is the time taken by the students to complete a route. However, this, along with the remaining variables (like the percentage of correct answers), should be used for the calculation of scores (as opposed to using time as a single factor for score calculation), as seen above. The reason for it is so as to avoid random answers just for the sake of being the quickest, which ultimately would turn the route into a race.

3.3 Global Teams and Challenges

Games are seen as a social activity by most teenagers [30] and this can be used to enhance the experience and engagement of a gamified application.

We propose a feature that creates a light social component, inspired by recent video games like PokemonGO that gives the player the possibility to choose one of three teams to be a part of. These teams do not affect the gameplay in a major way, but give the players something to argue about.

Other example is the Splatfest game mode in Splatoon and Splatoon 2. This mode allows each player to choose one of two options, dividing the community in two teams. At the end of each month, a team win based on the number of players that voted on the team and on the performance of those players in the game. The rewards given to the winning team are not game changing but that does not hinder this event's popularity.

The proposed feature is similar to Splatfest in the sense that each user of the MathCityMap app could choose a team and from time to time a team would be chosen as the winner based on the amount of completed routes of the members of said team.

This feature does not interfere with the flow of the App making its implementation relatively easy and could help to give a more global and social component to the application.

4   Conclusions

In this paper, we presented the results of a study on the effects of shallow gamification in the mathematical trails application MathCityMap, which is being developed as part of the MoMaTrE Erasmus+ project. The study showed that the introduction of shallow gamification elements have at most a small impact on motivation, as measured by motivation questionnaires, but successfully influenced performance parameters. Especially the leaderboard gamification increased the speed of task resolution and lowered the number of incorrect answers per task. Furthermore, the study indicates that the impact of gamification is gender dependent. So, while the full promised potential of gamification was not reached, there remains the question if deeper gamification can improve these type of results. With the goal of shifting motivation to a more intrinsic nature, we propose to introduce both narrative arcs associated and interlaced with the trails and meta-team and challenge creation. The effects of those gamification techniques in the MathCityMap application will then be tested.

Acknowledgements. This work was partially supported by the Erasmus+ European project MoMaTrE, EC Project Number: 2017-1-DE01-KA203-003577 and Fundação para a Ciência e a Tecnologia (FCT) with reference UID/CEC/50021/2013.

References

1. Ryan, R.M., Deci, E.L.: Intrinsic and extrinsic motivations: classic definitions and new directions. Contemp. Educ. Psychol. **25**(1), 54–67 (2000)
2. Deterding, S., Dixon, D., Khaled, R., Nacke, L.: From game design elements to gamefulness: defining gamification. In: Proceedings of the 15th International Academic MindTrek Conference: Envisioning Future Media Environments, pp. 9–15. ACM (2011)
3. Labouriau, I.S.: Instrução Personalizada na Matemática Universitária. Boletim da SPM **64**, 55–65 (2011)

4. Sheldon, L.: The Multiplayer Classroom: Designing Coursework as a Game. Cengage Learning, Boston (2011)
5. Tekinbas, K.S., Torres, R., Wolozin, L., Rufo-Tepper, R., Shapiro, A.: Quest to Learn: Developing the School for Digital Kids. MIT Press, Cambridge (2010)
6. Bogost, I.: Why gamification is bullshit. In: The Gameful World - Approaches, Issues, Applications, pp. 65–80. MIT Press (2014)
7. Santos, P.A.: Gamification of a university course. In: Proceedings of SciTecIN 2015, Sciences and Technologies of Interaction, Coimbra (2015)
8. Shoaf, M., Pollak, H., Schneider, J.: Math Trails. COMAP, Lexington (2004)
9. Blane, D.C., Clarke, D.: A mathematics trail around the city of Melbourne. Monash Mathematics Education Centre, Monash University (1984)
10. Ludwig, M., Jesberg, J., Weiss, D.: MathCityMap - a smartphone project to do math. University Library Dortmund (2013)
11. Wittmann, M.C., Flood, V.J., Black, K.E.: Algebraic manipulation as motion within a landscape. Educ. Stud. Math. **82**(2), 169–181 (2013)
12. Dicheva, D., Dichev, C.: Gamification in education: where are we in 2015? In: E-Learn: World Conference on E-Learning in Corporate, Government, Healthcare, and Higher Education, pp. 1445–1454. Association for the Advancement of Computing in Education (AACE) (2015)
13. Dickey, M.D.: Murder on Grimm Isle: the impact of game narrative design in an educational game-based learning environment. Br. J. Educ. Technol. **42**(3), 456–469 (2011)
14. Sigala, M.: The application and impact of gamification funware on trip planning and experiences: the case of TripAdvisor's funware. Electron. Mark. **25**(3), 189–209 (2015)
15. Iosup, A., Epema, D.: An experience report on using gamification in technical higher education. In: Proceedings of the 45th ACM Technical Symposium on Computer Science Education, pp. 27–32. ACM (2014)
16. Ibáñez, M.B., Di-Serio, A., Delgado-Kloos, C.: Gamification for engaging computer science students in learning activities: a case study. IEEE Trans. Learn. Technol. **7**(3), 291–301 (2014)
17. Armstrong, M.B., Landers, R.N.: An evaluation of gamified training: using narrative to improve reactions and learning. Simul. Gaming **48**(4), 513–538 (2017)
18. Morschheuser, B., Hamari, J., Werder, K., Abe, J.: How to gamify? A method for designing gamification. In: Proceedings of the 50th Hawaii International Conference on System Sciences 2017. University of Hawai'i at Manoa (2017)
19. Lieberoth, A.: Shallow gamification - testing psychological effects of framing an activity as a game. Games Cult. **10**, 229–248 (2015)
20. Intrinsic Motivation Inventory (IMI): the intrinsic motivation inventory. Scale description, http://selfdeterminationtheory.org/intrinsic-motivation-inventory/. Last Accessed 01 Oct 2018
21. Gurjanow, I., Ludwig, M.: Gamifying math trails with the Mathcitymap app: impact of points and leaderboard on intrinsic motivation. In: Aldon, G., Trgalova, J. (eds.) Proceedings of the 13th International Conference on Technology in Mathematics Teaching (ICTMT 2013), pp. 105–112, Lyon, France (2017)
22. Niederle, M., Vesterlund, L.: Gender and competition. Annu. Rev. Econ. **3**(1), 601–630 (2011)
23. Zender, J., Ludwig, M.: The long-term effects of MathCityMap on the performance of German 15 year old students concerning cylindric tasks. In: Proceedings of the Eleventh Congress of the European Society for Research in Mathematics Education, CERME 2011, 6–10 February 2019, Uitrecht (2019, in Press)

24. Bourgonjon, J., Valcke, M., Soetaert, R., Schellens, T.: Students' perceptions about the use of video games in the classroom. Comput. Educ. **54**(4), 1145–1156 (2010)

25. Essential video gamenews, p. 34. http://www.sell.fr/sites/default/files/essential_video_game_news_sell_2018-eng-hr.pdf. Last Accessed 01 Oct 2018

26. Quek, K.S.: Context for mathematical problem posing. In: Ee, J., Berinderjeet, K., Lee, N. H., Yeap, B.H. (eds.) New 'Literacies': Educational Response to a Knowledge-Based Society, Vol 1: Education, pp. 612–620. Educational Research Association of Singapore, Singapore (2000)

27. Muller, E.: Niagara Falls Math Trail. Department of Mathematics, Brock University (1993)

28. Lucas, P., Martinho, C.: Stay awhile and listen to 3buddy, a co-creative level design support tool. In: Eighth International Conference on Computational Creativity, ICCC, Atlanta (2017)

29. Hauge, J.B., et al.: Exploring context-aware activities to enhance the learning experience. In: Dias, J., Santos, P.A., Veltkamp, R.C. (eds.) GALA 2017. LNCS, vol. 10653, pp. 238–247. Springer, Cham (2017). https://doi.org/10.1007/978-3-319-71940-5_22

30. Lenhart, A., Kahne, J., Middaugh, E., Macgill, A.R., Evans, C., Vitak, J.: Teens, video games, and civics: teens' gaming experiences are diverse and include significant social interaction and civic engagement. In: Pew Internet & American Life Project (2008)

A Case Study of Deep Gamification in Higher Engineering Education

Heinrich Söbke$^{(\boxtimes)}$ (iD)

Bauhaus-Institute for Infrastructure Solutions (b.is),
Bauhaus-Universität Weimar, Weimar, Germany
heinrich.soebke@uni-weimar.de

Abstract. Gamification is often utilized to enhance the motivation to use digital learning tools. Usually, the effect of gamification alone is not sufficient to achieve sustainable self-directed occupation of students with digital learning tools. This statement is also confirmed by the authors' experiences from previous uses of quiz apps to impart factual knowledge. The presented study describes the use of gamification in a university course in Urban Water Management in a twofold approach. The first approach of gamification is a gamified quiz app, which offers matches as well as ranking lists and competitions. The second approach is the gamified integration of the quiz app into the didactic context. The didactic context is characterized by the voluntary use of the quiz app and meaningful incentives, such as substitution of preliminary assessment tests. Compared to previous experiences, students showed a high level of engagement. Research instruments are the usage data of the quiz app and data collection at four points in time with the help of standardized measurement instruments (QCM, EGameFlow, and expectation-value model). The results include outstanding engagement of students indicated by an average of 2,223 questions per student answered during the semester, a high degree of confidence in mastering learning tasks among students, and a comparatively high level of knowledge improvement and social interaction reported by students. Overall, the study demonstrates the huge impact of deep gamification by integrating gamification into the didactic context and encourages further systematic research of deep gamification of didactic contexts.

Keywords: Quiz app · Deep gamification · Instructional design ·
Higher education

1 Introduction

Gamification is defined as "the use of game design elements in non-game contexts" [1]. Especially educational contexts are an area of gamification application [2]. A key focus of gamification is the promotion of engagement [3]. Further, *shallow* and *deep gamification* are distinguished. Shallow gamification "can be seen as a layer that is put above and on top of the core processes, without changing their essence" while deep gamification "can be defined as introducing game elements that change the core processes of the activity" [4]. Deep gamification is considered to promote longer-lasting engagement than shallow gamification [5]. Examples show the effectiveness of deep

© Springer Nature Switzerland AG 2019
M. Gentile et al. (Eds.): GALA 2018, LNCS 11385, pp. 375–386, 2019.
https://doi.org/10.1007/978-3-030-11548-7_35

gamification in education, where a well-thought development of the didactic context as well as supervision by teachers is considered to be advantageous [6, 7].

Multiple-choice questions have been long established for assessment purposes [8, 9]. In addition, the so-called *testing effect* [10], which is triggered by repeated retrieval from memory, qualifies multiple-choice questions as medium for learning [11–13]. The omnipresence of mobile devices, such as smartphones and tablets, enables the spread of quiz apps, which are a means to gamify multiple-choice question-based learning. Quiz apps used for entertainment purposes are very popular due to high game enjoyment [14]. Various quiz apps or multiple-choice question-based apps have been developed for learning purposes and are offered on a commercial basis, e.g., [15–17]. Furthermore, quiz apps are subject of research as experimental prototypes, e.g., [18, 19], and as apps resulting from scientific projects, e.g., [20]. For example, motivation-increasing effects on students have been proven (e.g., [21]) as well as learning-enhancing effects [22].

However, despite the great potential, own experiences suggest that quiz apps in higher education do not elicit imperatively sufficient motivation to foster long-lasting engagement [23–25]. The observed reluctance to play may be promoted by the decreasing susceptibility to game elements with increasing age of students in favor of higher goal orientation [26].

This article describes a twofold gamification-based approach to foster engagement in a didactic context. First, a quiz app as a gamified learning tool is assumed to contribute game enjoyment. Second, the gamified integration of the quiz app in the didactic context should elicit further motivation. Both approaches are combined to generate engagement of students in the didactic context by complementing extrinsic and intrinsic motivation. Following a design-based research approach, the design of the didactic context is based on earlier studies of the authors of quiz apps as learning tools. The comparatively high age of the students, the unattended and self-directed use of the mobile quiz app and especially the twofold gamification-based approach itself characterize a didactic context, which, to our knowledge, has not yet been investigated. The article is structured as follows: Sect. 2 describes the didactic context and Sect. 3 presents the study design. The results are described in Sect. 4 and discussed in Sect. 5. The concluding section summarizes conclusions and further work.

2 Didactic Context

The course *Urban Water Management* is part of the Bachelor's study program *Civil Engineering* of the authors' institution. The course is concluded with a written final test, which consists of dimensioning tasks for water infrastructure facilities, such as wastewater treatment plants. Since the winter semester 2013/14, various quiz apps have been used to deepen the factual knowledge presented in the lectures. To encourage students to learn during the semester, the factual knowledge is tested in eight short digital tests spread over the semester. Each of these tests consists of five multiple-choice questions randomly selected from a question pool. The question pool contains 317 questions on 12 knowledge areas (on average 26 questions per knowledge area). In order to be admitted to the examination, students must pass six of these so-called admission tests with 75% each. An admission test must be taken within 14 days of the end of each lecture. The admission tests can be prepared either with the lecture script or with the help of the quiz app, as the content of the respective questions is similar. To retain the quiz apps' game character, students are not obliged to use the quiz app.

Previous studies had shown a relatively rapid decline in engagement to use the quiz apps. In some cases, the quiz apps were only used to explore the questions and their answers, to document them and then to use the documentation for learning in a time-optimized manner [27]. For the current study during the winter semester 2018 a quiz app (see Fig. 1) was used, which had proven its efficacy in the corporate didactic contexts of two home loan banks [28].

The didactic context presented shows two major structural differences compared to the previous studies: On the one hand, asynchronous matches are played against fellow students according to the principle of *QuizClash* [29]: in three rounds the opponents must each answer four questions on a knowledge area that can be chosen out of three knowledge areas. This game mechanic should stimulate social interaction between players. Social interaction is considered as particularly beneficial for the motivation of students and thereby for learning processes (e.g., [25]). The second difference is that the quiz app provides ranking lists for clearly defined metrics. This includes the number of matches won and the number of correctly answered questions. In the previous studies, students were ranked based on abstract features such as points [24], whose rules of achievement often remained unclear to players [27].

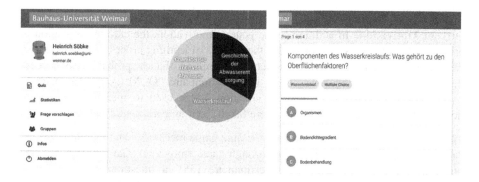

Fig. 1. Screenshots of the quiz app: knowledge area selection (left) and sample question (right)

Another important feature of the quiz app are competitions: one competition was announced for each knowledge area. For a competition, all questions of the specific knowledge area answered correctly in the time of the competition (14 days) are counted (including repeated correct answers). The two students with most correctly answered questions were considered to have passed the corresponding admission test. Both ranks were rewarded with a so-called *free ticket*, if at least 30 questions were correctly answered. The minimum number of questions correctly answered was introduced to avoid having to grant free tickets for only low utilization of the quiz app. In general, the competitions should counteract the motivation that usually decreases with time: each competition should trigger a motivation boost. The time of the competition was set parallel to the response time of the admission tests. The parallelism should prevent tactical activities of the students, e.g., students who passed the admission test would be less motivated to take part in the competition following the admission test.

In addition, a group incentive was offered: mock exams are very popular among students for preparing the final test. Per se, students are provided with three mock exams. Depending on students' engagement in the quiz app, further exams were offered. Upon reaching the marks of 100, 300 and 600 completed matches of all students, an additional mock exam was rewarded.

3   Study Design

Based on the defined didactic context and the findings of the previous studies the research questions and measurements have been chosen as follows.

General Motivation of Students. In the previous studies, often an effort-optimizing behavior of the students, which was driven by the goal of passing the final test, could be observed. This raised the question of the general motivation of students: Are students extrinsically motivated by the completion of the course or are they interested in the content of the course? To clarify this question, the students were asked for their expectations for the course and their values according to Eccles' expectation-value model [30, 31]. Translated questionnaire items from [32] were used and adopted to the didactic context. Comparison values were taken from [33].

Current Motivation. In addition to the general motivation, the current motivation in learning situations is also important for the success of learning processes. For example, learning processes are hindered by students' assumption of a low probability of success for the concrete learning tasks. Thus, the questionnaire "QCM: A questionnaire to assess current motivation in learning situations" was used to measure the current motivation [34]. Comparison values were taken from an earlier study [27].

Game Enjoyment. The quiz app uses the quiz game mechanics and therefore has the claim to generate intrinsic motivation through game enjoyment. Game enjoyment was measured using the EGameFlow questionnaire [35], a questionnaire specifically designed to measure learners' enjoyment of serious games. The German translation of the items and comparison values were taken from [36].

The usefulness of the measurements chosen depends on the point in time of measurement. For example, collecting the general motivation at the beginning of the study period is appropriate, while the game enjoyment should be evaluated right after using the quiz app. In addition, an overall assessment and suggestions for improvements are suitable to be collected after the end of the quiz app use. The data collection was therefore carried out at four points in time (see Table 1). In Questionnaires (Q) 2 and 3, the QCM was intended as an alternative for non-users of the quiz app.

Table 1. Data collection: point in time and type of collected data (Q: Questionnaire)

Q #	Point in time	Types of collected data
Q 1	Start of the semester	General motivation, QCM
Q 2	Admission test no. 5	EGameFlow (for quiz app users), alternatively QCM
Q 3	After admission test no. 8	EGameFlow (for quiz app users), alternatively QCM
Q 4	Before the final test	General motivation, overall assessment & suggestions for improvement

4 Results

4.1 Usage Data

All 14 students regularly used the quiz app (i.e. at least once per admission test) during the lecture period from the beginning of October 2017 to the end of January 2018 and answered 31,112 questions (2,223 questions per student on average (s = 1356, median: 1714.5)). Eight students answered between 1000 and 2000 questions. A good third (5) of the students are among the above-average users of the quiz app, who have strived for the top ranks in almost every competition.

The percentage of correctly answered questions was 76% and varied between 59% and 86% per student. The correlation coefficient between the total number of answered questions and the proportion of correctly answered questions had a value of 0.67 (to 0.7 mean correlation, 0.7–0.9 high correlation).

A competition for free tickets was observed, in which almost one third of the students participated. In total, only 9 of the 14 students were rewarded with at least one free ticket. Of these, three students earned 7, 6 and 4 free tickets each. Another three students were successful twice or once. The above-average users already identified by the number of answered questions can therefore also be identified by the metric of the number of free tickets granted. For the free tickets, 80 to 230 questions had to be correctly answered; the original limit of 30 questions was always clearly exceeded.

The students finished 565 matches. In doing so, they won two of the three mock exams. The total number of matches started was 2993. Only every fifth match was finished. In the interviews, it became clear that partly the cancellation of matches was deliberately used to maintain the player metric of the percentages of matches won. Secondly, the most frequent reason mentioned in Q 4 for the cancellation of matches was the missing of time restrictions (challenges must be answered within 24 h, every further round within 72 h).

Thirteen of the 14 students achieved admission to the examination without crediting free tickets (six students passed six admission tests, five students passed seven admission tests, and two students passed all tests). The number of admission tests passed could have been larger, as four students skipped one of the last two tests: they could be sure that they had already passed the admission test due to a misconfiguration of the test environment. In the previous studies, it was found that students do not take admission tests once admission to the final test has been permitted. Therefore, in the previous studies, the results of admission tests no. 6 to no. 8 were only revealed after completion of admission test no. 8.

4.2 Study Design Adjustments

Guided Interview. After the first admission tests, it was observed that some students who had used the quiz app little had passed the admission tests with excellent results. The first assumption was that students with a reliable command of the factual knowledge to learn had taken the admission tests for their fellow students. To prove this assumption, the fifth admission test was taken during a personal meeting of the supervisor with each student, followed by a guided interview about the didactic context and concluded by Q 2. The admission test results did not fall short of those previously provided, and the assumption had to be rejected. Further result of the guided interviews was that the students took the admission tests with considerably less stress than a final test. On a scale from 1 (no stress) to 10 (highest stress), they put the average stress of the admission tests at 4.0, while a value of 7.4 was given for the final test.

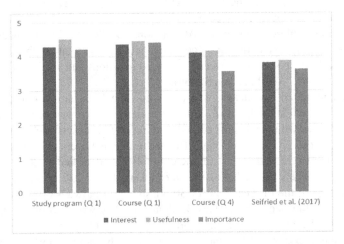

Fig. 2. Value categories of the value-expectancy model [30] (5-point Likert scale)

Admission Test Substitution. At the end of the semester, informal discussions with the students revealed that some students collected questions and answers from the quiz app and documented them on a cloud drive in preparation for the admission test. Documented questions were made then available to the fellow students. These indications were supported by declining activity in the quiz app. The public accessibility of questions and answers enables targeted short-term but unsustainable preparation ("bulimia learning") for the admission tests. In order to set a counterincentive here, an offer was made for admission test no. 8 that the admission test could be substituted by the correct answering of at least 120 questions on the topic. This offer was then fulfilled by three students, including one student who was previously not an above-average user of the quiz app.

4.3 General Motivation

The items of the value-expectancy model were collected twice. Firstly with regard to the course in particular and secondly with regard to the study program in general. Both item sets were included in Q 1 at the beginning and in Q 4 at the end of the study. For the items that contribute to motivation (intrinsic values, usefulness and importance) comparatively [33] high values were measured (see Fig. 2). The results confirm the observation that the students of the Civil Engineering study program are generally highly motivated. Decreasing values at the end of the course (Q 4) are in accordance with the literature [33]. Overall, there seems to be hardly any lack of general motivation.

4.4 Current Motivation (QCM)

The results of the QCM (see Table 2) show high values for the categories *Probability of success* and *Anxiety*. Category values of *Challenge* and *Interest* can be considered as good. Noteworthy is the comparison with the values from a previous study [27]: in the previous study, values of *Challenge* and *Interest* were on average one point lower, while *Probability of success* was determined more than one point lower. At the same time, very low values of *Fear of failure* were measured. The values were probably too low to spur students on to more activities. The generally lower standard deviations measured in this study may indicate a higher acceptance of the rather soberly designed quiz app compared to the comic style of the app used in the previous study. Taken together, the results of the QCM are consistent with the degrees of usage of both apps: In this study, a very high usage was observed, while the app of the former study was used only sporadically.

Table 2. QCM Categories: Mean values (5-point Likert scale)

Category	Q 1 (N = 14) $\bar{x}$ (s)	Comparison (N = 16) [27] $\bar{x}$ (s)
Challenge	3.41 (1.06)	2.29 (1.20)
Interest	3.51 (1.15)	2.56 (1.28)
Probability of success	4.32 (0.72)	3.00 (1.52)
Anxiety	2.37 (1.29)	1.75 (1.25)

4.5 EGameFlow

The EGameFlow categories (see Fig. 3) show values that are within the range of comparison values. Higher values indicate higher game enjoyment. In the category *Social Interaction* the quiz app has by far the best value, in the category *Knowledge Improvement* it also has the best value, only in the category *Feedback* the quiz app received the worst value. The high value of *Social Interaction* could be caused by the game mechanics of matches against fellow students. Improving knowledge can be perceived by the students through the feeling of success of answering recurring questions. The low value of *Feedback* could be due to the lack of absolute feedback for the student to master a knowledge area. Instead, answering a question correctly can be followed by answering the question incorrectly again, raising doubts in the student about learning progress. Assuming that the comparison values are to be regarded as typical, the quiz app achieved good values for game enjoyment.

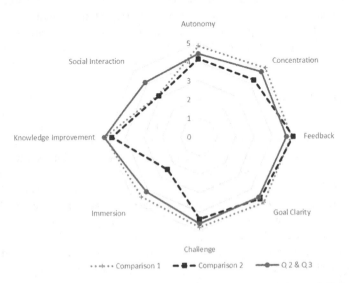

Fig. 3. EGameFlow: Category values (Comparison 1: [35], mean values of all four studies, comparison 2: [36])

4.6   Further Results

Q 4 included items for a final assessment of the quiz app. In particular, students were asked for their main motivational elements to use the app (see Table 3). As expected, the main motivational element was the preparation for the assessment tests. Not so expected was gaming enjoyment as the second highest rated motivational element. The group incentive received higher approval than the individual incentives (free tickets). This corresponds to the respective effect: while the mock exams benefited each participant, it turned out that - with one exception - the free tickets had no effect. The lowest approval was given to typical gamification elements: competition and ranking lists.

Table 3. Students' ratings of motivational elements (5-point Likert scale)

Motivational aspect	Rating
Ranking lists	2.5
Competition	2.5
Individual incentives (free tickets)	2.5
Group incentives (mock exams)	3.8
Training for admission tests	4.2
Gaming enjoyment	4.2
Pleasant feeling of learning work done	3.5
Common activity with fellow students	2.2
Alternative learning source to lecture script	3.0

5   Discussion

The case study of a twofold gamification approach described here shows many positive results. However, there are also findings that have to be considered in the further development of the didactic context. For example, the guided interviews pointed to rivalries for a top position in the ranking lists. A few students complained that matches were deliberately abandoned when the opponent no longer had a chance of winning. Although, competitions had a reoccurring motivating effect, competition between students did not have a community-building effect. In general, competition as design element of the didactic context should be investigated further, as the literature cannot provide clear guidance either (e.g., [37]). Furthermore, the students rated the questions as not necessarily relevant for the final test. However, this should not be seen as a problem of the gamification approach. Rather, the differences in content between lectures and final test - which are prepared in additional exercises - are reflected. A solution to this problem can also be achieved by another effect: the multiple-choice questions referred to factual knowledge. A recent study shows that the retrieval of procedural knowledge leads to higher learning effects [38]. Since the majority of the learning objectives of the course considered here are aimed at procedural knowledge, an adaptation of the questions should be considered.

Formally, the number of 14 students is too small to make representative statements. The given statistics are only of partial meaningfulness, even if the values appear reasonable compared to the comparative values. In order to increase the number of subjects, the study will be repeated in the same design in the winter semester 2019. Also, worth mentioning is the high proportion of almost 50% of students in the consecutive Master's program, who had to take the course as a compulsory subject. Experience has shown that these students are comparatively high motivated. On the other hand, motivation achievable through game mechanics decreases with increasing age of students [26]. This has already been observed in one of the earlier studies [24]. To simplify matters, it is therefore assumed that the two opposite effects outweigh each other.

Certainly, many elements of the didactic context such as ranking lists, matches and incentives have already been described on their own before. However, the results of the didactic context in its entirety may be seen as empirical confirmation of the theoretical foundations.

6 Conclusions

Overall, the case study shows a successful use of a quiz app in a demanding didactic context. Based on high general motivation, the included learning tasks were approached with an equally high engagement. The high level of the motivation is underlined by the noteworthy engagement - measured by the number of questions answered - of the students. The high level of engagement was achieved on the one hand with the game enjoyment of the quiz app leading especially to social interaction and knowledge improvement. On the other hand, the gamification of the didactic context contributed to the engagement, too. As main elements of gamification can be named the free choice to use the quiz app and the individual and group incentives. Nevertheless, there is further need for optimization, which concerns among other things the knowledge areas of the questions (i.e. extension to procedural knowledge) as well as the regulation of the competition thinking of individual students. It must also be clarified to what extent the didactic context can be transferred to other subject areas and how the didactic context works as a recurring element in several courses of the study program. In summary, the case study is an example of the successful combination of didactic context and gamification with the aim of increasing engagement and the means of assigning gamification elements with real-world significance. Since core elements of the course have been affected, the term *deep gamification* is applicable. Further research with the aim of a systematic overview of the manifestations and effects of deep gamification in higher education would increase the impact of deep gamification as powerful approach to design didactic contexts.

References

1. Deterding, S., Dixon, D., Khaled, R., Nacke, L.: From game design elements to gamefulness: defining gamification. In: Proceedings of the 15th International Academic MindTrek Conference: Envisioning Future Media Environments, pp. 9–15. ACM, New York (2011)
2. Hanus, M.D., Cruz, C.: Leveling up the classroom. In: Gamification in Education, pp. 583–610. IGI Global
3. Marczewski, A.: Defining gamification – what do people really think? https://www.gamified.uk/2014/04/16/defining-gamification-people-really-think/
4. Santos, P.A.: Deep gamification of a university course. In: Conference Proceedings SciTecIN 2015 Sciences and Technologies of Interaction 12–13 November 2015 Coimbra, Portugal. Departamento de Engenharia Electrotécnica Polo II da Universidade de Coimbra (2015)
5. Marczewski, A.: Thin Layer vs Deep Level Gamification. https://www.gamified.uk/2013/12/23/thin-layer-vs-deep-level-gamification/

6. Lees-Czerkawski, C.: Applying Game Design to a Medical Study Aid. http://www. gamasutra.com/blogs/CharlesLeesCzerkawski/20120118/9261/Applying_Game_Design_to_ a_Medical_Study_Aid.php
7. Bellotti, F., et al.: A gamified short course for promoting entrepreneurship among ICT engineering students. Proceedings - 2013 IEEE 13th International Conference on Advanced Learning Technologies. ICALT 2013, pp. 31–32 (2013)
8. Haladyna, T.M., Rodriguez, M.C.: Developing and Validating Test Items. Routledge, New York (2013)
9. Thor, A., Pengel, N., Wollersheim, H.: Digitalisierte Hochschuldidaktik: Qualitätssicherung von Prüfungen mit dem E-Assessment-Literacy-Tool EAs.LiT [Digitized university didactics: Quality assurance of examinations with the E-Assessment-Literacy-Tool EAs. LiT]. In: Igel, C., et al. (eds.) Bildungsräume 2017, pp. 179–184. Gesellschaft für Informatik, Bonn (2017)
10. Agarwal, P.K., Karpicke, J.D., Kang, S.H.K., Roediger, H.L., McDermott, K.B.: Examining the testing effect with open- and closed-book tests. Appl. Cogn. Psychol. **22**, 861–876 (2008)
11. Wiklund-Hörnqvist, C., Jonsson, B., Nyberg, L.: Strengthening concept learning by repeated testing. Scand. J. Psychol. **55**, 10–16 (2013)
12. Wiklund-Hörnqvist, C., Andersson, M., Jonsson, B., Nyberg, L.: Neural activations associated with feedback and retrieval success. NPJ Sci. Learn. **2**, 12 (2017)
13. Larsen, D., Butler, A.C.: Test-enhanced learning. In: Walsh, K. (ed.) Oxford Textbook of Medical Education, pp. 443–452. Oxford University Press, Oxford (2013)
14. Söbke, H.: Space for seriousness? In: Chorianopoulos, K., Divitini, M., Hauge, J.B., Jaccheri, L., Malaka, R. (eds.) ICEC 2015. LNCS, vol. 9353, pp. 482–489. Springer, Cham (2015). https://doi.org/10.1007/978-3-319-24589-8_44
15. Socrative.com: Socrative, http://www.socrative.com
16. Quizlet LLC: Simple free learning tools for students and teachers | Quizlet. http://quizlet. com/
17. Quitch.: Quitch - Learning at your fingertips. https://www.quitch.com/
18. Roppelt, B.: Gamification in der Hochschullehre durch eine Quiz-App [Gamification in university teaching using a quiz app] (2014)
19. Ferreira, A., Pereira, E., Anacleto, J., Carvalho, A., Carelli, I.: The common sense-based educational quiz game framework "what is it?" In: Proceedings of the VIII Brazilian Symposium on Human Factors in Computing Systems. pp. 338–339. Sociedade Brasileira de Computação, Porto Alegre, Brazil, Brazil (2008)
20. McClean, S.: Implementing PeerWise to engage students in collaborative learning. Perspect. Pedagog. Pract. **6**, 89–96 (2015)
21. Pechenkina, E., Laurence, D., Oates, G., Eldridge, D., Hunter, D.: Using a gamified mobile app to increase student engagement, retention and academic achievement. Int. J. Educ. Technol. High. Educ. **14**, 31 (2017)
22. McDaniel, M.A., Agarwal, P.K., Huelser, B.J., McDermott, K.B., Roediger, H.L.: Test-enhanced learning in a middle school science classroom: The effects of quiz frequency and placement. J. Educ. Psychol. **103**, 399–414 (2011)
23. Söbke, H., Weitze, L.: The challenge to nurture challenge. In: Wallner, G., Kriglstein, S., Hlavacs, H., Malaka, R., Lugmayr, A., Yang, H.-S. (eds.) ICEC 2016. LNCS, vol. 9926, pp. 15–23. Springer, Cham (2016). https://doi.org/10.1007/978-3-319-46100-7_2
24. Weitze, L., Söbke, H.: Quizzing to become an engineer - a commercial quiz app in higher education. In: Pixel (ed.) Conference Proceeding. New Perspectives in Scienze Education, 5th edn., Florence, pp. 225–230. Libreriauniversitaria it Edizioni (2016)

25. Söbke, H., Weitze, L.: Students' choices. In: Dias, J., Santos, P.A., Veltkamp, R.C. (eds.) GALA 2017. LNCS, vol. 10653, pp. 105–114. Springer, Cham (2017). https://doi.org/10. 1007/978-3-319-71940-5_10

26. Koivisto, J., Hamari, J.: Demographic differences in perceived benefits from gamification. Comput. Hum. Behav. **35**, 179–188 (2014)

27. Söbke, H., Reichelt, M.: Sewer Rats in Teaching Action: An explorative field study on students' perception of a game-based learning app in graduate engineering education. CoRR. abs/1811.0 (2018)

28. IT Finanzmagazin: Quiz-App – Wissenszuwachs durch Gamification: Wüstenrot qualifiziert 1.400 Außendienstler [Quiz App - Gamification increases knowledge: Wüstenrot qualifies 1,400 sales representatives] (2016)

29. FEO Media AB: QuizClash | Challenge your friends! http://www.quizclash-game.com/

30. Eccles, J.S., Adler, T.F., Futterman, R., Goff, S.B., Kaczala, C.M., Meece, J.L., et al.: Expectancies, values, and academic behaviors. In: Spence, J.T. (ed.) Achievement and achievement motives, pp. 75–146. Freeman, San Francisco (1983)

31. Wigfield, A., Eccles, J.S.: Expectancy – value theory of achievement motivation. Contemp. Educ. Psychol. **25**, 68–81 (2000)

32. Steinmayr, R., Spinath, B.: Konstruktion und erste Validierung einer Skala zur erfassung subjektiver Schulischer Werte (SESSW) [Construction and first validation of a scale for the recording of subjective school values]. Diagnostica **56**, 195–211 (2010)

33. Seifried, E., Kriegbaum, K., Spinath, B.: Veränderung der veranstaltungsbezogenen Motivation über ein Semester und die Rolle von veranstaltungsbezogenen Erwartungen [Change in course-related motivation over a semester and the role of course-related expectations.]. In: Seifried, E. and Spinath, B. (eds.) paepsy 2017 11. - 14. 9. in Münster - Arbeitsgruppe Motivation im Hochschulkontext: Entwicklung und beeinflussende Faktoren (2017)

34. Rheinberg, F., Vollmeyer, R., Burns, B.D.: QCM: a questionnaire to assess current motivation in learning situations. Diagnostica **47**, 57–66 (2001)

35. Fu, F.L., Su, R.C., Yu, S.C.: EGameFlow: a scale to measure learners' enjoyment of e-learning games. Comput. Educ. **52**, 101–112 (2009)

36. Eckardt, L., Pilak, A., Löhr, M., van Treel, P., Rau, J., Robra-Bissantz, S.: Empirische Untersuchung des EGameFlow eines Serious Games zur Verbesserung des Lernerfolgs [Empirical investigation of the EGameFlow of a serious game to improve learning success]. In: Bildungsräume 2017, pp. 285–296. Gesellschaft für Informatik, Bonn (2017)

37. Nebel, S., Schneider, S., Rey, G.D.: From duels to classroom competition: social competition and learning in educational videogames within different group sizes. Comput. Hum. Behav. **55**, 384–398 (2016)

38. Agarwal, P.K.: Retrieval practice & Bloom's taxonomy: Do students need fact knowledge before higher order learning? J. Educ. Psychol. (2018). https://doi.org/10.1037/edu0000282

Introducing NarRob, a Robotic Storyteller

Agnese Augello$^{(\boxtimes)}$, Ignazio Infantino, Umberto Maniscalco, Giovanni Pilato, and Filippo Vella

ICAR-CNR, Via Ugo La Malfa 153, 90146 Palermo, Italy
{agnese.augello,ignazio.infantino,umberto.maniscalco,
giovanni.pilato,filippo.vella}@icar.cnr.it

Abstract. In this work we introduce NarRob, a robot able to engage in conversations and tell stories, by accompanying the speech with proper gestures. We discuss about the main components of the robot's architecture, and some possible education experiments that we are planning to carry out in real scholastic contexts.

Keywords: Storytelling · Social robots · Chatbots · Social practices

1 Introduction

Nowadays, the use of robots in schools is increasing and their employment can lead to several advantages: they can operate as smart teaching platforms, assistants, or co-learners [1]. They represent attractive and amusing tools, capable of catching the attention of the students, while supporting the teacher in the learning activities. At the same time, the benefits coming from storytelling are well known, it contributes to improving students expertise, listening and reflection skills social awareness and also to increase their emotional vocabulary [2–4]. Several robotic storytellers [5,6] have been proposed to support the learning process of pupils and many studies have been conducted to analyze the perceptions of robots during this activity as well as the effects on students learning. In [7] the effectiveness of social robots employed in interactive, narrative tasks has been analyzed. The experiments were focused on measuring story recall and emotional interpretation of students, comparing single vs. group students - robot interaction. In that case the robot acted as an interactive puppet. The ability to process the semantic content of a story enriching the speech with proper gestures is essential in the storytelling process to add a proper expressiveness to the narration avoiding a trivial text reading.

The expressiveness and the ability to show emotions is basilar to obtain more engagement [8]. As an example, in [9] it is analyzed the use of bodily expressions in robots to facilitate a mood induction process of the story and to improve the storytelling experience.

In this work we introduce a storytelling robot, that we named NarRob, able to interact with users and telling stories, designing possible activities to perform in

M. Gentile et al. (Eds.): GALA 2018, LNCS 11385, pp. 387–396, 2019.
https://doi.org/10.1007/978-3-030-11548-7_36

classrooms. The work describes the main components at the basis of the robot's behaviour, aimed at providing a more active role to the robot in storytelling, with respect to a common use of robots as passive tools in educational contexts.

The proposed architecture allows the robot to manage the activity by interacting verbally with the student, adapting his expressions according to the semantic and emotional contents of the stories. The architectural choices are supported by previous investigations [10] on which behavioural features contribute to a greater perception of expressiveness in the well known Pepper Aldebaran robotic platform[1]. The work is motivated by the belief that a greater autonomy of the robot and its expressiveness adaptation could have more impact on the learning process of the students as explained in the planning of the learning activities. After a description of the system architecture (Sect. 2), two possible educational experiments that we are planning to carry out in real scholastic contexts will be discussed (Sect. 3).

2   NarRob Architecture

NarRob has the ability to analyze the content of a story and associate meaningful gestures and expressions to the verbal content. It is endowed with a repository of stories, together with some basilar knowledge about them, such as the structure, the author, the genre, the main characters. This knowledge, formalized in an ontology, is exploited by a chatbot module. It is also endowed with a repository of gestures, acquired by a direct observation of the same gestures, performed by humans.

The core of the NarRob architecture, depicted in Fig. 1, is the chatbot module that allows him to converse with users during the storytelling activity and, if necessary, to extract the information stored into the ontology. The *Words To Expression* component, is used by the robot to examine the text of a story in order to extract some important concepts that can be emphasized by using not-verbal, communicative signs, such as gestures or emotional expressions. The *Gestures Acquisition* component is used to learn, by observation, a set of gestures to use during the storytelling, while the *Gestures Synchronization* component allows the robot to synchronize the gestures selected by the *Words To Expression* component with the text of the story. We use the Aldebarans Pepper robot as robotic platform. Pepper is equipped with a tablet that is particularly suitable for the storytelling activity, since it can be used to show contents such as some images correlated to the story and the concepts that the students can learn or consolidate through this activity. The components of the architecture are described in the following sections.

2.1   Chatbot Module

The robot exploits a chatbot module to interact with the user, structuring the storytelling practice according to three main phases. In a first phase, the robot

---

[1] https://www.softbankrobotics.com/emea/en/robots/pepper.

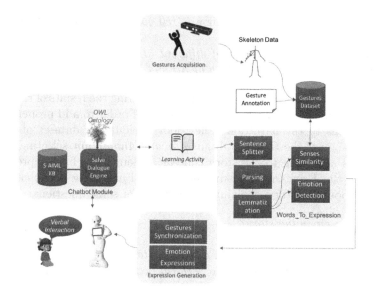

Fig. 1. NarRob architecture

can receive a specific request among a set of possible stories for the current activity, or it can pro-actively select the story by using some information acquired during the dialogue (for example the preferences of the student about literature genres or the category of stories best suited for the user age). In this phase, it can also give brief explanation about the main genres, and the structures characterizing the stories. In a second phase, the robot narrates the story, and finally, there is a questions/answers phase, used to evaluate the competence of the students.

The chatbot module is implemented by using the SALVE framework [11]. The framework relies on a KB described by an enhanced AIML mark-up language, called S-AIML, and a rule engine, allowing for the interpretation of events and the interaction management according to typical practices of interaction. According to the conversation, the robot can query the ontology to obtain specific information; in particular an OWL[2] ontology has been created to formalize the main concepts related to the storytelling domain, such as literature genres (e.g. fantasy, epic, adventure, ...), and age categories and information about the stories, such as the historical period, the form (poetry or prose, ...), the presence of a message, the main characters, the author and so on.

The chatbot uses the ontology to personalize the answers according to the story and to check the correctness of students answers to specific questions. In what follows, we report an example of interaction with the robot. In a first phase the robot acquires information to profile the user, and, as a consequence, select a story.

---

[2] W3C Web Ontology Language (OWL).

R: Hi I am NaoRobot and I am here to tell you a story. How old are you?
User: Ten
NarRob: I know many stories of different literary genres. I bet that you like fantasy. I'll tell you the story of Ali and the magic carpet.

After this phase, the robot tells the story, exploiting the results of the analysis performed by the *Words To Expression* module in order to add proper gestures and expressions to the narration. The robot exploits the dataset of gestures, created by means of the *Gestures Acquisition and Annotation*, selecting the most suitable ones according to the story content, generating a final expressiveness by means of the *Expression Generation* module. Finally, the robot can start a discussion about the story, explaining it and ask for some questions.

R: Did you enjoy the story?
User: Yes
NarRob: As you should know, in a fantasy story there is a magic element that allows the main character to perform extraordinary actions. What is the magic element in this story?
User: The carpet. NarRob: What kind of emotion was felt by the main character at the end of the story?
User: Joy.

2.2   Gestures Acquisition and Annotation

We have created a dataset of gestures by observing human movements with a standard RGB-D device. Relying on the gestures classification introduced by McNeill [12], we consider *iconic* and *metaphoric* gestures, focusing on the description of concrete actions or abstract ideas. A Kinect camera is used to capture the skeleton of humans performing the selected gestures during several repetitions of the same dynamic posture. The human tracked skeleton, allow us to have the three-dimensional position of each relevant joint, and to compute the corresponding robot's joints angles. The gestures are normalized to have a predefined duration interval and manually annotated according to their particular meaning.

2.3   Words to Expression

This module operates in two main phases. In the first, it detects the verbs that are best candidates to be translated in a gesture, by segmenting the text in sentences, parsing each sentence to detect the verbs and finds their lemmas. In the second phase, the detected words are compared with the annotations of the gestures according to a semantic similarity. In particular, it is obtained a score $s \in [0,1]$ by computing the shortest path linking two senses in the WordNet "is-a" taxonomy [13]. For the sake of simplicity we have just considered the most frequent sense for each lemma. If the semantic similarity is below a given threshold T_{sim}, whose value is experimentally determined, the verb is ignored and no specific gesture is performed by the robot. Otherwise, it is executed the action corresponding to the highest similarity between the detected verb in the sentence and that one present in the list of actions that can be performed by the robot. If the highest value is associated with two or more actions, a random choice process is executed.

Moreover, an emotion detection module presented in [14], is used to detect if there is a basic emotion related to that particular chunk of text that is being expressed.

The module has an effect on robot's communicative channels that can be easily correlated by a human observer to some emotions, such as the color of its LEDs, the speed of its speech, and the head inclination [15–17]. This adaptive talking behaviour is managed by the *Emotion Expression* component of the *Expression Generation* module. For the emotional labeling, we have considered the six Ekman basic emotions: *anger, disgust, fear, joy, sadness* and *surprise*, exploiting a well known lexicon derived from the Word-Net Affect Lexicon [18] and applying the procedure that has been introduced in [14], which is briefly summed-up below.

The emotion detection is based on the Latent Semantic Analysis (LSA) [19] paradigm and it is based on the assumption that any text chunk d can be coded as a point in a Data Driven "conceptual" space, by computing a vector $\mathbf{d}$ whose i-th component is the number of times the i-th word of the vocabulary appears in d. The vector $\mathbf{d}$ is therefore mapped into a reduced-dimensionality "conceptual" space induced by LSA.

At the same time, the emotional lexicon has been used to create a set of emotionally related subset of words leading to a cloud of about 3300 vectors acting as "beacons" that have been used to map a text from the conceptual space to the emotional space.

In particular, we have six sets $E_{anger}, E_{disgust}, \cdots, E_{surprise}$ of vectors constituting the sub-symbolic coding of each one of the aforementioned subsets of words identifying a basic emotion. The generic vector belonging to one of the sets is mapped in the same "conceptual" space as well as any sentence s of the story that has to be told.

Once the sentence s is mapped into the "conceptual" space, it is possible to compute its emotional fingerprint as reported in [14] by exploiting the vectors which are associated to each one of the six E_i sets.

The emotional space is a six-dimensional hypersphere where all the sentences are mapped, and each region of this hypersphere is associated to a set of emotional manifestation of the robot.

The element of the emotional fingerprint of s having the highest value determines the main emotion expressed by the sentence. A minimum value of threshold $Th_e \in [0, 1]$ is experimentally fixed in order to determine neutral sentences.

2.4   Expression Generation

Gestures Synchronization. To synchronize the movement execution with the pronunciation of the corresponding verb we consider the synchronization schema depicted in Fig. 2. For the sake of simplicity, we avoid overlapping situations (see for example the second row of Fig. 2), and the execution of a new movement starts only if the previous one is completed (as in the third row of Fig. 2).

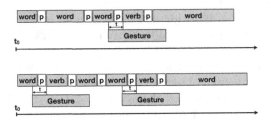

Fig. 2. Two different situations: a single verb with a single movement and two verbs not overlapped movements.

To manage this situation, if there are two verbs with two associated gestures, and the duration of the first movement lasts so long that it overlaps with the beginning of the second movement, only the first movement is executed; otherwise both the movements are accomplished by the robot. To synchronize a movement with an associated verb which is pronounced by the robot, we compute the timing of the speech and the starting of the associated action at the desired moment. Let d_{wi} be the duration of the i-th word in the sentence, d_{vi} be the duration of the i-th verb, d_{mi} be the duration of the i-th movement and p be the length of the silence between two words the start time t_{vi_s} of the word in the speech time-line can be obtained as:

$$t_{v_s} = \sum_{i=1}^{N} d_{wi} + N * p \tag{1}$$

where N is the number of words that precede the verb. The end time of the verb is

$$t_{v_e} = t_{v_s} + d_v \tag{2}$$

Starting from these considerations, different synchronization hypotheses can be made:

- the movement begins together with the starting time of the verb and then $t_{m_s} = t_{v_s} = \sum_{i=1}^{N} d_{wi} + N * p$;
- the movement ends with the ending time of the verb and then $t_{m_s} = t_{v_e} - d_m$;
- the movement is centered with the duration of the verb and then $t_{m_s} = t_{v_s} + \frac{t_{v_e} + t_{v_s}}{2}$;
- the movement starts a time δ before/after the starting time of the verb and then $t_{m_s} = t_{v_s} - \delta$.

Each one of the previous solutions could be considered a valid alternative to synchronize a gesture with the corresponding verb, but there is a solution that produces results more realistic and similar to what happens in human beings. The movement execution anticipates by 0.3 s the verb pronunciation, since it has been shown that the mean of the distribution of the starting times of gestures with respect to the word to which they refer is about -0.3 s [20].

Emotion Expression. The emotion detected by the *Words To Expression* module is here exploited to affect the robot's communicative behaviour. This component relies on three sub-modules, an Eyes Lighting Controller that converts the emotion into a facial expression, specifying the color and the intensity of each eye LEDs, a Speech Synthesizer that tunes voice parameters, such as pitch and speech rate, according to the emotion, and a Gestures Generator that generated a body expression by changing the postures of arms, hands and head. A detailed description of these modules can be found in [10].

3 Planning of a Real Experimentation in Learning Contexts

In the previous sections, we have summarized the main modules at the heart of the NarRob architecture. The premises were that (1) an adaptation of the behaviour to what is said by the robot can be perceived as a greater expressiveness and (2) the more expressiveness will have a robotics storyteller, the more effective could be in educational storytelling.

The first point is supported by a previous evaluation [10] of the expressiveness of a Pepper robot obtained adapting the robot's gestures, voice intonation and eyes color according to the emotional content of the text. With respect to the [10] implementation, we substituted the emotion detection module considering the approach described in Sect. 2.3 to detect the six basic Ekman emotions [14]. Currently, we are testing the basic abilities of NarRob on a collection of short stories retrieved on some websites of stories and learning activities for kids[3].

In a in-progress study, similar to the work reported in [10], we are checking if the NarRob is able to associate meaningful gestures to stories, as well to change the expressions according to the emotions detected in the text. Table 1 reports some examples of how the emotions and actions are associated with the first sentences of the famous story *Ali and the magic Carpet*.

For what concerns the second point of the list, it will be evaluated after an experimentation in a real settings with students of primary schools. We will focus on students aged between seven and nine years, in order to test the system with children who are old enough to avoid the issues related to the language comprehension and who, at the same time, can still find engaging the storytelling activities. In what follows, we discuss two possible learning activities, taking

---

[3] http://www.english-for-students.com/Short-Moral-Stories-for-Kids.html
http://learnenglishkids.britishcouncil.org/en/.

Table 1. Emotions and gestures associated to some sentences of a story

Sentence	Emotion	Gesture
One very hot day Ali finds a carpet in his uncle's shop	Joy	to_find
'What's this?' Suddenly the carpet jumps!	Surprise	no_action
It moves and flies off into the air	Fear	to_go, to_fly
'Hey!'	Joy	no_action

inspiration from the suggestions discussed in [2], aimed respectively to improve social awareness and the emotional vocabulary of children.

Our research design will have the goal to verify whether the enrichment of the robot's behavior and storytelling with the gestures and expressions produced by the system have a significant impact on the educational objectives of the two activities. To this end, the story narration will be performed by the robot in two conditions; in the former, the features introduced in previous paragraphs will be disabled, while in the latter the system will work in its complete configuration. After the story narration, a specific evaluation phase for each learning activity will be carried out.

3.1 Storytelling to Improve Social Skills

The storytelling can be finalized at the improvement of the students social skills and social awareness. For such an aim, it will be planned an activity loosely inspired to the concept of social story, introduced by Carol Gray to help people with autism spectrum disorders (ASD) to develop a greater social understanding [21]. Such activity can be performed by the robot to introduce social situations that could be complex for a child, simplify their understanding with the help of the narration. In this activity, the robot can exploit the information organized in his knowledge about social practices, routinized behaviors typically and habitually performed by people, that determine their purposes, expectations and behavior [11]. By relying on such a model of social practice, the robot, through the storytelling activity, can teach kids to manage the social context in a more efficient way, explaining information about what is happening in the story, who is involved and with which role, what is important to do in the different circumstances. The story can evolve according to the choices of the kids, in order to better show what happens when the expectations of the characters are not confirmed, focusing on the emotions of the characters during the evolution of the story. Then, after the storytelling, the robot will interact with the student to test the social awareness of the student about the situations described in the story using the same approach proposed by the Revised Behavioral Assertiveness Test for Children (BAT-RC) [22]. Another factor that could be investigated is the use of the Pepper tablet to show animations related to the story; the hypothesis is that it can further improve the learning of concepts and the attention of the children [23].

3.2   Improving the Emotional Vocabulary

This activity is based on another suggestion of [2], about the possibility to build and improve the emotion vocabulary of a kid. After the narration of a story with a rich emotional content, the robot will ask to the student some questions aimed at the evaluation of a correct differentiation about the emotions in the story. This interaction will be supported by the tablet of the robot. In particular, a set of cards related to the main emotions will be shown on the tablet and the robot will ask the kid to select a card related to the emotion that a specific character has felt in a particular situation of the story. When the kid selects a card, other cards will be shown on the tablet, and the robot will ask the students to select other cards that can be related to the main emotion of the character. The choices of the kid are analyzed and evaluated during the cards game, and, after the evaluation, the robot will show the cards grouped according to their emotional family, so to enrich the vocabulary of the student.

4   Conclusion and Future Works

In this work, we presented NarRob, a social robot that can collaborate with teachers in storytelling activities with the aim of improving the emotional and social skills of students. The robot has the abilities to analyze the text of a story in order to detect some emotional content and to associate gestures and expression to the narration. The aim is to obtain a not predefined, engaging and entertaining narration with any type of text. Future works will regard a concrete evaluation of the system by performing a experimentation with a group of students.

References

1. Pandey, A.K., Gelin, R.: Humanoid robots in education: a short review. In: Goswami, A., Vadakkepat, P. (eds.) Humanoid Robotics: A Reference, pp. 1–16. Springer, Dordrecht (2016). https://doi.org/10.1007/978-94-007-7194-9_113-1
2. Eades, J.: Classroom Tales: Using Storytelling to Build Emotional, Social and Academic Skills Across the Primary Curriculum. Jessica Kingsley Publishers, London (2005)
3. Smeda, N., Dakich, E., Sharda, N.: The effectiveness of digital storytelling in the classrooms: a comprehensive study. Smart Learn. Environ. 1, 6 (2014)
4. Jenkins, M., Lonsdale, J.: Evaluating the effectiveness of digital storytelling for student reflection. In: ICT: Providing Choices for Learners and Learning. Proceedings ASCILITE Singapore (2007)
5. Mutlu, B., Forlizzi, J., Hodgins, J.: A storytelling robot: modeling and evaluation of human-like gaze behavior. In: 2006 6th IEEE-RAS International Conference on Humanoid Robots, pp. 518–523, December 2006

6. Kory, J., Breazeal, C.: Storytelling with robots: learning companions for preschool children's language development. In: The 23rd IEEE International Symposium on Robot and Human Interactive Communication, pp. 643–648, August 2014

7. Leite, I., et al.: Narratives with robots: the impact of interaction context and individual differences on story recall and emotional understanding. Front. Robot. AI **4**, 29 (2017)

8. Striepe, H., Lugrin, B.: There once was a robot storyteller: measuring the effects of emotion and non-verbal behaviour. In: Kheddar, A., et al. (eds.) ICSR 2017. LNCS, vol. 10652, pp. 126–136. Springer, Cham (2017). https://doi.org/10.1007/978-3-319-70022-9_13

9. Xu, J., Broekens, J., Hindriks, K., Neerincx, M.A.: Effects of a robotic storyteller's moody gestures on storytelling perception. In: 2015 International Conference on Affective Computing and Intelligent Interaction (ACII), pp. 449–455. IEEE (2015)

10. Rodriguez, I., Manfré, A., Vella, F., Infantino, I., Lazkano, E.: Talking with sentiment: adaptive expression generation behavior for social robots. In: The 19th International Workshop of Physical Agents (WAF) (2018)

11. Augello, A., Gentile, M., Dignum, F.: Social agents for learning in virtual environments. In: Bottino, R., Jeuring, J., Veltkamp, R.C. (eds.) GALA 2016. LNCS, vol. 10056, pp. 133–143. Springer, Cham (2016). https://doi.org/10.1007/978-3-319-50182-6_12

12. McNeill, D.: Hand and Mind: What Gestures Reveal About Thought. University of Chicago Press, Chicago (1992)

13. Lingling, M., Runqing, H., Junzhong, G.: A review of semantic similarity measures in wordnet. Int. J. Hybrid Inf. Technol. **6**(1), 1–12 (2013)

14. Pilato, G., DAvanzo, E.: Data-driven social mood analysis through the conceptualization of emotional fingerprints. Proc. Comput. Sci. **123**, 360–365 (2018). 8th Annual International Conference on Biologically Inspired Cognitive Architectures, BICA 2017 (Eighth Annual Meeting of the BICA Society), held August 1–6, 2017 in Moscow, Russia

15. Feldmaier, J., Marmat, T., Kuhn, J., Diepold, K.: Evaluation of a RGB-LED-based emotion display for affective agents, arXiv preprint arXiv:1612.07303 (2016)

16. Johnson, D.O., Cuijpers, R.H., van der Pol, D.: Imitating human emotions with artificial facial expressions. Int. J. Soc. Robot. **5**(4), 503–513 (2013)

17. Bänziger, T., Scherer, K.R.: The role of intonation in emotional expressions. Speech Commun. **46**(3), 252–267 (2005)

18. Strapparava, C., Mihalcea, R.: Learning to identify emotions in text. In: Proceedings of the 2008 ACM Symposium on Applied Computing, SAC 2008, pp. 1556–1560. ACM, New York (2008)

19. Landauer, T.K., Foltz, P.W., Laham, D.: An introduction to latent semantic analysis. Discourse Process. **25**(2–3), 259–284 (1998)

20. Holzapfel, H., Nickel, K., Stiefelhagen, R.: Implementation and evaluation of a constraint-based multimodal fusion system for speech and 3D pointing gestures, January 2004

21. Gray, C.: The New Social Story Book. Future Horizons, Arlington (2000)

22. Ollendick, T.H., Hart, K.J., Francis, G.: Social validation of the revised behavioral assertiveness test for children (BAT-CR). Child Fam. Behav. Ther. **7**(1), 17–34 (1985)

23. Ayala, A.: The animated stories for autism. Ph.D. thesis, Division TEACCH University of North Carolina

CreaCube, a Playful Activity
with Modular Robotics

Margarida Romero[1(✉)], Dayle David[1(✉)], and Benjamin Lille[2(✉)]

[1] Laboratoire d'Innovation et Numérique pour l'Education,
Université Côte d'Azur, Nice, France
Margarida.Romero@unice.fr,
dayle.david@etu.univ-cotedazur.fr
[2] CRIRES, Université Laval, Quebec City, QC, Canada
Benjamin.Lille.1@ulaval.ca

Abstract. Programmable toys are blurring the lines between serious games and educational robotics solutions. In this study, the CreaCube activity is analysed using Cubelets modular robotics based on the Learning Mechanics and Game Mechanics (LMGM) framework. The CreaCube playful activity is used to analyse the creative problem-solving process through a playful activity made from interconnectable electronic cubes. The resolution of the CreaCube activity involves the manipulation and assembly of cubes to build a vehicle that moves independently from an initial point to a final point. After describing the Crea-Cube activity from the perspective of the LMGM framework, the discussion is developed in relation to creative problem solving.

1 Introduction

Gaming technologies have evolved in many ways in the past few years. On one side, game platforms have evolved to allow users to be creators of some game components (game levels, characters and artefacts). On the other side, some gaming platforms such as the "make, play, discover" Nintendo LABO have introduced modules allowing the players to create artefacts, which combine maker education techniques [7, 9] with augmented and virtual reality. In this context, educational robotics has the potential to engage learners in a playful activity. This exploratory study analyses the potential of Cubelets modular robotics to engage learners in a playful activity and try to identify the different strategies of problem-solving adopted by the participants within a challenge named CreaCube.

2 Educational Robotics as a Playful Activity

Educational robotics (ER) is often discussed as a playful activity [5, 16] in which learners can manipulate tangible artefacts which provide (delayed) feedback on their actions. Moreover, some educational robots are described as having a "playful appearance" [11: 99]. Educational Robotics (ER) has been analysed within Digital game-based learning (DGBL) in various studies. Eguchi and Shen [8] analyse CoSpace

© Springer Nature Switzerland AG 2019
M. Gentile et al. (Eds.): GALA 2018, LNCS 11385, pp. 397–405, 2019.
https://doi.org/10.1007/978-3-030-11548-7_37

Educational Robotics from the perspective of the gaming experience, in particular, in terms of the flow state of the player [6] that is experienced when using this 3D simulation for educational robotics. When analysing the children-robot experience, Shahid, Krahmer and Swerts [14] observe they have more fun playing with a robot than playing alone, but still have more fun playing with other children than playing with a robot.

3   CreaCube, a Playful Activity with Modular Robotics

The CreaCube activity aims to engage the player in a playful challenge to evaluate his/her creative problem-solving skills. The player is exposed to unknown cubes which need to be explored to achieve the game's objective: create an autonomous vehicle reaching the finish point [13].

CreaCube activity has been designed as a game in which the player is engaged towards the objective of creating a vehicle able to move in an autonomous way from a starting red point to a finish black point. The game components are four modular robotic cubes, selected from the *Cubelets* set [3]. *Cubelets* are classified as build bots composed of modular parts [4]. Once the player has read the game rules, the robotic cubes are presented separately (not connected) in front of the player. The player should grasp the cubes and explore them to understand their features and advance and experiment different constructions to find a solution.

The game activity can be modelled as a finite-state machine between the different states of the CreaCube activity. The figure below introduces the CreaCube game states.

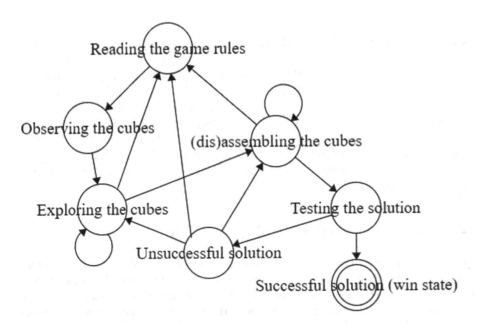

Fig. 1. CreaCube game activity as a finite-state machine.

The CreaCube activity is composed of a set of states and transitions, which are similar to those of the Escape Machine [15] and other "building objects-to-think-computationally-with" [15: 282] (Fig. 1).

3.1   CreaCube States of the Game

Reading the Game Rules. The CreaCube game rules are introduced to the player before introducing the game components. The CreaCube research facilitators give the player a paper containing the game rules and invites the player to read them and inform when (s)he is ready to start the CreaCube game (Fig. 2).

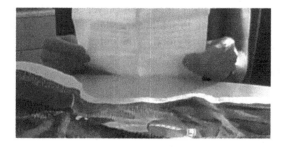

Fig. 2. A player reading the CreaCube game rules.

Providing hardcopy game rules helps the researchers to identify when the player is not sure of the objectives. When the player is unsure of the game rules, (s)he can grab the hardcopy to read them again. The game rules are the following: "You're invited to create a vehicle using four items. The vehicle should move in an autonomous way from the red point at your right to the black point at your left." In the next paragraph, it is made explicit that "You are not limited in time, but you can decide to stop the game at any moment" and "We cannot help you during the game".

Observing the Cubes. Once the player informs that (s)he is ready to play, the Crea-Cube research facilitator remove the cover of the cubes and the red point (right to the player) and the black point (at the left of the player). Once the cubes are made visible, the player observes them before grabbing them. While in some cases, the player takes time before grabbing the cubes, in other cases the player grabs the cubes very quickly. Therefore, the time it takes to observe (without manipulation) varies depending on the subject.

Exploring the Cubes. After the cubes are made available, the player can pick them up to further explore. In some cases, the exploration is made one cube at a time in a systematic way while in other cases, the exploration is less structured, and the subject takes more time with some of them. In this phase, some players identify the cube with the wheels (white cube), the cube with the battery (dark blue cube) and the cube with the sensors (black cube) (Fig. 3).

Fig. 3. A player starting to explore the cubes.

Assembly and Disassembly of the Cubes. The player assembles and takes apart the cubes to create a "vehicle" aiming to achieve the game objective of going from the red point to the black point. By (dis)assembling the cubes, the player has the potential to observe the effects of the different combinations of the cubes on the behaviour of the assembled modular robot.

Testing the Solution. The player has assembled four cubes and places (his/her/their) "vehicle" at the red point to test the solution. Based on the outcome of the solution, it is considered successful or unsuccessful.

Unsuccessful Solution. When the "vehicle" does not succeed in moving autonomously from the red point to the black point, the player should engage in other solutions by (dis)assembling the cubes into a new form.

Successful Solution or Win State. A solution is successful when the player has assembled the four cubes in a way (there are multiple solutions) that the cubes move autonomously from the red point to the black point (Fig. 4).

Fig. 4. A player found a solution to the CreaCube activity.

The first time a player succeeds in the CreaCube game, (s)he is invited to play again. The second attempt aims to identify at which point the player has learnt and reflects on the features of the cubes during the first attempt, but also, at which point (s)he attempts to solve the problem by creating a different solution or trying to reproduce exactly the first solution.

3.2 CreaCube Playful Activity

CreaCube game could be solved in different ways but is nearly impossible to solve at the first attempt when the player has never manipulated Cubelets modular robotics cubes before. Cubes exploration is required to ensure the player develops an understanding of the features of each cube and the relations between the cubes when connected. The CreaCube game requires the player to engage in creative exploration, trying to understand the role of each cube and develop a strategy to solve the game. These game learning and learning mechanics [1] are considered optimal to solve the game in a reflexive way, in which the player aims to understand the game and the features of the robotic cubes. Nevertheless, some players engage in trial-and-error behaviours, at different degrees of intensity and duration. To observe if players solve through trial-and-error or a developed understanding of their trials, the research facilitators ask them to play the CreaCube game twice. In the next section is introduced the analysis of the CreaCube activity under the lens of the Learning Mechanics and Game Mechanics (LMGM) framework [1].

4 The CreaCube Activity Under the Perspective of the Learning Mechanics and Game Mechanics (LMGM) Framework

The CreaCube game is constituted from the affordances of the Cubelets cubes chosen for the activity (battery, wheels, distance sensor and invertor), the game rules providing constraints, and a game objective to the player. The CreaCube play phase is the time when the player is interacting with the cubes in order to achieve the game objective. Through the play phase, the player is confronted by the intricacies of the mechanics and design of the CreaCube game rules and the Cubelets cubes affordances. The gaming experience is the way the CreaCube player feels during and after the play activity. While players report different degrees of difficulty and time duration to achieve the CreaCube activity, they report (spontaneously) the playfulness of the CreaCube activity. Next section analyses further CreaCube's mechanics according to the LMGM framework [1] in the next section.

4.1 Learning Mechanics and Game Mechanics (LMGM) Framework

According to Arnab and collaborators "overall, the Learning Mechanics and Game Mechanics (LMGM) model aims at providing a concise means to relate pedagogy intentions and ludic elements within a player's actions and gameplay" [1]. Game mechanics involve a certain degree of interaction between the player and the game artefact or other people involved in the game activity. Retroactivity is a key aspect of the game mechanics as a mechanism of interaction, allowing the learner to advance within the game [10]. The LMGM framework has been developed within the

NoE GALA and refined subsequently [12]. LMGM is organised around Bloom's thinking levels [2]. The table below also introduce the LMGM within the CreaCube activity (Fig. 5).

Game mechanics	Thinking skills level during CreaCube	Learning mechanics
Designing; Ownership; Status/Titles; Strategy/planning	**Creation:** The player engages into the creation of an "autonomous vehicle" which could be considered as a creative challenge because of the open-ended nature of the task in which the learner has different degrees of creative freedom to achieve a win state through different solutions. • Creation mechanics in CreaCube: *Planning and strategy*	*Accountability; Ownership; Planning; Responsibility*
Action points; Assessment; Collaboration; Communal discovery; Game turns; Pareto optimal; Resources management; Rewards/penalties; Urgent Optimism	**Evaluation:** Cubelets allows the player to evaluate the success of the solution when testing the built solution. As other educational robotics solutions, Cubelets allows the player to evaluate the success of the solution when testing the built solution. • Evaluation mechanics in CreaCube: *Hypothesis.*	*Assessment; Collaboration; Hypothesis; Incentive; External motivation; Reflect/Discuss*
Feedback; Meta-game; Realism	**Analysis:** The player should analyse the features of each of the cubes, but also the relation between the cubes when assembled. • Analysis mechanics in CreaCube: *Experimentation.*	*Analyse; Experimentation; Feedback; Identity; Observation; Shadowing*
Capture/Elimination; Competition; Cooperation; Movement; Progression; Selecting/Collecting; Simulate/Response; Time pressure	**Applying:** The player should use all the cubes to achieve the game objective. • Applying mechanics in CreaCube: *competition and time pressure* are experienced mostly by adult players despite the CreaCube activity is not designed for developing these mechanics.	*Action/Task; Competition; Cooperation Demonstration Imitation; Simulation*
Appointment; Cascading information Questions and answers Role-play; Tutorial	**Understanding:** The player should understand the game rules to achieve the game objective. However, the player does not have all the prior knowledge of the robotic cubes to solve the problem without going to the application/analysis/evaluation/creation levels.	*Objectivity; Participation; Questions and answers Tutorial*
Behavioural Momentum Cut-scenes/Story Goods/Information Pavlovian Interaction Tokens; Virality	**Retention:** The CreaCube player could engage in trial-and-error interactions and have Pavlovian feedback which can help retain the best assemblies. However, there is no possibility to remain at this stage because the CreaCube game requires the application/analysis/evaluation/creation levels. • Retention mechanics in CreaCube: *creative exploration.*	*Discover; Explore; Generalisation Guidance; Instruction; Repetition*

Fig. 5. Learning Mechanics—Game Mechanics (LM-GM) [1] and CreaCube activity according to the Bloom's thinking skills level.

4.2 CreaCube Game Mechanics and Learning Mechanics

The CreaCube game requires the player to engage in creative exploration (explore learning mechanics), try to understand the role of each of the cubes (hypothesis learning mechanics) and develop a strategy to solve the game (strategy game and learning mechanics). Below is a description of the main game mechanics and learning mechanics engaged in the CreaCube activity.

Strategy/Planning Game Mechanics. The Cubelets should be assembled considering the balance of the structure but also considering features on each cube.

Hypothesis Learning Mechanics. The manipulation of the cubes should lead the player to develop a hypothesis that reflects his/her understanding of the expected behaviour of each Cubelets (e.g. the battery cube should be on) and when assembled with others (e.g. red cube should be situated before the black distance sensor cube to make the structure move).

Experimentation Learning Mechanics. The CreaCube player should experiment with the Cubes to understand their behaviour. Different structures should be experimented to understand the balance and movement within the cubes.

Competition. Despite the CreaCube task not being designed for a *competition game mechanic*, adult players still experience a certain *competition game dynamic* when trying to do their best and not appear foolish when playing the game.

Time Pressure. The CreaCube game rules make it explicit that the game has no time limits. Nevertheless, despite the CreaCube task not being designed for a *time pressure game mechanic*, adult players experience a certain *time pressure game dynamic* when trying to do achieve the task in the fastest way possible.

Explore. The creative exploration aims to understand the artefact, its attributes and functions, to be able to manipulate the artefact and solve the problem. The CreaCube game activity could help researchers analyse creative exploration in the context of a problem-solving activity using parts of modular robotics unknown to the participant. The CreaCube activity helps also providing an after-task feedback to the participant making him/her more aware about his/her problem-solving strategies.

4.3 CreaCube and Creative Problem-Solving

The 85 participants of this exploratory study were between 6 and 60 year-old. Each participant was video-recorded individually. Video observation shows a lot of inter-individual differences not only among different age groups but also among the age groups. However, it seems that children and adults have different ways of solving the problems they face. Indeed, children facing any problem would tend to change the shape of their construction (intended to be an "autonomous vehicle"), while adults would tend to change the place of cubes and not the general shape of the vehicle. One of the hypotheses to be deepened is that the way participants solve the problems they encounter depends on their level of superficial (or more systematic) way of having explored the cubes a priori and their understanding of the functions of each cube. Also, at the end of each activity, a few questions were asked to participants about their understanding of the roles of each robotic cube, whether they were trying to make the same vehicle during the second activity or about their main difficulties.

5 Discussion

The analysis of the CreaCube game activity is developed in this study under the lens of the Learning Mechanics and Game Mechanics (LMGM) framework [1]. Through the CreaCube activity, it is possible to evaluate problem solving skills while being in a playful activity. The CreaCube game is open-ended which allows to observe different degrees of creative problem solving [13]. The CreaCube activity is not only a game to study problem-solving but also an educational game helping them to demystify educational robotics while playing with the Cubelets modular robotics.

Educational robotics (ER) is discussed in prior studies as playful activities in relation not only to the appearance of the ER artefacts but also to the child-robot interaction engaged during the ER activities. In this study, the analysis of the CreaCube activity goes further by being based on the LMGM framework [1]. The CreaCube LMGM engages the player within the different thinking skills levels of Bloom [2] from retention to creation. Thus, the CreaCube game design is based on creative exploration, experimentation, hypotheses and strategy/planning game mechanics, and learning mechanics. Despite these mechanics, the way adult players experience the task leads researchers to observe two game dynamics which were not intended within the CreaCube task design: competition and time pressure. Despite the CreaCube game rules explicitly stating that time is not limited, adult players put pressure on themselves both in terms of internal competitiveness (trying to do their best) and time completion (trying to achieve CreaCube's objective the fastest possible).

References

1. Arnab, S., Lim, T., Carvalho, M.B., et al.: Mapping learning and game mechanics for serious games analysis. Br. J. Edu. Technol. **46**(2), 391–411 (2015)
2. Bloom, B.S., Davis, A., Hess, R., Silverman, S.B.: Compensatory Education for Cultural Deprivation. Holt, Rinehart and Winston, New York (1965)
3. Buibas, M., Sweet III, C.W., Caskey, M.S., Levin, J.A.: Intelligent modular robotic apparatus and methods. Google Patents (2016)
4. Catlin, D., Kandlhofer, M., Holmquist, S.: EduRobot taxonomy a provisional schema for classifying educational robots (2018)
5. Conchinha, C., Osório, P., de Freitas, J.C.: Playful learning: educational robotics applied to students with learning disabilities. In: 2015 International Symposium on Computers in Education (SIIE), pp. 167–171. IEEE (2015)
6. Csikszentmihalyi, M.: Flow, The Psychology of Optimal Experience, Steps Towards Enchancing the Quality of Life. Harper & Row, Publishers, Inc., New York (1991)
7. Dougherty, D.: The maker movement. Innovations **7**(3), 11–14 (2012)

8. Eguchi, A., Shen, J.: Student learning experience through CoSpace educational robotics: 3D simulation educational robotics tool. In: Cases on 3D Technology Application and Integration in Education, pp. 93–127. IGI Global (2013)
9. Fleming, L.: Worlds of Making: Best Practices for Establishing a Makerspace for Your School. Corwin Press, Thousand Oaks (2015)
10. Koster, R.: A Theory of Fun for Game Design. O'Reilly Media, Sebastopol (2013)
11. Misirli, A., Komis, V.: Robotics and programming concepts in early childhood education: a conceptual framework for designing educational scenarios. In: Karagiannidis, C., Politis, P., Karasavvidis, I. (eds.) Research on e-Learning and ICT in Education, pp. 99–118. Springer, New York (2014). https://doi.org/10.1007/978-1-4614-6501-0_8
12. Proulx, J.-N., Romero, M., Arnab, S.: Learning mechanics and game mechanics under the perspective of self-determination theory to foster motivation in digital game based learning. Simul. Gaming **48**(1), 81–97 (2016)
13. Romero, M., DeBlois, L., Pavel, A.: Créacube, comparaison de la résolution créative de problèmes, chez des enfants et des adultes, par le biais d'une tâche de robotique modulaire. MathémaTICE (61) (2018)
14. Shahid, S., Krahmer, E., Swerts, M.: Child-robot interaction: playing alone or together? In: CHI 2011 Extended Abstracts on Human Factors in Computing Systems, pp. 1399–1404. ACM (2011)
15. Weller, M.P., Do, E.Y.-L., Gross, M.D.: Escape machine: teaching computational thinking with a tangible state machine game. In: Proceedings of the 7th International Conference on Interaction Design and Children, pp. 282–289. ACM (2008)
16. Zawieska, K., Duffy, B.R.: The social construction of creativity in educational robotics. In: Szewczyk, R., Zieliński, C., Kaliczyńska, M. (eds.) Progress in Automation, Robotics and Measuring Techniques. AISC, vol. 351, pp. 329–338. Springer, Cham (2015). https://doi.org/10.1007/978-3-319-15847-1_32

Posters

Augmented Reality Gamification
for Human Anatomy

Antonina Argo[1], Marco Arrigo[2(✉)], Fabio Bucchieri[3],
Francesco Cappello[3], Francesco Di Paola[4], Mariella Farella[2],
Alberto Fucarino[3], Antonietta Lanzarone[1], Giosuè Lo Bosco[5,6],
Dario Saguto[3], and Federico Sannasardo[5]

[1] Department Pro.SAMI - Forensic Medicine,
University of Palermo, Palermo, Italy
[2] Institute for Educational Technologies, Italian National Research Council,
Palermo, Italy
marco.arrigo@itd.cnr.it
[3] Department of Experimental Biomedicine and Clinical Neuroscience,
University of Palermo, Palermo, Italy
[4] Department of Architecture, University of Palermo, Palermo, Italy
[5] Department of Mathematics and Computer Science,
University of Palermo, Palermo, Italy
[6] Department SIT, Euro-Mediterranean Institute of Science
and Technology, Palermo, Italy

Abstract. This paper focuses on the use of Augmented Reality technologies in relation to the introduction of game design elements to support university medical students in their learning activities during a human anatomy laboratory. In particular, the solution we propose will provide educational contents visually connected to the physical organ, giving also the opportunity to handle a 3D physical model that is a perfect reproduction of a real human organ.

Keywords: Augmented Reality · Gamification · Mobile learning · Medicine · Human anatomy

1 Introduction

Usually, anatomy is the first subject faced by university students enrolled in medical faculties. Although it is undoubtedly fascinating, there are not a few difficulties that students have to face during the study of anatomy. The benefits of studying anatomy are not important exclusively during the university career, but they are fundamental in many disciplines and in particular the numerous surgery specialization, that receives a huge benefit from having an excellent previous background in anatomical knowledge [1, 2].

Dissection is among the supports dedicated to the study of human anatomy. The advantages obtained from the use of this technique are innumerable, and they cover numerous areas such as the increase of direct student knowledge by practical skills, creating the "life-death" experience that could result more traumatic if lived only later [3]. Despite the widespread use of human dissection during the history of medicine, direct anatomy teaching by dissection has become gradually rarer over time. Clearly, this deficiency undermines the possibilities of learning and training of new students so that working to develop equally valid alternatives from an educational point of view becomes a duty [4]. As a matter of fact, today, the teaching tools in Medicine are based on classic anatomy books and atlases, with the growing support of web-based virtual 3D atlases as well as Virtual Reality models. The use of such technology has turned out to be an excellent innovative instrument for students because it creates a transformative learning experience, making it possible to visualize gross and microanatomical features from a 360-degree perspective [5]. However, a major drawback of these technologies evidenced by students is the inability to fully appreciate the differences within a real-life sized organ or between two different organs.

Moreover, the rapid progress and diffusion of mobile and wireless technologies and Augmented Reality (AR) offer a unique opportunity to develop innovative methods of learning becoming ubiquitous in education [6, 7].

In this paper, we introduce an advance of an AR mobile educational system we have presented in our previous contribute [8] where we have carried out a gamification process in relation to some interactive exercises like quizzes and simulations in order to enable users to have a fellfield learning experience on the 3D human organ model enriched with dynamic virtual content.

2 System Details

As specifically described in [8], the system we have designed consist of three main modules: server, content designer and a mobile AR interface. The server manages all interactions between the other two modules and maintains the educational contents database. It also includes a built-in database of human organ 3D models that are a virtual representation of real human organs. Following [9, 10], to achieve proper virtual representation of the models, we have carried out an accurate digital acquisition with latest generation instruments and consequently the data-processing. This database was used to map the models for AR recognition steps, to anchor the educational tags and also to reproduce the real human organs with a 3D printer. Instead, the content designer module is used, by the professor, to produce "education tags" enriched with 3D coordinates relative to a virtual representation of the physical organ model. Then, students will access the anatomy education contents and play exercises using the developed mobile AR application. Starting from [8] in the next sub-section we will introduce improvement and new features on AR Mobile module.

2.1 Mobile AR Module Advances

The user interface was designed for a mobile device like Apple iPad, and we developed a mobile AR application that students will use during their study sessions. The AR layer is used to show over a physical model the didactical contents loaded from the "educational tags" database, as well as, to propose interactive quizzes and simulations in order to check the acquired knowledge. A gamification process was carried out integrating some game design elements into a set of exercises designed to improve the learning of the human anatomy. Because our interest was focused on how to improve learning efficacy instead of assessing, according to [11, 12] trials and errors serve to build up professional skills also considering that they have no fatal consequences. Moreover, in the exercise module, an on-screen feedback mechanism was also developed. Based on the work by Johnson et al. [13] we implemented two types of feedback: outcome feedback that provides the student with information about his performance and learning progress and process feedback that directs the student to reach the correct answers. Using these feedbacks students can be supported in evaluating their own preparation identifying the gaps to be filled. In particular, the feedback is provided in the form of hints, error flagging, correct/incorrect response, with a range of levels of help, so that students can continue to access educational contents also when they are playing the exercises. Specifically, until now, four types of exercises have been designed; one of which (the Correct flow) is related only to the heart organ:

- *Correct flow*: Considering the heart as an organ on which to test the acquired knowledge, the student must trace the correct path of blood within the organ. The system will check if the "touched" tags are correct and will provide positive or negative feedback to the student.
- *Answer the quizzes*: the student has to answer quizzes whose correct answer corresponds to one of the "educational tags" visible on the screen (Fig. 1). Through feedback, s/he can receive suggestions and know if the answer given is correct or not.
- *Dissection*: the student has to identify in which part of the organ the required dissection must take place by plotting on the screen the correct path that the scalpel must perform.
- *Memory*: the student will have to place the "educational tags" in the right place by dragging them on the screen.

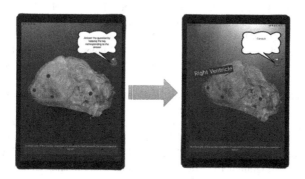

Fig. 1. Interactive quizzes

3 Conclusions

In this paper, we introduce an AR mobile educational system that implements a gamification process characterized by some interactive exercises like quizzes and simulations. Our work highlights the potentiality of mobile AR and gamification in a medical learning context. We think that the gamification process is able to substantially improve the learning experience of the students. We are going to validate such feature by introducing our tool during the ordinary anatomy lessons, starting from the month of October 2018. In this release, we have used open source software for the annotation part, and we plan to develop a proper software model devoted for this purpose. The AR mobile application has been developed for the IOS platform, but we plan to provide it also for other mobile OS such as Android.

References

1. Turney, B.W.: Anatomy in a modern medical curriculum. Ann. R. Coll. Surg. Engl. **89**(2), 104–107 (2017). https://doi.org/10.1308/003588407X168244
2. Maresi, E.A., Argo, A.M., Spanò, G.P., Novo, G.M., Cabibi, D.R., Procaccianti, P.G.: Anomalous origin and course of the right coronary artery. Circulation **114**(22), e609–e611 (2006). https://doi.org/10.1161/CIRCULATIONAHA.106.634667
3. Azer, S.A., Eizenberg, N.: Do we need dissection in an integrated problem-based learning medical course? Perceptions of first-and second-year students. Surg. Radiol. Anat. **29**(2), 173–180 (2007)
4. Saguto, D., et al.: Survey on the demand of Sicilian physicians for a specific training on human cadavers and animals. EuroMediterranean Biomed. J. **13**(3), 9–14 (2018)
5. Yammine, K., Violato, C.: A meta-analysis of the educational effectiveness of three-dimensional visualization technologies in teaching anatomy. Anat. Sci. Educ. (2014). https://doi.org/10.1002/ase.1510
6. Arrigo, M., Kukulska-Hulme, A., Arnedillo-Sánchez, I., Kismihok, G.: Meta-analyses from a collaborative project in mobile lifelong learning. Br. Educ. Res. J. **39**, 222–247 (2013). https://doi.org/10.1080/01411926.2011.652068
7. Adams Becker, S., Cummins, M., Davis, A., Freeman, A., Hall Giesinger, C., Ananthanarayanan, V.: NMC Horizon Report: 2017 Higher Education Edition. The New Media Consortium, Austin (2017)
8. Arrigo, M., et al.: HeARt mobile learning. In: Gómez Chova, L., López Martínez, A., Candel Torres, I. (eds.) Proceedings of EDULEARN18, 10th International Conference on Education and New Learning Technologies, pp. 10899–10905 (2018). ISBN: 978-84-09-02709-5
9. Di Paola, F., Milazzo G., Spatafora, F.: Computer aided restoration tools to assist the conservation of an ancient sculpture. The colossal statue of Zeus enthroned. In: International Archives of Photogrammetry, Remote Sensing and Spatial Information Sciences, XLII-2/W5, Ottawa, Canada, pp. 177–184 (2017)
10. Di Paola, F., Pizzurro, M.R., Pedone, P.: Digital and interactive learning and teaching methods in descriptive geometry. Procedia Soc. Behav. Sci. **106**, 873–885 (2013)
11. Graafland, M., Schraagen, J., Schijven, M.: Systematic review of serious games for medical education and surgical skills training. Br. J. Surg. **99**(10), 1322–1330 (2012)

12. Spielberg, B., Harrington, D., Black, S., Sue, D., Stringer, W., Witt, M.: Capturing the diagnosis: an internal medicine education program to improve documentation. Am. J. Med. **126**(8), 739–743 (2013)
13. Johnson, C.I., Bailey, S.K.T., Van Buskirk, W.L.: Designing effective feedback messages in serious games and simulations: a research review. In: Wouters, P., van Oostendorp, H. (eds.) Instructional Techniques to Facilitate Learning and Motivation of Serious Games. AGL, pp. 119–140. Springer, Cham (2017). https://doi.org/10.1007/978-3-319-39298-1_7

Digital Games as Tools for Enhancing Statistics Instruction in the Early Years: A Teaching Intervention Within a Grade 2 Mathematics Classroom

Maria Meletiou-Mavrotheris[1]([⊠]), Loucas Tsouccas[1],
and Efi Paparistodemou[2]

[1] European University Cyprus, 1516 Nicosia, Cyprus
m.mavrotheris@euc.ac.cy
[2] Cyprus Pedagogical Institute, 2238 Nicosia, Cyprus

Abstract. Digital games hold a lot of promise as tools for improving mathematics and statistics instruction in the early school years. The current article presents a case study that explored the potential of well-designed, mobile educational game apps for enhancing early statistics education. A teaching intervention took place in a rural Grade 2 (ages 7–8) primary classroom in Cyprus, which aimed to integrate mobile game apps Electric Company Prankster Planet and Kahoot! within the mathematics curriculum, so as to support learning of key ideas related to data collection, analysis and tabular and graphical representation. The main insights gained from the study indicate that appropriate exploitation of digital games can motivate young children and help them internalize important concepts related to data analysis and probability.

Keywords: Educational games · Game-based learning · Statistics education

1 Introduction

In recent years, statistics education researchers (e.g., [1]), have been experimenting with new instructional models focused on inquiry-based, technology-enhanced learning and on statistical problem-solving. One promising approach lately explored is the potential for digital games to transform statistics instruction. Although there only few published studies on game-enhanced statistics education, the general thrust of the evidence in the existing literature is positive ([2]).

Acknowledging the educational potential of educationally sound games for enhancing statistics instruction in the early years, this case study focused on the integration of well-designed, mobile educational game apps within the early statistics classroom. A teaching intervention took place in a rural Grade 2 (ages 7–8) primary classroom in Cyprus, and exploited the affordances of the mobile game apps Prankster Planet and Kahoot! for supporting learning of key concepts related to data collection and analysis.

M. Gentile et al. (Eds.): GALA 2018, LNCS 11385, pp. 414–417, 2019.
https://doi.org/10.1007/978-3-030-11548-7_39

2   Methodology

2.1   Research Design: Scope and Context of Study

The teaching intervention took place in a Grade 2 classroom with 18 students, and lasted for 80 min (two teaching periods). The class teacher selected the topic of *Data Collection, Analysis, and Representation*, and developed a lesson plan and accompanying teaching material which were aligned with the learning objectives specified in the curriculum, and incorporated the use of mobile game apps. He shared the lesson plan with the researchers for comments and suggestions, and revised it based upon received feedback. Next, he implemented the lesson plan in his classroom, with the support of the research team, and afterwards prepared a reflection paper where he shared his observations on students' reactions during the teaching intervention, noting what went well and what difficulties he faced and making suggestions for improvement.

Central to the intervention was the game app The Electric Company Prankster Planet, available on Android and iOS platforms. Prankster Planet is based on the Emmy Award-winning PBS KIDS TV series The Electric Company, and it targets children aged 6–10. It features eight unique quests with math curriculum woven throughout that children have to complete to save Earth from the Reverse-a-ball machines of Prankster character Francine, that are scrambling up all the words on Earth and are causing a lot of confusion. Children complete a series of data collection, representation and analysis challenges in order to shut down all eight machines hidden in the jungles, cities, junkyards, and underground world of Prankster Planet. The app features side-scrolling play and exploration in a 2D platformer world, an avatar creator with many customization options, a rewards system to encourage repeat play, and the option of collaborative play. The online gaming platform Kahoot! was also used during the lesson.

2.2   Data Collection and Analysis Procedures

The researchers observed closely and videotaped the lesson, kept field notes, and collected student work samples. Qualitative data were also obtained from the reflection papers written by the teacher at the end of the lesson. The collected data were first examined globally and brief notes were made to index them. Selected occasions from videotapes were viewed several times and transcribed. The transcribed data, along with other data collected in the study, were analyzed to identify and understand students' interactions with the game apps and each other, and the ways in which these interactions influenced their motivation and learning of statistical ideas.

3   Results

The observation of the teaching intervention indicated that the specific teacher had the necessary skills and competencies for teaching this topic and similar statistical topics using tablets and game apps. He selected appropriate game apps and exploited them to organize teaching in a constructive, learner-centered way, so that his young students would have the opportunity to work together in constructing statistical concepts and processes. Specifically, in several activities, children collaborated to build joint understanding of the new concepts they had just encountered. For example, to respond to some of the Prankster Planet questions, they worked together to understand and interpret pie-charts, which had never been mentioned in class before (see Fig. 1). Moreover, the process of assessing their learning process was transferred from the teacher to the students themselves. Instead of standing in front of the classroom, the teacher moved around to the different groups and offered assistance whenever necessary.

Fig. 1. A pair of students interpreting a pie-chart in Prankster Planet

As expected, the game-based nature of the lesson was well received by students and increased their motivation. In the discussion that took place at the end of the intervention, children expressed their enthusiasm about the games they engaged with during the lesson, *"because they gave [them] the chance to play and learn at the same time"*. Although expressing a preference for *"the game where [they] had to prevent the Lady from changing the letters"* (i.e. Prankster Planet) which they found to be *"more adventurous"*, they also liked the game on Kahoot! because it was set up as a contest.

In the reflection paper he wrote after the teaching intervention's completion, the teacher also noted that he was very impressed by the fact that the lesson ended up being so successful. He pointed out that the use of games led to an effortless involvement of all children, and contributed substantially to the achievement of the learning objectives, but also to ensuring fruitful cooperation among learners and the collaborative construction of knowledge in a creative and enjoyable way. Lastly, use of technology worked exactly as he had anticipated, providing the opportunity to introduce in the classroom activities with added value, that could not otherwise be implemented.

While the classroom experimentation further strengthened the teacher's belief that use of game apps can help create motivational and more conducive to learning environments, it also helped him to build more realistic expectations about what games' instructional integration might entail in practice. He recognized that games are not a panacea, and that their incorporation into the curriculum does not guarantee improved learning. He mentioned various challenges and drawbacks to digital games' incorporation in the mathematics classroom, including time constraints, difficulties in locating high-level games, the risk of the learning objectives being neglected for the sake of playfulness, and language issues for non-native English speakers. He stressed the key role of educators not only in choosing appropriate digital games, but also in *"coordinating classroom activities appropriately so as to keep children focused on the achievement of the learning objectives"*, and in facilitating learning by providing scaffolding.

4 Conclusions

In accord with the research literature (e.g., [2, 3]), our research indicates to teachers, researchers and mathematics curriculum developers that it is possible to teach statistical concepts and processes integrated within the early the mathematics curriculum in more constructive ways, by utilizing appropriate game apps to promote more inquiry-based, student-centered pedagogical approaches. Use of educationally sound game apps like the Prankster Planet and Kahoot!, encourages young learners to co-construct statistical concepts and procedures, collaboratively engage in exploration of virtual worlds, and in authentic problem-solving activities, and can help them to eventually become reflective and self-directed learners ([4]). These digital games reinforce student independence, ingenuity, creativity, personalized learning, as well as collaborative learning.

Of course, digital games' success as a tool for learning statistics ultimately depends on the abilities of teachers to take full advantage of their educational potential. In this study, the class teacher's knowledge and pedagogy contributed towards the creation of an engaging environment in which students were encouraged to experiment with statistical ideas, using the mobile game apps' environment as a tool.

A serious drawback of this case study is the lack of a rigorous research design that would have allowed the drawing of robust conclusions and generalizations. Further and deeper investigation into the use of mobile game apps to teach and learn statistical and mathematical concepts in the early years of schooling is warranted and timely.

References

1. Meletiou-Mavrotheris, M., Paparistodemou, E.: Developing young learners' reasoning about samples and sampling in the context of informal inferences. Educ. Stud. Math. **88**(3), 385–404 (2015)
2. Boyle, E.A., et al.: A narrative literature review of games, animations and simulations to teach research methods and statistics. Comput. Educ. **74**, 1–14 (2014)
3. Kyriakides, A.O., Meletiou-Mavrotheris, M., Prodromou, T.: Mobile devices in the service of students' learning of mathematics: the example of game application A.L.E.X. in the context of a primary school in Cyprus. Math. Educ. Res. J. **28**(1), 53–78 (2016)
4. Van Eck, R., Guy, M., Young, T., Winger, A., Brewster, S.: Project NEO: a video game to promote STEM competency for preservice elementary teachers. J. Teach. Knowl. Learn. **20**, 277–297 (2015)

Improving Learning Experiences Through Customizable Metagames

Ioana Andreea Stefan[1] ⓘ, Jannicke Baalsrud Hauge[2,3](✉) ⓘ,
Ancuta Florentina Gheorge[1], and Antoniu Stefan[1] ⓘ

[1] Advanced Technology Systems,
Str. Tineretului Nr 1, 130029 Targoviste, Romania
{ioana.stefan, anca.gheorghe,
antoniu.stefan}@ats.com.ro
[2] BIBA – Bremer Institut für Produktion und Logistik GmbH,
Hochschulring 20, 28359 Bremen, Germany
baa@biba.uni-bremen.de
[3] Royal Institute of Technology, Mariekällgt. 3, 15181 Södertälje, Sweden
jmbh@kth.se

Abstract. Since game-based learning require much planning and careful design, and also tailoring the learning content to game structures, the uptake of game-based learning activities remains limited, as their construction often requires a significant amount of time, and the reuse capabilities of such activities are minimal. This paper describes how the different components of a gamified lessons path can be adapted and reused. In order to ensure the reusability of the different learning paths, a set of minigame templates has been used.

Keywords: AT-CC · Minigame · Reuse · Beaconing

1 Introduction

The shift toward student-centric teaching requires uptake of new methodologies and teaching practices. Gamification and gaming technologies offer opportunities in line with the new demands [1] and can be used in order to achieve "learning at the speed of need through formal, informal and social learning modalities" [2], which is the definition of pervasive learning. "The purpose of adaptation is to optimize the relationship between the learning requirement and course content, hence, the learning outcome could be obtained with minimum time and interaction expended on a course" [3]. However, while the intention of the adaption of a lesson plan towards fitting individual needs is to increase the learning outcome and as Muhammed et al. write thus to spend less time for the student, the effect on the teacher side is in an increase in effort. Consequently, the teacher will often experience an overload of work.

Therefore, the deployment rate and their proper insertion in meaningful curricula are still quite low. In addition there is certain reluctance towards the use of games, and difficulties in adapting and integrating such learning tools in a simple and time efficient way [4]. For digitalized learning paths, the re-use of components can contribute to reducing this extra workload. As stated in [6] the goal of reuse strategies is to facilitate

© Springer Nature Switzerland AG 2019
M. Gentile et al. (Eds.): GALA 2018, LNCS 11385, pp. 418–421, 2019.
https://doi.org/10.1007/978-3-030-11548-7_40

the reuse of components, assets and knowledge. Technically, systematic software-reuse enables robust, faster and less costly design, development and implementation processes. The key benefits of reuse are: better allocation of resources; enhance error handling; enable standards compliance; and time compression.

The BEACONING project aims to foster a personalized learning experience and provide teachers a tool that makes adaption and customization of lessons plans easier, while focusing on the personalization of the learning units to specific student needs [5]. In order to ensure the reusability of the different learning paths, we use a set of templates and a taxonomy described in [7]. This paper focuses on how the different components of a gamified lessons path can be adapted and reused.

2 Reusing a Gamified Lesson Path

The Beaconing Platform provides several minigame templates that can be used to tailor the learning content to specific subjects, needs and contexts. A minigame is a short, modular, game-based activity that can be used to create learning paths.

A minigame, "*Catch the intruder*", has been created using the Authoring Tool for Context-aware Challenges (AT-CC) developed by Geomotion, Spain. The component provides two minigame templates for location-based activities: "Treasure Hunt" and "Follow the path" and it is one of the most innovative components of the project. The AT-CC uses geolocation technologies and promotes creative learning by participation in outdoor educational activities.

"*Catch the intruder*" has been customized to include three other minigames that have been used to test the students:

- Two minigames, "*It's elemental*" and "*Molecularium*", that have been created using the minigame templates "Drag IT" and "Match IT" developed by SIVECO, Romania. The minigames are based on drag and drop actions. When using these templates two main restrictions have been identified: the content that teachers can create can be associated only with the images available in the case of the "Drag IT" minigame template, or with the images and text available in the case of the "Match IT" minigame template.

- The minigame "*Atomix*" that have been created using the "Generic Quiz – Multiple choice" minigame template developed by Imaginary, Italy. This is a minigame where students must check the correct answer from a given list. To make the minigame more interesting and more challenging teachers can insert images to give hints for the answer.

These four minigames were used to create several versions of GLPs to showcase their reuse potential (Fig. 1):

(1) **A GLP with a location based game and three minigames.** This is a complex GLP that is recommended due to its novelty and interactivity, as it includes both outside and/or classroom activities. Students had to discover who stole an important research paper. They had to find the intruder and the documents stolen by visiting different locations in the city of Targoviste.

Fig. 1. The narrative content for a location

After playing the location-based minigame, students are further evaluated through three minigames, which are integrated into the narrative flow presented in the location-based minigame to streamline and enhance the user experience:

- *It's elemental.* In this minigame, students must discover the missing elements from the periodic table. Based on the initial template, the minigame has been customized to be finished within 120 min and additional information was provided when the player reached the third location in the location-based game.
- *Atomix.* In this minigame, students had to give correct answers to five questions about the characteristics and atomic structure of five periodic elements. No time limit had been customized for this minigame, Some of the questions provided hints for the answer.
- *Molecularium.* Students have to match the name of a chemical product with its graphical representation. As a hint, students could use the chemical formula provided in the name, in order to identify the molecule.

(2) **A GLP with only one location-based game.** Unlike the GLP presented above that customized existing minigame templates, this GLP has been created reusing the structure of the GLP described above and it included only the location-based minigame, ending the game flow at the first activity. Teachers can opt to shorten an existing GLP, thus reducing the time required to customize the learning experience, while enabling students to enjoy activities outside the classroom.

(3) **A GLP with a location-based minigame and one minigame.** Teachers can opt to customize the GLP to include only two minigames, thus benefiting of the outside the classroom activities and being able to further evaluate the knowledge the student has acquired through a second minigame.

There are other options to reuse a GLP. For example, the **extension and/or improvement of the learning content of the GLP.** This gives teachers the opportunity to create a GLP and improve it or customize it based on the feedback they get from their students. Another option could be the reuse of the narrative content of the GLP or the customization of the learning content of the minigames.

3 Discussion and Conclusions

Among the key issues identified by [8] we highlight the following: (1) The lack of time available to teachers to familiarize themselves with a game, and the methods of producing the best results from its use; (2) The amount of irrelevant content or functionality in a game, which could not be removed or ignored.

The Beaconing Project addresses these challenges and provides authoring tools that facilitate the customization of game-based learning activities. The teachers have the opportunity to reuse games they are familiar with and customize them to fit certain components of the curriculum, as well as specific learner needs. This significantly reduces the time requires to create engaging learning experiences, and enables teachers to use game features that support a certain learning activity. The paper presents a GLP created using tools developed in the Beaconing project and discusses several means to reuse and customize it. Future work includes testing of the customization capabilities, in order to further improve the user experience.

References

1. Ştefan, A., et al.: Approaches to reengineering digital games. In: Proceedings of the ASME 2016 International Design Engineering Technical Conferences & Computers and Information in Engineering Conference, IDETC/CIE (2016)
2. Pontefract, D.: Learning by Osmosis (2013). http://www.danpontefract.com/learning-by-osmosis/
3. Muhammad, A., Zhou, Q., Beydoun, G., Xu, D., Shen, J.: Learning path adaptation in online learning systems. In: 2016 IEEE 20th International Conference on Computer Supported Cooperative Work in Design (CSCWD), pp. 421–426. IEEE, United States (2016)
4. Hauge, J.B., et al.: Deploying serious games for management in higher education: lessons learned and good practices. In: EAI Endorsed Transactions on SG (2014)
5. Hauge, J.M.B., Stefan, I.A., Stefan, A.: Exploring pervasive entertainment games to construct learning paths. In: Munekata, N., Kunita, I., Hoshino, J. (eds.) ICEC 2017. LNCS, vol. 10507, pp. 196–201. Springer, Cham (2017). https://doi.org/10.1007/978-3-319-66715-7_21
6. Hauge, J.B., et al.: Serious game mechanics and opportunities for reuse (2015)
7. BEACONING project: D3.3 Learning Environment System Specification (2017). https://beaconing.eu/wp-content/uploads/deliverables/D3.3.pdf
8. Rushby, N., Surry, D.: Wiley Handbook of Learning Technology. Wiley, Boca Raton (2016)

Predicting Cognitive Profiles from a Mini Quiz: A Facebook Game for Cultural Heritage

Angeliki Antoniou[✉][ID]

University of Peloponnese, 22100 Tripolis, Greece
angelant@uop.gr

Abstract. Games are used in cultural heritage to engage visitors, to function as learning tools, or even advertise a venue. However, games can be also used for quick profiling purposes to overcome the cold start problem of personalized museum applications. A profiling game aiming to extract users' cognitive profiles was developed and tested with real users. The game follows the principles of pop psychology quizzes. The results of the game showed its potential in correctly predicting the cognitive profiles of users with average success rate around 90%. Being an entertaining and engaging way to involve visitors with diverse needs, games and especially profiling have a clear place in cultural heritage and should be investigated further. Our future work will focus on games that will try to predict different personality aspects, like Big Five dimensions.

Keywords: Games · Cultural heritage · Profiling · Cognitive profiles

1 Games in Cultural Heritage

Games are used in cultural heritage since they are considered good learning tools that can increase visitor motivation and allow visitors to engage deeper with the informative material, that can include images, texts, problem solving tasks, etc. [1, 2]. In addition, museum games were found to increase the potential of creating personal narratives and also to transform the visitor from a passive receiver of information to an active cultural explorer [3].

Furthermore, it is not only the heterogeneity among cultural spaces, cultural content and types of games that significantly increases complexity, but also among visitors. Visitors comprise a very diverse crowd with different needs and expectations. Personalization of content is increasingly popular [4] and visitor models that link individual preferences with cultural content need to be created. Nevertheless, in many cultural spaces visitors might only visit once and the time constraints imply that personalization under these conditions might be highly challenging. In other words, what content do we offer to new visitors of whom we have no previous information about their preferences and needs? In this light, games are also considered as a tool with great potential to create effective visitor profiles which have been used in the past as ways to extract visitor profiles and quickly disseminate cultural content on social media [5]. Thus, the present work investigates the potential of a specifically designed game (mini quiz) to create visitor profiles and (especially) to extract personality characteristics of the visitors.

© Springer Nature Switzerland AG 2019
M. Gentile et al. (Eds.): GALA 2018, LNCS 11385, pp. 422–425, 2019.
https://doi.org/10.1007/978-3-030-11548-7_41

A mini game/quiz was designed to be used in social media in order to advertise a small archaeological museum in the Arcadia region in Peloponnese. However, the game questions and theme had a generic character in order for it also to be used by other similar venues in the region. The mini game was developed for two main reasons: (a) to function as advertising games and increasing the digital visibility of the venue in social media and (b) to allow quick user profiling.

The game/quiz is called "Who is your guardian Goddess?" and its purpose is for the user to find her guardian goddess in antiquity by answering short questions. 12 questions are used, all deriving from Myers and Briggs Type Indicator (MBTI), a personality assessment test mainly used by industries for personnel selection [6]. The MBTI was chosen since it has been used in previous works for profiling games with good results [5]. However, although the original test uses at least 64 items in (short version) and 222 (full version) with 5 possible answers for each question, the mini game only uses 12 questions with 2 possible answers (3 questions per MBTI dimension as a minimum requirement for the elicitation of user profiles). The mini game imitates the very popular pop psychology quizzes available on Facebook (goo.gl/2zPamY).

In each screen, the user can provide an answer to a simple question (only two possible options). After answering 12 questions the user reaches her results screen and see the protective Goddess that corresponds to her personality. There were 16 goddesses used as possible answers, each corresponding to a specific cognitive profile. Mythological stereotypes for the personality of the different goddesses were used in order to match them with the 16 cognitive profiles of users. The results were matching the actual MBTI descriptions of the cognitive profiles. In this way, the player gets an answer that describes her cognitive characteristics and the museum system gets the necessary information in order to built a user profile that can be later used during the museum visit to provide personalized cultural content.

Thus, currently using 12 items and only 2 possible answers per question in the developed game, the research questions are:

- Does this game provide reliable cognitive profile results?
- What is its success rate with regards to the actual MBTI test?
- Can it be used as a quick profiling tool for cultural heritage?

The game can be found at: http://pilot3.crosscult.uop.gr/gameProfiler/ and it is available in two languages (English and Greek).

2   Method

Social media were used (i.e. Facebook) to ask people to participate in the study. In total there were 85 participants (33 men and 52 women) with an age range from 18 to 62 years. This study followed a within subjects design meaning that all participants had to play the game and also answer a free version of the MBTI questionnaire (short version with 64 items). The MBTI online free version that was used can be found at: http://www.humanmetrics.com/cgi-win/jtypes2.asp. This particular version was chosen because it is rather short and it would keep the cognitive load of participants low, thus increasing the chances of completing the tasks [7]. The present study follows the principles of an e-study, meaning that there are many advantages, like low cost, easy access to volunteers but also disadvantages like volunteer bias, generalizability of results and the possibility of a high dropout [8]. Therefore, an online short version of the MBT test was appropriate for use. Half of the users played the game first and then the test followed and the other half of the users answered the test first and then the game followed. All participants had to send the researchers an email with their game results as well as their MBTI results. The collection of the data for the study started on Saturday 13 May 2017 and ended on Tuesday 25 July 2017 (80 days).

3   Results

When the game results were compared to the MBTI test's results, it was observed that there were similar patterns between them. Each MBTI dimension was studied separately and it was found that the game predicted 56 Extraverts and the test 62, 29 Introverts (game) and 23 were found with the test, the game also found 38 people high in intuition and the test 59, 47 Sensors were found from the game and 26 from the test, 43 Thinkers found with the game and 34 with the test, the game found 42 Feelers and the test 51, the game also found 55 Judgers and the test 60, and finally the game predicted 30 Perceivers whereas the test 25. Based on these numbers the games' success rate was calculated. In particular, the dimension Extraversion – Introversion (E-I) was correctly predicted with the game 92.9% of times, the dimension Intuition – Sensing (N-S) 75% of times, the dimensions Thinking-Feeling (T-F) 89% and the dimension Judging-Perceiving (J-P) 94%. Since we wanted to correctly predict MBTI dimensions from only 12 questions, the values of the two conditions should not differ significantly. Indeed, when the two conditions were statistically compared, no significant difference was found, $x2(49) = 56$, $p = 0.229$.

4   Discussion and Conclusions

The findings of the present study showed a very high success rate of the game predicting the users' cognitive profiles. With an average number of 88% success rate, the game seems effective in quickly providing information for building user profiles. With only 3 questions per dimension, the game was able to correctly predict the cognitive profile of the majority of participants. Knowing personality characteristics of users of different systems can be a valuable tool in profiling and personalization of content. Going beyond cultural heritage such games can be used in other domains like education. As also mentioned above, the present work followed the methodology of an e-study, implying that we should be conscious regarding the generalizability of the results. The game is intended solely for social media use and therefore, an e-study on social media was appropriate since it targeted similar types of audiences (i.e. social media users that play such games). However, the present game will be also tested with museum visitor in situ at the Archaeological Museum of Tripolis in autumn 2018 and the results will be compared. Moreover, the number of profiling games that actually predict the personality of the user is limited, so it is very important to concentrate on the personality games that have already been created and need improvement. Thus, a further study on the "Who is your guardian Goddess?" game is essential, in order to further enhance the success rate. Finally, the present work used one test (MBTI), which is widely used and popular with the industry. Nevertheless, our future work includes a game, which is already implemented but not tested, relying of psychometric tests like the Big Five [9]. The Big Five has a strong theoretical background and it provides different types of information that might be very useful in a cultural heritage visit, like openness to new experiences, etc. Therefore, the second profiling game is underway and user testing is also expected in autumn 2018.

Acknowledgments. This work is supported by CrossCult: "Empowering reuse of digital cultural heritage in context-aware crosscuts of European history", funded by the European Union's Horizon 2020 research and innovation program, Grant# 693150. I would also like to thank Ms Bampatzia for game implementation and Ms Maipa for data collection.

References

1. Bellotti, F., Berta, R., De Gloria, A., D'ursi, A., Fiore, V.: A serious game model for cultural heritage. J. Comput. Cult. Herit. **5**(4, Article 17), 27 pages (2013). http://dx.doi.org/10.1145/2399180.2399185
2. Mortara, M., Catalano, C.E., Bellotti, F., Fiucci, G., Houry-Panchetti, M., Petridis, P.: Learning cultural heritage by serious games. J. Cult. Herit. **15**(3), 318–325 (2014)
3. Coenen, T., Mostmans, L., Naessens, K.: MuseUs: case study of a pervasive cultural heritage serious game. J. Comput. Cult. Herit. **6**(2, Article 8), 19 pages (2013). http://dx.doi.org/10.1145/2460376.2460379
4. Ardissono, L., Kuflik, T., Petrelli, D.: Personalization in cultural heritage: the road travelled and the one ahead. User Model. User-Adap. Inter. **22**(1–2), 73–99 (2012)
5. Antoniou, A., et al.: User profiling: towards a facebook game that reveals cognitive style. In: De Gloria, A. (ed.) GALA 2013. LNCS, vol. 8605, pp. 349–353. Springer, Cham (2014). https://doi.org/10.1007/978-3-319-12157-4_28
6. Briggs-Myers, I., McCaulley, M.H.: Manual: A Guide to the Development and Use of the Myers-Briggs Type Indicator. Consulting Psychologists Press, Palo Alto (1985)
7. Frick, A., Bächtiger, M.T., Reips, U.D.: Dimensions of internet science (2001)
8. Reips, U.D.: Internet-based psychological experimenting: five dos and five don'ts. Soc. Sci. Comput. Rev. **20**(3), 241–249 (2002)
9. Costa Jr., P.T., McCrae, R.R.: Revised NEO Personality Inventory (NEO-PI-R) and NEO Five-Factor Inventory (NEO-FFI) Manual. Psychological Assessment Resources, Odessa (1992)

Rapid-Play Games for Evaluating Future Technology

Robert Seater$^{(\boxtimes)}$ ⓘ, Joel Kurucar$^{(\boxtimes)}$ ⓘ, and Andrew Uhmeyer$^{(\boxtimes)}$ ⓘ

Massachusetts Institute of Technology Lincoln Laboratory,
Lexington, MA 02421, USA
{Robert.Seater,Joel.Kurucar,Andrew.Uhmeyer}@ll.mit.edu

Abstract. We introduce the HIVELET (Human Interactive Virtual Experimentation for Low-burden Evaluation of Technology) approach that uses rapid-play digital games to collect quantitative and qualitative data on the effectiveness, acceptance, and impact of future and emerging technologies. The core principle is for the player to alternate between two modes: selecting candidate capabilities with a game theoretic limiting pressure, and executing a simulated mission using those selections in a virtual environment. Alternating between the two modes allows us to collect quantitative data on performance and preferences, improve the trustworthiness of qualitative feedback, and increase the chance of discovering novel uses. We report on preliminary results from applying the HIVELET in a military context.

Keywords: Technology evaluation · Experimental results ·
Requirements analysis · Gamification

1 Introduction

Many technology programs are doomed to fail from the start if the capability needed is misjudged. In the current state of Research, Development, Test, and Evaluation (RDTE), these failures are usually identified late in the process and are costly to mitigate [1,2]. Recognizing which technologies will be useful before they have been developed, prototyped, and field tested is the main challenge that motivates our research. Asking users what they want is a problematic approach as experts tend to misjudge and fail to explain their decision making rational [3]. Since the design space is massive and complex, approaches like crowd-sourced creativity [4] and wargaming [5] provide utility. Our approach is a mixture of how games are typically leveraged in academic research and military wargaming contexts.

In a military context, wargaming typically offers qualitative feedback to inform planning, prediction, and rehearsal [6,7]. By contrast, research focused games are often cast as experiments that provide quantitative measures for analysis [8,9]. Game theory has been applied in a number of gaming contexts [10,11]. While mathematically superior, these approaches are not well suited for dealing

© Springer Nature Switzerland AG 2019
M. Gentile et al. (Eds.): GALA 2018, LNCS 11385, pp. 426–430, 2019.
https://doi.org/10.1007/978-3-030-11548-7_42

with the full range of human complexity. Additionally, rapid-play games are not a novel concept in entertainment game design, but they are rare in the context of non-entertainment games. Many design techniques developed for physical and digital games over the last 20 years demonstrate the ability to reliably capture complex strategic and social dynamics in a short play session in concise and abstract formats [12,13]. A more complete set of related work can be provided by the authors upon request.

2 Approach and Experimental Design

Rapid-play games have been used by our Laboratory in a range of domains, including public health, chemical and biological defense, emergency management, naval missile defense, air traffic control, and security operations [14,15]. To enable the desirable level of data collection, rapid-play games must be short, accessible, and flexible. The HIVELET approach (Human-Interactive Virtual Exploration for Low-Burden Evaluation of Technologies) focuses early-stage concept exploration. HIVELET combines a market-based selection with rapid-play digital simulations to collect quantitative data, improve qualitative feedback, and crowd-source the ingenuity of human experts (Fig. 1).

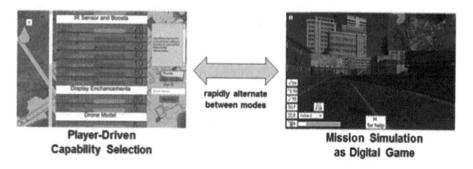

Player-Driven Capability Selection   **Mission Simulation as Digital Game**

Fig. 1. The HIVELET approach has players alternating between two modes capability selection (left) and mission simulation (right).

Capability selection gives players freedom to select different combinations of candidate capabilities, allowing them to formulate and explore novel strategies. The selection mode provides a counter pressure to prevent a player from simply choosing all available capabilities. The selection mechanism forces players to think critically about what capabilities they really need and to prioritize them by utility. Players judge not just if it is useful, but if it is useful enough to justify a cost.

Mission simulation gives players a chance to try their selected capabilities in a scenario to get feedback about their effectiveness and to build intuition about what did or did not work well. The mission simulation is a rapid-play game so that the player can make multiple attempts within a single sitting to explore different strategies, build intuition through iteration, and generate performance and behavior data for analysis.

After completing the mission simulation the player continues to alternate between the two modes, forcing them to combine abstract thinking about capability value with concrete feedback and intuition about how they performed in a mission. Data collected during the game on player preferences, behaviors, and performance and can be used in quantitative analyses that complement the qualitative feedback provided by participants in post-gameplay discussions and surveys. Researchers can vary the mission parameters to see how players change their preferences and strategies. It must be noted that the technology options were chosen to demonstrate the methodology and are not actual technologies being considered by our U.S. Department of Defense sponsor.

We used the HIVELET approach to analyze how small unmanned aerial vehicles (UAVs) might integrate into tactical infantry missions. The mission simulator uses the Unity3D game engine to render a three-dimensional real-time first-person virtual environment. The game modeled 29 capabilities, such as radio-frequency (RF) sensors and UAV cameras. We conducted experiments using 36 participants. Each participant attended a two and half hour session including one hour of training, one hour of competitive gameplay, and 30 min of discussion and paperwork. During the competitive gameplay hour, participants cycled between capability selection and mission simulation as many times as able. Capabilities were purchased using a random-price market.

3 Results

Our initial goal was to identify most valued capabilities, on the assumption that those are of high actual utility. We collected each players technology selections and prices over 263 recorded plays and ranked capabilities by frequency of selection and aver-age price paid. Clear patterns emerged, such as the real-time drone camera, drone robot arms, and autonomous collision avoidance were consistently ranked within players top five technologies and purchased at any price while the drone paint job and slight improvements to infrared sensors where consistently ranked in the bottom 15 technologies and only purchased at low prices.

By comparing the frequency and price rankings, we infer which capabilities players truly valued; for example, the drone camera, live map, and drone robot arms were clearly valued items for the modeled scenario as they are frequently bought and bought at any price. Further analysis was conducted on combinations of capabilities and clear synergies and redundancies emerged. Preliminary experimentation indicates that the HIVELET approach can produces the necessary data to evaluate these types of relationships with a relatively low burden on participants.

Furthermore, we conducted analysis to determine if the data provided by the HIVELET approach was meaningful. These analyses included convergence, external consistency, internal consistency, novel lessons, individual impact, and demographic sensitivity. While our preliminary results provided insights into all of these categories, we will only discuss the most significant two for brevity.

We analyzed convergence in order to determine if players were able to learn the games interface, formulate a strategy, revise the strategy, and build a cohesive opinion. We say that a players scores converged if the standard deviation of their scores stayed below a threshold and that their preferences converged if the number of changes between three consecutive plays was below a threshold. For player score 62% of participants converged. For player preference convergence, 32% of participants converged. We only consider players who played enough cycles to calculate convergence and these metrics do not account for cases where a player converges and then later diverges.

External consistency is important since we want some confidence that players are behaving and performing in the simulated environment in a manner similar to the real world. Some of that validation must be done qualitatively, since we are inherently studying future situations that have never occurred. Qualitatively, participants with 20+ years of military experience self-reported that the game felt like a real mission, made them make realistic tradeoffs, and was credible in its measures of mission success. Quantitatively, we can measure how a players self-reported preference during the post-game survey compare to their implied valuation based on in-game actions. We observed strong alignment from all players, even those with few plays.

Additional results on the remaining analysis (internal consistency, novel lessons, individual impact, and demographic sensitivity) can be provided upon request.

4 Conclusion

While the sample size (36 participants generating 263 total plays) limits the strength of some conclusions, these are positive preliminary results that suggest HIVELET has a role to play in RDTE. In a short period of time (two and half hours per participant), players were able to learn a new game, formulate opinions about the modeled capabilities, build strategies around those capabilities, and express their opinions through the in-game market. Our findings support that the opinions expressed are consistent, realistic, and potentially novel.

References

1. Dixon, A., Henning, J.: Nett Warrior Gets New End-User Device (2013). http://www.army.mil/article/107811/. Accessed 20 Sept 2018
2. Hern, A.: US marines reject BigDog robotic packhorse because it's too noisy. The Guardian (2015). https://www.theguardian.com/technology/2015/dec/30/us-marines-reject-bigdog-robot-boston-dynamics-ls3-too-noisy. Accessed 20 Sept 2018
3. Klein, G.: Sources of Power: How People Make Decisions. MIT Press, Cambridge (1998)

4. Terwiesch, C., Ulrich, K.T.: Innovation Tournaments: Creating and Selecting Exceptional Opportunities. Boston Harvard Business Press, Boston (2009)
5. Allen, G., Chan, T.: Artificial Intelligence and National Security. Study on behalf of the US Intelligence Advanced Research Projects Activity (IARPA). Belfer Center for Science and International Affairs, Cambridge MA (2017). http://www.belfercenter.org/sites/default/files/files/publication/AI %20NatSec%20-%20final.pdf. Accessed 20 Sept 2018
6. U.S. Naval War College: War Gaming. U.S. Naval War College, Newport (2017). https://www.usnwc.edu/Research-and-Wargaming/Wargaming. Accessed 20 Sept 2018
7. Burns, S., Del la Volpe, D., Babb, R., Miller, N., Muir, G. (eds.): War Gamers Handbook: A Guide for Professional War Gamers. U.S. Naval War College, Newport (2013)
8. Kato, P.M., Cole, S.W., Bradlyn, A.S., Pollock, B.H.: A video game improves behavioral outcomes in adolescents and young adults with cancer: a randomized trial. Pediatrics **122**(2), e305–e317 (2008). https://doi.org/10.1542/peds.2007-3134
9. Suarez, P.: Games for a New Climate: Experiencing the Complexities of Future Risks. Boston University Frederick S. Pardee Center for the Study of the Longer-Range Future Task Force Report, Boston MA (2012)
10. Liu, A.: Decentralized Network Interdiction Games. Air Force Research Laboratory: AF Office Of Scientific Research (AFOSR)/RTA2, Arlington VA (2015)
11. Allain, R.J.: An Evolving Asymmetric Game for Modeling Interdictor-Smuggler Problems. Naval Postgraduate School, Monterey (2016)
12. Burgun, K.: Clockwork Game Design. Focal Press, Burlington (2015)
13. Elias, G.S., Garfield, R., Gutschera, K.R.: Characteristics of Games. MIT Press, Cambridge (2012)
14. Gombolay, M.C., Jensen, R., Stigile, J., Son, S., Shah, J.: Apprenticeship scheduling: learning to schedule from human experts. In: Proceedings of the International Joint Conference on Artificial Intelligence (2016)
15. Seater, R., Rose, C., Norige, A., McCarthy, J., Kozar, M., DiPastina, P.: Skill Transfer and Virtual Training for IND Response Decision Making: Game Design for Disaster Response Training. MIT Lincoln Laboratory Technical Report 1207, Lexington MA (2016)

Serious Games as Innovative Approach to Address Gender Differences in Career Choice

Pia Spangenberger[1]([⊠]), Linda Kruse[2], and Felix Kapp[3]

[1] Technische Universität Berlin, Berlin, Germany
pia.spangenberger@tu-berlin.de
[2] The Good Evil GmbH, Cologne, Germany
linda@thegoodevil.com
[3] Technische Universität Dresden, Dresden, Germany
felix.kapp@tu-dresden.de

Abstract. Serious games have been recognized as an innovative approach to introduce instructional content of subjects at school [14]. In German middle school career choice is part of the curricula to introduce different career options and, at best, providing individual advice. Unfortunately, career choices of girls are still influenced by missing confidence in their abilities, role conflicts as well as resistant discrimination and harassment in the technology field [3, 11]. Women are also still underrepresented in the game industry, however, the number of female players is constantly rising [7]. Considering this, serious games seem to be a promising approach for girls to learn about career choice. The following paper will combine career choice findings and game design to present the German serious game "Serena Supergreen and the Broken Blade" - a point-and-click adventure aiming at promoting girl's self-concept and interest in technology associated tasks. Results of a qualitative content analysis concerning girl's perception of the game will be presented.

Keywords: Serious games · Career choice · Girls

1 Gender Differences in Digital Games

In the last couple of years, the discussion about women and digital games has risen. It has been observed that gender difference exists concerning the question, what kind of games women and men play, how women are represented in video games as well as if they perceive games differently [6]. And, although the game industry is still a strong male-dominated domain, the number of female game consumer and developers is growing [7]. However, the number of women developing games remains low, leading to the assumption, that most games might not fit women's aspirations. Since, video games had made their way into the classrooms and are used for learning and to support students to reach developmental goals such as career choices, this issue becomes more important. Serious Games should be beneficiary for both boys and girls equally. In alliance with this background information, two questions arise, (a) how should a game for career choice look like - considering gender differences, and by that, (b) how can it

© Springer Nature Switzerland AG 2019
M. Gentile et al. (Eds.): GALA 2018, LNCS 11385, pp. 431–435, 2019.
https://doi.org/10.1007/978-3-030-11548-7_43

support especially girls in their career choice in the field of technology? These two questions were addressed within the development of the serious game "Serena Supergreen and the Broken Blade" - a point-and-click adventure aiming at promoting girl's self-concept and interest in technology associated tasks.

2   Serious Games to Support Girl's Career Choice

Serious games are interactive, based on defined rules, have a clear goal, and provide feedback to the players [14]. However, the resulting entertainment or fun at serious games is used to convey content in the areas of training, education, health, or attitudinal change [14]. There are already several reviews on the effects of serious games on the learning process and the learning outcome. The meta-analysis by Wouters and colleagues [14] found that serious games can have positive effects on learning, but in certain contexts they do not necessarily have to be more motivating than traditional teaching methods. Boyle and colleagues [1] have analysed 129 studies on serious games with the result that the most common improvements occur in knowledge acquisition and understanding, as well as emotional and motivational effects. Several studies have shown that serious games increase motivation in the learning process [e.g., 10, 13]. Previous research on serious games also has shown that the games can have very different effects depending on the learning content and the playing characteristics. In the U.S. games like Minecraft or the Sims have already been detected to engage girls in career choice [5]. However, there are only a few serious games, that have been developed explicitly to support girl's career choice. Two examples are the browser game Sitcom by the Donau University Krems and the game MINT-Land by the ETH Zurich. Sitcom stands for "Simulation IT-Careers for WOMEN" and was developed as part of an EU funded project in 2006 [15]. The aim of the game is to use simulation and interactive games to interest girls between the ages of 12 and 16 for technical or scientific studies. The career simulation game enables girls to accompany a woman's day-to-day work in one of the professions and solve work-related tasks. The game MINT-Land was completed in 2011 and was also intended to arouse the interest of female players in scientific and technological questions and to illustrate the everyday relevance of mathematics, computer science, natural sciences and technology [4]. Although MINT-Land is not primarily intended for career orientation, it pursues the long-term goal to motivate more girls choosing a specific career.

3   The Game Serena Supergreen and the Broken Blade

In order to address career counselling, we designed the serious game Serena Supergreen and the Broken Blade. The major goal of the serious game is to promote girl's interest in technical vocational educational training. The story of the point-and-click adventure takes the player on a mission to earn money for a vacation on an island. The player's character "Serena", has to master technical tasks during her mission. She is supported by her two best friends and receives feedback on her tasks through other male and female non-player characters. As Johnson and colleagues [8] point out, feedback in serious games can have different learning outcomes for girls and boys, stressing girls might profit more strongly from feedback than boys. Thus, the feedback strategies implemented in the game help to master the tasks and are central to building the players trust in her own abilities. In preparing the game, we also let girls vote to decide about the looks of the main characters. This motion is in consonant with finding's in career choice literature, that the identification with a role model is very important to ascribe a certain activity to oneself [11]. The game starts on a very low technical level and after mastering the first technical tasks successfully, they get more challenging at the end. Since girls' value social impact of engineering and technology higher than their male peers [2], the tasks contain learning objectives regarding renewable energies such as repairing a solar plant or a rotor blade of wind power plant. To secure that all chosen technical tasks are part of technical vocational training, German curricula of professions such as electronic technician or system mechanic have been analyzed. The first evaluations of the game used in classrooms showed that Serena Supergreen has a positive influence on the interest in technology and the assessment of one's own abilities in the field of technology [12].

4 Perception of Serena Supergreen by Girls and Boys

Since its launch, the game has been evaluated in various contexts. For this article, we used a sample of 132 (f = 60, m = 72) students at the age of 13 to 15 years of three different middle schools in Germany. A questionnaire was handed out after playing the game at each school (playtime between 2 to 4 h). To evaluate the question, whether or not Serena Supergreen is perceived differently by boys and girls, and, by that, can contribute to girl's career choice, we analyzed open question text material using a qualitative content analysis approach [9]. The questionnaire contained an open question in the category "enjoyment". We analyzed the text material following the assumption, that the game Serena Supergreen offers individual approaches for girls to master technical tasks. As a result of the following coding process we identified different gender specific perceptions. Answering the question, what was the most exiting element within the game, girls most frequently pointed out "mastering new tasks" (18x), "problem solving" (15x) and "the island" (6x), referring to the final quest about renewable energies. As Hannah (15) describes, *"I like about the game, that it is so realistic and you always master new tasks. You can put yourself well into the story."* Or as Tina (15) points out, *"I always liked it when new tasks came up. The difficulty made it more demanding."* Boys instead most frequently pointed out "fixing machines" (10x) and "rescuing the monkey" (6x). As Bryan (15) describes, *"I like most about the game, printing the gear using the 3D printer, switching a light bulb in the pet shop and soldering the solar device."*

5 Discussion and Conclusion

In previous studies serious games have been ascribed an effect in learning outcomes if they are methodically well developed. However, games characteristics are valued differently by boys and girls. The serious game Serena Supergreen and Broken Blade was explicitly developed to foster girl's interest in the field of technology. The results of our qualitative content analysis of text material answered by 132 students showed that questioned girls described the mastery experience as most enjoyable characteristic of the game, followed by societal impact (problem solving and renewable energies). Thus, we stress, that the game design considered gender differences in career choice by designing technical quests as enjoyable especially for girls. To support girl's career choice by a serious game, we recommend, (a) to implement mechanisms to strengthen self-efficacy in mastering technology related tasks, (b) the learning content and the game characteristics should be developed as closely as possible with the target group, and, (c) provide social value, which has been identified as important to girl's when choosing a career in the field of technology. In future research these findings should be further investigated.

References

1. Boyle, E.A., et al.: An update to the systematic literature review of empirical evidence of the impacts and outcomes of computer games and serious games. Comput. Educ. **94**, 178–192 (2016)
2. Canney, N.E., Bielefeldt, A.R.: Gender differences in the social responsibility attitudes of engineering students and how they change over time. J. Women Minor. Sci. Eng. **21**(3), 215–237 (2015)
3. Eccles, J.S.: Understanding women's educational and occupational choices: applying the Eccles et al. model of achievement-related choices. Psychol. Women Quaterly **18**(4), 585–609 (1994)
4. ETH Zürich: Kinderleichte Spitzenforschung. http://www.ethlife.ethz.ch/archive_articles/1108198_scientifica_1_mf/. Accessed 19 Aug 2011
5. Hayes, E.R., King, E.M.: Not just a dollhouse: what The Sims2 can teach us about women's IT learning. Horiz. **17**(1), 60–69 (2009)
6. Hartmann, T., Klimmt, C.: Gender and computer games: exploring females' dislikes. J. Comput. Mediat. Commun. **11**(4), 910–931 (2006)
7. International Game Developer Association: Developer Satisfaction Survey 2017. Summary Report (2018)
8. Johnson, C.I., Bailey, S.K.T., Van Buskirk, W.L.: Designing effective feedback messages in serious games and simulations: a research review. In: Wouters, P., van Oostendorp, H. (eds.) Instructional Techniques to Facilitate Learning and Motivation of Serious Games. AGL, pp. 119–140. Springer, Cham (2017). https://doi.org/10.1007/978-3-319-39298-1_7
9. Mayring, P.: Qualitative content analysis. In: Flick, U., von Kardorff, E., Steinke, I. (eds.) A Companion to Qualitative Research, pp. 266–269. Sage, London (2004)
10. McGonigal, J.: Reality is Broken: Why Games Make Us Better and How They Can Change the World. Penguin, New York (2011)
11. Seron, C., Silbey, S.S., Cech, E., Rubineau, B.: Persistence is cultural: professional socialization and the reproduction of sex segregation. Work. Occup. **43**(2), 178–214 (2016)

12. Spangenberger, P., Kapp, F., Kruse, L., Hartmann, M., Narciss, S.: Can a serious game attract girls to technology professions? Int. J. Sci. Gend. Technol. **10**(2), 253–264 (2018)
13. Virvou, M., Katsionis, G., Manos, K.: Combining software games with education: evaluation of its educational effectiveness. Educ. Technol. Soc. **8**(2), 54–65 (2005)
14. Wouters, P., van Nimwegen, C., van Oostendorp, H., van der Spek, E.D.: A meta-analysis of the cognitive and motivational effects of serious games. J. Educ. Psychol. **105**, 249–265 (2013)
15. Zauchner, S., Zens, B., Siebenhandl, K., Jütte, W.: Gendersensitives Design durch partizipative Mediengestaltung: Evaluationskonzept zur Entwicklung eines Online-Rollenspiels für Mädchen. In: Schachtner, C., Höber, A. (eds.) Learning Communities, pp. 247–258. Campus Verlag, Münster (2008)

The AHA Project: An Evidence-Based Augmented Reality Intervention for the Improvement of Reading and Spelling Skills in Children with ADHD

Giuseppe Chiazzese[1] , Eleni Mangina[2] , Antonella Chifari[1] ,
Gianluca Merlo[1] , Rita Treacy[3], and Crispino Tosto[1(✉)]

[1] Consiglio Nazionale delle Ricerche, Istituto per le Tecnologie Didattiche,
Palermo, Italy
{giuseppe.chiazzese,antonella.chifari,gianluca.merlo,
crispino.tosto}@itd.cnr.it
[2] University College Dublin, Dublin, Ireland
eleni.mangina@ucd.ie
[3] WordsWorth Learning Limited, Dublin, Ireland
rita@wordsworthlearning.com

Abstract. Students with Attention Deficit Hyperactivity Disorder (ADHD) experience difficulties in maintaining focused attention and remaining on-task and often have comorbid Specific Learning Difficulties (SLD). Given the characteristics of ADHD, interventions for the SLDs should be designed to enhance students' motivation and engagement. Augmented Reality (AR) can improve students' outcomes by enhancing attention and motivation. In this direction, the ADHD-Augmented (AHA) project implements an evidence-based intervention, supported by AR, to improve reading and spelling skills for children diagnosed with ADHD.

Keywords: ADHD · Augmented Reality · Reading and spelling ability

1 Introduction

Digital learning solutions provide interesting opportunities to all students and, in particular, to those with special educational needs. Specifically, Augmented Reality (AR) can enhance students' motivation and attention thus promoting better academic achievements [1, 2]. Typically, students with Attention Deficit Hyperactivity Disorder (ADHD) experience difficulties in maintaining focused on cognitive *stimuli* and often go off-task [3]. Moreover, levels of motivation and academic engagement have been found to be lower than those of children without the ADHD diagnosis and explain the relationship between ADHD symptoms and academic achievement [4, 5]. A comorbid diagnosis of a Specific Learning Difficulty (SLD) (e.g. reading and spelling difficulties and writing difficulties) is also common [6] and tailored instructional interventions should be designed since maintaining students' motivation and engagement in the educational activities is generally challenging. The ADHD-Augmented (AHA) pilot

© Springer Nature Switzerland AG 2019
M. Gentile et al. (Eds.): GALA 2018, LNCS 11385, pp. 436–439, 2019.
https://doi.org/10.1007/978-3-030-11548-7_44

project [7] attempts to develop an evidence-based intervention, supported by the use of AR, to resolve or reduce reading and spelling difficulties for children with diagnosed with ADHD.

2   The AHA System

The AHA web-based system integrates the existing WordsWorthLearning© Programme (WWL) [8] with AR solutions and functionalities of the Web Health Application for Adhd Monitoring (WHAAM) [9], as shown in Fig. 1. WWL is a web-based tool developed to improve reading and spelling skills in individuals aged from 6 years to adulthood. WHAAM is a web-based service for monitoring students' problem behaviours across different settings. The AR solutions developed on the basis of an effective literacy programme is expected to produce an incremental impact on reading and spelling skills *via* its effect on students' engagement with the task.

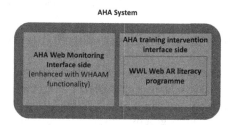

Fig. 1. The AHA system

The AHA system is comprised of two main interfaces (Fig. 1). The **AHA Training interface,** which allows children to access to the WWL activities supported by AR contents. AR can be accessed from desktop, iPad or mobile phone using a camera and is designed to catch students' attention thus facilitating the reading and spelling training. The AR contents includes (1) a AR WWL marker to visualise the AR objects (as shown in Fig. 2); (2) a set of AR charts for consonants and vowels; and (3) a set of AR flashcards. The vowel and consonant charts are used throughout the WWL tasks and use AR to provide 3D examples of letters and their sound symbol association (Fig. 2). The AR flashcards have reduced functionalities since no sound is related to the AR object and no rotation is possible. The **AHA Web monitoring interface** provides teachers and parents with a dashboard including the monitoring facilities to evaluate their children's engagement with the WWL task and their performance in AR-WWL. The AHA dashboard is constantly updated from data received automatically from the WWL AR programme. Specifically, in the toolbar for each child, four icons allow the access to different functionalities:

- WWL Account, to monitor the child's progress on the WWL activities;
- Case Data, to monitor the child's results on the pre and post literacy assessment tests of reading and spelling skills;

- Observations, provides teachers and parents with an interface to measure the level of academic engagement (off-task behaviour) and results from the last observation made;
- Data analytics, to monitor student's progress through several charts: scores at WWL evaluation questionnaires (per level), time spent on WWL activities (weekly and per level), and change in off-task behaviour (per session).

Fig. 2. WWL AR content

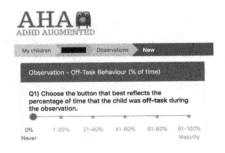

Fig. 3. Slider for off-task behaviour rating

3 The AHA System as an Evidence-Based Intervention

The research design aims at evaluating the effectiveness of the AR WWL intervention. To this purpose, at least 100 children with ADHD (4th to 6th class) will be recruited from Irish primary schools. A pre- and post-test design [10] will be used: children will be assigned to two intervention groups (AR-WWL vs. traditional WWL) and one control group (without WWL). Aims of the study are to evaluate the effect of AR on children's reading and spelling abilities and the level of engagement with the learning activities. Reading and spelling abilities are measured through the Neale Analysis of Reading Ability (NARA-II) [11] and the Vernon Graded Word Spelling Test [12]. With regard to children's engagement with the WWL activities, Direct Behaviour Rating (DBR) [13] is used to assess off-task behaviour. An observer rates on a Likert-type scale the occurrence of off-task behaviour in terms of percentage of time of the entire observation period. In addition to the assessment of overall off-task behaviour, ratings of motor, verbal, and passive off-task behaviours are obtained [14]. Each child in both intervention groups will be observed during each session for 15 min. At the end of the observation, the observer rates the occurrence of each type of off-task behaviour using a slider interface tool (as shown in Fig. 3). The research will be conducted obtaining an informed consent from all participants according to UCD's Human Research Ethics Committee approval and GDPR compliance.

4 Conclusion

The main idea of the AHA pilot within the prospect of future mixed reality educational spaces [15], is based on the hypothesis that the creation of AR 3D objects [16] for an existing online literacy programme can produce an incremental beneficial effect on children's reading and spelling skills *via* its positive impact on students' levels of engagement with the task. The results will provide the basis for further development of emerging technologies for digital learning solutions that can support the teaching and learning process of children with ADHD reducing issues related to their concentration problem. Moreover, the digital behavioural monitoring facilitates the creation of a working team close to the child (parents, teachers, and therapists) that can support and monitor the learning process, improve the home-school communication and collaboration, and assist in the adaption of a tailored approach to ADHD challenges. The results of the pilot will provide recommendations and a roadmap for policy makers, institutions, educators, and language specialists in terms of usage of AR digital technologies in classroom and home settings to facilitate the academic success of students with ADHD.

References

1. Akçayır, M., Akçayır, G.: Advantages and challenges associated with augmented reality for education: a systematic review of the literature. Educ. Res. Rev. **20**, 1–11 (2017)
2. Chen, P., Liu, X., Cheng, W., Huang, R.: A review of using augmented reality in education from 2011 to 2016. Innovations in Smart Learning. LNET, pp. 13–18. Springer, Singapore (2017). https://doi.org/10.1007/978-981-10-2419-1_2
3. Rapport, M.D., Kofler, M.J., Alderson, R.M., Timko Jr., T.M., DuPaul, G.J.: Variability of attention processes in ADHD: observations from the classroom. J. Attention Disord. **12**(6), 563–573 (2009)
4. Demaray, M.K., Jenkins, L.N.: Relations among academic enablers and academic achievement in children with and without high levels of parent-rated symptoms of inattention, impulsivity, and hyperactivity. Psychol. Sch. **48**(6), 573–586 (2011)
5. Volpe, R.J., et al.: Attention deficit hyperactivity disorder and scholastic achievement: A model of mediation via academic enablers. Sch. Psychol. Rev. **35**(1), 47 (2006)
6. DuPaul, G.J., Gormley, M.J., Laracy, S.D.: Comorbidity of LD and ADHD: implications of DSM-5 for assessment and treatment. J. Learn. Disabil. **46**(1), 43–51 (2013)
7. http://aha.ucd.ie
8. WordsWorthLearning Ltd. https://www.wordsworthlearning.com/
9. Web Health Application for ADHD monitoring. https://www.whaamproject.eu/
10. Kazdin, A.: Research Design in Clinical Psychology, 4th edn. Allyn & Bacon, Needham Heights (2003)
11. Neale, M.D.: Neale Analysis of Reading Ability – Revised. NFER-Nelson, Windsor (1997)
12. Vernon, P.E.: Graded word spelling test, revised and restandardized by Colin McCarty and Mary Crumpler. Hodder Education, UK, London (2006)
13. Chafouleas, S.M., Riley-Tillman, T.C., Christ, T.J.: Direct behaviour rating (DBR) an emerging method for assessing social behaviour within a tiered intervention system. Assess. Effective Interv. **34**(4), 195–200 (2009)
14. Shapiro, E.S.: Academic Skills Problems. The Guilford Press, New York (2011)
15. Campbell, A., Santiago, K., Hoo, D., Mangina, E.: Future mixed reality educational spaces. In: Proceedings of IEEE Future Technologies Conference, pp. 1088–1093 (2016)
16. Mangina, E.: 3D learning objects for augmented/virtual reality educational ecosystems. In: Proceedings of 23rd International Conference on Virtual System & Multimedia (VSMM) (2017)

User Preferences for a Serious Game to Improve Driving

Pratheep Kumar Paranthaman, Francesco Bellotti[✉], Riccardo Berta,
Gautam Dange, and Alessandro De Gloria

DITEN, University of Genoa, Via Opera Pia 11A, 16145 Genoa, Italy
pratheephw@gmail.com, gautam.dange2007@gmail.com,
{franz, riccardo.berta, adg}@elios.unige.it

Abstract. As automotive games are gaining interest, there is a lack in literature on specifications, user needs and requirements. We collected information from potential users on some basic features about two types of games for improving the driver performance: driver games and passenger games. In a survey with 18 respondents, both the typologies have been considered appealing, with drivers more interested in assessing performance and having suggestions, passengers in having fun. The greatest difference involves the requirement that a driver game should avoid distraction. Thus, the set-up phase should be doable when the vehicle is stopped, the visual feedback, if any, should be very limited (e.g., color spots), and most of the feedback should be provided through the audio channel. Passenger games might have more complex plots, with chance factors, and also support social interaction, for instance with passengers of other vehicles.

Keywords: Serious games · Mobile computing ·
Usability survey · User interfaces · Internet of Things ·
Games and infotainment · Smart cars · Vehicle safety

1 Introduction

Automotive games are getting ever more interest (e.g., [1, 2]). However, published experience report usability problems [3] and little is available on user needs and requirements. This paper focuses on information from users about serious games (SGs) for improving driver performance. Use of the game itself can be clearly a source of distraction. On the other hand, playing in the field, during the actual user activity, is an important factor, that is being explored in the emerging "reality-enhanced" (RE) SG genre. We focus on two types of games: Driver game (DG) and Passenger game (PG) [4]. In both cases, the game is fed by drive data collected through vehicular or personal device sensors, the difference is given by the target users.

© Springer Nature Switzerland AG 2019
M. Gentile et al. (Eds.): GALA 2018, LNCS 11385, pp. 440–444, 2019.
https://doi.org/10.1007/978-3-030-11548-7_45

2 Design Considerations and Research Questions

2.1 Player Motivation

The gameplay must motivate users and keep them on track to improve performance. This leads to our first research question. RQ1: How can we motivate users in gameplay?

Several projects are testing the deployment features of games in vehicles [5]. However, the process of implementation comes with various questions concerning the ease of use, safety, and motivation. Also, it is necessary to understand the game design parameters, user preferences, and deployment analysis; then only a solid framework can be determined for creating a suited user experience.

2.2 Game Logic and Impact

One reason for the drawback is, the transportation industry is more sensitive with regards to driver safety and distraction. When a driver is given a secondary task (such as learning), the focus from the primary task (driving) gets distracted, and hence that could cause a mishap [6]. On the other hand, when deploying a minimal gaming interface (e.g., [7, 8]), the user involvement decreases over a period of time because the interface remains passive (certain elements of passive gaming are observing, listening, etc.) for the users. If we make games more reactive and induce active gameplay then again it might lead to distraction. Having this considerations in mind, the second research question (RQ2) emphasizes the need for designing a suited game logic. RQ2: How can we design a game logic to foster games for improving mobility quality?

3 Preliminary User Survey

The user survey focuses on the two mentioned game types: DG and PG [4]. In general, we are interested in understanding whether the distinction between DG and PG is reasonable, and whether the two types of games make sense. The test comprised 18 users, who were students/workers at the University of Genova (Age - mean: 28.2, stdev: 5.5).

In the DG part, the questionnaire comprised four questions related to activities and user expectations for gaming while driving (see Fig. 1). For each question, users could choose more than one answer. From the results, we argue that a game should have usual interaction modalities, essentially audio, with limited set-up, doable, when the vehicle is still. Results on the main reason for gaming seem to suggest that real-time feedback is assessed better than post-trip more detailed information (events displayed on the map), and that self-improvement is valued more than competitions/comparisons with other drivers. We thus see the need for an entertaining game and, overall, for a precise, real-time analysis, with coaching capabilities.

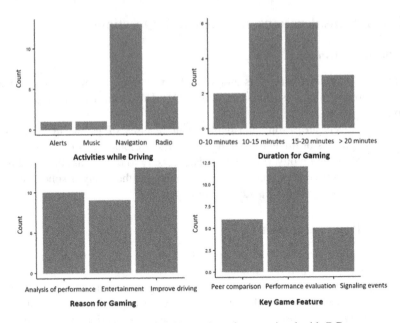

Fig. 1. User preferences questionnaire associated with DG

It seems that the game needs to be passive (i.e., the user does not interact with the game HMI). On the other hand, timely feedback (e.g., audio) is typically needed for a game. We thus argue that DG should rely essentially on real-time audio feedback, while giving the opportunity to the driver to access more detailed information later. This post-trip phase, however, does not seem to be particularly appealing, while most of the effect is expected during the actual game. But how to engage the driver? This approach does not preclude levels, nor score, and we thus believe that a proper design should lead to compelling DG implementations (entertainment is anyway a requested and distinctive feature). Proper mechanics for coaching (possibly also in real-time) are needed, as performance improvement was indicated as the most important motivator for a DG.

The second part was devoted to the PG (Fig. 2). Target users are the passengers, who play a game whose gameplay is influenced by the driving performance of the vehicle on which they are on. The game needs more entertainment, and the player attention can be devoted more to the game. Thus, more fun could be added through interactivity. In PG, driver performance could be one of the game factors, together with the player ability. Driver performance, for instance, could enhance (or decrease) an avatar energy or weapon force in a combat game. Respondents – despite being passengers - show a clear interest on analysis of the driver performance, this calls for appropriate mechanics to precisely and timely indicate how the driver behaves and could improve performance.

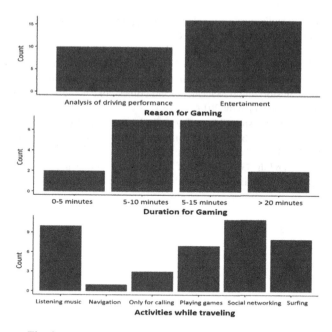

Fig. 2. User preferences questionnaire associated with PG

4 Conclusions

The survey showed interest for both the PG and DG typologies, with drivers more interested in performance and feedback, passengers in fun. The greatest difference concerns that a DG should avoid user distraction. Thus, the set-up should be doable when the vehicle is still, the visual feedback, if any, should be very limited (e.g., color spots), and most of the feedback should be audio. PGs might have more complex plots, with chance factors, and support for social interaction, (e.g., with other vehicles passengers). In both types, the duration should not increase the workload. Despite neglecting some factors (e.g., privacy), we think that our findings could be useful for future research.

References

1. Krome, S., Walz, S.P., Greuter, S., Holopainen, J., Gerlicher, A., Schleehauf, M.: Exploring game ideas for stresslessness in the automotive domain. In: Proceedings of the 2014 Conference on Interactive Entertainment, pp. 36:1–36:3 (2014)
2. Bellotti, F., et al.: TEAM applications for collaborative road mobility. IEEE Trans. Ind. Inform. (in press). https://doi.org/10.1109/tii.2018.2850005
3. Broy, N., et al.: A cooperative in-car game for heterogeneous players. In: Proceedings of the 3rd International Conference on Automotive User Interfaces and Interactive Vehicular Applications, pp. 167–176. ACM, New York (2011)

4. Dange, G.R., et al.: Deployment of serious gaming approach for safe and sustainable mobility. In: IEEE Intelligent Vehicles Symposium (IV) (2017)
5. McCall, R., Koenig, V.: Gaming concepts and incentives to change driver behaviour. In: The 11th Annual Mediterranean Ad Hoc Networking Workshop (Med-Hoc-Net) (2012)
6. Road accidents, stabbings, and car racing: Pokemon Go is madness redefined. http://indiatoday.intoday.in/story/injuries-accidents-and-crimes-pokemon-go-is-madness-redefined/1/714903.html. Accessed 17 Nov 2017
7. Why driving slowly and responsibly can actually be fun. https://www.washingtonpost.com/news/innovations/wp/2014/06/20/why-driving-slowly-and-responsibly-can-actually-be-fun/?utm_term=.0cab031415d0. Accessed 17 Nov 2017
8. Car2Go's EcoScore and the Gamification of Driving – Jay Goldman. https://jaygoldman.com/car2go-s-ecoscore-and-the-gamification-of-driving-d6415ea1045e. Accessed 16 Nov 2017

Video Games and Attitude Change – Can We Reliably Measure This? The Challenges of Empirical Study Design

Lukáš Kolek[1], Vít Šisler[1(✉)], and Cyril Brom[2]

[1] Faculty of Arts, Charles University, Prague 116 38, Czech Republic
lukaskolek@live.com, vit.sisler@ff.cuni.cz
[2] Faculty of Mathematics and Physics, Charles University,
Prague 121 16, Czech Republic
brom@ksvi.mff.cuni.cz

Abstract. The aim of this paper is to address methodologically the challenges that arise when measuring attitude changes toward video game content. Drawing on findings from two pilot studies ($N = 18, 25$) and field notes from an ongoing empirical study ($N = 140$), we have identified three key challenges: reliability of measurement of attitudes, standardization of game experience for each participant, and measurement of attitudes toward socially sensitive topics. In this paper, we outline our research design that tried to address these challenges. In particular, we propose modifying the game, used as a research tool, to maintain player agency while ensuring all players engage with the measured phenomena. We also recommend using the concept of attitude strength in order to measure effectively attitudes toward socially sensitive topics. Overall, this paper provides preliminary insight into research on video games and attitude change within the field of digital game-based learning.

Keywords: Attitude change · Czechoslovakia 38–89: Borderlands ·
Explicit and implicit attitudes · Serious game · Representation of history

1 Introduction

Video games give players agency and, to varying degrees, control over their experiences. This subsequently affects emotions. They are also one of the few media that allows players to feel guilty because of the decisions they make during the game [1]. Both interactivity and emotional impact have the potential to affect attitudes [2].

However, the effect of video games on players' attitudes is still a scarcely researched domain. There is only limited evidence on how playing video games impacts short- and long-term changes in attitudes toward content depicted in these games [3]. The aim of this paper is to address methodologically the challenges of empirical study design measuring the impact of video game playing on attitude change. We will draw on findings from two pilot studies (N = 18, 25) and field-notes from our ongoing empirical study (N = 140).

© Springer Nature Switzerland AG 2019
M. Gentile et al. (Eds.): GALA 2018, LNCS 11385, pp. 445–448, 2019.
https://doi.org/10.1007/978-3-030-11548-7_46

This study is part of a larger empirical study on the effects of a historical game *Czechoslovakia 38–89: Borderlands* on players' attitudes toward historical content; namely, the expulsion of Sudeten Germans from Czechoslovakia after WWII.

2 Reliability of Measurement of Attitudes

In order to assess players' attitudes toward game content reliably, the following three issues must be taken into account. (a) The most common technique for measuring attitude change is self-reports assessing explicit (conscious) attitudes. However, when dealing with socially sensitive topics, participants may tend to avoid giving an undesirable impression. They may present themselves in a way that seems to gain social approval or have respectable characteristics [4]. As such, self-reports may suffer from participants' impression management [5]. Therefore, we also recommend indirect attitude measurements which do not possess these limitations. They access implicit (subconscious) attitudes: usually through measuring participants' response times for their evaluation of attitude objects [6, 7].

(b) Participants' moods may affect attitudes and possible changes thereto [8]. Hence, assessing participants' positive and negative affects before every attitude measurement may reveal important correlations, e.g. through Positive and Negative Affect Schedule (PANAS) [9].

(c) Attitude persistence and formation are still debated among social psychologists [10]. Empirical evidence suggests that participants' implicit attitudes can be affected by exposure to stimuli related to the measured phenomena immediately before attitude measurement [11]. As a result, the research design should also include a delayed post-test: at least several weeks after the intervention in order to measure long-term attitude change.

3 Standardization of Game Experience for Each Participant

The interactive nature of video games provides players with relative freedom of choice. However, researchers must deal with limited control over different players' experiences. This issue must be considered when selecting a game. In our case, we chose as our research tool the serious game *Czechoslovakia 38–89: Borderlands*. It is a narrative, adventure game based on historical research and personal testimonies. The game was chosen deliberately since we are its developers. We identified all the dialogue options containing information about the expulsion of the Sudeten Germans (i.e. the key information messages). We purposefully redesigned the dialogue options, so that players could pass through the game in different ways. However, at some point, they all naturally encountered the key information messages. In this way, we managed to create a standardized gaming experience for each player during multiple sessions of our experiment; and without apparent limitations on the player's agency.

4 Measurement of Attitudes Towards Socially Sensitive Topics

Attitudes do not serve only as a guide to how to behave toward a given object, but they also have a symbolic function which is affected by our self-perception and our values [6]. The topic of the expulsion of Sudeten Germans from Czechoslovakia still arouses passion and has the potential for in-group bias among our Czech participants. Therefore, we used the concept of attitude strength [13]: assuming that if attitudes are stronger, they are also more stable over time and across various situations [12]. Stronger attitudes are more accessible, extreme, less ambivalent and held with a high level of conviction [13]. They also possess high levels of ego- and issue-involvement and knowledge base [6]. All these indicators allowed us to identify possible irregularities in attitude change caused by in-group bias.

5 Final Research Design

As a result of dealing with the above-mentioned challenges, we created the following research design. It used pre-test/post-test design with a second delayed post-test one month after the intervention. The number of participants (M^{age} = 20.6) ranged from 3 to 11 for each session. They were recruited through sites offering short-term jobs.

We had one experimental and one control group (n = 73, n = 67). The experimental group was exposed to a modified version of *Czechoslovakia 38-89: Borderlands*, while participants in the control group played the fantasy game *Trader of Stories* [14]. During the first phase of data collection, we gathered data on participants' initial positive and negative affects using PANAS. Then we evaluated participants' initial implicit attitudes through the Single Category Implicit Association Test, SC-IAT [15], which is derived from the Implicit Association Test, IAT [7]. IAT compares relative attitudes toward two complementary attitude objects (e.g. female and male, war and peace, etc.). As we intended to measure implicit attitudes toward only one historical concept, SC-IAT was more suitable. Next, we collected data on explicit attitudes using two questionnaires. In the first one, participants evaluated the expulsion of the Sudeten Germans using a five-point semantic differential scale with seven bipolar adjectives. In the second one, explicit attitudes were assessed through ten evaluative statements (with 7-point Likert items).

After the pre-test phase, participants were exposed to two 30-min interventions of playing *Czechoslovakia 38–89: Borderlands* separated by a 10-min pause.

The post-test phase of data collection followed the same pattern as the pre-test phase. Then, we collected qualitative data from our participants through focus groups.

We organized a delayed post-test three to five weeks after the intervention. In it, we followed the same pattern from the pre-test but with one additional questionnaire focusing on participant activities during the previous month related to the expulsion. At the end of the delayed post-test session, we again collected qualitative data through focus groups: this time examining participants' relations to the borderlands.

6 Discussion

Data from the main empirical study was still being analyzed at the time of writing this paper. However, preliminary results and the results of our pilot study [12] suggest there is viability and internal validity for our research design. Qualitative feedback did not indicate any systematic or random errors in our measurements.

Acknowledgments. This study was supported by the project PRIMUS/HUM/03 at Charles University and by the project FF/VG/2017/115 of the Faculty of Arts at Charles University. Vít Šisler's work was further supported by the European Regional Development Fund Project, "Creativity and Adaptability as Conditions for the Success of Europe in an Interrelated World" (No. CZ.02.1.01/0.0/0.0/16_019/0000734) and the Charles University Program, Progress Q15.

References

1. Farber, M., Schrier, K.: The limits and strengths of using digital games as empathy machines. MGIEP Working Paper 5, 1–35 (2017)
2. Oh, J., Sundar, S.S.: How does interactivity persuade? An experimental test of interactivity on cognitive absorption, elaboration, and attitudes. J. Commun. **65**(2), 213–236 (2015)
3. Soekarjo, M., Oostendorp, H.V.: Measuring effectiveness of persuasive games using an informative control condition. Int. J. Serious Games **2**(2), 37–56 (2015)
4. Albarracín, D., Johnson, B.T., Zanna, M.P.: The Handbook of Attitude. Psychology Press, New York (2014)
5. Tedeschi, J.T.: Impression Management Theory and Social Psychological Research, 1st edn. Academic Press, Michigan (1981)
6. Vogel, T., Wanke, M.: Attitudes and Attitude Change, 2nd edn. Routledge, New York (2016)
7. Greenwald, A.G., Farnham, S.D.: Using the implicit association test to measure self-esteem and self concept. J. Pers. Soc. Psychol. **79**(6), 1022–1038 (1995)
8. Wegener, D.T., Petty, R.E., Klein, D.K.: Effects of mood on high elaboration attitude change: the mediating role of likelihood judgments. Eur. J. Soc. Psychol. **24**, 25–43 (1994)
9. Watson, D., Clark, L.A., Tellegen, A.: Development and validation of brief measures of positive and negative affect: the PANAS scales. J. Pers. Soc. Psychol. **54**(6), 1063–1070 (1988)
10. Schwarz, N., Bohner, G.: The construction of attitudes. In: Tesser, A., Schwarz, N. (eds.) Blackwell Handbook of Social Psychology, pp. 436–457. Blackwell, Oxford (2001)
11. Banaji, R.B., Greenwald, A.G.: Blindspot: Hidden Biases of Good People, 1st edn. Delacorte Press, New York (2013)
12. Kolek, L., Šisler, V.: Representation of history in computer games and attitude change: empirical study design. In: Pivec, M., Grundler, J. (eds.) CONFERENCE 2017, ECGBL, vol. 11, pp. 829–834. Academic Conferences and Publishing International Limited, Reading (2017)
13. Petty, R.E., Krosnick, J.A.: Attitude Strength: Antecedents and Consequences, 1st edn. Psychology Press, New York (1995)
14. Rudowski, M.: The Trader of Stories. http://traderofstories.blogspot.com. Accessed 15 Aug 2018
15. Karpinski, A., Steinman, R.B.: The single category implicit association test as a measure of implicit social cognition. J. Pers. Soc. Psychol. **91**(1), 16–32 (2006)

Author Index

Printed in the United States
By Bookmasters